THE COLLECTED
WORKS OF
JEREMY BENTHAM

General Editor

F. Rosen

CONSTITUTIONAL LAW

The essays which Bentham collected together for publication in 1830 under the title of *Official Aptitude Maximized; Expense Minimized*, written at various times between 1810 and 1830, deal with the means of achieving efficient and economical government. In considering a wide range of themes in the fields of constitutional law, public finance, and legal reform, Bentham places the problem of official corruption at the centre of his analysis. He contrasts his own recommendations for good administration, which he had fully developed in his magisterial *Constitutional Code*, with the severe deficiencies he saw in English practice. The core of the volume consists of four major essays directed against the principles and policies of four leading statesmen: Edmund Burke, George Rose, Robert Peel, and Lord Chancellor Eldon. Of particular concern to Bentham were the abuses sanctioned by the judges and their officials in the Westminster Hall courts, which, he argued, resulted in the denial of justice to the majority of the population. In this volume, Bentham not only displays the precise logical reasoning for which he is well known, but also his considerable skills as a rhetorician of reform.

The Collected Works of Jeremy Bentham

The new critical edition of the works and correspondence of Jeremy Bentham (1748–1832) is being prepared and published under the supervision of the Bentham Committee of University College London. Despite his importance as jurist, philosopher, social scientist, and leader of the Utilitarian reformers, the only previous edition of his works was a poorly edited and incomplete one brought out within a decade or so of his death. Eight volumes of the new *Collected Works*, five of correspondence, and three of writings on jurisprudence, were published between 1968 and 1981 by the Athlone Press. Further volumes are published by Oxford University Press. The overall plan and principles of the edition are set out in the General Preface to *The Correspondence of Jeremy Bentham* vol. 1, the first volume of the *Collected Works* to be published.

OFFICIAL APTITUDE MAXIMIZED; EXPENSE MINIMIZED

edited by
PHILIP SCHOFIELD

CLARENDON PRESS · OXFORD
1993

Oxford University Press, Walton Street, Oxford OX2 6DP

Oxford New York Toronto
Delhi Bombay Calcutta Madras Karachi
Kuala Lumpur Singapore Hong Kong Tokyo
Nairobi Dar es Salaam Cape Town
Melbourne Auckland Madrid
and associated companies in
Berlin Ibadan

Oxford is a trade mark of Oxford University Press

Published in the United States
by Oxford University Press Inc., New York

British Library Cataloguing in Publication Data
Data available

Library of Congress Cataloging-in-Publication Data
Data available
ISBN 0–19–820403–5

1 3 5 7 9 10 8 6 4 2

Typeset by Joshua Associates Ltd, Oxford
Printed in Great Britain
on acid-free paper by
Bookcraft Ltd, Midsomer Norton, Bath

PREFACE

The Bentham Committee wishes to thank the Economic and Social Research Council whose generous grant allowing for the appointment of an editor and half-time Research Assistant has made possible the preparation of the present volume. The Committee is indebted to the British Academy and University College London for their continuing support. Thanks are also due to the Esmée Fairbairn Charitable Trust and the John Ellerman Foundation for financial assistance.

The editor wishes to thank the following repositories for permission to quote from manuscripts in their possession and for assistance in tracing rare volumes: University College London Library; the British Library; the Bodleian Library; Lincoln's Inn Library; the National Library of Ireland; Yale University Library; Harvard Law School Library; the University of Western Ontario Library; and the Bibliothèque Publique et Universitaire, Geneva. Special thanks are extended to the staff of University College London Manuscripts and Rare Books Library, and in particular to Miss G.M. Furlong, for their kind help and attention.

I am indebted to Professor F. Rosen, the Director and General Editor of the Bentham Project, for his careful reading of the completed text, but more generally for his continuing guidance, encouragement and support. Especial thanks are due to Ms Jane Haville for her invaluable assistance: in her capacity as Research Assistant, she has been actively involved at every stage of the production of the volume, from transcribing manuscripts and researching references, to preparing the computer-encoded text and reading the proofs. I am also particularly grateful to my other colleagues at the Bentham Project: to Dr Janet Semple for gathering information for the purposes of annotation; to Dr Stephen Conway and Dr Cyprian Blamires for their scholarly help and advice on a whole range of points and queries; and to Mrs Evelyn Hannah for general secretarial assistance. I should like to thank them collectively for creating such a supportive and friendly atmosphere within which to work.

Thanks are also due to Professor J.H. Burns for reading the Editorial Introduction and for his help on a whole variety of matters; to Ms Catherine Pease-Watkin for her meticulous work in preparing the collations; to Mr David Shields for typing the text onto computer disk; to my wife, Kathryn, for volunteering to help with page-numbering the subject index; to Catherine Fuller for helping to prepare the name index and other typing work; and to Miss Monica Lim for typing the subject index and the collations. I gratefully acknowledge the help received in the elucidation of certain references in the text from the following scholars: Professor J.H. Elliott, Mr A.H. Griffiths, Mr A.D.E. Lewis, and Dr R.W. Sharples.

P.S.

CONTENTS

CONTENTS

CONTENTS

CONTENTS

CONTENTS

SYMBOLS AND ABBREVIATIONS

Symbols

| | | Space left in manuscript.
[to]   Word(s) editorially supplied.
[?]   Reading doubtful.
[. . . ?]   Word(s) proved illegible.

Abbreviations

Apart from standard abbreviations the following should be noted:

Bowring	*The Works of Jeremy Bentham*, published under the superintendence of . . . John Bowring, 11 vols., Edinburgh, 1843.
UC	Bentham papers in the Library of University College London. Roman numerals refer to boxes in which the papers are placed, arabic to the leaves within each box.
BL Add. MS	British Library Additional Manuscript.
CW	This edition of *The Collected Works of Jeremy Bentham*.
1830	*Official Aptitude Maximized; Expense Minimized: as shewn in the several papers comprised in this volume*, London, 1830.
1817 EITHER	'Defence of Economy against the late Mr. Burke', *The Pamphleteer*, vol. ix, no. xvii (1817), 3–47.
OR	'Defence of Economy against the Right Hon. George Rose', *The Pamphleteer*, vol. x, no. xx (1817), 281–332.
1825A	*Observations on Mr. Secretary Peel's House of Commons Speech, 21st March, 1825, introducing his Police Magistrates' Salary Raising Bill. Date of Order for Printing, 24th March, 1825. Also on the Announced Judges' Salary Raising Bill, and the Pending County Courts Bill*, London, 1825.
1825B	'Observations on Mr. Secretary Peel's House of Commons Speech, 21st March, 1825, introducing his Police Magistrates' Salary Raising Bill. Date of Order for Printing, 24th

	March 1825. Also on the Announced Judges' Salary Raising Bill, and the Pending County Courts Bill, *The Pamphleteer*, vol. xxv, no. 1 (1825), 405–43.
1825C	*Indications respecting Lord Eldon, including History of the Pending Judges'-Salary-Raising Measure*, printed 1825 [this version does not contain the Postscript].
1825D	*Indications respecting Lord Eldon, including History of the Pending Judges'-Salary-Raising Measure*, London, 1825.
1826	'Indications respecting Lord Eldon, including History of the Pending Judges' Salary-Raising Measure', *The Pamphleteer*, vol. xxvi, no. li (1826), 1–55.
1826 *Extract*	*Extract from the proposed Constitutional Code, entitled Official Aptitude Maximized, Expense Minimized*, London, [1826].
MS del.	Word(s) deleted in manuscript.
MS orig.	Original manuscript reading.

EDITORIAL INTRODUCTION

Bentham first conceived the idea of publishing a collection of essays—the 'pasticcio' as he called it—towards the end of 1824, in order to illustrate his own ideal of constitutional law, captured in the aphorism 'aptitude maximized, expense minimized', and contrast it with practice under the British constitution, which he believed to be based on the opposite principle of minimizing aptitude and maximizing expense. Such a volume would complement the detailed administrative provisions which he had been drafting since 1822 for his *Constitutional Code*, the major endeavour of the final decade of his life. These two works are therefore closely related both chronologically and thematically. Bentham quickly settled the core essays for the pasticcio, but new materials were added and others discarded before the eventual publication of *Official Aptitude Maximized; Expense Minimized* in June 1830, shortly after the publication of Volume I of *Constitutional Code*. The pasticcio contained eleven Papers, written at various times between 1810 and 1830, of which only two, the 'Preface' and 'On Public Account Keeping', had not been previously published. In the process of drafting the printed Papers of the volume, Bentham composed a considerable number of manuscripts which have hitherto remained unpublished. These have been fully surveyed for the present edition, and have yielded the essays included in the three Appendices.

HISTORY OF THE WORK

The history of each of the component Papers will be considered in more detail below, but in the first place it seems appropriate to give a brief overview of the development of the volume itself. Towards the end of 1824, Bentham had been approached by Richard Smith, who was in the process of editing the work published in the following year as *The Rationale of Reward*, based in part on Bentham's manuscripts and in part on the second volume of Étienne Dumont's recension, *Théorie des peines et des récompenses*.[1] Smith asked Bentham whether

---

[1] *The Rationale of Reward*, London, 1825 (Bowring, ii. 189–266); *Théorie des peines et des récompenses*, ed. Étienne Dumont, 2 vols., London, 1811 (this was itself based on MSS written by Bentham in the 1770s and 1780s).

Richard Smith, a collector of stagecoach duties at the Stamp and Taxes Office, went on to edit

any of his views on the subject of reward had changed since he had written the material which Dumont had incorporated into *Théorie des peines et des récompenses*. Bentham responded by drafting 'Corrections to *The Rationale of Reward*', which he decided not to include in Smith's volume, but instead to place in a separate volume of his own, along with other tracts illustrating his thinking on matters of official economy and reward.[1] An extract from his proposed *Constitutional Code* (as well as a table of the contents of the whole work) would contrast his own ideas with English practice as he had exposed it in two pamphlets written in 1810, but only published in 1817, 'Defence of Economy against Edmund Burke' and 'Defence of Economy against George Rose'.[2] He would complete the volume with a preface or conclusion, in which, amongst other themes, he would discuss the imposition of legal fees at the discretion of judges, a topic briefly noticed in 'Defence of Economy against Burke'. Concentrating in particular on the machinations of Lord Chancellor Eldon,[3] Bentham gradually expanded this material until, by the summer of 1825, he had developed it into a long, separate essay, 'Indications respecting Lord Eldon'.[4] Meanwhile, he found time to compose a detailed commentary on a speech of the Home Secretary, Robert Peel,[5] made in the House of Commons on 21 March 1825, proposing to raise the salaries of metropolitan police magistrates.[6] By July 1825, the pasticcio had taken recognizable shape: its contents were to include the material extracted from *Constitutional Code*, 'Corrections to *The Rationale of Reward*', and the essays on Burke, Rose, Peel and Eldon.[7]

In 1826, Bentham published *Extract from Constitutional Code* as a separate pamphlet,[8] but then neglected the pasticcio until he drew up

thirteen works for the Bowring edition (see Bowring, x. 548n). Pierre Étienne Louis Dumont (1759–1829), Bentham's Genevan editor and translator, produced several recensions of Bentham's work.

[1] See Bentham's 'Remarks' in *The Rationale of Reward*, pp. iv–vi (Bowring, ii. 191).

[2] See pp. xxvi–xxviii below for further details. Bentham took the views of Edmund Burke (1729–97), MP for Wendover 1765–74, Bristol 1774–80 and Malton 1780–94, Paymaster-General 1782, 1783, as representative of the Whig party, and those of George Rose (1744–1818), MP for Launceston 1784–8, Lymington 1788–90 and Christchurch 1790–1818, Secretary to the Treasury 1782–3, 1783–1801, Vice-President of the Board of Trade and joint Paymaster-General 1804–6, Vice-President of the Board of Trade 1807–12, Treasurer of the Navy 1807–18, as representative of the Tory party.

[3] John Scott (1751–1838), first Baron and first Earl of Eldon, Lord Chancellor 1801–6, 1807–27.

[4] See pp. xxx–xl below.

[5] Peel (1788–1850), Home Secretary 1822–7, 1828–30, First Lord of the Treasury and Chancellor of the Exchequer 1834–5, First Lord of the Treasury 1841–6.

[6] See pp. xxviii–xxix below.

[7] See Bentham's draft 'Preliminary Advertisement' for the pasticcio of 15 July 1825 at UC cxiv. 168. An abandoned plan of the same date is at UC cxiv. 169.

[8] See pp. xxii–xxiii below.

a plan on 18 January 1828.[1] He had by now probably decided to omit his 'Corrections to *The Rationale of Reward*', though the rest of the volume remained substantially unaltered.[2] He went on to organize some material for the preface, and then in the spring and summer of 1828 made a further, more sustained, attempt to draft not only a projected conclusion to the whole volume, but also new material on the subject of retrenchment.[3] At the same time he was organizing material for an additional supplement to 'Extract from Constitutional Code'. These efforts, however, came to nothing, and it was not until the spring of 1830 that Bentham finally prepared the pasticcio for the press. He was perhaps stimulated by the publication of Volume I of *Constitutional Code* in April 1830, but he seems to have been particularly excited by Peel's intention, announced in the House of Commons, to commute into salaries the fees of office holders in the Common Law Courts as a preliminary to more wide-ranging legal reform.[4] He drafted the 'Preface' to the pasticcio and a new essay, 'On Public Account Keeping', and added a further extract from *Constitutional Code* dealing with the militia. Together with 'Extract from Constitutional Code' (which Bentham divided into three Papers), the 'Table of Contents' for the whole of the *Code*, and the essays on Burke, Rose, Peel and Eldon, these completed the eleven Papers of *Official Aptitude Maximized; Expense Minimized*, when it appeared in June 1830.

Corrections to The Rationale of Reward

Bentham's 'Corrections' to Richard Smith's edition of *The Rationale of Reward* did not appear in the pasticcio when it was eventually

---

[1] He did claim in April 1827 that the pasticcio was 'in a state to be published at any time', though admitted that he still had to make 'a contemplated addition or two': see Bentham to Robert Peel, 7 April 1827, BL Add. MS 40,393, fos. 148–9.

[2] Bentham's plan for the pasticcio of 18 January 1828 is at UC cxii. 65. He retained 'Extract from Constitutional Code' and the essays on Burke, Rose, Peel and Eldon, but proposed to add three further papers: 'Retired Allowances, or say Pensions of Retreat'; 'Militia—its usefulness'; and 'Boards—their abolition'. Bentham of course did include an extract on the militia in the pasticcio, while he dealt with boards in *Constitutional Code*: see *Constitutional Code*, vol. I, ed. F. Rosen and J.H. Burns, Oxford, 1983 (*CW*), Ch. IX, §3, pp. 173–86. The plan contains references to 'Corrections to *The Rationale of Reward*' (which had dealt with pensions of retreat) and the material on 'Droits of Admiralty' (see p. xxv below), but they do not appear in the proposed list of contents.

[3] This included the essays on retrenchment and remuneration reproduced below in Appendices B and C respectively.

[4] Peel had been given leave to bring in a Bill to this effect on 18 February 1830 (see *Parliamentary Debates* (1830) xxii. 650–63), but it was his further reference to it in a debate on the Welsh Judicature Bill on 9 March 1830 (ibid., xxiii. 67–8) that seems to have caught Bentham's attention (see Bentham to Peel, 13 March 1830, BL Add. MS 40,400, fos. 94–5). The measure was enacted on 23 July 1830 as 11 Geo. IV and 1 Wil. IV, c.58.

published, yet it was through this project that the idea of producing a collection of essays on the theme of official economy occurred to him. Smith, when preparing *The Rationale of Reward* for publication, had asked Bentham whether he now disagreed with any of the opinions expressed in the work, and whether he would like to make any insertions in the new version in the form of footnotes. In the 'Remarks by Mr. Bentham', inserted as a preface to *The Rationale of Reward*,[1] he declined to make any comment there, but referred to 'a sequel' on which he was working:

In that production may be seen, not in description only, but *in terminis*, the arrangements, which, after from forty to fifty years for reflection, exhibit the practical—I do not say the *now practicable*—result of the principles of yours [i.e. *The Rationale of Reward*]: and *that*, cleared (forgive my saying so) of what now shows itself to me as dross.

Bentham had in mind the detailed administrative provisions on official economy which he intended to publish in the form of an extract from his proposed *Constitutional Code*. He explained that the phrase 'Official Aptitude maximized; Expense minimized' not only formed the title of the proposed extract, but also of a collection of essays of which it would form a part.[2]

Send your readers, if you have any, to that work. There, with official economy, and official education, they may see national growing out of it— added, and *that* without need of additional description or expense. There, confronted with Radical, they may see Whig and Tory economy, and take their choice. I say Whig and Tory; for these two are one.

The contrast would of course be provided by 'Defence of Economy against Edmund Burke', representing Whig 'economy', and 'Defence of Economy against George Rose', representing Tory 'economy'. Bentham's 'Remarks' must have been written prior to his letter to Dumont of 14 December 1824,[3] in which their general tenor is repeated. Significantly however, he proposed a further topic for the pasticcio:

a pointed and personal attack against one of the main roots of evil in this land, by way of preface, for having in the most impudent manner persevered in a state crime of the highest magnitude discussed in one of those defences, and for which were there here any the least responsibility on the part of the higher functionaries he would long ago have been turned out and punished.

---

[1] *The Rationale of Reward*, pp. iv–vi (Bowring, ii. 191). A *précis* of the contents of Book I of the work, in the hand of a copyist, is at UC cxliii. 130–45.

[2] In the event, the aphorism did indeed form both the sub-title of *Extract from Constitutional Code* and the title of the pasticcio.

[3] Bentham to Dumont, 14 December 1824, Dumont MSS, Bibliothèque Publique et Universitaire, Geneva, 74, fos. 46–9.

This 'attack', directed against Lord Chancellor Eldon, concerned the legal fees imposed at the discretion of judges, which Bentham had noticed in 'Defence of Economy against Burke', and which at length developed into 'Indications respecting Lord Eldon'.[1]

As he explained in his 'Remarks', and as the surviving manuscripts confirm, Bentham in the main concentrated on three passages in *Théorie des peines et des récompenses*: the first dealing with 'Catherine the Great's Table of Ranks';[2] the second with the exclusion of corruption by emoluments; and the third with pensions of retreat.[3] Bentham made an initial attempt to compose his 'Corrections' in late October and early November 1824. This material is very fragmentary, consisting of a series of short drafts which scarcely amount to any coherent text. Several drafts deal with the theme of excluding corruption by emoluments,[4] others with pensions of retreat,[5] but only one with the Scale of Ranks.[6] Nevertheless these are the earliest manuscripts which Bentham wrote specifically for the pasticcio, and they even contain a short comment on the legal fees levied by Eldon and the other judges on their own authority.[7] Bentham again turned his

---

[1] See pp. xxx–xl below.

[2] The Table of Ranks had in fact been introduced in Russia in 1722 by Peter the Great (1672–1725), Tsar of Russia from 1682 and Emperor from 1721, but had been confirmed by Catherine II (1729–96), Empress of Russia from 1762, in the Charter of Nobility of 1785.

[3] For the passages in question see *Théorie des peines et des récompenses*, ii. 7–9, 182–6, 187–9 (Bowring, ii. 194, 244–5, 245–6 respectively). Bentham used Dumont's first French edition of 1811 (see the page references in the headings on the MSS). The material on 'Pensions of Retreat' in *The Rationale of Reward* was in fact written by Dumont: see Dumont's note in *Théorie des peines et des récompenses*, ii. 187n (Bowring, ii. 245n).

[4] These drafts are headed 'Gold no antiseptic': see UC cxliii. 74 (24 October 1824); cxliii. 78–9 (28 October 1824); cxliii. 75 (29 October 1824); cxliii. 77 (29 October 1824); cxliii. 80–1 (30 October 1824); cxliii. 67–72 (31 October 1824); and cxliii. 73 (31 October 1824). UC cxliii. 75–81 were at some stage placed together and numbered sequentially by Bentham; the sequence was copied in June 1825 (see UC clxii. 119–26).

[5] See UC cxliii. 97 (20 October 1824); cxliii. 98 (20 and 29 October 1824); cxliii. 82–3 (24 October 1824), of which there is a copy at cxliii. 128–9 (21 June 1825); cxliii. 89–91 (27 October 1824); cxliii. 92–6 (27 October 1824); cxliii. 99 (27 October 1824); cxliii. 76 (28 October 1824); cxiv. 42 (29 October 1824); and cxiv. 50 (29 October 1824).

[6] UC cxliii. 66 (22 October 1824), of which there is a copy at cxliii. 63 (22 October 1824). In addition, a few sheets headed 'Cabinet Parties. Oppressionists and Depredationists' are at UC cxii. 44, cxiv. 162, 185 (5 November 1824); a sheet of 'Miscellaneous Amendments' is at cxliii. 65 (20 October 1824), with a copy at cxliii. 64 (n.d. October 1824); while a sheet of 'Rudiments' at cxiv. 64 (25 October 1824 and 4 March 1828) contains a list of some of the passages in *Théorie* on which Bentham wished to comment, together with notes on pensions of retreat, on the 'Conclusion of the whole Pasticcio' and on the proposed additional supplement to Ch. IX, §17 of *Constitutional Code* dealing with 'Aptitude is as Opulence' (see pp. xxiii–xxv below).

[7] See UC cxliii. 97 (20 October 1824) and cxliii. 92–6 (27 October 1824), sub-headed 'Equity fee encrease'. Bentham also referred to the subject at UC cxliii. 99 (27 October 1824) and cxiv. 185 (5 November 1824). There is, moreover, a sequence at BL Add. MS 33,551, fos. 101–6 (14–15 November 1824), headed 'Principles of Official Economy', which deals with the sinister implications of the law of blasphemy.

attention to *The Rationale of Reward* in June 1825, after completing the main body of the text of 'Indications respecting Lord Eldon', just as he was about to go on to compose the bulk of the Postscript to that work. This material is more exclusively concerned with the Russian Scale of Ranks and with pensions of retreat, there being three separate drafts on the former topic,[1] and three on the latter.[2] By this stage Bentham may have decided to publish a fairly limited version of his 'Corrections', consisting only of two sections composed of two sequences which had been copied. The first section, taken from material written in June 1825, dealt with 'Catherine and her Scale of Ranks', and the second section, taken from material written in October 1824, with 'Pensions of Retreat'.[3] Soon afterwards, he may have decided to exclude the 'Corrections' altogether from the pasticcio[4]—he had, of course, apparently done so by the time he drew up the list of contents on 18 January 1828.[5]

Preface

On several occasions between his conception of the volume in late 1824 and its eventual publication in the summer of 1830, Bentham drafted or organized material meant either for a preface or conclusion to the pasticcio, in which he introduced and discussed the main themes of the several Papers. The gradual emergence of 'Indications respecting Lord Eldon' from endeavours in late 1824 and early 1825

---

[1] UC cxliii. 110 (22 June 1825); cxliii. 111–15 (22–3 June 1825); and cxliii. 116–18 (23–4 June 1825), of which there is a copy at cxliii. 104–9 (n.d. June 1825). These copied sheets are part of a longer sequence (UC cxliii. 100–9), for which the original MSS corresponding to the first four sheets have not been traced.

[2] UC cxiv. 43–7 (19 June 1825); cxiv. 48–9 (25 June 1825); and cxliii. 84–8 (25–6 June 1825), of which there is a copy at cxiv. 51–6 (27 June 1825). A much later sequence on this topic is at UC cxiv. 61–3 (4 January 1827). Bentham at this time also had copies made of some of the October 1824 material, all of which he headed 'Pensions of Retreat', even though some of it belonged to the 'Gold no antiseptic' material: thus UC cxliii. 75–81 are copied at clxiii. 119–26 (n.d. June 1825) and clxiii. 82–3 at cxliii. 128–9 (21 June 1825). The original MS from which UC cxliii. 127 (21 June 1825) was copied has not been traced.

[3] See UC cxliii. 100–9 and cxliii. 119–26 respectively. There is, however, a sequence of 33 marginal summary paragraphs, for which no text appears to survive, but which apparently dealt with pensions of retreat, and which Bentham may also have intended to include: see UC cxiv. 32–4 (20 June 1825).

For Bentham's normal working practice, and the relationship between the text, marginal summaries and marginal summary sheets, see pp. xlvii–xlviii below.

[4] See his comment of 11 July 1825 at UC cxliii. 119 (the first sheet in the copy of the proposed §2): 'Matter supposed better omitted than inserted.'

[5] See pp. xvi–xvii above. Bentham did however think some of the material still worth referring to: notes at UC cxliii. 100, 127, 128 show that he reviewed the material in early 1828.

to draft a general introductory essay will be discussed below.[1] Bentham next attempted to produce a preface in January 1828, when he organized a long sequence of material from manuscripts originally intended for *Constitutional Code*, and written at various times over a period of more than two years. The earliest of these manuscripts were written in March 1825,[2] and a more substantial group in July 1825,[3] but the bulk of the material dates from April and July 1827.[4] Bentham organized the material in the following manner. Taking the corresponding marginal summary sheets,[5] he numbered the marginal summary paragraphs in sequence from 1 to 83, and then added short sub-headings. Finally he transferred some of these headings with the numbers of the appropriate marginal summary paragraphs to his plan of 18 January 1828.[6] While most of the original shorter drafts from which Bentham composed this sequence are coherent in themselves, the resulting consolidated text is fragmentary and repetitive. It seems unlikely that Bentham ever intended to publish this material in this form—perhaps the exercise was meant to help him clarify and draw together his ideas. Bentham made several more attempts to compose a preface or conclusion to the pasticcio between May and August 1828, when he wrote a series of short drafts.[7] At some stage,

---

[1] See pp. xxx–xl below.

[2] UC cxiv. 164–6 (25 March 1825), in the hand of a copyist. The corresponding marginal summary sheet is at UC cxiv. 159 (25 March 1825). This material, originally headed 'Preface for the Extract from the Constitutional Code', appears to be an early draft of the 'Introductory View' (see pp. xxii–xxiii below). A fragment from a draft 'Preliminary Advertisement' for the 'Extract' is at UC cxiv. 167 (13 July 1825). The marginal summaries for this sheet have also been copied at UC cxiv. 159.

[3] UC cxiv. 168, 170–7 (15 and 18 July 1825). The corresponding marginal summary sheet is at UC cxiv. 158 (15 July 1825).

[4] UC cxiv. 195–203 (28 April 1827), cxiv. 192–4, 204–7 (27–8 July 1827): in addition, one sheet at cxiv. 191 is dated 24 November 1827. The corresponding marginal summary sheets are at UC cxiv. 158 (15 July 1825), 160 (24 November 1827) and 161 (28 April 1827). Bentham also brought together two further short sequences. The first is composed of UC cxiv. 178 (30 June 1827), 179 (7 August 1827) and 180 (22 May 1827): the marginal summaries have been copied at cxiv. 161. The second is composed of UC cxiv. 181–2 (n.d. September, 3 October 1826) and 183 (19 July 1826): the marginal summaries have been copied at cxiv. 158.

[5] i.e. UC cxiv. 158–61.

[6] See UC cxii. 65. Following the enumeration of the marginal summary paragraphs, the order of the rearranged material is as follows: UC cxiv. 168, 170–7, 181–3, 164–7, 191–207, 178–80. An unmarginalized sequence, and therefore not incorporated in the rearranged text, headed 'Official Aptitude. Preface or Conclusion', and dealing with the retrenchment of pensions, is at UC cxiv. 188–90 (14 May 1827). A further unmarginalized sequence, also headed 'Official Aptitude. Preface or Conclusion', on the subject of 'Retrenchment', is at UC cxii. 85–7 (9 May 1827).

[7] See UC cxii. 25–42, 48–64, 177–81. The wrapper enclosing UC cxii. 23–64 (28 May 1828) is headed: 'Rudiments for a Conclusion of or Preface to the whole Pasticcio.' In chronological order, the various drafts are as follows: UC cxii. 58, 60 (25 May 1828); cxii. 48 (25, 28 May 1828); cxii. 50–1, 53, 49, 52, 55, 54, 56, 59 (27 May 1828); cxii. 45 (28 May 1828); cxii. 57 (31 May 1828); cxii. 61–4 (5 June 1828); cxii. 26–9 (8 June 1828); cxii. 30 (11 June 1828);

Bentham organized some of this material into a longer sequence, but the resulting text lacks coherence.[1]

The final group of manuscripts consisting of general introductory or concluding material dates mainly from the end of April 1830.[2] Though intended as a 'Conclusion', rather than a 'Preface',[3] these manuscripts tackle similar themes to those of the published 'Preface', which forms Paper I of the pasticcio, and possibly represent early drafts for it. No manuscripts corresponding to the published 'Preface' survive, but it was almost certainly written about this time.[4]

Extract from the proposed Constitutional Code, entitled Official Aptitude Maximized, Expense Minimized, On the Militia and *Constitutional Code:—Table of Contents*

Papers II–IV of the pasticcio were taken from the pamphlet *Extract from the proposed Constitutional Code, entitled Official Aptitude Maximized, Expense Minimized*,[5] which Bentham originally published in 1826.[6] The *Extract* consisted of an 'Introductory View', followed by

cxii. 31 (14 June 1828); cxii. 177–81 (15–16 June 1828); cxii. 25 (29 June 1828); cxii. 32 (13 July 1828); cxii. 33–4 (20 July 1828); cxii. 35–6 (24 July 1828); cxii. 37–40 (29 July 1828); cxii. 41 (15 August 1828); and cxii. 42 (17 August 1828). An earlier but related fragment is at UC cxii. 322 (4 March 1828). There are also several sheets of 'Collectanea', mainly newspaper extracts, from 1828 and 1830, at UC cxiv. 213–20.

[1] UC cxii. 44–5 are paginated A1–2; cxii. 48–53 are B1–6; cxii. 54 is C1; cxii. 55 is D1; cxii. 56 is E1; cxii. 57 is F1; cxii. 58–60 are G1–3. UC cxii. 44 (5 November 1824, 22 June 1825) was originally written for 'Corrections to *The Rationale of Reward*'.

[2] A fragment discussing the essays on Peel and Eldon is at UC cxii. 336–8 (23 April 1830); a sequence discussing Peel and law reform at cxii. 339–50 (various dates between 20 and 30 April 1830), with related fragments at cxii. 351 and 352 (29 April 1830); and a sequence on 'Depredationists and Oppressionists' at cxii. 353–6 (28 April 1830). In addition, two sheets written on 13 March 1830, sub-headed 'Conclusion?', are at UC cxii. 332–3 (a fragment dated 10 June 1828 is attached to the latter). There are also marginal summary sheets at UC cxii. 69 (23 March 1830), headed 'Preface', and cxii. 67 (17 April 1830), headed 'Preface or Introduction', but for which no corresponding text appears to survive.

[3] All of the sheets at UC cxii. 336–56 carry the sub-heading 'Conclusion' (UC cxii. 336–9 also bear the sub-heading 'Preface' or 'Preface—Introduction'). Bentham noted at the top of UC cxii. 336: '☛ 25 Apr. Put this at the close of the whole. Even after tit. *Retrenchments*.' At this stage, Bentham still apparently intended to include an essay on retrenchment (see p. xliii below).

[4] Bentham took the decision to prepare the 'Preface' for publication on 15 April 1830: see p. xliii below.

[5] The MSS written for the *Extract* (whose sub-title was of course the same as the title of the pasticcio) often bear the heading 'Official Aptitude', even though Bentham ultimately intended them for *Constitutional Code*, as do those written specifically for the pasticcio and not meant for publication elsewhere, such as the material for the preface, and the essays on public account keeping, retrenchment and remuneration.

[6] The title page is mis-dated MDCCCXVI.

the proposed Ch. IX, §§ 15−18 (including the 'Concluding Instruction to the Public Opinion Tribunal') of *Constitutional Code*. Both the 'Introductory View' and the extract from *Constitutional Code* were republished in the pasticcio, though the former was omitted from *Constitutional Code* itself.[1] There are, however, some discrepancies between the content of the three versions, and the order in which it appears.[2] Both the original *Extract* and the pasticcio contained the 'Introductory View', Ch. IX, §§ 15−17 and the 'Concluding Instruction to the Public Opinion Tribunal'. The *Extract* also contained the first three articles of a projected § 18; these articles were omitted from the pasticcio, presumably because in the meantime Bentham had composed a completely new § 18 with which he replaced them in *Constitutional Code* itself.[3] At the end of the 'Concluding Instruction' in the pasticcio, Bentham added a Supplement to § 16, followed by a Supplement to § 17 (this latter Supplement is separately paginated and entitled 'Further Extract from proposed Constitutional Code'). This arrangement was followed in Volume I of *Constitutional Code* as published by Bentham in 1830,[4] except for the addition of five articles to the end of § 17 (Arts. 37−41),[5] and therefore preceding the two Supplements.[6] In the pasticcio, Bentham divided the 'Extract' into three Papers: Paper II consisted of the 'Introductory View'; Paper III of §§ 15−17, 'Concluding Instruction to the Public Opinion Tribunal' and the Supplement to § 16; and Paper IV of 'Further Extract from proposed Constitutional Code', in other words the Supplement to § 17. The present volume includes the 'Introductory View', but excludes the extracts from *Constitutional Code*, which will be found in their place in that work.[7]

The surviving manuscripts reveal that at some stage Bentham had intended to publish an additional extract to follow the 'Further Extract' or Supplement to § 17.[8] During 1826, 1827 and 1828, he

---

[1] Note that Volume I of *Constitutional Code*, though only published in 1830, had been printed in 1827.

[2] For full details see *Constitutional Code*, I (*CW*), pp. xxxix−xl, xliii, 297n.

[3] See ibid., p. 364n. The text of the three articles from the version of § 18 in the *Extract* is reproduced in ibid., Collation D, p. 523.

[4] *Constitutional Code*, I (*CW*) follows Bowring in placing the Supplements immediately after the sections to which they appertain.

[5] There are discrepancies in the article numbers of the different versions: unless otherwise noted, the references follow the enumeration adopted in *Constitutional Code*, I (*CW*).

[6] See ibid., p. 345n.

[7] See ibid., Ch. IX, §§ 15−17, pp. 297−364, and Collation D at pp. 520−8. A *précis* of the contents of the 'Introductory View', in Bentham's hand, dated 25 April 1830, is at UC cxii. 67.

[8] i.e. to follow Ch. IX, § 17, Art. 59, at p. 362 of *Constitutional Code*, I (*CW*).

drafted a considerable amount of material,[1] from which he organized two sequences in particular. Both of these, of which the first carries the heading 'Objection 6. Aptitude is as opulence',[2] and the second 'Objection 7. Mischievousness of reduction experienced',[3] continue the 'Objections' to the public examination and pecuniary competition systems introduced in the Supplement to § 17.[4] Soon after bringing together the material dealing with 'Objection 6', Bentham decided not to include it as an integral part of the 'Extract', though he reserved judgment as to whether it might appear elsewhere in the pasticcio. In a note of 28 May 1828,[5] he explained:

On a review of the from 15 to 18 pages in MS for so long a time designed to be added in Official Aptitude to the Supplement to Ch. IX. § 17 Locable who[6] as per the print of Constitutional Code, it has been judged that it wanders too far from the list of Objections to the probationary and pecuniary-competition principles to be inserted into the matter of that list: insomuch that if employed at all in the pasticcio (the Miscellany in question) it should constitute a separate paper, under some such title as 'Further Illustrations of the axiom forming under the existing system the test of and security for Official Aptitude—namely Aptitude is as opulence.'

☛ Quere. Might not this paper be made the last in the whole *pasticcio*, for the purpose of its not being sold, but only given away to particular persons?

---

[1] This material, variously headed 'Aptitude is as opulence', 'Acceptableness', 'Mischief of reduction experienced', 'Subordination Grades', 'Examination' and 'Pecuniary Competition', is at UC xxxiv. 313–15; xxxix. 194–6, 201–38; cxii. 46–7, 182–218, 220–2, 319–21; cxiv. 35–40, 65–6, 68–86, 92–127, 184, 186–7, 200–10. Bentham also inserted two sequences originally written under the heading of 'Constitutional Code Rationale' (for this essay see *First Principles preparatory to Constitutional Code*, ed. P. Schofield, Oxford, 1989 (*CW*), pp. 227–331) into the material for 'Aptitude is as opulence': see UC cxii. 223–5 (24 September 1822) and cxii. 226–8, xxiii. 34 (27 October 1822). The corresponding marginal summary sheet is at UC cxii. 70 (this has been dated 24 September 1822, but this evidently refers to the date on the text sheets, and not the date when the marginal summaries were copied). Other sheets apparently intended for addition to the Supplement to Ch. IX, § 16 are at UC xxxix. 197–200, cxii. 43. Bentham also considered writing an essay, either for the pasticcio or as an addition to the *Extract*, on the subject of 'Degrees, as in Universities, their uselessness', but did not get beyond the title: see UC cxiv. 212 (13 August 1827). Much of this material was originally headed 'Constitutional Code', and then re-headed 'Official Aptitude': this referred to the title of the *Extract*, and not the pasticcio.

[2] See UC cxii. 183–96 (11 September 1826, 6, 8, 14 March, 25 April, 25–6 May 1828). On the first sheet of this sequence, in a note dated 23 May 1828, Bentham directed: '☛ This follows immediately from what is in print. p. 470.' The page number refers to the 1830 edition of Volume I of *Constitutional Code*. In the margin, the following note is in the hand of John Bowring (1792–1872), Bentham's disciple and literary executor: 'This should be printed with Official Aptitude as a sequel.' There are further notes in Bowring's hand at UC cxii. 188, 190, 191, 192, 198 and 207, but there is no indication of the date he surveyed this material.

[3] See UC cxii. 198–207 (12 March, 23–4 September 1826, 7 March, 29 May 1828).

[4] See *Constitutional Code*, I (*CW*), Ch. IX, § 17, Arts. 50–9, pp. 350–62.

[5] See UC cxii. 182.

[6] An error for 'Located how'.

Bentham had further doubts as to the need of publishing the material dealing with 'Objection 7', since it had possibly been superseded by a passage already printed in *Constitutional Code*.[1] Bentham also drafted a sequence on Droits of Admiralty with a view to inserting it in the *Code*.[2] Moreover, he considered the topic for inclusion in the pasticcio,[3] and went so far as to review the material when preparing the pasticcio for publication.[4] However, neither this, nor any other of the proposed additions, appeared either there or in *Constitutional Code*. A similar fate befell a short Supplement for §15 of *Constitutional Code* which Bentham composed in the spring of 1830, and which he entitled 'Mode of connection between service, or say duty, and reward'.[5]

A second extract from *Constitutional Code* which Bentham did insert in the pasticcio as Paper IX was on the subject of the militia. Bentham had mentioned the militia in his plan of 18 January 1828,[6] by which time he was in the midst of composing a lengthy discussion of the topic for Ch. X of the projected Volume II of *Constitutional Code*, a chapter which he printed in 1830 but did not publish. He did, however, publish an extract of fifteen articles in the *Morning Herald* of 27 April 1829, and this he republished, with a different introductory paragraph, in the pasticcio. The present volume includes this short introduction, but excludes the extract from *Constitutional Code*, which will be found in its place in that work.[7]

The final Paper in the volume was the 'Table of Contents' for *Constitutional Code*. As early as 25 March 1825,[8] Bentham suggested that a table of the titles of the chapters and sections of *Constitutional Code* would be incorporated with the *Extract*. In the 'Introductory View' of

---

[1] See his note of 29 May 1828 at UC cxii. 197: 'Quere whether the demand for the matter of this *Objection 7* is not already superceded by the matter of Art. 44 or 8, pp. 453. 454 (Supplement to §17. Located how) in the Constitutional Code?' i.e. Ch. IX, §17, Art. 49 at pp. 349–50 of *Constitutional Code*, I (*CW*).

[2] UC cxii. 323, 325, 324, 326–30 (28 February, 25–6 April, 1–2 May 1827). The sequence, which includes an unnumbered sheet after UC cxii. 330, was intended as a note to *Constitutional Code*, I (*CW*), Ch. IX, §17, Art. 56, p. 357. Related fragments are at UC cxiv. 87 (28 February 1827), cxii. 331 (10 May 1828) and cxii. 334 (20 April 1830).

[3] See Bentham's note to this effect of 4 March 1828 added to the plan of 18 January 1828 at UC cxii. 65.

[4] See Bentham's notes of 19 April 1830 at UC cxii. 328 and 329.

[5] The first draft, which would have comprised an additional sixteen articles (i.e. Arts. 58–73), is at BL Add. MS 33,549, fos. 143–5, 153–5 (12 March 1830), with a marginal summary sheet at fo. 184 (16 April 1830), and the second at fos. 146–52 (18 April, 1 May 1830). A related fragment, consisting of a draft of Art. 58, is at UC xxx. 174a (12 March 1830). Bentham refers to this material in the 'Preface' of the pasticcio: see pp. 15–16n below.

[6] See p. xviin above.

[7] See *Constitutional Code*, Ch. IX, §3, Arts. 21–35 (Bowring, ix. 345–8).

[8] See UC cxiv. 164.

the *Extract* reference is made to the Table being 'hereunto annexed',[1] so Bentham had at least intended it to appear there.[2] The Table presumably appeared with Volume I of *Constitutional Code* when this was printed in 1827, and certainly did so when it was published in 1830. Despite its enumeration as Paper XI, the 'Table of Contents' was in fact bound facing the title page of the pasticcio. The present volume excludes the 'Table of Contents', which will be found in its place in *Constitutional Code*.[3]

Defence of Economy against the Right Honourable Edmund Burke and *Defence of Economy against the Right Honourable George Rose*

From the first conception of the pasticcio, Bentham decided to include the two 'Defences of Economy', which he had drafted as long ago as 1810, but only published in 1817. These essays were commentaries on relatively short extracts from Edmund Burke's *Speech on Oeconomical Reformation*, which had been delivered in the House of Commons on 11 February 1780, and had then appeared in pamphlet form,[4] and from George Rose's *Observations respecting the Public Expenditure, and the Influence of the Crown*, published in 1810.[5] Very little is known about the drafting of these two essays, beyond what Bentham reveals in the respective 'Advertisements'.[6] It is possible that the appearance of Rose's pamphlet stimulated Bentham into producing his attack on what he saw as 'Tory economy', and this in turn led him to consider 'Whig economy' as it had been propounded by Burke. Bentham himself only says that the essays were written in 1810, and more specifically that 'Defence of Economy against Rose' was written in April and May of that year,[7] and that they were meant as 'a sequel to a

---

[1] See p. 23 below.

[2] It is however missing from the surviving copy of the *Extract* in the British Library, shelf-mark 6025. bb. 5.

[3] See *Constitutional Code*, I (*CW*), Table 1, prefixed to p. 1.

[4] *Speech of Edmund Burke, Esq. Member of Parliament for the City of Bristol, On presenting to the House of Commons (On the 11th of February, 1780) A Plan for the Better Security of the Independence of Parliament, and the Oeconomical Reformation of the Civil and other Establishments*. Bentham used the third edition of the pamphlet (published in 1780); his own marked copy is in the British Library, shelf-mark 08138. dd. 50 (4).

[5] Bentham used the second edition of the pamphlet (also published in 1810).

[6] See pp. 41–7, 97 below.

[7] There is however no reference in Bentham's surviving correspondence to the essays at this time, nor do there appear to be any surviving manuscripts which can be directly linked to them, apart from UC cvi. 231–5 (26 July 1810), with a corresponding marginal summary sheet at cvi. 230 (29 July 1810), which are enfolded in a wrapper headed 'Prefatoria for Defence of Economy, or New Edition to Fragment on Government' (see *A Comment on the Commentaries and A Fragment on Government*, ed. J.H. Burns and H.L.A. Hart, London, 1977 (*CW*), Introduction,

tract of no great bulk, having for its title *Hints respecting Economy*'.[1] His attention was 'called off', and the three papers left 'lying upon the shelf'.

Bentham seems to have put aside the two 'Defences' until the autumn of 1816, when his interest in publishing them, but without 'Hints respecting Economy', was reawakened. He looked over the manuscripts at the end of October and beginning of November 1816,[2] at the same time negotiating with the editor of *The Pamphleteer*, Abraham John Valpy (1787–1854), to see if he would consider them for publication. Bentham's motives for publishing the essays are unclear, though he may have been stimulated by the impending publication of *Plan of Parliamentary Reform*[3]. He did, however, explain his decision to exclude 'Hints respecting Economy':

The Defences of Economy were preceded by a part in which my principles are stated. But I do not expect to find that part ready for the press: and even if it were besides that it would make the whole affair too bulky it would not so well suit the Pamphleteer: not being so *piquant* as these attacks upon personages promise to be.[4]

Valpy quickly decided to accept 'Defence of Economy against Burke', for a week later Bentham, having made a few revisions and decided on the division of the sections and their titles, was returning the manuscripts to Koe, for him to pass on to Valpy. He drafted a short 'Advertisement or Preface' which, he said, would explain the failure to publish 'Hints respecting Economy'.[5] This he finally sent to Koe on 27 November 1816, with the comment: 'It has been a sad bore to me, but seemed a necessary one.'[6] The 'Defence of Economy against Burke', along with the 'Advertisement', was published in *The Pamphleteer* in January 1817.[7] Meanwhile, in the same month, apparently at Valpy's

p. xxxiin). It is possible that more details will emerge when a full survey is undertaken of the unpublished 'Parliamentary Reform' writings of 1809–10, to which the essays seem to be related.

[1] Both essays contain a number of references to 'Hints respecting Economy', but it was never published, nor do any MSS for it appear to survive.

[2] Bentham was at his Devonshire retreat, Ford Abbey, at this time. On 27 October 1816, he asked his secretary, John Herbert Koe (1783–1860), at Queen's Square Place, Bentham's home in Westminster, to send the two 'Defences' to him: see *The Correspondence of Jeremy Bentham*, vol. viii, ed. S. Conway, Oxford, 1988 (*CW*), p. 558.

[3] *Plan of Parliamentary Reform, in the form of a Catechism, with reasons for each article, with an Introduction, shewing the necessity of radical, and the inadequacy of moderate, reform*, London, 1817 (Bowring, iii. 433–557).

[4] See Bentham to Koe, 8–9 November 1816, *Correspondence* (*CW*), viii. 562.

[5] Bentham to Koe, 16 November 1816, ibid., 563–4.

[6] Bentham to Koe, 27 November 1816, ibid., 568. A sheet from this draft, headed 'Advertisement to Defence of Economy', but with the text crossed through, is at UC cxxviii. 2 (17 November 1816).

[7] *The Pamphleteer*, vol. ix, no. xvii (1817), 3–47.

behest, Bentham also decided to publish 'Defence of Economy against Rose' in *The Pamphleteer*.[1] This was being printed at the beginning of June 1817,[2] and was published in September 1817.[3]

Bentham had found that the principles espoused by both the Whig and the Tory statesman were in effect the same: they justified the extortion, for the benefit of the monarch and aristocracy, of the maximum amount of wealth possible from the rest of the people. These principles were in direct contradiction to his own, later put forward in *Extract from Constitutional Code*, which aimed to minimize the expense of government, as well as to maximize the aptitude of its officials. The characterization of English practice as 'things as they are', and of his own *Constitutional Code* as 'things as they ought to be', was a recurrent theme of Bentham's writings on constitutional law. It is not surprising that when planning the contents of the pasticcio, he should wish to highlight the contrast: 'Defence of Economy against Burke' therefore appeared as Paper V, and 'Defence of Economy against Rose' as Paper VI.[4]

Observations on Mr. Secretary Peel's House of Commons Speech, 21st March, 1825, introducing his Police Magistrates' Salary Raising Bill. Date of Order for Printing, 24th March 1825. Also on the Announced Judges' Salary Raising Bill, and the Pending County Courts Bill

Bentham was prompted to draft the essay which appeared as Paper VII by the speech made by the Home Secretary, Robert Peel, in the House of Commons on 21 March 1825, introducing a measure to increase the salaries of the metropolitan police magistrates and to limit their appointment to barristers of at least three-years' standing. The essay seems to have been written in early April 1825. The only surviving draft, written on 5–6 April 1825, is incomplete,[5] and considerably shorter than the printed text. Nevertheless, Bentham had already decided to organize the text around the versions of Peel's

---

[1] Bentham to Koe, 25 January 1817, *The Correspondence of Jeremy Bentham*, vol. ix, ed. S. Conway, Oxford, 1989 (*CW*), p. 8.

[2] Bentham to John Quincy Adams, 7 June 1817, ibid., 17.

[3] *The Pamphleteer*, vol. x, no. xx (1817), 281–332. Bentham however was complaining towards the end of November 1817 that he had still not seen any copies of 'Defence of Economy against Rose': see Bentham to Koe, 16 and 22 November 1817, *Correspondence* (*CW*), ix. 120, 123.

[4] The criticism of English practice was of course continued in 'Observations on Peel's Speech' and 'Indications respecting Lord Eldon'.

[5] See UC xi. 167–79.

speech which appeared in *The Times* and *Morning Chronicle* of 22 March 1825, and to append these to the essay. Moreover, the two major themes which he took up in the draft were both fully developed in the printed text: the first, that Peel had not proved his claim that the existing police magistrates were deficient in appropriate aptitude; and the second, that the alleged deficiency in attendance would not be remedied by the proposed measure, the increase in salary of £200 a year. These sheets clearly contain the embryo of the longer final essay, though for the printed text he added discussions firstly of judges' salaries, prompted by the notice given by Richard Martin (1754–1834) in the House of Commons on 2 April 1825 of his intention to introduce a bill to raise the salaries of judges, and secondly of the protracted attempts to establish a network of County Courts to deal with small debts. It is quite possible that Bentham drafted only one more version of 'Observations on Peel's Speech'. Since Bentham's practice was to destroy the drafts of material which he had printed himself, this would explain the fact that very few sheets of manuscript survive. In the event, the essay was published as a separate pamphlet in May 1825,[1] and later that year in *The Pamphleteer*.[2]

Over the next few years, Bentham was involved in a correspondence with Peel on a variety of topics related to legal reform, including the issue of judges' and police magistrates' salaries.[3] Bentham even went into print: his five letters published in the *Morning Herald* in the spring of 1828 under the pseudonym of Parcus[4] were in large part directed at Peel. These touch on many of the themes discussed in the essays included in the pasticcio, while some of the surviving related manuscripts, which include drafts for further letters, are headed 'Official Aptitude'. The Parcus letters seem to be closely related to Bentham's attempts in 1828 to compose a preface or conclusion to the pasticcio, but there is no evidence that Bentham ever intended to incorporate the letters themselves in it.

---

[1] Publication was announced in the *Morning Chronicle* of 13 May 1825. The pamphlet was sixty-two pages long, printed by C.H. Reynell, Broad Street, Golden Square, and published by John and H.L. Hunt, Tavistock Street, Covent Garden.

[2] *The Pamphleteer*, vol. xxv, no. 1 (1825), 405–43.

[3] See Bentham to Peel, 14 January 1827, BL Add. MS 40,391, fos. 83–6; Peel to Bentham, 3 February 1827, UC xi. 253; Bentham to Peel, 26 March 1827 (draft), UC xi. 263.

[4] Letter I (7 April 1828) 'Peel, Bentham, and Judges' Salaries'; Letter II (15 April 1828) 'Peel and Munificence;—Bentham and Niggardliness'; Letter III (8 May 1828) 'Peel, Tenterden, Bentham, and Law Reform'; Letter IV (28 May 1828) 'Written Pleadings Pickpocket Lies'; Letter V (29 May 1828) 'Inquiry-Splitting and Reform-Quashing Commission Jobs'. Related MSS are at UC xi. 292–331; lxxxv. 33, 43–186; cxii. 1–20, 135–8; cxiv. 128–40, 142–51; and BL Add. MS 33,549, fos.119–26 (March–July 1828).

*Indications respecting Lord Eldon, including History of
the pending Judges'-Salary-Raising Measure*

Paper VIII, 'Indications respecting Lord Eldon', is the full-scale development of a comment made in a note in 'Defence of Economy against Burke', concerning the increase of legal fees sanctioned by an Order of the Court of Chancery issued on 26 February 1807 by Lord Chancellor Erskine[1] and the Master of the Rolls, Sir William Grant,[2] which Bentham presumably picked upon when reviewing this essay for the pasticcio.[3] Bentham had originally intended to discuss this issue in a preface, either to the 'Defences of Economy' or to the pasticcio as a whole, but in the process of drafting, the material expanded into a lengthy pamphlet whose main purpose was to expose the machinations of Lord Chancellor Eldon and force his resignation from office. The composition of the 'Indications' can be roughly divided into three stages: first, from December 1824 to March 1825, when Bentham intended to include his comments on Eldon in some sort of preface;[4] second, from the middle of April to the middle of June 1825, when Bentham developed the 'Indications' as a discrete essay;[5] and third, from the middle of June to the beginning of August 1825, when Bentham drafted additional material for inclusion in a Postscript.[6]

Bentham had raised the question of judges imposing legal fees on their own authority in material written towards the end of October 1824 on the subject of pensions of retreat for the projected 'Corrections to *The Rationale of Reward*'.[7] He seems to have decided that the topic was worthy of more detailed treatment, and that he would consider it either in a preface to the pasticcio as a whole, or perhaps more particularly in a preface to the 'Defences of Economy'. The

[1] Thomas Erskine (1750–1823), first Baron Erskine, Lord Chancellor 1806–7.

[2] Grant (1752–1832), Solicitor General 1799–1801, Master of the Rolls 1801–17.

[3] For the passage see pp. 61–2n below. Bentham had a transcript made on 15 December 1824: see UC cxiv. 163. For the Chancery Order see 'Indications respecting Lord Eldon', §III, p. 212 below.

[4] The surviving MSS are usually headed 'Official Aptitude' or 'Defence of Economy': see UC xix. 33, 43–70, 73–83, 85–9, 92–113, 131–3. A related sheet of 'Rudiments' is at UC xix. 19a (15 December 1824).

[5] The surviving MSS are usually headed 'J.B. v. Eldon' or 'Indications': see UC xix. 28–9, 31, 71–2, 90–1, 114–19, 148–82, 195–6, 198–248. Related marginal summary sheets are at UC xix. 20–4. An undated and mutilated sheet at UC xix. 147 probably belongs with this material.

[6] The surviving MSS are usually headed 'Indications. Postscript': see UC xix. 138–42, 183–4, 186–94, 249–436. In addition, 'Collectanea' of various dates, mainly extracts from newspapers, are at UC xix. 1–2, 18, 25–7, 30, 32, 84, 120, 123–30, 134–7, 143–6, 185, 197.

[7] See p. xix above.

earliest surviving manuscripts which can be related to this intention were written on 11 December 1824.[1] These sheets, along with several others written intermittently during the following few weeks which carry the heading 'Comments'[2] or 'Official Aptitude. Preface',[3] contain fragmentary notes and ideas for possible development. This material makes frequent reference to Eldon, as well as to many of the themes which were later more fully developed in the 'Indications', but does not form a coherent text. The earliest surviving sequence of any length, written on 28 December 1824, consists of an 'Introduction' entitled 'Matchless Constitution—how far an entity, how far a non-entity. Main pillar, Lord Eldon—His political character and exploits'.[4] These themes however are scarcely developed, and the sequence appears to have been abandoned. Bentham made a further attempt to draft an introduction for the whole pasticcio on 26 January 1825.[5] Having repeated the substance of his 'Remarks' in *The Rationale of Reward*,[6] Bentham went on to explain the genesis of the 'Indications'.

In the course of a glance cast upon the earliest of the two tracts which regards Burke,[7] a Note was found to which some recent incidents gave a degree of importance too great to admitt of its remaining involved, and as it were buried, in the surrounding matter for want of special notice. This is the note which has for its subject-matter a case in which, by a confederacy between two Law functionaries, the power of legislation, by laws operating a denial of justice, by taxes imposed for their own benefit, was openly assumed and exercised. If any act of depredation coupled with anti-constitution insubordination could, under such a form of government as the English, be worth notice, the improvement thus made upon Ship-money[8] seemed even then one of the number. By recent occurrences, no small interest has been added to that, no small additional light thrown upon the texture of the existing Chaos. There may be seen the illegal act exercised:

---

[1] UC xix. 44–5. They are headed 'Defence of Economy. Preface', and sub-headed 'Comments. Anti-Eldoniana'. An earlier fragment, headed 'Defence of Economy against Rose. Concluding Note', at UC xix. 43 (12 November 1824), does not take up the issue of legal fees.

[2] UC xix. 46 (12 December 1824); xix. 48 (24 December 1824); xix. 49 (24 December 1824); xix. 47 (28 December 1824); xix. 51 (28 December 1824).

[3] UC xix. 63 (15 December 1824); xix. 64 (17 December 1824); xix. 65 (17 December 1824); xix. 60 (22 December 1824); xix. 61 (22 December 1824); xix. 62 (22 December 1824); xix. 59 (30 December 1824); xix. 66 ([. . . ?] January 1825); xix. 67 (7 January 1825). See also UC xix. 58 (15 December 1824), which carries the main heading 'Official Aptitude. Preface', but also the sub-heading 'Comments. Anti-Eldoniana', and xix. 50 (30 December 1824), which is headed 'Constitutional Code', but contains notes on Eldon.

[4] UC xix. 52–7.

[5] UC xix. 68–70.

[6] See pp. xviii–xix above.

[7] i.e. 'Defence of Economy against Burke'.

[8] The ancient tax revived in 1634 by Charles I (1600–49), King of England, Scotland and Ireland from 1625, but declared illegal by the Ship Money Act of 1640 (17 Car. I, c.14).

now may be seen, and from the same bench, with the addition of others, the illegality of the act confessed and in the same breath the act exercised and persistence in it declared; by a Chancellor of Great Britain, avowedly seconded and imitated by other Judges, legislative power openly assumed and the powers of Parliament set at nought.

There stands the position: comes now the proof.

Though the draft is abandoned at this point, Bentham clearly intended to follow it with an essay along the lines eventually developed in the 'Indications'.

For some time thereafter Bentham's attempts to draft material remained spasmodic. The most substantial sequence, dated 8 February 1825,[1] discussed a theme that Bentham in the end decided to exclude from the 'Indications': the resignation of Charles Runnington (1751–1821) from the office of Chief Commissioner of Insolvency in 1819.[2] According to Bentham, Runnington had been forced to resign because he had imposed fees upon suitors without authority from Parliament. Yet this was precisely what Eldon had done—'what did he but copy the example that had been set him by Lord Eldon?' However in this case, the abuse had become notorious, and a scapegoat was required, so Runnington was sacrificed, and an 'alledged' remedy—increasing the number of the commissioners—not an effective one, applied.[3] In the early months of 1825 Bentham was nevertheless busily acquiring information and material for his exposure of Eldon.[4] For instance, having perused the sixth volume of Vesey's *Chancery Reports*,[5] he composed on 13 March 1825 a commentary on remarks made by Eldon in 1801 on the law of bank-

---

[1] UC xix. 85–9, 73–83. Other fragments from about this time, mainly concerned with bringing about Eldon's resignation from office, are at UC xix. 99 (7, 23 February 1825); xix. 92 (8 February 1825); xix. 93–5 (8 February 1825); xix. 96–8 (10 February 1825).

[2] Runnington's conduct in the Insolvent Debtors Court had been investigated by the Select Committee on Acts respecting Insolvent Debtors. Their Report, which noted that Runnington had established a system of fees, 'a considerable share of which he has appropriated to himself', recommended that all fees in the Court should be abolished, and that three Commissioners should be appointed in place of one (see *Commons Sessional Papers* (1819) ii. 321–536, especially 325–6, 467–8). Runnington, it seems, in consequence resigned and the Court was restructured according to the Committee's recommendations (see 1 Geo. IV, c.119).

[3] Another theme left undeveloped in the printed text—the expense of having documents authenticated by the Great Seal and the related profits arising to officials—was dealt with in a draft of 5 March 1825 at UC xix. 33–7.

[4] In particular from his former secretary, John Herbert Koe, who by this time was a practising barrister, but also from Henry Bickersteth (1783–1851), later Baron Langdale, a Chancery lawyer and subsequently Master of the Rolls, and Samuel Hawtayne Lewin (d. 1840), a Sworn or Sixty Clerk in the Court of Chancery (see the correspondence at UC xix. 5–17, 121–2, 124b and BL Add. MS 33,546, fos. 38, 41–2).

[5] Francis Vesey, Jun., *Reports of Cases argued and determined in the High Court of Chancery*, vol. VI, London, 1803: see especially pp. 1–5, 429–34.

ruptcy,[1] and on the following day on the passage from Eldon's remarks of 8 August 1801 in the case of *Ex-parte* Leicester.[2] This latter sequence is significant in that it contains in embryo the substance of the published 'Indications'. Bentham points out that 'to exercise a dispensing power over acts of Parliament—to give effect to it when it suits his purposes, to disobey and frustrate it when it stands in the way of his purposes' was, with Eldon, 'a settled principle'. Eldon's remarks revealed a 'design to assume arbitrary power', with the extortion of money for its object. Moreover, Bentham incorporated into this draft information he had gathered on the history of Eldon's 'principle' from James Lowe's *Observations on Fees in Courts of Justice*, which he had also just been reading.[3] The government which had allowed its authority to be trampled upon by Eldon, claimed Bentham, was not his dupe, but his accomplice:

It sits still and, if it has not actually employed him, willingly and purposely suffers him clandestinely and irregularly to do with the minimum of trouble that which fear or shame or indolence would have prevented it from doing openly by its own authority and with its own hands.

He went on to suggest that the 'leprosy' had spread to the other Westminster Hall benches—public evidence showed that it had spread to the Court of the Exchequer, and he surmised that it had extended to King's Bench and Common Pleas as well.

Just as the essay was beginning to take recognizable shape, Bentham seems to have turned his attention elsewhere, in part to the drafting of 'Observations on Peel's Speech'. Bentham's return to Eldon and the question of legal fees at the end of April 1825 marked, however, the second stage in the development of the essay, for instead of incorporating the material in a preface to the pasticcio, he began to draft it as a discrete work.[4] Moreover, for the first time, he

---

[1] UC xix. 131–3. In a further fragment, entitled 'Not influenced by the money—Impossible?', Bentham suggests that Eldon's proposal for affidavits to prevent bankruptcy fraud was motivated by the profit he would thereby acquire: see UC xix. 112–13 (16 March 1825).

[2] UC xix. 100–11. The theme is developed in 'Indications respecting Lord Eldon', §IX, pp. 224–5 below.

[3] Bentham's comments on this pamphlet, which had been printed in 1822 but remained unpublished, and of which Bentham had acquired an incomplete copy through Koe, are at UC xix. 38–42 (10 March 1825). For Bentham's use of it see 'Indications respecting Lord Eldon', §X, pp. 225–30 below.

[4] Two sheets headed 'Official Aptitude. Preface. Eldon', and sub-headed 'Comments' (originally 'Beginning') are at UC xix. 71–2 (22, 24 April 1825), but thereafter the MSS are usually headed 'J.B. v. Eldon' or 'Indications'. The earliest sheet with the heading 'J.B. v. Eldon', at UC xix. 114 (26 April 1825), appears to be a fragment from a sequence now lost dealing with the Chancery Order of 26 February 1807. The decision to develop the material on Eldon in a separate essay, and not as part of a general preface, may therefore have been taken at this time.

devoted great energy and a considerable proportion of his time to the project. It is quite possible that Bentham made a complete draft of the essay at the end of April and beginning of May. The surviving manuscripts from this period are mainly either fragmentary or contain drafts for sections which were eventually excluded from the printed text. They do however include a substantial early draft for §§ VIII–XII of the printed text,[1] although a long preceding sequence of fifteen pages appears to have been lost or destroyed, or possibly incorporated into the final draft.[2] Comparing this draft with the printed text, Bentham considerably expanded §§ VIII and X–XII, though he shortened § IX, which contained his comments on Eldon's remarks in *Ex-parte* Leicester. There also survives a projected 'Continuation' to this draft (i.e. to § XII of the printed text) entitled 'Infection spread: Runnington', which takes up the theme of Runnington's resignation from the Insolvency Court.[3]

The final draft of the 'Indications' was probably written around the middle of May 1825. The manuscripts which survive from this time can be divided into two groups: the first is material which Bentham appears to have discarded from the final text, because he decided either to re-write it or simply to exclude it (that these are the only manuscripts which survive is consistent with Bentham's habit of destroying manuscripts which he published himself); and the second is material intended for a 'Supplement' or 'Conclusion' to the essay. Amongst the first group of manuscripts, one short sequence, apparently written as part of the final draft, but then excluded from the

---

[1] UC xix. 148–62 (30 April–1 May 1825). UC xix. 148–57 form '§ 7. The illegality was avowed by him [Eldon] while continuing it', the substance of which corresponds to §§ VIII–X in the printed text, and xix. 158–62 form '§ 8. By him the other Chief Judges were purposely infected with the same corruption', which corresponds to §§ XI–XII. A sheet is missing between UC xix. 148 and 149: this probably contained a copy of the report made by Koe of the case 'Donnison v. Currie' (see 'Indications respecting Lord Eldon', § VIII, p. 222 below), which was presumably transferred to a later draft. A further sheet is missing between UC xix. 158 and 159: this probably contained a copy of the case 'In the matter of Salisbury' from R.V. Barnewall and E.H. Alderson, *Reports of Cases argued and determined in the Court of King's Bench*, vol. V, London, 1822 (see 'Indications respecting Lord Eldon', § XII, pp. 231–2 below), which was again presumably transferred to a later draft. A further fragment which is possibly part of this draft is at UC xix. 196, 195 (27 April 1825), paginated 42–3 respectively. This is sub-headed '§ 11. The illegality avowed. Abbot', and seems closest in sense to part of § XII of the printed text. Other fragments which may also be related to this draft are at UC xix. 115 (28 April 1825), discussing William Hawkins' exegesis of the Common Law on bribery and corruption in his *Treatise of the Pleas of the Crown* (this is dealt with in §§ VI–VII of the printed text), and xix. 116 (28 April 1825), discussing the Act of 1822 (3 Geo. IV, c.69) enabling the Judges to impose fees on their own authority (dealt with in § XIII of the printed text).

[2] UC xix. 148–62 are paginated 16, 18–31 respectively.

[3] UC xix. 117–19 (1 May 1825). A related fragment on Runnington is at UC xix. 90–1 (27 April 1825). Bentham did not in the end incorporate this material into the main sequence.

printed text,[1] is the earliest material which carries the heading 'Indications respecting Lord Eldon'. Other material which Bentham seems to have re-written was intended for the introductory section to the 'Indications'. Two drafts survive, of which the first is headed 'Occasion—Subject—Object—Facts'.[2] Bentham here outlines the evils of a fee system supported by sinister interests, and proposes 'the entire substitution of salary to fees in the case of all Officers employed in judicature, especially under the Westminster Hall Judges'. The title of the second draft, 'Facts indicated—facts real or supposed—subjects for enquiry by a competent tribunal',[3] matches closely that eventually adopted in §I of the printed text.

The second group of manuscripts, mainly fragmentary, was intended for a 'Supplement' or 'Conclusion' to the 'Indications'.[4] A plan of 22 May 1825 shows that Bentham proposed to write a further four sections for this Supplement: '§16 or 1. Amendment proposed—Buy off all fees. §17 or 2. Mr Robinson's Judges' Salary-raising Speech. §18 or 3. Lord Eldon's Commission of enquiry, and Commissioners. §19 or 4. Mr Brougham's Antiseptic plan.'[5] The numbering of these additional sections suggests that by this date Bentham's draft contained fifteen sections, though it should be pointed out that his

---

[1] See UC xix. 163–7 (16 May 1825), paginated 26–30 respectively. The first sheet carries the following note of 25 May 1825: 'Quere whether to employ?' The sequence consists of an imaginary dialogue between Eldon and the Chairman of a House of Commons Committee enquiring into Eldon's conduct in regard to the levying of fees. In the final sheet, Bentham remarks: 'Mr Lowe, be it remembered, at the beginning of this section, is stated as a gentleman capable of giving, in relation to these doubts of Lord Eldon's, instructive information'. This places the sequence at the end of §X of the printed text, in which Bentham introduces Lowe. Moreover, Bentham goes on to say that he will discuss the case of Salisbury in the next section but one, which he actually does in §XII of the printed text.

Two further sheets which may have belonged to the final draft are at UC xix. 230 and 229b (17 May 1825), paginated '35' and '38' respectively. These sheets are both sub-headed '§10. Swindling, profit by', and seem therefore related to §XIV of the printed text (of which Bentham's running-heading is 'Swindling connived at and profited by').

[2] UC xix. 168–75, 177, 176 (22–3, 25 May 1825). The first sheet of the sequence is missing. The corresponding marginal summary sheets are at UC xix. 22–3 (23 May 1825).

[3] UC xix. 178–82 (25 May 1825). At the head of the first sheet, Bentham noted: 'Supposed Superceded.'

[4] UC xix. 200 (17 May 1825), xix. 199 (18 May 1825) are sub-headed 'Conclusion'; xix. 201 (19 May 1825), xix. 214 (20 May 1825) are sub-headed 'Supplement'; xix. 198 (18 May 1825) is sub-headed 'Supplement' and 'Conclusion'. The only coherent sequence, at UC xix. 201–4 (19 May 1825), deals with the Royal Commission on Chancery practice established in 1824.

[5] See UC xix. 226. The title of §17 refers to the speech delivered by Frederick John Robinson (1782–1859), later first Viscount Goderich and first Earl of Ripon, Chancellor of the Exchequer 1823–7, in the House of Commons on 16 May 1825 on the proposal to increase the salaries of judges; and that of §19 appears to refer to the motion made in the House of Commons on 20 May 1825 by Henry Peter Brougham (1778–1868), later first Baron Brougham and Vaux, that the proposed salaries of the puisne judges be reduced and that their promotion to the Chief Justiceships be prevented (see *Parliamentary Debates* (1825) xiii. 804–12).

enumeration is often misleading.[1] Bentham noted that §§16 and 17 should be 'postponed' until the next session of Parliament, and that §18 should be 'discarded'. In the event, Bentham made little progress with the proposed §18:[2] none at all with §19; while the subject-matter of §16 was taken up in §3 of the Postscript,[3] and §17 briefly in §§IV and XVI of the printed text.[4] Nevertheless some material does survive for these latter two sections. A short sequence on 'Robinson's Speech' deals with the denial of justice caused by legal fees, and the iniquities of leaving offices in the gift of Judges while abolishing their sale.[5] In a draft for the projected §16, sub-headed 'Buy off the fees', Bentham recommended the payment of ample compensation to those who profited by legal fees, thereby placing some limit to the amount of depredation which might be committed by them.[6]

There is, finally, a draft (27 May 1825) and copy (10 June 1825) of the section titles of the 'Indications'.[7] This suggests that the final draft of the text had been substantially completed by the end of May, and presumably a fair copy was prepared soon afterwards. Indeed, in a letter to Sir Francis Burdett (1770–1844) of 12 June 1825, Bentham mentions that the text was at that moment being printed, and that he hoped to be able to send him the first ten sections on the following day, with the rest to follow soon afterwards.[8] Even at this late stage, however, Bentham was considering some adjustments and additions. Most significantly, it seems likely that §XIX was drafted around this time.[9]

---

[1] Moreover, as noted below, there is evidence that Bentham at a later stage altered the ordering of §§XII–XVIII; therefore, even if he had written fifteen sections, it is unclear whether these would correspond to the first fifteen sections of the printed text.

[2] Only the few sheets mentioned above, i.e. UC xix. 201–4, deal with this topic.

[3] See Appendix A, pp. 307–33 below.

[4] See pp. 213, 251 & n below.

[5] UC xix. 205, 207–12 (18–19 May 1825). Related fragments are at UC xix. 213 (22 May 1825) and xix. 206 (31 May 1825). The relative merits of the sale and gift of offices is discussed in Appendix A, Postscript §3, pp. 307–33 below.

[6] See UC xix. 215–25 (21 May 1825). A later fragment on this topic is at UC xix. 237 (9 June 1825).

[7] The draft, in the hand of Richard Doane but bearing substantial emendations by Bentham, is at UC xix. 29 and the copy at xix. 28. The draft reveals that §§II and X were later additions to the text, and that the sections published as XII–XVIII were originally ordered 14, 15, 17, 13, 18, 16 and 12 respectively. A similar list of the section titles appears in §I of the printed text (see pp. 205–6 below).

Doane (1805–48) had entered Bentham's service in 1819 to be trained as his amanuensis, and remained with him until 1831: he entered the Inner Temple in 1824 and was called to the bar in 1830.

[8] Bentham to Burdett, 12 June 1825, Bodleian Library, MS Eng. lett. d. 97, fos. 8–9. Two days later, Bentham had received this first part of the printed text: Bentham to Burdett, 14 June 1825, ibid., fo. 10.

[9] On the draft plan (UC xix. 29), §19 is entitled: 'How the last hand is putting, or has been put, to the Judge and C⁰· Joint Stock Company's concern by Mr Robinson's Judges' Salary-raising

The only surviving sheet of manuscript for this section, containing the draft of the note and accompanying sub-note dealing with perjury, is dated 14 June 1825.[1] The whole of the first nineteen sections had been printed soon afterwards, since a review appeared in the *Morning Chronicle* of 18 June 1825.[2] Note that this version of the pamphlet, which did not contain the Postscript, appears to have been privately circulated by Bentham, but was not published.[3]

The third and final stage, therefore, in the drafting of the 'Indications', from the middle of June to the beginning of August 1825, saw Bentham working on additional material for the Postscript. The stimulus for the two sections which were printed and published came from the two pamphlets particularly discussed in §1,[4] and from Eldon's speech in the House of Lords on 27 June 1825 in the debate on the increase of judges' salaries, on which §2 forms a commentary. These sources provided Bentham with additional 'indications'. His initial strategy may have been to insert the matter he thought pertinent into §II of the main text,[5] but the material soon expanded into a separate section. An initial draft, an emended copy, and a second copy containing further emendations survive for §1 of the

Scheme.' On the fair copy (UC xix. 28), however, Bentham inserted a new §19, entitled 'Character Evidence', which corresponds to §XIX in the printed text, while the section on the salary-raising scheme was re-numbered §20. This projected §20 did not appear in the printed text (the theme is developed in Appendix A, Postscript §3, pp. 307–33 below). The new §19 was therefore added to the list of contents after 10 June 1825.

[1] See UC xix. 31 (the corresponding printed text is at p. 266n below). Other potential additions or amendments were written under the heading of 'Joint-stock', and therefore related to §XVII of the printed text. The most substantial sequence is at UC xix. 240–7 (12 June 1825), but a few other fragments survive: xix. 231 (6 June 1825); xix. 239 (12 June 1825); and xix. 248 (13 June 1825). This material deals with the limits to which the profits from fees could be increased, the need to replace the fee system with salaries, and the opposition which any such proposal would meet from the confederacy of sinister interests. A further batch of material, in a very fragmentary form, is headed 'Swindling continued' and therefore related in content to §XIV of the printed text. One sheet, UC xix. 227, dates from as early as 29 May 1825, but the remainder were written on 9–10 June 1825: see xix. 228 (in the hand of a copyist), xix. 232–3, xix. 234, xix. 235–6, and xix. 238.

[2] It is unclear how the text came to the newspaper since Bentham claimed that the article appeared 'without authority or expectation' on his part (see Postscript §2, p. 275 below).

[3] It was eighty-five pages long and printed by C.H. Reynell, Broad Street, Golden Square, for John and H.L. Hunt, Tavistock Street, Covent Garden.

[4] Namely *Review of the Delays and Abuses occasioned by the Constitution and Present Practice of the Court of Chancery; with practical hints as to the remedy: in a Letter to the Commissioners of Inquiry*, London, 1825, and *A Letter to the Right Honourable Robert Peel; upon the delays in the Court of Chancery. By a Member of Gray's Inn*, London, 1825.

[5] The earliest surviving sheet, at UC xix. 229a (6 June 1825), containing a draft outline of §1 of the Postscript, is headed 'Samples Inserenda'. It should be noted that Bentham at first intended his commentary on Eldon's speech to form §1 of the Postscript, and 'Samples continued' to form §2. For the sake of clarity, the final enumeration is adopted here.

Postscript,[1] while a draft and emended copy survive for § 2.[2] Apart from minor differences in punctuation and capitalization, the final emended copies for both sections bear a very close resemblance to the printed Postscript. It is possible that a further fair copy of this material, now lost, was made and sent to the printer. However it seems more likely that these very sheets were sent, since one of them contains an instruction for the printer.[3] Bentham would have been unlikely to add this to a manuscript he did not intend the printer to see. Moreover, the instruction reveals that the manuscripts were sent to the press on 22 July 1825, the same day apparently that the final copies of both sections were at least surveyed, if not corrected, by Bentham.[4] It seems unlikely that there would have been sufficient time to make a further fair copy. If this is the case, the survival of these manuscripts is highly unusual in that Bentham almost invariably destroyed both drafts and copies of the material he himself sent to the printer. The full version of the pamphlet, containing the nineteen sections of the main text and two sections of the Postscript, was finally published at the beginning of August 1825.[5] When the pamphlet was republished at the beginning of 1826 in *The Pamphleteer*, the Postscript was excluded.[6]

Between late June and early August 1825 Bentham drafted other material for the Postscript which he did not print or publish, but from which the two sections which appear below in Appendix A have been extracted.[7] His earliest attempts, however, remained largely un-

[1] The draft is at UC xix. 138–42 (6, 8 June 1825), the emended copy at xix. 249–53 (9–10 June 1825), and the second copy at xix. 270–4 (n.d. July 1825).

[2] The draft is at UC xix. 254–69 (3, 7–9 July 1825), and the copy at xix. 275–93 (n.d. July 1825). The draft is incomplete to the extent that an extract from the *Morning Herald* of 2 December 1824 (see pp. 281–4 below) has been removed and placed in the copy (see UC xix. 284–5). A related fragment, very heavily crossed through, is at UC xix. 194 (2 July 1825). A further fragment, containing comments on Eldon's speech of 27 June 1825, but also touching on some of the themes developed in §4 of the Postscript, is at UC xix. 328–30 (19 July 1825).

[3] See UC xix. 275. In the instruction, Bentham informs the printer that the text for a note which he wished to insert 'will be sent tomorrow July 23ᵈ.' The draft for this note, which was not in fact printed, is at UC xix. 332 (22 July 1825). The text is reproduced at p. 274n below.

A draft for a further proposed note, which also remained unprinted, is at UC xix. 331 (21 July 1825), with an emended copy at xix. 398 (n.d. July 1825). The text is reproduced at p. 281n below.

[4] See UC xix. 270 and 287 which have been so dated by Bentham.

[5] Publication was announced in the *Morning Chronicle* of 2 August 1825. The pamphlet was 110 pages long (unlike the version which appeared in the pasticcio, the whole pamphlet was continuously paginated), printed by C. and W. Reynell, Broad Street, Golden Square, and published by Robert Heward, Wellington Street, Strand.

[6] See *The Pamphleteer*, vol. xxvi, no. li (1826), 1–55.

[7] For the MSS used in the text see the Table of Manuscripts, p. xlix below. Some related fragments are referred to in editorial footnotes accompanying the text. The MSS are usually headed 'Indications', and sub-headed 'Postscript'.

developed. On 30 June 1825, for instance, he wrote two sequences entitled 'J.B.'s Apology for attacking Judges'.[1] He felt compelled to answer the criticism that by undermining respect for the judges, he was undermining obedience to their mandates, and thus the security of the people 'for every thing that is dear to them'.[2] His response was that any reverence felt towards judges under the present legal system would only encourage them in pursuing their own sinister interests to the detriment of the general interest, and thereby exclude any reform. The main benefit of his 'exposure' of the judges lay in 'destroying the weight of their authority in so far as opposed to any such changes as may be necessary to prevent their continuance' in their practices of extortion. Similarly incomplete was material headed 'Writs of Error'.[3] This again touches on the evil effects of the reverence offered to judges, as well as the question of the sale and gift of legal offices remunerated by fees, but concentrates on the debate in the House of Lords on 28 June 1825 on the measure for preventing frivolous Writs of Error (enacted as 6 Geo. IV, c.96), and in particular Eldon's objection to the measure on the grounds that, even though Writs of Error were an evil, their abolition would produce greater evil still.

Bentham went on, nevertheless, to compose the material presented here as §4 of the Postscript.[4] He wrote the second part of the section on 11 July 1825, and the preceding part a few days later.[5] Bentham was perhaps stimulated to write this section by reading the pamphlets he discusses,[6] but perhaps also by the recognition of the need to propose some way of achieving legal reform now that his 'exposure' had been made. About the same time, he began to compose material in response to the debates in Parliament concerning the judges' salaries Bills, and in particular the intention of ministers, in judicial offices in general, to leave present incumbents in possession of their fees, and not to abolish fees on the death of incumbents

---

[1] UC xix. 304–7 and xix. 295–302 respectively.

[2] See Bentham's note of 11 July 1825 at UC xix. 298: 'This may be revised for defence of J.B. in case of an attack on him upon this ground.' The point had been made by Edward Burtenshaw Sugden (1781–1875), later first Baron Saint Leonards, in his *A Letter to John Williams, Esq. M.P. In reply to his observations upon the abuses of the Court of Chancery*, London, 1825, pp. 3, 20. Bentham discusses this pamphlet in §4 of the Postscript, pp. 333–41 below.

[3] Drafts on this subject are at UC xix. 191–3 (29 June 1825); xix. 186–90 (1 July 1825); and xix. 183–4 (2 and 7 July 1825).

[4] Bentham originally intended this to form §3 of the Postscript, but when reviewing the material on 19 July 1825 he indicated that it was 'to be revised and printed as the concluding Section' (see UC xix. 318).

[5] See the Table of Manuscripts, p. xlix below.

[6] Namely *A Letter to the Right Honourable Robert Peel; upon the delays in the Court of Chancery. By a Member of Gray's Inn*; Sugden, *A Letter to John Williams*; and *An Inquiry into the Causes of the Delay, attending proceedings in the Court of Chancery*, London, 1824.

but to transfer them to the account of the public.[1] Under the general heading of 'Warning—Gift worse than Sale', he composed an initial draft on 12 July 1825,[2] and a second draft on 23 July 1825,[3] before writing the more extensive body of material which is presented here as §3 of the Postscript. Though a plan for this section, drawn up by Bentham on 26 July 1825,[4] includes many of the themes discussed in the surviving manuscripts, the ordering is difficult to reconcile with them. The organization of the text is therefore conjectural, based in part on the dates of drafts and page numbers, but most importantly on internal evidence. In his introduction, Bentham puts forward four propositions, for each of which some relevant material survives. The text has therefore been structured around these four points. Bentham decided not to publish this additional material until the new session of Parliament:[5] by the time Parliament reassembled on 2 February 1826, he presumably had more pressing concerns, and these manuscripts remained undisturbed.

On Public Account Keeping

The final essay in the pasticcio to be drafted was Paper X, 'On Public Account Keeping'. A controversy had arisen when a Treasury Commission established to investigate the practice of keeping accounts in government departments had produced both a majority and dissenting minority report.[6] Though Bentham admitted that he was no expert on the technical terminology of account-keeping (indeed it was the fact that the terminology of account-keeping was so technical that Bentham identified as the root of the problem), the whole issue of government record-keeping had been of great concern to him when drafting *Constitutional Code*.[7] Bentham's interest in the controversy seems to have been awakened by reading Sir Henry Brooke Parnell's

---

[1] See UC xix. 333 (23 July 1825). By the time Bentham was writing, the Bills incorporating these measures (6 Geo. IV, cc.82–4) had received the Royal Assent: see 'Indications respecting Lord Eldon', §I, p. 205n below.

[2] UC xix. 308–9, 311–12, 374, 313–16. This draft is incomplete. Moreover, UC xix. 374 was at some stage removed by Bentham, and inserted into another sequence headed 'Transference', dealing with the problems of transferring the profits of fees from the functionaries receiving them to the account of the public: see xix. 371–5 (12, 27, 30 July, 1 August 1825).

[3] UC xix. 333–7. The title of this sequence, 'Warning—intended system of abuse anticipated', has been adopted for the section title in the text. Related fragments are at UC xix. 339 (24 July 1825); xix. 356 (24 July 1825); xix. 338 (25 July 1825); and xix. 355 (25 July 1825).

[4] UC xix. 294.

[5] See his note at UC xix. 308: '☛ Postpone this to near the meeting of Parliament?'

[6] See 'On Public Account Keeping', p. 293n below.

[7] See *Constitutional Code*, I (*CW*), Ch. IX, §7 Statistic function, pp. 218–67.

work, *On Financial Reform*, which had been published early in 1830, and which supported the introduction of the Italian or double-entry system of book-keeping.[1] At the end of March and beginning of April 1830, Bentham drafted two long letters to John Charles Herries on the subject, in which he offered his services in drawing up a non-technical language for use in government accounts.[2] The themes he developed there were taken up in the material drafted for the pasticcio, probably in early May 1830. Though no draft which corresponds to the printed text survives, there does exist material for two, presumably earlier, drafts.[3] The first draft, consisting of a sequence of seven manuscript sheets, seems complete in itself.[4] The organization of the second draft is more complex. Bentham in the first place composed a 'Preface' consisting of two sheets,[5] and then wrote two further sequences to replace the second of these sheets.[6] Finally he drafted a further sequence of seven sheets to follow on from either of the alternatives.[7]

On Retrenchment and *On the mode of Remuneration as between Salary and Fees*

At the end of May and beginning of June 1828, Bentham turned his attention to the related themes of government retrenchment and

---

[1] Bentham's marked copy of this work is in the British Library, shelf-mark Cup. 403. a. 37: his inscription is dated 23 February 1830.

Parnell (1776–1842), later first Baron Congleton, Secretary at War 1831–2, Treasurer of the Navy 1835–6, Paymaster-General 1835–41, had been Chairman of the Select Committee on Public Income and Expenditure of 1828 whose recommendation had led to the establishment of the Treasury Commission.

[2] See UC x. 222–43 (31 March, 3, 9 April 1830) and x. 244–9 (12 April 1830) respectively: it is unclear whether copies of either of these were sent.

Herries (1778–1855), Chancellor of the Exchequer 1827–8, Master of the Mint 1828–30, President of the Board of Trade 1830, had considerable expertise in government finance, and had been an active member of Parnell's Select Committee.

[3] See UC cxii. 357–85. Most of these sheets carry the main heading 'Official Aptitude', and are sub-headed 'Book-keeping' or 'Italian Book-keeping'. The undated wrapper enclosing this material carries the following description: 'Official Aptitude &c. Paper 9. On Public Account-keeping.' It is possible that this essay replaced the projected essay on retrenchment as Paper IX, to be displaced in turn by the extract on the militia (see p. xlvn below).

[4] UC cxii. 369–75 (5 May 1830). The corresponding marginal summary sheet is at UC cxii. 357 (7 May 1830).

[5] UC cxii. 359, 365 (7–8 May 1830). A copy of UC cxii. 359, with emendations in Bentham's hand, is at UC cxii. 358, 364 (8 May 1830).

[6] Firstly, UC cxii. 376–8 (8 May 1830); and secondly, cxii. 361–3 (9 May 1830), which appears to be abandoned.

[7] UC cxii. 379–85, 368 (9 May 1830): the first and last of these sheets are sub-headed 'Conclusion'. The final sheet contains a few notes but no text. In addition, there are related fragments at UC cxii. 366 (7 May 1830); cxii. 367 (8 May 1830); and cxii. 360 (17 May 1830, though this may be a slip for 7 May 1830).

official remuneration, with a view to inserting essays on these subjects in the pasticcio. In the event, Bentham did not publish this material, but since it includes two essays which are relatively complete and coherent, they are included in the present edition in Appendices B and C. Bentham had been planning an ambitious and wide-ranging essay on the subject of retrenchment as early as 15 March 1828, when he had drawn up a list of 'Subject-matters or say sources of retrenchment' to be inserted 'at the end of the Official aptitude Pasticcio'.[1] He listed the following topics for possible consideration: 1. the Militia; 2. Retired allowances; 3. Diplomatic Agents; 4. Boards; 5. Colonies or Colonial Military Establishments; 6. Droits of Admiralty; 7. Remuneration—Salary or Fees; and finally 8. 'On Retrenchment—what modes eligible etc.' The essay composed by Bentham between 2 and 9 June 1828, and presented below in Appendix B, corresponds to this final topic.[2] Bentham initially organized the material into one continuous sequence.[3] He then drew up a plan of the material on 9 June 1828,[4] by which time he had decided to exclude two sequences of text. One sequence, on the disappointment-prevention principle,[5] is repetitive of matters discussed elsewhere in the essay, and has therefore also been excluded from the present text. The other sequence deals with the history of the principle of utility,[6] but because of its interest and coherence, it has been reinstated in its original place in the text. The plan of 9 June 1828 divides the remaining material into twelve sections. The section titles are followed by the appropriate marginal summary paragraph numbers. These have been collated with the text sheets, by means of the marginal summary sheets, and the appropriate text assigned to each section.[7]

---

[1] See UC cxii. 23. A further sheet containing notes on judges' salaries and pensions, sub-headed 'Retrenchment. Superannuation', is at UC cxii. 66 (18 March 1828).

[2] The relevant MSS are at UC lxi. 58–66, cxii. 139–76. The corresponding marginal summary sheets are at UC cxii. 71–4, 77, 79–80: cxii. 80 is copied at cxii. 78, with additions by Bentham. A related sequence, headed 'Retrenchment. Introduction', is at UC cxii. 88–91 (10 June 1828).

[3] UC cxii. 139–69, lxi. 58–66, cxii. 170–6 are paginated 1, 1*, 2–5, 5*, 6–38, 41–7 respectively. Pages 39–40 have not been traced.

[4] See UC cxii. 68.

[5] UC lxi. 58–66 (7–8 June 1828). The corresponding marginal summary sheet is at UC cxii. 74 (7 June 1828). At some stage Bentham transferred these sheets from the 'Official Aptitude' material to that intended for his 'Law Amendment' project.

[6] UC cxii. 146–54. The corresponding marginal summary sheets are at UC cxii. 72, 77 (3 June 1828). Bentham considered this sequence to be 'a digression from the subject of *Retrenchment*', and thus proposed that it 'be discarded from that subject' (see his note at UC cxii. 146). A separate plan for this material, attached to UC cxii. 71, divides the essay into two chapters, each with two sections, and makes substantial alterations to the order. However, since this new order renders the text incoherent, it has not been adopted. Bentham may have intended to replace this sequence with UC cxii. 145, which is reproduced at p. 346n below.

[7] For the MSS used in the text see the Table of Manuscripts, p. xlix below.

When Bentham finally came to prepare the pasticcio for publication in the spring of 1830, he reviewed this material but decided not to use it,[1] instead drafting new material on the subject of retrenchment. He made little progress, composing a total of four short drafts, each of which is probably incomplete, plus a few fragments.[2] On 15 April 1830, however, he took the decision to exclude any full-scale treatment of retrenchment from the pasticcio, because of the delay which would otherwise result in its publication, though he mentioned the possibility of including it in a second edition. He decided instead to concentrate on preparing the 'Preface' to the whole pasticcio.[3] Bentham may still have intended to publish a short essay on retrenchment, much more limited in scope than the scheme envisaged in March 1828. On 22 April 1830, he noted his earlier intention to include in the pasticcio 'a short survey of the whole Official Establishment with a view to retrenchment', but that he had other urgent matters to complete. 'On the present occasion', he continued, 'I shall content myself with throwing out the following hints which—by any person so inclined—may be taken in hand.'[4] In the event, not even this attenuated version appeared in the pasticcio.

Both immediately before and immediately after drafting the essay on retrenchment, Bentham turned his attention to the relative merits of paying officials by salary or by fees.[5] The earliest draft was apparently

---

[1] UC cxii. 146–51, 153–4 each carry the note, 'Not for 1830'; UC cxii. 161–3, 170–6, each carry the note, 'For 1830?', to which Bentham has answered 'No' on the last two sheets.

[2] 1. UC cxii. 119–27 (28 March 1830), with related fragments at cxii. 92 (26 March 1830) and cxii. 117–18 (27 March 1830), deals principally with ecclesiastical retrenchment. 2. UC cxii. 93–5 (14 April 1830), with a related fragment at cxii. 96 (14 April 1830), is general introductory material. 3. UC cxii. 97–106 (22 April 1830), with a related fragment at cxii. 129 (15 April 1830), deals with retrenchment in the ecclesiastical establishment, the army and the navy, 'distant dependencies' and 'Foreign Mission expenditure'. A further sequence on 'Foreign Mission Expence', in the hand of an amanuensis but apparently dictated by Bentham, is at UC cxii. 128, 130–4 (11 April 1830). 4. UC cxii. 107–16 (27 April 1830) is general introductory material.

[3] See Bentham's note at UC cxii. 95: 'While writing this, took a resolution not to delay the publication of the *pasticcio* any longer: but to defer any addition to a 2ᵈ· future contingent Edition.

'Particularly as the subject of retrenchment would render it necessary to carry the examination over the whole of the Official Establishment with *et cæteras*.

'Only to fit up the *Preface* for immediate publication.'

Since no second edition of the pasticcio ever appeared, or ever seems again to have been contemplated, the projected essay on retrenchment remained unpublished.

[4] See UC cxii. 97, which carries the sub-heading 'Paper 9. On Retrenchment'. Other sheets amongst this material also headed 'Paper 9' include UC cxii. 106 (22 April 1830) and cxii. 107–10, 112–16 (27 April 1830).

[5] See UC cxii. 252–61, 263–318; cxiv. 152–5, 211. The corresponding marginal summary sheets are at UC cxii. 244, 246–51, and sheets containing rudiments and plans at cxii. 245, 262. Many of these sheets are headed 'Official Aptitude. Remuneration—Salary or Fees?' This topic is listed as point 7 on the plan of 15 March 1828.

written at the end of May 1828,[1] but the bulk of the surviving material was written in the middle of June 1828. There are two drafts from this period, each with its own plan.[2] The earlier draft consists of three separate sequences of manuscript,[3] but in comparison with the scheme envisaged in the plan, it appears to be very incomplete. The later draft is much fuller and closely matches the corresponding plan: it therefore forms the basis of the text presented below in Appendix C.[4] The essay has been organized with reference to the plan, the numbering of the sections on the text sheets, and of course the sense. The titles for the sections are taken from the text sheets where these exist;[5] otherwise, the titles for §§ 8, 9 and 11 are taken from the plan, and that for § 3 from the marginal summary sheet. There is some discrepancy however between the order and content of the essay suggested by the plan and that suggested by internal evidence. According to the text,[6] Bentham intended to include a discussion of 'Good effects looked for' from the fee system. One of these 'good effects', that 'the burthen imposed rests on an individual to whom the service performed by the functionary is rendered', is not mentioned on the plan. The other 'good effect', alacrity, corresponds with the proposed subject-matter of § 11 on the plan, but no text sheets for this section appear to survive. Other text sheets have been lost, or were never written.[7] Nevertheless the text retains its coherence and continuity.

[1] Only a copy for this survives: see UC cxii. 252–61 (24–5, 29 May 1828). Two sheets (UC cxii. 257–8), as well as the marginal summary paragraphs, are in the hand of Bentham's nephew, George Bentham (1800–84), and the remainder in the hand of his amanuensis, John Flowerdew Colls (1801–78); some of the headings and dates are in Bentham's hand, and he has made one correction to the text (at UC cxii. 259). The corresponding marginal summary sheet is at UC cxii. 248 (12 June 1828). A plan for this draft is at UC cxii. 262 (17 May 1828). In a note of 28 May 1828, written on the verso of the wrapper enfolding UC cxii. 252–304, Bentham commented: 'Matter revised . . . but now proposed to be eliminated so as to form a separate Paper of the *Pasticcio*, or to be suppressed altogether.' This perhaps represents a decision to separate the material on remuneration from that on retrenchment, instead of incorporating it into the more wide-ranging work envisaged in the plan of 15 March 1828.

[2] The plans for these drafts, marked 'Ordo 1°' and 'Ordo 2°' respectively, are both at UC cxii. 245 (12 June 1828).

[3] 1. UC cxii. 305–11 (11–12 June 1828). The corresponding marginal summary sheet is at UC cxii. 244 (11 June 1828). 2. UC cxii. 312–15 (12 June 1828). The corresponding marginal summary sheet is at UC cxii. 247 (n.d. June 1828). 3. UC cxii. 316–18 (12 June 1828). The corresponding marginal summary sheet is at UC cxii. 246 (12 June 1828).

[4] For the MSS used in the text see the Table of Manuscripts, p. 1 below. The corresponding marginal summary sheets are at UC cxii. 249–51 (13–15, 17 June 1828). A further short sequence discussing the evils of the fee system is at UC cxiv. 211, 152–5 (20 July 1828).

[5] It should be noted that the titles for §§ 2, 4–8 and 10 on the text sheets correspond closely to those given on the plan.

[6] See § 1, p. 369 below.

[7] The text sheets for § 3 have not been located; the copy of the marginal summaries at UC cxii. 250 (15 June 1828) is reproduced in an editorial footnote (see p. 371n below). There is no evidence that any material was ever written for §§ 9 and 11.

A further small group of manuscripts, drafted in January 1828, but related to the remuneration theme, concerns the office of Secondary in the Sheriff's Courts of London and Middlesex.[1] Bentham recommends that the fees payable to the Secondary should be abolished and replaced by salary, and that the office be sold by auction and its accounts made public. This material is marked for inclusion in the projected Conclusion to the pasticcio, but though written very soon after Bentham had drawn up his plan for the volume on 18 January 1828,[2] it is not specifically mentioned there.

At the end of April 1830, Bentham reported that the pasticcio was 'now passing through the press', and that he already had 'the greatest part' of it, though some of it still had to be printed.[3] Yet despite his resolution on 15 April 1830 not to delay publication any longer, he went on to draft the essay on public account keeping and also seems to have decided to add the extract on the militia. This explains his remark in the 'Preface' of 'some change having been made in the list of the Papers originally intended to be inserted' in the pasticcio.[4] By the middle of June 1830 Bentham was distributing copies of the volume,[5] and finally published it towards the end of the month.[6] According to accounts which Bentham received from the publisher, Robert Heward, ninety-seven copies of the volume were boarded and sewn, of which five were sold in 1830 and eight in 1831.[7]

[1] UC cxii. 229–36, 238, 237 (21 January 1828). The corresponding marginal summary sheet is at UC cxiv. 157 (21 January 1828). A further draft at UC cxii. 239–43 (5 July 1828) is also sub-headed 'Secondary's Office', but the text is entitled 'Fallacies employed in support of waste and depredation—Mutual-laudation fallacy', and deals with the motives which rulers and their supporters impute to their own actions.

[2] UC cxii. 65.

[3] See Bentham to Adolphus Hauman, 30 April 1830, Osborn Collection, Yale University Library (printed in Bowring, xi. 42–3).

[4] See p. 5n below. It seems most likely that in the first place Bentham intended the essay on retrenchment to form Paper IX. At the beginning of May, Bentham drafted the essay on account keeping and decided that this should form Paper IX instead. Finally, he decided to include the extract on the militia as Paper IX, which meant that the essay on account keeping became Paper X.

[5] See Daniel Whittle Harvey to Bentham, 16 June 1830, BL Add. MS 33,546, fo. 426; Sir James Graham to Bentham, 19 June 1830, Bowring, xi. 51.

[6] In his letter to Daniel O'Connell of 23 June 1830, Bentham reported that the pasticcio was 'on the point of being published': see National Library of Ireland, MS 13,648 (3).

[7] BL Add. MS 33,553, fos. 301–2, 309–10. The price of the volume was 14 shillings.

TEXT

The Printed Text

The present edition of *Official Aptitude Maximized; Expense Minimized* corresponds as closely as possible with the style and conventions, including spelling, capitalization, punctuation, the use of italics and other devices, of the printed text published by Bentham in 1830. There are some minor variations: double inverted commas indicating quotations are replaced here with single inverted commas (consequently, single inverted commas usually indicating quotations within quotations are replaced with double inverted commas); the symbols used in the 1830 edition to indicate Bentham's own footnotes and subfootnotes are replaced here with suprascript letters (editorial footnotes are indicated by suprascript numerals); and Bentham's square brackets are replaced with braces. Moreover, in the 1830 edition, each Paper is separately paginated (except for 'Defence of Economy against Burke' and 'Defence of Economy against Rose' which are paginated sequentially, and 'Indications respecting Lord Eldon' in which the Postscript is separately paginated), whereas this edition is continuously paginated. Where appropriate, the running headings from the 1830 edition have been adopted on the recto page; for the sake of clarity, the short title of the Paper usually appears on the verso page, even where this is not the case in the 1830 edition. Editorial apparatus is confined to the use of square brackets to indicate editorially inserted words: in these cases, and where text has been excluded, the original reading is indicated in an editorial footnote. On occasion, a variant from one of the earlier published versions of the texts has been preferred: in these cases, the 1830 reading is indicated in an editorial footnote.

Of the eleven Papers which comprised the volume as published in 1830, only two, the 'Preface' and 'On Public Account Keeping', had not been previously published. Of the other Papers, four, 'Extract from Constitutional Code', 'Supplement to the Extract' (both from *Extract from Constitutional Code*), 'On the Militia' and 'Constitutional Code:—Table of Contents' (which was originally prefixed to the title page) are not reproduced here, but will be found in *Constitutional Code*, Volumes I and II. The texts may be reconstructed by reference to the respective collations in those volumes. Variations between the 1830 edition and the earlier published versions of the remaining five Papers are indicated in the Collations:[1] the essays on Burke, Rose,

---

[1] See pp. 393–437 below.

Peel and Eldon each appeared in *The Pamphleteer*, and the latter two as discrete pamphlets; the 'Introductory View' to *Extract from Constitutional Code* was published in 1826 as part of that pamphlet. The volume was republished in the Bowring edition of Bentham's *Works*,[1] but as this is entirely derivative from the 1830 text, a collation has not been deemed necessary.

A copy of the 1830 volume located in the Library of University College London contains several notes in Bentham's hand.[2]

The Manuscripts

As is commonly the case with works whose publication Bentham himself superintended, the manuscripts which formed the final drafts of the bulk of the texts no longer exist. However a considerable number of related manuscripts do survive, and some of them are published in the Appendices. By far the greater part of this manuscript material is in Bentham's own hand, written on single sheets of foolscap ruled with a wide margin and with a double line at the top for the date and the heading. Many of the text sheets contain numerous additions (usually interlinear, but sometimes marginal), deletions and emendations. Bentham's habit at this time seems to have been to date the sheets and write a sequence of several sheets of text, to read it over and make corrections, and then to write summaries of the content in the margin.[3] The marginal summaries were written in the form of short paragraphs and numbered consecutively. These marginal summary paragraphs were then copied out onto separate sheets (marginal summary sheets) by Bentham's amanuensis—in the case of this material, usually John Colls. The marginal summary sheets also bear occasional additions and emendations in Bentham's hand. The marginal summary sheets are written on single sheets of foolscap ruled into four columns with a double line at the top for the date and the heading. Bentham did not add marginal summaries to a large number of the text sheets which he wrote, while marginal summary sheets corresponding to some of the marginal summaries on

---

[1] See Bowring, v. 263–386. This version was edited by John Hill Burton (1809–81), author and historian of Scotland.

[2] The first, on the fly-leaf at the conclusion of 'Observations on Peel's Speech', refers to 'exemplifications of Police Magistrates' inaptitude'; the second, at §IX of 'Indications respecting Lord Eldon', deals with 'instances of legislation by Chancellors'; and the third, on the fly-leaf at the end of the volume, refers to a newspaper report of a reduction of official salaries in Hesse-Darmstadt. See UC Bentham Collection, shelf-mark 2. O. 3.

[3] Note, however, that Bentham appears to have delegated the composition of a large proportion of the marginal summaries for this material to George Bentham.

the text sheets were either never made or have not survived. It should be noted that the marginal summary paragraphs were not intended for publication, unlike the marginal headings incorporated in some of the earlier works,[1] but rather seem to have been used by Bentham for purposes of reference. Additionally a few sheets containing notes, aphorisms and general principles, and others containing plans, are usually written on double sheets of foolscap, each sheet again being ruled into four columns.

Some of the manuscripts are found in paper wrappers on which Bentham has inscribed a descriptive heading. These headings are sometimes detailed and specific, where the number of manuscripts is small and they comprise one continuous sequence, and at other times more general, where the number of manuscripts is larger and the content more wide-ranging. These wrappers were presumably used by Bentham as a rough contents index, allowing him to find and organize his material more easily. However, some of the wrappers have been misplaced, and are therefore not always a reliable guide to the content of the material they enfold.

A few general points should be made in regard to the organization of the texts reproduced here in the Appendices. The manuscripts for the essays 'On Retrenchment' and 'On the mode of Remuneration' (Appendices B and C respectively) are in reasonably good order, but those for §§ 3–4 of the Postscript to 'Indications respecting Lord Eldon' (Appendix A) are in a state of some confusion, and considerable reliance has therefore been placed on internal evidence. In general, the internal organization of each part or section has been ascertained by paying regard, where applicable, to the dating and pagination of sheets of text, the numbering of marginal summary paragraphs and of course the sense. Difficulties arise from the existence in some cases of several drafts for the same part or section, not to mention other isolated and abandoned fragments on the same theme. Usually the later draft has been preferred as representing Bentham's more mature consideration of the subject-matter in question. The location and date of any alternative draft or any other related manuscript not included in the text has been indicated in the Editorial Introduction above or, where appropriate, in an editorial footnote accompanying the text. On other occasions, no draft for a particular section was ever written or else has not survived. For the manuscripts used in this edition, reference should be made to the Table of Manuscripts below.

---

[1] See for instance *An Introduction to the Principles of Morals and Legislation*, ed. J.H. Burns and H.L.A. Hart, London, 1970 (*CW*).

Table of Manuscripts

Appendix A
Indications respecting Lord Eldon
Postscript

Section	MSS (UC)	Date (1825)
3	xix. 367–70[1]	26–7, 29 July
	xix. 350–4[2]	27 July
	xix. 340–5, 348, 346–7, 349	26, 28 July
	xix. 358–66[3]	27 July, 1, 3, 5 August
	xix. 405–6, 404	1 August
	xix. 407–10[4]	3–4 August
	xix. 411–12	4 August
	xix. 414–17	7 August
4	xix. 318	15 July
	xix. 319–23	19–20 July
	xix. 324–7[5]	11 July

Appendix B
On Retrenchment

Section	MSS (UC)	Date (1828)
1	cxii. 139–41	2 June
2	cxii. 142–4, 146–54	2–3 June
3	cxii. 155–7	3–4 June
4	cxii. 158	4 June
5	cxii. 159–60	4 June
6	cxii. 161–3	4 June
7	cxii. 164–5	4, 6 June
8	cxii. 166–9	6 June
9	cxii. 170–2	8–9 June
10	cxii. 172–3, 175	9 June
11	cxii. 173–4, 176	9 June[6]
12	cxii. 174	9 June

[1] This material is copied at UC xix. 376–9 (30 July 1825).
[2] This material is copied at UC xix. 427–32 (n.d. August 1825).
[3] This material is copied at UC xix. 418–26 (9 August 1825).
[4] This material is copied at UC xix. 433–6 (n.d. August 1825).
[5] The whole section is copied at UC xix. 390–7, 399–403 (19 July 1825).
[6] This sheet is evidently mis-dated 9 July 1828.

Appendix C
On the mode of Remuneration as between Salary and Fees

Section	MSS (UC)	Date (1828)
1	cxii. 263–5	13 June
2	cxii. 266–8	14–15 June
3	——[1]	
4	cxii. 269–73	14 June
5	cxii. 280	16 June
6	cxii. 281	16 June
7	cxii. 282–93	16–18 June
8	cxii. 278–9, 274–7	16–18 June
9	——[2]	
10	cxii. 294–304	12, 15, 19 June[3]
11	——[4]	

Presentation of the manuscript-based Text

It has been editorial policy to reflect as far as possible the manuscript sources on which the texts in the Appendices to this volume are exclusively based, but without the sacrifice thereby of clarity and sense. Bentham's spelling and capitalization have in most instances been retained, though editorial discretion has been exercised with regard to his punctuation, inconsistent and sparse as it often is. Punctuation marks have been adjusted and supplied where clearly indicated by the sense or required for the sake of clarity, but not in cases where this might involve a dubious interpretation of the meaning. The words and phrases underlined by Bentham for emphasis have been rendered in italics, as have all foreign words and phrases, some of which Bentham underlined and some of which he did not. In general, standard abbreviations have been retained, though some abbreviated words have been expanded into their full form (thus 'do.' is rendered as 'ditto').

The manuscripts contain many deletions, additions and emendations, representing Bentham's later corrections to the text. The final alternative reading is usually given in the text. Original readings

---

[1] No text for this section has been found. The copy of the corresponding marginal summaries is reproduced at p. 371n below.
[2] No text for this section has been found.
[3] UC cxii. 304 is evidently mis-dated 9 June 1828.
[4] No text for this section has been found.

have usually not been indicated. Where there is no text corresponding to some part of the marginal summary, the marginal summary is reproduced in an editorial footnote. Unless otherwise indicated, these passages are taken from the original in Bentham's hand on the text sheet, and not from the copy on the marginal sheet. Square brackets in the text are reserved for editorially inserted words: if these replace a word or phrase in the manuscript, Bentham's original is given in an editorial footnote. Round brackets are those supplied by Bentham. Perpendicular strokes indicate a gap or blank space in the manuscript.

Bentham's own footnotes are indicated by suprascript letters and editorial footnotes by suprascript numerals, with a separate sequence for each page of the text.

OFFICIAL APTITUDE MAXIMIZED;
EXPENSE MINIMIZED:
AS SHEWN IN THE SEVERAL PAPERS COMPRISED IN THIS VOLUME.

CONTENTS OF THIS VOLUME.

PREFACE.

To the whole of the matter, which, under nine or ten different heads[a], is now, in the compass of one and the same volume, published under the same general title,—belongs one and the same design, and, it is believed, one and the same result. But, it being composed of no fewer than (besides this) nine different papers, published mostly at different times, on different occasions, and under titles by which no intimation of such unity of design is conveyed,—it has occurred that that design may in no small degree be promoted, by holding up to view, in this Preface, the way in which they are regarded as being respectively conducive and contributory to it.

The work, from which they take their common origin, was an all-embracing system of proposed Constitutional Law, for the use of all nations professing liberal opinions: Volumes, three; the first of which, after having been some years out of the press, is at this time now first published.[1] Of this work, a main occupation was, of course, the shewing by what means the several members of the official establishment—in other words, the public functionaries, of the aggregate body of whom, what is called the *Government* is composed—might be rendered, in the highest degree well qualified, for rendering to the whole community the several services which are or ought to be looked for at their hands: or say, for giving fulfilment to that, which is or ought to be the end of their institution:—namely, the maximization of the happiness of the whole community under consideration.

In any one of these forms of words, may be seen expressed the whole of the benefit in view.

---

[a] Since this Preface was committed to the press, some change having been made in the list of the Papers originally intended to be inserted; hence some uncertainty and mis-statement in the *numerical* designation of them.[2] But, as by reference to the list of contents, things may be set right, the benefit of correction would not (it has been thought) pay for the trouble.

---

[1] The first volume of *Constitutional Code* had been printed in 1827, but was only published about the beginning of April 1830, shortly before *Official Aptitude Maximized; Expense Minimized*: see *Constitutional Code*, vol. I, ed. F. Rosen and J.H. Burns, Oxford, 1983 (*CW*), pp. xxxix–xli.

[2] There were, of course, eleven papers included in the volume. Bentham does not include the 'Preface' itself in the enumeration of the Papers which follows, while Paper IX, 'On the Militia', and Paper X, 'On Public Account Keeping', were late additions to the volume (see the Editorial Introduction, p. xlv above).

But, in the very nature of the case, connected with this *benefit*, is a *burthen*, without which the attainment of this same benefit is, in all places, and at all times, utterly impossible. Of this burthen the principal and most prominent part, being of a pecuniary nature, is designated and presented to view by the word *expense*.

Hence it is—that, with the object designated by the words *Official aptitude*, becomes inseparably associated the object designated by the word *expense*.

Of whatsoever *benefit* comes to be established, the *net* amount will be—that which remains after deduction made of the amount of the *burthen*.

A notion, which, in the course of this inquiry, whether really entertained or no, I had the mortification of seeing but too extensively endeavoured to be inculcated, was—that the net amount of the benefit reaped would, in this case, increase, and as of course, with the amount of the burthen imposed: and—to speak more particularly, that the aptitude of official men for their several situations would, in a manner of course, receive increase with, and with every practicable degree of exactness in proportion to, the expense employed in engaging them to enter upon, and continue in, their respective situations.

On the contrary, for my own part, the more closely I looked into the matter, the more thoroughly did I become persuaded—not only that this opinion is erroneous, but that the exact reverse of it is the real state of the case.

In regard to each of these so intimately connected objects—maximization of official aptitude, and minimization of official expense—to show by what means the best promise of the obtainment of them might be afforded, was of course an object of my inquiries. From the words *Official aptitude maximized, expense minimized*—from these five words might this design receive its expression: and, of the design or purpose of this work, might intimation be thus afforded by its title. But, in addition to *this*, a further idea, which it is my wish to see associated with these words, is—that of these two states of things—these two mutually concomitantly desirable objects—one bears to the other the relation of *cause* to *effect;* for, that from the same arrangement from which the expense so employed will *experience diminution*, the aptitude in question will, in the natural order of things, *receive increase:* in a word, that *cæteris paribus*, the less the expense so bestowed as above, the greater, not the lesser, will be the aptitude.

Now for the painful part of this inquiry:

Never, to any subject-matter,—considered as a source of happiness or unhappiness, or both,—have my labours on any occasion been directed, but with a view to the giving increase to the net amount of happiness. But, so intimately blended and intermingled, throughout the whole field, are those two fruits of human action,—never could the sweet be brought to view, but the bitter would come into view along with it: and, as the sweet would, in great measure, come into view and be reaped without effort,—the consequence was—that in clearing away the bitter consisted the great part of the labour necessary to be employed. In such part of the field,—for obtaining, of the *bitter*—in a word, of the unhappiness—produced by deficiency in the aptitude—a perception sufficient to put me in search after the most effectual mode of supplying that same deficiency,—a very slight glance would commonly suffice. But, this object accomplished, then has come the task of shewing the needfulness of the research that had been made: shewing this, by shewing the bitterness of the fruit with which the whole field was overrun, and the magnitude of the evil, actually and continually coming into existence, from the want of the supposed discovered appropriate and effectual remedy.

Painful (I may truly say) has, on every occasion, been this part of my task: for, never has it happened to me to witness suffering, on the part of any creature, whether of my own species or any other, without experiencing, in some degree or other, a sensation of the like nature in my own nerves: still less possible has it been to me to avoid experiencing the like unpleasant situation, when it has happened to myself to have been contributory to that same suffering.

Yet, without bringing to view the evil,—utterly incomplete would have been the good, produced by the invention and description given of the remedy: for, by all those, whosoever they were, by whom, for the sake of the benefit derived by them from the evil, the existence of the evil would of course be denied, and their endeavours applied to the keeping it out of view,—correspondent ill-will, harboured towards those by whom this source of the good is endeavoured to be dried up, is a necessary consequence.

Here then, in connection with every particle of the good endeavoured and supposed to be done,—come *three* distinguishable particles of evil: evil, from the contemplation of the suffering endeavoured to be prevented; evil, from the contemplation of the suffering, producible, on the part of the evil-doer, by the application made of the remedy; evil, apprehended from the desire of vengeance, produced, in the mind of the evil-doer, by the loss of his accustomed benefit.

Happily, it follows not in this case that, because the particles of evil bear in number to those of the good the ratio of three to one, they must in the aggregate be superior in value to the good. Happily: for, if such were the consequence,—scarcely where, between man and man, contention had place, would good to any net amount be ever produced.

Moreover, a few hints there are, to which, coupling together two considerations, namely, that of the extent of their usefulness, if any they have, and the narrowness of the space into which they may be compressed, I could not refuse admittance: and, for such admittance, no other place than the present could be chosen with any advantage.

Disappointment-prevention, or say *non-disappointment*, principle. For the purpose of *retro-susception* or say *resumption*, as well as for that of original distribution,—in this principle may be seen the chief and all-directing guide. In this may be seen, on the ground of utility and reason, the foundation of the whole law of property, *penal* branch as well as *civil*. In another place[a] application has already been made of it, to the subject of what is called *real property*:—and thereby explanation given of it. In the present volume may be seen ulterior application made of it, and explanation given to it: namely, in the immediately ensuing Paper, intituled *Introductory View*.[1]

In the train of it come now a few proposed rules and observations:—

1. Rule I.—So long as expenditure continues running through any pipe or channel, which can be stopped without production of disappointment—disappointment to *fixed* expectations already formed,—forbear to stop it, in any pipe or channel by the stoppage of which such disappointment will be produced.

2. Rule II.—On this occasion, by appropriate delineation draw a clear and express line of demarcation between *fixed* and *floating* expectations.

Every solicitor, who sends a son of his to one of the Inns of Court, *expects* to see that same son on the Chancery Bench with the seals before him; as the Lord Bathurst, of Queen Ann's creation, saw his.[2]

---

[a] *{Another place}*—Westminster Review for 1826, No. XII.[3]

---

[1] See p. 36 below. For a fuller discussion of the disappointment-prevention principle see Appendix B, 'On Retrenchment', pp. 342–67 below.

[2] Allen Bathurst (1684–1775) was created Baron Bathurst in 1712 by Anne (1665–1714), Queen of Great Britain and Ireland from 1702, and was raised to an Earldom in 1772 by George III (1738–1820), King of Great Britain and Ireland from 1760: his son Henry Bathurst (1714–94), created Baron of Apsley in 1771, who succeeded as second Earl Bathurst on his father's death, was Lord Chancellor 1771–8.

[3] Bentham's review of James Humphreys, *Observations on the actual State of the English Laws of Real Property, with the Outline of a Code*, London, 1826, first appeared in the *Westminster Review*, vol. vi, no. xii (1826), 446–507, but was published in 1827 as a separate pamphlet entitled *On Mr. Humphreys' 'Observations on the English Law of Real Property', with the Outline of a Code*. It

Behold here a specimen of *floating* expectations: correspondent to *fixed expectations* in ordinary language, are *vested interests* in technical language.

Rule III.—The amount of the sum proposed to be *retrenched* being given, and the amount of suffering of every sufferer by it being the same, the less the number of the sufferers by it the better.

Application. Case supposed: In the department in question, mass of expenditure proposed to be retrenched, 1000*l.* a year: one sum of 1000*l.* a year forms the salary of *one Commissioner* of a Board: another sum of 1000*l.* a year, the aggregate of the salaries of *ten Clerks*. These situations, all eleven of them, are, on examination, deemed needless: but, without production of disappointment they cannot, any one of them, be struck off. Direction in consequence: strike off the one Commissioner, rather than the ten Clerks, or any one or more of them.

4. Rule IV.—Remember always,—that, on both sides, the amount of the provision probably obtainable by each such dismissed functionary, in lieu of what he thus loses, requires to be taken into consideration.

5. Example of a channel of expenditure capable of being stopt up, without disappointment of fixed expectation, this: namely, Salaries of the ostentatious class of functionaries sent on *foreign missions:* Secretaries of Legation, Consuls, and Vice-Consuls, not included. Offers of service at reduced salaries to every diversity of amount— offers of gratuitous services, not to speak of offers of purchase—let all such offers be called for and received, before choice is made. Of purchase? Yes. For, if a fit man there be, who, instead of being paid for taking upon him the burthen, is willing to pay for the permission to bear it,—why, even against any such offer should the door be closed?

As to the general indication afforded, of aptitude for a political situation, by the proof given, of *relish* for it by the smallness of the sum required for taking it, or the largeness of the sum ready to be given for it,—see on this head what is said in Paper III—*Extract from the Constitutional Code*.[1]

6. Note, that—by striking out any individual, in whose instance *fixed* expectation, either of *continuance* in possession, or of *acquisition* of possession, has place,—nothing is gained, upon the whole, by the community of which he forms a part. Not more is the community

was republished at Bowring, v. 387–416 as 'Commentary on Mr. Humphreys' Real Property Code'.

[1] See *Constitutional Code*, I (*CW*), Ch. IX, § 15, Arts. 3–6, pp. 298–9, for the relationship between relish and aptitude. Pecuniary competition is discussed most fully at Ch. IX, § 17, pp. 337–62.

thus benefited,—than, by the removal of a weight from one side of a ship to another, the ship is lightened.

7. As often as, at the public expense, money is given in the name of *indemnification*, complete or incomplete, for loss, sustained by him without his default,—so often is acted upon a principle, the reverse of that which would produce the disappointment of a fixed expectation, by the uncompensated extinction of a profit-yielding office.

To apply this observation to the matter of the present volume. In the three first of these Papers will be seen nearly the whole of the *sweet* part of the compound task: in the four next will be seen predominating the bitter.[1] The first thing done will consist accordingly in laying down, all along, what, in my view of it, is *right;* that, to this, as a standard, for the purpose of detection and exposure, may all along be applied that which, in my view, is *wrong*.

As to the ninth of these Papers,—of the subject of it (the *Militia*) the extent is comparatively narrow,—and the relation of it to the rest must wait for its explanation till some other matters have been brought to view.

Occupied principally in shewing how the aptitude in question *may* be maximized and the expense minimized, and that by every diminution effected in the expense, augmentation may be given to the aptitude—are the three first and the eighth of the ensuing papers:[2] occupied in shewing that in fact, on the part of the rulers of the British Empire in its whole vast mass, and of the English part in particular of them, the endeavour has been, and continues to be, and so long as the form of government continues to be as it is, never can cease to be—to maximize the expense and minimize the aptitude—occupied in the establishment of this position, are the remaining numbers; that is to say, the 4th, 5th, 6th, and 7th of these same Papers.[3]

Specially connected with one another will be seen to be Papers 4 and 5;[4] mutually connected in like manner with one another, Papers 6 and 7.[5]

In Papers 4 and 5, may be seen occupied the leading minds of the two parties between which the statesmen of those days respectively were divided, years 1780 and 1810,—occupied in the endeavour to obtain the approbation of the community, for principles, by which, if carried into practice, not an atom of the fruits of human labour over and above what is necessary to bare existence, would be left in the

---

[1] i.e. Papers II–IV (Bentham divided 'Extract from Constitutional Code' into three papers) and V–VIII respectively.

[2] i.e. Papers II–IV and IX.

[3] i.e. Papers V–VIII.

[4] i.e. Papers V and VI.

[5] i.e. Papers VII and VIII.

hands by the labour of which it was produced. So much for principles:—or if another word be more agreeable, *theory*.

In Papers 6 and 7 may be seen—with what consummate consistency and perfection those same principles have been, and down to the present time continue to be, carried into practice: to how enormous and endless an amount has been swelled the mass of expense, employed under the notion of securing appropriate aptitude on the part of the head functionary in one of the departments; namely, in that of *Justice;*—and the degree of perfection, in which, in that same instance, the quality of *inaptitude* has had place: and how effectual the provision that has been made, for addition altogether boundless to that same expense.[1] Moreover, in Paper 7[2] may be seen—how, by the head functionary in another department, namely that of the Home-affairs—not only was support given to the system of predatory exaction, and thereby of expense, just mentioned,—and to the continuance of the official inaptitude also just mentioned,—but in his own department an addition, with (it is believed) unexampled wantonness, made, to the expense of offices subordinate to his own, and thereby to his own emolument; coupled with the inexorable establishment of a set of regulations, having for their most obvious and incontestable effect, not to say their avowed object, the exclusion of every efficient cause, and assignable presumptive proof, of official appropriate aptitude. Sole qualification required, eating and drinking; qualification decidedly rejected—of the several powers belonging to the very office in question, the habitual exercise.

Thus then may be seen—not only restricted, but by every day's practice continually confirmed and acted upon,—the theory to which expression may be given by the words—*official expense and official inaptitude, both maximized*.

When, in the career indicated by the words *expense maximized, aptitude minimized*, the ruling powers have proceeded for a certain length of time,—it will sometimes happen—that, by the fear of seeing their power drop from under them, they will be induced to stop; and even not simply to make a *stand*, but actually to make a *retreat;* and that this retreat, when applied to expense, will be declared under the name of *retrenchment*.

All this while, the original opposite design,—the design of advancing in that same career,—continues, of course, in unabated force. For, the same cause which first gave birth to it, will, so long as man is man, make it grow with his growth, and strengthen with his

---

[1] This in fact is the subject-matter of Paper VIII.

[2] To be consistent with his own enumeration, Bentham should have referred here to 'Paper 6'. His reference is to Paper VII.

strength.[1] The design, however, not being altogether so acceptable to the people at whose expense, as it is to their rulers by whom, it is entertained and pursued,—hence the endeavour to impress on the minds of the people—instead of the apprehension of its existence—the opposite confidence. But, such is the force of truth, and of the nature of things, that whenever a design of this sort really has place, so it is that, by means of the very endeavours employed to dispel the apprehension of it, it is liable to be brought to light.

Whether, in the several instances of Edmund Burke[2] and George Rose[3] this result has not had its exemplification,—is among the questions, on which the reader will have to pronounce, should his patience have carried him through Papers the 4th and 5th.[4]

Not unfrequently, those who, by delusive arguments, are labouring to inculcate an erroneous opinion, have, by those same or some other considerations, been themselves involved in the like delusion; such is the influence exercised on the judgment by the affections. In the mind of George Rose, the existence of the power of self-deceit, in quantity more or less considerable, presented itself to me (I remember) as not improbable: in the mind of Edmund Burke, not a particle. In the mind of George Rose (means for observation not being wanting) there seemed to me to be no small portion of downright honesty and goodness of intention; in that of Edmund Burke, nothing better than matchless artifice.

To return to the subject of *retrenchment*. Just now, a shew of a design of this sort having been made, and in that track even some short steps taken,—among the topics, for some time proposed to be included in this miscellany, was that of *retrenchment*. But, after some progress made in relation to it, came into view, what ought to have presented itself from the first; namely, that the field of *retrenchment* is no other than the whole field of *expenditure:* the only difference being—that the points of view, in which that same field has to be contemplated, are, on the two occasions, opposite. This being borne

---

[1] See Alexander Pope, *Essay on Man*, ii. 133–6:

> As Man, perhaps, the moment of his breath,
> Receives the lurking principle of death;
> The young disease, that must subdue at length,
> Grows with his growth, and strengthens with his strength.

[2] Edmund Burke (1729–97), statesman, MP for Wendover 1765–74, Bristol 1774–80 and Malton 1780–94, Paymaster-General 1782, 1783.

[3] George Rose (1744–1818), statesman, MP for Launceston 1784–8, Lymington 1788–90 and Christchurch 1790–1818, Secretary to the Treasury 1782–3, 1783–1801, Vice-President of the Board of Trade and joint Paymaster-General 1804–6, Vice-President of the Board of Trade 1807–12, Treasurer of the Navy 1807–18.

[4] i.e. Papers V and VI.

in mind, time and space were seen joining in putting a peremptory *veto* upon any regular progress in that track: any progress, presenting, upon the face of it, any pretension to the character of a comprehensive one.[1]

Seeing however, as above, one supposed proper seat and source of retrenchment—the *militia*, in relation to which what had occurred to me had already assumed a determinate shape,—the quantity of space occupied by it being but small, admittance (it seemed) need not be refused to it. It forms accordingly the matter of Paper 9.

8. What is the *Navy* good for? Answer: to help defend Colonies. What are *Colonies* good for? Answer: to help support the *Navy*. Quere, what part of the national expenditure is kept up on the ground of this circle?

9. On the question—by the metropolitan country shall this or that distant dependency be kept up,—there are two *sides*—two *interests*—that require consideration: that of the metropolis herself and that of the dependency. To *Great Britain and Ireland*—say in one word to *Brithibernia*—would it be matter of advantage or disadvantage to surrender the dominion of *British India* to the inhabitants, as it surrendered to the inhabitants the dominion of the new Anglo-American United States? On the question whether it would be for the advantage of *Brithibernia*, much might be said on both sides. On the question, as applied to the nation of British India,—in the minds of those who have read the documents, and in particular the work of the so well-informed, intelligent and incontestably well-intentioned Bishop Heber,[2]—scarcely can there be a doubt. By the withdrawal of the English regiments from British India, in what respect or degree would Hindoos or Mahometans profit? Answer: In much the same as did the ancient *Britons* by the withdrawal of the *Roman* legions.

10. If, in the case of the several European powers, and other civilized nations and governments, security against *one another* were all that were sought for, at the hands of *standing armies* and *permanent navies*,—no less effectually might this security be procured and retained, by proportional *diminution* than by proportionable *augmentation*. But, by all of them, permanent military force, in one or

---

[1] Bentham's essay 'On Retrenchment', written in June 1828, is reproduced in Appendix B, pp. 342–67 below. However the material referred to here is a further series of MSS headed 'Retrenchment', written in March and April 1830, at UC cxii. 92–134. Bentham apparently made the decision not to include a full-scale treatment of this subject in the pasticcio on 15 April 1830. For further details see the Editorial Introduction, p. xliii above.

[2] See Reginald Heber, Bishop of Calcutta, *Narrative of a Journey through the Upper Provinces of India, from Calcutta to Bombay, 1824–1825, (with notes upon Ceylon,) an Account of a Journey to Madras and the Southern Provinces, 1826, and Letters written in India*, 2 vols., London, 1828.

both branches, whether needed or not, is prized at any rate as an instrument of security for themselves against their own subjects: security by means of intimidation: and security by means of delusive show and corruptive influence.

11. Now for *dead weight*. After having so much too long had its *habitation*, it has at length received its *name*. It was on the shoulders of the good woman who used to figure upon a halfpenny,[1] *a wen*, or a *millstone* about her neck: either emblem may serve. But should the first be preferred, let not *imagination* take place of reason,—and, turning her back on the herein-above-proposed non-disappointment principle,—go on to say, *immedicabile vulnus ense recidendum est*.[2]

12. Millstone or wen—it is among the blessings for which Brithibernia stands indebted to *Matchless Constitution*. In the Anglo-American United States, no such excrescence is known. Pensions, in compensation for wounds received,—and thence for the encouragement necessary to the engaging of men to expose themselves to such casualties,—Yes. But, pensions of retreat,—pensions for widows or orphans,—remuneration mis-seated or extravasated, in these or any other shapes,—none. As to extravasated remuneration, see Paper III, *Extract from Constitutional Code*.[a]

13. Exactly as necessary, exactly as reasonable, are pensions of retreat, et cætera, at public expense, for official men,—as for professional men they would be, or for artists, or for tradesmen, or for labouring men engaged in any other profit-seeking occupations.

14. Once upon a time,—in the Senate House of Gotham—a motion was made, to impose upon everybody a tax, and put the whole produce of it into everybody's pocket. Hear him! hear him! hear him!

[a] {*Mis-seated and extravasated.*}[3] To men conversant in the medical branch of art-and-science, the use and importance of *nosology* is no secret. Be the disorder what it may,—to it how can any cure, under it how can any relief, be administered,—unless it be *spoken* of? And, how can it be spoken of with best effect, unless a name, and that an appropriate and characteristic one, be given to it? As little to the practitioners in the body politic is this a secret, as to those in the body natural. But, under *matchless* constitution, the practitioners—having and being actuated by an interest at daggers drawn with that of the patient,—hence every idea and every expression, which contributes to throw light on the nature of the disorder, is, in proportion to the strength and clearness of that light, necessarily and uniformly odious: hence the endeavours to cause it to be regarded as ridiculous.

---

[1] The image of Britannia appeared on the reverse of the halfpenny.

[2] A corrupt rendering of Ovid, *Metamorphoses*, i. 190–1, 'immedicabile corpus ense recidendum est', i.e. 'the incurable body must be pruned with the sword'.

[3] See *Constitutional Code*, I (*CW*), Ch. IX, § 15, Arts. 39–48, pp. 306–8.

was the cry. The motion passed by general acclamation.[1] Quere, of the Gotham senate-house what was the distance from St. Stephen's?[2]

15. Account to be taken. Account of the annual amount per head, of an average pauper on the Aristocratical pauper list called the Dead Weight, in each of its several classes, from the 50*l.* a year class to the 4000*l.* a year class inclusive, compared with the expense of the Democratical pauper list called the *Poor Rates*. Quere, how much longer will the real poor—the vast majority of the community—endure to see five hundred times as much thus bestowed upon one of their *betters* (and such betters!) as is bestowed upon one of themselves?

One of these days, two comparative accounts will be made up by authority; one, of the expense bestowed upon the democratical class of paupers; the other of the expence bestowed upon the aristocratical. How much, if anything, does the aggregate of the last-mentioned expense fall short of that of the former? Next to nothing. Think too of the length of *time*, taken by the one and the other, for arrival at their present magnitude. Calculate the length of time, at the end of which, while the democratical continues stationary, the aristocratical pauper-list will have out-run the interest of the national debt, as much as that same interest has out-run the annual sum applied to the maintenance of Government!

Look at him! there he sits! Prince of the Aristocratical pauper-list, at this moment![3] Conservator of everything that is evil! Implacable enemy of every new thing that is good! Loaded with the spoils—of the injured, the afflicted, the helpless, the orphan, and the widow!

What is the number of Clerks, who after any number of years' faithful service, would not, with less compunction, be turned a-drift pennyless, than this man deprived of the addition thus made to so many hundred thousand pounds, accumulated by the delay, sale, and denial of justice[a].—By disturbing the peace, for the purpose of

---

[a] Mode of connection between official service and official remuneration. In the character of a *Supplement* to the section, on Official Remuneration, as reprinted in the extract from the Constitutional Code,[4]—matter under this head has for some time past been collecting.[5] But, no great progress in it had been made, when the observa-

---

[1] The village of Gotham in Nottinghamshire was proverbial for the folly of its inhabitants.

[2] i.e. the House of Commons, which met in what had originally been St. Stephen's Chapel in the Palace of Westminster.

[3] John Scott (1751–1838), first Baron and first Earl of Eldon, Lord Chancellor 1801–6, 1807–27, who, as ex-Chancellor, enjoyed a pension of £4,000 per annum (see 'Defence of Economy against Burke', §III, pp. 57–8n below).

[4] i.e. *Constitutional Code*, I (*CW*), Ch. IX, §15, pp. 297–310.

[5] Drafts of this 'Supplement', which remained unpublished, are at BL Add. MS 33,549, fos. 143–5, 153–5 (12 March 1830), with a marginal summary sheet at fo. 184 (16 April

tion was also made, that *this* is but one modification, of the manner of bringing into coincidence the line of conduct prescribed by private interest, and that prescribed by public duty; and that—to complete the problem, what was requisite was the establishing the correspondent closeness of connection between maleficence on the one part, and punishment on the other part:—punishment, together with the several other *remedies*, which the nature of things admits of:—namely, satisfactive, suppressive, and preventive. Desirable and requisite is this coincidence in the case of official men,—true: but not more so than in the case of all other persons whatsoever.

These things observed, what was further observed was—on the other part, that the head to which this disquisition belongs is that of *Nomography* in general. But, in the collection of matter under this head, considerable progress had been already made.[1] The art-and-science of clothing, in the best adapted form, the several modes of giving expression to the dictates of the *will*, may be considered as a hitherto unobserved branch of *Logic:* the branch of art-and-science as yet designated by the name of *Logic*, being, as to its subject-matter, confined to the dictates of the *understanding*—a faculty not exactly the same with the *will*, though not far distant from it.

Nomography—(from a Greek word which signifies *law*, and another which signifies *to write*, or say *give expression to*)—is an appellation, which presented itself as capable of being made to serve, with most convenience, for the designation of the *logic of the will*. True it is, that between the will operated upon, and the will operating upon it, degree of relation in respect of *power*, there are three: namely, superiority, equality, and inferiority; and that, in the case of *nomography*, the relation borne by the operating will to the will operated upon, is no other than that of superior to inferior: and, as in the case where the will operating is that of the *superior*, the mode of address has its appropriate denomination; namely, in private life *command*, in political life, *law, ordinance*, and so forth,—so has it in the case where it is that of an *equal;* as for example, *proposal* or *proposition*; so likewise in the case where it is that of an *inferior;* as for example, *petition*, not to mention other appellations of a less decided character.

These things notwithstanding,—no sufficient cause presented itself to view, for considering the matter of this branch of art and science, as distributed under those denominations corresponding to the arithmetical distinctions, or for looking out for any other denomination than this of *nomography*; Why? *Answer:*—1. Because, in comparison of the occasions on which the expression of will receives the name of *law*, those on which it receives the two other denominations, are, when taken together, so much less important: the interest at stake being so much less considerable: 2. Because the *motives*, or say *inducements*, by which *compliance* (the effect aimed at) is produced, are not, in those cases, at bottom so different, as to a first glance they will be apt to appear to be: 3. Because, in respect of the rules, having for their object and effect the securing the coincidence between the mode of conduct which it is the desire of the operating *will* to produce on the part of him whose will is operated upon, and the conception thereby entertained of that same will, the difference in the several cases is comparatively inconsiderable. Supposing the assortment of rules for this purpose correct and complete as applied to *law*,—nothing, or next to nothing, will require to be done, in the view of providing rules for those two *other* cases.

1830), and fos. 146–52 (18 April, 1 May 1830). For further details see the Editorial Introduction, p. xxv above.

[1] Bentham's writings on this subject were posthumously edited by Richard Smith and published as 'Nomography; or the Art of Inditing Laws', in Bowring, iii. 231–95.

plundering the property, of families;—by setting children against parents, and parents against children;—by giving, of his own single authority, origination, execution, and effect, to institutions so shockingly immoral, that neither he nor any other man in his place, would have dared so much as attempt to introduce the proposal of them, into either House of Parliament?

Of one of the states of things, held up to view in and by the *Defence of Economy against Burke*, namely, the state of the Crown Lands, a curious enough and highly instructive application may be made, to the now existing state of things, in the same quarter, as brought to light in and by the admirable speech so lately made in the Honourable House,

Should the papers thus denominated arrive at a state in which they will have been deemed fit to see the light,—it will then be seen—in what a variety of ways the effects of *imperation* in its two shapes, positive command, or say jussion, on the one hand, and prohibition, or say inhibition, on the other, are producible. Consequence of this variety, difference—in some cases between the effect intended, and the effect produced; in other cases, between the effect *appearing* to be intended, and the effect *in reality* intended. Cause of the difference—in the first case, want of discernment; in the other case, discernment applied to a sinister purpose.

Here then, in the political melo-drama, are so many *dramatis personæ*, who enter upon the stage in masquerade. Prohibition, disguised under the cloak of Positive Command; Positive Command or Permission, under the cloak of Prohibition; Permission, Remuneration and Encouragement, under the cloak of Punishment. Of this masquerade, under the head of *Indirect Legislation*, some intimation may be seen given, as long ago as the year 1802, in the *Traité[s] de Legislation Civile et Pénale*,—in what is said of the effect of *fixed penalties*, in the Introduction to Morals and Legislation, titles *Properties desirable in a lot of punishment*, and *Proportion between Crimes and Punishments*,—in what is said under the head of *Blind fixation, &c.* in the *Petition for Justice*, Device the 8th;[1] and in the work still in the press, intituled *Equity Dispatch Court Bill*, § 6. *Judge's Powers*.[2]

---

[1] See respectively *Traités de législation civile et pénale*, ed. Étienne Dumont, 3 vols., Paris, 1802, iii. 1–199; *An Introduction to the Principles of Morals and Legislation*, ed. J.H. Burns and H.L.A. Hart, London, 1970 (*CW*), pp. 165–86; *Justice and Codification Petitions: being forms proposed for signature by all persons whose desire it is to see Justice no longer sold, delayed, or denied: and to obtain a possibility of that Knowledge of the Law, in proportion to the want of which they are subjected to Unjust Punishments, and Deprived of the Benefit of their Rights*, London, 1829, pp. 85–92 (see Bowring, v. 437–548 for the whole work, and v. 470–2 for the passage in question).

[2] The first eight sections of this work were printed, but not published, by Bentham. An extended version, entitled 'Equity Dispatch Court Bill; being a Bill for the institution of an experimental judicatory under the name of the Court of Dispatch, for exemplifying in practice the manner in which the proposed summary may be substituted for the so called regular system of procedure; and for clearing away by the experiment, the arrear of business in the Equity Courts', was first published in Bowring, iii. 319–431. The section referred to here is at Bowring, iii. 345–76. Bentham however may have had in mind the summary of this material which he published as *Equity Dispatch Court Proposal: containing a plan for the speedy and unexpensive termination of the suits now depending in Equity Courts. With the form of a petition, and some account of a proposed Bill for that purpose*, London, 1830 (Bowring, iii. 297–317). The passage in question is at pp. 39–41 (Bowring, iii. 311).

by Mr *Whittle Harvey*.[1] Estimated annual value of the Crown Lands obtained by *Somers* when Lord Chancellor, for his own use, year the 7th William the Third, A.D. 1695, or thereabouts, 2,100*l.* per annum.[2] Of what remained after this grant,—produce, upon an average of fifteen years ending in 1715, 1,500*l.* a year, and no more; according to Mr Secretary Rose's pamphlet, intituled '*Observations respecting the Public Expenditure and the Influence of the Crown. 2nd Edition*. 1810.'[3] Of the present remnant of that same remnant, annual value, according to various estimates, made by various members, varying between 500,000*l.* and 800,000*l.* Motion being made for a Committee of the Honourable House[a] to enquire by what means this portion of the national property 'might be made most available for the public service,' what was the course thereupon taken by the Honourable House? *Answer:*—That which, without the imputation of rashness, a man might, by the wager of 'ten thousand pounds to one penny,' have pledged himself for its taking: It declined giving the Honourable Mover the trouble of any ulterior enquiry. 'No enquiry' was the language: bring '*Your charge;*' that is to say—call for the *punitive* remedy, and not either the *preventive*, or the *suppressive*. Hear and

---

[a] March 30, 1830. Motion for 'a Select Committee to enquire into the Land Revenues of the Crown, under the management of the Commissioners of Woods and Forests, and to report their opinion as to the means by which they may be rendered most available for the public service.'

---

[1] In the House of Commons on 30 March 1830, Daniel Whittle Harvey (1786–1863), radical MP for Colchester 1818–20, 1826–34 and Southwark 1835–40, proposed a motion, 'That a Select Committee be appointed to take into consideration the State and Management of the Land Revenues of the Crown which are under the Superintendence of the Commissioners of His Majesty's Woods, Forests, and Land Revenues, and to report upon the most efficient means of rendering the same available to the exigencies of the Country' (*Commons Journals*, lxxxv. 244). For the debate see *Parliamentary Debates* (1830) xxiii. 1055–1110.

[2] The articles of impeachment brought in 1701 by the House of Commons against John Somers (1651–1716), first Baron Somers, Lord Keeper of the Great Seal 1693–1700, Lord Chancellor 1697–1700, stated that he 'begg'd and procured, for his own Benefit, many great, unreasonable, and exorbitant Grants of several Manors, Lands, Tenements, Rents, Hereditaments, and Revenues belonging to the Crown', including the manors of Rygate and Howleigh worth over £12,000 per annum. In reply, Somers stated that the value of the manors was 'far short' of this sum, and that the value of other grants (which were made in 1697, and not 1695) was £2,100 per annum (see Francis Hargrave, *A Complete Collection of State Trials, and Proceedings for High-Treason, and other Crimes and Misdemeanours*, vol. V, 4th edn., London, 1777, cols. 349–52). Bentham discussed this matter further in 'Defence of Economy against Burke', §III, pp. 57–8n below.

[3] Rose gave this information at p. 34n of his *Observations respecting the Public Expenditure, and the Influence of the Crown*, 2nd edn., London, 1810. His own source was *Commons Journals*, xx. 520, which contains a table of 'Produce of sundry Small Branches and Casualties paid into the Exchequer, on the Civil List, from Christmas 1699 to Lady-day 1715'. Bentham made further references to this matter in 'Defence of Economy against Burke', §III, p. 58n, and 'Defence of Economy against Rose', §XII, p. 148n below.

determine without evidence; we being determined that you shall have none.[1]

To this case, as to all others, applies one of the fundamental, characteristic, and distinctive principles of Matchless Constitution; namely, the *Judica-teipsum*[2] principle. To enquire into the conduct of the Servants of the Crown belongs not to any men but themselves.

[1] Harvey's motion was rejected by 98 votes to 46.
[2] i.e. 'judge yourself' or 'self-judication'.

EXTRACT FROM THE PROPOSED CONSTITUTIONAL CODE, ENTITLED OFFICIAL APTITUDE MAXIMIZED, EXPENSE MINIMIZED.[1]

---

[1] In the pasticcio, the title page was printed after the 'Introductory View', rather than before it as in 1826 *Extract*. For the text of the extract itself see *Constitutional Code*, I (*CW*), Ch. IX, §§ 15–17, pp. 297–364, and the Collation at pp. 520–8.

INTRODUCTORY VIEW, &c.

THE following tract,[1] as the title of it imports, has for its subjects the appropriate aptitude of public functionaries, and the expenditure employed at the charge of the people in engaging persons to subject themselves to the obligation of rendering the correspondent services. It is composed of four sections,[2] detached from the ninth of the thirty chapters, or thereabouts, of a proposed Constitutional Code, the entire of which, wanting little of completion, will be published as soon as circumstances permit. A table, composed of the titles of the chapters and sections of it, is hereunto annexed.[3]

The class, composed of the members of the official establishment taken in its several branches, was the only class in contemplation when the plan here delineated was taken in hand. In the progress of the work, the idea occurred that, supposing the plan well adapted to its purpose in the case of the class thus distinguished, it might be so, in no small degree, in the case of any other persons whose situation in life would, without any particular view to office, admit of the expenditure of the quantity of time and mental labour, which, with that view, is here proposed to be employed. But, what further may require to be said in relation to this secondary, and as it were collateral, subject, will be rendered more intelligible, by being postponed till after everything which belongs to the primary, and sole relevant, subject, has been brought to view.

Such being the *subjects*, now as to the *objects*, or say *ends in view*. These are, as the title of these pages intimates, maximization of the degree of appropriate aptitude in all its branches on the part of the functionary in question, and minimization of the expense employed in the creation and purchase of that same aptitude.

In this same title, a proposition fully expressed is—that, in the plan to which it gives denomination both these objects are endeavoured to be accomplished: a proposition not so fully, if at all expressed, but which will be seen maintained, is, that the accomplishment of the financial object, far from being, as seems but too generally supposed, at variance with that of the intellectual and moral, is, on the contrary,

---

[1] i.e. Papers III and IV.

[2] The 1826 *Extract* contained an early version of Ch. IX, § 18, which was not included in the published first volume of *Constitutional Code*, nor in the version of the *Extract* published in the pasticcio, in addition to the three sections (15–17) which were published. See the Editorial Introduction, pp. xxii–xxiii above.

[3] i.e. Paper XI, for which see *Constitutional Code*, I (*CW*), Table 1, prefixed to p. 1.

in no small degree, capable of being made conducive to it. A notion but too extensively entertained is—that, whatsoever quantity[1] of public money is employed in engaging individuals to step into official situations, relative aptitude in proportionate degree will follow as a matter of course: and that, for example, if, in the case of a chief judge, for 5,000*l.* a year salary, you get a certain quantity of appropriate aptitude, double the salary, and, without anything further, you double the aptitude. Such, at any rate is the opinion which, in England, whether inwardly entertained or not, is outwardly and generally acted upon.

With this opinion, that which gives direction to the here proposed arrangements, so far from harmonising, approaches more[2] nearly to the reverse: in so much that, supposing a number of competitors, so far as instruction will go, endowed with equal degree of aptitude,—a man, who, if any such there be in the situation in question, is willing to take upon himself, without emolument in any shape, the performance of the duties of an office, is likely to perform them better, than another man who would not undertake it for less than 5,000*l.* a year: or even better than he himself would have done, if, on stipulating for that same sum, he had obtained it. In the course of the section entitled *Remuneration*, being the first of the four sections of which this tract is composed, this opinion, together with the grounds on which it rests, may be seen developed.[3]

First comes the *appropriate aptitude:* and the problem is how to *maximize* it.

When, for the performance of a certain work, an *individual* finds himself in need of a helper, before he fixes upon any one, he naturally puts questions to any one that offers,—questions having for their object the obtaining satisfaction, as to the relative aptitude of the candidate: if, instead of *one* only, a number more than one presented themselves, he would, as far as time permitted, put those same questions to them all: and, in the putting of these questions, he would address himself to them separately, or all at the same time, as he found most convenient. In either way, by so doing, he would *examine* them; he, the *examiner;* they, the *examinees*. In private would the examination be of course performed in this case; for, on this occasion, of no person other than the individual himself, would the interest or convenience be in view: by publicity, if obtainable, he would, and in proportion to the number of persons present, be embarassed, and in no way benefited.

---

[1] 1826 *Extract*, 1830 'whatsoever, quantity'.
[2] 1826 *Extract*, 1830 'harmonising approaches, more'.
[3] See *Constitutional Code*, I (*CW*), Ch. IX, § 15, pp. 297–310.

To the *functionary in chief*, who, for aiding him in the business of his department, feels the need of helpers in the businesses of the several sub-departments, their aptitude cannot in the nature of the case be a matter of indifference. His property will not, it is true, as in the case of the individual, be at stake upon the aptitude of his choice. His *property*, no; but his reputation, yes. If the subordinate chosen be to a certain degree unapt, the reputation of the superordinate will suffer in two distinguishable ways: by the badness of the work done under his orders, and by the weakness, or something worse, evidenced by the badness of the choice.

Under these circumstances, what can he do? For making, in his own person, any such examination as that which the individual, as above, has it in his choice to make, power is altogether wanting to him, for time is altogether wanting. To some person or persons other than himself, he must therefore have recourse for the formation of his opinion, and the determination of his choice. Who, then, shall they be? If, in each instance, the reporter, who in this case will be the recommender, be this or that individual,—what is *not* certain is,— that the giver of the advice will have had any better grounds for the choice than the asker: what *is* certain is, that he will not have had so great an interest in the goodness of the choice. For the goodness of *his* choice, the individual employed is not responsible to anybody but himself: the functionary is responsible to everybody. In so far as he is proof against the temptation to serve his own particular interests and affections at the public expense, his wish will, therefore, be, to see located, in each situation, the individual in whose instance the maximum of appropriate aptitude has place. Unable as he is of himself to perform the examination, the persons to whom it will be his desire to assign the task will, in consequence, be those, in whom the maximum of appropriate aptitude with relation to this same task, is to be found. By this most general description the next most general description is settled: they will be the persons that are most distinguished in the character of *instructors* in the several branches of art and science in which it is requisite the persons to be located should be proficients.

In regard to the *number* of the persons present, the examination must, in this case, be either private or public. Which shall it be? Private, it might or might not be as satisfactory as if public, to *himself;* to the public, it would not be. But, supposing him wise, it would not be so satisfactory, even to himself. For, the more complete the cognizance taken of the proceedings of these examiners by the public, the stronger the inducement they would have, each of them, for rendering his proceedings as well adapted to the purpose as it was in his power to render them. Thus, then, we have the maximum of publicity as a necessary condition to the maximum of appropriate aptitude: of appropriate aptitude—in the first place on the part of the examin*ers*, in the next place, on the part of the examin*ees*, in their quality of persons locable in the several situations, say in one word, *locables*. Evidenced by the answers will be the aptitude of the *examinees:* by the questions, that of the *examiners*.

Such, then, should be the *examination judicatory*. As to the *examinees*, by the opinion expressed by the votes of the members of this same judicatory, they will at any rate be placed in the list of persons more or less qualified for being located in the several official situations: as to their respective degrees of aptitude, in the judgment of the judicatory taken in the aggregate, they can be expressed by the several individual members. As to the manner in which the deduction may be made, it will be seen in § 2, of which *Locable who*, is the title.[1]

Next subject, the *expense*: problem, how to *minimize* it. First expense, that of the instruction: next expense, that of remuneration for the services to be rendered by those by whom the instruction has been received.

For the instruction there must be the necessary apparatus of instruction: lands, buildings, furniture for every branch: appropriate implements according to the nature [of][2] each branch.

For administering the instruction there must, moreover, be instructors, and, for the instructors, subsistence, and remuneration in quantity sufficient to engage their services. As to the pockets from whence the expense is drawn, so far as regards subsistence—bare subsistence, together with the apparatus—they must, in the first place, be those of the public, for in this way alone can the sufficiency of it be secured. This being thus settled, such part of the remuneration as is over and above bare subsistence, —from what source shall it be drawn? Answer: from the pockets of those by whom alone the most immediate benefit from the instruction is reaped: those, to wit, by whom it is received. From *them* it cannot come, without being accompanied with willingness, and followed by retribution; and the quantity of it will of itself increase in exact proportion to the number of those benefited by it: in which case it will, in the same proportion, *be a bounty upon industry* on the part of the instructors. Drawn from persons other than those by whom the immediate benefit is reaped, it would neither be accompanied with willingness, nor followed by retribution. And, if it were, as it naturally would be, a fixed sum—a

[1] The second section of the *Extract*, i.e. *Constitutional Code*, I (*CW*), Ch. IX, § 16, pp. 310–37.

[2] 1826 *Extract*, 1830 'af'.

sum not depending for its quantity on the exertions of the instructor to whom it is given—it would be a *bounty upon idleness*.

Next comes the expence of the remuneration to the intended functionaries; remuneration for the time and labour requisite to be expended on their part; before location, in qualifying themselves for rendering their several official services; after location, in the actual rendering of those same services.

For this purpose, the nature of the case presents three distinguishable modes: 1. In compliance with appropriate calls, offer to take a less salary than that which has been proposed; 2. Offer to pay a price for it; 3. Offer to submit to its being reduced to a certain less amount, and then to pay such or such a price for it, after it has been so reduced. The two first modes are simple; the third, a compound of the two: all these will have to be considered.

A point all along assumed is—that, in each office there is but one functionary: in a word, that no such implement as a *board* has place anywhere. Assumed, and why? Answer: for these reasons: All advantages that can have been looked for from a *board* are better secured by other means: in particular, by maximization of publicity and responsibility; and because the exclusion of this instrument of intrigue and delay is not less essential to aptitude than to economy. Moreover, these reasons may, as will be seen, be applied with still greater profit, to the judiciary, than to the executive, branch of government.

After all, neither by the intellectual competition, nor by the pecuniary competition, nor by both together, can the individuals, by whom the situation shall be filled, be finally determined. For the formation of this determination, there will still be need of some one person, or set of persons, in quality of *locator* or *locators*. By reasons, the essence of which is contained in the word *responsibility*, the choice has, in this case likewise, been determined in favour of number *one*.

This one person can be no other than the functionary in chief, under whose direction the functions belonging to all the several situations in question are to be exercised. As to his choice, it cannot but be influenced, not to say directed, by information which the examinations have put the public in possession of, as to the merit of the respective candidates; but, it will not, because it cannot, be determined by any positive rule. By all that has been done, or can be done, towards divesting the power—the *patronage*, (for that is the name of it,) of the quality of *arbitrariness*,—it will not therefore be by any means divested of value, or sunk beneath the acceptance of a person competent to the task of exercising it.

In the annexed table of chapters and sections, will be seen a list of the several ministerial situations to be filled.[1] *Prime minister* will be the natural appellation, of him by whom those are thus filled, and by whom the exercise of the functions respectively belonging to them is directed. In §3, intituled *Located [how]*,[2] will be seen how this consummation is proposed to be effected.

But, once more as to the *instructors*. After whatsoever may have been done for engaging them, remains still the question—*where* can they be obtained? Three sources of obtainment, and no more, does the nature of [the] case afford: they must be *found* at home, they must be *made* at home, or they must be *imported* from abroad. In each of these three modes, *invitation* is necessary. *Formation* is, in this case, an operation pre-eminently tedious: and the *formators*, where shall they be found? To find or make them would be to remove a smaller, by a greater difficulty. Different, according to the circumstances of the community in question, will, in this particular, manifestly be the eligible course.

Now as to the collateral subject, *national* education, and the assistance which the arrangements proposed for the instruction of official functionaries would give to it. What is manifest here is, that whatever is good, as applied to functionaries, will not be otherwise than good, as applied to non-functionaries: whatever promotes useful instruction in any shape in the one case, will promote it in that same shape, in no less degree, in the other. The only difference is—that, in the case of *national* education, that is to say, in the case of a youth educated at the charge of his parents,—for occupations other than the exercise of a public function,—there will be no service for the public to buy, no salary for the public to sell: and, the taking the benefit of the instruction provided will, on the part of each individual, be—not matter of necessity, as in the case of an official situation, but matter of choice. It was of course with a view to office alone, that the idea occur[r]ed, of bringing to view the several branches of instruction, that appeared requisite to give to public men the best qualification possible for the several classes of offices.[3] But, as far as it goes, this same exhibition will be of use, with a view to no small variety of private occupations. When proposing for his child this or that occupation, the parent will find in this table, if not a sufficient body of infor-

---

[1] In 'Constitutional Code.—Table of Contents' (Paper XI), under Ch. XI Ministers Severally, Bentham listed thirteen ministers: Election, Legislation, Army, Navy, Preventive Service, Interior Communication, Indigence Relief, Education, Domain, Health, Foreign-relation, Trade, and Finance.

[2] 1826 *Extract*, 1830 '*law*'. The third section of the *Extract*, i.e. *Constitutional Code*, I (*CW*), Ch. IX, §17, pp. 337–64.

[3] See ibid., Ch. IX, §16, Art. 15, pp. 314–15.

mation, a memento, at least, reminding him of the need of his satisfying himself as to what are the branches of instruction to which the mind of his child shall be directed, and of his looking out accordingly for an appropriate set of instructors.

As to instructors,—of whatsoever degree of aptitude will have been given to persons of this class, for the purpose of the instruction to be given by them to functionaries, the benefit will be open to non-functionaries: they who are able and willing to instruct the one, will not be less so to instruct the other.

So much as to *aptitude*. And as to *expence*,—of the expenditure necessary to the instruction of functionaries, a part, more or less considerable, will have been employed in the obtainment of means of instruction, which, without detriment to the one, may be employed in the instruction of the other. Of all such means the non-functionary class may have the benefit, without paying for it, any further than in their quality of members of the whole community, they had necessarily been made to pay, along with all others, for the instruction of the functionary class.

To a plan of this sort, various objections will of course present themselves. These, as far as they could be anticipated, are here collected, and such answers as seemed sufficient, subjoined.

For conveying a general conception of them, the few words following may, in this page perhaps, suffice.

I. Objection to the publicity of the examination.—*Timid aptitude excluded.*

II. Objection to the probationary period proposed for the instruction.—*Time, thence aptitude, insufficient.*

III. Objections to the pecuniary competition:—

1. Pecuniary responsibility diminished—thence corruption and depredation probabilized.

2. *Venality established.*

3. *Unopulent classes excluded, and thus injured.*

In the perusal of the here proposed arrangements, one thing should all along be borne in mind. The *sort* of government supposed by them is a representative democracy: the *time* in question that of the infancy, not to say the birth, of the state in that same form: such being the state of things, in which, in the largest proportion, the information endeavoured to be conveyed, could have any chance of being listened to.

But, in the several subordinate situations, even supposing the highest to be filled by a monarch, not inconsiderable is the number of those of the proposed arrangements, which, in the eyes even of the monarch himself, might be not altogether unsuitable. For, setting aside any such heroic endowment, as that of sympathy for the people under his rule,—to a monarch, however absolute, neither can appropriate aptitude on the part of his official servants, nor frugality in respect of the pay allotted to them, be naturally unacceptable. The more completely security, in all its shapes, is given to the subject many, the greater is the quantity of wealth they will acquire; and, the greater the quantity they acquire, the greater is the quantity that can be extracted by him from them, for his own use: in particular, for the maintenance of his *standing army*—that high-pressure, high-priced and most supremely prized, engine, which is at once an instrument of supposed security for the timid, of depredation for the rapacious, of oppression for the proud, of boasting for the vain, and a toy for the frivolous and the idle: and, as to frugality, the less is expended in the comfort of any part of the subject many, the more is left for the fancies of the ruling one.

Setting aside the case of a pure aristocracy,—a form of government no where exemplified to any considerable extent,—one only form there is, in which maximization of official aptitude, and minimization of expense, are of course objects of congenial horror to the rulers. This is that, the composition of which is a mixture of monarchy and aristocracy, with a slight infusion of democracy in the shape of a sham-representative body, in the formation of which the subject many have a minute share. In this state of things, expense of official emolument is maximized, and why? That the possessors may be pampered by the receipt of it, the people intimidated by the force kept up by it, corrupted by the hope of it, and deluded by the glitter of it. Aptitude is, at the same time, minimized, and why? Because, if the contents of the cornucopia were distributed exclusively among the most apt, those junior partners of the all-ruling one, with their dependents and favourites, would have little or no share in it.

Four distinguishable sorts of matter may be seen pervading the whole texture of this extract: the *enactive*, the *expositive*, the *ratiocinative*, and the *instructional*. Of these, the enactive, the expositive, and ratiocinative, have already been exemplified in the three-volume work, intitled, 'Traités de Legislation Civile et Penale,' being the first of four works published in French, from the author's papers, by M. Dumont.[1] Had the political state, to the circumstances of which the

---

[1] See 'Promulgation des Lois. Promulgation des Raisons des Lois', in *Traités de législation*, iii. 273–321, which contains an example of an article from Bentham's proposed Penal Code: the enactment is followed by 'Observation générale' and 'Commentaire raisonné sur la Loi'. The other recensions of Bentham's works edited by Dumont were *Théorie des peines et des récompenses*, 2 vols., London, 1811; *Tactique des assemblées législatives, suivi d'un traité des sophismes politiques*, 2 vols., Paris, 1816; and *Traité des preuves judiciaires*, 2 vols., Paris, 1823. After this

codes in question were to be adapted, been, as mathematicians say, a *given quantity*,—the *instructional* might not perhaps have been brought into existence: at any rate, it would not have occupied anything near the quantity of space, which it will be seen to occupy here. But, the indeterminateness of these circumstances impossibilized, on many occasions, the giving to the matter the form of a positive enactment, capable of standing part of the text of the law, as in the case of a code emanating from authority. Necessitated was therefore the expedient, of employing, instead of determinate expressions, general descriptions,—for the purpose, of conveying such idea as could be conveyed of the matter of the provision, which the nature of the case presented itself as demanding. By the *instructional* matter is accordingly meant the sort of matter, the purpose of which is the giving instructions to the legislator, if the tide of events should ever carry into that situation a man, or body of men, to whom it seemed good, to give to such part of the matter as could not here be expressed *in terminis*, a character conformable in principle, to those parts, for which an expression thus completely determinate, has already been proposed.

Such being the distinctive characters of the parts in question, by some minds, it was thought, it might be found a commodious help to conception, if, as often as they presented themselves, applicable indication were given of them throughout, by prefixing to each portion of matter its appropriate denomination as above. To any person, to whom these additaments appear useless, they need not offer any annoyance,—for he has but to pass them by, and read on, as if no such words were there.

Of a code, to which the stamp of authority had been affixed, these distinctions would afford a commodious method of exhibiting so many authoritative abridgments: abridgments of the only sort, on which any safe reliance can be placed. By the enactive part, if published alone, the most condensed of all the abridgments would be presented; by appropriate types and figures of reference, intimation of the existence of the omitted matter might be conveyed, without any sensible addition to the bulk of it. In another edition, might be added the expositive matter; in a third, the expositive and the ratiocinative in conjunction.

In England, a highly laudable disposition has of late shown itself, and from a quarter from which it might be followed by effect:—a disposition to raise the language of the legislator to a level, in respect

'Introductory View' was written, Dumont also produced *De l'organisation judiciaire, et de la codification*, Paris, 1828.

of propriety, somewhat nearer than that which it occupies at present, in comparison with the worst governed among other civilized nations, whichsoever that may be.[1] A design so extensively useful, would indeed stand but an indifferent chance of being carried into effect, if the fraternity of lawyers, professional as well as official, could not find adequate inducement for giving it their permit. But neither is such toleration altogether hopeless. What that particular interest requires, is—that the rule of action shall continue in such a state, that, without their assistance, comprehension of it, to a degree sufficient for the regulation of conduct, should, to all other members of the community, continue impossible. But, such is the excess to which the bulkiness and disorderliness of it have been carried;—such, in consequence, even to themselves, the difficulty of stowing it and keeping it stowed in the mind, in a state capable of being applied to use as wanted;—that, for their own relief under that difficulty, the risk of rendering the oracle too extensively and effectually comprehensible, may perhaps appear not too great to be hazarded.

This being supposed,—a result, that seems not altogether out of the sphere of possibility, is—that even those to whom the *matter* of all such codes as those here exemplified is—it need not be mentioned by what causes—rendered the object of insurmountable abhorrence,—the *form*, as far as regards *arrangement* and *expression*, may, in a degree more or less considerable, be regarded as a subject for adoption. To any person by whom it may have happened to be viewed in this light, the intimation conveyed by the words *enactive, expositive*, and *ratiocinative*, may perhaps appear not altogether devoid of use. In the case of the series of codes to which the present extract belongs,[2]—in proportion as the *matter* presented itself, the *form* in which it might be presented, it was thought, to most advantage, came along with it. Thus it was, that, as they were committed to paper, explanations, belonging to the head of *form*, became so many materials for a short disquisition, which may perhaps be submitted to the public in a separate state.[3] But, even from the small specimen here exhibited, it may be perhaps in some sort conceived, how great would be the contribution to condensation, as well as precision, if the expedient were employed, of substituting to the continued repetition of a portentous pile of particulars, that of a single general expression, in which they were all contained: the import of that expression

[1] Bentham seems to have had in mind the measures being adopted by Peel to consolidate and reform important areas of criminal and private law.

[2] Bentham conceived *Constitutional Code* as part of his Pannomion, or complete code of laws, which would also include Penal, Civil and associated Procedural Codes.

[3] Presumably the writings on 'Nomography': see 'Preface', pp. 16–17n above.

having, once for all, been fixed,—fixed, by an appropriate exposition, in the ordinary mode of a definition *per genus et differentium*,—or, where that is inapplicable, in such other mode as the nature of the case admitted of.

Between the several sorts of matter, distinguished from each other as above,—the actual separation, it cannot but be observed, has not, with any approach to uniformity, been, on this occasion, made. In one and the same article, two, or even more, of these species, will not unfrequently be found exemplified. In an authoritative code, this want of symmetry might, supposing it worth while, [be][1] remedied. In the present unauthoritative work, the difficulty of separating the proposed *enactive*, and the *instructional* from each other, was found so great, that the necessary labour and time (which would have been neither more nor less than that of writing the whole anew), was felt to be too great, to be paid for by any possible use. In like manner, in other instances, the *ratiocinative* will be seen blended with the *enactive*. In an authoritative code, the labour might, perhaps, in this case, though this does not appear altogether clear, be paid for by the use: for example, for the purpose of an authoritative *abridgment*, such as the one above proposed. But, in the present unauthoritative sketch, a mixture of the *ratiocinative* presented itself as desirable, not to say necessary, were it only to the purpose of humectating the dryness of the enactive matter, and diminishing the aversion, which a set of arrangements, so repugnant to commonly-prevailing notions and affections, would have to encounter, if inducements to acquiescence were not in some shape or other mixed up with it.

In a *civil*, or say a *right-conferring* code (for *civil* expresses so many different things that it expresses nothing), and in a *penal*, or say a *wrong-repressing* code, especially if made for a *given* political state, the separation would be a work less difficult than it has been found in the present one: accordingly, in the *Traités de Legislation*, it may, in both instances, be seen effected.[2]

In that part of the present proposed code, which regards the *judiciary establishment* the heads of which may be seen in the annexed table, the separation will be found much less imperfect.[3]

Another particular, which will naturally call forth observation, is the practice of adding to the numerical denomination of a section when

---

[1] 1826 *Extract*, 1830 'he'.

[2] In *Traités de législation*, Bentham's example of this separation of different sorts of matter was taken from the proposed Penal Code alone: see p. 30n above.

[3] According to 'Constitutional Code.—Table of Contents' (Paper XI), Bentham intended to deal with the judiciary in Chs. XII–XXV. For a reconstruction of the relevant text by Richard Doane (1805–48) see Bowring, ix. 454–612, where Ch. XXIII is omitted and the remaining Chapters renumbered accordingly.

referred to, the[1] *title* by which it is characterised. In authoritative codes an additament of this sort is not however without example. In the present unauthoritative sketch it has been matter of necessity. By the author, nothing he writes, in the character of a proposed code [of][2] law, can ever be regarded as perfected, so long as he lives: in the proposed code in question, alteration after alteration have, in great numbers, at different times, been actually made: further alteration after further alteration will continually be contemplated: and wherever, in regard to an entire *article*, either insertion or elimination have place, all the articles which follow it in the same section will require a fresh numerical denomination, and the anterior reference, if preserved, will be found delusive: and so in the case of *sections* or *chapters*.

Into what is new in point of form, a further insight will, it is hoped, ere long, be given, by another and larger preliminary extract from the present Constitutional Code: to wit, the *judiciary* part above alluded to.[3] The *enactive* matter, combined with what seemed the indispensable portion of the other sorts of matter, is already in a state fit for the press, as likewise a considerable portion of the *ratiocinative* and *instructional*, in a detached state. From the annexed table of the titles of chapters and sections for the whole, an anticipation more or less extensive may be formed of the instruments, which have been contrived for the purpose of *compression*, and may be regarded as a sort of *condensing engines*: a principal one may be seen composed of the general word *function*, followed by the several specific adjuncts attached to it. In several of its parts the matter of this same *judiciary* code could not be determined upon, without correspondent determinateness being given to correspondent portions of the *procedure* code: a code for this purpose is in such a state of forwardness, that all the principal and characteristic points are settled, and nothing remains to be done, but the reducing to appropriate form some portion of the matter which has been devised.[4]

In this work will be included, as far as circumstances admit, an all-comprehensive *formulary*, exhibiting forms for the several written

---

[1] 1826 *Extract*, 1830 'to the'.

[2] 1826 *Extract*, 1830 'or'.

[3] Bentham only printed two short passages, comprising Ch. XII, §§ 5 and 32 respectively, both entitled 'Extract from proposed Constitutional Code'. They were published in *Lord Brougham Displayed: including I. Boa Constrictor, alias Helluo Curiarum; II. Observations on the Bankruptcy Court Bill, now ripened into an Act; III. Extracts from proposed Constitutional Code*, London, 1832 (Bowring, v. 549–612), but neither was incorporated into the version of *Constitutional Code* prepared by Doane for the Bowring edition.

[4] Though not published in his own lifetime, Bentham's writings on judicial procedure were later edited by Doane and published as 'Principles of Judicial Procedure, with the outlines of a Procedure Code' in Bowring, ii. 3–188. For the relationship of the Constitutional and Procedure Codes see *Constitutional Code*, I (*CW*), pp. xxxv–xxxvii, 38n.

instruments of procedure; in particular the instruments of *demand* and *defence*, for suits of all sorts; as also forms for the *mandates* required to be issued by the judge, on the several occasions, for the several purposes: and for each mandate an appropriate *denomination* has of necessity been devised. On this occasion, as on every other, the endeavour has all along been to render the instrument of designation as characteristic as possible of the object designated. *Summonition mandate* will accordingly be seen taking place of *subpœna; Prehension and adduction* mandate of *capias* and *habeas corpus:* and, in lieu of *adduction*,—as the purpose requires, will be subjoined *abduction, transduction, sistition, sequestration, vendition*, and so forth; an appellation, such as *prehension*, and *vendition mandate*, for example, may, it is hoped, be found by lay-gents to constitute no disadvantageous substitute to *fieri facias* or *fi fa:*—to *lay-gents*, that is to say, to all human beings, but those whose interest it is that every thing by which human conduct is undertaken to be regulated, should be kept to everlasting in as incomprehensible a state as possible.

Demand paper will, in like manner, for all occasions taken together, be seen substituted, to the aggregate, composed of *action, mandamus, bill, indictment, information, libel*, and so forth: *defence paper*, to *plea, answer, demurrer*, and so forth: for, if artificial injustice has its language, so has natural justice. But time and space join in calling upon conclusion to take place of digression.

With the regret that may be imagined, does the reflection occur— that, as far as regards the diction, there are but too many political states, in which the above-mentioned views, supposing them approved of, could not be carried into any such full effect, as in those in which the language in use is the English: for, with the exception of German, there exists not, it is believed, any where that language, which will lend itself, anything near so effectually as the English, to the formation of such new appellatives as will be necessary to precision and condensation: in particular the French, which, not-withstanding its scantiness, unenrichableness, and intractability— still seems destined to continue—say who can how much longer—the common language of the civilized world.

For a particular purpose, the present extract has been sent to press, before the proposed code to which it belongs, and in which it is designed to be inserted, could be completed. Hence it is that, but for this information,—the numerical figures, in the titles to the several sections, might be taken for so many *errata*, or have the effect of giving to the whole publication the appearance of a fractional part of a work that has been lost.

This same circumstance will serve to account for the *headings* of the pages.[1]

It may not here be amiss to observe, that of the bulk of the work in its complete state, no judgment can be formed, from the space occupied by the three first of these four sections.[2] The *enactive* part of the first four chapters together, for example, does not occupy so large a space as does the least of these same three sections.

Amid so much innovation, a short caution may be not altogether unseasonable. In the frugality here recommended, no *retroaction* is comprised. By the taking away of anything valuable, either in possession, or even, though it be but in expectancy, so it be in fixed expectancy, whether on the score of remuneration, how excessive soever, or on any other score,—pain of *frustrated expectation*—pain of disappointment is produced. In the import of the above words *fixed expectancy*, is contained whatever is rational and consistent with the *greatest happiness principle*, in the pertinacity, manifested by the use of the English parliamentary phrase, *vested rights:* and note—that by forbearing to apply the alleviation which, by the defalcation in question might be given, in respect of the public burthens, to persons of all classes taken together, no such pain of disappointment is produced.

As little ought it to pass unheeded, that, supposing a high-paid functionary divested of a certain portion of wealth thus misapplied, he is not, by a great many, the only sufferer: with him will be sufferers all persons of all classes, in proportion as their respective means of expenditure were derived from his. Supposing, indeed, the over-pay derived from *crime*—obtained, for example, by false pretences, by this supposition the case is altered. But, add the supposition, that all by whom the punishment should be ordained, or that all by whom a part should be taken in the infliction of it, are sharers in the guilt, then comes the question—By whom shall be cast the first stone?[3] An Englishman need not look far to see this supposition realised. Prudence might in this case join with sympathy, in the constructing a bridge of gold, for carrying to the land of safety all opponents. Only at the expense of those, who would otherwise have been, but never will have expected to be, receivers,—can *retrenchment*, on any other ground than that of *punishment*, be, except in case of public insolvency, without hesitation, justified.

---

[1] The running headings on the recto leaves gave the short title 'Const. Code', the chapter and section number and the section title; those on the verso gave the short title 'Official Aptitude Maximized, &c.'

[2] i.e. §§ 15–17: for the 'fourth' section, § 18, see p. 23n above.

[3] See John 8: 7.

On the occasion of the ensuing proposed arrangements, mention of divers periods of years has of necessity been made. It might have been some help to conception, if, on the occasion of this or that train of suppositions, a determinate day could have been fixed, for the commencement of each period. This, however, could not be done. For different countries, different days would have been requisite. For this country, —England to wit, —the day may be fixed by imagination with something like precision. The day for the commencement of this Code with the stamp of authority on the first page of it, is the day which will give commencement to the hundred and first year, reckoning from the day on which the author will have breathed his last. In the mean time, to those who have the faculty of extracting amusement from dry matter, it may serve as a second Utopia,[1] adapted to the circumstances of the age. Of the original romance, it may, however, be seen to be—not so much a continuation as the converse. In the Utopia of the sixteenth century, effects present themselves without any appropriate causes; in this of the nineteenth century, appropriate causes are presented waiting for their effects.

END OF THE INTRODUCTORY VIEW.

[1] The 'first Utopia' was that of Thomas More, published in 1516: see *The Complete Works of St. Thomas More*, vol. 4, ed. E. Surtz and J.H. Hexter, New Haven and London, 1965.

DEFENCE OF ECONOMY
AGAINST THE
RIGHT HONOURABLE
EDMUND BURKE.
FIRST PRINTED IN JANUARY 1817.

ADVERTISEMENT.

THE paper here presented to the reader under the title of *Defence of Economy against the Right Honourable Edmund Burke*, together with another containing a *Defence* of the same more useful than welcome virtue *against the Right Honourable George Rose*, were written as long ago as in the year 1810. At that time the joint destination of the two papers was—to form a sequel to a tract of no great bulk, having for its title *Hints respecting Economy*.[1] For its subject it had taken the whole of the official establishment, and for its objects two intimately connected practical operations, viz. *minimizing official pay*, and *maximizing official aptitude:* operations the mutual subservience of which, in opposition to the universally convenient, universally received and acted upon, and in truth but too natural opinion, of their incompatibility, was maintained. The circumstance, by which the publication of it, and in some degree the completion of it was suspended, was the expectation of obtaining certain documents, which in the way of exemplification and illustration afforded a promise of being of use. Meantime the turn of affairs produced some incident or other, by which the author's attention was called off at the moment to some other quarter; and thus it is that altogether the three papers have been till now lying upon the shelf.

As to the two objects in question, so it was, that the plan, which had presented itself to the author as that by which both of these objects might be secured, and the only one by which either of them could be so in any degree approaching to perfection, having the misfortune to find itself reprobated with one voice by the two distinguished statesmen abovementioned, the removal of the impediment opposed by so strong a body of authority, presented itself of course as an object of endeavour altogether indispensable.

In the order at that time intended, a statement of the principles which had presented themselves as claiming the direction of practice would have preceded the examination here given of the principles which it was found necessary to combat: hence the reference which may here and there be found to portions of matter, which neither in any other place in which they could be referred to have made, nor in this place can make, their appearance. By a change in the order thus originally intended, that one of the two defences which will here be

---

[1] For this work see the Editorial Introduction, pp. xxvi–xxvii above.

41

found (for in the present receptacle there was not room for the other)[a] cannot, it will therefore be evident enough, but appear under more or less of disadvantage. But to the rendering them perfectly intelligible as far as they go, it did not seem, that to either of them any of the matter which belonged to that by which they had been designed to be preceded was necessary: and, by the forms of warfare, especially considering the situation and character of the person against whom it was unavoidably directed, the attention of many a reader (it has been supposed) may be engaged, whose perseverance would not carry him through the dry matter of a sort of didactic treatise, the principles of which are in a state of irreconcilable hostility to the personal interest of that class of persons which forms the subject of it, to which it cannot but look for the greatest number of its readers, and without whose concurrence, how far so ever from being accompanied with any degree of complacency, it could not at any time be in any degree carried into effect.

At the time when these papers were penned, not any the slightest symptom of official regard for public economy was it the author's good fortune to be able anywhere to recognise; everywhere it seemed an object of contempt: of contempt not only to those who were profiting by, but to those who were and are the sufferers from, the want of it. Under this impression, the wonder will rather be how the author's perseverance could have carried him so far into the subject as it did, than how it should happen that by the sense of a slight deficiency, the suspension should have been commenced, and, by a series of intervening avocations, have been continued. At present, in this respect, for a time at least, matters seem to have undergone some change. Surely enough, if it does not at the present, small indeed must be its chance of obtaining any portion of public attention at any future point of time. But should it happen to the two, or either of them, to obtain any portion of favourable regard, the more favourable, the greater will be the encouragement afforded for the labour necessary to the bringing the plan to that degree of maturity which would be necessary to its producing any assignable effect in practice.

Short as it is, in the intimation above given of the nature of the plan, one circumstance will already be but too undeniably visible, viz. that not only without any exception in respect of the first of its two connected objects, viz. *minimizing official pay*, but likewise, and with very little exception in respect of the other, viz. *maximizing official*

---

[a] This tract was first printed in the *Pamphleteer* (No. 19.)[1]

---

[1] This note was added for 1830. 'Defence of Economy against Burke', with which this 'Advertisement' originally appeared, was in fact published in vol. ix, no. xvii of *The Pamphleteer*.

aptitude, nothing can be more irreconcilably opposite to the particular interest of that class of persons, without whose concurrence no effect whatever could be given to it. Yes; even in respect of this latter object: for, if, in the instance of every office, so odd an effect as that of an exclusion put upon all who were not the very fittest for office, or even upon all who were flagrantly[1] unfit for it, were to be the result, an exclusion would thus be put upon all those, and[2] their connections, and the connections of those connections, and so on, for whom gentlemen are most anxious, because in every other way they find it most difficult, to provide. But if on the part of the plan in question the objection is grounded on the opposition of interests, and consequent unwillingness were to be regarded as a proof of impracticability, it would be a proof, not only that in government nothing good *will* ever be done, but moreover that in government in general, and in our own in particular, of all the good that *has* ever been done, the greater part has *not* ever been done. Among the points on which government turns, some there are relative to which the interest of the ruling few, be they who they may, coincides with the universal interest; and as to all these points, in so far as it happens to them to know what that same universal interest is—as to all these points, gentlemen's regard for that same universal interest may be reckoned upon without much danger of error, or much imputation on the score of credulity. Unfortunately, under most governments, and under this of ours in particular, other points there are, in which that partial and sinister interest is in a state of implacable hostility with the universal interest:[3] and of this unfortunate number are the two just mentioned: and so far as this hostility has place, so far is the universal interest, as being the least condensed, sure of being overpowered by, and made a constant sacrifice to, that which is most so.

In this state of interests, the subject-many may deem themselves particularly happy, when, to make up a provision worthy of the acceptance of a member of the ruling few, nothing more than the precise amount of that same sum, with the addition of the expense of collection, is taken out of the pockets of the subject-many. An unfortunately more common case is—where for each penny put into the privileged pocket, pounds to an indefinite number must be, and are accordingly, taken out of all pockets taken together: from privileged ones in this way with more than adequate compensation, unprivileged, without anything at all. Thus it is, that, while *wars* are made to make *places*, places are made to secure commencement or

[1] 1817, 1830 'were not flagrantly'.
[2] 1817, 1830 'for whom, and'.
[3] 1830 'interst:'.

43

continuance to wars: and, lest this should not be enough, distant dependencies—every one of them without exception productive of net loss—are kept up and increased. Yes; productive of *net loss:* for this is as uncontrovertibly and universally the case, as that two and two make four; for which reason no man who has a connection to provide for, or to whom power and glory, might, majesty, and dominion, in the abstract, are objects of concupiscence, can endure to hear of it.

As to war, so long as in the hands of those who have speech and vote in parliament, or of their near connections, offices are kept on foot with emolument in such sort attached to them, as to be materially greater in war than in peace, who is there that will venture to affirm that, of a parliament by which an arrangement of this sort is suffered to continue, the conduct is in this respect less pernicious in effect, or when once the matter has been brought to view, less corrupt in design, than it would be if in that same number the members of that same body were by masses of money to the same value, received under the name of *bribes*, engaged by one another or by any foreign power, clandestinely or openly, thus out of an ocean of human misery to extract so many of these drops of comfort for themselves? In both cases the same sums being pocketed—pocketed with the same certainty, and under the same conditions—in what particular, except in the language employed in speaking of them, and in that chance of punishment and shame which would have place in the one case, and has not in the other, do these two cases present any the smallest difference? Tell us, good Sir William! Tell us, good your Lordship, Lord of the freehold sinecure![1] exists there any better reason, why emoluments thus extracted should be retained, than why bribes given and received to the same amount, and by the same means, without disguise, should, if received, repose in the same Right Honourable pockets?

In a certain sensation called *uneasiness*, Locke beheld, as his Essays tell us, the cause of everything that is done.[2] Though on this occasion, with all his perspicuity, the philosopher saw but half his

[1] Presumably an allusion to Sir William Scott (1745–1836), created Baron Stowell in 1821, Judge of the High Court of Admiralty 1798–1828, and his brother, Lord Chancellor Eldon, respectively. The administration of Prize Law by the Court of Admiralty, and, as he saw it, the encouragement it thus gave to war, was a topic of particular concern to Bentham: see *First Principles preparatory to Constitutional Code*, ed. P. Schofield, Oxford, 1989 (*CW*), p. 257; *Constitutional Code*, I (*CW*), Ch. IX, § 17, Art. 56, p. 357. As Lord Chancellor, Eldon had an enormous quantity of patronage at his disposal.

[2] See John Locke (1632–1704), *An Essay concerning Human Understanding*, ed. P.H. Nidditch, Oxford, 1975, Book II, Ch. XXI, § 29, p. 249: 'The motive to change, is always some *uneasiness*: nothing setting us upon the change of State, or upon any new Action, but some *uneasiness*.'

subject (for happily neither is pleasure altogether without her influence): sure it is that it is in the rougher spring of action that any ulterior operation, by which the constitution will be cleared of any of its morbific matter, will find its immediate cause.

Yes:—in the returning back upon the authors some small portion of the uneasiness which the sufferers have so long been in the experience of—in this necessary operation, for which the constitution, with all its corruptions, still affords ample means—in this, if in anything, lies the people's hope.

The instrument by which the God *Silenus* was made into a poet and a prophet[1]—it is by this, if by anything, that noble Lords and Honourable Gentlemen will be fashioned into philosophers and patriots: it is by this, if by anything, that such of them whose teeth are in our bowels, will be prevailed upon to quit their hold.

Submission and obedience on the one part, are the materials of which power on the other part is composed: whenever, and in so far as, the humble materials drop off, the proud product drops off along with them. Of the truth of this definition, a practical proof was experienced in 1688 by King James, in the case of England and Scotland:[2] in 1782 it was experienced by King George and his British Parliament, in the case of Ireland.[3] In the character of ancient Pistol eating the leek,[4] in that same year was the first Lord Camden seen and heard in the House of Lords by the author of these pages demonstrating, by the light of an instantaneous inspiration, to ears sufficiently prepared by uneasiness for conviction, the never till then imagined reasonableness of the termination of that system, under which that island was groaning, under the paramount government of a set of men, in the choice of whom it had no share;[5] in the same character, in the event of a similar expediency, might his Most Noble Son be seen

---

[1] i.e. by force. Silenus, a mythological deity, would exercise the gift of prophecy only if forced to do so: he might be bound with chains of flowers while in a drunken sleep, and then compelled to prophesy and sing.

[2] James II (1633–1701), King of England, Scotland and Ireland from 1685 to 1688, was forced to flee the country in December 1688: he was later declared by the English Convention Parliament to have abdicated, by the Scottish Convention Parliament to have forfeited, the throne.

[3] In 1782 the legislative independence of the Irish Parliament from the British Parliament was effectively secured by the repeal of the Declaratory Act of 1719 (22 Geo. III, c.53), and confirmed in 1783 by the passing of a Renunciation Act (23 Geo. III, c.28). This constitutional relationship continued until the Union of the three kingdoms at the beginning of 1801.

[4] See *Henry V*, V. i, where Pistol, having earlier mocked the leek which Fluellen was wearing in his hat, is forced by Fluellen to eat it.

[5] Charles Pratt (1714–94), first Baron and first Earl Camden, Chief Justice of Common Pleas 1761–6, Lord Chancellor 1766–70, Lord President of the Council 1782–3, 1784–94, spoke in favour of Irish legislative independence in the House of Lords on 17 May 1782 (see *Parliamentary History* (1782–3) xxiii. 44–6).

in one House,[1] and his Right Honourable Grand Nephew in the other,[2] holding in hand, the one of them a Bill for the abolition of sinecures, useless places, needless places, and the overpay of useful and needful places; the other a Bill for such a reform in the Commons House of Parliament, as may no longer leave the people of Great Britain, in a number more than twice as great as the whole people of Ireland, in a condition, from which the people of Ireland were liberated as above at the instance of the learned founder of an illustrious family, which was, in one instance at least, not ill taught: in a word, such a reform as by divesting the ruling few of their adverse interest, by which so long as they continue to grasp it, they are rendered the irreconcilable enemies of those over whom they rule, will leave to them no other interests than such as belong to them in common with the people, who are now groaning under their yoke.

What belongs to the only effectual remedy which the nature of the case admits of, viz. a *restoring* change (for such in no small degree it would be) in the constitution of the House of Commons—may perhaps be spoken to elsewhere: it belongs not directly to this place. What does belong to it is the nature of the principles established on the subject of public expenditure: principles not only acted upon but avowed: not only avowed but from the connected elevations, the alas! but too closely connected elevations, the mount of the houses and the mount of financial office, preached. In these principles, it was long ago the fortune of the author to behold causes of themselves abundantly adequate to the production of whatever sufferings either are felt or can be apprehended: and if it be without any great demand for our gratitude, yet will it be seen to be not the less true, that to two distinguished statesmen, one of whom is still in a condition to answer for himself, we are indebted for the advantage of beholding these

---

[1] John Jeffreys Pratt (1759–1840), second Earl and first Marquis Camden, Lord Lieutenant of Ireland 1795–8, Secretary for War and Colonies 1804–5, Lord President of the Council 1805–6, 1807–12, had in 1780 been appointed one of the Tellers of the Exchequer, an office from which, by 1808, he received an annual income of £23,000 (see Third Report of the Committee on Public Expenditure, *Commons Sessional Papers* (1808) iii. 427). An unsuccessful attempt was made in the House of Commons on 7 May 1812 to limit his income from the office (see *Parliamentary Debates* (1812) xxiii. 73–88). However at the beginning of 1817 (after Bentham had written this passage) he voluntarily relinquished the profits and emoluments arising from the Tellership, retaining only the salary of £2,700 per annum which had been allotted to the four Tellerships as each vacancy occurred by Burke's Economical Reform Act (23 Geo. III, c.82).

[2] Robert Stewart (1769–1822), second Marquis of Londonderry, styled Viscount Castlereagh 1796–1821, Foreign Secretary 1812–22, was 'grand-nephew' of Camden in the sense that his step-mother, Lady Frances Pratt (d. 1833), second wife of Robert Stewart (1739–1821), first Baron Londonderry, first Viscount Castlereagh, and first Earl and first Marquis of Londonderry, was Camden's eldest daughter. Castlereagh, as leader of the House of Commons, was closely identified with the government's hostility to any proposals of wide-ranging reform.

same principles in a tangible shape; in that tangible shape in which they have been endeavoured to be presented to view, in two separate yet not unconnected tracts: viz. in the present *Defence of Economy*, and in the other with which it is proposed to be succeeded.

Nov. 1816.

TITLES OF THE SECTIONS.[1]

---

[1] This title page was added for 1830.

DEFENCE OF ECONOMY
AGAINST BURKE.

SECTION I.
BURKE'S OBJECTS IN HIS BILL AND SPEECH.[1]

I BEGIN with Mr. Burke: and this, not only because, as compared with that of any living statesman, the authority of a departed one unites the advantages that are afforded to authority of the intellectual kind by *anteriority* and by *death;* but because it seems but natural that, in the delivery of his own opinions, the junior and survivor should have drawn upon his illustrious predecessor, for such assistance, if any, as, in the way of argument, he may have regarded him[self] as standing in need of.

Such, as they will be seen to be, being the notions advanced by the orator—such their extravagance—such their repugnance even to the very measure they are employed to support, what could have been his inducements, what could have been his designs?—questions these, in which, if I do not much deceive myself, the reader will be apt to find at every turn a source of perplexity in proportion as the positions of the orator present themselves to view, stripped of those brilliant colours, by the splendour of which the wildest extravagances and the most glaring inconsistencies are but too apt to be saved from being seen in their true light.

In the hope of affording to such perplexity what relief it may be susceptible of, I shall begin with stating the solution which the enigma has suggested to my own mind:—showing what, in my view of the ground, was the plan of the orator's campaign—what the considerations by which he was led thus to expose his flanks, laying his principles all the time so widely open to the combined imputations of improbity and extravagance. Here then follows the statement by way of *opening*. On the mind of the intelligent and candid reader, it will

---

[1] On 11 February 1780 Burke had introduced his Civil Establishment Bill into the House of Commons. His proposals for economical reform included the eventual limitation of the annual sum available for pensions and the abolition of a number of sinecures and other offices thought to be superfluous, including the Colonial Secretaryship, the Board of Trade and a host of offices in the Royal Household. The Bill, after some initial success, was finally defeated in the House of Commons on 23 June 1780. Burke's introductory speech was published as *Speech of Edmund Burke, Esq. Member of Parliament for the City of Bristol, On presenting to the House of Commons (On the 11th of February, 1780) A Plan for the Better Security of the Independence of Parliament, and the Oeconomical Reformation of the Civil and other Establishments*, London, 1780.

make no ultimate impression any farther than as to his feelings, the charge stands in each instance sufficiently supported by the evidence.

Needy as well as ambitious, dependent by all his hopes on a party who beheld in his person the principal part of their intellectual strength, struggling, and with prospects every day increasing, against a ministry whose popularity he saw already in a deep decline,[1] the orator, from this economical scheme of his, *Bill* and *Speech* together, proposed to himself, on this occasion, two intimately connected though antagonising objects; viz. immediate depression of the force in the hands of the adversary, and at the same time, the eventual preservation and increase of the same force in the hands of the assailants, in the event of success, which on the like occasions, are, by all such besiegers, proposed to themselves, and, according to circumstances, with different degrees of skill and success pursued.

For the more immediate of the two objects, viz. *distress of the enemy*, it was, that the bill itself was provided; and to this object nothing could be more dexterously or happily adapted. Opposition it was certain of: and whatsoever were the event, advantage in some degree was sure. Suppose the opposition completely successful, and the whole plan of retrenchment thrown out together: here would be so much reputation gained to the promoters of the measure, so much reputation lost to the opponents of it. Suppose the plan in any part of it carried, in proportion to the importance of the part so carried, the reputation of its supporters would receive an ulterior increase: while that of its opponents, the weakness betrayed by them increasing in proportion to the conquests thus made upon them, would in the same proportion experience an ulterior decrease.

But as it is with the war of hands so it is with the war of words. No sooner is the conquest effected, than the weakness of the vanquished becomes in no inconsiderable degree the weakness of the conquerors: of the conquerors who from assailants are become possessors. To this eventual weakness an eventual support was to be provided.

To this service was his *speech* directed and adapted: we shall see with what boldness, and—in so far as the simultaneous pursuit of two objects in themselves so incompatible, admitted—with what art.

Such in truth were the two objects thus undertaken to be recommended—recommended at one and the same time—to public favour: a practical measure, (the measure, brought forward by his

---

[1] Burke was of course one of the principal spokesmen at this time for the Rockingham Whigs, who had been in opposition since 1766. The administration of Frederick North (1732–92), second Earl of Guilford, styled Lord North 1752–90, Chancellor of the Exchequer 1767–82, First Lord of the Treasury 1770–82, was under severe pressure because of the critical situation in the American War of Independence.

bill) a measure of practice, and in the same breath a set of *principles* with which, necessary as they were to the main and ulterior purpose, the measure, so far as it went, was in a state of direct repugnancy.

The problem therefore, with which his ingenuity had to grapple, was—so to order matters as that the economical measure should be pursued, and even if possible carried, with as little prejudice as possible to the necessary anti-economical principles.

Of principles, such as these, which have been submitted to the reader,[a] of principles really favourable to frugality and public probity, of principles in which waste and corruption would equally have found their condemnation, in whatever hands—in the hands of whatever party—the matter of waste and means of corruption were lodged,—of any such principles the prevalence would, by its whole amount, have been in a proportionable degree unfavourable to the orator's bright and opening prospects. Once in possession of the power he was aiming at, the only principles suitable to his interests, and thence to his views, would be such principles as were most favourable to the conjunct purposes of waste and corruption. So far as was practicable, his aim would therefore be, and was—to preserve for use the principles of waste and corruption in the event of his finding himself in possession of the matter and the means—to preserve them, in undiminished, and, if possible, even in augmented, force.

For this purpose, the only form of argument which the nature of the case left open to him was, that of *concession* or admission. Such, accordingly, as will be seen, was the form embraced by him and employed.

By the portion, comparatively minute as it was, of the mass of the matter of waste and corruption, of which his bill offered up the sacrifice, his *frugality* and *probity* were to stand displayed: by the vast, and as far as depended upon his exertions, the infinite mass preserved—preserved by the principles let drop, and as it were unwillingly, and as if wrung from him by conviction in his *speech*, his *candour*, his *moderation*, his *penetration*, his *discernment*, his

---

[a] Of the matter of these principles a portion more or less considerable would probably be found in that part which concerns *Reward*, of the work not long ago (1811) published in French by Mr. Dumont, under the title of *Théorie des Peines et des Recompenses*, from some of the author's unfinished manuscripts.[1]

---

[1] See the second volume of *Théorie des peines et des récompenses*, which Richard Smith translated into English as *The Rationale of Reward*, London, 1825 (Bowring, ii. 189–266). Smith also translated the first volume as *The Rationale of Punishment*, London, 1830 (Bowring, i. 388–525).

wisdom,—all these virtues were, in full galaxy, to be made manifest to an admiring world.

All this while an argument there was, by which, had there been any lips to urge it, this fine-spun web, with purity at top and corruption at bottom, might have been cut to pieces. If of the precious oil of corruption a widow's cruise full, and that continually drawn upon,[1] be so necessary as you have been persuading us to believe, why, by any such amount as proposed, or by any amount, seek to reduce it?

True; *had there been any lips to urge it*. But, that there were no such lips, was a fact of which he had sufficient reason to be assured: to urge it, probably enough, not so much as a single pair of lips:—to listen to it, most assuredly, not any sufficient number of ears: and where ears to listen and eyes to read are wanting, all the lips in the world to speak with, all the hands in the world to write, would, as was no secret to him, be of no use.

Thus then, by the craft of the rhetorician, were a set of principles completely suited to his purpose—principles by a zealous application of which, anything in the way in question, howsoever pernicious, might be done—anything however flagrantly pernicious defended—collected together as in a magazine ready for use: a magazine too the key of which was in his own pocket, and with an adequate assurance, that on the part of no enemy whom he and his need care for, would any attempt ever be made to blow it up.

Suppose now the orator seated at the treasury board—the Marquis of Rockingham on the seat of the first Lord, looking great and wise, the orator himself thinking and writing, and speaking, and acting in the character of Secretary.[2] Let him fill his own pockets, and those of his favourites and dependants, ever so rapidly, ever so profusely, no man can ever say to him, *You have belied your principles;* for, as will be seen, so long as there remained in the country so much as a penny that could be taken in a quiet way, his principles were such as would bear him out in taking it.

All this while, honourable gentlemen on the other side might have grumbled, and would of course have grumbled. *Undeserved! undeserved!* would have been the exclamation produced by every penny wasted. But *Well-deserved! well-deserved!* would be the counter-cry all the while: and, the *ayes* being in possession, the ayes would have it.

---

[1] See the story of Elijah and the widow of Zarephath, 1 Kings 17: 8–16.

[2] Burke was private secretary to the First Lord of the Treasury, Charles Watson-Wentworth (1730–82), second Marquis of Rockingham, during his first administration from July 1765 to July 1766. During Rockingham's second administration, from March 1782 until his death in July 1782, Burke took office as Paymaster-General.

Unprincipled! unprincipled! would be an interjection, from the utterance of which honourable gentlemen would by their principles—their real principles—their operating principles—not their principles for show—but their principles for use—be on both sides alike (as lawyers say) *estopped*.

As to the principles thus relied upon by the orator, they will be seen to be all of them reducible to this one, viz. that as much of their property, as by force or fraud or the usual mixture of both, the people can be brought to part with, shall come and continue to be at the disposal of him and his;—and that, for this purpose, the whole of it shall be and remain a perpetual fund of premiums, for him who on each occasion shall prove himself most expert at the use of those phrases, by which the imaginations of men are fascinated, their passions inflamed, and their judgments bewildered and seduced; whereupon he, this orator, whose expertness in those arts being really superior to that of any man of his time (to which perhaps might be added of any *other* time) could not but by himself be felt to be so, would in this perpetual *wrestling-match* or *lottery*, call it which you will, possess a fairer chance than could be possessed by any other adventurer, for bearing off some of the capital prizes.

SECTION II.
METHOD HERE PURSUED.

THUS much as to the purpose pursued by the orator in this part of his speech. A few words as to the course and method pursued in the view here given of it.

The passages to which the development of the principles in question stand consigned, are contained, most if not all of them, in that part of the speech which in the edition that lies before me occupies, out of the whole 95 pages, from 62 to part of 68 inclusive. This edition is the third—year in the title page, 1780;[1] being the year in which the bill was brought in; and, as between edition and edition, I know not of any difference.

My object is to present them to the reader in their genuine shape and colour, stripped of the tinsel and embroidery with which they are covered and disguised.

For this purpose the course that happened to present itself to me was—dividing the text into its successive component and distinguishable parts,—to prefix to each such part a proposition of my

---

[1] Bentham's own marked copy of the pamphlet is in the British Library, shelf-mark 08138. dd. 50 (4).

own framing, designed to exhibit what to me seemed the true and naked interpretation of it. Next to this interpretation, that the best and only adequate means for forming a correct judgment on the correctness of it, may not in any instance be for a moment wanting to my reader, comes the correspondent passage of the text: viz. that passage in which, as appeared to me, the substance of the interpretation will be found to be more or less explicitly or implicitly contained.

Lastly follow in general a few observations, such as seemed in some way or other conducive to the purpose of illustration, and in particular as contributing, and in some instances by means of extraneous facts, to justify the preceding interpretation, and clear it of any suspicion of incorrectness to which at first view it might seem exposed.

In some instances the truth of the interpretation will, I flatter myself, appear as soon as that portion of the text which immediately follows it has been read through; in other instances, two or three such extracts may require to have been read through, before the truth of the interpretation put upon the first of them has been fully proved; in others again, this or that extraneous fact may to this same purpose seem requisite to be brought to view, as it has been accordingly, together with a few words of explanation or observation, without which the relevancy of the facts in question might not have been altogether manifest.

As to the *order* in which the propositions here succeed one another, should it present itself to the reader, as differing in any respect from that by which a clearer view of the subject might have been exhibited, he will be pleased to recollect, that the order thus given to the effusions of the rhetorician, is the order given to them by himself; and that by their being exhibited in this order of his own choosing, the thread of his argument is delivered unbroken, and the parts of it untransposed.

Having thus before him two sets of principles, one of them in the preceding part[1] suggested by a perfectly obscure, the other, in this present part, laid down by a transcendantly illustrious hand, the reader will take his choice.

---

[1] i.e. the unpublished 'Hints respecting Economy'.

SECTION III.

PROPOSITIONS DEDUCED FROM BURKE'S ECONOMY SPEECH.[a]
1. *Concerning Public Money—What the proper Uses of it.*
Propositions 1, 2, 3.

Proposition 1. On condition of employing, upon occasion, in conversation or elsewhere, the word *reward*, in phrases of a complexion such as the following: viz. 'furnishing a permanent reward to public service,'[b] public money ought, at the pleasure of Kings and Ministers, to be habitually applied to the purpose of making the fortunes of individuals; and that in such manner as to raise their families to a state of grandeur and opulence.

Proposition 2. To this power of parcelling out the property of the public among the nominees of Kings and Ministers, there ought to be no limit: none to the quantity capable of being thus put into the hands of each nominee; none to the whole quantity of public property thus disposed of.

Proof. 'Whoever (says he) seriously considers the excellent argument of Lord Somers[1] in *the Banker's case*,[2] will not he bottom himself upon the very same maxim which I do? and one of his *principal grounds* for the *alienability* of the domains in England, contrary to the maxim of the law in France, he lays in the constitutional policy of *furnishing a reward to public service;* of making that reward the *origin of families*, and the foundation of *wealth* as well as of *honours*.'

---

[a] 'Speech on presenting on the 11th of Feb. 1780, A Plan for the better security of the independence of parliament and the economical reformation of the civil and other establishments.' Dodsley, 1780, 3d Edition. The part from which the following extracts are made is contained in pages from 62 to 68 inclusive.

[b] Page 63.

---

[1] As Bentham goes on to point out, the 'argument' in question was advanced not by Somers, but by Sir John Holt (1642–1710), Chief Justice of King's Bench 1689–1710.

[2] It had been the practice of Charles II (1630–85), King of England, Scotland and Ireland from 1660, to borrow money from bankers on the security of the taxes and hereditary revenue. Repayment, which had ceased with the Stop of the Exchequer in 1672 (see p. 59n below), had been resumed in 1677 when, by letters patent, the bankers were granted annuities charged on the hereditary excise. These payments however fell into arrears, so that by 1688 interest had only been paid up to Lady Day 1683. Following the Glorious Revolution, the bankers petitioned the Court of Exchequer for payment of these arrears. It was urged against them that the grant was invalid because it had been made by letters patent and not by Act of Parliament, but the Court decided in their favour: on appeal to the Court of Exchequer Chamber, in November 1696, the decision was reversed by Somers, with Holt dissenting, on the ground that the case was not cognizable in the Court of Exchequer, but that the correct procedure was by petition of right. Finally the original decision was affirmed by the House of Lords in January 1700. Bentham's account of the case is at pp. 57–60n below.

Then, to the word *England*, comes a note, which says 'Before the Statute of Queen Anne, which limited the alienation of land.'[1]

Observations.

Proof. At the time of this 'excellent argument of Lord Somers,' (7th Will. 3.) the whole of this domain was alienable; alienable to the utmost farthing; and, so faithfully and efficiently had it been applied to this its destined, and as we are desired to persuade ourselves, properly destined purpose, as to have brought the subject matter of it to that state, of which a description may be given in the words of the existing Committee on Finance.[a]

'The right of the crown over its own demesne lands was formerly (say they, 3d Report, p. 127.)[2] as complete as its power of conferring offices; and yet the use which was made of that part of its prerogative, occasioned Parliament frequently to interpose; and particularly, after the crown had been greatly impoverished, an act passed whereby all future grants, for any longer term than thirty-one years, were declared void.'

'The misfortune (continue they) is, as Mr. Justice Blackstone remarks,[3] that the act was made too late, after every valuable possession of the crown had been granted away for ever, or else upon very long leases.'

Such was the observation suggested by the case to Mr. Justice Blackstone; viz. that '*it was made too late.*'

But, according to the *excellent argument* of the excellent Lord Somers, it was made *too soon;* for the use of it,—the 'principal' use,—at least if the excellent Mr. Burke is to be believed, was, in the conception entertained on the subject by the excellent Lord Somers, the supplying the requisite matter for this 'constitutional policy' to operate upon;—viz. 'the constitutional policy of furnishing a per-

---

[a] This was in March, 1810.[4]

---

[1] Burke, *Speech on Oeconomical Reformation*, pp. 62–3. There are some minor inaccuracies in the rendering of this and other passages from Burke's *Speech on Oeconomical Reformation*. The italics, unless otherwise noted, are Bentham's. The statute was 1 Ann., sess. 1, c.7.

[2] For the Third Report, dealing with 'Pensions, Sinecures, Reversions', see *Commons Sessional Papers* (1808) iii. 257–459, and for this particular passage iii. 275 (this is p. 127 of the Report). There are some minor inaccuracies in the rendering of the passage.

[3] Sir William Blackstone (1723–80), first Vinerian Professor of English Law at Oxford University 1758–66, MP for Hindon 1761–8 and Westbury 1768–70, Justice of Common Pleas 1770, 1770–80, Justice of King's Bench 1770: see his *Commentaries on the Laws of England*, 4 vols., Oxford, 1765–9, i. 277.

[4] The Committee on Public Expenditure, which had been appointed in February 1807, continued to sit until 1812, in which time it produced thirteen Reports.

manent reward to public service; of making that reward the origin of families; and the foundation of wealth as well as honours.'

Now of this Statute of Queen Anne (as far as it went) the effect was to *counteract* the 'constitutional policy,' and render it together with the excellent '*maxim*' on which the excellent law Lord is said to have '*bottomed himself*,' incapable of being pursued; and, to a plain and un-law-learned understanding, they cannot both be good, viz. the *policy* and the *statute:* the *policy* by which the alienation of the property in question for that purpose was prescribed, and the *statute* by which the alienation of that same property, for that or any other purpose, was prohibited.[a]

[a] After all, it was not by the '*excellent*' Lord Somers that this profundity of policy was, or, considering the side taken by him, could consistently have been displayed. It was to another '*excellent*' law Lord, though not noble Lord, viz. the Lord Chief Justice *Holt*, that the glory of it should have been ascribed.

'Rewards and punishments' (says he) 'are the supporters of all governments:—and for that reason it is that there ought to be a power in all governments to reward persons that deserve well':[a]—proof sufficient to the excellent Lord Chief Justice that it was no more than right and fitting, that it should always be, and so long as anything was left, remain in the King's power, to give away, to any body he pleased, whatsoever part of the people's money he could contrive to lay his hands on.

'But it is objected' (says the excellent Lord Chief Justice) 'that the power in the King of alienating his revenues may be a prejudice to his people, to whom he must recur continually for supplies.' But to this objection, the excellent Chief Justice had his answer ready. 'I answer' (says he) 'that the law has not such dishonourable thoughts of the King, as to imagine he will do any thing amiss to his people in those things in which he has power so to do.'[1] Reason sufficient with the excellent Chief Justice to trust the King, thus in the lump, with the arbitrary and uncontrolled disposal of men's properties;—reason not less sufficient might it have been, for trusting the same royal person, on the same terms, with their liberties and their lives. This was *Whig Common Law*. What more could a King have had or wished for, from *Tory Common Law?*

This theory then, which, to the views of our Orator being so convenient, was in the judgment of the Orator so '*excellent:*'—this theory was the theory—not of the excellent Lord Keeper, but of the excellent Lord Chief Justice. Not that by this mistake of John for Thomas any very material injustice was done to the excellent Lord Keeper; for, in this instance, if anything was wanting in *theory* (not that any such deficiency appears) it was made up in *practice*.

To the profits of the office—those profits, for an eventual supplement to which even Lord Eldon required, or at least obtained, not more than a floating 4,000*l.* a

[a] Modern Reports, Vol. 5, pp. 54, 55. 7 Will. 3d. The Banker's case.[2]

[1] Thomas Leach, *Modern Reports, or, Select Cases adjudged in The Courts of King's Bench, Chancery, Common Pleas, and Exchequer*, vol. V, 5th edn., London, 1794, p. 54. There are some minor inaccuracies in the rendering of the passage.

[2] See ibid., p. 55, where Holt is reported: 'And there ought to be a power in all governments to reward persons that deserve well; for rewards and punishments are the supporters of all governments. . . .'

year,[1] these profits not being sufficient for '*making reward the origin of that family;*' for affording to it a sufficiently broad '*foundation of wealth as well as of honours,*' a pension for life of 4,000*l.* a year was added: 4,000*l.* a year *then* equal at least to 12,000*l.* a year *now*. This, as not being in fee, being still insufficient, an estate,[a] which *was* and *is* in fee, was added: an estate which according to his own admission and valuation made for the purpose, was producing at that time no more than a poor 2,100*l.* a year, if the statement thus given in general terms by the learned and noble grantee for the purpose of his defence against an impeachment is to be taken for correct: how much at present is best known to some noble or not noble proprietor or other, related or not related, into whose hands it has passed.

But this 4,000*l.* a year, and this 2,100*l.* a year and this 12,000*l.* a year more or less, these et cæteras, were they, any of them, ever *begged* for by the excellent Lord? Oh no: so he himself expressly assures us:[2]— begged for, no more than the Teller-ship was begged for by Mr. Yorke.[3] These are of the number of those gracious designs, which till the very moment of their taking effect, are never known of. While the eyes of the Right Honourable person are, as usual, fixt on heaven, the grant is slipped into his pocket, and when, putting in his hand by accident, he feels it there, his astonishment is not inferior to his gratitude.[b]

Note that for no such expence as this, in so rare an article as wisdom, was there any the smallest need. In the time of Charles the 2nd (the Bank of England not as yet

---

[a] The Manor or Manors of *Rygate* and *Howleigh*, which according to the Tory House of Commons were at that time worth *upwards* of 12,000*l.* but according to the noble and excellent defendant 'far short' of that 'value:' though how far short he was not pleased to say: also divers other good gifts the amount of which became the matter of so many disputes, which, the impeachment of the excellent Lord not having come to a trial, was never settled.—V. State Trials, Vol. 5, pp. 350, 351, 352.[4]

[b] Of the relative quantity of the slice thus taken, relation being had to the quantity left, some conception may be formed from a note of Mr. Rose's in his 'Observations respecting the public expenditure and the influence of the crown.' 2nd Edition, 1810. 'In 15 years, to 1715, the whole income from crown lands (says he) including rents, fines, and grants of all sorts, was 22,624*l.* equal to 1,500*l.* a year.'—Journals of H. C. Vol. XX. p. 520.[5]

---

[1] By Act of Parliament (39 Geo. III, c.110), Eldon's pension upon retirement as Lord Chancellor was to be £4,000 per annum.

[2] The articles of impeachment accused Somers of having 'begg'd and procured' the grants in question: in response he denied 'that he did ever beg, or use any Means to procure any Grant whatsoever from his Majesty for his own Benefit' (Hargrave, *State Trials*, v. 349–50).

[3] Charles Philip Yorke (1764–1834), Secretary at War 1801–3, Home Secretary 1803–4, First Lord of the Admiralty 1810–12, having defended the conduct of the Walcheren expedition of 1809 in the House of Commons on 25 January 1810, was offered, and in the following month was appointed to, a Tellership of the Exchequer by Spencer Perceval (1762–1812), Chancellor of the Exchequer 1807–12, First Lord of the Treasury 1809–12.

[4] For the charges brought against Somers with regard to his procuring grants from the Crown see 'Preface', p. 18n above. Bentham's account of the charges is slightly confused. In addition to the manors of Rygate and Howleigh (which the House of Commons claimed were worth over £12,000, but which Somers said were worth 'far short' of that sum) and other grants (which Somers said were worth £2,100 per annum), he was accused of obtaining 'an annual Pension or Allowance from the Crown' of £4,000. In reply, Somers stated that a similar pension had been granted to several of his predecessors. (See Hargrave, *State Trials*, v. 349–52).

[5] See 'Preface', p. 18n above.

born or thought of) money to the amount of 'above a million' (a vast sum in those days) part their own, part that of their *customers*, having been lent to the King by a set of *bankers*, was by him the said King converted to his own use: in court English, '*the Exchequer was shut up.*'[1]

In a succeeding reign, viz. that of King William,[2] the question was, whether there was power in the crown, sufficient for applying a particular branch of its revenues in part restitution of the profit of this robbery. Yes, says this Lord Chief Justice: for the branch in question (a new one—a portion of the Excise) was given to the King in exchange for an old branch, viz. the branch called '*wards and liveries.*' Whoever has an estate *in fee* may alienate it; in the '*wards and liveries*' the King had an estate in fee! the Excise was by Act of Parliament given to him in lieu of those '*wards and liveries:*' and what is more, by the express words of the act, he was and is empowered to alien it.[3] This, supposing the construction put upon the act not inconsistent with the words of it, might, one should have thought, have sufficed for argument. But this would not have sufficed to shew the learned Lord's acquaintance as above with the depths of policy: nor yet the '*honourable thoughts*' entertained of the King by the law:—and so, *ex abundantiâ* the sage reasons that have been seen, were added.

Whatsoever money the King could contrive to lay his hands upon, *that* the virtuous Whig Chief Justice was content to see him waste. Why? For this plain reason: because 'the law has not'—(i.e. he, his predecessors and colleagues had not) any such dishonourable thoughts of the King 'as to imagine he will do anything amiss to his people in those things in which he has power so to do.'

And what was the incident that called forth their effusion of faith and confidence? It was that of a King having robbed his subjects: robbed them of so much money—and for what? to hire men with, for robbing in conjunction with their enemies[a]—for robbing and murdering their allies.[b]

Now therefore in my humble conception of the matter, whosoever it was that went *thus far*, whether it was the excellent Lord Keeper, whether it was the virtuous and intrepid Whig Chief Justice went so far, it is no very easy matter to imagine how the learned colleagues of the Chief Justice, or any of them, should (as Edmund Burke says they did) 'go further:'[4] and that for any imaginable set of existing circumstances, for any imaginable purpose of *accommodation, convenience, reward of merit, reward of*

---

[a] The French.
[b] The Dutch.

---

[1] In accord with the secret Treaty of Dover 1670, Charles II was committed to join the French in hostilities against the Dutch. In anticipation of the declaration of war in March 1672, the Stop of the Exchequer on 2 January 1672, instigated by Thomas Clifford (1630–73), first Baron Clifford, member of the Cabal and Lord High Treasurer 1672–3, by which repayments to government creditors were suspended, was conceived as a means of raising revenue for the armed forces.

[2] William III (1650–1702), King of England, Scotland and Ireland from 1689.

[3] For Holt's argument to this effect see *Modern Reports*, V, p. 54: 'I hold, that King Charles the Second might charge this branch of his revenue; and my reason for my opinion is but short. It is, because the king was seised of an estate in fee of this revenue; for to such an estate a power of alienation is incident. And I take it to be the intent and the express words of the act, that the king should have a right and liberty of alienating and charging this estate.' The Act in question was 12 Car. II, c.24.

[4] Burke, *Speech on Oeconomical Reformation*, p. 63: 'The other judges who held the same doctrine, went beyond Lord Somers with regard to the remedy, which they thought was given by law against the crown, upon the grant of pensions.'

Proposition 3. The progress of this revolution ought not to be stopped, till it has received its consummation as above described, i.e. so long as any part of the property of the public (understand of the people) remains unapplied to the purpose of giving effect to this 'maxim' with its 'constitutional policy;' viz. 'the furnishing a permanent reward to public service: of making that reward the origin of families, and the foundation of wealth as well as honours.'

Proof. (Observations.) For, already, at the time of this excellent argument, had this quiet and gradual revolution made such progress, that within a trifle, the domain in question,—a mass of property originally sufficient for the peace establishment of the country—had been thus disposed of.

There remained, it is true, and still remains, in part at least as yet undisposed of in the same constitutional way, the private property of individuals.

But a principle adequate to this purpose, had already been established—established by the same or another provident set of hands—and, at the same time of this excellent oration still continued to be

eminent services, and so forth—not to speak of reasonable, useful, and honest purposes,—it went far enough of all conscience.[1]

Of these 'honourable thoughts' one effect was to reduce to such a state of debility the learned thinker's learned imagination, as to disable it from representing to him as *possible*, a state of things which his memory, if consulted upon the occasion, could not but have represented to him as realized, and that no more than seven years before: that state of things expressed—the half of it by the lawyer's word *abdication*, the whole of it by the people's word *revolution*, but for which (I mean the revolution) his master could not have been a King, nor himself a Lord Chief Justice.[2] This master of his was now King: and now, whatsoever power the King has, is become incapable of being used amiss; misuse being in such hands either the same thing as use, or (what comes to the same thing) converted into use.

This is the way the sort of a thing called common law is made. Not content with exercising the *power* which he *has*, nothing will serve a man but he must display the *wisdom* which he has *not*: he bewilders himself and raves: and his ravings as often as it happens to them to suit the interest or the humour of those that come after him, these ravings of his become law.

Principles and practice together, nothing could be better matched: practice found by the excellent Lord Keeper, principles by the excellent Lord Chief Justice.

Note that while lawyers as well as favourites were thus fattening (for the reign of William, though a reign of salvation for England and for Europe, was a reign of waste and favouritism) the state, for want of common necessaries, was continually on the brink of ruin: expense unprecedented, ways and means scanty, deficiencies abundant, losses distressing, credit at death's door.

---

[1] 1830 'concience.'

[2] The Glorious Revolution of 1688–9, by which James II was deposed and the Crown offered to William and Mary of Orange.

acted upon; yes, and still continues to be acted upon, under the eye and cognizance, and without censure from the above mentioned existing committee, by which a diamond from this same excellent oration has, without acknowledgment, been picked out,—picked out and employed in giving additional lustre to the jewel for which we are indebted to their hands.[a]

[a] Burke, p. 62, in the paragraph immediately preceding the one above quoted:—'I know, too, that it will be demanded of me how it comes, that since I admit these offices' (sinecures) 'to be no better than pensions, I chose, after the principle of law had been satisfied,' (meaning the principle, with how little propriety soever it can be termed a principle of law, the principle of policy and humanity, that forbids the abolition of them, though it be by the legislature, to the prejudice of existing rights of property, i.e. without adequate compensation) 'I chose to retain them at all.' This being the question, now reader, whether you have, or have not, read Part I. of this Tract, Chapter 3, *On Sinecures*,[1] be pleased to observe the answer—'To this, Sir, I answer, that conceiving it to be *a fundamental part of the constitution of this country*, and of the *reason of state* in every country, that there must be *means of rewarding public service*, these means will be incomplete, and indeed wholly insufficient for that purpose, if there should be no further reward for that service than the *daily wages* it receives during the pleasure of the Crown.'

Thus far Edmund Burke: and thus far, and without inverted commas, or any other token of adoption, the existing Committee on Finance, (3rd Report, p. 126)[2] substituting only for the words—'*To this, Sir, I answer, that conceiving*' the words 'at the same time regarding.'[3]

Here we see what, according to the logic of the rhetorician, constitutes a sufficient reason why the quantity of annual emolument in question should not be put into the shape of *pension*, but be continued in the shape of Sinecure. And this is the flourish which, with the question between Sinecures and Pensions before their eyes, the Committee copy: and though like the Orator in the way of *concession*, exhibit not the less in the character of a 'fundamental part of the constitution of this country.'

This principle consists in the *habit*, which under common law, is the same thing as the *power*, of creating *offices*, with fees annexed to the same, and receivable by the officers successively invested with the same: of creating these fee-gathering offices, or what comes to the same thing, annexing more and more fees to offices of this sort already created; fees, that as *taxes*, are exacted by the sole authority of some official person or persons, without allowance, special or general, from the representatives of the people in Parliament.

This principle may be seen flourishing to this day, and with unabated vigour; for so long as the word *tax* is not mentioned, and instead of a contribution to a *tax*, the money levied is called *a fee*, and instead of the pocket of the public, the pocket it goes into is that of the imposer, and the assembly in the composition of which the people have some share have no share in the imposition of it, nothing can exceed the acquiescence and complacency with which the good people of this country, as well as

---

[1] i.e. Ch. 3 of 'Hints respecting Economy'.
[2] See *Commons Sessional Papers* (1808) iii. 274 (this is p. 126 of the Report). There are some minor inaccuracies in the rendering of the passage.
[3] i.e. in the Report, Burke's original words 'To this, Sir, I answer, that conceiving' have been replaced with the phrase 'at the same time regarding'.

its Parliament, are content to view it; especially when the tax thus imposed, is imposed upon that class of the community which is composed of the distressed members of all the other classes, and by so fast a friend to the rights of the people and to *liberty*, and to *Juries*, and to the laws which forbid the *levying money* upon the people without consent of Parliament, and to the *Magna Charta* which forbids the *delaying of justice*, and to the *Magna Charta* which forbids the *sale of justice*, and to the *Magna Charta* which forbids the *denial of justice* (whether by putting a price upon it beyond what they have to give, or otherwise)[1] as the Noble Ex-Chancellor, then Chancellor, legislating with the advice and consent of his Right Honourable Subordinate,[2] whose experience in equity business found such a contrast to that of the Common-Law-Learned Novice.[a]

Thus, from this Table, it appears, that of the four great Westminster Hall Courts, there is not one in which the principle of taking the property of the distressed to make fortunes for Court favourites, or, in the Orator's language, to '*make it the origin of families and the foundation of wealth and honours*,' was not applied,—not one in which the application of it is not to this very day continued. A natural question here is—how in so great a length of time it comes to have made so small a progress? The answer is—that in the hands of the King, this mine having, soon after its discovery, been worked too openly and too rapidly, the consequence was, that the thus working of it received the check we hear so much of, and care so little about;[3] and that from that time it was given up to those useful servants of his, whose professional dexterity was now become necessary to enable a man, when working under the Rose,[4] to make a living profit out of it.

The earliest instance, of which any effect or memory is now remaining is, as the

---

[a] No. I. List of Law Sinecures, granted in *fee*, with the masses of *emolument* respectively attached to them: gleaned and put together from the Reports of the Finance Committee of the years 1797–8 and 1807–8: distinguishing as well the different descriptions of the Offices and Officers in question, as the different masses of emolument respectively received at the two different periods, as exhibited by the two committees: with references to the Nos. of the Appendixes and Pages of the two Reports; the Reports being—of those of the committee of 1797–8, the [27]th,[5] and of those of the committee of 1807–8, the 3d.[6]

---

[1] See Magna Carta, c.40 (1215), c.29 (1225): 'To no one will we sell, to no one will we refuse or delay right or justice.' (*English Historical Documents 1189–1327*, ed. H. Rothwell, London, 1975, pp. 320, 345.)

[2] An increase of costs in the Court of Chancery had been sanctioned by an order of 26 February 1807 signed jointly by Thomas Erskine (1750–1823), first Baron Erskine, Lord Chancellor 1806–7, and the Master of the Rolls, Sir William Grant (see further p. 65n below and 'Indications respecting Lord Eldon', §§III–VII, pp. 212–21 below). At the time of his appointment, Erskine was said to know nothing of equity, whereas Grant (1752–1832), Solicitor General 1799–1801, Master of the Rolls 1801–17, had considerable experience both as a practitioner and a judge.

[3] i.e. Magna Carta.

[4] i.e. in strict confidence.

[5] 1817, 1830 '29'.

[6] The Reports deal with 'Courts of Justice' and 'Pensions, Sinecures, Reversions': see *House of Commons Sessional Papers of the Eighteenth Century*, ed. S. Lambert, 145 vols., Wilmington, Delaware, 1975, cxi. 41–315, and *Commons Sessional Papers* (1808) iii. 257–459 respectively. The information presented in the table is generally correct; significant discrepancies are recorded in editorial footnotes.

§III. DEDUCTIONS FROM BURKE'S SPEECH

1797–8 No.	Page	1807–8 No. Page	Description as per 1797–8.	Description as per 1807–8.	Annual Sums received as per 1797–8	1807–8.
			(1)	I. COURT OF CHANCERY.	£	£
1 K.7	84,5	72 280	1. Keeper or Clerk of His Majesty's Hanaper in Chancery, Earl of Northington, and his heirs, during the lives of (see next column.)	1. Hanaper, Clerk of; sisters and co-heiresses of the Earl of Northington.	1,811a	2,070
2 K.3a K.3b	62–3[1]		(2) 2. Register of the Court of Chancery, Duke of St. Albans, or Drummond, his Mortgagee, (see Vezey, Jun. V. 433.)[2]	2. No mention.	640	
			(3)	II. COURT OF KING'S BENCH.		
3 L.16	160–1	72 [280][3]	3. Comptroller of the Seals of the Courts of King's Bench and Common Pleas, his Grace the Duke of Grafton.	2. Seal Office of King's Bench and Common Pleas, Duke of Grafton.	400	2,886
			(4)	III. COURT OF COMMON PLEAS.		
4 M.[4]14	190–1	72 281	4. Hereditary Chief Proclamator, J. Walker Heneage.	4. Chief Proclamator, Arabella Walker Heneage, Widow.	100	100
5 M.1	172–3	72 281	(5) 5. Custos Brevium, C.[B].[5] Honourable Lady Louisa Browning, one-[sixth];[6] Hon. Lady Robert Eden, one-sixth; [Jos^h][7] Hankin, Esq. Tenant by the Curtesy, one-third; Edward Gore, Esq. in right of his Wife, Lady Mostyn, one-third.	5. Custos Brevium, Honourable Louisa Browning, Sir Fr. M. Eden, Lady B. Mostyn, Joseph Hankin.	455	929
			(6)	IV. COURT OF EXCHEQUER.		
6 N.29	[238][8]	72 281	6. Hereditary Chief Usher of the Exchequer, with the Appurtenances thereof, John Walker Heneage.	6. 'Chief Usher, Arabella 'Walker Heneage, in fee, 'under Grant from Henry 'II. as well as the other 'office.'	133 &c. b	137

Reference to the Reports of the Finance Committees.

No. (1) 1797–8, K. 7. p. 84, 85—1807–8. No. 72. p. 280.
No. (2) 1797–8, K. 3a, K. 3b, p. 62, 63—1807–8. No mention.
No. (3) 1797–8, L. 16. p. 160, 161—1807–8, No. 72, p. 280.
No. (4) 1797–8, M. 14. p. 190, 191—1807–8, No. 72, p. 281.
No. (5) 1797–8, M. 1. p. 172, 173—1807–8, No. 72, p. 281.
No. (6) 1797–8, N. 29. p. 238, 239—1807–8, No. 72, p. 281.

a Gross 1994*l*. The beneficial interest is not in fee: the reversion was granted to a pair of Thurlows in June 1792.—27th Finance Report, 1797–8. p. 84.

b 'Viz. an ancient allowance of 5d. a day, (called *diet money*) during the time the Court is open, which is uncertain.'—27th Finance Report, 1797–8, N. 29 (a) p. 238.

[1] Appendix K.3a is at p. 62, and K.3b at pp. 63–9.
[2] A dispute had arisen concerning the reversion of the Register of the Court of Chancery. The case, Drummond v. The Duke of St. Albans, which was decided in favour of the plaintiff, was reported in Francis Vesey, Jun., *Reports of Cases argued and determined in the High Court of Chancery*, vol. V, London, 1801, pp. 433–40.
[3] 1817, 1830 '180'.
[4] 1830 omits full stop.
[5] 1817, 1830 'P'.
[6] 1817, 1830 'eighth'.
[7] 1817, 1830 'John'.
[8] 1817, 1830 '238–9'.

Table shows, of as early a date as the reign of *Henry the Second*.[1] Soon after him came *King John*, whom, besides his *Magna Charta*,[2] so many details that have come down to us on record prove to have kept an open shop for the sale of the commodity which went by the name of *justice*, and in which the prices were not *then* in any sort, as *at present* they are in some sort, fixed. In King John's reign comes this *Magna Charta*, and thenceforward, so far as concerned the sort of *'public service'* rendered by the *Gavestons*, the *Spencers*, and the *Mortimers*,[3] this source of *'permanent reward to public service'* was nearly dried up; and for what few drops have here and there been collected by the successors of those accomplished Gentlemen, they have been forced to enter into a sort of partnership with the Gentlemen of the Long Robe.

Had it not been for the obstruction just mentioned, the present amount of that part of the produce of the *stamp duties* which is levied upon those who are distressed whether by or for want of the commodity sold under the name of *justice*, would have composed but a part, and that a small one, of that part of public money which would have followed the fate of the Crown Lands, under and by virtue of the principle thus maintained by Holt and fattened upon by Somers.

I say, but a small part: for had the mine continued in individual hands, with the power and capital of the King openly employed, as under King John, in backing them, it would have continued to be worked with that zeal and consequent success, by which labour in private is, so much to its advantage, distinguished from labour on public account: and supposing any remnants of it, as of the Crown Lands, to be still remaining, the Percevals of the present day,[4] instead of being occupied in the augmentation of those taxes on distress for the benefit of rich and poor together, defending inch by inch, and not always without loss, those parts of the produce which stand appropriated to the enrichment of the rich, would have been exclusively employed in the more agreeable occupation of giving additional breadth to '*the foundation of wealth as well as honours*' upon the plan here sketched out by Edmund Burke, and with as little reserve or mystery as was found necessary by King John, in the halcyon part of his days.

In the Court of Chancery there exists a set of men called from their number *the sixty clerks*, whose situation is something compounded of or intermediate between, that of an *officer of the court* and that of an *attorney*.

---

[1] Henry II (1133–89), King of England from 1154.

[2] Magna Carta was first issued in 1215 by John (1167?–1216), King of England from 1199.

[3] These figures were prominent in the intrigues and upheavals which characterized the reign of Edward II (1284–1327), King of England from 1307. Piers Gaveston, Earl of Cornwall, a favourite of Edward II, was executed in 1312 by rebellious barons, headed by Thomas, Earl of Lancaster (c.1277–1322). Hugh le Despenser the Elder (1262–1326), Earl of Winchester, was a minister and supporter of Edward II, while his son, Hugh le Despenser the Younger, was another favourite of the King. Having defeated and executed Lancaster in 1322, the Despensers effectively ruled the country until 1326, when they were themselves seized and put to death by Queen Isabella (1292–1358), Edward II's wife, and her paramour, Roger Mortimer (1287?–1330), Earl of March. Isabella and Mortimer then imprisoned the King, forced him to resign the crown, and subsequently had him murdered in September 1327. They ruled the country in the name of his son and successor, Edward III (1312–77), who eventually established his independence by executing Mortimer in November 1330.

[4] Probably an allusion to Sir Philip Perceval (1605–47), who, amongst other offices, held those of General Feodary of Ireland, Escheator of Munster, Commissioner of Survey into Land Titles in Tipperary and Cork, and Clerk of the Commission for the Remedy of Defective Titles. Using his official position, and exploiting uncertainties in titles to Irish estates, he acquired about 100,000 acres of land in grants from the Crown.

They are *officers of the court*, inasmuch as, through an intermediate nomination, they are nominated by a subordinate *judge* of the court (the Master of the Rolls) and inasmuch as in every cause the parties on each side are obliged to employ one or other of them; they are *attornies*, inasmuch as they are *agents* of the *parties*, and, on each side of a cause, the party or parties, through the medium of their respective attorneys, (called here solicitors) have their choice which of them to employ.

In the same court there exists another set of men called the *six clerks*, whose situation seems to be purely that of an officer of the court. To each of these *six clerks* belongs the nomination of *ten* out of the *sixty clerks;* which nominations he either sells or gives, which ever mode of disposition happens in each instance to be most for his advantage.[a]

Of these six clerks, the nomination belongs to the Master of the Rolls for the time being: which nomination, like the Lord Chancellor and Chief Justices of the King's Bench and Common Pleas, he in like manner either sells or gives, according to the mode of disposition, that happens to be most to his advantage.

The greater the annual value of a *sixty clerk's* place, the greater the value of the place of a *six clerk* who has the gift or sale of it. The greater the value of a *six clerk's* place, the greater the emolument of the place of the Master of the Rolls who has the gift or sale of it.

By order of the Court of Chancery, dated 26th February, 1807, signed by the Lord Chancellor, *Lord Erskine*, and by the Master of the Rolls, *Sir William Grant*, by whose advice and assistance he states himself as acting therein, a new '*schedule of fees*,' is established and authorized to be taken by each one of those sixty clerks: — fees described in so many articles, 43 in number, and the amount avowedly increased in the instance of each article.[1]

A prior instance had been found in which in like manner, viz. by a law enacted in the same way by the joint authority of the two judges, bearing the same offices, money had in this way, about the middle of last century, been levied upon those children of distress called *suitors* without consent of parliament.[2] Coupled with *power*, *sinister interest* begets *precedent*, and precedent *begets*, or rather precedent *is law*.

Of the two modes in which, without consent or privity of parliament, law is made by the sole authority of the King's nominees in the character of *judges*, this (it must however be confessed) is beyond comparison the least mischievous; it not involving, as the other does, the attribute of uncognoscibility, and the tyranny of an ex post facto law.

---

[a] Harrison's Chancery. I. 61. Ord. Can. 83.[3]

---

[1] See p. 62n above, and 'Indications respecting Lord Eldon', §III, p. 212 below.

[2] See 'Indications respecting Lord Eldon', §V, pp. 217–18 below.

[3] Joseph Harrison, *The Accomplish'd Practiser in the High Court of Chancery, shewing The whole Method of Proceedings, according to the present Practice, from the Bill to the Appeal inclusive*, 7th edn., ed. John Griffith Williams, 2 vols., London, 1790, discusses the Six Clerks at i. 75–6 and the Sworn Clerks (or Sixty Clerks) at i. 76–7 (Bentham seems to have been using a different edition). The Order of Chancery to which Bentham refers (though why here is unclear) is as follows: 'All office copies made by [the Sworn Clerks] of proceedings in the court, are to contain fifteen lines in every sheet, and six words in every line, written orderly: and the same are to be signed with the name of the Six Clerk to whose division they belong, by himself or his deputy, or otherwise the same shall not be read, or otherwise made use of in court' (ibid., 76).

SECTION IV.
CONCERNING TITLE TO REWARD.
Proposition 4.

IN the course of the disposition thus made of the whole property of Government, with the growing addition of the whole property of the people, the plea of its having for its use and object the furnishing a reward to public service, ought never to be any other than a false pretence: at any rate nothing ought ever to be done to prevent its being so.

Proof. (Observations.) Four modes of disposing of the public money, under the notion of reward for public service—extraordinary public service—all of them in frequent use—lay open to the rhetorician's view. 1. Remuneration by *Act of Parliament.* 2. Allowance out of *secret service money.* 3. *Pensions* granted by the Crown *without concurrence of parliament.* 4. *Sinecure offices* granted by the Crown *without concurrence of parliament.*

In the case of Remuneration by act of Parliament, every thing is open to *view;* every thing is open to *discussion;* 1. The nature and *reality* of the *service* supposed to have been performed. 2. The *part taken by the person* in question in the rendering of that service. 3. The *importance* of the *whole* service and of the *part* taken by him in the rendering it. 4. The *magnitude* of the proposed *reward.*

In the case of remuneration out of *secret service money,* all these particulars are left in darkness; and in time of *war,* and thence at all *other* times (since there are none in which the approach or danger of war may not be imminent) it being necessary that in the hands of the administration there should exist means of purchasing services, such as under any apprehension of disclosure would be unobtainable: hence a fund for this purpose ever has been, and ever ought to be, on foot.

In the case of *pensions,* some of the above four particulars are open to *discussion:* two of them, and two only, *are* open to view; viz. 1. The *person on whom* so much of that matter, viz. *Money,* which is in use to be applied, and in this case is applied, to the purpose of remuneration, has been bestowed. 2. The *quantity* of that matter thus *bestowed.* What is *not* open to view is whether it is under the *notion* of his having rendered *any* public service, that the money has been bestowed; much less whether such notion, supposing it really entertained, be in any degree *just* or no.

In[1] the case of *Sinecures,* he saw all these helps to misapplication

---

[1] 1817, 1830 '4. In'. Since Bentham failed to enumerate the previous three paragraphs, the paragraph number has been suppressed.

having place, and as compared with the case of *pensions*, acting in much greater *force*. In the case of a pension, what is bestowed constitutes a new article, put upon an already existing list: a list, which if not already public, is liable to become so at any time;—a list, which in the mean time, whether made known or not to the *public*, cannot but be kept constantly in view by various members of administration, if it were only lest the fund on which it is settled should be overloaded;—a list such, that no fresh article can ever be placed on it, without producing a fresh *sensation*, as constituting a manifest addition to the mass of public burthens; and in relation to which it is impossible, but that to many persons the question must occur—on what *grounds*, and with what *propriety*, has this addition been made?

In the case of sinecures, not one of these spurs to attention had, in *his* view, any more than they have at present, any existence. Sinecure list, none: no, nor so much as a future possibility of making out any such thing, without a course of intricate inquiry, such as even now, in the fourth year of the sitting of a second Finance Committee,[1] has not been completed. A sinecure office falling vacant, the vacancy is in case of this inefficient, as in the case of any efficient sort of office, filled up in course; filled up under no other impression than the general one, viz. that in the list of offices, as often as one name drops out, another must according to usage be put in the room of it.

In two different situations, he saw the same set of hands, viz. those of the servants of the Crown, habitually employed in disposing of the property of the public, whether to the purpose, real or supposed, of remuneration, or to any other purpose. In two different situations, viz. out of parliament and in parliament; in parliament, since without their concurrence, even in parliament, no such power can under the established rules be exercised. Of this difference, what is now, what in his view could have been, the consequence? Disposed of *in* parliament, the money had never been disposed of, but that to the misapplication of it there had been *some* check, though how far from being so effectual a one as might be wished, is but too notorious. Disposed of, *out of* parliament, as in the shape of a sinecure emolument, the misapplication of it had never experienced, nor in the nature of the case was capable of experiencing, any check whatever. It is in this shape that we see him defending it.

Of this state of things, the consequence was and is as obvious and natural as the existence of it is incontestable. When, at the expense of the people, on the ground of service rendered to the people, a case can, it is supposed, be made, be it ever so weak a one, recourse is had

---

[1] The Committee on Public Expenditure had been first appointed in 1807.

to parliament, and parliament is the hand by which the favour is bestowed. When no such case can be made—when the very mention of public service might be regarded as mockery and insult, when the annihilation of the precious matter thus bestowed would be a public blessing, a secret hand acting out of parliament, is the hand occupied in such service: windfalls are waited for, Tellerships are bestowed.

Whatever you want in force of *reason*, make up in force of *assertion*. Whatever is wanting in *merit*, make up in *eulogy*. Maxims these the use and value of which are perfectly understood by sophists of all classes.

Our Rhetorician goes on. '*It* is indeed' (meaning by *it* the principle which prescribes the dividing the substance of the people among great families, and families that are to be made great by such means) 'it is indeed the only genuine, unadulterated origin of nobility.' Peculation the only genuine and unadulterated origin of nobility! What a character of nobility! What a plea for the House of Lords! What a lesson to the people!

'It is' (continues he) 'a great principle in Government; a principle at the very foundation of the whole structure.'[1] O yes, such a principle exactly as a running stream would be, running under the foundation of a structure erected on a quicksand.

SECTION V.
CONCERNING VIRTUOUS AMBITION, GRATITUDE, AND PIETY.
Propositions 5, 6, 7, 8.

Proposition 5. WHEN ambition is virtuous, nothing but money is capable of acting with effect as an incitement to it; power in whatever shape—power of management—power of patronage; dignities, honours, reputation—respect, by whatever cause created, are all without effect.

Proof. 'Indeed no man knows' (continues the rhetorician) 'no man knows when he cuts off *the* incitements' ('*the* incitements,' i.e. the sole incitements) 'to a virtuous ambition, and the just rewards of public service, what infinite mischief he may do his country through all generations. Such saving to the public may be the worst mode of robbing it.'[2]

---

[1] Burke, *Speech on Oeconomical Reformation*, p. 63.
[2] Ibid.

'The incitements;' meaning those alone which are composed of money. For thereupon comes a panegyric on the virtue of money; an eulogium composed of a string of phrases, which in the common-place book of a university poem-maker, might, if the subject of the poem were the virtues of money, perform the sort of service performed to genius in the bud in that useful manual called the *Gradus ad Parnassum*,[1] under the head of *synonyms* or *phrases*.

'The means for the repose of public labour'—'The fixed settlement of acknowledged merit'—'A harbour into which the weather-beaten vessels of the state ought to come; a retreat from the malice of rivals, from the perfidy of political friends, and the inconstancy of the people.'[2]

How pitiable under this view of it, must be the condition of every man, who without a certainty of raising a family into overgrown opulence at the expense of the people, employs his time, or any part of it, in any branch, at least in any of the higher branches, of the public service!—of every member of parliament, at least (for to honourable gentlemen of this description do the regards of the rhetorician appear on this occasion to have confined themselves) of every member of parliament who ventures his bark in any such stormy latitude, without the certainty of a 'harbour' in the shape of an auditorship, or a cut-down Tellership at least!

Storms and tempests forsooth! Yes, such as we see on canvas at Covent Garden, and hope to see again at Drury Lane.[3] Labour as severe almost as what is undergone on the Cricket Ground, or at the Card Table, and standing about as much in need of remuneration at the expense of the people: labour such as, without receiving the value of a farthing from any hand that did not itself cheerfully take the money out of its own pocket, *Mr. Gale Jones* and his company would have undergone, and continued to undergo, if the Honourable House could have prevailed upon itself to suffer them: labour far short of that which on the same ocean the newspaper reporters were in the habit of undergoing, and if Mr. Yorke and his honourable and worthy nephew had suffered them, would have continued to undergo, without

---

[1] A dictionary of Latin prosody used in schools for the teaching of Latin verse, published in several London editions from the end of the seventeenth century.

[2] See Burke, *Speech on Oeconomical Reformation*, p. 63: 'The crown, which has in its hands the trust of the daily pay for national service, ought to have in its hands also the means for the repose of public labour, and the fixed settlement of acknowledged merit. There is a time, when the weather-beaten vessels of the state, ought to come into harbour. They must at length have a retreat from the malice of rivals, from the perfidy of political friends, and the inconstancy of the people.'

[3] Drury Lane theatre had been burnt down on 24 February 1809; the theatre was rebuilt and eventually reopened on 10 October 1812.

ceasing:[1] and even (how 'incomplete' soever, 'and indeed wholly insufficient for that purpose;' 'for that public service must' (as Mr. Burke says) 'be those means of rewarding' that 'public service')[2] yes, even without 'further reward for that service than the daily wages received during pleasure:'[3]—daily labour beyond comparison more compulsory, more assiduous, more severe, than that which, besides so many contingent sweets, has present honour for a sweetening to it;—daily labour without pension of retreat, without provision for superannuation; provision, actual or eventual, for widows or mistresses, children or grandchildren, uncles or aunts, brothers or sisters, nephews or nieces; without power either of management or patronage, without either possession or prospect of honour, dignity, reputation or respect in any shape.

Proposition 6. So as the place be permanent, the hope of receiving it, how large soever the mass of emolument attached to it, '*does not operate as corruption*'—does not produce '*dependence*.'

Proof. 'Many of the persons who in all times have filled the Great Offices of State, have' (says he) 'been younger brothers, who had originally little, if any fortune. There ought to be' (continues he) 'some power in the Crown of granting pensions out of the reach of its own caprices.'—Caprices! The hand by which the whole property of the people is thus to be disposed of, has it then its caprices? O yes, for the moment, and for the purpose of the argument. What is it that it may not happen to a thing to *have* or *not* have, for the purpose of the argument? 'The intail of dependence' (continues he) 'is a bad reward of merit.'

'I would therefore leave to the Crown,' says he (viz. to the '*caprices*' of the Crown) 'the possibility of conferring some favours, which, whilst they are received as a reward, *do not operate as corruption;*'[4]—

---

[1] On 2 February 1810, Charles Yorke secured the exclusion of strangers (including newspaper reporters) from the debate on the Walcheren expedition in the House of Commons. John Gale Jones (1769–1838), radical politician, on 19 February published a placard decrying the exclusion as an attack upon the liberty of the press. Yorke responded immediately by complaining in the Commons of a breach of privilege, which led to Jones' imprisonment in Newgate, where he remained until the House rose on 21 June. The identity of the 'honourable and worthy nephew' is unclear, though Yorke's brother, Joseph Sydney Yorke (1768–1831), at this time MP for St. Germans, supported the ministry over the Walcheren expedition.

[2] Bentham's rendering of Burke's speech is obscure here. In the passage in question (*Speech on Oeconomical Reformation*, p. 62), Burke states: 'conceiving it to be a fundamental part of the constitution of this country, and of the reason of state in every country, that there must be means of rewarding public service, those means will be incomplete, and indeed wholly insufficient for that purpose, if there should be no further reward for that service, than the daily wages it receives during the pleasure of the crown'.

[3] 1830 omits closing speech mark.

[4] 1830 omits closing speech mark. Burke, *Speech on Oeconomical Reformation*, p. 63.

as if, to this purpose, call it good, call it a bad one, a pension might not be made to operate with the same effect as a sinecure, both being equally for life.

Proposition 7. When a man is in parliament, whatsoever be the conduct of the servants of the Crown, and whatsoever be the quantity of money he may gain or hope to gain by giving them his indiscriminating support, virtue requires that, to protect him against the charge of corruption, he be provided with the plea of *gratitude;* which plea pleaded, acquittal follows of course.

'When men receive obligations from the Crown through the pious hands of a father, or of connections as venerable as the paternal, the dependencies' (says he) 'which arise from them are the obligations of gratitude, and not the fetters of servility. Such ties' (continues he) 'originate in virtue, and they promote it.'[1]

Proposition 8. When a man happens to have children, 'piety' on his part consists in filling their pockets with public money.

Proof. The epithet 'pious' applied with so much unction to paternal hands thus occupied.

Observations. In the Wolf's Bible, piety would indeed naturally enough consist in providing lamb, as much as she could lay her paws upon, to feed her cubs with. But in the Shepherd's Bible, at least the Good Shepherd's Bible, piety will probably be found rather to consist in keeping the lambs from being disposed of to such pious uses.[2] The orator, though not a no-popery-man, was fond of his Bible, and here we have a sample of the uses he was fond of making of it.

SECTION VI.
CONCERNING PARTY-MEN AND THEIR PRINCIPLES.
Propositions 9, 10.

Proposition 9. MEN, who have at any time joined together in the way of party, ought not ever, any one of them, to differ from any other; nor therefore to act, any one of them, according to his own conception of what is right. Sinecures, if not absolutely necessary, are highly conducive at least, and thence proportionally useful, to the purpose of preventing all such differences.

Proof. 'They' ('such ties' as above) 'continue men' (says he) 'in those habitudes of friendship, those political connections, and those political principles' (we have seen what principle) 'in which they began

---

[1] Ibid., pp. 63–4.
[2] See John 10: 11–14.

life. They are antidotes against a corrupt levity, instead of causes of it.'[1]

Observations. Sinecures, according to this account of them, seem to be as necessary to secure fidelity at the expense of sincerity in parliament, as *test oaths* and subscriptions are to secure various good things, at the expense of reason or sincerity there and elsewhere.

Two things here call for notice, the proposed *end* and the proposed *means*. Proposed *end*, each man's persevering in the *principles* (whatever is meant by *principles*) in the professions and habits, right or wrong, in which he '*began life;*' i.e. which it happened to him to have imbibed from the instructors under whom it had happened to him to be placed, and the society in which it had happened to him to have lived. Proposed *means;* his having got into his hands as much public money as his parents and other connections could contrive to put into them by means of sinecures. *Means* and *end,* it must be acknowledged, are not ill matched.

Proposition 10. On a change of Ministry, were it not for the sinecures, the *comers-in* would cut the throats of the *goers-out;* whereupon 'the *sons*' of the goers-out would '*cringe*' to the same *comers-in* (now ins) and '*kiss their hands.*'

Proof. 'What an unseemly spectacle would it afford, what a disgrace would it be to the commonwealth that suffered such things, to see the *hopeful son of a meritorious minister* begging his bread at the door of that treasury from whence his father dispensed the happiness[2] and glory of his country? Why should he be *obliged to prostrate his honour, and to submit his principles* at the levee of some *proud favourite,* shouldered and thrust aside by every impudent pretender, in the very spot where a few days before he saw himself adored?—*obliged to cringe* to the author of the calamities of his house, and to *kiss the hands* that are *red* with his father's blood? No, Sir;—these things are unfit, they are intolerable.'[3]

Observations. And so there are, it seems, such things as proud favourites. But if so, what sort of food is their pride fed upon? Sinecures? And if so, is not one of these *proud favourites* on every occasion a dangerous rival to the hopeful son of a meritorious minister? But the plan was—that there should be enough of them for every body: and thus every thing would be as it should be.[4]

---

[1] Burke, *Speech on Oeconomical Reformation*, p. 64.

[2] Burke 'dispensed the œconomy of an empire, and promoted the happiness'.

[3] Burke, *Speech on Oeconomical Reformation*, p. 64.

[4] An echo of Blackstone's phrase, 'Every thing is now as it should be', made in the context of a discussion of the offence of heresy at *Commentaries on the Laws of England*, iv. 49, but which Bentham took to be characteristic of Blackstone's attitude to the British political system as a whole.

SECTION VII.
CONCERNING MINISTERS AND THEIR DUTY TO THEMSELVES.
Propositions 11, 12, 13, 14.

Proposition 11. The danger of a man's being too bountiful to himself, when, in and by the adjudication of reward claimed on the ground of service said to have been rendered to the public, he is allowed to be judge in his own cause, affords no reason, at least no conclusive reason, against the allowing him to act in that character.

'As to abuse,' (says he) 'I am convinced, that very few trusts in the ordinary course of administration, have admitted less abuse than this. *Efficient ministers have been their own paymasters.* It is true. *But their very partiality has operated as a kind of justice;* and still it was service that was paid. When we look over this Exchequer List, we find it filled with the descendants of the Walpoles, of the Pelhams, of the Townsends,[1] names to whom this country owes its liberties and to whom his Majesty owes his Crown.[a] It was in one of those lines that the immense and envied employment he now holds, came to a certain Duke,' ('the Duke of Newcastle,'[2] says a note) 'whose dining room is under the House of Commons, who is now probably sitting quietly at a very good dinner directly under us, and acting *high life below stairs*,[3] whilst we his masters are filling our mouths with unsubstantial sounds, and talking of hungry economy over his head.'[4]

For merited wealth and honour he declares his '*respect:*' 'respect' which accompanies it 'through all its descents, through all its transfers, and all its assignments.' In plain English, the object of his

---

[a] Their co-operation within doors by hundreds, and without doors by millions, he would have us believe, having had no share in the business, or at least no merit in it. These men stand up in a *room* (*absit verbo invidia*)[5] and pronounce a set of phrases, and by these men alone (we are desired to believe) by these men alone it is, that every thing that is done, is done.

---

[1] Prominent Whig families who were closely associated with the Hanoverian regime.

[2] Henry Fiennes-Clinton, afterwards Pelham-Clinton (1720–94), ninth Earl of Lincoln and second Duke of Newcastle-under-Lyne.

[3] These italics are Burke's. Newcastle had since 1751 held the lucrative office of Auditor of the Exchequer. The dining room of his official residence, which was in the Palace of Westminster, and was later allocated to the Speaker of the House of Commons, was presumably in the vaults of St. Stephen's Chapel.

[4] Burke, *Speech on Oeconomical Reformation*, p. 65. In the following paragraphs, Bentham discusses the continuation of the passage: 'But he is the elder branch of an ancient and decayed house, joined to, and repaired by the reward of services done by another. I respect the original title, and the first purchase of merited wealth and honour through all its descents, through all its transfers, and all its assignments.'

[5] i.e. 'I say it without boasting.' Livy, *Ab Urbe Condita*, IX. xix. 15.

respect is wealth itself, whatever hands he sees it in. As for '*original title*,' and '*first purchase*,' and the epithet '*merited*' prefixed to '*wealth*,' all this is for decency and delusion. For as to *merited*, the orator's notion about merits have surely by this time become sufficiently apparent.

And as to *title*, what is it that on the subject of title, specific title, so much as asserted, not to speak of proved, he ever drops so much as a hint of his looking upon as requisite? No: with him, to the purpose of approbation, though without reason, as in a lawyer's point of view, to the purpose of protection, for the best reason, possession of wealth, acquired at the public expense, is regarded as proof of title: and that proof not only presumptive and provisional, but conclusive.

As for *transfer* and *assignment*—wealth sure enough is *transferable* and *assignable*. But *merit?* is *merit* too a subject of bargain and sale? A manor? yes. But *manners*, those '*manners*' which, in the language of *Edward the Third's* chancellor 'maketh man,'[1] are these manners with an *e*, appendages and appurtenances that by the attraction of cohesion adhere to, and are rendered inseparable from, the manors with an *o?*

Wealth or power, wherever you see them, '*prostrate*' yourself before them: '*cringe* to' them, and though they be '*red with*' your '*father's blood*,' '*kiss the hands*' that grasp them. This is what you are '*obliged*' to do: and that which is matter of obligation, how can it be matter of blame? Such are the precepts which call for the observance of that pupil whose preceptor is Edmund Burke.

After the predilection he thus declared, predilection for *vicarious reward*, in short for any thing that can afford to political rapacity a colour or a cloak, to complete the system of corruption and tyranny, what more can be wanting than a like declaration in favour of *vicarious punishment?*

Observations. 'But' (continues the orator) 'he is the elder branch of an ancient and decayed house, joined to, and repaired by the reward of services done by another.'[2] Thus far the orator.

'*Done by another.*' Yes, done by George the Second's[3] old favourite the minister Duke of Newcastle, whose culinary profusion and poli-

---

[1] This was the motto of William of Wykeham (1324–1404), Bishop of Winchester from 1367, and Chancellor of England 1367–71 under Edward III, and again 1389–91 under Richard II (1367–1400), King of England from 1377 to 1399.

[2] The second Duke of Newcastle, already Earl of Lincoln by direct descent, had received the dukedom under special remainder on the death of his uncle, Thomas Pelham-Holles, formerly Pelham (1693–1768), second Baron Pelham, first Earl of Clare, first Duke of Newcastle-upon-Tyne and first Duke of Newcastle-under-Lyne, Secretary of State for the Southern Department 1724–46, 1746–8, Secretary of State for the Northern Department 1748–54, First Lord of the Treasury 1754–6, 1757–62, Lord Privy Seal 1765–6.

[3] George II (1683–1760), King of Great Britain and Ireland from 1727.

tical inaptitude were alike proverbial, whose inefficiency the efficiency of the first Pitt had for such a length of time to struggle with, and whose services consisted in the sacrifice made of his patrimony to his palate and his pride.[1]

'I respect' (continues the rhetorician) 'the original title, and the first purchase of merited wealth and honour through all its descents, through all its transfers, and all its assignments. May such fountains never be dried up! May they ever flow with their original purity, and fructify the commonwealth for ages.'[2]

May such fountains never be dried up! exclaims the ejaculation, poured forth with fervency, with almost the solemnity, and with at least the sincerity, of a prayer. *'May such fountains never be dried up.'* As if he had not all this while in full view a fountain of this sort, the patrimony of the Crown, all but dried up, and that almost a century before the utterance of this prayer: as if any thing could operate more speedily, or more effectually, towards the drying up of all such fountains, than the acting up to those laws of profusion to the keeping of which it was the object of this prayer to incline men's hearts.

Proposition 12. If it be admitted that the masses of emolument, respectively attached[3] to the great *efficient* offices, are not excessive, this admission will be sufficient to justify the possessors of them in putting into their pockets additional masses of emolument to an unlimited amount, on condition of creating or keeping on foot *inefficient* offices, to which such additional masses of emolument shall respectively stand attached.

Proof. 'If I were to give judgment' (says he) 'with regard to this country, I do not think the great offices of the state to be overpaid.[4] When the proportion between reward and service' (resumes he) 'is our object, we must always consider of what nature the service is, and what sort of men they are, who are to perform it. What is just payment for one kind of labour, and full encouragement for one kind of talents, is fraud and discouragement to others.'[5]

[1] Newcastle had entered into a coalition ministry in 1757 with William Pitt (1708–78), later first Earl of Chatham, in order to prosecute the Seven Years' War. Despite outstanding military success, the ministry collapsed in 1761, in large part due to the hostility of the new King, George III. Newcastle's reputation for incompetence made a stark contrast with Pitt's reputation as a great war minister and national hero. As Bentham suggests, Newcastle seems to have expended a considerable amount of his own money, about £300,000, as a result of his official commitments. He was moreover famed for the banquets which he provided for his tenants and dependents.

[2] Burke, *Speech on Oeconomical Reformation*, p. 65.

[3] 1830 'attatched'.

[4] Bentham omits the following sentence from the quotation at this point: 'The service of the public is a thing which cannot be put to auction, and struck down to those who will agree to execute it the cheapest.' He discusses it in §XI, pp. 91–3 below.

[5] Burke, *Speech on Oeconomical Reformation*, p. 66.

Observations. True enough. But what is it to the purpose? and what is it that it amounts to? and what is it that by volumes of phrases thus floating in the air would be proved?

'*Not overpaid.*' For the purpose of the argument let it pass.

'*Not overpaid!*' Admitted. But does it follow that they are *under-paid?* 4,000*l.* a year, or 6,000*l.* a year not excessive? Good: but does it follow that 23,000*l.* a year, or that 38,000*l.* a year must be added?

Proposition 13. To justify the leaving to the possessors of public offices, in an unlimited number, the power of putting each into his own pocket, and into the pockets of his relatives, and friends, and dependents, and their respective descendants, such supplemental masses of emolument, each to an unlimited amount, it is sufficient to point out one office and *one class* of offices, which present a reasonable claim to larger masses of emolument than what are attached to the rest.

Proof. 'Many of the great officers have much duty to do, and much expense to maintain.'

'A Secretary of State, for instance, must not appear sordid in the eyes of Ministers of other nations.'

'Neither ought our Ministers abroad to appear contemptible in the Courts where they reside.'

'In all offices of duty' (continues he) 'there is almost necessarily a great neglect of all domestic affairs. A person in high office can rarely take a view of his family-house. If *he* sees that the *state* takes no detriment, the *state* must see that *his* affairs should take as little.'[1]

Proposition 14. In the case of a real efficient office, no mass of emolument which either is or can be attached to it, ever is or ever can be too great.

Proofs. 'I am not' (says he) 'possessed of an exact measure between real service and its reward.'

'I am' (continues he) 'very sure that states do sometimes receive services, which it is hardly in their power to reward according to their worth.'

'I do not' (continues he) 'think the great efficient officers of the state to be overpaid:' he, Edmund Burke, who in so many words, has just been saying, 'If I knew of any real efficient office which did possess exorbitant emoluments I should be extremely desirous of reducing them. Others' (continues he) 'may know of them. I do not.'[2]

Observations. Of the sincerity of this declaration, no question need be made. If so it had been, that any such office, '*possessing emolu-*

---

[1] Ibid., pp. 66–7.
[2] Ibid., p. 66.

76

ments,' which in his eyes were *'exorbitant,'* had been known to him, a *'desire,'* and *that* an *'extreme'* one, 'of reducing' those exorbitant emoluments would have been the result of such *knowledge*. But in his eyes no such emoluments could be exorbitant. Therefore in his breast the formation of such desire must, notwithstanding the extreme desire he could not but have had to form such a desire, have been impossible.

At that moment, and for the purpose of the argument, such was the ignorance of Edmund Burke that he 'was not possessed of,' i.e.[1] he knew not of 'an exact common measure between real service and its reward.' But except Edmund Burke, no man is thus ignorant, any more than Edmund Burke himself could be at any other time than that in which such ignorance had its convenience.

Between *'real service and its reward'* the exact common measure is the least quantity of the matter of reward that he who is able to render the service consents to take in return for it. This is the measure of all *prices:* this is the measure of the value of all good things that are at once valuable and tangible. This is the measure of the value of all *labour*, by which things tangible are produced: as also of all labour by which, though nothing tangible is produced, valuable service in some other shape is rendered. This was the *common measure*, by which the exact value had been assigned to the *coat* he had on his back. This was the exact common measure of the value of those real services which had been rendered him by the person or persons by whom his coat had by means of one kind of brush, and his shoes by means of two others, been qualified for their attendance on the lips, by which this brilliant bubble was blown out.

But (says the sophist, or some disciple for him) there is no analogy (says he) between the service rendered to the public by a Minister of State, and the service rendered to one individual, by another individual, who removes extraneous matter from his coat, or puts a polish upon his shoes.

O yes there is—and to the purpose here in question, analogy quite sufficient.

1. They stand upon the same ground (the two services) in point of *economy*. There is no more economy in paying 38,000*l.* a year for the wearer of the coat, if he can be had for nothing, than in paying 20*l.* for a coat itself, if it[2] can be had for 10*l.*

For the wearer of the coat—I mean, of course, for his services: his *services;* I mean his services to the public, if so it be that he be capable of rendering any.

---

[1] 1830 'i,e.'
[2] 1830 'he'.

But the misfortune is, that when once the '*reward* for service' has swelled to any such pitch, any question about the service *itself*—*what* is it? what does it consist in? *who* is it that is to render it? what desire, or what *means* has *he* of rendering it? of rendering to the public *that* sort of service, or *any* sort of service? Any question of this sort becomes a joke.

Where Sinecures, and those 'high situations' in which they have now and then become the subjects of conversation among 'great characters,' are taken for the subject of conversation among little characters in their low situations, questions and answers are apt to become giddy, and to turn round in a circle. What are Sinecures of 38,000*l.* a year good for? to maintain the Sinecurists. What are the Sinecurists good for? to maintain the Sinecures. Thus on profane ground.—Thus again, on sacred ground. What are Bishopricks good for? to support Bishops. What are Bishops good for? to support Bishopricks.

2. So again as to probability of *efficiency*, and meritoriousness on the part of the *service*. Competition—preference given to the best bidder among candidates bidding upon each other, under the spur applied by that incentive—competition, affords in the instance of the party chosen, a better chance of fitness for the office and its services, than will in general be afforded by preference given, either without a thought about fitness for the *service*, or about *merit* in any other shape, or with thoughts confined to such merit of which *Parliament* is the only theatre, and in the composition of which, obsequiousness is the principal ingredient, and that an indispensable one. But of this proposition the truth, it is hoped, has been rendered sufficiently apparent elsewhere.[a]

SECTION VIII.
CONCERNING GRATUITOUS SERVICE, AND THE PROFLIGACY INVOLVED IN IT.
Propositions 15, 16.

Proposition 15.—IF a man were to decline receiving at the public expense, money which it were in his power to receive without danger either of punishment or of disgrace, it would be a conclusive proof that his designs were to endeavour to filch money from the public, in some

---

[a] Part I.[1]

[1] i.e. 'Hints respecting Economy'. For Bentham's mature discussion of competition for office see *Constitutional Code*, I (*CW*), Ch. IX, § 17, pp. 337–62.

mode that would subject him to danger in one or other of the two shapes, or in both.

Proof. 'I will even go so far,' (says he, p. 67) 'as to affirm, that if men were willing to serve in such situations' (viz. offices of duty, '*all offices of duty,*' p. 66) 'without salary, they ought not to be permitted to do it. Ordinary service must be secured by the motives to ordinary integrity. I do not hesitate to say, that, *that* state which lays its foundation in rare and heroic virtues, will be sure to have its super-structure in the basest profligacy and corruption. An honourable and fair profit is the best security against avarice and rapacity; as in all things else, a lawful and regulated enjoyment is the best security against debauchery and excess.'

Observations. '*If men were willing to serve in such situations without salary, they ought not*' (says he) '*to be permitted to do it.*' Here we have the theory—the waste-and-corruption-defending Sophist's theory. What says experience? In Part I. of this tract[1] may be seen a list, nor that yet a complete one, of men of various classes serving in such situations; and not merely without salary, but without neat emolument in any shape: and as for the not permitting them to do so, whether in[2] such *non-permission*, in whatsoever manner effected, whether by prohibition or otherwise, there would be any, and what use, let the reader, if any such there be, on whom this rhapsody has passed for reason or for reasoning, learn from it, if he be able.

'*Ordinary services*' (says the orator) '*must be secured by the motives to ordinary integrity.*' In Part I.[3] the reader, it is hoped, has already seen, that for the securing of ordinary service, to furnish any motive what-ever, is not in the nature of Salary: that in so far as ordinary service comes to be rendered, it is by apprehension of eventual *punishment* that it is produced, that all that by salary can ever be done towards the production of it, is by engaging a man to subject himself to such eventual punishment; and that, if so it be, that without salary, he is content to subject himself to such eventual punishment, the service (it being ordinary service) is not merely *as* likely, but *more* likely, to be produced *without* salary than *with* it.

'*That state which lays its foundation in rare and heroic virtues,*' says the orator, meaning (for there is nothing else to which the word '*virtues*' can have any application) the disposition manifested by him, who 'without salary is willing to serve in such situations.' Now, in a disposition of that sort, though there be great use, there is nothing that can bear the name of virtue. For (as is sufficiently proved by

---

[1] i.e. 'Hints respecting Economy'.
[2] 1830 'in in'.
[3] i.e. 'Hints respecting Economy'.

every morsel a man puts into his mouth, and every draught or sip he takes) so it is, that out of mere *utility*, even though it rise to the height of absolute *necessity*, no such thing as *virtue* can be made. Not that in these 'situations,' or any of them, whether 'served in,' with[1] or 'without salary,' virtue rising even to heroism may not perhaps by accident be displayed: but any such accidental display is quite another business.

Now, if even by actual service in such situations, no 'virtue' at all is displayed, or, by the man himself, who thus serves, is so much as conceived to be displayed, whether in the mere willingness so to serve there be any room for 'rare or heroic virtue,' may be left to any reasonable person to pronounce.

Proposition 16. In any office of duty, 'to be willing to serve without salary,' is to pretend to 'rare and heroic virtue,' and is a 'sure' indication of 'the basest profligacy and corruption.'

Proof. 'In all offices of duty,' (says he, p. 66) 'there is almost necessarily a great neglect of all domestic affairs. A person in high office can rarely take a view of his family house.'—'I will even go so far as to affirm,' (continues he, p. 67) 'that *if men were willing to serve in such situations without salary*, they ought not to be permitted to do it. I do not hesitate to say,' (continues he) 'that, that state which lays its foundation in *rare and heroic virtues* will be *sure* to have its superstructure in *the basest profligacy and corruption*.'[2]

Observations. The Office of *Member of the House of Commons*—the Office of Delegate of the people in Parliament—*is* that, or is it not, in the number of his 'Offices of Duty?' Is that, or is it not, in the number of his 'high Offices?' Members of the House of Commons as such—the Members of the House of Commons taken together—have they not, in conjunction with their duty, more *power* than the Members of Administration taken together? In the Members of the House of Commons taken together, do not the Members of Administration taken together, behold their *Judges*, to whom, for their conduct as such they are continually accountable, and by whom, under the *form* of an *address* to the King, they are in *effect* displaceable? This assertion then, to the absurdity of which men are to be made to shut their eyes by the violence, the unhesitating and audacious violence,

---

[1] 1830 adds opening speech mark before 'with'.

[2] 1817, 1830 insert the following paragraph at this point, but this is an evident mistake since it repeats what is said in the first paragraph of the *Observations* to Proposition 15, p. 79 above: '*Observations*. In Part I. of this publication, [i.e. 'Hints respecting Economy'] may be seen a list, though by no means a complete one, of offices '*willingly served*,' not only without salary, but even without emolument; as also a list of others, by and for the obtainment of which, men are found who are willing to be out of pocket.'

with which it is endeavoured to be driven down their throats—try it, try it in the first place, upon the Members of the House of Commons.

A Member of the House of Commons, who, in that his office, *'is willing to serve without salary, ought not to be permitted to do it.'* Whoever does serve on any such terms, is a most *base and corrupt profligate*.

From this charge of base and corrupt profligacy, having for its proof the fact of a man's performing public duty without salary, the *impossibility* of obtaining any portion of this his specific against corruption, may, it is hoped, according to the orator's system, serve in the character of an *extenuation*, in a case where the inability is real and unaffected.

But within the compass of his knowledge, what man, public or private, can be at any loss to find public men—men of distinguished talents—men even of distinguished eloquence—who in that very station have served, and for a long continued course of years, with as much assiduity as it is possible for men to bestow, even for and with the most overflowing measure of reward? serving and toiling with an assiduity equal to that of the most assiduous minister all the time, yet without factitious reward in any shape, all the time having at command rewards to the highest amount, and even at the public expense?

Of these base and corrupt profligates, as Edmund Burke called them, and would have persuaded us to think them, I had even began a list, none of them unknown even to Edmund Burke, when I was stopped at once by a concurring cluster of considerations: the personality of the detail, my own incompetency for it, the room it would have occupied, and, as it seemed to me, the superfluity of it.

As between individual and individual, that without expectation of money or money's worth, in any shape, in return, it may not happen to an individual to render a service to another, nay, even to persevere as towards him in a course of service of any length and degree of constancy, and this, too, without any sort of prejudice to probity, not to speak of base and corrupt profligacy, is surely more than any man, even the orator himself, was ever heard to assert: why not then to the public at large—to that all comprehensive body, of which individuals taken together are component parts?

For the labour or the self-denial necessary to the rendering the service to the individual, pure sympathy, pure of all self-regarding considerations, is frequently the sole, and being at the same time the efficacious, is thereby the self-sufficient motive. But when the public is the party to whom the service is rendered; in this case, in addition to whatsoever emotion of sympathy is called forth by the contemplation of the welfare of this aggregate body, in aid of that purely social spring of action, comes the prospect of gratification to the self-regarding affection, *love of reputation*, accompanied or not with the love of that *power*, which, whether put to use or not, reputation brings with her in her hand.

Besides the shape in which he would receive payment for the service, if no more than a single individual were the better for it, he who renders service to the public receives, or at least may not unreasonably expect to receive, payment for it, in those two other shapes besides. Yet, in the eyes of the orator, if he is to be believed, so unnatural and incredible is the disposition to be on any occasion content with this treble payment, that should any such disposition find any man to manifest it, what the orator[1] is quite 'sure' of, and insists upon our believing, is, that that man belongs to the list of 'base and corrupt *profligates*.' Such is his sincerity, or such his knowledge of human nature.

After an answer thus conclusive, it may be matter of doubt, whether the inanity of the arguments, considered with reference to the state of things the orator saw at that time before him, be worth touching upon.

As in a magic lantern, the scene shifts every moment under his hands. On the occasion in question, to be of any considerable use, the view taken, it was necessary, should embrace the whole field of official emolument—the whole field of office. So, in his hands, but a page or two before it accordingly did. Now, and without warning, the extent of it is shrunk, perhaps to that of half a dozen offices, perhaps to that of a single office. To a single office confined it must be—to a single office, viz. that of the chief Minister, if, of the plan of *hypocrisy* he speaks of, the sort of despotism he speaks of is, in case of success, to be the consequence.

'Unfair advantage to ostentatious ambition over unpretending service,'—'invidious comparisons,'—'destruction of whatever little unity and agreement may be found among Ministers:'[2]—all these words, what is it they amount to? words, and nothing more.

Realized they might be—all these supposed disasters; and still, on the part of the people, the question might be—What then? what is all that to us? how is it that we should be the worse for it?

1. Says A, I don't want all this money. Says B, I do. Here the thing

---

[1] 1830 'orator'.

[2] See Burke, *Speech on Oeconomical Reformation*, p. 67: 'If any individual were to decline his appointments, it might give an unfair advantage to ostentatious ambition over unpretending service; it might breed invidious comparisons; it might tend to destroy whatever little unity and agreement may be found among ministers.' See further §X, pp. 86–90 below, for Bentham's comments on this passage.

which A is ambitious of is power, and power only: the thing coveted by B is the same power, with the money into the bargain. On the part of A, where now is the ostentation, where the ambition, more than on the part of B: and, if there were, where would be the specific mischief of it in any tangible shape?

2. *Invidious comparisons!* What is choice without *comparison?* and if invidious meant any thing, where is the comparison, which being made for the purpose of choice, is *not* invidious? What is parliamentary debate, what is any debate, but a topic of invidious comparisons?

3. *Destruction of unity and agreement among Ministers!* According to circumstances, such destruction is either a misfortune or a blessing. Misfortune to be sure it is, and nothing else, with reference to the ten or a dozen persons spoken of: but with reference to the people and their interests, a 'destruction' of this sort is perhaps the most efficient, though it be but a casual, check upon misrule. In case of that system of misconduct, which it is so constantly their interest, and almost constantly in their power to persevere in, it affords the only chance—of *punishment* it cannot be said; for of *that* never, for this last half century, has there been any chance,—but of exposure. And in this character, the people, thanks to able instructors, begin to be not altogether insensible to its value.

But a Government in the quondam *Venetian* style[1]—a Government, in which, under the guidance of upstart Machiavelism, titled and confederated imbecility should lord it over King and people, and behind the screen of secrecy, waste, oppression, and peculation, should find themselves for ever at their ease; such was the Utopia of Edmund Burke.

To dispose men, if it be possible, to distinguish from solid argument, empty froth, such as this of Edmund Burke's, to distinguish it, and, whenever found, to cast it forth from them with the scorn which is its due, such has been the object; such, if they have had any, has been the use, of these four or five last paragraphs.

SECTION IX.

A PROPHECY, AND BY BURKE—THE KING WILL SWALLOW UP THE WHOLE SUBSTANCE OF THE PEOPLE.

Proposition 17.—The King, with the advice and consent of Lords and Commons, will '*infallibly*,' one of these days, possess himself of the whole property of the country.

---

[1] The government of Venice under the Doges was often characterized as a corrupt and closed oligarchy.

Proof. 'For,' (says he, p. 67) 'as wealth is power, so all power will *infallibly* draw wealth to itself by some means or other: and when men are left no way of ascertaining their profits but by their means of obtaining them, those *means*,' (continues he, but the argument, it will be seen, required him to say, those 'profits') 'will be increased to infinity. This is true' (continues he) 'in all the parts of administration as well as in the whole.'

Observations. These doctrines, I mean of the exposure thus made of them, the use is, to show what extravagances imagination is apt to launch into, where, to bring down an *ignis fatuus* for the defence of an indefensible proposition, it mounts without rudder or compass into the region of vague and aërial generalities.

The result, to any such extent as that in which, for the purpose of the moment, the sophist tried, or pretended, to regard it as infallible, is as far, let us hope, from being in any degree a probable one, as at another time he would have been from speaking of it as such.

In the situation of Chief Minister, or in any other situation, if, by means of an artifice, which, long before it had travelled any considerable length in the tract of success, must have become transparent and visible to the whole people, it depended upon a single individual to possess himself of the whole '*power*,' and by means of it the whole 'wealth' of the country, what is it that should have prevented this conquest of the whole *wealth* from having been achieved, achieved ages ago, by those who have had the whole power in their hands?

To the *power*, that exists in the hands of the members of the sovereignty as such—to this power is to be ascribed as to its cause, the aggregate mass of the several portions of the matter of wealth, which, in their *individual* capacities, are at any given point of time respectively possessed by them. To the power itself there are not any legal limits: there ought not to be any. But to the aggregate mass of wealth actually possessed by them, how excessive soever, limits there always are: limits comparatively narrow: and, at all times, seeing what that *mass* is, we see what those limits are. The King, with the advice and consent of the Lords and Commons, might, if such were his pleasure, might, viz. by act of Parliament, take into his hands the whole wealth of the country, and share it between himself and them. Nothing could be more correctly lawful: but, as few things would be more manifestly *inexpedient*, it is what never has been done, and what nobody sane or insane is afraid of seeing done.

Not but that the advances made towards this point of consummation have been somewhat nearer than could have been wished: and in this way, as in every other, in the eyes of those who profit by what is *wrong*, 'whatever is is right:' yes, and not only *right*, but *necessary*.

But of the necessity where lies the proof? Here, as elsewhere, it lies in the existence of the *practice:* which where the thing to be proved is the necessity of that same practice, is, according to the logic of *practical* men, proof abundantly sufficient.

Pressing on the people with so heavy a pressure as this vast portion of their burthen does, on what *ground* is it that it is concluded to be, to wit, in the whole of it, necessary? On this ground, viz. that it is— that in the whole of it, it is—*customary*. And how came it to be customary? Because those whose *interest* it was to make it as great as possible, as great as the people would endure to see it made, found they had *power*, and without preponderant inconvenience, in the shape of danger to themselves, viz. from discontent on the part of the people, to make it what it is.

This *power*, the word power being here taken in the *practical* sense, is all that, to the purpose here in question, has ever been attended to. As to *need, demand* in respect of *public utility*, of that utility which is such with reference to the interest of the whole people, *need* or *necessity* in *this* sense, never is—never has been—felt to be worth a thought.

As to all those things, in respect to which it is the interest of rulers that the mode of Government should be bad, it of course always has been, and of course always will be, as bad as, in their judgment, the people will quietly endure to see it.

This Economy Bill of Edmund Burke, for example, was it produced by *virtue*, by *public spirit*, on the part of Edmund Burke? No: nor so much as by policy alone—if by policy be meant any *spontaneous* policy on his part, how personal soever and pure of public spirit. Towards the production of this measure, such as it is, *prudence*, meaning apprehension of nearer inconvenience, howsoever assisted by *policy*, meaning hope of more or less distant *power*, with its concomitant sweets, operated, and with no small force as it should seem, on his mind. The proof is in certain *petitions* which he speaks of.[1]

As to these '*petitions*,' they are such as could not have been all of them of his *calling forth*, at least not all of them of his *dictating*, since some of them were troublesome to him. Amongst the things called for by them was, in the instance of several of them, the thing which in this place is more particularly in question, viz. '*the reduction of exorbitant emoluments to efficient offices*.' This, though spoken of by him as an article, '*which seems to be a specific object in several of the petitions*,' is an

---

[1] A series of petitions calling for economical reform, most notably that from the county of Yorkshire, had been presented to the House of Commons in the few days prior to Burke's speech.

object with which he expressly declares himself *'not able to inter-meddle.'*[a]

SECTION X.

THE orator continues—'If any individual were to decline his appointments, it might' (continues he, p. 67) 'give an unfair advantage to ostentatious ambition over unpretending service; it[1] might breed invidious comparisons; it might tend to destroy whatever little unity and agreement may be found among ministers. And, after all, when an ambitious man had run down his competitors by a fallacious show of disinterestedness, and fixed himself in power by that means, what security is there that he would not change his course, and claim as an indemnity ten times more than he has given up?'

To these arguments, such as they are, against gratuitous service, my answer, so far as regards the plan above alluded to, is a simple and decisive one. To the plan of adequate salary, coupled with sale so far as applicable, for the account of the public, with the benefit of com-

---

[a] That the thread of the rhetoric may be under view in its entire state, and without a break, here follows the whole passage:—

'Sir, I think myself bound to give you my reasons as clearly and as fully, for stopping in the course of reformation as for proceeding in it. My limits are the *rules of law; the rules of policy;* and the *service of the state*. This is the reason why I am not able to intermeddle with another article, *which seems to be a specific object in several of the petitions;* I mean the reduction of exorbitant emoluments to efficient offices. If I knew of any real efficient office which did possess exorbitant emoluments'—(continues he) and then comes the profession of the hypothetical and hypocritical wish to reduce them, as above.[2]

'*Rules of law,'*—'*rules of policy'*—'*service of the state'*—all these quiddities may here be seen held up to view, as so many distinct limits, serving as bars to reformation, let down, on this occasion, for the particular purpose of stopping the reduction of exorbitant emoluments: precious bars composed of rhetorical jargon, void of meaning. '*Rules of law,'*—no attempt to bring forward any such rule: nor could any such attempt have been other than an absurd one. '*Rules of law?'* Yes, to a judicatory. But to the legislator, what sort of a *bar* can that be, which is removed or broken through of course, at every step he takes.

'*Rules of policy'* and '*the service of the state'*—the same idea; as, in a strolling company, the same performer brought on upon the stage, twice over in two different dresses.

---

[1] 1830 omits 'it'.
[2] Burke, *Speech on Oeconomical Reformation*, p. 66. Bentham discusses the continuation of the passage in §VII, Proposition 14, pp. 76–8 above.

petition they have not, any of them, any application. For *'ostentation,'* under that plan there is no room: the retrenchment, whatever it may amount to, being to all competitors matter of necessity, to none more than another matter of choice: and if it be in this ostentation, that the two other alleged mischiefs, whatever they may be, meant to be denoted by the words *'invidious comparison,'* and *'destruction of unity,'* have their supposed source, the *ostentation* being out of the case, so will these other supposed mischiefs be likewise.

Here (to speak in his own words) there would be no such *'declining'*—no such *'unfair advantage'*—no such peculiarly *'invidious comparison'*—no such mischievous *'destruction of unity and agreement'*—no such *'running down of competitors'* (for one and the same call would be given to all competitors)—no such *'self-fixation'* of one man alone *'in power,'* and by means peculiar to himself.

'And after all' (continues he, as above) 'and after all, when an ambitious man had run down his competitors by a fallacious show of disinterestedness, and fixed himself in power by that means, what security is there that he would not change his course, and claim as an indemnity more than he has given up?'

Gratuitous official service—and, under the name of gratuitous official service, reduction of official emolument being the object still contended against, here we have a quite new argument. Till now, it was in other shapes, though indeed in all manner of shapes other than that of frugality, that, in case of any such reduction, the service was to suffer: now it is in the shape even of frugality itself. Whatsoever a man (the sort of man in question) gives up in appearance, in reality (says our sophist) he will take to himself *'ten times more.'*

To the above proposed plan of retrenchment, the objection, such as it is, has not, it must have been seen already, and for the reasons already given, any the slightest application. But even with reference to the then existing state of things, what could be more extravagant?

On the part of the orator, suppose on this occasion any the smallest particle of thought, and at the same time of sincerity, what must have been the opinion entertained by him of the state of government in this country, and how profound at the same time his indifference to it? The state of government such, that on so easy a condition as the giving up a mass of lawful emolument for a time, a man might *make sure* of gaining, in the way of 'base profligacy and corruption,' *ten times* 'as much' in the long run! and this sort of speculation, promising and feasible enough, not only to be *worth* guarding against, but to be *necessary* to be guarded against, and that at such an expense as that of making an all-comprehensive addition to the mass of official emolument! and this too an addition without bounds!

Oh no! (cries the orator) not *make sure*, those were no words of *mine: 'claim'* was *my* word, 'claim' and nothing more. Oh yes, Mr. Orator, *'claim'* was indeed the *word* you used; but *make sure* was the *idea* it was your object to convey by it: for, sure enough, where public money is the subject, it is only by what a man *gets*, and not by what he *claims*, and *without getting* it, that any mischief can be done.

In writing, no man ever weighed his words in nicer scales; no author ever blotted more. To find, for each occasion, a set of words that shall comprehend two meanings, one for *attack*, another in case of necessity for *retreat* and *self-defence;* such throughout is the study of the rhetorician, whom devotion to a party reduced to that species and degree of servitude, with which sincerity is incompatible. In this sinister art no man ever laboured more—no man surely ever made a greater proficiency—no man, one may venture to say, ever made so great a proficiency as this Edmund Burke.

Here we have a picture (shall we say) or a plan of Machiavelism, sketched out by his own hand. In itself it is but a loose sketch, for, by anything like a complete and correct draught, too much would have been brought to view. But in its exact shape, no small part, and in outline the whole, was already in his own breast. Nor, so far as concerned his own portrait, was it from fancy but from the looking-glass that he drew.

The Treasury Bench—the Castle of Misrule—stood before him. Sham-Economy, an instrument of 'Young Ambition,' the ladder by which it was to be scaled. Already the ladder was in his hand. A bill for *'independence'* and so forth—and for *'economical reformation'* and so forth—was the name—the wordy name—he had found for it.[1]

At the end of a long contest, the ladder performed its service. But when the fortress was in his hands, a buttress was deemed necessary to enable him to maintain his ground. The buttress fell, and he in it, and along with it; the buttress fell, and great was the fall thereof.[2]

And what was this buttress? Few readers can be at a loss for it.

Four years after, when under the pressure of the mass of corruption, in the hands of the secret advisers of the Crown, they betook themselves for relief, he and his party, not to the legitimate influence of the people, as it would have been manifested in an equalized representation, accompanied with the exclusion of dependent votes, but *to a counter mass* of corruption, to be drawn from the East Indies—it was to the *'fallacious show of disinterestedness'* made by this his *Economy Bill*, already carried and turned into an Act, that he trusted

---

[1] Burke's pamphlet was, of course, entitled 'A Plan for the Better Security of the Independence of Parliament, and the Oeconomical Reformation of the Civil and other Establishments'.

[2] An echo of Matthew 7: 27.

for that blind support, which he had looked for at the hands of a supposed blinded people. The result is known to everybody.[1]

As to the picture we here see him drawing, it was at the time of his thus drawing it, half history, half prophecy: the prophetic part left unfinished, as everything in the shape of prophecy must necessarily be.

The picture dramatised, the characters and other objects in it, might stand as follows:

1. *'Ambitious man,'* Edmund Burke.

2. *'Fallacious show of disinterestedness:'* the show made by this *Economy Bill* of his with the inconsiderable retrenchments (60,000*l.* a year, or some such matter) effected by it.

3. *'Competitors run down'* by means of it (in addition to the force derived from other sources, such as the unpopularity and ill success of the American war, together with the exertions of arbitrary vengeance in the case of Wilkes, &c.) Lord North and his Ministry then in power, with the secret advisers of the Crown for their support.[2]

4. Instrument attempted to be made *for the 'fixing himself in power,'* Burke's East India Bill: a steadiment, containing in it a sort of pump, contrived for drawing from the East Indies the matter of *wealth*, to be applied in the character of matter of *corruption*, by hands of his own choice, to the purpose of engaging a sufficient number of workmen for the fixing him and his party as above, to wit, with such a force of resistance as it should not be in the power of the secret advisers of the Crown, with all the assistance they could get from the people, to overcome.

As to the particular *'course,'* which, for the purpose of reaping the

---

[1] The 'buttress' was the East India Bill, drafted largely by Burke, and introduced into the House of Commons in November 1783 by Charles James Fox (1749–1806), at that time Foreign Secretary. The proposed measure was denounced as an attempt by Fox and the Whigs to appropriate for themselves the patronage of the East India Company. George III took advantage of the suspicions aroused to dismiss the Fox-North Coalition in December 1783 and to appoint William Pitt the Younger (1759–1806) at the head of a new administration. Burke's proposals for economical reform of 1780 had been passed, with amendments, by the second Rockingham administration and received the Royal Assent in July 1782 (22 Geo. III, c.82).

[2] North's administration, in office from 1770 to 1782, was eventually forced to resign when military defeat at the Battle of Yorktown resulted in the effective loss of the American colonies. John Wilkes (1725–97), MP for Aylesbury 1757–64 and Middlesex 1768–9, 1774–90, posed as a champion of popular liberty against arbitrary power after he had been expelled from the House of Commons in January 1764, and subsequently convicted in his absence (he had fled to France) of blasphemy and seditious libel and then declared an outlaw. His cause became even more celebrated when in 1768 he returned to England and, being elected to Parliament for the county of Middlesex on four occasions, the House of Commons each time declared his election invalid. The administrations which bore the brunt of the Wilkite disturbances however were those of Grenville (1763–5) and Grafton (1768–70), rather than that of North. The Whig fear of the secret advisers of the Crown found its classic exposition in Burke's *Thoughts on the Cause of the Present Discontents* of 1770 (see *The Writings and Speeches of Edmund Burke*, vol. II, ed. P. Langford, Oxford, 1981, pp. 251–322).

fruits of his conquest, had this machinery of his succeeded, it might have happened to him to take, and with the word *indemnity* in his mouth, the quantity of public money he might *have claimed*, —so it is, that his grand instrument of steadiment and '*fixation*' having failed, all these, together with so many other *quondam* future contingencies, remain in darkness inscrutable. But, supposing the indemnity no more than '*ten times*' the amount of the sacrifice, still would it have fallen short, as anybody may see, of the ground prepared for it by this his speech.

Some years after, viz. about the year 1790, a decent quantity of public money, even though not in office, he did contrive to get:[1] but forasmuch as for this donation there was a pretence made out of a Pamphlet,[2] with the help of which the embers of war between Britain and France were blown into a flame, and, for security against anarchy, the good people of Great Britain driven, as far as by his pious endeavours thay could be driven, into the arms of despotism, so it was, that the bread of *sinecure*—the sacred *show-bread*, destined and appropriated to the Chief Priests of the Temple of Corruption—was not, any part of it, profaned and diverted to this use: reward in the ordinary shape of *pension* being regarded as applicable to, and sufficient for, this ordinary service.[a]

[a] 'This rule,' (continues he, p. 67) 'this rule,[3] like every other, may admit its exceptions. When a great man has some one great object in view to be achieved in a given time, it may be absolutely necessary for him to walk out of all the common roads, and if his fortune permits it, to hold himself out as a splendid example. I am told' (continues he) 'that something of this kind is now doing in a country near us. But this is for a short race: the training for a heat or two, and not the proper preparation for the regular stages of a methodical journey. I am speaking of establishments, and not of men.'[4]

As to the splendid example he was here alluding to, it was that of *Necker;* and here, as the sequel showed, the orator was completely in the wrong. What he could not make himself believe, or at least could not bear that others should believe, was, that this training of Necker's (meaning the serving in the office of Finance Minister without salary) could last for more than '*a heat or two.*' It lasted however during the whole of his '*journey*' nor that an '*unmethodical*' one. He did more than serve the public without being paid for it: he trusted the public, that child of his own adoption, with his own money—with the greatest part of his own money: and that public—that '*base and profligate,*' though, in a pecuniary sense, not in general *corrupt*, trustee of his, betrayed its trust.[5]

---

[1] After Burke's resignation from the House of Commons in 1794, Pitt awarded him a Civil List pension of £1,200 per annum back-dated to January 1793, and in September 1795 further granted him two annuities charged on the West Indian revenues.

[2] i.e. *Reflections on the Revolution in France* first published in 1790 (see *The Writings and Speeches of Edmund Burke*, vol. VIII, ed. L.G. Mitchell, Oxford, 1989, pp. 53–293).

[3] i.e. the rule that 'if men were willing to serve in such situations without salary, they ought not to be permitted to do it'.

[*See opposite page for n. 4 and n. 5.*]

SECTION XI.

BURKE'S OBJECTION TO THE APPLICATION OF THE PRINCIPLE
OF COMPETITION TO THIS PURPOSE—ITS FRIVOLOUSNESS.

AFTER denying that the great efficient offices are overpaid, 'The service of the public' (continues he) 'is a thing which cannot be put to auction, and struck down to those who will agree to execute it the cheapest.'[1]

Cannot! Why *cannot* it? Upon the face of it, the proposition bears not so much as the colour of reason; nor in the sequel is either substance or colour so much as attempted to be found for it. Of *possibility*, what is the sort of evidence that in this case he would require? Would *fact* have been regarded as admissible? 'The service of the public *is* a thing, which,' a year afterwards, after the orator had been in, and out again, Pitt the Second did *'put up to auction'*—*'did strike down to those who would agree to execute the cheapest:'* and this to such an extent, that, in comparison of the saving thereby effected, whether money or improbity be the article considered, the utmost saving so much as projected by this our sham-reformer, shrinks into insignificance.[a]

This, it is true, the pseudo-reformer had not as yet witnessed. But there was nothing in it that was not in the most perfect degree obvious: what difficulty there was in the business consisted not in the *thinking* of it, but in the *doing* of it.

But what the sophist trusted to was the word *auction*, and the sentiment of ridicule which, if applied to the subject in question, he hoped to find prepared for the reception of it in men's minds. Mention

[a] Viz. in the instances of Loans, Lotteries, and Victualling contracts.—See Mr. Rose's Observations, &c. pp. 26 to 31.[2]

---

[4] Burke, *Speech on Oeconomical Reformation*, pp. 67–8.

[5] Jacques Necker (1732–1804), at first Director of the Royal Treasury and then Director General of Finances, but effectively in charge of French finances from 1776 to 1781, had declined to draw any salary. In 1778 he deposited 2 million livres of his own money in the Royal Treasury, which, upon his dismissal from office, he left on deposit there as a mark of his confidence in the Royal finances. However this money, along with his other goods, was sequestered by the National Assembly in 1793, a decision confirmed by the Directory in 1796. A part of the sum was eventually returned to Necker's daughter, Anne Louise Germaine de Staël (1766–1817), after the Restoration in 1815.

[1] Burke, *Speech on Oeconomical Reformation*, p. 66.

[2] Rose calculated that in the seventeen years from 1793 to 1809 there had been a saving of £8,220,000, on average £483,000 per annum, from Pitt's practice of open competition for loans; a saving of £28,250 per annum through the practice of purchasing army stores through Commissioners of Victualling (see *Observations respecting Public Expenditure*, pp. 26–31); and that these and various other measures had resulted in total savings of £2,590,000 per annum (see ibid., pp. 38–9).

the word *auction*, the image you present is that of a man with a smirk upon his countenance mounted on the burlesque of a pulpit, with a wooden hammer in his hand, expatiating upon the virtues—sometimes of statues and pictures, sometimes of chairs and tables.

The hyperboles employed by orators of that class while expatiating on the virtues of the vendible commodities consigned to their disposal, are, as he in common with every body else must have remarked every now and then, such as while in some parts of the audience they produce the desired impression, excite in the minds of others the idea of the ridiculous.

But no panegyric that was ever bestowed by any such orator on the picture or the screen of a Marquis or a Duke, had more of exaggeration in it than the pictures which this vender of puffs was so expert at drawing, naming them after this or that one of his most noble patrons and originals. His piece of still life, called the Marquis of Rockingham—his Duke of Portland,[1] into the picture of which a Kneller or a Reynolds[2] would have put more thought than Nature and Art together had been able to force into the original—that original whose closest resemblance to a picture that had thought in it was the property of being vendible—that puppet, whose wires after playing for a time so easy, ran rusty at last under the hand of Mr. Canning[3]—viewed through the raree-show glass of Edmund Burke, these and so many other *'great characters'* appeared no less fit for their *'high situations'* than the Counsellers of King *Solomon*, when, with Punch for their interpreter, on the drawing up of the curtain, they are displayed in the act of paying tributes of wisdom to the wise.[4]

Competition.—This word would not, as *auction* so well did, serve the sophist's purpose. To the word *competition* no *Smirk* stands associated—no pulpit—no hammer. *Competition*—a power, the virtues of which had already been so well displayed by Adam Smith, not to

---

[1] Rockingham and William Henry Cavendish Bentinck (1738–1809), third Duke of Portland, were successively leaders of the Whig party.

[2] Sir Godfrey Kneller (1646–1723) and Sir Joshua Reynolds (1723–92) were two of the most celebrated portrait painters of their age, both of whom enjoyed the patronage of royalty and nobility.

[3] George Canning (1770–1827), Foreign Secretary 1807–9, 1822–7, First Lord of the Treasury and Chancellor of the Exchequer 1827. Bentham may be alluding to Canning's unsuccessful attempts in 1809 to persuade Portland, the head of the administration, to remove Castlereagh from the War Office and thus place the management of the war more firmly in his own hands. This eventually led to the celebrated duel between Canning and Castlereagh on 21 September 1809, and both their resignations from office.

[4] King Solomon was a minor character in the Punch and Judy puppet show. No account of the scene referred to by Bentham has, however, been traced.

speak of Sir James Stewart.[1] In *competition* he beheld that security against waste and corruption which would have been mortal to his views.

SECTION XII.

CONCLUDING OBSERVATIONS.—BURKE, WHY THUS EXAMINED.

ERASMUS wrote an elogium on *Folly:*[2] but Erasmus was in jest: Edmund Burke wrote an elogium—he wrote *this* elogium—on *Peculation:*—and Edmund Burke was serious.

In thus exhibiting the orator in one of those fits of extravagance to which he was but too subject—in exhibiting the orator's own figure, according to the monstrous caricature we have seen him drawing of himself, viz. that of a man, in whose estimation nothing but money has any value—a man by whom all breasts that have anything in them that is not sordid, are to be marked out as fit objects of abhorrence,— let me not be accused of wasting time and paper.

It is out of this his book—meaning always such parts of it as are found suitable, that our statesmen of the present day may be seen taking their lessons. It is out of this his garden of sweet flowers that the still existing Finance Committee, and without acknowledgment, have culled, as we have seen, a chaplet wherewith to decorate their brows.[3] It is in this his school, that by another Right Honourable Teacher of Economy,[4] that maxims have certainly been found, and to all appearance learnt, which we shall come to presently.[5]

Had the purpose of his argument, or of his life, required it—here, in this very place, instead of declaiming and writing *for* money, and trying to persuade men that nothing but money is of any value, the orator might, and naturally would, have declared *against* money,— shown in the way that so many other declaimers have shown, that it is of no value, that it is even worse than useless, and that without '*the basest profligacy and corruption*' no man—no public man at least—can ever get, or try to get, any of it.

---

[1] Adam Smith (1723–90), *An Inquiry into the Nature and Causes of the Wealth of Nations*, ed. R.H. Campbell and A.S. Skinner, 2 vols., Oxford, 1976 (first published in 1776); Sir James Steuart (1712–80), *An Inquiry into the Principles of Political Oeconomy: being an Essay on the Science of Domestic Policy in Free Nations*, 2 vols., London, 1767.

[2] Desiderius Erasmus (1466–1536), *Moriæ encomium*, written in 1509, privately published in Paris in 1511. Translated into English by Sir Thomas Chaloner (1521–65), it was published in London in 1549 as *The Praise of Folie*.

[3] See §III, p. 61n above.

[4] i.e. George Rose.

[5] See 'Defence of Economy against Rose', pp. 91–155 below.

In exaggerations, improbity or folly may behold a use on either side; but to common honesty, nothing is here needful but common sense.

Money is a good thing; a very good thing indeed: and, if it were not a good thing, scarce would any thing else be: for there are few good things which a man may not get by means of it: get, either in exchange for it, or (what is still better) even without parting with it.

But the misfortune is, that from us the people, for paying orators of the class of Edmund Burke, it is not to be had without our being forced to part with it: and if the orator suffer in case of his not having it, in case of his never having got so much of it as he could have wished, we the people, who, after having had it, find ourselves, for the use and benefit of the orator, forced to part with it, suffer still more.

Thence it is, that if there be anything else, which, the people not feeling themselves forced to part with it, the orator can persuade himself to be satisfied with, so much the better. Upon this plan, every body is satisfied; orator and people both: whereas, upon the orator's plan, only one of the parties is satisfied, viz. the orator; the orator, who is the agent and spokesman of *the ruling few;* while the other party, viz. we the people, are suffering and grumbling, and as it should seem not altogether without reason; for we are *the many;* and in our number consists our title to regard: a very unpretending title, but not the less a good and sufficient one.

DEFENCE OF ECONOMY AGAINST THE RIGHT HONOURABLE GEORGE ROSE.

FIRST PRINTED IN SEPTEMBER 1817.

ADVERTISEMENT.

WHILE committing to the press so free an examination as this will be found to be, of Mr. Rose's declared *principles*, as published by him on the subject of public expenditure, there would, as it strikes me, be something ungenerous at least, if not unjust in the omission, were I not to make acknowledgment, as, without any communication, direct or indirect, with the Right Honourable Gentleman, I hereby do, of such proofs of due regard for economy as by incidents falling exclusively within my own observation have been furnished by his *practice*. Of the measures alluded to—two in number—both were in a very considerable degree important: one of them, in respect of extent as well as difficulty, pre-eminently so: and, on both occasions, in his instance as well as that of Mr. Pitt, by such tokens, as in the nature of the case could not have left room for doubt in the mind of any person in any situation, it fell in my way to be assured that a real regard for economy, forming a striking contrast with the mixture of waste, corruption, and dark despotism which in one of the two cases has since been exemplified, was an actuating motive: and that with the spontaneously expressed desire of receiving those suggestions, which, had not circumstances above their control stood in the way, would accordingly have been received, any such design on the parts of either of them, as that of giving on the particular occasions in question, any such increase as, on one of those occasions has since been given, to corruptive influence, was plainly incompatible.[1]

As to the tract itself, with the exception of a few inconsiderable verbal alterations, which the nature of the case necessitated, it is exactly in the state in which it was written; which was in[2] the months of April and May, 1810.

---

[1] One of the measures referred to here by Bentham was perhaps the establishment of fee funds, which Pitt had progressively extended to the offices of the Secretaries of State in 1795, the Navy Board in 1796, the War Office in 1797 and the Admiralty in 1800, whereby fees and other allowances were replaced by fixed salaries. The increase of fees in the Court of Chancery, discussed in 'Defence of Economy against Burke', §III, pp. 61–5n above, and 'Indications respecting Lord Eldon', §§III–VII, pp. 212–21 below, was then 'the mixture of waste, corruption, and dark despotism' with which it formed 'a striking contrast'. The other measure was perhaps the Panopticon, whose adoption, Bentham was convinced, had been vetoed by George III.
[2] 1830 'in in'.

DEFENCE OF ECONOMY
AGAINST ROSE.

SECTION I.
INTRODUCTION.

HAVING taken my leave of the departed orator, I have now to pay my obeisance to the surviving statesman; who, though in the line of politics not always conjoined with him, will, in the track of principle, be on the ground here in question, found, as there has already been occasion to observe, separated from him by no great distance.

For principles such as on this same ground may serve as a standard for comparison, I must, on this occasion, as on that other, take leave to refer the reader to these closely compressed thoughts, which are about to take their chance for obtaining a small portion of his notice.[1]

For the convenience of such persons whose taste or whose disposable time shrinks from any such mass as would be formed in the union of all *three* papers, I detach in advance these two parts from that which had been intended to precede them. But forasmuch as throughout this *third* part, reference, either express or tacit, is all along unavoidably made to the principles laid down in the postponed part, and enforced by that by which this one has now lately been preceded;[a] I find myself in this respect reduced to the necessity of supposing, or at least writing as I should do, if I supposed the postponed, as well as the already published part, to have already made its experiment upon the reader's patience.

In the production of *Edmund Burke*, the quantity of matter taken for the subject of examination, was that which happened to be contained between the 62d and 68th pages, both inclusive. Within the pages designated by the same numbers, happens to be contained the only part of Mr. Rose's work, to which the like tribute of unremitted attention has on the present occasion been paid.

A coincidence rather more material, is—that of the *discrepancy*, not to say the *repugnancy*, which in this instance as in *that*, will, if I do not greatly deceive myself, be seen to have place. By the one architect as

---

[a] In the *Pamphleteer*, No. XVII. January 1817.[2]

---

[1] i.e. to the unpublished 'Hints respecting Economy'.
[2] i.e. 'Defence of Economy against Burke', pp. 39–94 above.

98

by the other, to the same virtue, viz. *economy*, a temple erected in the first part, beaten down in the second.[a]

SECTION II.

MR. ROSE'S PLEAS IN BAR TO ECONOMY.
Plea 1.— Vastness of the Expenditure.

1. THE first of his pleas thus pleaded, in bar to any defalcations that might be proposed to be made from the mass of public burdens, is that which, with that ingenuity which will not pass unobserved, has been made out of the very magnitude of the mass.

'The whole revenue of Great Britain,' says the Right Honourable Gentleman (p. 62) 'is more than 60,000,000*l*. a year; the charge on which of 242,000*l*. for pensions and sinecure employments at home and abroad, is between three farthings and one penny in the pound. By the extinction, therefore, of all sinecures and pensions, a person paying taxes to the amount of 50*l*. a year, would save about 4*s*.; such a saving,' continues he, '*we* (who are *we?*) are far from thinking should be treated as trifling or insignificant, it would ill become *the author* to do so: on the other hand, how infinitely short would this fall of the expectation that has been held out.

'But if,' continues he, 'from the total sum received from *sinecures, places*,[1] *and pensions*, deduction were made of such as have been given as rewards for public services, the amount would be very greatly reduced; pensions to foreign ministers in particular, whose appointments are hardly in any instance sufficient for their maintenance.'[2]

It is to '*sinecures and pensions*' alone, that this argument has, by the ingenious author, been applied, to the extra pay of over-paid places,

---

[a] As to the *method* pursued in the present instance—whether it was that by the statesman in question, no such elaborate art, having *here*, as there, been employed in wrapping up peccant matter in splendid language—or in short, howsoever it happened, so it has happened that the course taken on that occasion by the commentator, so far as concerns the prefixing *interpretations* to *text*, has not been pursued here. But, to avoid all design, as well as charge of mis-representation, the same care that was taken there has been continued here, viz. that of not hazarding in any instance any thing in the shape of a *comment*, without laying at the same time before the reader, in the very words, whatever passage served or contributed to form the ground of it.

---

[1] Rose 'sinecure places'. The rendering of this and other passages from Rose's *Observations respecting Public Expenditure* contain some minor inaccuracies; major discrepancies are recorded in editorial footnotes. The italics, unless otherwise noted, are Bentham's.

[2] Rose, *Observations respecting Public Expenditure*, pp. 62–3.

not: but, applying as it does to both branches of expenditure, and with equal force, it would be wronging the argument not to give to both of them the full benefit of it.

Now, true it is, that were this argument to be received in the character here proposed for it, it would, it must be confessed, be a very convenient one, and save others in abundance. For every 4*s.* a year which you wish to give away without any public use, contrive to spend 50*l.* a year, for which such a use or the appearance of such a use can be found, and your justification is then made.

Meantime, some reasoners there are, to whom the contrary inference would appear the more reasonable one: unnecessary or even necessary, the heavier the mass of our burdens is already, the less able are we to bear any addition to it, or even this or that existing part of it.

In my own view of the matter, I must confess the consideration of the magnitude of the mass, is a consideration to which, on a question such as the present, there can be no necessity nor any great use in recurring.

Whatsoever it be that at the expense of the people, is by the trustees of the people, given to this or that individual without equivalent, and that an adequate one, I mean without either receiving or reasonable expectation of receiving on account of the public a preponderate advantage, is so much *waste*,—and if given with eyes open to the misapplication of it, so much *peculation*.

When by *indictment* a man is prosecuted for theft, or by bill in equity for a breach of trust in the way of peculation, that of the pecuniary circumstances of the party to whose prejudice the act of dishonesty has operated, any account should be taken, is never looked upon as necessary, or so much as admissible. And not being so on that individual scale, I see not why it should be so on this all-comprehensive scale.

But if so it were, that I found myself under an obligation of bringing this topic to view, it seems to me, that in the vastness of the existing burdens, I should be more apt to view an argument for decreasing it, than either for giving increase to it, or so much as keeping it from decrease.

The misfortune is, that without being thus expressed, this consideration has in experience operated, and with too much effect, in disposing the people to acquiesce without remonstrance, under unnecessary pressure. Turn over the book of history, you will find that the heavier the burdens have been with which the people have been loaded, the greater the facility that has been found for rendering the load still heavier: or, what comes to the same thing, look backward, and you will find that the [less][1] considerable the load they had been accustomed to, the greater was the difficulty that was experienced in persuading them to submit, though it were but for a year or two, to any addition to it.

If as the facility of engaging them to submit to increased burdens increased, the suffering produced by those burdens diminished, this disposition of mind would be as desirable as it is natural: but unfortunately this is not the case. By heaping law taxes upon law taxes, and law fees upon law fees, you may ruin a thousand families one year, two thousand the next year, and so on: and, the greater the number that are thus ruined, the better enabled and the better satisfied will the man of finance and the man of law be to go on receiving more and more: it will be to both of them, as it has been to both of them, and *to both in one, a motion of course;* but it does not appear, or (to speak intelligibly to learned gentlemen) *non constat,*[2] that when the number thus ruined is two thousand, the affliction is to each or any of them lighter than when the number was but one thousand.

For forming a gag to stop complaints in the mouth of the party tormented, as well as a *callus* to case the heart of the tormentor, precedent is indeed a mighty good thing; and the more manifold the precedent the more effective the gag, as well as the harder the callus: and the latter use is that to which these several pleas against economy, and this first plea in particular, seems more especially destined and adapted. The misfortune is, that by the callus formed round the one heart, the affliction that rends the other is not assuaged.

Oh, but sir, (cries somebody) what is it you are about all this while? and how sadly have you been misrepresenting the Right Honourable Gentleman! Here are you imputing to him this sad purpose, and that immediately after having read and passed over (fie upon you!) a paragraph in which he tells you *himself* the purpose he had in view, and that a very different one.

True it is that I have read that paragraph; but as to the purpose spoken of in it, I feel myself under a sort of embarrassment which I shall proceed to state.

'The opinion already alluded to,' (says the paragraph, p. 62) 'as prevailing *to a certain extent,* that if sinecures and pensions were entirely suppressed, the burdens of the country would be *instantly lightened to a great amount,* and by some entertained that they would

---

[1] 1817, 1830 'more'. The evident sense of the passage requires 'less'.

[2] i.e. 'it is not evident', a legal phrase meaning that an alleged inference is not deducible from given premises.

in that case be *removed altogether*, renders it *necessary* that a comparison should be made of the before-mentioned total, (viz. of sinecures and pensions) large as it is, with the amount of the taxes raised upon the people.'

Now then—what is *expressly* averred here, is—that an opinion to the purpose in question is '*prevailing to a certain extent*.'

What seems to be insinuated—I should rather say—what from the idea of '*necessity*' thus brought to view, some readers might be apt to imagine, is—that the purpose the Right Honourable Gentleman had in view, was only the setting the *people* right in respect of this supposed prevalent error, and not the persuading the imposers of public burdens to consider the enormity of the mass as affording an argument for not diminishing it.

Now then, as to this supposed error: what seems to me is, that it must have been in some vision or some dream, and no where else, that any person not in the care of a keeper, could have presented themselves to the conception of the Right Honourable Gentleman, as entertaining it. The interest of the debt paid without money—the expense of the army defrayed without money—the expense of the navy defrayed without money—all this, not to speak of anything more, must have been believed by any person, in whose mind any such opinion should prevail, as that if sinecures and pensions were suppressed, the burdens of this country would be removed altogether.

Another thing that passes my comprehension is, how should it be that, supposing them to have found '*to a certain extent*,' whatever that extent be—that is to a certain *number*, whatever that number be, a set of people among whom any such opinion was prevalent, how it should be that it should have entered into their conception, otherwise than in dream or vision, as above, that for the purpose of setting right any such people, and weaning them from their error, there could be either necessity or use, in bringing forward any such ingenious and accurate calculation as that which has just been seen, and which he was thereupon immediately about to treat us with: as if, supposing the existence of any such swine, such pearls could be of any the smallest use to them![1]

If to so Right Honourable a Gentleman anything could be attributed, that would bear any such appellation as that of *artifice*, (no, I will not call it *artifice*, I will call it *astutia*—and then everything will be as it should be) what, on an occasion such as this, one should be tempted to suppose, is, that the agreement thus brought forward, and put in front of the battle, was the result of a *consultation* with some learned, or quondam learned, as well as Right Honourable or Honourable

[1] An echo of Matthew 7: 6.

Gentlemen, profoundly learned in that superior and purer branch of the law called *equity;* one of the rules of which is, that in the drawing of the initiative instrument called *a bill*, to entitle yourself to ask a question of the defendant, you must, in the first place, impute to him the having told some story or other, no matter how extravagant, which he never told, to serve him in the character of a *'pretence'* for defrauding the orator (your client) of his due; he himself neither having heard of the defendant's ever saying such thing, nor believing him to have ever said it; which falsehood having thus with all due regularity been come out with, serves by way of licence, as well as introduction, to whatsoever other falsehoods, mixed with whatsoever truths, it may have been deemed convenient to introduce.

SECTION III.
PLEA 2.—NEED OF PROVISION FOR DECAYED NOBILITY, &C.

2. THE next plea is that which is founded on the alleged necessity of making provision for noble and respectable families fallen into decay.

'The pension list' (continues the Right Honourable Advocate, p. 63) 'also contains provisions for[1] *noble and respectable families* fallen into decay; this is, however,' (continues he) 'an exertion of *national generosity*, if not of *justice*, which *the most scrupulous economist* will hardly consider as improper. Something' (continues he) 'must certainly be allowed for mere favour; but when the instances are *clearly improper*, (and it is not meant to contend there are no such) they are at least open to public animadversion, as they are now *regularly laid before parliament*, and printed from time to time, *which certainly affords a considerable, if not an effectual check against abuse.'*[2]

Thus far the Right Honourable Gentleman. For my own part I am doomed to fall into sad disgrace with him. The conception entertained by him of any *'the most scrupulous'* sort of person, in the character of an *'economist,'* is far outstripped by me. Under what denomination it may be my lot to fall in his black dictionary, I know not; if it were that of Jacobin or Leveller, it would be no surprise to me.

Of the sort of *justice*, which can so much as *permit*, not to speak of *commanding*, any such disposal of public money, I have no conception, nor yet of generosity, unless it be of that pernicious and hypocritical sort, which gratifies itself at the expense of justice.

[1] Rose 'for the branches of'.
[2] Rose, *Observations respecting Public Expenditure*, pp. 63–4.

My protest is in the first place against the *principle;* as being founded on oppressive extortion, and breach of trust; as affording encouragement to extravagance, and to every vice that is fed by extravagance; as being still unjustifiable, even though there were a certainty of its not having either vice or extravagance for its consequence any more than for its cause.

My next objection is to the *amount;* as being without limit; as scorning all limit: and being of itself capable of effecting a revolution in the state of *property*, if it did not, in a revolution in the state of *power*, find a preventive remedy.

I. In the first place, as to *principle*.

Now, to a provision of the sort in question, what is it that, according to the Right Honourable Gentleman's law, is to constitute a man's title? It is '*decay;*'—mere decay;—the having *fallen into decay;* i.e. the being at the time in question in a state of indigence. Mark well, that to indigence at that degree, to which the next degree is death, or at least disease, his argument does not look; for indigence in that shape, provision is made already—made, to wit, by the species of tax called the *Poor Rates:* a tax which, even by the Right Honourable Gentleman himself, on whose feelings public burdens sit thus lightly, has never been spoken of as a light one.

This provision then is not the sort and degree of provision he has in view: of the sort and degree of provision which he has in view, what more adequate or unexceptionable description can be given, than that which has been given in and by his own words? for '*noble*' families then, it must be *noble*, for '*respectable*' families, it must be *respectable*.

Against provision of even the scantiest kind, an objection that by many has been regarded as a peremptory one, is, that it operates as a provision for idleness and extravagance. By myself any more than by the Right Honourable Gentleman it has never been regarded in that light; not seeing that so long as it is confined to what is absolutely necessary to keep a person alive and free from disease, and given on condition of working, where work can be made profitable (and beyond this I undertake not for the defence of it) subsistence is capable of acting to any preponderantly formidable extent in that character: and considering that, without some such provision, multitudes there are, that by infirmity, the result of infamy, or decrepitude, or disease, would without any default of their own, be exposed to perish, and would accordingly perish, by lingering disease or famine.

But by any such provision, neither the *generosity* of the Right Honourable Gentleman, nor so much as his *justice* is to be satisfied;

104

for *noble* families, satisfied it never can be by any thing less than a *noble* provision: for *respectable families* by any thing less than a *respectable* one.

In the provision already made by law—a provision neither limited, nor, unfortunately for the country, capable of being limited—some have viewed a gulph capable, of itself, of swallowing up one of these days the whole produce of national industry. Of any such disaster I have not for my own part any serious apprehension; but, of the *generosity* of the Right Honourable Gentleman, or by whatever other name this article in the catalogue of his virtues be to be called, of this virtue, if once admitted to operate, and in the character of a *principle* set the law to practice, I cannot but regard this catastrophe as an inevitable consequence.

II. For now let us think a little of the *amount:* and to this the Right Honourable Gentleman has not attempted to set any limits. Vain indeed would have been any such attempt; the principle scorns all limits. Taken by itself, nobility, had *that* been the only source of demand on this score, would not have scorned all limits. Noble families, for example, so many:—in each family, generations reckoning downwards from each peer, to be regarded as still *noble*, so many:—minimum of the pension to each individual in a state of decay, according to the rank occupied by the family in the scale of the peerage, is so much.—Here would have been one exercise for the Right Honourable Gentleman's skill in figures.

But neither for the Right Honourable Gentleman's *generosity*, nor for his *justice*, is it enough, that for *noble* families in decay a *noble* provision be thus kept up; for *respectable* families in the same state there must moreover be a *respectable* one. Here all powers of calculation, even those of the Right Honourable Gentleman, would find themselves at a stand.

For the moment, let me take the liberty of proposing for them an analogous, though a somewhat different exercise.

By the taxes, as they stand at present—(I presume it is out of taxes, and not out of heaven-dropped manna or heaven-dropped quails, that, according to his plan, the *noble* and the *respectable* provision would be to be made)—by the taxes, as they stand at present, a certain number of families are every year pressed down from a state of independence into a state of pauper and parochially-supported indigence. Now then, for every branch of a noble and respectable family, which by the noble or respectable provision respectively, is kept above indigence, meaning, that which to the noble or respectable family would have been indigence, how many branches that, without being either noble or respectable, or as yet independent, would be pressed down into that which really is indigence. If *thought* be too much to ask for, a *calculation* of this sort from a right honorable hand, in which figures are so plenty and so much at command, might, at any rate, be not undeserving, it is hoped, of a few figures.

Another exercise for the mathematics of the Right Honourable Gentleman. The *respectable* families, let them for the moment be laid out of the question—let the calculation still confine itself to the *noble* ones.

After observations taken of the rate of the increase given to nobility by his still present Majesty,[1] or even of that part of it that was given with the advice of the Right Honourable Gentleman's departed hero,[2] let him, with *Cocker*[3] in his hand, carry on the increase through a portion of future contingent time. Considering that neither Scotland nor Ireland, nor any thing that is noble in either kingdom, can on this occasion be left out of the account, let him inform us what are the number of years that will have elapsed antecedently to that point of time at which the amount of the provision made on his plan for *noble decay*, will have outstripped that of the provision at the same time made for ignoble indigence.

'Oh, but you are confounding *classes*—you are confounding *species*. This is the way with you *jacobins* and you *levellers*. You confound every thing. The noble and respectable families are of *one* species: the ignoble and unrespectable families are of *another*. The ignoble and unrespectable families are of the species that *are sent* to *Walcheren;* the noble and respectable families are of the species that *send them* there.[4] The families whose branches are to be preserved from decay, are those whose *feelings* have a right to be consulted: the families that are to be helped on in the road to ruin, are those whose feelings have no such right.'

A smile beams on the countenance of the Right Honourable Gentleman. He calls for his *extinct peerage:* he foresees his triumph: he beholds the confusion of the jacobin; when, at the end of the calculation, it has been made as plain as figures can make anything, how

[1] George III.

[2] William Pitt, who created eighty-seven British peers during his first administration (1783–1801) and five during his second (1804–6): see A.S. Turberville, *The House of Lords in the Age of Reform 1784–1837*, London, 1958, p. 45.

[3] *Cocker's Arithmetick*, first published in 1678, the work of the arithmetician Edward Cocker (1631–75), was for many years the standard introduction to the subject.

[4] The Walcheren expedition of 1809, dispatched to attack Antwerp and thereby divert French troops in order to relieve pressure on Austria, had been badly mismanaged, many troops dying from disease, and had finally been abandoned without achieving any of its objectives.

many centuries will have elapsed before any such outstripping can have taken place.

Well then; having, by the success of the operation thus performed upon the *noble* families, given vigour to his hand, let him try it upon the *respectable* ones.

What has just been seen, is what the Right Honourable Gentleman has not anywhere said. True;—but it is what (I fear much) from the beginning of his pamphlet to the end of it, is but too much like what he has thought.

'Something'—(says the Right Honourable Gentleman, such is his candour) 'something must certainly be allowed for mere favour.' Good sir, you already forget your own argument: it is all mere favour, or it is none. 'Decay,' not service; 'decay,' not merit in any shape, real or imagined, was your title: decay, by what cause soever produced, as well as in whatsoever quantity; produced by eating and drinking,—produced by carrying about seraglios in foreign missions,—produced by horse-racing,—produced by dice or E.O.; is decay less decay? Is nobility the less noble? Is respectability (I mean your sort of respectability—the respectability which consists in having or spending money of one's own or other people's) the less respectable?

Talk of justice and injustice. So long as any *one* individual is, whether on the score of *nobility*, or of *respectability*, preserved in this way from decay, it is not mere disfavour, it is no better than mere *injustice*, to refuse it to any *other*.

'But where the instances are clearly improper, and it is not meant,' continues the Right Honourable Gentleman, 'to contend that there are no such, they are at least open to public animadversion.' Good sir, once more your candour carries you too far. What *you* do not mean to contend for, I must, even I; indeed, sir, there are not any such *instances:* your principle admitted, there *cannot* be any.

'*They are at least open to public animadversion.*' Your pardon, sir; indeed they are not. *Individually* they are not: they are not common: to the 'public' two things altogether necessary to the purpose are wanting, viz. *information* and time. Mr. Brown has 1200*l.* a year: two Miss Vandals have 600*l.* Who knows who this Mr. Brown or those Miss Vandals are? At the moment when the necessity of providing for noble or respectable decay in the person or persons of this Mr. Brown or these Miss Vandals, has by some noble or right honourable person been whispered into the royal ear, the whisperer knows: but the next moment nobody knows. Even now there are more of them than the public patience can endure so much as to *count:* and shall we talk of *scrutiny?* More than can be so much as counted even now! and what shall we say when, your principle being in full operation, there are with us in England, as you know when there were in France, enough of them to fill a *red book*, and *that*, like the army list, no small book, of themselves.[1]

No, sir; individually open to public animadversion they are not, even now: much less at the time in question would they be. But in the lump, in the principle on which they are proposed to be multiplied, and that to infinity, they are *'open to animadversion:'* and on this consideration it is that the presumption, betrayed by the present weak and inadequate attempt at 'animadversion,' has found its cause.

On the *wing*, who can think to catch, who can so much as follow, all such wasps? But in the *egg*, if the people have but spirit enough, they may be crushed.

'Something' (says the candour of the Right Honourable Gentleman) 'must be allowed for mere *favour*.' Yes: and something must also be allowed for an affection of an opposite nature. This candour of his shall not go unrequited: it shall be paid for in the same coin. If *profusion* be, as it appears to be, all that is meant by 'the abuse,' a check that abuse 'certainly' has;—and that check but *too* 'certainly' is *'considerable,'* though unhappily it is far from being *'an effectual'* one. Of itself, *profusion*, were that the whole of the disorder, would have no check: but, complicated as it is with another disorder, *corruption*, in that other disorder, odd as the case may seem at the first mention of it, it does find a sort of a check: the *diarrhœa* finds in the *septic* diathesis a sort of astringent.

The paradox will disappear immediately. When it happened that the Right Honourable Gentleman, by whom the case of the *sprig* of *decayed nobility* or *respectability* had been submitted to *royal* 'generosity' or *royal* 'justice,' had been voting on the *improper* side, the instance (could any such hopeless intrusion be supposed on the part of the Right Honourable Gentleman) would be one of the *clearly improper* ones, and the decay would be left to its own natural course. When so it happened that on all occasions the patron had *properly* understood, as in duty, I mean in loyalty, every such patron is bound to understand, what on each occasion is the proper side, the decay would find its *proper* preservative, and the profusion would be left to the operation of that check, with the virtue of which the Right Honourable Gentleman is so nearly satisfied; I mean, that *'certainly considerable, if not effectual check' against abuse*, which is 'afforded' by the pensions forming, when the mischief is past remedy, part and

---

[1] The Red Book was the popular name for the *Royal Kalendar*, bound in red covers, published annually, and containing the names of holders of state offices. The equivalent in France under the *ancien régime* had been the *Almanach Royal*, which was succeeded in turn by the *Almanach National* and the *Almanach Impérial*.

parcel of that almost completely unintelligible, and effectually inscrutable, mass of information or non-information, which is 'now' '*so
regularly laid before parliament.*'

SECTION IV.

PLEA 3.—NEED OF SUBSISTENCE FOR OFFICIAL PERSONS.

3. A THIRD plea is that which is composed of the alleged non-excess,
or even insufficiency, of official incomes.

'If we look to official incomes, it will be found they are in most
cases' (says the Right Honourable Gentleman) 'barely equal to the
moderate, and even the *necessary* expenses of the parties: in many
instances they are *actually* insufficient for these.'[1]

Under the modest guise of a plea *against retrenchment*, we have
here a plea *for increase*, and that again an inexhaustible one.

In this plea, *two* points present a more particular call for observation.

[1.] One consists in the *indefiniteness* and thence in the *universality*
of the terms by which the *incomes* in question, and thence the
incomists are designated. By '*official incomes*,' unless some word of
limitation be annexed—and no such word is annexed—must be
understood *all* official incomes. Less than *all* cannot be meant; for, if
anything less be meant, the argument falls short of its undissembled
purpose. In most cases, scantiness being asserted, and in many,
insufficiency—and that even without a view to the single purpose of a
bare subsistence, whether there be any of these incomes that are
more than 'barely equal' to that object, is left to conjecture.

2. The other the word *necessary*, viz. in the application here made
of it to a mass of expenses that are to be defrayed at the public charge:
an aggregate composed of the several individual expenditures of all
these several official persons; and when the present Mr. Rose comes
to be in the situation (poverty excepted) of the late Mr. Pitt, let any
one calculate, whose skill in calculation is equal to the task, how many
are the hundreds of thousands, not to say the millions, a year, that
will depend on the construction of these two words.

To assist us in this calculation, an example, though unfortunately
but one, has been afforded us by the Right Honourable Gentleman:
and, so far as this carries us, it will appear that, even where by the
frugality of the Right Honourable Gentleman, it is confined to what is
'*necessary*,' (the inflexibility of this virtue not suffering it to rise to so

---

[1] Rose, *Observations respecting Public Expenditure*, p. 64.

high a pitch as even to be '*moderate*') what, in speaking of an official person, is meant by his *expense*, is composed of the official income, whatever it be, which he finds provided for it by law, together with a capital to the amount of between eight and nine years' purchase of it, or reckoning by the year, about 25 per cent. upon it, the person's own patrimony, if he happens to[1] have any, included or not included. But of this under another head.[a]

SECTION V.
PLEA 4.—NEED OF MONEY FOR MAKING FORTUNES FOR OFFICIAL PERSONS AND THEIR FAMILIES.

4. THE next plea is that which is founded on the alleged necessity of enabling persons in official situations—all persons in all official situations—to provide for their families at the public expense.

'May we not *then* venture to ask' (continues the argument from the passage last quoted)—'may we not *then* venture to ask whether it is *reasonable*, or whether it would be *politic*, that such persons should, after spending a great part of their lives with *industry, zeal, and fidelity*, in the discharge of trusts and public duties, be left afterwards without reward of any sort, and their families entirely without provision?'[2]

The skill of the Right Honourable Gentleman in *arithmetic* is above, far above, dispute; but, if we may venture to say as much, his *logic* seems to be not altogether upon a par with it.

His *antecedent*, as delivered in the last preceding sentence, is, that the 'official income' of the official man is 'in many instances insufficient,' even for his necessary expenses, meaning his necessary *current* expense; and in this next sentence the *consequent* or *conclusion* drawn, is that, in plain English and to speak out, he ought to be enabled to make his fortune always at the public expense; and that to so good a purpose, that after his decease his family may in respect of current expenses, so long as it continues, find itself—in what plight? in the same plight (we are left to conclude) or thereabouts, as its founder, the official man himself.

As to the being preserved as long as it lasts, preserved in all its branches, from decay, that any such provision would be short of the

---

[a] Chap. [10].[3]

---

[1] 1830 'to to'.
[2] Rose, *Observations respecting Public Expenditure*, p. 64.
[3] 1817, 1830 '9'. Pitt's expenditure is discussed in §X, pp. 132–42 below.

mark, though not to what degree short of the mark, is what we are assured of; for if the family of an official person be a respectable family, (and if not, what family can be a respectable one?) if this be admitted, 'trusts,' or no trusts, 'public duties,' or no public duties; the being kept in a state of perpetual preservation from decay is a right that, in the preceding paragraph, has been claimed for them by the Right Honourable Gentleman's *generosity*,' supported by his *justice*.

The form of the argument is indeed rather of the rhetorical than the logical cast— *May we not venture to ask?* The answer is, good sir, no apology—ask boldly; but ask one thing at a time. First, let us make up the deficiency in respect of current and present expenses, and as the supply we are to provide for these 'discharge[r]s of trusts and duties' is to keep pace with their expenditure—with the expenditure of each and every of them (for your 'generosity' makes no exception) '*may we not then venture to ask*,' on our parts, for a little breathing time? If so, then, after we have taken breath a little, will be the time for entering on the further employment you have found for us: viz. the making provision for the families of those official, and *therefore* meritorious persons, whose '*industry, zeal*, and *fidelity*,' as we have not the honour of being acquainted with them, it is impossible for us to dispute.

To this industry, zeal, and fidelity, the 'reward' which your generosity and justice, your reason and your 'policy' have in store for them, is doubtless to be proportioned: for otherwise those virtues of theirs would, as to a part of them more or less considerable, be left without reward—(virtue left without its reward!) and as, in the estimate to be formed of the degree in which these several virtues will, by the several official, and therefore meritorious, persons be displayed, your '*policy*,' under the guidance of your 'generosity,' will not find itself under any restraint; the quantity of the reward will be as little in danger of finding any such limits, as would pinch and straiten it.

The 'insufficiency' of their respective 'official incomes,' for the respective 'necessary expenses' of these officially industrious, zealous, and 'faithful' persons—as such is the title on which the 'generosity,' 'justice,' 'reasonableness,' and 'policy' of the Right Honourable Gentleman rests their right to have their 'necessary expenses' defrayed for them, and at the same time their fortunes made for them; and as no other man can be so good a judge of what is necessary for a man as the man himself is, there is a sort of comfort in the reflection—how small the danger is, that, upon the principles and plans of the Right Honourable Gentleman, virtue, in any such shape at least as that of 'industry, zeal, and fidelity,' (meaning always official ditto) will be left without its reward. Having got your official situation, you spend in it so much a year as you find necessary. Having so done, thus and *then* is it that you have entitled yourself to the benefit of the Right Honourable Gentleman's conclusion—his logical conclusion, embellished and put into the dress of a rhetorical *erotesis;*—that you are entitled to receive out of the taxes as much more as will secure to your 'family' that 'provision' which, in virtue of your '*industry, zeal,* and *fidelity,*' speaking without partiality, or with no other '*partiality*' than that which, according to the Head-Master[a] in the school of official economy is a kind of justice, it appears to you to deserve.

After so exemplary a pattern of diffidence as has been set by a Right Honourable Gentleman, whose grounds for confidence are so manifest and so unquestionable, a plain man who feels no such grounds, nor any grounds, for any such pleasurable sensation, can scarce muster up enough of it to put a question of any kind, for fear of being thought encroaching: but, if any one would save me harmless from that charge, I would venture to ask whether it may not have been by a too unqualified adherence to these principles, a too rigid adherence to these precepts, of the two great masters, and without taking the benefit of those precautionary instructions, which the prudence or even the example of one of them might, if sufficiently studied, have furnished them with, that their Right Honourable friend Mr. Steele, and the Honourable Mr. Villiers, and till the other day Honourable Mr. Hunt, and the Gallant General Delancy, and the '*industrious, zealous, and faithful*' Mr. John Bowles, with *his* et cæteras, and so many other et cæteras, were led into those little inaccuracies, which time after time have afforded matter of so much, though happily as yet fruitless, triumph to Jacobins, levellers, and parliamentary reformers?[1]

[a] Burke, p. 65.[2]

---

[1] Thomas Steele (1753–1823), MP for Chichester 1780–1807, Secretary to the Treasury 1783–91, Joint Paymaster-General 1791–1804, and close friend of Pitt, had appropriated two sums of public money for his private use in May 1799 and July 1800. The affair came to the attention of the Committee on Public Expenditure, which made it the subject of their First Report (see *Commons Sessional Papers* (1808) ii. 313–77). By the time this had been presented, Steele had repaid the money with interest and retired from public life. George Villiers (1759–1827), MP for Warwick 1792–1802, had been forced to resign as Paymaster of Marines in January 1810 because of the state of his official accounts, which appeared to be in massive arrears. The conduct of Joseph Hunt (1762?–1816), MP for Queenborough 1807–10, as Treasurer of the Ordnance, an office he held 1803–5 and 1807–10, formed the subject of the Twelfth Report of the Commissioners of Military Enquiry (see *Commons Sessional Papers* (1810) ix. 457–518). Having already resigned from office in January 1810, he was expelled from the House of Commons on 23 May 1810 on the grounds of embezzling public funds. Lieutenant-General Oliver De Lancey (c.1749–1822), MP for Maidstone 1796–1802, resigned from his post as Barrack Master General in November 1804, when the Commissioners for auditing the Public Accounts found he could not account for considerable sums of money entrusted to him

 [*See opposite page for n. 1 cont. and n. 2.*]

It is necessity alone, and not inclination, that in the performance of the task I have set myself in the school of economy, so frequently imposes upon me so great a misfortune as that of being seen to differ from so great a master as the Right Honourable Gentleman: and accordingly wherever I am fortunate enough to be able to descry between us anything like a point of coincidence, it is with proportionable eagerness that I lay hold of it, and endeavour to make the most of it.

His plan is—that 'official persons,' among whom, for the purpose in question, he includes (I presume) persons proposed or proposing themselves for official situations, should determine for themselves what mass of emolument is sufficient for their own expenses, and what for the expenses of their respective families, in present and in future. Now, thus far, this is exactly my plan. Thus far then we are agreed; but now comes the unfortunate difference.

My plan (it will be seen) is, that having formed his own calculations, each candidate, in taking his determination, should take it once for all: and moreover, that, as in the case of *stores*, in which instance, instead of skilful labour itself, the produce of skilful labour has, with such well-grounded approbation on the part of the Right Honourable Gentleman, been, ever since the time he speaks of,[a] regularly furnished for the public service, there should be a '*competition;*' whereupon that one of them, whose judgment concerning what is sufficient for *him and his*, is most favourable to the public interest, should (unless for, and to the extent of, special cause to the contrary) be accepted.

Thus far my plan. But, according to the Right Honourable Gentleman's, the accepted candidate, who without any such competition is to be accepted, viz. in consideration of that '*industry, zeal, and fidelity,*' which will be so sure of being found in him—this accepted candidate, after his calculation has been formed, and the office, with its emolument, taken possession of, is to have the convenience of remaining at

[a] Pp.29, 30.[1]

(see the First Report of the Commissioners of Military Enquiry, *Commons Sessional Papers* (1806) vi. 1–113). It is unclear why Bentham added John Bowles, the barrister and prolific pro-government and anti-radical pamphleteer, to his list of officials involved in pecuniary scandals.

[2] See Burke, *Speech on Oeconomical Reformation*, p. 65: 'Efficient ministers have been their own paymasters. It is true. But their very partiality has operated as a kind of justice; and still it was service that was paid.'

[1] Rose, *Observations respecting Public Expenditure*, pp. 29–30, describes how, 'at the very commencement of the last war' (in 1793), provisions for the armed forces had been purchased through competitive auction, reforming the previous practice whereby the Treasury had given 'beneficial contracts to persons selected from favor'.

liberty to correct by the light of experience (as we shall see[a] the illustrious chief and pattern of all official men did) any such errors as the calculation shall, from time to time, have been found to contain in it. By this practical test, having ascertained what is *'necessary'* for his own present expenses, he will have put himself in a condition to determine, and ought accordingly to stand charged with the *'trust and duty'* of determining, what further provision will be necessary for the *'necessary expenses'* of his family, considered in its several branches, present and future contingent, for and during the continuance of that portion of time called *future time*.

Another unfortunate difference is—that according to my plan, no exclusion, either express or implied, is put upon such candidates to whom it may happen to have property or income of their own: unable as I am to discover any such office, for the *'trusts and duties'* of which, any such property or income can reasonably be considered as constituting, in any point of view, a ground of disqualification, or to understand, how it can be that a hundred a year should, in the case of its being a man's own *private* money, go less far towards the defraying the *'necessary expenses'* of *him* and *his*, than if it were so much *public* money, received in the shape of official emolument out of the public purse. What, in regard to *my* official man, my plan accordingly assumes, is,—either that he has more or less property or income of his own, or (what in my view comes to much the same thing) what, if any thing, remains to the official situation, after the offer made by him, in relation to it, has been accepted, is, in his own judgment, sufficient for his *'expenses,'* *'necessary'* and unnecessary, upon every imaginable score.

Of this assumption, that which seems all along to have been proceeded upon by the Right Honourable Gentleman's plan, is exactly the reverse.

True it is, that no *disqualification Act*, excluding from official situations all such persons as shall have either property or income, is any where proposed by him;—no, nor is so much as any recommendation given by him to the wisdom of the Crown in the choice it makes of persons for filling these situations, to act as if a law to some such effect were in force. But, all along, the supposition proceeded and argued upon by him is,—that there exists not in the quarter in question, any such relatively superfluous matter: a state *'entirely without provision'* is the state in which *'afterwards,'* to wit, after *'a*

---

[a] Infra, §[10].[1]

---

[1] 1817, 1830 '9'. See §X, pp. 132–42 below.

great part of his life spent' by the official person 'in the discharge of trusts and duties,' his *'family'* is spoken of as being *'left:'* and it is upon this supposition that at least the *'policy'* of the Right Honourable Gentleman (not to speak of his humanity) grounds itself in the appeal it makes to that same endowment, which he beholds as fixed in the breasts of those Honourable persons for whose use this lesson of economy is designed. Would it be *'reasonable'?*—would it be *'politic'?*—are the questions which on this occasion he asks leave to *'venture to ask.'*

SECTION VI.
PLEA 5.—NEED OF MONEY FOR BUYING MEN OFF
FROM PROFESSIONS.

5. A FIFTH plea is composed of the alleged necessity of buying off men from private pursuits: in other words, of the want of 'wisdom' there would be in failing to allow to official men—to all official men—in the shape of official emolument, as much money, at the least, as any body can gain 'by trade or manufactures.'

'It would hardly' (says he, p. 64) 'be *wise*, on *reflection*, to establish a *principle*, which would have a *tendency* at least to exclude from the service of their country men likely to be useful to it. Great numbers of those who engage in trade and manufacture (than whom none are held in greater[1] estimation by the author) or who enter into various professions, frequently acquire very large fortunes' (very true indeed) 'and seldom, if they have talents and perseverance, fail to obtain independence. What fairness, justice, or reason, is there then in marking the character of the official man alone with disrespect, and himself as unfit to have reward in any case, beyond an annual stipend for his labour and services, just sufficient for his[2] current expenses, however faithfully and diligently he may have discharged an important trust for a long series of years?' 'Surely' (concludes he) 'it is not unwise or unreasonable that the public should be in a situation to *bid* to a limited extent for talents, in competition with other honourable and lucrative professions, and various branches of trade and manufactures.'[3]

Thus far the Right Honourable Author:—as for the obscure commentator, perplexity is once more his fate. The Right Honourable

---

[1] Rose 'higher'.
[2] Rose 'his necessary'.
[3] Rose, *Observations respecting Public Expenditure*, pp. 64–5.

Author speaks of a *principle:* a principle which, such as it is, he disapproves of. But what this principle is, the obscure commentator can no otherwise take his chance for declaring aright, than by a very random guess.

The omitting in the instance of an official person to make for his family a provision, such as *he* (the official person) or the Right Honourable Author, or somebody else (and who else?) shall pitch upon as being '*necessary,*' and, according to the just-described plan of estimation, *sufficient?* An omission to this effect is it the thing to which, by the style and title of a '*principle,*' the Right Honourable Gentleman, '*on reflection,*' means to attach the *censure* (for gentle and considerate as it is, it is still a *censure*)—attached to it, viz. by saying of it that 'it would hardly be wise'? Yes; this must be it; at any rate, it is the nearest approach to it that the perplexed commentator is able to make.

But of this *principle*, which '*it would hardly be wise to establish,*' though unfortunately we have no such specific and particular description, as (were it only to save us from wishing to see an unwise principle established) we cannot but wish for, we have at any rate a general description, viz. such a description as is given of it by the designation, its imputed *tendency;*—and that in so many words:—'a principle' (says he) 'which would have a *tendency* at least to exclude from the service of their country men likely to be useful to it.'

Now in this *principle*, if so it be that the perplexed commentator has succeeded in his humble endeavours to pierce the cloud that covers it; in this principle we have another measure of the quantity of emolument which on this single score, not to speak at present of any other—on this one account, viz. that of money to be employed in making the fortunes of their respective families, the Right Honourable Author, did it depend on him, would, in the situation of minister, annex to office,—annex to *every* office.

Let us distinguish what requires to be distinguished. What, under the last head, we learned, was one of the *purposes* for which the official emolument was necessary;—what, under this head, we receive, is a sort of standard of reference, from which the quantity of that necessary emolument may be estimated, and finally set down in figures. True it is that, on the present occasion, not that same purpose but a *fresh* purpose is named and brought to view; *there*, the purpose was, enabling the official man to make his family; *here*, it is—inducing a man, not as yet official, to become such by buying him off from other pursuits; from all pursuits, how lucrative soever, in any one of which, if not thus bought off, it might have happened to him to engage.

But, if the quantity allowed for this fresh purpose (viz. the *buying-off* purpose) be ample enough, (and the necessity of not being niggardly on this score will be no secret)—the consequence is, that by the help of a little economy, such as at the hands of so enlightened a professor of economy it might not be too much to venture to ask for, one and the same mass of money might be made to serve both purposes. The reason is—that on the occasion of the two purposes, two different *periods* are in question: viz. that of *possession*, and that of *expectancy*. When actually in possession, whatsoever it be that is necessary to a man, for the good purpose (whatever it be) which is in question (making a family, for example, and so forth) *that* it is that he must have in hand. But, *before* he has taken possession, and till he has taken possession, it is not necessary, how desirable soever on some accounts it might be, that at the public expense he should have any thing. So as you do but give him in prospect, and sufficiently secured, as much as, if in possession, would be, by ever so little, more than any man ever got into possession of by means of trade or manufactures—a million for example—that same million will, when the time comes, be accepted of, upon account at least, as and for the money necessary to make his family. Of this same million, the eventual *possession* being sufficiently secured, the bare expectation will suffice to buy him off from all trades and manufactures in the lump: so that in fact, if when measured according to the standard laid down by this *fifth* plea, the allowance made on the sum mentioned in plea the *fourth* be sufficiently liberal, the advantage mentioned in this same *fifth* plea is so much got for nothing.

Money, it must all this while be carefully kept in mind—*money* is the only sort of matter, which, according to the principles of our Right Honourable Author, is to the purpose here in question; viz. to the purpose of providing recruits for the official establishment, capable of officiating in the character of matter of *reward*. Even so substantial a thing as *power*—power of *management*—power of *patronage*,—*titles*,—*honours*, not to speak of any such empty bubble as *reputation*—all this, in the estimation of the Right Honourable Author, is, to the purpose here in question at least, without force or value.

Money, therefore, and in the same quantity as if there were nothing else that had any value, is the matter of which the *reward*, or whatever it be that is to constitute a man's inducement to engage in the service of the country, is to be composed.

But, as is very truly observed by the Right Honourable Gentleman, so it is, that in virtue of the money, the prospect of which they present to those who engage in them, there are not only 'other honourable and

lucrative professions,' but 'various branches of trade and manufactures,' that enter into 'competition' with the money, which, in the
character of official emolument, stands annexed to official service.

Equally true it is, that every instance, in which, in case of a man's
'engaging in any of those non-official lines of industry, and in particular in any branch of trade or manufacture, it might happen to him to
get more money than he could by official service, the difference,
whatever it may be, has' (to use the words of the Right Honourable
Gentleman) '*a tendency at least to exclude from the service of their country
men likely to be useful to it.*' True, on the other hand, it is, that the
character in which this 'tendency' operates, is not that of a *physical
bar:* no, nor so much as that of a *penal statute*. It is, however, in the
character of that sort of obstacle, the resisting force of which is in his
eyes so powerful, that the whole paragraph, with the whole of the
deobstruent force therein contained, is devoted to the sole purpose of
removing it; viz. by persuading those on whom it depends, so to order
matters, that by this 'discharge of trusts and duties' more money may
so be got by somebody or anybody, than can be got by anybody in the
exercise of any 'lucrative profession, trade, or manufacture.'

Now, then, to get the better of so troublesome a thing as this
'*principle* of *exclusion*,' and enable the '*service of the country*' to have as
good a chance as '*trade and manufactures*' have, for '*engaging men
likely to be useful to it*,' what is then to be done? two courses there are,
and in the nature of things but two, by which any such effect is capable
of being produced. One consists in lessening the quantity of money
capable of being gained in the way of trade and manufactures; the
other, in increasing the quantity of money capable of being gained in
the shape of official emolument in the way of official service.

To the quantity of money capable at present of being gained in trade
or manufactures there are no limits. A million or more one hears
spoken of as the amount of the money gained in this or that instance,
and even from no very considerable beginnings: of half that money or
thereabouts one hears of in numbers of other instances. Fixations of
this sort must remain exposed, not only to original uncertainty, but to
continual variation. By a select committee, with the Right Honourable
Gentleman at the head, this point, however, is one that needs not
despair of being settled: settled, if not with mathematical exactness,
at any rate with that rough degree of precision which is sufficient for
practice.

True it is, all this while, that on behalf of the public—that public
which he has thus taken under his protection—the sum which the
Right Honourable Gentleman requires for this purpose is but a
'*limited*' sum. To enable the public to maintain, on the occasion in

question, the proposed '*competition*' with so formidable a host of competitors as the '*other honourable and lucrative professions, and various branches of trade and manufactures,*' all he asks is—that it 'should be in a situation to bid to a *limited* extent.'

But, the *limits* here alluded to—at what point shall they be set? If set at a sum, the effect of which will leave to these rival pursuits so much as a '*tendency* to exclude from the service of their country men who are likely to be useful to it,' they will '*exclude,*' from the faculty of regulating practice on this head, the Right Honourable Gentleman, with those 'wise' principles of his which he is thus supporting against the *unwise* ones he complains of.

For a *maximum*, beginning with the highest situation, shall we, to make sure, say, for example, a couple of millions, to be laid up over and above '*his necessary current expenses,*' by an official person who, with that 'industry, zeal, and fidelity,' the union of which the Right Honourable Accountant gives him credit for, as a matter of course, shall, in that highest situation, have spent in the '*discharge of trusts and public duties a great part*'—say for example five and twenty years—of his life.

For our *maximum*, taking then these two millions, or even so scanty an allowance as a single million, and setting out from this point, shall we proceed downwards till, after the manner of that other *state lottery*, which is commonly so called, we have got for our lottery a number of prizes equal to the aggregate number of official situations?

This is what, '*on reflection,*' the '*wisdom*' of the Right Honourable Gentleman requires us to do, on pain of seeing '*established,* the principle,' against the 'exclusive tendency' of which we have been seeing him remonstrate so pathetically: this in short is what we *must* do, unless, embracing the only other branch of the alternative, and going to work in the other quarter, we set ourselves to restrict the quantity of money that a man shall be '*in a situation*' to gain by any of the '*various branches of trade and manufactures.*'

In the '*bidding,*' thus proposed by him '*for talents,*' if on his plan the public service is to have any chance of bearing off the prize or prizes, there remains therefore but one other expedient; and that is, the '*limiting,*' and thus eventually lessening, the quantity of the emolument which men shall have it in their power to make in trade or manufactures.

But this is what the Right Honourable Gentleman would never permit himself to endeavour at. For this would be to '*mark with* disrespect the character'—not now indeed 'of the official man,' but what in the Right Honourable Gentleman's estimation would be quite as improper a character thus to mark, viz. that of the *mercantile* man.

It would be to stigmatize by this invidious mark 'great numbers of those who engage in trade and manufactures:'—persons 'than whom none,' not even the official man himself, 'are by the author,' (as the Right Honourable Author is himself pleased to assure them) 'held *in higher estimation*.' This, then, is the objection to the setting limits to the sum, which a man shall be 'in a situation to gain by trade or manufactures:' and after an objection thus conclusive it were lost time to look for minor ones.

SECTION VII.
DIGRESSION CONCERNING THE VALUE OF MONEY.

SUCH, as we have seen, is the course one or other branch of which is, 'on reflection,' in the sight of the Right Honourable Author, so necessary, that the omitting to pursue it is considered by him as that which would have the effect of '*marking the character of the official man with disrespect;*' which to do would, as, in the way of interrogation, the Right Honourable Gentleman, with most incontestable propriety, observes, would be to act without '*fairness, justice, or reason*.'

Now as to '*disrespect*' for this *protégé* of the Right Honourable Gentleman—disrespect for him I do protest that I feel none. But, as to the allowing to him out of the taxes all that money which the '*generosity*' and '*justice*' and '*reason*' and '*policy*' and '*wisdom*' and '*fairness*' of his Right Honourable Patron lays claim to on his behalf—without knowing exactly what it is, thus much I know, that so expensive a proof of the absence of disrespect is more than I could afford to pay my share of: mine being one of the 'many instances in which *income*,' even though not '*official*,' is insufficient (to borrow the Right Honourable Gentleman's words) 'actually insufficient for *these*.'[1]

What I am therefore reduced to, is—the plea that my declining to do *that*, to the doing of which my limited means are so far from being sufficient, is not a mark of *disrespect* to any body; and by this plea, in so far and so long as it can be maintained, as I humbly conceive it may be to the very last, without disrespect to the Right Honourable Gentleman, I am determined to abide.

My notion of him (I mean the 'official man') is—that, besides *money*, there are other things that are capable of being objects of his regard: other things that are capable of engaging him to take upon himself the obligations of office, in the words of the Right Honourable

---

[1] See ibid., p. 64: 'If we look to official incomes, it will be found they are, in most cases, barely equal to the moderate, and even the necessary expences of the parties; in many instances they are actually insufficient for these.'

Author (of the value of which, when they are to be had, I am too fully sensible to take up with any other) to 'spend' even 'a great part of his life in the discharge of trusts and public duties:' and in proof of this, regarding *fact* as no bad proof of possibility, I have referred to several most conspicuous, and happily very extensive lines of practice.[a]

If it be by either of us,—if it be by any body,—that this same 'official man' is treated with 'disrespect,' I would venture to appeal to every man, in whose eyes there may be anything besides *money* that has a value, whether it is not, by the Right Honourable Gentleman himself, whose sympathy can so ill brook the imputation, and whose imagination paints to him a set of unreasonable people; a set of people, into whose company, spite of all protestations, I cannot but expect to find myself forced;—people who, being sworn enemies to this same officially 'industrious, zealous, and faithful' person, exercise themselves in 'marking his character with disrespect,' in despite of 'fairness, reason, and justice.' (p. 65.)

What the Right Honourable Gentleman *insists* upon—and in a manner much stronger than by *direct assertion*—what he insists upon in the way of *assumption*, is—that upon the mind of his official person there is nothing in the world but money that is capable of operating, whether in possession or expectation, with any adequate degree of efficiency, in the character of *'reward.'*

Now, in regard to this same sort of person, my notion is quite opposite:—quite opposite, and so determinately so, that the supposed contrariety of his disposition to the character given of him by the Right Honourable Gentleman, is all that that plan of mine, which has so often been alluded to, has to ground itself upon.

Money, money—nothing else, Sir, is of any value in your eyes....

Many things there are, Sir, besides money, that have their value in your eyes....

The first is the language in which this respectable person is addressed by the Right Honourable Gentleman, his declared patron. The other is the language in which he is addressed by the *obscure* man, his supposed enemy.

In which of these two modes of address is there most of *respect*, most of *'disrespect?'*—Gentle reader, judge between us.

For my part, the former mode of address is one that I could not prevail upon myself to use to any man; no, not even to the Right Honourable Gentleman himself; not even his own licence, clear as it

[a] Part I.[1]

___

[1] i.e. 'Hints respecting Economy'.

is,—not even his own express command would prevail upon me; neither *to* him, nor *of* him, could I prevail upon myself ever to say any such thing: for I do not, no, *that* I don't,—I would say it to his face—believe it to be true. I beg pardon for the seeming contradiction that I put upon what he says: I mean not anything of disrespect to him in this shape, any more than in the other. I mean not that, should he absolutely insist upon giving any such account of himself, he would, *at the moment*, be saying *that* of which he would be conscious of its not being true. All I mean is, that if such be his opinion of himself, he does not do himself justice: that, for want of leisure, engrossed as his attention has been by the 'discharge of trusts and public duties,' he has not looked closely enough into a subject—a human subject—which if he were to become a little better acquainted with it, than he appears as yet to be, might afford him more cause of satisfaction than he seems to be aware of.

Yes, on this ground, defend him I will, though it be against himself, and, fierce as his attack upon himself is, it is not pushed with so much skill, but that I will make him parry it.

For this purpose, I do insist upon it—I will take no denial—that he shall look once more at the last of his own pages but one. After reading, marking, and learning them, that 'the most degrading corruption of a statesman, or his friends, is indeed by the influence of money,' he will find it written—and that immediately after—that 'public men may be corrupted by *the love of power*, as well as by lust of gain.'[1] Now, then, if by this same love of power men may be '*corrupted*,' by this same love of power, (I say) they may be *operated upon;* and if operated upon to a *bad* purpose, so may they, and (let us hope) still more easily and effectively, to a *good* one: for when operated upon to a bad purpose, they must be strange men indeed if they do not find themselves operated upon, with how little force and effect soever, by some principle or other, in a *counter direction:* in a counter direction by some principle or other, call it *fear of disrepute*, call it *conscience*, call it what you please[a]—which they would find acting, not in *opposition* to, but in *concert* with, the love of power, in any case, in which the purpose, towards which it operated upon them,

---

[a] In the *Table of the Springs*[2] *of Action*, lately published by the author, all the principles in question may be found, with explanations.[3]

---

[1] Rose, *Observations respecting Public Expenditure*, p. 78.

[2] 1830 '*Spring*'.

[3] See *A Table of the Springs of Action* (first published in 1817) in *Deontology together with A Table of the Springs of Action and Article on Utilitarianism*, ed. A. Goldworth, Oxford, 1983 (*CW*), pp. 79–115.

and towards which it tended to direct their exertions, were a *good* one.

And is it really any opinion of the Right Honourable Gentleman's, that to the love of power it is impossible to act upon the mind of man in any direction but a *sinister* one? Impossible to act upon it with effect in any other way than by corrupting it?—No; *that* it is not: for if it were, he would shake off from his hands whatsoever, in the shape of power, he felt sticking on them; he would shake it off as he would a viper. Adieu all Treasurerships! adieu even all *Clerkships!* for to the *Clerkship*, even of *Parliament*, though no such troublesome appendage as that of *obligation* has ever been felt cleaving to it and incumbering it,[1] yet (not to speak of *money,—that* not being here in question) *power* enough, and in a variety of shapes, might be found thereunto appertaining, if a gentleman happened to be in a humour to make use of it.

Thus it is that in and by every line, I am labouring and toiling to prove, and if possible persuade gentlemen to be of opinion, that the sun shines at noon-day. But why? Only because in and by the argument of the Right Honourable Gentleman the contrary fact is assumed.

SECTION VIII.

PLEA 6.—NEED OF MONEY AS A STIMULUS TO OFFICIAL EXERTION.

A SIXTH plea, if I understand it right, consists in the alleged need of money for the purpose of serving in the case of official men in the character of a stimulus: to be applied, viz. to men of hereditary wealth and independence, to spur them on to the acquisition of talent, or else to be applied somewhere else, in order to enable us to do without them and their talents, by having better men in their stead.

Of this plea the account I am thus giving, is, I must confess, besides its not being quite so clear as I could wish, a little long-winded; but it is the best I am able to give. Meantime the reader will see whether he can make anything better of it.

'It has always been justly held' ([a]says the Right Honourable Gentleman) 'in a free country, and particularly in this, to be one of its greatest privileges, that the chief aristocracy, as far as relates to the

[a] P.65.

---

[1] Rose held the office of Clerk of the Parliaments from 1788 until his death in 1818: the duties, which included the production of the Journals, were executed by deputies.

management of its public concerns, *should be* an aristocracy of *talent* and of *virtue*, as well as of *rank* and of *property;* which principle would be *destroyed, if remuneration for public services should be withheld;* and the community would be deprived of all its advantages. Not only the great offices of state, but some others of most efficiency' (Secretaryships to the Treasury,[1] perhaps, for instance) '*must then be*' (meaning probably, *would in that case necessarily be*) 'confined to men of hereditary wealth and independence; and, with all the *proper* respect which *should be* entertained for such men, it must be allowed that, for the acquisition and improvement of talents necessary for the higher offices, the passing occasionally through the inferior situations, and that *principle of activity* which animates men in the attainment, so much more than in the mere possession, of power and station, are much more favourable than the *honours* claimable by descent alone.'[2]

The exertions made by the Right Honourable Gentleman, in the endeavours he uses to prevail upon himself, and enable himself, to pay whatever respect it may be '*proper*' to pay to men of a certain description, present an edifying spectacle. It is what he has been trying at, and labouring at throughout the whole course of his paragraph, (which, as the reader feels, is not a very short one) and after all without having any great success to boast of. Stationed, and for so long a course of time, close to the very door of the Cabinet, though not yet on the right side of it—seeing the *Duke of Portland* every day, seeing the *Earl of Liverpool*, seeing the *Lord Viscount Castlereagh*, son and heir-apparent to the Earl of Londonderry, seeing the *Earl of Westmoreland*, seeing the *Earl of Chatham*, seeing *Earl Camden*, seeing the *Lord Mulgrave*[3]—(seeing in a word almost everybody that is worth seeing) all of them not only 'men of hereditary wealth and independence,' but even nobles of the land—among all those great men there is not one, no not one, whom he has found it possible to 'hold in any higher estimation' than great numbers of those who engage in trade and manufactures. I mean antecedently to the exertions betrayed or displayed in this present paragraph; and how

---

[1] Rose was Secretary to the Treasury 1782–3, 1783–1801.

[2] Rose, *Observations respecting Public Expenditure*, pp. 65–6.

[3] These men were all members of the Cabinet in the Portland administration of 1807–9: Portland was First Lord of the Treasury; Robert Banks Jenkinson (1770–1828), second Earl of Liverpool, styled Lord Hawkesbury 1796–1808, was Home Secretary; Castlereagh was Secretary for War and Colonies; John Fane (1759–1841), sixteenth Earl of Westmorland, was Lord Privy Seal; John Pitt (1756–1835), second Earl of Chatham, was Master General of the Ordnance; Camden was Lord President of the Council; and Henry Phipps (1755–1831), third Baron Mulgrave (I), first Baron Mulgrave (GB) and later Earl of Mulgrave, was First Lord of the Admiralty.

small the progress is, which in this same paragraph he has succeeded in making, let this same paragraph itself declare.

His Majesty, for whom also the Right Honourable Gentleman (I will be bound for him) has all along been labouring, and with at least equal energy, to entertain *'all the proper respect which should be entertained for'* him, all these great men, his Majesty, or *those whose estate* (as the lawyers say) *he hath*, were, at one time or other, at the pains of decking out with *titles*, and even some of them with *ribbons:*[1] yet after all, and upon so good a judge of merit as the Right Honourable Gentleman—one moreover who has had such good and such near opportunities of observation—so inconsiderable has been the effect that has been produced at all this expense—that 'in the estimation' of the Right Honourable Gentleman, they are still so unfortunate, every one of them, as not to occupy any higher place, than is occupied by, alas! alas! 'great numbers of those who engage in trade and manufactures.'

Of the difficulties which he had to struggle with, in his endeavours to find or make any higher place for them, the magnitude is betrayed (shall we say?) or manifested, in every line: as is likewise, when all is over, the delicacy with which, to the very last, he avoided giving any direct expression to that conclusion, which having, in an unlucky moment, before the commencement of this paragraph, burst out unawares, had, throughout the whole course of it, been labouring once more to find vent and utterance.[2] Of all these great men, if we may take the word of so good a judge, there is nothing to be made without money; nor, if it were 'proper' to speak out, any great matter even with the help of it: especially in comparison of some other great men that he knows of, who, *'for the acquisition and improvement of talents'* necessary for the higher offices—including a consummate skill in the application of the four rules of arithmetic,[3] and without wasting time upon any such speculative and theoretical science as logic, have had the benefit of 'passing *occasionally'* (*pour passer le tems*, as the French say) 'through the inferior situations.'

When the antagonists whom the Right Honourable Gentleman has to contend with, are the offspring of his own genius, they give him little trouble.

In his 62d page we find him setting to rights a set of men (but whether these were 'among his reasonable and candid men' that he

---

[1] By the time Bentham was writing, George III had bestowed a British peerage on Mulgrave, and installed Portland, Westmorland, Chatham and Camden as Knights of the Garter.

[2] Presumably Rose's statement that 'none are held in higher estimation by the author' than 'those who engage in trade and manufacture'.

[3] i.e. addition, subtraction, multiplication and division.

had just been meeting with, I cannot take upon me to be certain)[1] a set of men, however, of some sort or other, according to whose conception, the *whole* amount of what is levied on the people by taxes, goes to pay 'sinecures and pensions:' from which, if true, it would follow that, on so simple a condition as that of suppressing these nuisances—taxes, those still greater nuisances, might be cleared away at any time. But that any such conception is a misconception, and 'consequently, although there were no sinecures or pensions, there would still be taxes,' he proves immediately beyond all dispute; and his antagonists, let them be ever so '*reasonable*,' have not a word more to say for themselves.

This misconception being set to rights in that his 62d page,[2] here again in his 66th page we find him employed in instructing and undeceiving another set of men, or perhaps the same set in another dress, who are for '*withholding remuneration*' (meaning nothing less than *all* remuneration, howsoever ashamed they may be to say so) 'for public services.'

A strange set of men they are whoever they are—and what is to be done with them? The course he takes with them (and if he does not convince them, he at least reduces them to silence) is, the setting them to think of a 'principle,' which he knows of, and which, if such 'remunerations[3] were withheld, *would*' (he says) 'be destroyed: and the principle once destroyed,' 'the community' (he concludes with an irresistible force of reasoning) '*would be deprived of all its advantages*.'

Now, if so it be that he really knows of any such men, it is pity but he had told us where some of them are to be seen: for as a raree-show they would be worth looking at. I, for my part, jacobin as I suppose I am,—I, for my part, am not one of them. And this too I am happily enabled to prove: having, for a particular purpose, proposed some good round sums to be disposed of in this way; and *that* according to another plan, in my opinion of which, every day I live confirms me.[4]

---

[1] Rose, *Observations respecting Public Expenditure*, p. 62: 'To what extent, or in what manner, it may be proper to press further retrenchments, the author has not the remotest intention of offering an opinion: his view has been clearly explained; and he trusts the statements will bring to the recollection of his readers what has been done for the attainment of objects of high importance, and of deep interest to the public, by shewing the present state of patronage and influence, compared with what it was in antecedent periods, which have been spoken of as "good times;" about which he is persuaded much misconception prevails at this day, even among reasonable and candid men.' The remainder of the paragraph is given in §II, p. 99 above.

[2] The passage to which Bentham refers, discussed in §II, pp. 99–103 above, is in fact at pp. 62–3.

[3] 1830 omits opening speech mark.

[4] Bentham's pecuniary competition system, which he appears to have developed in 'Hints respecting Economy' (see §IX, p. 129n below), but which he outlined most fully in *Constitutional Code*, I (*CW*), Ch. IX, §17, pp. 337–62.

Of the only sort of thing which in his account,—at least while this paragraph lasts,—is of any value, viz. *money*, my plan (I speak now of that which relates to the present subject) goes somewhat further than any other which it has happened to me to see, in reducing the quantity to be administered at the public expense: and yet not even in this shape do I propose to withhold it, except in so far as the public service would be performed, not only *cheaper* but *better* without it: and, be the Right Honourable Gentleman's '*principle*' what it may, I disclaim altogether any such destructive thought, as that of '*destroying*' it.

All this while, a difficulty, which has been perplexing me, is—that of comprehending what sort of an aristocracy this new sort is, the discovery of which has been made by the Right Honourable Gentleman, and to which, exercising the right which is acknowledged to belong to all discoverers, he has given the name of '*an aristocracy of talent and of virtue.*' Not that by any such description, if taken by itself, any great difficulty would have been produced, but that it is by the sort of relation, which is represented as subsisting between this sort of aristocracy and the sort of thing called *money*, that my perplexity is occasioned.

So far as money is concerned, '*virtue,*' according to what we have been used, most of us, to hear and read of at school, and at college, such of us as have been to college, consists, though not perhaps in doing altogether without money, at any rate in taking care not to set too high a value on it. But, *with* all its virtue, or rather *in virtue* of its very virtue, the aristocracy, which the Right Honourable Gentleman has in view, is a sort of aristocracy, of which the characteristic is, that they will not (the members of it) do a stitch without money: and in their eyes, 'remuneration' in any other shape is no remuneration at all: why? because in their eyes, to this purpose at least, nothing whatever but money is of any value.

We have seen who they are that must have been sitting for the Right Honourable Gentleman's Kit-Cat Club[1]—his '*aristocracy of rank and of property:*' where now shall we find the originals of his 'aristocracy of talent and of virtue?'

Consulting the works of *Dr. Beatson* and *Mr. Luffman*,[2] the only

---

[1] The Kit-Cat Club had been founded in the 1690s by Whig politicians and their associates. Sir Godfrey Kneller painted portraits of the forty-eight club members for Jacob Tonson (1656?–1736), the secretary, in whose villa the club meetings came to be held. The paintings had to be made three-quarter length in order to accommodate them to the low ceiling of the club dining-room, and such portraits came subsequently to be known as kit-cats.

[2] Both Robert Beatson (1742–1818) and John Luffman were compilers who published political reference works. Bentham perhaps had in mind Beatson's *A Chronological Register of both Houses of the British Parliament, From the Union in 1708, to the Third Parliament of the United Kingdom of Great Britain and Ireland, in 1807*, 3 vols., London, 1807, which contained informa-

channels, the periodical ones excepted, through which, in my humble situation, a man can form any conception concerning any such '*great characters,*' I can find no others but *Mr. Percival, Lord Eldon, Mr. Canning, Sir David Dundas,*[1] and a Gentleman (Right Honourable, I presume) who, in Mr. Luffman's Table of Great Characters, occupies at present his 15th column, by the description of '*Mr. G. Rose.*'

Meantime *money*,—meaning *public* money,—being in the Right Honourable Gentleman's system of ætiology, the *causa sine quâ non*, not only of '*virtue,*' but of that '*talent*' which is found in company with virtue, and being on that score necessary to the constitution of that *one* of the *two* branches of his aristocracy, if it has two, or of the *whole* of it, if it is all in *one*,—what I would submit to him is—whether the task which in entering upon this work, he appears to have set himself, will have been perfectly gone through with, till he has found means for securing to this *talent-and-virtue* branch of his '*aristocracy,*' a larger portion of his one thing needful than appears to have as yet fallen to its lot.

Running over, in this view, such parcels of the matter of remuneration as exceed each of them the amount of 10,000*l.* a-year (the only part of the *sinecure list* a man can find time for looking over and speaking to in this view), I find them all, or almost all of them, in possession of the '*rank-and-property*' branch: while the '*talent-and-virtue*'[2] branch, starved and hide-bound, has found itself reduced to take up with the other's leavings.

SECTION IX.

PLEA 7.—NEED OF MONEY FOR THE SUPPORT OF OFFICIAL DIGNITY.

A SEVENTH plea, and the last I have been able to find, consists in the alleged need of money for a purpose that seems to be the same with one, which in other vocabularies is meant by the words '*support of dignity:*'[a] in the words of the Right Honourable Gentleman (for, on

---

[a] Finance Committee, 1797–8; do. 1807–8.[3]

---

tion on members of both Houses of Parliament, and an earlier version of Luffman's *A Table, Exhibiting the Sixteen Administrations of Great Britain and Ireland, during the Reign of King Geo: III*, London, 1816, whose fifteenth column recorded Rose's position as Treasurer of the Navy.

[1] Sir David Dundas (1735–1820), Commander-in-Chief of the Army 1809–11.

[2] 1830 '*talent—and virtue*'.

[3] The phrase 'support of dignity' has not been traced, though Bentham may have had in mind the following sentence from the Thirtieth Report of the Finance Committee of 1798 on the Civil Government of Scotland (*Commons Sessional Papers of the Eighteenth Century*, cxii. 268), which was repeated in the Third Report of the Committee on Public Expenditure of 1808 (*Commons*

pain of misrepresentation, the very words must be taken where words are everything) '*preservation of a certain appearance*.'

'It is true' (continues he) 'that magnanimity and genuine patriotic ambition will look for a nobler reward for their services than the emoluments of office; but in the present state of society, *a certain appearance* is essential to be *preserved* by persons in *certain stations*, which cannot be maintained without a liberal provision.'[1]

From this paragraph, one piece of good news we learn, or should learn at least, if it could be depended upon, is—that the time is now come when '*magnanimity and genuine patriotic ambition will look for a nobler reward for their services than the emoluments of office*.' So late as the moment when the last hand was put to the Right Honourable Author's last preceding paragraph, this moment of magnanimity was not yet arrived: down to that moment, had '*remuneration*' (meaning as afterwards explained, in the shape of *emolument*) been withheld, '*principle*,' of some kind or other, would have been destroyed—and so forth.

Fortunate is this change for the country, and in particular, not a little so for the somewhat deficient plan here, by an unofficial hand, ventured to be proposed.[a] Here then we have it;—and from such high and competent authority,—that besides emolument, there is a something, which, in the character of '*reward for their services*,' '*magnanimity and genuine patriotic ambition*' '*will look for:*' and (what is better still) this unspecified something is capable of being received not only in the character of a *reward*, but in the character of a reward of '*a nobler*' sort than emolument—that *sine quâ non*, without which, till this paragraph of the Right Honourable Gentleman's was concluded, or at least begun upon, nothing was to be done.

Having this, I have all I want, and (as will be seen, and as I hope has even been seen already) even more than I mean, or have any need to use.

Unfortunately for me, no sooner has the Right Honourable Gentleman's wisdom and candour and discernment obtained from him, and

---

[a] The plan here, as elsewhere alluded to, is the plan, the publication of which was suspended as above.[2]

Sessional Papers (1808) iii. 266): '[The Committee] are no less sensible of the Delicacy with which another Branch of the Expenditure should be touched, as it concerns the Munificence and Bounty of the Sovereign, applied to the Encouragement of Learning and Religion, to the Remuneration of national Services, in the rewarding of public Merit, and in the Support of those Branches of noble and respectable families, which the Policy and Principles of the British Constitution cannot suffer to fall into Indigence.'

[1] Rose, *Observations respecting Public Expenditure*, pp. 66–7.
[2] i.e. 'Hints respecting Economy'.

for my use, this concession,—than some others of his virtues, I know not exactly which, join hands and take it back again: and, though no otherwise than by *implication*, yet—so necessary to his argument is this implication—that, if he had taken it back in *direct* words, he could not have done more than he has done, if so much, towards depriving me of the benefit of it.

'But,' (continues he, and now comes the retractation) 'a *certain* appearance is essential to be preserved by persons in *certain* stations, which' (meaning probably '*which*¹ *appearance*) 'cannot be maintained without liberal provision.'

'In *certain* stations, a certain appearance'—Nothing can be more delicate,—nothing at the same time more commodiously *uncertain*,—than this double *certainty*. Meantime, if, in the meaning of the whole paragraph there be anything certain, it appears to me to be this: viz. that on behalf of '*the magnanimity and genuine patriotic ambition*' which the Right Honourable Gentleman has taken under his protection, what he claims is—that, in the account *debtor* and *creditor*, as between service and reward, this reward which, not being emolument, is *nobler* than emolument, (meaning by *nobler*, if anything at all be meant by it, that which, in *their* estimate at least, is *worth more*) is to be set down as *worth nothing*: and accordingly, that the quantity of the matter of reward, which each official person is to have in *the less noble*, but *more substantial* and tangible shape, is to be exactly the same as if there were no other reward, either in their hand, or within their view.

To my plan however, with its weak means of support, so necessary is the concession thus plainly, though but for the moment, made by the Right Honourable Gentleman, that with my good will, he shall never have it back again. *Power* then has its value: *reputation* has its value: and this, for the moment at least, has been admitted by Mr. Rose. By Mr. Rose's evidence—by the weight of Mr. Rose's authority—I have proved it. And now is my time for triumphing. For though neither he, nor any other Right Honourable Gentleman, ever took his seat in any moderately full *House of Commons*, nor ever attended a *Quarter Sessions*, without seeing before him gentlemen in numbers, whose conduct afforded a still more conclusive evidence of the same fact, than any verbal testimony they could have given, even though it were in black and white,—(*magistrates*, by the labour they bestow without emolument in the execution of their office,— *members*, by the expense which, lawfully or unlawfully they have been at in obtaining their *unemolumented* seats)—yet such is the weight of

---

¹ 1830 omits closing speech mark.

his authority, and to my humble plan, so strong the support it gives, that, having seized the fortunate moment, and got possession of the evidence, I can do no less than make the most of it.

Now then (say I) whatever it be that these valuable things are worth, so much, in the account as between *reward* and *service*, let them be set down for: nor shall even the ingenuity of the Right Honourable Gentleman enable him to object any want of *'fairness'* to my estimate, leaving, as my plan does, to his *protégé* (the proposed official person himself) to make out his own estimate:—to fix his own value upon the *non-emolumentary* part of his reward. The more he chooses to have in the *more 'noble'* shape, the less may he be content to receive in the *less* noble shape: how much he will have of each rests altogether with himself: and, so long as,—with its *bitters* in one hand, and its *sweets* in the other,—the office cannot upon my plan be put into his hands without his own consent, what ground for complaint anybody can make for him, is more than I can see.

'Certain appearance?' For what *purpose* is it that this *certain appearance*, whatever it be, is so 'essential to be preserved?'—Is it for *commanding respect?*

In *common* arithmetic—in the sort of arithmetic that would be employed in a plain man's reasoning, be the article what it may—respect or anything else—if there be divers sources or efficient causes of it,—*money*, for instance, and *power* and *reputation*,—to command the necessary or desirable quantity, whatever be that quantity, the more you have from any one source, the less you need to have from the others, or from any other.

'In the present state of society' (for it is to *that* that the Right Honourable Gentleman calls for our attention) unfortunately for us vulgar, this arithmetic,—this vulgar arithmetic,—is not the arithmetic of *'high situation:'* it is not the arithmetic of *St. James's:* it is not the arithmetic of the *House of Lords:* it is not the arithmetic of the *House of Commons;* it is not the arithmetic of the *Treasury:* it is not the arithmetic of *Office*,—of any office, by which a more *convenient* species of arithmetic can be employed instead of it. In particular, it is not (so we learn, not only from this paragraph, but from the whole tenor of the work of which it makes a part) the arithmetic of the *Navy Treasurer's Office*.[1] According to this *higher* species of arithmetic, the more you have been able to draw from *any one* of these same sources, the more you stand in need of drawing from *every* other. *Power*, not *indigence*, is the measure of demand.

Have you so many hundred thousands of pounds in money? having

---

[1] Rose was Treasurer of the Navy at the time Bentham was writing, and held the office until his death in 1818.

this money you have *power*. Having this *money* with this *power*, it is '*essential*' you should have dignity. Having this dignity, you have that which requires money—more money—for the '*support*' of it. *Money, Power, Dignity; Money, Power, Dignity*,—such, in this high species of arithmetic, is the everlasting circulate.

Are you in a '*certain station?*'—Whatsoever you have *power* to spend, and at the same time *inclination* to spend, this is what the Right Honourable Treasurer is ready to assure you, it is '*indispensably necessary*' you should spend. This is what, if your patience will carry you to the next section of this humble comment, or to the next page of the Right Honourable text, you will see stated by the Right Honourable '*discharger of trusts and public duties,*'—and in terms, of which, on any such score as that of want of distinctness or positiveness, no just complaint can be made.

SECTION X.

PLEA 8.—CONCERNING THE LATE MR. PITT'S EXPENDITURE—THE IMPROPRIETY OF ECONOMY HOW FAR PROVED BY IT.

IMMEDIATELY upon the back, and as it should seem for the more effectual ascertainment, of this so unfortunately uncertain, though double certainty, comes the grand example already above referred to:[1] that one example,—in which we are to look for whatsoever explanation is to be found, for whatever is not inexplicable, in the Right Honourable Author's theory. And this example proves to be the rate, and quantum, and mode of expenditure (private expenditure) observed and here stated by the Right Honourable Gentleman in the instance of the late Mr. Pitt.

'That great statesman' (says he[a]) 'who was "poor amidst a nation's wealth," whose ambition was patriotism, whose expense and whose economy were only for the public, died in honourable poverty. That circumstance' (continues he) 'certainly conveys no reproach upon his memory; but when he had leisure to attend to his private concerns, it *distressed* him seriously to reflect that he had debts, without the means of paying them, which he could not have avoided incurring, except from a *parsimony* which would have been called meanness, or by accepting a remuneration[2] from the public, which his enemies would have called rapacity; for he had no expense of any sort that was

[a] P.67.

---

[1] See §IV, pp. 109–10 and §V, pp. 113–14 above.
[2] 1830 'renumeration'.

not *indispensably necessary*, except in *improvements* in his country residence, where his house was hardly equal to the accommodation of the most private gentleman.'

That the logic of our Right Honourable Author is not altogether so consummate as his arithmetic, is a suspicion that has been already hazarded: and here perhaps may be seen a confirmation of it.

The proposition undertaken by him to be proved was a pretty comprehensive one; its extent not being less than the entire field of office, considered in respect of the several masses of official emolument comprised in it. This it was that he took for his *subject:* adding for his *predicate*, that these incomes were and are not one of them sufficient,—not one of them, *all things considered*, sufficient to all purposes.[a]

For proof of this his *universal* proposition, in so far as it is in the nature of *example* to afford proof, he gives us *one* example: *one* example and but one. The one office, in the instance of which, if insufficiency of emolument be proved, such insufficiency is to be accepted as proof, and that *conclusive*, of equal or proportionable insufficiency in the case of all the rest, is the office of *Prime Minister:* an office, the emolument of which is composed of the emolument attached to *two* offices, which, when the parliamentary seat of the official person is in the House of Commons, have commonly been, and in the instance of the said Mr. Pitt were, holden in *one* hand.[1]

To complete the Right Honourable Author's argument, there remains for proof but one other proposition, and *that* is—the insufficiency of this compound mass of emolument in the instance of the said Mr. Pitt: and the medium of proof is composed of this fact; viz. that, being so in possession of this mass of annual emolument, he the said Mr. Pitt spent all this money of his own, together with no inconsiderable mass,—amount not mentioned,—of other people's money besides.

Assuming, what nobody will dispute, that Mr. Pitt died in '*poverty*,' that which by his Right Honourable Friend is observed and predicated of this poverty, is, that it was '*honourable*' to him: which being

---

[a] 'If we look to official incomes, it will be found they are, in most cases, barely equal to the moderate, and even the necessary expenses of the parties: in many instances they are actually insufficient for *these*. May we not then venture to ask, whether it is reasonable, or whether it would be politic, that such persons should, after spending a great part of their lives with industry, zeal, and fidelity, in the discharge of trusts and public duties, be left afterwards without reward of any sort, and their families entirely without provision?'—p. 64.

---

[1] Pitt held the offices of First Lord of the Treasury and Chancellor of the Exchequer during both his ministries, 1783–1801 and 1804–6.

admitted or not admitted, the Right Honourable Gentleman's further observation, that it 'certainly conveys no reproach to his memory,' shall, if it be of any use to him, be admitted or not admitted likewise.

Had this been all, there would certainly at least have been no *dishonour* in the case: a man who has no family, nor any other person or persons, having on the score of any special relation, any claim upon his bounty, whether it be his choice to expend the whole of his income, or whether it be his choice to lay up this or that part of it, nobody surely can present any just ground for complaint.

But, in addition to that which was his own to spend or save, Mr. Pitt having spent money of other people's in round numbers to the amount of 40,000*l.* more: and this mode of expenditure having in so unhappy a way been rendered notorious, rich and poor together having been forced to contribute to make up to this division of the rich the loss they had been content to run the risk of,[1] something was deemed adviseable to be said of it.

In strictness of argument, some readers there may be perhaps, in whose view of the matter it might be sufficient here to observe—that, admitting the fact, unhappily but too notorious, of Mr. Pitt's spending other people's money—admitting this fact in the character of a proof, and that a conclusive one, that the mass of emolument attached to the *two* offices he filled was not sufficient for the *one* official person by whom those two offices were filled, the proof would not extend beyond that one pair of offices: and, the number of offices being unhappily to be counted by thousands, perhaps even by tens of thousands, and this highest of offices, in point of *power*, differing more widely from the general run of offices than perhaps any other that could have been found, the proposition has much the air of remaining in rather worse plight, than if nothing in the character of proof had been subjoined to it.

On this footing might the matter perhaps be found to stand, if viewed in a point of view purely and drily logical. But, forasmuch as, notwithstanding,[2] or rather by reason of, its profuseness, the expenditure of this one official person is by his Right Honourable Friend held out as an example; not merely as an example for illustration, but as a pattern for imitation:—for imitation by official persons in general,—for imitation in respect of the quantum of emolument necessary to be allotted out of the taxes, and attached to their respective offices,—an observation or two shall here be hazarded, respecting the conclusiveness of the Right Honourable Author's argument with reference to this collateral and practical part of it.

---

[1] On 3 February 1806 the House of Commons voted £40,000 for the payment of Pitt's debts.
[2] 1830 'notwitstanding,'.

The *wry neck* of the hero having in this way rendered itself too conspicuous to be concealed by any artifice, what was left to the panegyrist was to make a *beauty* of it. The expense of this repair has surely not been inconsiderable: for here it is not logic only, but morality and policy that have been made to share in it. Our assent being secured for so unexceptionable a proposition, as that, in the circumstance in question, *poverty is honourable*, the next contrivance is to slip in and get the benefit of our assent extended to one other proposition, viz. (as if there were no difference) that *spending other people's money was honourable;* and thus it is that our approbation is to be engaged for the practice and policy of giving encouragement to such *honourable* conduct, by tokens of parliamentary approbation bestowed at the public expense.

'*Necessary,*' with its conjugate '*necessity*' and its near of kin '*essential,*' are words of no small convenience to the Right Honourable Gentleman: of such convenience, that *that* thing (it should seem) could not be very easy to be found, which the same, being convenient to official persons in official situations, is not, by and in virtue of such convenience, under and by virtue of the Right Honourable Author's system of ontology, rendered '*necessary.*'

Even to a man, who had not quite so much as 8,000*l.*[1] a year of his own to spend,[a] a mode of expenditure, which, in whatsoever degree *convenient*, would (one should have thought) have presented the least satisfactory claim to the appellation of *necessary*, is that which consists in spending money of other people's.

Two rocks the reputation of the hero found his course threatened by: two rocks, *meanness* and *rapacity*, one on each side: and the expenditure of other people's money—this was the harbour in which, to avoid this *Scylla* and this *Charybdis*, he took refuge.

Had the expenditure of the hero been confined to the sum which by the competent authorities had been deemed sufficient, such limitation

---

[a] As first Commissioner of the Treasury,
       including additional salary —— £5,032 11 0
   As Chancellor of the Exchequer —— 1,897 15 1

                    Net receipt together —— £6,930 6 1

15th Report from the Select Committee on Finance, 1797, Appendix C. page 20. Add house rent, coals, and candles.[2]

---

[1] This seems to be a slip for '7,000*l.*'
[2] See *Commons Sessional Papers of the Eighteenth Century*, cix. 54–5. From 1792 Pitt enjoyed a further income from his office of Lord Warden of the Cinque Ports: see p. 137n below.

would, from the justice of the Right Honourable Panegyrist himself, notwithstanding his *'just partiality,'*[1] have received a gentle reprimand couched under the term *'parsimony,'* and his imagination has found somebody else to call it *meanness;* had he for those *extraordinary* services which we hear so much of, *'accepted'* as 'a remuneration from the public,' any of those *sinecures*, which, in such unhappy abundance, he saw lavished on men who could not produce so much as the pretence of even the most *ordinary* service; the same industrious and fruitful imagination has found him friends, in the character of 'enemies,' to *'call it rapacity:'*—to avoid this charge of meanness it is, that he places himself in a state of dependence under traders of various descriptions,—the butcher, the baker, the fishmonger, not to speak of the political intriguer;—to avoid the charge of rapacity it is, that what he obtains from those people, he obtains from them on the pretence of meaning to pay them, knowing that he has not wherewithal, and nobly, constantly, and heroically determined never to 'accept' it.

As to distress—while the distress confined itself to those plebeian breasts, this Right Honourable breast knew no such inmate: but when 'some debts pressed so severely upon him as to render it necessary for some of his most private and intimate[2] friends to step in and save him from immediate inconvenience,'[3] when, in plain English, he had or was afraid of having executions in his house, then it was that the distress became contagious—then it was that 'it distressed him seriously to reflect that he had debts.'

When, of a *necessity*, or of anything else, the existence is asserted by a Gentleman, and as of his own knowledge, and that so Right Honourable a Gentleman,—an obscure person—who, having no such honour, nor any chance of producing persuasion, by any other means than such as his own weak reason may be able to supply—has after, and notwithstanding all this form of assertion, the misfortune to feel himself still unsatisfied, it is natural to him to look around him for whatever support may anywhere be to be found:—Parliament—the opinion of parliament—should it be found on his side, will *that* stand him in any stead?

Such as we have seen is the opinion of Mr. Rose. But parliament—on this same point, what is it that has been the opinion of parliament? Why the opinion of parliament is—that, what Mr. Pitt *had* was suffi-

---

[1] Bentham appears to have taken this phrase from Burke, *Speech on Oeconomical Reformation*, p. 65: 'their very partiality has operated as a kind of justice'. For the passage see 'Defence of Economy against Burke', §VII, p. 73 above.

[2] Rose 'private and most intimate'.

[3] Rose, *Observations respecting Public Expenditure*, p. 67n.

cient: that more than he had was *not* necessary:—was not of that *'indispensable necessity'* which has been brought on the carpet, by the zeal, assisted by the imagination, of Mr. Rose.

Unfortunately for the Right Honourable Panegyrist—unfortunately for his opinions—unfortunately for his assertions—this point, this very point—did, and on the very occasion he speaks of—come under the cognizance and consideration of parliament. The emolument which is found annexed to these two offices, both of which had been held at the same time by Mr. Pitt,—this emolument, had it been deemed insufficient for the 'official man' in question—viz. for the *species* of official man,—would thereupon of course have received an augmentation: in the instance of this official person, the subject would have received those marks of attention, which have so frequently been asked for, and so constantly been given for asking for,[1] in the case of the judges.[2]

Was it that by the case of this distinguished individual, any demand was presented, for any greater mass of emolument than there was likely to be an equally cogent demand for, in the case of any successor of his in the same situation? It seems not easy to conceive a case, in which, all things considered, that demand can ever be so small. True it is, his private fortune was, his station in life considered, barely sufficient for independence. But, he had no wife—no child:—he was in *deed*, as well as in *law*, completely single: and, in the Right Honourable Gentleman's own arithmetic,—which, on this head, differs not much, it must be confessed, from the vulgar arithmetic,— the demand for money, on the part of the father of a family, is as the number of persons it is composed of.

Over and above his 8000*l.* a year, augmented during half his political life, by his sinecure, to 12,000*l.*[3] what is it that he could want money for?—more money (for *that* is *here* the question) than would be wanted by or for any of his successors in power and office? Was it to buy respect and reputation with?—Deserved and undeserved together, no man in his place, unless it was his father, ever possessed a larger share of those valuable commodities, than this second *William Pitt*. Had he been in the case of the good-humoured old

---

[1] 1830 'asking, for'.

[2] Since the Glorious Revolution of 1688, the salaries of judges had been increased by statute in 1758 (32 Geo. II, c.35), 1779 (19 Geo. III, c.65), 1799 (39 Geo. III, c.110) and 1809 (49 Geo. III, c.127).

[3] In 1792 Pitt was appointed Lord Warden of the Cinque Ports, from which he received a gross annual salary of over £4,000, but from which, after the deduction of duties and taxes and salaries to subordinates, he received a net income of just over £3,000: see the Fifteenth Report of the Finance Committee of 1797, *Commons Sessional Papers of the Eighteenth Century*, cix. 54–5. Pitt's total official net income was therefore not quite £10,000 per annum.

driveller, who gave so much trouble to Pitt the first, and whom his Majesty's grandfather was so loth to part with or suffer to be elbowed,[1]—in that case there would have been on his part a great deficiency in those essential articles; and if, like *seats*,[2] they had been an object of purchase, and public money the proper sort of money to be employed in the purchase, no small quantity of such money would, in that case, have been necessary.

In the way of experiment—in the endeavour to make this purchase, money, though the man's own, and not public money, was, in the Duke's case, actually employed, and in memorable and still-remembered abundance: but how completely the experiment failed, is at least as well remembered.

To return to the deficiency of the sort in question, supposed to have been, on the more recent occasion, displayed in the same place: this deficiency then,—such as it was and still is—Parliament, in the case of Mr. Pitt, did not, so long as he lived, think fit to supply: at any rate left unsupplied. What was done was—the giving a mass of public money—to the amount of 40,000*l.* or thereabouts—among a set of people, names undisclosed, but said to be the deceased minister's *creditors*. Friends remembered their friendships: enemies, now that the enemy was no longer in their way, forgot their enmity: friends and enemies vied in sentimentality—vied in generosity—always at the public expense: and a justification, yea and more than a justification, was thus made, for the cases of the still *future-contingent* widow of Lord Grenville, and the then *paulo-post* FUTURE widow of Mr. Fox.[3]

Should it here be asked why those trustees of the people chose to saddle their principals with the payment of debts, for which they were not engaged, and the necessity of which they themselves could not take upon themselves to pronounce,—my answer is—that if anything in the shape of an *efficient, final*, or *historical* cause will satisfy them, plenty may be seen already:—but if by the word *why* anything like a *justificative* cause—a *rational* cause—a good and sufficient *reason*—be meant to be asked for, I for my part know of none. At the same

---

[1] i.e. the first Duke of Newcastle, who held high office almost continuously during the reign of George II. See also 'Defence of Economy against Burke', §VII, pp. 74–5 above.

[2] By the end of his career, Newcastle had been able to control the nominations of about twelve members of the House of Commons (see L. Namier, *The Structure of Politics at the Accession of George III*, 2nd edn., London, 1957, p. 9).

[3] Anne, Baroness Grenville (1772–1864), daughter of Thomas Pitt (1737–93), first Baron Camelford, was to receive a pension of £1,500 per annum after the death of her husband, William Wyndham Grenville (1759–1834), first Baron Grenville. Elizabeth Bridget Blane, alias Armistead (1751–1842), had received a pension of £1,200 per annum on the death of her husband, Charles James Fox, in September 1806, a few months after Parliament had voted to pay Pitt's debts.

time, for the support of the proposition that stands on my side of the argument—it being the negative—viz. that for no such purpose as that of encouraging and inducing Ministers to apply to their own use the money of individuals, can it ever be necessary, that money raised by taxes should be employed—for the support of any proposition to this effect—so plain does the proposition seem to me, that neither can I see any demand for a support to it in the shape of a *reason*, nor in truth should I know very well how to go about to find one. Not thus clear of all demand for support is the side taken by the Right Honourable Gentleman. By his vote and influence whatsoever on that occasion was done, having been supported and encouraged, on him, in point of consistency, the obligation is incumbent:—He stands *concluded*, as the lawyers say, in both ways: on the one hand, not having ventured to propose any correspondent addition, or any addition at all, to be made to the mass of emolument openly and constantly attached to the office, he is *estopped* from saying that any such extra expenditure was necessary:—on the other hand, having, in the case of the individual by whom that expenditure was made, concurred in the vote and act[a] passed for filling up at the public charge, the gaps made by that same expenditure in the property of other individuals, he stands convicted by his own confession of concurring in charging the public with a burthen, the necessity of which could not be so much as pretended.

On this occasion 'may we not venture to ask,' whether this may not be in the number of those cases, in which Gentlemen, Honourable Gentlemen, under the guidance of Right Honourable, have, in the words of our Right Honourable Author, been '*misled by mistaken ideas of virtue?*' (p. 77.)[1]

Be this as it may, by this one operation which is so much to the taste of the Right Honourable Gentleman—(not to speak of so many other Right Honourable, Honourable, and even pious Gentlemen)—two distinguishable lessons may they not be seen given—two distinguishable lessons given to so many different classes of persons, standing in so many different situations? One of these lessons, to wit, to Ministers; the other to any such person or persons whose situation might enable them to form plans for fulfilling their duty to themselves, by lending money to Ministers.

To Ministers an invitation was thus held out, to expend upon

---

[a] 46 Geo. III. c. 149. sect. 15.[2]

---

[1] Rose, *Observations respecting Public Expenditure*, p. 79 (not p. 77): '[public men] may be misled even by mistaken ideas of virtue'.

[2] The clause which granted the sum of money required for the payment of Pitt's debts.

themselves, in addition to whatever money is really necessary, as much more as it may happen to them to be disposed so to employ, of that which is not necessary.

Thus far as to the *quantum:*—and as to the *mode*, by borrowing money, or taking up goods of individuals, knowing themselves not to have any adequate means of repayment, and determining not to put themselves into the possession of any such means.

To persons at large, an invitation was at the same time held out to become *intriguers;* and, by seizing or making opportunities of throwing themselves in the way of a Minister, to supply him with money, more than he would be able to repay on demand, and having thus got him in a state of dependence, to obtain from his distress—always at the expense of the public—good gifts in every imaginable shape: *Peerages*—*baronetcies*—*ribbons*—*lucrative offices*—*contracts*—assistance in parliamentary *jobs*,—good things, in a word, of all sorts, for which, no money being paid or parted with, neither the giver nor the receiver would run any the slightest risk of being either punished, or in any other way made responsible.

By a *loan*, though, for example, it were but of 5000*l.* if properly timed—and that on both occasions—first as to the time of the administering the supply, and then as to the time of pressing for repayment, *that*, may it not every now and then be done, which could not have been done by a gift of 10,000*l.*? How often have not *seats*, for example, been in this way obtained—and this even without any such imputation as that of the sin, the venial sin, of Parliamentary simony?

In virtue of the invitation thus given by the magnanimity and generosity of Parliament,—an invitation open at all times to the acceptance of persons to whom it may happen to find themselves in the corresponding situations—who is there that does not see, how snugly the benefit of bribery may be reaped on both sides, and to any amount, without any of the risk?

A banker is made a Lord—why is a banker to be made a Lord? What is it that the banker ever did, that he is to be made a Lord? A merchant is made a Lord? Why is a merchant to be made a Lord? What is it that the merchant ever did, that he is to be made a Lord?[1]— These are among the questions which are in themselves as natural, as the answers, true or untrue, might be unpleasant to some and dangerous to others.

We have heard, many of us, of the once celebrated *Nabob of Arcot*

---

[1] Bentham perhaps had in mind two in particular of Pitt's creations: Robert Smith (1752–1838), created Baron Carrington (I) in 1796 and Baron Carrington (GB) in 1797, belonged to a banking family; Noel Hill (1745–89), created Baron Berwick in 1784, was the grandson of a Shrewsbury draper.

and his *creditors:* and the mode in which their respective debts were, to an as yet unfathomed extent, contracted: those debts, which, in so large a proportion, and to so large an amount, just and unjust together, in name the expiring Company, and in effect the whole body of the people, have paid, or, spite of the best possible discrimination, will have to pay.[1]

By the example set, and lesson held out, by the *virtue* of the Right Honourable Gentleman, and his Right Honourable and Honourable coadjutors, the policy of Arcot was it not thus sanctioned and imported into Great Britain? *Ministers, plunge your hands as deep as you can into other people's pockets: intriguers, supply profuse and needy Ministers with whatever they want, and make the most of them: we will be your sureties; our care it shall be, that you shall not be losers.*

Against the opinions of so many great characters—such has been my temerity—over and over again have I laboured to prove, I know not with what success, that *money* is not the only coin in which it may happen to a public man to be willing to take payment of the public for his labour: and that *power* and *reputation*,—though they will not like shillings and half-pence, go to market for butter and eggs,—yet, like Exchequer Bills, within a certain circle, they are not altogether unsusceptible of a certain degree of currency. Of the truth of this proposition, the Mr. Pitt in question affords at least one instance.

It proves indeed something more: for, in so far as purposely forbearing to receive what it is in a man's option to receive, is tantamount to paying,—it proves that, in the instance in question, the value of these commodities was equal to that of a very considerable sum of money: in round numbers, worth 40,000*l.*—at any rate worth more than 39,000*l.*

Not that in the eyes of the hero, money had no value: for it had much too great a value: it possessed a value greater than the estimated value of common honesty and independence.

He loved money, and by much too well: he loved it with the love of *covetousness.* Not that he hoarded it, or put it out to usury. But there are two sorts of covetous men: those who covet it to keep it, and those who covet it to spend it: the class he belonged to was this *coveting-and-spending* class.

---

[1] Mohammed Ali Khan Walajah (1717–95), Nawab of Arcot, the titular ruler of the Carnatic, but a client of the East India Company, had run up huge debts, owed both to the Company and to individual Company servants. Under a plan adopted by the East India Company in 1784, the debts had been paid off by 1804. It was then discovered that the Nawab had incurred a massive new debt, whereupon a Commission was appointed to investigate the affair (see the local and personal Act 46 Geo. III, c.133). Four Reports had already been produced by the time Bentham was writing, and a further twenty-two were to follow before the matter was finally closed in 1830. The Company was 'expiring' in that its Charter had to be renewed in 1813.

Yes:—*that* he did:—Pitt the second did love money: and not his own money merely, but other people's likewise: loving it, he coveted it; and coveting it, he obtained it.

The debt which he contracted, was so much money coveted, obtained, and expended, for and in the purchase of such miscellaneous pleasures as happened to be suited to his taste. The sinecure money which he might have had and would not have, was so much money expended in the shape of *insurance money* on account of power: in the purchase of that *respect* and *reputation*, which his prudence represented as necessary to the preservation of so valuable an article against storms and tempests from above. Sinecure money to any given amount the hero could have got for himself with at least as much facility as for his Right Honourable Panegyrist; but the *respect* and the *reputation* were defences, which in that situation could not be put to hazard. Of the battles he had to fight with the sort of *dragons* commonly called *secret advisers*, this bare hint is all that can be given by one who knows nothing of any body or any thing: his Right Honourable *Achates*,[1] by whom he must (alas! how oft!) have been seen in a tottering and almost sinking attitude,—more particulars could doubtless be given, by a great many, than by a gentleman of his discretion it would . . . (unless it were in a posthumous *diary*, for which posterity would be much obliged to him) be '*useful on his sole authority*' . . . '*to*[2] *enter into any detail of.*'[3] It was to enable virtue to rise triumphant out of all these trials, that the amount of all this sinecure money was thus *expended*, and without having been *received*.

SECTION XI.
CONCERNING INFLUENCE.

On the subject of *Influence* (p. 74)[4] what the Right Honourable Gentleman *admits*, is—that owing to the greatly increased revenue, and all the other augmented and 'accumulated business of the state,'

---

[1] In ancient mythology, Achates was the faithful companion of Aeneas: see Virgil, *Aeneid*, i. 312. The allusion here is to Rose.

[2] 1817, 1830 omit opening speech mark.

[3] Rose, *Observations respecting Public Expenditure*, p. 74: 'On the more extensive consideration respecting the charges to be incurred for the great branches of the public service, whatever strong opinions the author entertains on the subject, it is not meant to enter into any detail here, as it would not be useful, on his sole authority, to do so. . . .'

[4] Ibid., pp. 75–6 (not p. 74): 'The greatly increased revenue, and all the other augmented and accumulated business of the state, have unavoidably occasioned some increase of patronage; but the influence created by such means is infinitely short of what has been given up by the measures of œconomy and regulation to which recourse has been had, especially when the description and value of the employments created is compared with those abolished. . . .'

some increase has, though 'unavoidably, been occasioned in it,' viz. by 'increase of patronage.' At the same time, notwithstanding this increase, yet, in point of practice, the state of things if we may trust to his conception, is as exactly as if there were no such thing at all as influence. How so?—why, for this plain reason, viz. that 'the influence created by such means is *infinitely* short of what,'—viz. 'by the measures of economy and regulation to which recourse has been had'—'has been given up.'

Thus far the Right Honourable Author. But in the humble conception of his obscure commentator, the question between the two quantities, one of which is, in the hands of the Right Honourable Accountant, multiplied by one of those figures of rhetoric, which, in aid of the figures of arithmetic, are so much at his command—multiplied in a word to '*infinity*'—this question is not, on the present occasion, the proper one. In regard to *influence*, the question which with leave of the public, the obscure commentator would venture to propose—as and for a more proper one, is—whether, for any existing particle of this influence any preponderant use can, in compensation for the acknowledged evil consequences of it, be found? and if not, whether there be any and what quantity of it left remaining, that could be got rid of? Understand, on each occasion, as being a condition universally and necessarily implied—without prejudice in other respects,—and *that* preponderant prejudice—to the public service.

As to these points, what appears to me,—with submission, is—that, without travelling out of this the Right Honourable Gentleman's own work, an instance might be found of a little sprig of influence, which, without any such preponderant prejudice to *Mr. Reeve's tree* might be pruned off.[1]

This work of his (I mean Mr. Rose's) has for its title '*Observations respecting the Public Expenditure, and the Influence of the Crown.*'

But unfortunately,—as, in due place and time, the candour of the Right Honourable Gentleman himself, in effect, acknowledges, these

---

[1] See John Reeves' (1752–1829) pamphlet, published anonymously, *Thoughts on the English Government. Addressed to the Quiet Good Sense of the People of England. In a series of letters. Letter the First*, London, 1795, pp. 12–13: 'In fine, the Government of England is *a Monarchy*; the Monarch is the antient stock from which have sprung those goodly branches of the Legislature, the Lords and Commons, that at the same time give ornament to the Tree, and afford shelter to those who seek protection under it. But these are still only branches, and derive their origin and their nutriment from their common parent; they may be lopped off, and the Tree is a Tree still; shorn indeed of its honours, but not, like them, cast into the fire.' On 26 November 1795, the House of Commons condemned the pamphlet as a seditious libel (*Commons Journals*, li. 119). The 'little sprig of influence' was presumably Rose's own sinecure of Clerk of the Parliaments.

observations of his—and from so experienced an observer—are *all on one side*.[1]

On the subject of expenditure, out of 79 pages, 61 have been expended in showing us what retrenchments have been made, and how great they are. Are they indeed so great? So much the better: but even yet, considering that if we may believe the Right Honourable Gentleman himself, (p. 62) the whole revenue of Great Britain is '*more than* 60,000,000*l. a year,*' let the retrenchments have been ever so great, the demand for further retrenchment, wheresoever it can be made, without preponderant prejudice to the public service, seems by no means to be superseded.

Subject to that necessary condition, is there any such further retrenchment practicable? This is exactly what the Right Honourable Gentleman has not merely avoided, but positively refused to tell us.

From first to last, this work of his has, according to the author's own account of it, but one aim; and that is, by showing how great the retrenchments are, that have been made already, to stop our mouths, and prevent our calling for any more. Is it then true, that in this way all has been done that ought to be done? Even this not even in terms ever so general, will he vouchsafe to tell us. 'To what extent or in what manner it may be proper to press further retrenchments, the author' (says he, p. 62) 'has not the remotest intention of offering an opinion: his view has been clearly explained.'

Looking for the explanation the clearness of which is thus insisted on, I find it, if I do not mistake, in his last preceding page but one, viz. in p. 60, in which, speaking of this his work by the name of 'the present publication,'—'In endeavouring to set right the public opinion on this subject, the performance of an act of justice to *any*[2] administration, is' (he says) 'but a *small part* of its use; a much *more important* consideration is, its effect in producing that salutary and reasonable *confidence*, which gives the power of exertion to the government, and that concurrence which seconds its exertions among the people.'[3]

Thus far the Right Honourable Author. For my own part, if my conception concerning a government's title to confidence be not altogether an erroneous one, this title depends in no inconsiderable degree on its disposition '*to press further retrenchments:*' (p. 62) I mean

[1] This phrase does not appear in Rose's *Observations respecting Public Expenditure*. Bentham perhaps had in mind the phrase 'in one point of view' which appears at p. 5: 'It is with an intention to a discharge of that duty to the country, that the following accurate statement of the measures which have been already adopted towards the attainment of the objects above alluded to, in one point of view, is made. . . . ' The context however will hardly support Bentham's construction.

[2] The italic is Rose's.

[3] Rose, *Observations respecting Public Expenditure*, pp. 60–1.

of course, in so far as, in the judgment of that government, they are not otherwise than '*proper*' ones. Yet this the Right Honourable Gentleman—a member of this same government, and that in the very next rank to the highest, and receiving (besides sinecure money) no less than 4,000*l*. a year for being so,[1] peremptorily—and as we have seen of his own accord,—refuses to do.

He will not do any such thing: and why not? On this point we might be apt to be at a stand at least, if not at a loss, were it not for the lights with which, in another page (p. 74)[2] the Right Honourable Author himself has favoured us. His 'opinions' on the subject, he there acknowledges, are '*strong ones;*' but strong as they are, or rather because they are so strong, he will not let us know what they are; because '*on his sole authority*,' that is, unless other opinions that in the scale of office stand yet higher than his, concurred with his, '*it would not be useful:*'—there would be *no use* in it. No use in it? what! not on a subject of such vital importance—when for the declared purpose of 'setting right the public opinion on this subject,' a Right Honourable Author, who knows all about it, takes up the pen, can it be that there would be no use in speaking what he thinks is right? and as much of it as he has to speak? No use in his speaking impartially?—in speaking on both sides, and on all sides, what he thinks?

But not to go on any further in thus beating the bush, may we not in plain English venture to ask—at the bottom of all his delicacy, can any other interpretation be found than this, viz. that by those, for whose defence and for whose purposes, and to come to the point at once—under whose *influence* this work of his was written, his speaking as he thinks, and what he thinks right—his speaking out on both sides, would it in his own persuasion have been found not endurable?

If so, here then we have a practical illustration and development of a number of preceding hints. Here we see the character—here we see one effect and use—of that '*aristocracy of talent and virtue*' with which, in the account of remuneration, nothing but money will pass current,—nothing but money is of any value,—and which constitutes so necessary an addition to the '*aristocracy of rank and property.*'

Here we see what is, and what we are the better for, the fruit of 'that principle of activity,' (p. 66) which animates men in the attainment, so much more than in the mere possession, of power and station, 'and of that amusement, which, for the acquisition and improvement of talents necessary for the higher offices, gentlemen

---

[1] Rose's annual salary as Treasurer of the Navy was about £4,300.
[2] See §X, p. 142n above.

have given themselves, in passing *occasionally* through the inferior situations.'[1]

'Of the *unpopularity* and *ridicule* that has so often been attempted to be fixed on the word *confidence*,' the Right Honourable Gentleman has, as he is pleased to inform us, according to his own statement (p. 61) had '*some experience*.'[2] One little item, to whatsoever may have been the stock laid up by him of that instructive article, he may find occasion to make. To that sort of *confidence* which is '*unthinking and blind*,' this 'unpopularity and ridicule,' he appears to look upon as not altogether '*inapplicable*,' nor consequently the sort of '*attempt*' he speaks of, viz. that of fixing it on the word *confidence*, as altogether incapable of being attended with success.

But can any thing be more '*unthinking and blind*' than that confidence, which should bestow itself on an official man, howsoever Right Honourable, who, in treating of a subject confessedly of high national importance, and after furnishing, in favour of one side, whatsoever information his matchless experience, his unquestioned ingenuity, his indefatigable industry, can rake together,—and feeling, on the other side of his mind '*opinions*'—and those '*strong* ones,'[3] nor doubtless unaccompanied with an adequate knowledge of facts—of those facts from which they receive their existence and their strength,—should refuse—deliberately, and peremptorily, as well as spontaneously, refuse—to furnish any the least tittle of information from that other side.

Eloquent and zealous in support of profusion, mute when the time should come for pleading in favour of retrenchment, not without compunction let him behold at least one consequence. Destitute of all competent, of all sufficiently qualified, of all officially qualified, advocates—deserted even by him who should have been its Solicitor-General, thus it is that the cause of *Economy* is left to take its chance for finding here and there an advocate among low people, who have never been regularly called to this high *bar:* interlopers, who, destitute of all prospect of that 'remuneration' which is the sole '*principle of activity that animates men in the attainment of power and station*,' (p. 66) destitute of the advantage of '*passing occasionally through even the inferior situations*,' (p. 66) are destitute of all '*talent*,' destitute of all '*virtue*'—and whose productions, if, for the purpose of the argument they could for a moment be supposed capable of contri-

---

[1] See § VIII, p. 124 above.

[2] Rose, *Observations respecting Public Expenditure*, p. 61: 'This is stated, with some experience of the unpopularity and ridicule that has been so often attempted to be fixed on the word Confidence, applicable only to that which is unthinking and blind.'

[3] See ibid., p. 74 and §X, p. 142n above.

buting, on the ground here in question, anything that could be conducive to the public service, would, one and all, be so many effects without a cause.

SECTION XII.
CONCERNING PECUNIARY COMPETITION—
AND THE USE MADE OF THE PRINCIPLE.

BEFORE the subject of *influence* is dismissed, a word or two may, perhaps, have its use, for the purpose of endeavouring to submit to the consideration of the Right Honourable Panegyrist an article of *revenue*, viz. *crown lands*, which neither on his part, nor on the part of his hero, seems to have received quite so much attention as could have been wished.

To the purpose of the present publication, a circumstance that renders this article the more material, is—that it may contribute to render more and more familiar to the eye of the reader a *principle*, on a due estimation of which the plan hereafter to be proposed depends for every thing in it, that either promises to be in its effect eventually useful, or is in its application new.

Economy and *purity*—reduction of expense, and reduction of undue influence—in these may be seen the two distinguishable and distinguished, though intimately connected, objects, to which, speaking of the principle of *competition*, our Right Honourable Author speaks of it as having meant to be made subservient, and as having accordingly been made subservient, in the hands of Mr. Pitt (p. 26.)

'Mr. Pitt' (he informs us, p. 25)[1] 'looking anxiously to reforms,

---

[1] Because of the many omissions and discrepancies in the rendering of this passage (Rose, *Observations respecting Public Expenditure*, pp. 25–6), it is reproduced here in full: 'Mr. Pitt, however, did not confine his views to what might be done by official arrangements, but, looking anxiously to reforms, wherever they could be made, he effected many more considerable savings to the public than those we have enumerated, and at the same time sacrificed an influence as Minister, much more dangerous than any possessed by the Crown, because more secret and unobserved; the extent of it, indeed, could be known only to himself, and to those immediately in his confidence. We shall state the measures to which we allude in their order, beginning with LOANS AND LOTTERIES; which used invariably to be settled by bargains made between the Chancellor of the Exchequer and a certain number of persons, selected by him: then shewing the profit to the public, by putting an end to the practice of making *private contracts* with persons intended to be favoured, for supplying the troops on foreign stations with provisions and money, and sometimes for furnishing ships, as already alluded to; and closing this part of the account with the profit derived from the mode irrevocably established respecting *the renewals of crown leases*. In each of which cases the influence diminished was not only extensive, but was obviously in its nature much more objectionable than any that could be acquired by the disposal of offices; as the effect of the former was secret and unobserved, whereas the latter is apparent and generally known.'

147

effected many even considerable savings—and at the same time sacrificed an influence as minister, much more dangerous than any possessed by the crown, *because more secret and unobserved;* the extent of it indeed could be known only to himself and to those in his immediate confidence. We shall state' (continues he) 'the measures—in their order, beginning with loans and lotteries,—proceeding with *private contracts*, and closing this part of the account with the profit derived from the mode irrevocably established respecting *the renewals of crown leases*. In each of which cases the influence diminished was not only extensive, but was obviously in its nature more objectionable than any that could be acquired by the disposal of *offices;* as the effect of the former was *secret and unobserved*, whereas the latter is apparent and generally known.'

Thus far the Right Honourable Author: a word or two now from his obscure commentator.[1]

Coming to crown lands (p. 34) 'The last head of saving by management' (says he) 'is under that of the estates of the Crown. The Act of the 1st of Queen Anne,[a] continued at the beginning of each succeeding reign, for limiting grants of crown lands to 31 years, put a stop to the actual alienation of the property of the crown;[2] but, in its operation, had the effect of greatly adding to the influence of it, and certainly afforded no protection whatever to its revenues, as will be seen in the note below.[b] In reigns antecedent to that of Queen Anne, when grants were perpetual, the persons to whom they were made became immediately independent of the crown, and not unfrequently gave very early proofs of that independence: whereas, by the measure adopted on the accession of the Queen, every grantee, or the person representing him, became dependent on the Minister for a renewal of his lease, for which applications were generally made at such times,

---

[a] 1 Anne, st. 1. c.7.[3]
[b] In 15 years, to 1715, the whole income from Crown lands, including rents, fines, and grants of all sorts, was 22,624*l.* equal to 1,500*l.* a year. Journals of H.C. vol. xx. p. 520; and in 7 years, to 1746 was 15,600*l.*, equal to 2,228*l.* a year.—Journals, vol. 25, p. 206.[4]

---

[1] In fact Bentham offers no comment, but passes straight on to a further passage.
[2] The original clause in 1 Ann., sess.1, c.7, 'An Act for the better Support of her Majesty's Houshold, and of the Honour and Dignity of the Crown', was confirmed in the equivalent acts at the beginning of the reigns of George I (1 Geo. I, sess.1, c.1), George II (1 Geo. II, sess.1, c.1) and George III (1 Geo. III, c.1).
[3] The footnote is Rose's.
[4] The footnote is Rose's. See 'Produce of sundry Small Branches and Casualties paid into the Exchequer, on the Civil List, from Christmas 1699 to Lady-day 1715', *Commons Journals*, xx. 520; 'An Account of the Produce, into the Exchequer, of the several Duties and Revenues applicable to the Uses of his Majesty's Civil Government', ibid., xxv. 206.

and on such occasions, as were thought to afford the best hope of their being attended to, on terms favourable to his interest.

'Under this system Mr. Pitt, on coming into office, found the whole landed property of the Crown, and the income arising from it, in every way, very little exceeding 4,000*l.* a year.

'*He therefore after long inquiries, and most attentive consideration*, applied a remedy in 1794, when an Act was passed,[a] by which it is provided that no lease shall be renewed till within a short period of its expiration, nor till an actual survey shall have been made by two professional men of experience and character, who are required to certify the true value of the premises to the Treasury, attested on their oaths. *No abuse can therefore take place*, nor any *undue favour be shown*, under the provisions of this law, *unless surveyors of eminence* in their line shall *deliberately perjure themselves*, or a Treasury shall be found bold enough to grant leases, or renew them, at a less value than shall be certified to them, which could not escape immediate detection, as there is a clause in the act requiring an account to be laid before Parliament annually of what leases or grants shall have been made in the year preceding; for what terms or estates; the annual value, as returned on oath by the surveyors; the annual value of the last preceding survey; what rents shall have been reserved, or what fines paid; and upon what other considerations such leases shall have been respectively made.[1]

'More strict provisions to guard against any evasion of the law could *hardly* have been devised.'[2]

Thus far our Right Honourable Author.

Where, having determined with himself to obtain for public property the best price that is to be had, Mr. Pitt pursues that principle, my humble applause follows him: but when, without sufficient reason he turns aside from that or any other principle, then my applause stops: applause, whatever in that case perseveres in following him, will be of that sort which comes from copartners and panegyrists.

When government annuities were the commodity to be disposed of, then it was that it was the choice of Mr. Pitt to have the best price: then it was that, choosing to have the best price, he adopted the mode and the only mode by which that effect can be produced.

---

[a] 34 Geo. III. c. 75.[3]

---

[1] Rose '"of what leases or grants . . . respectively made."' This is clause XXI.
[2] Rose, *Observations respecting Public Expenditure*, pp. 34–6.
[3] The footnote is Rose's, and refers to 'An Act for the better Management of the Land Revenue of the Crown, and for the Sale of Fee Farm and other unimprovable Rents'.

When leasehold interests in Crown lands were the commodity to be disposed of, then it was that it was not the choice of Mr. Pitt to have the best price. Then it was accordingly that, for fear of having the best price, care was taken *not* to employ the mode, the only mode by which any such effect can be produced.

To avoid giving birth to the undesirable effect in question, the expedient employed was (we see) an 'actual survey, made by two professional men of experience and character, who are required to certify the true value of the premises to the Treasury, attested on their oaths.'

'Under the provision of this law,' one thing the Right Honourable Gentleman endeavours to persuade us of (p. 35)[1]—is, that 'no abuse can take place, nor undue favour be shown.' Why not? Because (says he) no such effect can take place 'unless surveyors of eminence in their line shall deliberately perjure themselves or'—something else which he mentions shall take place, and which, admitting the improbability of it, I shall not repeat here.

As to *perjury*, the *word* is a *strong word*, and to the purpose of causing the reader to suppose that the security provided by it is a *strong security*, more conducive than any real lover of sincerity can be well pleased to find it. But, from the pen of a veteran in *office*, and in *offices*, and in *such* offices, to whom it cannot be altogether unknown, to how prodigious an extent the people of this country are made deliberately and habitually to perjure themselves; and how fond, under the guidance of priests and lawyers, the legislation and jurisprudence of this same country have been, of causing men, always without any the smallest use, deliberately to perjure themselves[a]—it is not without pain that a man who has any real dislike to perjury can behold this security held up to view in the character of a *real* one.

Cases there are (it is confessed with pleasure) in which this alleged security is an efficient one: as for instance, where testimony to a matter of fact is to be given, *vivâ voce*, in an open judicatory, and under the check of cross-examination: not that even in that case it is to the ceremony that the efficiency would be found ascribable, but to the cross-examination, and the publicity, with or without the eventual punishment. But in the case *here* in question, not one of all those

[a] See 'Swear not at all,' &c. by the Author: printed 1813: now (1817) just published.[2]

---

[1] These phrases are in fact at p. 36.

[2] *'Swear not at all:' containing an exposure of the needlessness and mischievousness, as well as anti-Christianity, of the ceremony of an oath*, London, 1817 (Bowring, v. 187–229).

elements of efficiency is to be found. The sort of perjury which the Right Honourable Gentleman endeavours to make us take for a punishable offence, suppose it, for argument's sake, committed— was ever one instance known of a man being prosecuted for it as for perjury? Great would be my surprise to hear of any such case. Would so much as an indictment lie? I have not searched, nor to the present purpose does it seem worth while. Gross indeed must be the case, strong and clear; stronger and clearer than it seems in the nature of the case to afford—the proof by which, upon any such indictment, conviction must be produced.

Few, it is evident, are the sorts of articles—lands, houses, or any other such articles, coming under the head of *crown lands*, being unquestionably not of the number—few, about the value of which it may not happen to 'surveyors of eminence, experience, and character' to entertain real differences of opinion; and moreover, and without the smallest imputation on that '*character*,' much more without the possibility of suffering as for *perjury*, to agree in assigning such a value, as to a very considerable amount—according to circumstances, say 5, 10, 12, 15, 20, 50 per cent. (in short one knows not where to stop) greater or less than what in their opinions respectively is the true one.

The real value of the premises is the joint result of some half dozen (suppose) of circumstances on each side: whereupon on one side (suppose again) this or that little circumstance, somehow or other, fails of being taken into the account. Unless the human understanding were that perfect kind of machine which every body acknowledges it not to be, who could think of speaking of it as importing so much as a speck upon a man's character, that any such little oversight has taken place? Meantime the profit by the oversight may amount to thousands of pounds in any number.

Unfortunately for *Economy*, still more unfortunately for *Uncorruption*, the sort of contract here in question is one of those in which, with a pre-eminent degree of force, interest and opportunity join, in securing to the subject of valuation, a false or under-value. What the one party, viz. the proposed lessee wants, is money: what the other party—the 'discharger of duties and public trusts' wants, is *influence*. If the valuation be deficient, then, in proportion to the deficiency, both parties have what they want. Under a state of things so favourable to mutual accommodation, let any one, who feels bold enough, undertake to set a limit to the loss liable to be produced to the public by the substitution of this mode of sale, to the only one which is capable of finding out the real value. In a *fancy* article, such as a villa, or a site for a villa, cent. per cent. may be below the difference. Ten

151

per cent.—to put, for argument's sake, a certain amount for an uncertain one—will surely be regarded as a very small allowance.

In this ten per cent. then may be seen the amount of the *saving*, or the acquisition, call it which you please, which on the occasion in question might have been made to the public, and was not made.

Thus much as to *revenue*. Then as to *influence*, 'some judgment,' as Mr. Rose observes (p. 37) 'may be formed by observing, that of the persons holding crown leases when the act was passed, upwards of *eighty were* Members of one or the other House of Parliament; and it is hardly necessary to add' (continues he) 'that in the cases of *other lessees*, the parties, who might have the means of doing so, would naturally resort to solicitations of friends for obtaining the Minister's favour.'

Now, in the picture thus drawn of the state of the case, as it stood at *that* time—drawn by so experienced and expert a hand—so far as concerns *influence*, I, for my own part, till some distinct ground of difference is brought to view, cannot but see a picture equally correct of the state of the case as it stands at this moment: at this moment, viz. after and notwithstanding—not to say by reason of—the reform thus lauded. So far indeed as concerns revenue, I cannot doubt but that a very considerable change—and so far as it goes, a change for the better, has been made: a change, for the amount of which I take of course the account given of it by Mr. Rose.[1] But, so far as concerns *influence*, what I should not expect to find is that any change, worth taking into account, had taken place. '*Eighty*,' according to the Right Honourable Gentleman, is the number of *Members* so circumstanced at that time; *eighty*,—or rather from that increasing division, which landed property, where it will serve for building, or even for sites of villas, naturally admits of, *more* than eighty—is the number which I should expect to find at present; not to speak of *expectants*, for whom, where the purpose of the argument requires it, the Right Honourable Arguer knows so well how to take credit. For convincing an Honourable or Right Honourable Gentleman of the superiority of one ministry over another, ten per cent. upon any given sum will not, it is true, serve so effectually in the character of a persuasion, as thirty per cent.: but wherever the ten per cent. suffices, the abolished twenty per cent. would have been but surplusage, since thirty per cent. could do no more. The case of the villa contiguous to Chelsea Hospital—a case which, though it happened so long ago as the last session, is not

---

[1] See Rose, *Observations respecting Public Expenditure*, pp. 36–7: 'Under this management the revenue arising from the estates of the Crown has increased, in the fifteen years since the law took effect, from 4,251l. to 63,862l. and will go on improving till it amounts to about 400,000l. . . . The profit from this arrangement is already, as stated above, annually 59,611l.'

yet, it is hoped, altogether out of recollection—may serve, and as well as half a hundred, for clearing and fixing our ideas on this subject.[1] From that case may be formed some judgment, whether the impossibility of 'abuse and undue favour' is quite so near to complete, as it would be for the convenience of the Right Honourable Gentleman's acknowledged purposes that we should believe it to be.

All this while a circumstance which has contributed in no small degree to that composure and tranquil confidence, of which my readers, if I happen to have any, may on this occasion have observed the symptoms, is—a surmise in which I have all along been indulging myself,—viz. that between the opinions of the Right Honourable Author and those of his obscure commentator there does not, on this occasion, exist *at bottom* any very considerable difference.

'More strict provision to guard against any invasion[2] of the law could *hardly*' (says the Right Honourable Author) 'have been devised.' But it will be for the reader to judge, whether the law in question be quite so well guarded against evasion, as, by this saving word *hardly*, the argument of the Right Honourable Gentleman is guarded against any such impertinent charge as that of having said the thing that is *not*. Neither on this nor on any other occasion, could it easily have escaped a sagacity such as his, that a mode of sale, the sure effect of which is to perpetuate a constantly *inferior* price, is not quite so favourable either to increase of revenue or to diminution of influence, as a mode of sale, the sure effect of which is—to obtain, on each occasion the *very best* price.

Pecuniary competition—Auction—having, and in other instances to so great an extent—by this same hero, and with the special applause of this same panegyrist been employed, as and for the best contrived mode or instrument for obtaining, for such articles as government has to dispose of, the very best price—having been applied, and with so much success, in the case of government annuities—having been applied, and with so much success, in the case of contracts for stores[3]—(for when there is no fraud, it is in form only and not in effect that, in this case, there is any difference between *competition* and *auction* in the common acceptation of the word)—and moreover in the case of the very sort of article here in question—in the case of

---

[1] In the House of Commons, on 13 April 1809, Sir Francis Burdett (1770–1844), radical MP for Westminster, suggested that the leasing of land by Chelsea Hospital to enable a house to be built was 'a great and serious abuse'. For this and further debates on the subject on 14 and 20 April and 5 May see *Parliamentary Debates* (1809) xiv. 21–3, 33–45, 107–13, 392–400.

[2] Rose 'evasion'.

[3] See Rose, *Observations respecting Public Expenditure*, pp. 25–34, where the savings made by Pitt in each of these two areas are discussed.

lands—sale of leasehold interests presenting themselves to view in every newspaper, and even *letting by auction* in the first instance, having nothing new in it, it would be a most instructive explanation, to us whose station is *without doors*, if in his next edition the Right Honourable Author would have the goodness to inform us, how it happened, that when in the course of her voyage, Economy had reached the latitude of the *crown lands*, she all of a sudden stopped short, and, instead of the best instrument for fishing out the best price, took up with so weak and ill-contrived an one. Is it that in the case of lands, *auction* is less well adapted than in the case of goods to an obtainment of the best price?—less well adapted to the obtaining that best price for leasehold interests in *lands*, to be paid for in money, than for *money* to be paid for in *goods?* On the contrary, in the case of goods, to be supplied to government by contract, as in the case in question, with the benefit of competition, the Right Honourable Gentleman, if not already informed, might with little difficulty be informed of cases upon cases, in which the rigour of the principle of competition receives a very convenient softening, from expedients which have no application in the case of lands.

In default of such full and authentic lights, as nothing short of the *experience*, joined to the condescension, of the Right Honourable Gentleman, would afford us, it may be matter of amusement at any rate, if of nothing better,—to us whose station is on the *outside* of the curtain,—to figure to ourselves, in the way of guess and pastime, what, on the occasion in question, may have been passing *behind* it.

Before so desirable a head of reform as that in question could be brought even into the imperfect state dressed up as above by the ingenuity of our Right Honourable Author, '*long inquiries, and most attentive consideration*' (we are informed by him, p. 35) took place. Of these '*long inquiries*,' no inconsiderable portion, if one who knows nothing may be allowed to guess, were naturally directed to so desirable an object, as that of knowing what, in case of a change of the sort proposed, the *eighty* members, of whom we have seen him speaking, would be disposed to think of it: and of the '*attentive consideration*,' no inconsiderable portion (it is equally natural to suppose) was bestowed upon the *objections*, which an *innovation* of this sort could not but have given birth to in so many Honourable and Right Honourable minds.

With a set of hobgoblins, known among school boys by the collective appellation of the *secret advisers of the crown*—and of whom certain *sceptics* (such has been the growth of infidelity!) have of late (it seems) been found *Arians* or *Socinians* enough to question the existence,—our author's hero, there cannot be any doubt, supposing them always to have had existence, must have had to fight, on this, as on many other occasions, many a hard battle. Of such warfare, the result, on the occasion here in question, seems to have been a sort of compromise. To restraint upon the dilapidation of the revenue, *Fee, Faw, Fum* could be, and accordingly were brought to submit;—and thus it was, that sale, grounded on collusive valuation, was substituted to absolute gift. To the diminution of influence, *Fee, Faw, Fum* could not and would not be brought to submit: they would have gone off to *Hanover* or to *Hampshire* first:[1]—and thus it was that sale, grounded on collusive valuation, was preferred to sale *for the best price*.

---

[1] The British monarch was of course also the ruler of Hanover, while Rose had close connections with Hampshire. His principal residence was Cuffnells, near Lyndhurst, Hampshire, and he was MP for the Hampshire boroughs of Lymington from 1788 to 1790 and Christchurch from 1790 until his death.

OBSERVATIONS ON MR. SECRETARY PEEL'S HOUSE OF COMMONS SPEECH,

21st MARCH, 1825,

INTRODUCING HIS

POLICE MAGISTRATES' SALARY RAISING BILL.

Date of Order for Printing,

24th March, 1825.

ALSO ON THE

ANNOUNCED JUDGES' SALARY RAISING BILL,

AND THE

PENDING COUNTY COURTS BILL.

OBSERVATIONS, &c.

1. Clauses, six: of minor importance, the four last: of major, the two first: whereof the second for establishing the measure: the first (the preamble) for justification of it.[1]

Measure, 200*l.* a year added to the salaries of the existing thirty Police Magistrates.[2] Original salary, 400*l.*—see below.[3] Last year but two, (3 G.IV. c.55.) so says clause 1,—200*l.* added to it.[4] Already comes the demand for as much more.

A reason is wanted—and such an one as shall amount to a justification. Ready at hand is a complete one, and not less concise than complete; one single word—*expediency*. 'And whereas it is *expedient* to encrease the said salary.'[5] The House has *standing orders*—Parliament has standing *reasons:* at any rate it has this one, and this one is the standing representative of all others. To the wise, and from the wise, this one word is sufficient.

For this second 200*l.* it is all-sufficient; whether it might have served equally for the first, time[6] for search is wanting. But I would venture a small wager, that on that occasion it did so serve: it will serve equally well for any number of others. It is made of stretching leather. It *works well*, and wears well: it will be as good a thousand years hence as it is at present. That which is *expedient* is *expedient*. What can be more *expedient* than *expediency?* . . . . I could not refrain

---

[1] The 'Police Magistrates' Salary Raising Bill', whose full title was 'A Bill to amend an Act for the more effectual Administration of the Office of Justice of the Peace, in and near the Metropolis', had been introduced into the House of Commons on 21 March 1825 by Robert Peel (1788–1850), Home Secretary 1822–7, 1828–30, First Lord of the Treasury and Chancellor of the Exchequer 1834–5, First Lord of the Treasury 1841–6. It contained a preamble plus five enactive clauses, giving the 'six clauses' to which Bentham refers (see *Commons Sessional Papers* (1825) iii. 359–62). Two further clauses having been added in committee, the Bill received the Royal assent on 20 May 1825 (6 Geo. IV, c.21). The Secretary of State's power to raise magistrates' salaries to £800 was conferred by the first clause.

[2] In fact, there were only twenty-seven police magistrates: three each at Bow Street, the Thames Police Office, and the seven offices established by the Metropolitan Justices Act of 1792 (for which see below). Bentham is repeating the figure given by Peel (see p. 202 below).

[3] See p. 170 below.

[4] This Act, 'for the more effectual Administration of the Office of a Justice of the Peace in and near the Metropolis, and for the more effectual prevention of Depredations on the River Thames and its Vicinity, for Seven Years', passed in 1822 (of which 6 Geo. IV, c.21 was the amendment), merely confirmed the yearly salary of the Justices at £600. A stipendiary magistracy had first been established by the Metropolitan Justices Act of 1792 (32 Geo. III, c.53); the stipend had originally been set at £400, but had been raised to £500 in 1802 (42 Geo. III, c.76) and to £600 in 1814 (54 Geo. III, c.37 and c.187).

[5] This phrase is in the preamble. The italic is Bentham's.

[6] 1825A, 1825B, 1830 'first. Time'.

looking. I should have won my wager. The *expediency* reason is not indeed applied exclusively to the salary-raising clause (No. 6.), but it shines in the preamble; and in that clause the lustre and virtue of it extends to all the others.[1]

According to usage, the sum is left in blank in the Bill: according to usage, the blank is filled up by the eloquence of the Minister.

After having thus done the one thing needful, and stamped the measure with intelligibility, he might not perhaps have done amiss, had he left the justification of it to the wisdom of Parliament, as above.

That injustice may be completely avoided, misrepresentation as far as possible, the *Times* and the *Morning Chronicle*—two of the most accredited sources of information—have, upon this occasion been drawn upon, and the matter divided into numbered paragraphs; and, for the grounds of the respective observations here hazarded, reference has, by means of the numbers, been made to those several paragraphs.[2]

Original salary, 400*l.* a year (see below.)[3] Last year's addition, 200*l.* a year.[4] Existing, what? 600*l.* Magistrates, thirty. Aggregate of the addition, 6000*l.* a year: aggregate of the now proposed addition, another 6000*l.* a year; together, 12,000*l.* Nature of the demand clear enough: not to speak of *reason*, which seems altogether out of the question: not so the alleged *grounds* of it. To tread them up has been *tread-wheel* work.—Result, what follows.

Evils proposed to be remedied, deficiencies: 1. deficiency in appropriate intellectual aptitude: 2. deficiency in time employed in attendance. As to aptitude, during the 400*l.* a year (so says No. 2.) incompetence total. Thus far aptitude: the same certificate may, without much stretch of inference, be made to apply to quantity of attendance. These are the evils for which the second 200*l.* a year, multiplied by 30, is to suffice as a remedy. The first dose was administered two or three years ago: already it has been found insufficient, else why apply for another? But that which a single dose cannot effect another dose may; and if this does not, others and others after them are at hand from the same shop.

For the remedying of these evils, the reality of them being supposed, begin as above and end as above, the means provided by the wisdom of Parliament.

---

[1] The preamble to 3 Geo. IV, c.55 begins, 'Whereas it is expedient that the Provisions of an Act made in the last Sessions of Parliament . . . should be continued and amended. . . .'

[2] See pp. 199–202 below.

[3] See p. 170 below.

[4] Presumably the addition which Bentham assumed had been made in 1822 (not 1824).

That wisdom having thus exhausted itself,—for ulterior remedies, how little so ever needed, comes, as will be seen, an additional supply, provided by administration: provided, by the genius of Lord Sidmouth,[1] who invented them; by the magnanimity of Mr. Peel, who disdained not to adopt them. They are—future exclusion of all non-barristers: ditto of all Barristers of less than three years' standing.[2] I speak here, and of necessity, of the two Secretaries, late and present. For it is by Mr. Peel and his successors in that office, if by anybody, that these remedies are to be applied. Parliament is to know nothing of them: Parliament is not to be trusted with the application of them.

Viewing all this wisdom and virtue through the medium of the *greatest happiness principle*, (a principle which has been accused of giving to financial objects rather a yellow tinge) I have the misfortune of seeing the whole speech in a considerably different point of view— 1. The alleged evils—the inaptitude, and the non-attendance— neither of them proved by it. 2. Supposing the disorder proved; the supposed remedy, Parliamentary and ministerial, as above, inefficient to any good purpose; efficient to a very bad purpose; but both these evils, though not proved by the Right Hon. Secretary, I admit, and, as it seems to me, probabilize, the existence. 3. At the same time, of both. 4. So doing, I venture to propose a remedy, which, for reasons assigned, seems to me a promising one—and the only one which the nature of the case admits of, without some change in the whole judiciary system, such as in part has been, and with large amendments, will again be, submitted to the public, but which it would be altogether useless, as well as impracticable, to insert here.

Alleged evil 1.—Deficiency in appropriate aptitude. Here I take upon me to say *not proved*. Here I am all confidence. *Subpœna* in hand, I call on the Right Hon. Secretary. In No. 11. stands his evidence—'Present Police Magistrates' (per *Times*) 'of the highest personal respectability.' Per *Morning Chronicle*—'their knowledge, experience, and respectability'—(all 30 of them)—'and their services had already proved the importance of the duties they had to fulfil.' Per *Times*, again—'they performed their duties' (and *that* not only to the satisfaction of the Right Hon. Secretary, but) 'to the great satisfaction of the country.'

---

[1] Henry Addington (1757–1844), first Viscount Sidmouth, Speaker of the House of Commons 1789–1801, First Lord of the Treasury and Chancellor of the Exchequer 1801–4, Lord President of the Council 1805, 1806–7, 1812, Lord Privy Seal 1806, Home Secretary 1812–22.

[2] The qualifications of candidates for the police magistracy had not been regulated by law, but it had been the practice of both Sidmouth and Peel to appoint barristers of at least three-years' standing.

This being unquestionable, what is become of the evil, and what need can there be of a remedy?

What a scene is here! The Right Hon. Gentleman at daggers drawn with himself! How to account for it? One way alone I can think of, and it is this: the force of his eloquence overpowered his memory. While, with so much pathos, he was lamenting, on the part of a certain set of persons, the deplorable want of aptitude,—he forgot that, before he sat down, he had to deliver, in behalf of the self same persons, a certificate of accomplished aptitude. When at last the time had come for the delivery of this certificate, he had already forgot how large a portion of his speech had been employed in giving contradiction to it. To answer the purpose for which they are made, what must be the complexion of the assertions of inaptitude uttered with such entire confidence? They must be at once true and false: true, for the purpose of proving the necessity of the additional bonus; false, for the purpose of entitling these thus meritorious and actually existing persons (for this slides in *sub silentio)* to receive, before any of their future contingent colleagues have been in existence to receive it, a full share of the benefit of it. Admit him to be in possession of the power of giving truth to a self-contradictory proposition, the Right Hon. Secretary proves this his *probandum*, and thus far justifies his measure: refuse him this accommodation, he stands self-confuted, and his argument is somewhat worse than none.

Were ministerial responsibility anything better than a word, the task the Right Hon. Gentleman had charged himself with, was (it must be confessed) rather a delicate one. English punch, according to the Frenchman in the Jest Book, is a liquor of contradiction:[1] a compound of a similar complexion was that, which, on occasions such as the present, a situation such as the Right Hon. Secretary occupies, gives him in charge to mix up, for the entertainment of Honourable House. Except in the case of an underling whose character is too offensively rotten not to make it matter of necessity to suffer him to be thrown overboard, for all official men in general—high and low— there is but one character: a general character for excellence, tinged here and there with a little difference of colour, corresponding to the nature of the department. The idea looks as if it were taken from the old chronicles: where, with decent intervals, one portrait serves for half a dozen worthies: one town for the same number of towns, and so

---

[1] The source for this jest has not been traced, though Bentham explains the allusion more fully at UC clxvii. 222 (31 January 1821): 'We have an old jest-book story of a Frenchman's account of the English beverage called punch. There was the brandy to make it strong; there was the water to make it weak: there was the lemon juice to make it sower; there was the sugar to make it sweet: in a word, it was the liquor of contradiction.'

as to battles and executions. Time and labour are thus saved. This universal character puts one in mind of an ingenious document I have seen, sold under the title of the Universal Almanac. A copy of it has been supposed to be bound up with every Cabinet Minister's copy of the Red Book. Like a formula for convictions, it might be inserted into each particular, or into one general Act of Parliament. Subscription to it, and oath of belief in it, in relation to all official persons whose salaries had risen or should hereafter rise to a certain amount, might be added to the Test and Corporation Acts:[1] and, without need of troubling the legislature, Lord Chief Justice Abbot,[2] or Lord Chief Justice Anybody, would hold himself in readiness to fine and imprison every man who should dare to insinuate that any such person that lives, or that ever has lived, or that ever shall live, is, has been, or ever can be, deficient in any one point belonging to it.

Without violation of this standing *character rule*, he saw how impossible it was, that any the slightest shade of inaptitude, actual or possible, in any one of its modes, could be laid upon the character of any one of the existing incumbents. 'With the character of all of them, all who heard him,' (see No. 11.) 'were acquainted.' Remain, according to Parliamentary usage, the only persons with whom any such liberty could be taken—their future-contingent, and thence as yet unknown successors.

Here however comes something of a difficulty. Evil as above—disorder as above—inaptitude in some shape or other: remedy as above, of the preventive stamp, the 200*l.* a year. Good: supposing disorder or danger of it. But where is the room for it, where there is neither the one nor the other? Sole reason, the word *invidious*.[3] Invidious it would be, and that being the case, 'poor economy'—'so poor,' (says No. 8.) 'that there could not be a worse'—to refuse to those gentlemen whom every body knows, that which will be given, to those of whom, without disparagement it must be said, that they are gentlemen whom as yet nobody knows.

So much as to *aptitude:* and the alleged, and by the same person at the same time denied, deficiency in it. Remains as another, and the only remaining subject-matter of deficiency, the article of *time*—time employed in official attendance. This, too, is another delicate topic. Standing so near to aptitude, and, in particular, to the moral branch of

---

[1] The Corporation Act of 1661 and Test Act of 1673, which required the swearing of oaths, in principle excluded non-Anglicans from public offices, though in practice annual indemnity acts were usually passed in favour of Protestant Trinitarians. The Acts were repealed in 1828.

[2] Charles Abbott (1762–1832), first Baron Tenterden, Justice of Common Pleas 1816, Justice of King's Bench 1816–18, Chief Justice of King's Bench 1818–32.

[3] This word does not in fact appear in the reports of Peel's speech.

it, nothing determinate in relation to it could be hazarded: allusion, insinuation, yes: but nothing that applied to any body. 'Great increase of population.' (No. 1. *Morning Chronicle*) 'The duties of the office would require constant attendance' (No. 5. *Morn. Chron.*)—'almost constant attendance.'—(No. [5].[1] *Times*.)—Hereupon comes the same troublesome question as before. This constancy of attendance, is it not then paid by the present gentlemen? Answer, as before, yes and no: and, to secure it at the hands of their future colleagues and successors, comes the necessity of the same sweet security—the 200*l.* a year: this 200*l.* a year to be given, and without condition, not only to those unknown persons, but moreover, and in the first place, on pain of hearing the word 'invidious,' and bearing the stigma of 'poverty,' given also to the existing Gentlemen, in whose instance there is so much, and so little, need of it.

So much for the Right Hon. Secretary's two evils, and his proof of their existence. Now for his two ministerial remedies in aid of the 200*l.* a year parliamentary one:—1. exclusion of all but Barristers; 2. exclusion of all Barristers but three-year old ones. Problem, which his rhetoric or his logic, or what is sometimes more powerful than both, his silence, has undertaken for the solution of—how to prove, that, by these two exclusions, added to the 200*l.* a year,—appropriate aptitude, moral, intellectual, and active, adequate to the situation, together with adequate plenitude of attendance, will be produced.

By this policy, he secures, to this class of his *protegés* the aptitude, proved by the right to the name of *Barrister*. Now then what are the qualifications, the sole qualifications, of the possession of which any proof whatever is given by the right to bear this name? Answer: Being of full age; payment of a certain sum in fees and taxes, and, on a certain number of days sprinkled over a surface of five years, eating and drinking in a certain place, or therein making believe to eat and drink. Sum: between one and two hundred pounds; place, the hall of an Inn of Court; number of days, twenty in every year; total number of days, a hundred. As to the *making believe*, this option must not be omitted: nor yet the hour—four, or half-past four; for neither the hour nor the fare accord well with the taste of the class of persons for whom, it will be seen, the 800*l.* is destined.

As if this security were not strong enough, now mounts another upon the shoulders of it. After five years employed in the above exercises, then comes a *repose* of three years more; for not less indeed than these three years more, must this class of the Right Hon. Secretary's *protegés* have borne the name of *Barrister:* but, as to the

---

[1] 1825A, 1825B, 1830 '4'. 1825A, 1830 omit closing speech mark following 'attendance.'

exercises of eating and drinking, if it be agreeable to the gentleman to perform them, he is no longer burthened with any limitation in regard to place. The Right Hon. Minister in the pathetic part of his speech (No. 4.) asks a question: May logic, in the person of an obscure individual, be permitted to do the like? Comparatively speaking (for I mean nothing more)—service for five years, (the usual time), as clerk to an attorney, would it not be a security, though not so dignified, somewhat more efficient? The clerk could not be altogether ignorant of law without his master's suffering for it. The master, therefore, has some interest in causing him to learn it; the clerk, in learning it. But more of this further on.

The security is of Lord Sidmouth's invention: so his Right Hon. Successor assures us: and much inferior authority might have sufficed to command belief. It is just the sort of security, that the genius of his Noble and Learned Oracle,[1] or of Mr. Justice Bailey,[2] or of Mr. Justice Park,[3] might have devised: of all these luminaries the collective wisdom was perhaps expended upon it. For all these luminaries, the name of barrister, with three years' wear of it, was security sufficient: and, if he is sincere, Lord Sidmouth's Successor looks no deeper than to names.

So much better in their eyes is a nominal security than a real one, that when a real one offers, it is deliberately put aside. (No. 6.)

The design of the Right Hon. Secretary found the class of country gentlemen standing in its way: a class, before which Ministers, not to say Kings themselves bow, was not to be lightly dealt with. Something in the way of compliment to them was indispensable; the compliment, however, was unavoidably of a somewhat ambiguous character, as, not being eminent lawyers, they could not serve the purpose. Inaptitude on their parts, relative inaptitude at least, it was necessary should somehow or other be insinuated.

As to this matter, if *absolute* inaptitude would content the Right Hon. Gentleman, my feeble suffrage would see no very cogent reason against joining itself to his: but, as to comparative inaptitude, in the case in question,—comparative in relation to his three years old, and theretofore *perhaps*, eating and drinking Barristers, so far I cannot go with him. For, not only country gentlemen at large, but country Magistrates—nay, and such country Magistrates as have been in use to perform—and that for whatsoever length of time—the duties of this very office—such are those he puts from him. This being

---

[1] Eldon.
[2] Sir John Bayley (1763–1841), Justice of King's Bench 1808–30, Baron of the Exchequer 1830–4.
[3] Sir James Alan Park (1763–1838), Justice of Common Pleas 1816–38.

decided, for extinguishing all pretensions to appropriate aptitude on their part, the purpose of his argument required a dyslogistic epithet. *Routine* is accordingly the epithet, by which the whole of the business they have been accustomed to is characterised. Yet, make the least of it, it at any rate composes the greatest part of the business of the very office from which he is excluding them: one more look, and, as you will see that the business they have been accustomed to, has [been], in the instance of many of them, and may, if he will vouchsafe to adopt them, be, in the instance of all these children of his adoption, made to comprise the whole of it. Such being the candidates whom he puts aside as unfit for the business, what are the objects of his embrace? Three years old Barristers, altogether unused to business of any kind; unless eating and drinking, or making believe to eat and drink, is business. To a person who has never dined, or made believe to dine, at an Inn of Court hall, all this may seem exaggeration, to say no worse. *I* speak not only from observation, but from experience.[1] Such is my good fortune, never as yet have I been convicted of perjury: nobody has ever given me anything for saying this: my evidence is therefore good evidence; and it applies not less to the making believe to eat and drink, than to the actual exhibition of those so perfectly conclusive, and exclusively receivable tests of aptitude for the office of Magistrate. Thus the matter stood sixty years ago, and thus I am assured, by equally competent witnesses, it stands still. Let it not be said, the place being a law place, the conversation turns of course upon law. There being no conversation upon anything, there is no conversation upon law; for, unless you happen to be already acquainted with him, you have no more conversation with your messmate, than if he were at the antipodes.

To complete his demonstration of the superiority of his three years old Barristers without any experience, to a quondam country Gentleman with thirty years of appropriate experience, the Right Hon. Secretary brings exemplification from the Building Act,[2] and tells Honourable House of a case under it which (says No. 7.) had occupied 'a couple of days, during which surveyors had been examined on both sides.' Now, in a case of this sort, what is there that should render even an experienced Magistrate less competent than an equally experienced Barrister? What has it to do either with equity or with common law? Country Magistrates, who, not a few of them, are themselves builders—who, all of them, are accustomed to order buildings

---

[1] Bentham had been admitted to Lincoln's Inn in 1763, and called to the bar after reaching his majority in 1769. He lived in chambers in Lincoln's Inn from this date until 1792 when he inherited his father's house in Queen's Square Place, Westminster.

[2] 14 Geo. III, c.78.

to be built—built with perhaps a little of their own money, and sometimes with rather too much of other people's—what should hinder them from being at least as well conversant with the subject, as the most learned inhabitant of Lincoln's Inn Old-buildings? Here, for law is an Act of Parliament, nothing more: for fact, evidence about something that should or should not have been done under that same Act. The *days* thus employed, what would they have been to the purpose, if, instead of two, there had been twenty of them?

At the winding up of his speech, (No. 10.) to place above all contradiction the indispensableness of the 200*l.* a year, comes a trope—the word *refuse*—which seems to bid defiance to all endeavours to descry anything in it beyond the intensity of the desire to give birth to the indispensable effect.

Barristers—all Barristers in the lump—are, by this figure of speech, divided into two classes: those who will serve for 600*l.* a year, and those who will not serve for the 600*l.* but will for the 800*l.* As to the meaning, it is indeed intelligible enough: not so, by any means, the grounds of it. That it were so is, however, rather to be wished: for, those—all those, who would be content that the [200]*l.*[1] a year, public money, which the Right Hon. Secretary is thus buying creatures with, should be saved—all those, Barristers as they are, are branded with the common name of *refuse*. Such is the contempt, the undisguised, the thus loudly proclaimed contempt, in which sincerity, I mean always comparative sincerity, is held by this one of our head guardians of public morals. Insincerity is among the qualities professed to be possessed by Barristers: the only one which is sure to be possessed by any of them. Now then, true it is, that no reason can be alleged for supposing, that, so far as *disposition* goes, those who get least business are behind-hand in this endowment, with those who get most: but disposition is one thing, practice is another: and the less a man has manifested of it, the more deep-drawn is the contempt which he receives on his head at the hands of the Right Hon. Secretary, from the bucket lettered with the word *refuse*.

Meantime, here stands a strange mystery. Refuse—were there ever such a plenty of it, would the hand of Mr. Peel pick it off the dunghill, and place it on high—this refuse? Forbid it, consistency, at least. For who is it that prophecies it of him? Is it not Mr. Peel himself? But shall he be suffered thus to deal by himself? Shall Amyntas murder Amyntas?[2]

---

[1] 1825A, 1825B, 1830 '600'. Presumably Bentham meant to say £200, since this is the amount which would be saved by employing barristers who would serve for £600 per annum.

[2] The quotation occurs in *The Lamentations of Amintas for the death of Phillis. Paraphrastically translated out of Latine into English Hexameters, by Abraham Fraunce*, London, 1596, iv. 26. This

One possible solution remains, and but one. On the part of a Barrister, willingness to serve in the office of Police Magistrate for so little as the 600*l.* a year, is not merely evidence of his inaptitude for that office, but conclusive evidence. This meaning, however strange, being intelligible enough,—we have thus far something tangible to examine. For, supposing none but refuse willing to serve, refuse he must take up with, or have none: and thus, it being Hobson's choice, there is no inconsistency either in his making it, or in his avowing the making it. But suppose enough willing who are *not* refuse, what matter is it how many there are who *are* refuse? Will he, then, having good and bad before him, both in plenty, take in hand the bad, putting aside the good?

The stock of difficulties is not yet exhausted. Comes now a point for him to settle with certain gentlemen. Of the thirty gentlemen at present serving in this situation, *four* I see, who, by his own account (No. 11.) are serving, and for these three years, or thereabouts, have been serving, at the low price. None of them, I hope, were born in Ireland, or in the United States: if yes, there may be danger in the case. 'Sir (they may say to him, one after another) do you mean to call me *refuse*?' One consolation is, that refuse, as according to him they are (as per No. [10].)[1] they are not the less included in his certificate (No. [10].)[2] of universal aptitude. This, with the assurance of the additional 200*l.* may, it is hoped, soften them. Was it for this that the 200*l.* was extended to those, in whose instance experience, if he is to be believed, has demonstrated that for any other purpose it was not needed?

One lumping assumption there is, upon which the whole strength of his argument rests. Faintness of prospect, such as to induce a man in the profession to take up with 600*l.* a year certain, charged with moderate labour, is conclusive evidence of his not being fit, either for the profession of Barrister, or for the office of Police Magistrate. How brisk are the Right Hon. Secretary's conclusions! Involved in the assumption is this—that all who have not actually a certain quantity of the business in question, or at least a strong assurance of it, are unfit for it. Now then how stands the matter in point of fact? In a prodigious degree more than any other, this profession is always overstocked. In this same profession, the quantity of business that shall be deemed sufficient to produce a refusal of the office, with the 600*l.* a year—let the fixation of it be left even to him—for one who is in possession of it there may be two, or more likely a much greater multiple of one, that

was a translation of Thomas Watson's Latin poem, *Amyntas*, which had been published in 1585, itself based on Torquato Tasso's play *L'Aminta*, written in 1573 and published in 1580.

[1] 1825A, 1825B, 1830 '1'.
[2] 1825A, 1825B, 1830 '6'.

are *not* in possession of it. Here then, according to his own reckoning, for one who is *not* refuse, there will be the two, the three, the half dozen (where shall we end?) who *are* refuse: and yet, as above, of this refuse, for aught he can know, numbers there are in any proportion, whose aptitude is at the highest pitch, and who yet, if they have either common prudence, or disposition to follow so many examples as are before them, will not disdain to pick up the supposed disgraceful pittance. Let me not be accused of taking an undue advantage of an unguarded word. Substitute the tamest word the language furnishes, the arguments remain the same.

Mean time, who does not know that there are certain points of aptitude, in respect of which a man may be very indifferently qualified for making his way at the bar; and yet, perhaps, be but so much the better qualified for the exercise of the functions of the office in question, being, as they are, with Mr. Justice Bailey's leave be it spoken, the functions of the judge.[1] Rhetoric is the leading talent of the Barrister; logic, of the judge: and between the two, the strife is not much less fierce than, according to the poet, between liberty and love.

Be this as it may, almost every body knows—and a man must be a Secretary of State, or at least a Cabinet Minister, not to know—that in this profession, above all others, success depends upon accident, at least as much as upon aptitude:—that it has for its proximate cause a certain opinion in the heads of attornies: and that, if external circumstances, altogether independent of inward endowments, do not concur in the generation of this opinion, a man may unite the rhetoric of a Murray[2] with the logic of a Dunning,[3] and, at the end of a long life, die, like Serjeant Kemble the Reporter, without ever having clasped, to his panting breast, the blessing of a brief.[4]

Nor yet are we out of our wood. For, still remains one topic, to thicken the perplexity. It is that of the *length of standing*—the yet remaining one of the three branches of the Right Hon. Secretary's security for aptitude. To render a barrister an object of his choice, three years (says No. 3.) must be his length of standing. Now then of the number *three* thus applied, what was the design? to extend the number of admissible candidates, or to narrow it? The too young or the too old—for the exclusion of which of these unapt classes was it

---

[1] For Bayley's distinction between police offices and courts of justice see pp. 187–8 below.

[2] William Murray (1705–93), first Baron and first Earl of Mansfield, Chief Justice of King's Bench 1756–88.

[3] John Dunning (1731–83), first Baron Ashburton, Solicitor General 1768–70, Chancellor of the Duchy of Lancaster 1782–3.

[4] Joseph Keble (1632–1710), a barrister who had no practice, but who had occupied himself by producing reports (considered in Bentham's time as worthless) of cases in King's Bench.

intended? The too young—says the wording, abstractedly considered: the too old—says the word *refuse*, and the sort of argument conveyed by it. For, these are they, who, by their willingness to accept of so low a price as the 600*l.* have given the requisite proof of inaptitude:—of their despair of Barrister business;—and consequently of their inaptitude for the office of Police Magistrate. Thus incompetent (says the argument) are the old Barristers run to seed.—Turn now to the three year olds. In the breasts of all this blooming youth, no such self-condemning and inaptitude-proving despair, can have had time to form itself. At this short standing,—unless here and there a special pleader, who has shown himself by practice under the bar, be an exception,—no practice, no expectation—consequently no disappointment.[1] Expectation! How should there have been any? After these three years, how long (shall we say) continues the time for *junior openings*, which require nothing but a few words got by heart, and half-guinea *motions of course*, which require not even that?—sources not furnishing, upon an average, the tenth part of the supposed disdained 600*l.* Now then comes the comparison. To these men, in whose instance, by the admission, or rather by the assertion, of the Right Hon. Secretary, the probability is, that they have had no appropriate experience worth mentioning,—to these men is to belong the exclusive chance of being chosen for the office: while those, who may have appropriate experience, in any quantity not incompatible with the choice of 600*l.* a year for life, charged with the already very moderate, and naturally still decreasing labour, which will be seen presently,—are for that reason to be regarded as being proved in hopeless degree unapt, and on that ground are to be excluded from all chance.

'But you have forgot' (says somebody) 'the wonder-working 200*l.* a year.'—Not I indeed. But, forasmuch as, in the case of the three year olds, it is to create aptitude out of nothing,—I see not why it should find less difficulty in creating it, in the instance of the twenty or twenty-three year olds, to whose stock of the requisite materials no limitation can be assigned, short of that which is applied by an assurance of more than the 600*l.* a year by professional practice.

To prepare Honourable House for the reception of the above logic and the above rhetoric, Right Hon. Secretary sets out, I see, with history. Original salaries, 400*l.*; result per *Times* (No. 2.) 'incompetence:' per *Morning Chronicle*, 'total incompetence.' Cause and proof of the incompetence, manifest: out of twelve (the original

---

[1] 1825A, 1830 'disapointment.'

number) barristers, no more than *three*.[1] Being Barristers, these three should naturally have produced a five-and-twenty per cent. discount from the totality of the incompetence; but *perhaps* they were of the *refuse* sort: and grant him but this, the exception, being thus only apparent, gives strength rather than weakness to his sweeping rule. Here too sincerity compels me to be totally recalcitrant: major, minor, conclusion—to nothing can I accede. Incompetence, neither proved nor probabilized: power of the first 200*l.* a year to increase competence (supposing a deficiency of it) denied by me: supposing it admitted, need of the proposed second 200*l.* a year for producing competence, denied again: the actual production of it having been so triumphantly proved by me, as above: proved by the most irrefragable of all testimony—his own evidence.

Proof of the incompetence of the original nine,—*non-Barristership.* With so concise, and at the same time so satisfactory a proof, especially to the Barrister part of the audience,—at this stage, of his history in union with his logic, the Right Hon. Secretary might perhaps have done as well, had he not only begun, but ended: not much strength, it is believed, will either of these his supports, receive from the particulars. The year of the establishment being 1792,—the nine are all of them, by this time, gathered to their fathers; indeed, the Right Hon. Gentleman's urbanity considered, the sentence thus passed on them proves as much. From such a quarter, a more drastic condemnation,[2] unless it were by the word *refuse*, can scarcely be imagined. But they had not risen (poor gentlemen!) to the rank of those, the feelings of whose surviving relatives can make claim to the protection of Lord Chief Justice Abbott;[3] and, if they had, it is not against a Secretary of State, nor even against a member of Hon. House—speaking in his place—that it could be afforded.[4] Instead of the sweet satisfaction of seeing fine and imprisonment inflicted on the gainsayer,—they must therefore, under their affliction, put up with such poor support, as an obscure and unpaid ex-Barrister of the refuse class has it in his power to give.

With an exception (of which presently) of no one of the devoted nine do I remember anything. The sort of *character evidence* which I

---

[1] The Metropolitan Justices Act of 1792 had in fact provided for a total of seven new police offices (in addition to Bow Street), each of which had three stipendiary magistrates, giving a total of twenty-one. Peel had presumably only extended his enquiries to a small proportion of them.

[2] 1825A, 1830 'condemation,'.

[3] An allusion to the prosecution of John Hunt for libel discussed at pp. 189–90 below.

[4] Parliamentary privilege exempted members of the House of Commons and House of Lords from liability for any words spoken in their place in Parliament.

have to adduce for them, is therefore none of it of that sort which is called *direct:* none of it more than *circumstantial*. Nor is it the worse for being so; for, as applied to character, the value of direct evidence, unless it be from some such person as a Secretary of State, may be judged from what is above, although it is from a Secretary of State.

To return to the history.—In regard to appropriate aptitude (*competence* I cannot keep to, since it includes, not to say exclusively denotes, acceptance at the hands of those to whom inaptitude is a recommendation)—in regard to appropriate aptitude, the question is between the nine defunct and reprobated original Magistrates, and the Right Hon. Secretary's Magistrates in *petto* or in *embryo*—his three year old Barristers. Of these, as yet unborn babes of grace— offspring of the imagination of the Right Hon. Secretary, the title to the quality of aptitude has been already disposed of: circumstantial evidence and proof presumptive of inaptitude,—want of experience in business, or more shortly—their not being *men of business*. Now then for my nine clients. The Right Hon. Secretary's list of them (No. 2.) has been seen: Major, one; Clergymen, three;—(oh fie! what after the Major?) Starch Dealers, two; Glasgow Trader, one. Now, with the exception of the three Clergymen (whom I shall leave to those so much more efficient advocates, of whom no gentlemen of their cloth can ever be in want—Magistrates for whom I cannot find any tolerable presumptive evidence of their having been men of business in any way)—of all the others I am bold to affirm that they had been men of business.

I will go further, and add,—nor is there any one of those occupations, experience in the business of which does not afford stronger presumption of aptitude—even in relation to the business of the office in question, than can be afforded by an utter want of all experience in any kind of business. The Major, being a Major, must have passed through the several grades—Ensign (or the equivalent) Lieutenant, Captain: and, in all of them, if commanding men by scores and hundreds is business—he must have been a man of business. The Starch Dealers, they too must have been men of business; for, buying and selling starch is doing business: and in that business, with whatever degree of success, they could not but have been exerting themselves, forasmuch as their subsistence depended upon it. All this too, in addition to their having been *bonâ fide eating* as well as *drinking;* to wit, from the hour they gave up the nipple, down to the time of their appointment; which is rather more than can be alleged in favour of the aptitude of the Right Hon. Secretary's *protegés*, unless it be the difference between the performing of those exercises at a man's own home, and the performing them in the hall of an inn of court: which difference, I cannot bring myself to regard as constituting, to the purpose in question, a very material one.

I come lastly to the Glasgow Trader. Being a trader, he too must have been a man of business. As such I might leave him; but, it having fallen in my way, to know in what ways, and in how conspicuous a degree, with reference to the business of this very office, he proved himself a man of business, I shall venture a few particulars. This man was *Patrick Colquhoun:* and, unless destroyed by the comparative smallness of his remuneration, his relative aptitude has stronger, as well as more incontrovertible proofs than can, I trust, be produced, not only by the Right Hon. Secretary's unknown *protegés* in embryo, whom even I look down upon as so many chits,—but even by the whole of the actually existing Barrister-Magistrates, produced by the additional 200*l.* a-year, to whom I make my bow, whoever they may be. Treatise (I mean) on the Police of the Metropolis, Treatise on Indigence, Treatise on the Office of Constable—and for ought I know, others (for I have not time to hunt for them) bearing most directly upon the business of this very office. As to the first mentioned—of the number of its editions I am afraid to speak, not having the last before me: the fifth, which I have in hand, is as early as 1797, and there must have been several others after it.[1] Into the merits of them I cannot afford to enter, this paper not being either a *Quarterly*, an *Edinburgh*, or a *Westminster Review:* nor, if I could, could I venture to put my judgment in competition with the single word *incompetence*, from the lips of the Right Hon. Secretary. I must leave them therefore to that evidence: and, if that evidence be not more probative, than any which the Right Hon. Secretary has adduced in favour of his future *protegés*, or even in favour of their existing predecessors and intended colleagues, I must give up my cause.

Evidence of this sort in abundance must be omitted. One lot is too pointed to be thus dealt with. To this Glasgow Trader, whatever may

---

[1] Colquhoun (1745–1820) had established himself as a merchant in Glasgow in 1766, and as Lord Provost, a position he held from 1782 to 1784, had instituted the Chamber of Commerce in 1783. Moving to London in 1789, he was appointed as a stipendiary magistrate in 1792, serving first at Worship Street, Shoreditch, and from 1797 at Queen Square, Westminster, until his retirement in 1818. He was author, amongst other publications, of *A Treatise on the Police of the Metropolis; containing a detail of the various crimes and misdemeanors by which Public and Private Property and Security are, at present, injured and endangered: and suggesting remedies for their prevention*, London, 1796 (there had been a sixth edition in 1800, and a seventh in 1806); *A Treatise on Indigence; exhibiting a general view of the national resources for productive labour; with Propositions for ameliorating the Condition of the Poor, and Improving the moral Habits and increasing the Comforts of the Labouring People, particularly the Rising Generation*, London, 1806; and *A Treatise on the Functions and Duties of a Constable; containing details and observations interesting to the public, as they relate to the corruption of morals, and the protection of the peaceful subject against penal and criminal offences*, London, 1803.

be the value of it, was the public indebted for the first addition made to the number of those offices, and the Right Hon. Secretary for a proportionable part of the patronage, to the value of which he is thus labouring to give increase. It was the addition[1] made by the Thames Police Act 39 and 40 Geo. III. anno 1800 ch. 87. Of this business, it fell in my way not to be altogether ignorant. A bill was necessary. Colquhoun had found the facts. I ventured to supply the law. I drew the bill, leaving out as much of the customary surplusage as I durst. In the procedure clauses, for giving execution and effect to the law, I ventured as far as I durst, and further than any one had ventured before. Incompetent as the performance could not but be, coming out of such hands, change of hands rendered its competence unquestionable. At my humble request, a Learned Gentleman of the first distinction (I know my distance better than to mention him) received it into his, and without the change of a word, it became law.[2] The plan had been formed by Colquhoun, in conjunction with I forget what body of mercantile men, who wanted a sort of Board of which he was to be at the head. The Board they did not get: but a present of 500*l.* testified their sense of his competence with relation to police business.[3] Such was the nameless Glasgow Trader: his name would not have been quite so suitable to the Right Hon. Secretary's purpose, as it is to mine.

As to the three Clergymen, leaving the question, as to their incompetence, to be settled by the Hon. Secretary with the Archbishops of Canterbury, defunct and living, the Lord Chancellors, and the

---

[1] 1825A, 1830 'adddition'.

[2] In June 1798, Colquhoun had been prominent in the establishment of the Marine Police Office, financed partly by government and partly by the West India merchants themselves, in an attempt to stop widespread pilfering from ships engaged in the West India trade. Following its initial success, Colquhoun attempted to persuade the government to put the Marine Police Office upon a statutory footing and extend its benefits to the whole port. Bentham drafted a bill (the MSS for his 'Summary View of a Bill for the more effectual prevention of depredations on the Thames' are at UC cl. 118–24, and a version is printed in Bowring, x. 330–3) which he hoped his step-brother Charles Abbot (1757–1829), first Baron Colchester, Speaker of the House of Commons 1802–17, would introduce into the Commons. In the event, however, the Thames River Police Act of 1800 (39 and 40 Geo. III, c.87) was introduced on 11 June 1800 by Henry Dundas (1742–1811), first Viscount Melville, Home Secretary 1791–4, Secretary for War 1794–1801, First Lord of the Admiralty 1804–5. For Bentham's involvement with Colquhoun and Abbot in this matter see *The Correspondence of Jeremy Bentham*, vol. vi, ed. J.R. Dinwiddy, Oxford, 1984 (*CW*), pp. 155–65.

[3] At a meeting held on 15 August 1800, the West India merchants voted their thanks to Colquhoun 'for his constant and unremitted attention to the duties of the Marine Police Institution, which has been of material benefit in preventing the numerous depredations on the River Thames; for his great assiduity in preparing a Bill for the establishment of a Thames Police Office, which has received the sanction of Parliament', and asked him to accept a piece of plate worth £500 in recognition of his services. See Ἰατρος, *A Biographical Sketch of the Life and Writings of Patrick Colquhoun, Esq. LL.D.*, London, 1818, pp. 29–30.

several Lord Lieutenants, I proceed to the remaining one of the two evils, for which the second 200*l.* a-year, as provided by him, is to operate as a remedy. This is—the deficiency in the article of *time:* the deficiency, if any, present or future, in regard to the quantity of time employed, or eventually about to be employed, by the Magistrates in question, in the fulfilment of their duties.

On this evil the Right Honourable Secretary touches, it should seem, with rather a tender hand: allusion and insinuation, rather than assertion, are the forms of speech I see employed. (Per No. 1.) In the business 'great increase:' cause, ditto, partly in acts of parliament, partly in population. Triumphant tenders of papers in proof of all these facts,—to which might have been added the existence of the sun at noon day.

Of the existence of the thus delicately-assumed evil,—at the hands of the Right Hon. Secretary I look in vain for other proof. From that most authentic source, somewhat less explicit is the evidence I see to the contrary. It is that which has been already seen: it is made of stretching leather: it is wide enough to be applied to whatever can be desired. By the thirty gentlemen, (who, it has been seen, are at once so competent, and, for want of the 200*l.* a-year, so incompetent)— these duties, as per No. 11, are performed to the great satisfaction of the country; and this, notwithstanding that, as per No. [5],[1] to prove the necessity of the Barrister part, almost constant attendance, he says, is required. Required? Good. But *by whom* was it, or anything like it, ever required?—a question somewhat more easy to put than to answer. By any such attendance, or anything like an approach to it, the place would be spoilt, and no gentleman would accept it: acceptance would of itself be proof of incompetence.

Now then, forasmuch as, in this office, according to the Right Honourable Secretary's opinion, an 'almost constant attendance' is required, and accordingly forms part and parcel of its duties;—and forasmuch as, without exception, these same duties are, according to this his evidence, actually performed—performed not merely to *his* satisfaction, but to the satisfaction of the country:—forasmuch as, I say, evidence of the existence of this one of his two evils, is, notwithstanding the prodigious pile of papers, with the mention of which he at once alarmed and satisfied the House, still to seek;—for this deficiency, though it is not in my power to provide a supply, it is not, I flatter myself, altogether out of my power, humbly to point out a course by which he may obtain it. True or false, newspaper statement is unofficial statement: unofficial statement is not admitted in

---

[1] 1825A, 1825B, 1830 '4'.

evidence, even when no man in Honourable House doubts, or will venture to express a doubt, of the correctness of it. Honourable House knows better than to admit, through such a channel, anything, however well attested, in the character of evidence. Yet are such statements,—unofficial and incompetent as they are,—made use of, every day, in the character of indicative evidence, for the elicitation of acknowledged evidence. This premised, I shall venture to copy from a newspaper a portion of a paragraph: humbly observing, that in every one of the offices in question there exist various persons, from any of whom, if it be agreeable to know it, Honourable House, and in it Right Honourable Secretary may learn at any time, whether, in this same newspaper statement, there be any and what portion and degree of truth, and how far the actual agrees with their 'required constancy of attendance.'

'We believe,' says the *Globe and Traveller*, as quoted in the *Examiner* of March 27, 1825,[1]—'we believe a Magistrate attends at each of the offices from 12 to 3, and looks in again in the evening. There are three Magistrates in an office, so that this duty is imposed upon each of them *twice* a week. We know that there is some business for which the *presence* of two Magistrates is necessary; but it is to be recollected that at almost all the offices, *volunteer* Magistrates are frequently in attendance. We are convinced that a very large statement of the time each Magistrate needs be in attendance, is—every other day, three hours in the morning, and twice a-week, two hours in the evening.'

In regard to this evil, if anything that comes from so incompetent a quarter could be heard, I could, I think, do something towards tranquillizing the Right Honourable Secretary. Aptitude is not quite so easily secured as asserted. But *attendance*—the maximum of possible attendance—every master-man; how humble soever in condition— every master-man that really desires it, has it. To the extent of his desires, the Right Honourable Secretary has it in his own individual office. With the assistance of Honourable and Right Honourable House, to the same extent, he may have it in the instance of every other public office without exception. If, then, in any instance, and in any degree, he fails to have it, it is because he does not desire, not because he is not able, to obtain it.

You may maximize attendance, and you may minimize it. The maximization problem has been solved, and with illustrious success, in the case of the children of the indigent, when worked upon a steam

---

[1] The report originally appeared in the *Globe and Traveller* on 23 March 1825. There are some minor inaccuracies in the rendering of the passage.

scale. As some are killed off, others succeed: and capital—the one and the only thing needful—accumulates. Examined in his place, or elsewhere, one Honourable Member of Honourable House could give, on this point, if I have not been misinformed, instructive information. His name, if I mistake not, begins with a P.[1]

Those whose will it is to minimize attendance might, if in the above newspaper report there be any approach to truth, receive instruction, if it be worth while, by applying to another P, no less a P. than Mr. Secretary Peel. But it is not worth while: those who understand nothing else, understand this. Everybody, man and boy, knows how to be idle, every man knows what it is to stand looking on, and helping, while others are idle. Every man knows what it is to pay, as well as to be paid, for doing work, and all the while seeing and leaving it undone. Other arts travel at their different paces. Under matchless constitution, the art of sinecurism is at its acmè.

In my small way, I have a manufactory of my own, in which, with the same sort of instrument (imagination), with which the Right Hon. Secretary has manufactured aptitude in the instance of his three-year-old Barrister-Magistrates, and for my own amusement (as the half-retired chimney-sweeper swept chimneys) I make judges. My judges are judges of all work, and of all hours. They do not, it is true, sit each of them, every day in every year, and on every day, every hour of the four-and-twenty; but, in each judicatory they, following one another, do all this. *When sleeps injustice, so may justice too*, said a voice to me in one of my dreams. My muse is but a hobbling one:—she has not been to school to the Laureat's: the *too* is somewhat of a botch: but I remember her so much the better. In one thing I endeavour to copy the Right Honourable Secretary's noble and learned friend—it is the quality so judiciously selected for his eulogium—consistency.[2] The

[1] Presumably Peel's father, Sir Robert Peel (1750–1830), MP for Tamworth 1790–1820, who, though no longer a member of the House of Commons, had actively promoted legislation for ameliorating the working conditions of children in factories. He had been responsible for the Cotton Apprentices Act of 1802 (42 Geo. III, c.73), the establishment in 1816 of a Select Committee to investigate child labour in factories, and the Factory Act of 1819 (59 Geo. III, c.66), which prohibited the employment of children under nine years of age, and stipulated that children under sixteen should work for no more than twelve hours a day.

[2] In the debate on the address on the King's Speech in the House of Commons on 3–4 February 1825, Henry Peter Brougham (1778–1868), later first Baron Brougham and Vaux, Lord Chancellor 1830–4, suggested that Eldon would sacrifice all principle rather than resign from office. Referring to Eldon, Peel responded: 'Of that eminent individual he could not speak in terms of adequate praise. He believed his name would go down to posterity, as that of a man of great and exalted merits, and that notwithstanding the failings imputed by some men to some of his acts, he would go down to posterity as being the most consistent politician who had ever held the great seal.' See *Parliamentary Debates* (1825) xii. 63–5, 105–6. Peel's remark is noted at UC xix. 66, and a copy of a squib on Peel's words, which appeared in the *Morning Chronicle* of 8 February 1825, is at UC xix. 129.

ends to which my Judicial Establishment, and my Procedure Code, in conformity to the Constitutional Code to which they belong,[1] are from beginning to end directed, are the ends of justice: under matchless Constitution, the ends to which the Judicial Establishment is, and the Procedure Code, if there were any, would be, directed,—are the ends of Judicature. What these are, it is not for me to presume to inform the Hon. Secretary: over and over again he must have heard them, amidst peals of laughter, or floods of tears, from his Learned and matchlessly-consistent Friend, before or after the second bottle.[2]

Such being the bill—such the ostensible and declared objects of it—such the evils asserted or insinuated—such the remedies provided—such the arguments employed in proof of the evils, and in recommendation of the remedies—what, after all, is the real object? The topic must not be omitted: though to few of the readers, if any, whose patience has brought them thus far, can anything on this head be regarded as much more needed, than were the Hon. Secretary's proofs of encrease of population and acts of Parliament.

Loss, by waste of public money, is in every instance an evil: in the present instance, loss in the article of aptitude is, in my view of the matter, a still greater evil. To the augmentation of aptitude, perfectly inoperative will be the 200*l.* a year: not so to the diminution of it. 1,000*l.* a year is a salary for a nobly related puisne, at one of the highest boards. I am fearful of mistakes, and have no time for searches. When Red Books had the salaries to them, 1,000*l.* if recollection does not mislead me, was the number attached to the office of Puisne Admiralty Lord.[3]

In the heaven of office, there are many mansions.[4] Of a Police Magistrate, the station cannot be altogether upon a level with that of an Admiralty Lord: but the 200*l.* a year will raise the lower office to a level next below that of the higher one. To a reverend youth—even to one born honourable, a spiritual benefice yielding 800*l.* a year is not altogether an object of disdain: eased, as above, of labour, though not so perfectly as in the other case, why should even this temporal one? Without some improvement, *attendance* is a burthen the lay incumbent can not be altogether eased of: *thought* he may be eased of without difficulty. When two Magistrates are necessary, there must

---

[1] Bentham dealt with the judicial establishment in the projected third volume of *Constitutional Code* (see Bowring, ix. 454–647). For Bentham's Procedure Code, and its relationship to *Constitutional Code*, see 'Introductory View', p. 34n above.

[2] Eldon was known for his love of port.

[3] Bentham was perfectly correct: the last *Royal Kalendar* to include details of the salaries of the Lords of the Admiralty, that of 1812, gave the sum as £1,000 per annum.

[4] An echo of John 14: 2.

be a non-honourable to yield *thought*, but the honourable will serve as well as the non-honourable to yield *auspices:* when one Magistrate suffices, the dignity of the honourable man will need no disturbance. But, the only case, in which burthens so degrading to honourable men will require to be imposed, is an extreme case. Naturally speaking, there will in general be unpaid Magistrates enough, to whom, for the time and trouble of attendance, the power and the amusement will afford sufficient compensation. One of these *suppléans*, the non-honourable, takes care to provide, each time, for his honourable friend and colleague. Thus is the labour of the honourable minimized: and, sadly have his non-honourable colleagues been deficient in what everybody owes to his rank, if the quantity of time actually employed in official duties is anything more than an impalpable one.

Here then, in short, comes the effect and use of this second 200*l.* The first did not bring the place within the sphere of the highly-connected class: the hope is—that the second will: it will, at any rate, form a basis for a third.

> 'What makes all doctrines plain and clear?
> 'About two hundred pounds a year.'

So stood the matter in Sir Hudibras's time.[1] But now the 200*l.* must have an ever increasing number of others to mount upon.

Seldom, if ever, do I endeavour to overthrow, without endeavouring at the same time to build up. For maximizing the chance in favour of every thing needful, I have a recipe of my own, and that exemplified upon the largest scale; the principle of it will be found in another part of this volume, or in one that will soon follow it.[2] Alas! what hopes can there be for mine? It is the very reverse of the Right Hon. Secretary's. It may serve him at any rate to laugh at. *His* plan excludes experienced Magistrates, admitting nobody but nominal Barristers. Now then comes the laugh:—the most efficient and approved of House of Commons arguments. *Mine* admits nobody but experienced Magistrates; excluding Barristers, nominal and real all together.

My plan serves at once for aptitude and attendance. As to aptitude,—for *that* I require, as a qualification, previous admission into the Magistracy, and thereafter, unpaid, but constant and adequately proved attendance, at some one of the existing offices;

---

[1] Samuel Butler, *Hudibras*, III. i. 1277–8.
[2] Bentham presumably had in mind his proposal for pecuniary competition discussed in 'Extract from Constitutional Code': see *Constitutional Code*, I (*CW*), Ch. IX, §17, pp. 337–62. More generally, for his proposals regarding the necessary qualifications for judges see *Constitutional Code*, Ch. XII, §XXVIII, at Bowring, ix. 525–9.

attendance for a certain length of time, say five years: to wit, when from the commencement of the plan that length of time has elapsed, and till then for as great a length of time as can be had.

Now for a contrast, between my experienced Magistrates, and the Right Hon. Secretary's unfledged Barristers, adding, if so it please him, any number of grey-headed ones.

1. As to moral aptitude, my Magistrates will have been engaged in the exclusive support of *right*,—or at least of what the *legislature* has pronounced *right*,—and the exclusive repression of *wrong*,—or at least of what the *legislature* has pronounced *wrong*. His Barristers will have been occupied either in nothing at all, or in what is so much worse than nothing, promiscuous defence of right and wrong, with the universal predilection for wrong, as being the best customer.

2. As to intellectual aptitude, composed as it is of appropriate knowledge and judgment, my magistrates will, for the whole of their unremunerated length of time, have been employed, on the very spot, in study, and occasionally in practice, in the very field for which it is proposed to engage their remunerated services; in the whole of that field, and in no other than that field, to their consideration will have been subjected, in all their varieties, all sorts of cases which can have grown up in that same field. The Right Hon. Secretary's Barristers, with their 800*l.* instead of 600*l.* a-year—how will they have been occupied? My answer has been seen already. The Right Honourable Secretary's answer the country will be grateful for, if he can find any. But they may have been not only Barristers, but Barristers in full practice, and all the while not knowing anything more of the business of a Police Magistrate, than if they had been all the while fighting as army officers. Of practising Barristers there are about as many equity as common lawyers. Now in a Police Magistrate's practice, what is there that has any thing in common with equity practice? Let him bestow a glance on the Table to *Maddocks's Equity*, and then on the Table to the last edition of *Burn's Justice*,[1] or whatever work has now supplanted it, and see whether this is not strictly true. To those abstracts I venture in kindness to refer him, long as the road through may seem to be, as being shorter than through the mazes of his walking dictionary.[2] Those he might get by heart, sooner than an intelligible answer from his oracle; a negative the oracle would not venture to give, and an affirmative he would not choose to give.

3. Lastly, as to appropriate *active* aptitude. On the part of my

---

[1] See the tables of contents in Henry Maddock, *A Treatise on the Principles and Practice of the High Court of Chancery*, 2 vols., London, 1815, and Richard Burn, *The Justice of the Peace, and Parish Officer*, 2 vols., London, 1755 (a twenty-fourth edition, in five volumes, was published in 1825).

[2] i.e. Eldon.

Magistrates it would be a maximum. By every motive they would be impelled to render it so. At the hands of the Barrister, what his Right Hon. Patron does not require, is activity in any shape; all he does require, is existence.

As to attendance, and the means of securing it, to a great degree it is already comprised in the active aptitude just spoken of. But, in whatever possible degree he chooses to have it, he may have it if he pleases: nobody who does choose to have it, ever fails of having it. I will not attempt to trouble him with particular proofs, and they are already in one of my waking dreams.[a] In manuscript they are already in another or two, and will ere long be in print, if I live.[b]

This plan would suit both classes. The expectant stipendiaries would not be disinclined to attend, since it would increase their chance of the preferment; the existing stipendiaries would not be disinclined to be *attended for*, since it would increase their ease. How much soever superior the 600*l.* a-year ones may be, to their exploded predecessors the 400*l.* a-year ones,—were they to leave the burthen of the day altogether to the still superior expectants, if such they should prove, the public would not, any more than these same parties, have, in this quiet arrangement, any reason to repine. Ahab had served Baal a little. Jehu hath served him much.[1] What prospect have I not opened! What an Epicurean heaven! Thirty 600*l.* a-year places, and all sinecures! So many temporal Prebends and Canonries! With such a *pot-pourri* of sweet arguments, what is there that could not be proved? Laughable and delectable all this—true: but would it be the less beneficial? Not it, indeed.—See Horace's Reports. *Ridentem dicere*, &c.[2]

Suppose not that it is upon this 6,000*l.* a-year alone that all this examination has been expended. The expense is but as a drop in the bucket. The reasoning on which it is supported is no such trifle: if

---

[a] Draft of a Judicial Establishment for the use of the French National Assembly, 1790 or 1791: printed and distributed, but not sold.[3]

[b] 1. Constitutional Code, Judiciary part. 2. Procedure Code preceded by the Judiciary part of the Constitutional Code.[4]

---

[1] See 2 Kings 10: 18.

[2] Horace, *Satires*, I. i. 24–5, 'quamquam ridentem dicere verum quid vetat?' i.e. 'and yet what is to prevent one from telling truth as he laughs?' Presumably 'Reports' is a slip for 'Satires'.

[3] See 'Draught of a Code for the organization of the Judicial Establishment', Ch. V, Title III, §III, pp. 6–7 and Ch. V, Observations, §VIII, pp. 53–5 (Bowring, iv. 356 and 378–9), in 'Draught of a New Plan for the organisation of the Judicial Establishment in France: proposed as a Succedaneum to the Draught presented, for the same purpose, by the Committee of Constitution, to the National Assembly, December 21st, 1789', printed 1790 (Bowring, iv. 285–406).

[4] See p. 178n above.

good for 6,000*l.*, not less would it be for 60,000*l.*, for 600,000*l.* or 6,000,000*l.* More than even this might, if duly looked into, be seen perhaps to stand upon no better grounds. Be this as it may; by any one in whom curiosity is strong enough, it may be seen how admirable a match it makes with that, on the ground of which Burke for the Whigs, followed by Rose for the Tories, proved, as another part of this volume will show,[1] the necessity of draining, out of the pockets of the productive classes, the last drop of the matter of wealth that could be squeezed out of them, consistently with the continuation of their existence. Practice, it is true, cannot be always rendered altogether co-extensive with theory; but, whether the theory actually pursued as a law by Government, under the really existing form of Government, and under the fictitious entity, called the *Constitution*, is not the thing actually avowed by both parties, may be seen without other trouble than the turning over a few leaves.

Mr. Martin, if eyes or *Morning Chronicle*, April 2, 1825, do not deceive me,—Mr. Martin, of Galway, treading in the Right Hon. Secretary's steps, and, with a copy of the above speech, I presume, in his memory,—stands engaged, on the 12th of May, to extend his protection to Judges, and I know not what besides.[2] While his protection was confined to the helpless and persecuted part of the creation, I followed the Honourable Gentleman at an humble distance. But, if nothing will serve him but the extending it to those bipeds with gowns and wigs, instead of feathers, whom I had almost called v——n, which would have been as bad as *refuse*,—to those whose every-day occupation is depredation, and every-day employed instrument a lie,—here I feel it impossible to go on with him. Were it my good fortune to be honoured with his confidence, I would beg him to stop where he is, and not suffer a hand admired (and vainly endeavoured to be made ridiculous) for its beneficence, to be converted into a cat's-paw: let those (I would say to him) let those who are to eat the chesnut put paws upon pates, and beg for it.

---

[1] See 'Defence of Economy against Burke' and 'Defence of Economy against Rose', pp. 39–155 above.

[2] The *Morning Chronicle* of 2 April 1825 reported that Richard Martin (1754–1834), MP for Galway 1801–12, 1818–27, known as 'Humanity Martin', and one of the founders of the Royal Society for the Prevention of Cruelty to Animals (1824), had 'given notice of the following motion, for the 13th of May next:—"To Increase the Salaries annexed to the Great Officers of State, and to High Judicial Situations of the Country, so as to render them more adequate to the labour and importance of the duties to be discharged, and more worthy of the justice and liberality of the nation."' Martin sponsored several unsuccessful bills for the protection of animals in the 1825 session: on 24 February he moved for leave to introduce a Bear-Baiting Prevention Bill, and on 24 March and again on 5 May and 28 June amendments to extend the Cattle Ill-Treatment Act of 1823 (3 Geo. IV, c.71). The salaries of the judges were increased by the three Acts which are discussed in 'Indications respecting Lord Eldon', pp. 203–89 below.

Let me not be mistaken. When I had like to have said v——n, what I had in view were fee-fed Judges: the only sort, alas! which matchless Constitution has yet bred: men, to whom, and so much more than to the man of finance, we are indebted for the so little less than universal denial of justice. If, instead of adding, he would substitute salaries to fees, I would consent to shut my eyes against the amount, howsoever extravagant it might prove.

The fees to be compounded for would have been—not only the fee avowedly extorted, but the unhappily so much more abundant stock surreptitiously received: received by these so erroneously supposed uncorrupt hands. They would be—not only the fees exacted by superintendants in their own name, but all those exacted under their authority, by respective subordinate holders of offices, of which they have the patronage. For, who is there that does not know that an office in a man's gift has a no less decided marketable value than an office of the same emolument in his possession? True it is that, compared with the value of the possession, the value of the patronage may be to any amount less: not less true is it, that it may also be, and that it not unfrequently is, fully equal. Let Lord Eldon say, how much less worth to him the many thousands a year he has put into his son's pocket are, than if it had been his own? Let Mr. Peel, if he feels bold enough, look into the documents, and tell us, in his place, how many those thousands are.[1]

To the number of the offices, the emolument of which a man can pocket with his own hand, there are limits: to the number of the offices, the emoluments of which he can thus pocket through other hands, there are no limits; and, in any number of instances, the *protégé's* life may be worth more than the patron's.

Who is there that does not know, that the value of an office to the incumbent is directly as the emolument, and inversely as the labour? Who is there that does not know, that to the patron the value of it is directly as the inaptitude of the *protegé* he has it in his power to put in and keep in it, since the more consummate this inaptitude, the less his choice is narrowed? Who is there, for example, that does not know, that it is to the union of these two characters that spiritual offices in particular are indebted for their transcendent value? Who is there that can deny, that while this mode of payment lasts, interest is, in all Judges, at daggers drawn with duty?—that it is from this cause that suits take up as many years as they need do hours, and as many pounds as they need do pence?

---

[1] Eldon's surviving son, William Henry John Scott (1795–1832), MP for Heytesbury 1818–20, Hastings 1820–6 and Newport I.o.W. 1826–30, held sinecures worth about £3,500 per annum: see 'Indications respecting Lord Eldon', Postscript, §2, p. 279n below.

Who is there that can deny, that it is from this cause that our system of judicial procedure is what it is? and that, through the whole texture of it, Judges having been the manufacturers,—delay, expense, and vexation, have been maximized, for the sake of the profit extractible out of the expense?

Yes: by such hands made, to no other end could it have been directed.

The Chief Justice of the King's Bench, has he not the nomination to the keepership of the prison named after his judicatory? If so, then to the profits of the bench are added the profits of the tap: and the money which Justice would have returned to the hands of the creditor, is extracted, through this channel also, into the pockets of the Judge.

Same question as to other chiefships,—whether, as between one and another, consistency in this respect, or inconsistency, is the rule: also of that which is about to be squeezed by jailor out of debtors and creditors, how much is, in advance, squeezed out of him by Judge: questions these, none of them surely unfit to be put by Mr. Peel before he gives his support to the Advocate of innoxious beasts and pre-eminently noxious Judges.

Originally, though pregnant with depredation and oppression as it could not but be, payment by fees was matter of necessity: for judicature was necessary before kings had money to pay salaries.

For these three-and-thirty years past, it has been without excuse.[1] The corruption continued has been continued with open eyes.

When the trade of *trading Justices* was put an end to—(this was the name then given to Middlesex Magistrates)—it was undoubtedly for this same cause; it was because, in their small way, they made and protracted suits, for the purpose of multiplying fees.

When this small branch of the trade was put an end to, it was by the self-same remedy, I am now venturing, with how little hope soever, to propose. So far as concerned corruption, success could not be more complete. Salaries were [substituted][2] to fees, and in that form the plague ended.

When fees had thus given place to salaries, what disorder there was took an opposite turn. While the fees flowed into the judicial pocket, there was too much activity: now that, if any come in, they take a different direction, if report is to be believed (see above p. [176][3]) there is not enough of it. Lethargic not excitative is now the character

---

[1] That is, since the Metropolitan Justices Act of 1792 provided for the appointment of stipendiary magistrates, and the payment of fees to a receiver.

[2] 1825A, 1825B, 1830 'substitutes'.

[3] Presumably Bentham means to refer to the attendance of the police magistrates as reported in the *Globe and Traveller* and *The Examiner*.

of the disease. Beyond comparison more mischievous than the lethargic is the excitative, though when the specific is applied, so much easier to cure.

If in the case of the trading Judges called *Magistrates* the remedy was needful, how much more bitterly needful is it not in the case of the trading Judges called *Judges?* Look to mischief, profit, temptation, check: look to the two fields of mischief; take measure of their extent.

Under the *trading Justices*, the delay manufactured may be reckoned by *days:* under the *trading Judges*, by *years*.

Under the *trading Justices*, expense imposed on suitors may be reckoned by *shillings:* under the *trading Judges*, by hundreds and by thousands of pounds.

Of the jurisdiction of the trading Justices, local field, Middlesex, with or without the now added three other home counties;[1] of the trading Judges, England: lo[gi]cal field, in both cases, far too irregular for measurement. Chaos bids defiance to the theodolite: what is sufficient is—that in the case of the trading Justices, the sum of the scraps is a trifle, compared with what it is in the case of the trading Judges.

Under the trading Justices, the *profits* of the trade may be reckoned by *hundreds* a year: under the trading Judges, by more than as many *thousands*.

Honourable Gentlemen, will they always be so weak as to believe, or so transparently insincere as to pretend to believe, that while the temptation afforded by the *hundreds* was irresistable, the temptation afforded by the *thousands*, was, is, or can ever be, without effect? Mr. Peel,—does he believe this? His noble, learned, and consistent Friend,[2] who, if you will believe him, is purity itself,—does *he* believe this?

Honourable Gentlemen,—will they always believe, or affect to believe, that it is in the power of a masquerade dress to change man's nature, and that a contagion which a coat could not resist, has been, and is resisted by a gown with a strip of fur sewed to it? Mr. Peel,— does he believe this? The noble, learned, and consistent Friend, who is faith as well as purity personified,—does he believe this?

So much for mischief—profit—temptation. Now as to *check*, in one sense of the word, *responsibility*.

The trading Justices had Judges over them: Judges, by whom,—if haply, in an extreme case, money could be raised sufficient to buy a

---

[1] By the Act of 1792, the new stipendiary magistrates had jurisdiction in Middlesex and Surrey, but by an Act of 1821 (1 and 2 Geo. IV, c.118) their jurisdiction was extended to Essex and Kent.

[2] Eldon (see p. 177n above).

hearing for a cry for punishment,—they might be punished:—Judges, who, though not fond of punishing any man with a King's commission in his pocket,—might thereupon, by fear of shame, be peradventure driven so to do, if the case were flagrant.

The trading Justices had Judges over them. To any practical purposes the trading Judges have none: head of them all is the Lord Chancellor: head over himself is Lord Eldon: over Lord Eldon in Chancery, Lord Eldon in the House of Lords. Charge him with creation or preservation of abuse—of delay, expense, vexation, uncertainty,—motive, either none at all, or the profit upon the expense;—he names the inquisitors by whom the inquisition is to be made. The rehearsal of this farce has been performed.[1] When the curtain comes to be drawn up—if there be hardihood enough to draw it up—will the plaudits of a plundered people welcome it?

Remains still untouched the effective responsibility. Impunity wanted much of being complete in the case of the trading Justices: it wanted nothing in the case of the trading Judges. Here the word *responsibility* is mockery. Action, none: indictment, none: pretence of impeachment, a cloak: consistently with legislation, impeachment is physically impossible. Time would suffice for rendering it so, even if accusers were to be found, and where is the inducement for accomplices to become, some of them informers, others of them Judges?

Thus much for impeachment. Address of both Houses is impeachment under another name.[2]

Trading Justices never *made law*. The trading Judges have always made it, continue to make it, and, so long as the pretended lawmakers suffer them—which they find no small convenience in doing—will never cease making it.

Yes: made it they always have, and above all things for the sake of the trade. Accuse them—you do so in the teeth of a law made by themselves to punish you for it.[3] The counterfeit and Judge-made law is even more effectual than a real one would be: for, on each occasion, it is moulded at pleasure: moulded by those who, having made it for the purpose, execute it.

Were I to see a Judge taking a bribe—should I tell of it? Not I, if I had common prudence. The person punished would be—not the Judge for taking the bribe, but I for telling of it.

---

[1] Bentham's allusion is to the Royal Commission appointed on 26 April 1824 to enquire into the practice of Chancery. Eldon himself was one of the Commissioners.

[2] The Act of Settlement of 1701 (12 and 13 Will. III, c.2) provided that judges were to be appointed during good behaviour (*quamdiu se bene gesserint*), and that they could only be removed upon the address of both Houses of Parliament.

[3] Presumably an allusion to the Common Law offence of libel.

Thus, and hence it is—that, on the part—not only of all Judges, but of all whom they delight to favour—including all whom 'the King delighteth to honour'[1]—virtue is consummate, character immaculate.

But why talk of imaginary things, such as *bribes*, when by the real things, called *fees*—fees made lawful by those who pocket them—the work of corruption—of sure and self corruption—is carried on; carried on in open day—carried on without fear or shame—in the face of the so long plundered, and though so often warned, yet still deluded people?

No: never surely was grosser delusion than that by which English Judges are exhibited as models of uncorruption. In whatsoever shapes they could practise it without danger, they have always practised it: and of this practice, their system of procedure, composed of depredation and denial of justice, has been the fruit. Never (it is said and truly) never was English Judge known to take a bribe. No, verily, for how should he? Bribery requires two: a receiver and a giver. Receiver a man cannot be without putting himself into the power of the giver. Since Bacon, no English Judge has been weak enough to do so;[2] and so there can be no receiver. This is seen by every body: and so there can be no giver. What, in England, should induce a Judge thus to expose himself, when, without exposing himself, he gets more in abundance than, in any other country, Judge ever did by anything he could do to expose himself? What should induce him to take, of this or that man, with fear and trembling, money in the shape of a bribe,— when, by money exacted by taxes, levied on all men without distinction, by force of a law made by his predecessors, or perhaps by himself,—he is permitted, under the name of *fees*, to pocket more money than Judge ever received elsewhere in the shape of bribes? Give a man whatsoever he would steal from you, you may prevent his stealing it: whatsoever a man desires to exact, give him power to exact it *by* law, you may prevent his exacting it *against* law. Of this sort is the antiseptic, the infallibility of which has received such ample proof in the case of English Judges.

As to bribery so called, what is the real preservative against it? Publicity:—that most efficient and sole safeguard, which these incorruptibles ever have been, and even now, with the eye of the public full upon them, never cease labouring to destroy. A judicatory on

---

[1] See Esther 6: 4–11.

[2] Francis Bacon (1561–1626), first Baron of Verulam and first Viscount Saint Alban, Lord Chancellor 1618–21, having been accused of taking bribes, was impeached in 1621. Found guilty, he was deprived of office, imprisoned in the Tower and fined £40,000. James I (1566–1625), King of Scotland from 1567, King of England and Ireland from 1603, pardoned him and effectively revoked the fine, but did not again employ him in state affairs.

which life and death depend, is not (if you will believe Judge Bailey) is not a *Court of Justice*. Why? because if you will admit this, a certain quantity of nonsense, with the word *prejudging* in it, may suffice for keeping the doors of it closed.[1] Admit this, and you may see the doors of the Westminster Hall judicatories equally closed. Give them this, you may do anything with them: with as little ceremony they will be ready to give up their own title to the appellation of *Courts of Justice*. Were they so to do, no contradiction would the position receive from me: all I should object to, is the practical conclusion drawn from it.

With Lord Eldon you will have little difficulty. He has long been working at the change. So frequently open are the doors of his closet,—to shut the door of his hitherto mostly open Court, will be, one of these days, a motion of course. They may however be thrown open now and then, for occasions of parade: whereupon Bar will be seen arguing while Court writes dockets, reads letters, or takes a nap.[2]

A kindred and eminently convenient policy is—the giving to chambers of judicature such a size and form, that no *lay-gents* can find entrance. True it is that by this device, ingenious as it is, the guardian influence of the Public-Opinion-tribunal cannot be entirely destroyed; for lawyers cannot be altogether prevented from becoming writers, and betraying the secrets of the Court. It may however, by this means, be in no inconsiderable degree weakened. How much more effectual instruments of this policy brick and mortar are, than rules of Court can be, is no secret. All that rules could do, is the rendering admission difficult: properly placed, brick and mortar render it impossible.

[1] The question of the legality of reporting proceedings at police offices was raised in the case of Duncan v. Thwaites and others (the proprietors of the *Morning Herald*), heard in the Court of King's Bench on 26–7 October 1824. In the judgment delivered by Chief Justice Abbott on 29 November 1824, such reports were held illegal on the grounds that they might prejudice a future trial, and that police offices were not necessarily open like Courts of Justice, but might be closed by the magistrate whenever he thought proper. Bentham perhaps had in mind the remark made by Justice Bayley at the trial on 26 October 1824. In response to a comment by counsel that 'the question fairly arose, whether a true account of proceedings at police-offices, in open courts, might not innocently be given to the world', Bayley stated: 'Then they should be courts which ought to be open—which, by law, the public have a right to enter—and not courts which are only open by the sufferance of the magistrate.' (See *The Times*, 27, 28 October and 30 November 1824.)

[2] See Bentham's note at UC xix. 47 (28 December 1824): 'Per Pearson, Indian Advocate General, through Macculloch (per Mill to J.B.) Universally understood that Eldon made no secret of his displeasure when speeches were purposely shortened—the wish was that the length might be maximized—to give him time for reading and docketing letters.' Bentham's immediate source then appears to have been James Mill (1773–1836), the philosopher, economist and historian. Mill seems to have heard the anecdote from John Macculloch (1773–1835), doctor, geologist, botanist and chemist, who in turn heard it from John Pearson (1771–1841), Advocate-General of Bengal 1824–40.

English Judges incorrupt indeed! Those who talk in this strain, what is it they can mean by it? Did they ever see or hear of a Judge who was not completely at the *command* of the Corruptor-General?[1] Places for sons, daughters' husbands, nephews, nieces' husbands, friends, and friends' friends—and, to crown all, coronet for self—None of these things are bribes: true: but are they the less irresistible? Are they the less corruptive? But why speak of *command?* Far short of the real strength of the corruption—of the corruptive longings, and consequent courtings, and consequent compliances with presumed desires,—comes the view which that word gives of it. From any such superior, to any such subordinate authority, no such explicit expressions of will ought to be, none accordingly ever are, issued. Issued? To what end need they be? In a situation of that sort, is there a Judge, is there a man, that needs to be told, what will displease, and what will please? To stand assured with sufficient certainty, not a step need any man stir from his own *home*.

Take, for example, the case of John Hunt. Among the titles of Majesty in this country, is that of *most excellent*. John Hunt, in his *Examiner*, says things which go to impugn that title. Lord Chief Justice Abbot punishes him for this, with loss of 100*l.* under the name of fine, and 90*l.* under the name of *costs:*[2] *costs*, of which the Honourable House could know at any time, if it chose to know, whether anything, and if anything, how much, directly or indirectly, goes into the pocket of the Chief Justice.

Now, then, of the thus punished words, wherein consisted the mischief? Oh! says his Lordship, or somebody for him, the feelings of the King were hurt by them. Hurt by them? How so? This same hurt—how came his Lordship to be so sure of it? This said Majesty that now is—did he ever tell him of it? Did he bespeak any such punishment? No: the questions answer themselves. To be thus assured, his Lordship had no further to look than into his own learned breast, and there he saw them; for, in that repository of fine feeling, what he could not fail to see clearly enough is, that had it happened to himself to hear a man speak in any such strain of his Lordship's

---

[1] i.e. the King.

[2] John Hunt (1775–1848), editor of *The Examiner*, had published Byron's poem, *The Vision of Judgment* (written under the pseudonym Quevedo Redivivus) in *The Liberal*, i (1823), 3–39, a literary periodical edited by his brother, James Henry Leigh Hunt (1784–1859). Hunt was tried in the Court of King's Bench before Chief Justice Abbott on 15 January 1824, in a private prosecution brought by the Constitutional Association, for libelling the memory of George III, and injuring the feelings of George IV (1762–1830), King of Great Britain and Ireland from 1820, and other members of the Royal Family. He was found guilty, and on 19 June 1824 sentenced, by Justice Bayley, to pay a fine of £100 and give security for good behaviour for five years.

father, he would have been indignant, and not sorry to see the blasphemer punished.

By the King that now is, or by anybody for him, does Lord Chief Justice Abbot, or Lord Chief Justice Any-body, need to be told, that obsequiousness to crowns is the road to coronets?

So much for power and glory. Now as to money. If ever there was a judge, on whose incorruptibility the sound of the trumpet was loud, it was the late Lord Camden. His Lordship was Lord High Chancellor. His son, on pretence of telling out public money, got out of it an income, which, when he gave it up (a bow upon paper is due to him for it) was worth 27,000*l.* a year to him.[1] So much for corruptive intercourse, in a case in which it is not bribery. Now for a case in which it would be bribery. Seven-and-twenty guineas in hand, suppose George the Third saying to the Lord Chancellor—'In this suit (naming it) which I have against such an one (naming him) give judgment so and so, and I will give you these seven-and-twenty guineas,'—would his Lordship have taken it?—Oh, fie! fie! what a thought!—This would have been no better than bribery. Multiply the twenty-seven by a thousand—multiply the product by so many years as the income lasted,—and, though assuredly nobody said what nobody had any need to hear, all is consummate purity.

So much for motives, and the influence of them on conduct: to know which, for the purpose of legislation, which is the purpose *here* in question, never do I look to anything but *situation:* of individuals I know just nothing, which is just what I want to know. Now as to mischievousness. Of the law thus made, the effect is, and, if it had any, the object was, to establish punishment for everything that can tend to place in an unfavourable light the character of any King that ever lived; while the whole treasury of reward is applied to the purpose of placing those jewels in the most favourable light possible. Probative force of the evidence being in both cases the same, suppression of evidence in favour of one side, is in effect exactly the same thing as forgery of it in favour of the opposite side. Mischievousness of the practice the same in both cases; wickedness of it the same, though the people as yet have not sufficiently learnt to see it.

Keep in force this law, and with a steady hand give execution and effect to it,—the will of Holy Alliance is done, and history, from being the food, is converted into the poison of the mind. Yes, all history. First, as to the supposed injured dead. The protection granted to the manes of the third George, shall it be refused to those of the second,

---

[1] See 'Defence of Economy against Burke', Advertisement, p. 46n above.

or those of the first? If yes, at what point, if at any, in the line of ancestry, shall it end? Then as to the supposed injured living: if thus wounded by the aspersions cast upon his Royal Father, can the King that now is[1] be indifferent to any such, or any other aspersion cast upon his Princely Grandfather, his Royal Great Grandfather, or his first Ducal, then Royal Great-great-grandfather, &c. &c.?[2] If not, then up go we to Egbert[3] and to Fergus,[4] and so on, through Woden,[5] to Japhet[6] and to Adam.[7] At which of all these points does Royal tranquillity commence?—that degree of tranquillity which will suffice to render truth and history unpunishable?

In this case, by the bye, may be seen, as well as in so many hundred other instances, how much more useful *Judge-made* law is to Parliament itself,—constituted as it is, and looking to the ends which, so constituted, it cannot but look to,—than even its own *Parliament-law* could be made. Parliament itself, would it thus dare to destroy the truth of history, and cut up political science by the roots? But innumerable are the things of this sort which it does every day by the hands of Judges; and which fear or shame would keep it from doing by its own.

These things (unless the last-mentioned one be an exception) being so manifest, and so almost universally acknowledged to be true, that, on account of their notoriety, the very mention of them is fastidious,—what less can follow, than that to all purposes to which corruptness is to the greatest extent mischievous, a state of constant corruptedness is the state in which every Judge has been that ever sat upon the English bench?

In cases between King and subject, in which the mischief of it consists in giving countenance and increase to depredation and oppression, for the benefit of [the][8] Monarch, his associates, and dependents,—the disease is incurable: its root is in the form of government. But in suits between subject and subject, in which the mischief consists in giving countenance and increase to

---

[1] Respectively George III and George IV.

[2] Respectively Frederick Louis, Prince of Wales (1707–51); George II; and George I (1660–1727), King of Great Britain and Ireland from 1714, who had succeeded as Elector of Hanover shortly before succeeding to the British throne.

[3] Egbert (d. 839), King of the West-Saxons from 802, who extended his influence over much of England.

[4] Fergus Mor, son of Earc (d. 501), the first Dalriad King in Scotland.

[5] The Anglo-Saxon deity, from whom most of the Anglo-Saxon royal families traced their descent.

[6] Japheth, one of the sons of Noah, the supposed ancestor of the Aryan race.

[7] According to the patriarchal theory of government advanced by Sir Robert Filmer (1588–1653) in his *Patriarcha*, published in 1680, Adam, as the first man, was also the first monarch.

[8] 1825A, 1825B, 1830 'his'.

depredation and oppression by Judges (the present Judges at all times excepted, whatever they have been, are, or will be) for the benefit of Judges, their associates, and dependents, the disorder is not incurable.

A few words more as to the remedy, but for which the disease would not have here been mentioned. The principle has been seen. The public are indebted for it to Lord Colchester. His was the original Middlesex Police Magistrate Act, 32 Geo. III. c. 53, anno 1792.[1] Time enough for amendment, the Bill found its way, somehow or other, into my hands. Time for scrutiny I could not afford. My approval was pure and simple. Sheridan opposed it in Honourable House.[2] Objection, encrease of patronage—a Whig complaint, never grudged when non-redress is sure: a few words might have dissipated it, but they were words that could not be heard there. Subject of the objection—either the *source* of the delegated power, or the *quantum* of it. Applied to the *source*, the objection (an unanswerable one) went to the form of government; it applied to every part, present and future, of the official establishment: applied to the *quantum*, it supposed a certain quantity of corruption needful: and, as such, requiring to be protected from censure by the word *influence:* all above needless; and, that it might be game for the Whig hunt, licensed to be hallooed at by its proper name. Applied to every future addition to the establishment, the objection sought the exclusion of every good, to the introduction of which,—and the perpetual continuance and increase of every evil, to the diminution of which,—any such addition should be necessary.

No such desire as that of applying a bar to the increase—to the addition of corruption to influence—was really entertained. In Honourable House the disposition to keep influence within its bounds, whatever they were, had place or it had not. If no, objection to increase was useless: if yes, cancelling an equal quantity of sinecure would afford the same general security, without depriving the public of the benefit of the particular measure.

To return to the true remedy: it was a specific. In the Finance Committee of 1797 and 1798—the groundwork of such economy as the form of government admits of—Lord Colchester applied it, and

---

[1] Charles Abbot, later Baron Colchester, who was first returned to Parliament in 1795, had no involvement in the passage of the Bill, which was in fact introduced by Francis Burton (1774–1832), MP for Oxford, and seconded by the Home Secretary, Henry Dundas.

[2] Richard Brinsley Sheridan (1751–1816), the Whig politician and dramatist, spoke against the second reading of the Bill on 17 April 1792: see *Cobbett's Parliamentary History* (1791–2) xxix. 1182–3.

with success, to some of the Administration Offices.[1] It stopped there. Judicial corruption was in an ark too sacred to be touched. In both Houses, whatsoever was Learned would have been in a state of insurrection. Learned Lords were above shame. Ministers were not above fear: so there the reform rested.

Since then the public mind has made some advance: whether sufficient for the substituting of justice to depredation and corruption, time will show.

To return to Mr. Martin and his new *protégés*. By his humanity he got nothing but ridicule: from his liberality he may hope better fortune. No Honourable Gentleman, who, for self, son, brother, cousin, or friend, has ever refreshed his eyes with a glimpse of the remuneration fund, can consistently harbour a doubt of the insufficiency of it. Whigs form no exception: for, though possession is not theirs at any time, expectancy is at all times. In the maximization of expense, it unites them in interest with Judges. With what aspect they behold the County Courts Bill[2] may be seen without looking at their eyes. Saving to suitors would be robbery to these their protectors, while in the patronage they have no share. Everything they say against it,—everything they can seek to clog it with,—is a certificate in favour of it. A measure with this object cannot have a stronger one.

By this his liberating scheme, who knows how many supporters he may not have brought over for his humanity scheme? How profound soever their contempt for their betters (for, when educated, as they sometimes are, and always may be, quadrupeds have the virtues without the vices of featherless bipeds) how profound soever their contempt—how complete soever their indifference,—men's hatred for these animals, can it, to any considerable extent, be greater than their love for themselves?

As to his instrument of purchase—his announced vermin-gorging

---

[1] Abbot was Chairman of the Commons Finance Committee of 1797–8. Their Reports gave support to the extension of fee funds (see 'Defence of Economy against Rose', Advertisement, p. 97n above), and as a result of their recommendations the fees of Customs officers were converted into salaries (see *Commons Sessional Papers of the Eighteenth Century*, cxiv. 9–22).

[2] Following the production of the Report from the Select Committee on the Recovery of Small Debts (*Commons Sessional Papers* (1823) iv. 183–264), a Bill to enable the easier recovery of small debts through County Courts had originally been introduced into the House of Commons by the Chairman of the Committee, John Charles Spencer (1782–1845), styled Viscount Althorp, later third Earl Spencer, on 30 May 1823, but consideration of the measure had been put off on 11 June 1823. He reintroduced it on 23 February 1824, whereupon it passed on 24 May 1824, before being defeated in the Lords on 14 June 1824. Althorp reintroduced it into the Commons for a second time on 8 February 1825, where it passed on 19 May 1825. It was then reconsidered by the Lords, who eventually again rejected it on 21 June 1825. One of the points at issue was whether compensation should be paid to officers in the Court of Common Pleas whose fees would be diminished by the measure.

Bill—he could not have chosen a more promising one. This measure is of the number of those, which even an Opposition Member may be admitted to carry, and in which success can scarce be dubious. Reasons are ready stationed in each Honourable breast. They stand upon a rock; and *Calculation* is the name of it. What will my share of the annual charge amount to? A few half-pence a-year—what I toss now and then to a beggar to get rid of him when he is troublesome. Thus much on the debtor side: now, *per contra* creditor. So many more thousands a year for my son, my nephew, my cousin, or though it were but my cousin's cousin, when his time comes, which it can scarce fail to do, for taking his seat in a certain place. For, calculation being settled in the head, then, from hand or lungs, comes the substance of the universally-received economico-mathematical truism—official aptitude is in the direct ratio of ditto remuneration:—a proposition, which, to render it really true, requires nothing but the substituting to the word *direct*, the word *inverse*. Thereupon comes a flower or two, such as the Right Hon. Secretary's rhetoric has just been seen scattering over the subject:—virtue, displayed and appealed to, generosity: dignified virtue displayed, in the penetration manifested, by seeing through the cloud which the word *economy* (pronounced with a shake of the head—'*poor economy!*') had, in the head of vulgar ignorance, thrown over the question. Natural and customary result,—'hear him! hear him!' from all quarters. Is anything ever said on the other side? If yes, it is for form sake, with a sort of faint, and as if self-condemning tone, nor even this but under the most satisfactory assurance, that the measure will not be hurt by it.

While upon this ground, I cannot pass over altogether an error, for such I am persuaded it is, on the part of Mr. Peel, as to a matter of fact, and which remained unnoticed before because foreign to the purpose. In England, according to him (No. 8.) Judges are worse paid than 'in almost any other country in the world.' Not that, even if admitted, the fact would serve his purpose. It would run counter to his purpose. For, if not the only incorruptible, English Judges (so almost everybody has hitherto been in the habit of saying) are of all in the world the most incorruptible. Well then—this incorruptibility—forasmuch as by what you are paying for it you have got it already,—why pay anything more for it? This question would be unanswerable, were it not for the argument *ad verecundiam:*[1] men, who perform so charmingly, can you be so ungenerous as to let them serve at an under price, when it would be so easy for you to give them a fair price? The

---

[1] i.e. 'to modesty': see Locke, *Essay concerning Human Understanding*, Book IV, Ch. XVII, § 19, pp. 685–6.

argument is worthy of the nursery, and perhaps has been inherited from it. The child is gorged with meat, but spies out cake, and cries for it. 'Dear sweet poppet (says grand-mother to mother) can you be so hard-hearted as to let it cry on, only to save a little bit of cake?'

So much for argument: now for fact. Talking with a Frenchman t'other day on this subject, 50*l.* a year, he assured me—50*l.* and no more, is the salary of that class of Judges, by which by far the greatest part of the business is done. 'Well, but don't they take bribes?'—'No such thing. On the contrary, the country is universally satisfied with them:' just what we have seen the Right Hon. Secretary assuring us of, in the case of the 600*l.* a year Magistrates. The Right Hon. Secretary, having it in charge to find his 600*l.* a year insufficient, its sufficiency notwithstanding, had somewhat of a bias upon his mind. According to the Right Hon. Secretary, with these his 600*l.* a year Magistrates, the country is universally satisfied. But then, as has been seen, though satisfied, he is at the same time dissatisfied with them: and besides, their aptitude being to be proved as well as disproved, he had something of a bias, though a shifting one, upon his mind. The Frenchman had no such bias. He is himself neither Judge, Magistrate, nor Lawyer; nor patron, with reference to any who are. He is a man of estate, birth, and connection; and, though all that, a man of information and discernment. It did not occur to me to cross-examine him as to fees: but, as what we were talking about turned upon what was the whole of the emoluments, I cannot but think that if there are fees, they are fees of which neither the magnitude can be encreased, nor yet the number extended, otherwise than by the satisfaction afforded by good judicature; and that, if any at all, the 50*l.* does not receive from them any such encrease as would affect the argument. I for my part would not give for them another 50*l.*

This, though, if it were anything to the purpose, it might surely serve for enquiry,—is not official. What follows is. Printed 'Register of Officers and Agents, &c. prepared at the Department of State.' Date of Congress Resolution, 27th April, 1816. Printed anno 1818, at Washington, page 18.[1] Judiciary of the United States Supreme Court. Chief Justice, dollars 4000; not so much as pounds 1000. No Equity, put above Law, to stop and overrule it. Compare this with Lord Eldon's 23,000*l.* a year (those who make least of it make this) with so

---

[1] See *A Register of Officers and Agents, Civil, Military, and Naval, in the service of the United States, on the Thirtieth Day of September, 1817; together with the Names, Force, and Condition, of all the Ships and Vessels belonging to the United States, and when and where built. Prepared at the Department of State, In pursuance of a Resolution of Congress, of the 27th of April, 1816*, Washington, 1818.

many other thousands for his son;[1] not to speak of the thousands a year salaries of the minor and common law Chiefships, and Puisneships, and Masterships, besides the ever corruptive fees. Before the words '*every other country*' stands indeed, in one of the Reports of the Right Hon. Secretary's Speech, (No. 8.) the limitative word '*almost:*' let any one judge whether it was not a prudential one.

A thing more to be wished than hoped for, is—that, in the Right Hon. Secretary's situation and those associated with it, Right Honourable Gentlemen and Noble Lords were a little more careful than they sometimes are, when speaking to facts, especially distant and complex ones, such as those in questions like this more especially. By Lord Liverpool, not many years ago, if recollection does not greatly deceive me—by Lord Liverpool it was declared and insisted upon, that in this country (population for population he could not but mean) the expense of the Official Establishment was less than in the United States.[2] Proceeding in this strain, had he entered upon particulars, the King (he would have had to say) costs this country less than the President does the United States. So much for first Treasury Lord. Right Hon. Secretary—would he, after speaking upon the particular branch of the expenditure now in hand, as he has done—would he, after Parliamentary enquiry into the facts, consent to pay the Judicial Establishment upon the same scale as it is paid, in that country, in which, to use his own phrase, it is so much less parsimoniously paid than in this? Not he, indeed! What is it (he would then turn upon us and ask) what is it to the purpose, what people do in other countries?—in countries in which the state of things is so different from what it is in our own? Is it for us to receive laws from other countries?

In a Committee of his own nomination, will he be pleased to elicit the evidence by which the correctness of this assertion of his will be proved? He knows better things. What use (he would ask) is getting up evidence from which nothing is to follow? Lord Liverpool—will he consent to assign, to the whole Official Establishment, the same rate of remuneration as that which [has]³ place in the United States?—

---

[1] According to Eldon himself, his income as Chancellor at this time was about £9,000 per annum, and that of his son, William Henry John Scott, from his offices about £3,000 (see Horace Twiss, *The Public and Private Life of Lord Chancellor Eldon, with selections from his correspondence*, 3 vols., London, 1844, ii. 556).

[2] An exact quotation has not been traced, though Bentham may have had in mind Liverpool's comment, in a debate on the abolition of sinecure offices in the House of Lords on 27 May 1816, that, 'The fact was, that there was no country where the salaries of great officers were so small, or had been so little augmented, as in this country.' See *Parliamentary Debates* (1816) xxxiv. 812.

[3] 1825A, 1825B, 1830 'his'.

General Government and particular States always included. To no such insidious proposal would his Lordship give acceptance. His love for the people and for economy is too sincere, to suffer him to pledge himself to an innovation, from which the dear people would have nothing to gain and so much to lose.

On pain of ignominy, a helpless radical must maintain, whether he will or no, some caution in regard to his facts: were he to make a slip, he would never hear the last of it. High situation places a man at his ease in regard to facts. As often as occasion requires, he may let fly insinuations or assertions, such as the above, and thenceforward hear no more of them than he pleases. Should any unpleasant use of them be endeavoured to be made, up comes the rule: 'No allusion to anything said in a former debate.' Good, if responsibility be good for nothing: not so clearly so, if responsibility be good for anything. So far as regards facts, it is a counterpart to that mendacity licence, which, in Scotch Reform and elsewhere, has been held up to view as one of the pillars and main instruments of English Judicature.[1]

Throughout this examination, I have never been altogether free from feelings of compunction, at the thoughts of the sort of liberty all along taken with the Author of the Special Jury Bill. On the present occasion, I found him doing as, in his place, every body else has done. On that other occasion, I see him taking a course peculiar to himself. Time does not at this moment permit me so much as to read the Bill. I cannot therefore, on the ground of any opinion of my own, venture to say a syllable of it. But, if it does but completely substitute, as I am assured it does, *lot* to *packing*, and is in other respects what it has been certified to be, by those whose discernment and love of justice I stand assured of, it will, by this one measure, ensure to him a stock of popularity and public confidence, such as I tremble but to think of.[2]

Should this measure be carried through, he must however content himself, as well as he can, with the reputation of probity: for as for that of consistency, it will quit him, and seek refuge in its chosen seat,

---

[1] See *Scotch Reform; considered, with reference to the Plan, proposed in the late Parliament, for the Regulation of the Courts, and the Administration of Justice, in Scotland: with Illustrations from English Non-reform*, London, 1808, pp. 19–20 (see Bowring, v. 1–53 for the whole work, and Bowring, v. 11 for the passage in question), where the 'mendacity licence' is defined as, 'to parties on both sides, a general permission of falshood, granted by the Judge, to extend so far forth as may be necessary to the giving birth and continuance to *malâ fide* demands and defences'.

[2] On 9 March 1825, Peel had introduced a Bill to consolidate the law relating to juries. The subsequent Act (6 Geo. IV, c.50) required juries to be appointed by ballot in criminal cases, though a select jury in civil cases was allowed if requested by both parties. For Bentham's views on special juries see *The Elements of the Art of Packing, as applied to Special Juries, particularly in cases of Libel Law*, London, 1821 (Bowring, v. 61–186).

the bosom of his Noble and Learned Friend.[1] Consistency being where it is,—how anything of this sort should have found its way into the Secretary of State's Office, is the mystery of mysteries!

One word more as to patronage. On the present occasion, it is to the lessening the value of it to the Honourable Secretary that my endeavours, such as they are, have been applying themselves. Yet, so far am I from grudging him any good thing obtainable without preponderant evil to the community—in the case of the County Courts Bill, no desire a man in his place can have, for feeling the patronage of it in[2] his own hands, can be more sincere than mine for seeing it there. Supposing the situation equally acceptable to the only class of expectants worth providing for, here is a stock of patronage worth at least three times as much as that other.

County Court Judges, thirty: salary of each, 800*l.*: this gives 24,000*l.* a year—thrice as much as the 6,000*l.*[3]

No hands can I find anywhere, which, in point of aptitude (matchless Constitution standing as it stands) would bear a thought in comparison of his. Lord Lieutenants?—they are so many invisible objects. In the High Court of Public Opinion, nobody will see them, nobody will know who they are. The Judge chosen by each will be chosen of the family most connected in the county, which is as much as to say, the most unapt that could be chosen. Armed as he is like any Achilles,[4] still the place of a Secretary of State is at the bar of public opinion, and he stands an object to all eyes. Here are mine, for example, weak as they are, yet better perhaps than none, thus watching him: could they keep running after thirty, or I don't know how many more, Lord Lieutenants?

Chancellors!—'aye—there's the rub.'[5] Sooner than see the patronage in the hands of the Model of Consistency, or even of any other English fee-fed Judge,—sooner, much sooner, would I see it added to the *porte-feuille* of the Chancellor of France.

---

[1] Eldon: see p. 177n above.

[2] 1825A, 1825B, 1830 'it is in'.

[3] In fact the Bill, as reintroduced by Althorp on 8 February 1825, provided for the establishment of twenty-one new courts, each of which would be presided over by a salaried Assessor (see *Commons Sessional Papers* (1825) i. 323–46). Bentham should of course have said that £24,000 was three times as much *again* as £6,000.

[4] The hero of the *Iliad*, who, according to legend, was dipped in the River Styx by his mother, Thetis, to make him invulnerable. Thereafter no weapon could harm him, except on the heel by which she held him as he was immersed.

[5] *Hamlet*, III. i. 65.

SPEECH *of Mr.* SECRETARY PEEL, *on introducing the Police Magistrates' Salary Increase Bill, 21st March, 1825. Extract reported in the Times and the Morning Chronicle, of the 22d:*—[1]

TIMES.
1.

He held in his hand papers, from which, if he chose to enter into any detail, he could prove to the satisfaction of the Committee, that since the Institution of Police Magistrates, the business which devolved on those individuals had, owing to various Acts of Parliament which had been passed, independently of the increase of population, greatly augmented. *Although that circumstance would of itself be a sufficient reason for increasing the salary of the magistrates*, he rested his proposition upon grounds which he hoped the Committee would consider even more satisfactory.

2.

When the Police Magistrates were first appointed, it was the practice to select individuals to fill the office who, he must say, were incompetent[2] to discharge the duties which devolved upon them. He found from the papers which had been laid upon the table, that out of twelve Police Magistrates appointed at a former period, there were only three Barristers, the rest were composed of a Major in the Army, a Starch Maker, three Clergymen, a Glasgow Trader, and other persons who, from their occupations,[3] could not but be considered as utterly unqualified to perform the duties of Magistrates.

MORNING CHRONICLE.
1.

He held papers in his hand, showing in the clearest manner the great *increase* that had taken place in the business of the Police Offices since their first institution, arising from the great increase of the population of the metropolis amongst other causes. It appeared from those papers, that since their first establishment, considerable additions had been made to the business of the Offices, by various Acts of Parliament, passed at different times, but he would lay his proposition upon stronger grounds.

2.

In the first instance, the salaries of the Magistrates amounted only to 400*l.* per annum, it was afterwards raised to 600*l.*, but, it was well known, that under the former regulation the persons appointed were totally *incompetent* to the duties. He found that of the twelve Magistrates first appointed, three were Barristers. One was a Major, three Clergymen, two Starch Dealers, and one Glasgow Trader.

---

[1] There are some minor inaccuracies in the rendering of the passages; more substantial discrepancies have been recorded in editorial footnotes. The italics are Bentham's. Peel's speech is also recorded in *Parliamentary Debates* (1825) xii. 1128–30.

[2] *Times* 'utterly incompetent'.

[3] *Times* 'previous occupations'.

199

3.

The law had fixed no limitation with respect to the previous education of persons appointed to the office of Magistrate, but he thought the Committee would be pleased to hear, that a limitation on that point had been *prescribed* by the Secretary of State. Neither his predecessor in office (Lord Sidmouth) nor himself had ever appointed a person to fill the office of Magistrate who had not been a Barrister of three years standing. That was a rule to which, in his opinion, it was *most desirable to adhere*.

3.

He thought the Committee would be pleased to hear, that though there was no limitation fixed by law to determine the eligibility of the persons to fill such offices, Lord Sidmouth and himself had confined themselves strictly to the appointment of *Barristers alone*, and had not nominated any to the office of Magistrate who were of less than *three years* standing. He would ask the Committee, under those circumstances,

4.

But in order to enable the Secretary of State to abide by that rule, and to carry it into practice, it was necessary to augment the present salary of Police Magistrates. He implored the House to consider, whether 600*l.* a year (the present salary) was sufficient to induce a Barrister to give up the emoluments of private practice, and the hope of preferment in his profession, to undertake the duties of a Magistrate,

4.

whether 600*l.* a year could be sufficient to tempt a professional man of *adequate abilities* to relinquish their hopes of rising at the Bar?

5.

which required their *almost constant attendance?* It could not, he thought, be considered an unreasonable proposition, that in future the Secretary of State should *be empowered* to give to each Police Magistrate the sum of 800*l.* per annum.

5.

The duties at the office would require his constant attendance, and the Committee, he thought, would not consider it unreasonable to *empower* the Secretary of State to grant them each a salary, not exceeding 800*l.* a year.

6.

He hoped that he should *not* be told, that individuals might be found who would be willing to undertake the magisterial duties for a less sum. It was very true that *such was the case*. He was constantly receiving applications from persons who were anxious to be appointed Police Magistrates. Those applications proceeded principally from *Country Magistrates*, who had discharged the duties of *their office ably and satisfactorily;* but whom nevertheless he did not think right

6.

It was true, he might be told, that there were many individuals now ready to accept those offices; but though that was certainly the case, they were most of them country *gentlemen*, who had discharged the duty of Magistrates in their respective counties, but that was no reason why they should be selected to fill the situation of Police Magistrates in the metropolis. He respected, as much as any man could, the unpaid magistracy of the country; but it did not follow, that

to appoint to be Police Magistrates in the metropolis. He held the unpaid magistracy in as high respect as any man, but he could easily conceive that a gentleman might, in consequence of the influence which he derived from local circumstances—the relations of landlord and tenant for instance—be able to discharge the duties of a Country Magistrate, in a satisfactory manner, who would be incompetent to undertake the important ones of a Police Magistrate.

because they were enabled by the weight of their character and influence to perform the ordinary routine duties of County Magistrates, they were competent to discharge the more arduous business of the police in this city.

7.

"Police Magistrates" was the name generally given to those magistrates to whom he alluded, but those persons were mistaken who supposed that the duties which they had to perform were merely executive. They were called upon to administer the law in a great number of complicated cases which were submitted to them. Out of some recent Acts of Parliament some very important questions arose, which the Police Magistrates were called upon to decide. Several nice cases had occurred under the Building Act.[1] He knew one case of that description which had occupied the attention of the magistrates *for a couple of days, during which surveyors had been examined on both sides*. He thought that a salary of 800*l.* a year was not more than a fair remuneration *for the practice which a Barrister must abandon when he undertook the duties of a Magistrate*.

7.

Many Acts of Parliament had increased the duties of those offices; important questions in civil causes often came before them, and under the Building Acts they were often obliged to hear the evidence of surveyors on each side, and to determine many points which required a considerable degree of legal knowledge. He would rather rest his proposition on that single statement, than enter into the details contained in the papers which he held in his hands.

8.

It appeared to him, that the individuals appointed to administer justice in this country were more parsimoniously dealt with than in almost any other country in the world. He thought this was poor economy, to give inadequate remuneration to individuals selected to administer justice, whether in the *highest office of judge*, or in the less important but still very important office of *Police Magistrate*.

8.

It appeared to him, that this country was more parsimonious in its provisions upon the administration of justice than any other, and he was sure that there could not be a worse economy than such saving, either with regard to the highest or to inferior officers.

[1] *Times* 'acts'.

9.

He might, he did not doubt, get persons—

9.

The great object should be to procure persons qualified to discharge the duties {hear, hear!}

10.

those persons *who could not succeed in their profession—the refuse of the bar*—to fill the office of Police Magistrate at a lower salary than he proposed to give— he could save 100*l.* or 200*l.* a year by such a proceeding, but the public would have cause to lament it.

10.

To tell them that they might take the *refuse of the bar*, would be to recommend a course which the public would soon have reason to lament. Upon those grounds he trusted that the Committee would not consider the addition of 200*l.* a year to their present salaries too much to remunerate them for the services of the Police Magistrates.

11.

The present Police Magistrates were of the highest personal respectability, and performed their duties to the great satisfaction of the country. They were thirty in number, *only four of whom were not barristers*. The Right Hon. Gentleman concluded with moving, 'That it is the opinion of the Committee that each Justice appointed, or to be appointed, under the Act for the more effectual administration of the office of Justice of the Peace, shall receive a salary[1] not exceeding 800*l.*'

11.

They were acquainted with the character of the individuals who filled those offices at present. *Their knowledge, experience, and respectability, were unquestionable.* They were thirty in number, and their services had already proved the importance of the duties they had to fulfil. The Honourable Gentleman concluded with moving a Resolution—'That each of the Justices appointed, or to be appointed, to the Police Offices of the Metropolis, shall be allowed a salary not exceeding 800*l.* a year, to be paid by one of his Majesty's Principal Secretaries of State.'

THE END.

[1] *Times* 'yearly salary'.

INDICATIONS RESPECTING LORD ELDON,

INCLUDING HISTORY OF THE PENDING JUDGES'-SALARY-RAISING MEASURE.

BY JEREMY BENTHAM, ESQ.
BENCHER OF LINCOLN'S INN.

INDICATIONS, &c.

§I. *Facts suspected.*[a] *Subjects of enquiry for the House of Commons.*

RESPECTING Lord Eldon, certain suspicions have arisen. The object of these pages is—to cause enquiry to be made, if possible, by the competent authority, whether there be any ground, and if yes, what, for these suspicions.

In general terms they may be thus expressed:—

1. That, finding the practice of the Court of Chancery replete with fraud and extortion, Lord Eldon, on or soon after his coming into office as Chancellor, formed and began to execute a plan for the screwing it up, for his own benefit, to the highest possible pitch; to wit, by assuming and exercising a power of taxation, and for that purpose setting his own authority above that of Parliament; which plan he has all along steadily pursued; and, if not the present *Judges' Salary-raising Measure*, 69, anno 1822, a late Act, to wit the 3rd Geo. IV. cap. 6 is the consummation of it.[1]

2. That, it being necessary, that, for this purpose, the other Westminster Hall Chiefs should be let into a participation of such sinister profit—to wit, as well for the better assurance of their support, as because the power of appointing to those offices being virtually in his hands, whatever is profit to them is so to him—the means employed by him tended to that effect also, and have been followed by it.

In relation to the whole scheme, conception may, perhaps, receive help, from a glance, in this place, at the titles of the ensuing sections. Here they are:

§2. Under Lord Eldon, Equity an instrument of fraud and extortion—samples of it.

___

[a] Objection. Among these so stiled *facts* are matters of *law*. Answer. The existence or supposed existence of a matter of law, is matter also of fact.

___

[1] Bentham's references are confused here. By 'a late Act', he appears to mean 3 Geo. IV, c.69, which authorized the Westminster Hall Judges to make regulations concerning the fees received by the officers of their respective Courts (see §XIII, pp. 238–42 below), whereas by the 'judges' salary-raising measure' he appears to refer generically to three closely related Bills. The salaries of the Master of the Rolls, the Vice Chancellor, the Chief Baron of the Exchequer and the puisne Judges and Barons, were increased by 6 Geo. IV, c.84, while the Chief Justices of King's Bench and Common Pleas were similarly provided for in 6 Geo. IV, c.82 and c.83 respectively, which also abolished the sale of offices in those Courts. Together, the Acts provided for the commutation of the fees received by the judges and newly appointed officials. They passed through Parliament in tandem and received the Royal Assent on 5 July 1825. The sentence should perhaps be properly read as follows: 'if not a late Act, to wit the 3rd Geo. IV. cap. 69, anno 1822, the present *Judges' Salary-raising Measure* is the consummation of it'.

§3. Anno 1807. Order by Chancellor and Master of the Rolls, augmenting fees, of offices in the gift of one of them.

§4. Profit to subordinates was profit to principals: so in course to successors.

§5. Contrary to law was this order.

§6. By it, increase and sanction were given to extortion.

§7. So, to corruption.

§8. How Lord Eldon pronounced the exaction contrary to law, all the while continuing it.

§9. How the Chancellor had laid the ground for the more effectual corruption of himself and the other chiefs (anno 1801).

§10. How the project was stopped by a Solicitor, till set a-going again, as per §3.

§11. How the other Chiefs were corrupted accordingly.

§12. How the illegality got wind, and how Felix trembled.

§13. How the Chancellor went to Parliament, and got the corruption established.

§14. How the Head of the Law, seeing *swindling* at work, stept in and took his profit out of it.

§15. How King George's Judges improved upon the precedent set by King Charles's, in the case of *ship-money*.

§16. How to be consistent, and complete the application of the self-paying principle.

§17. How Lord Eldon planned and established, by Act of Parliament, a Joint Stock Company, composed of Westminster Hall Chiefs, and other dishonest men of all classes.

§18. How the King's Chancellor exercised a dispensing power.

§19. Character evidence.

§II. *Under Lord Eldon, Equity, an instrument of fraud and extortion.*
Samples:—

A single sample will serve to show in what state Lord Eldon found this branch of practice, and that it stood not in much need of improvement at his hands: by a few more which follow, a faint yet for this purpose a sufficient idea, will be given of the improvement it has actually received under his care.

By the command of a father, I entered into the profession, and, in the year 1772 or thereabouts, was called to the bar.[1] Not long after, having drawn a bill in equity, I had to defend it against exceptions before a Master in Chancery. 'We shall have to attend on such a day,'

---

[1] Bentham was in fact called to the bar in 1769.

(said the Solicitor to me, naming a day a week or more distant,) 'warrants for our attendance will be taken out for two intervening days, but it is not customary to attend before the third.' What I learnt afterwards was—that though no attendance more than *one* was ever bestowed, *three* were on every occasion regularly charged for; for each of the two falsely pretended attendances, the client being, by the Solicitor, charged with a fee for himself, as also with a fee of 6s. 8d. paid by him to the Master: the consequence was—that, for every actual attendance, the Master, instead of 6s. 8d., received 1l., and that, even if inclined, no Solicitor durst omit taking out the three warrants instead of one, for fear of the not-to-be-hazarded displeasure, of that subordinate Judge and his superiors. True it is, the Solicitor is not under any *obligation* thus to charge his client for work not done. He is however sure of *indemnity* in doing so: it is accordingly done of course. Thus exquisitely cemented is the union of sinister interests.[a] So far as regards attendances of the functionaries here mentioned, thus is the expense tripled: so, for the sake of the profit on the expense, the delay likewise. And I have been assured by professional men now in practice, that on no occasion, for no purpose, is any Master's attendance ever obtained without taking out three warrants at the least.

So much for the state of the practice before Lord Eldon's first Chancellorship: now for the state of it under his Lordship's auspices.

Within the course of this current year, disclosures have been made in various pamphlets. One of the most instructive, is the one intitled 'A Letter to Samuel Compton Cox, Esq. one of the Masters of the Court of Chancery, respecting the practice of that Court, with suggestions for its alteration. By a Barrister. London, 1824.'[1] Extracted

---

[a] Of the result of the above-mentioned experience, intimation may be seen in the *Théorie des Peines et des Recompenses*, first published in French, anno 1811, or in B. 1, ch. 8, of the *Rationale of Reward*, just published, being the English of what regards *Reward* in French.[2]

These things and others of the same complexion, in such immense abundance, determined me to quit the profession: and, as soon as I could obtain my father's permission, I did so: I found it more to my taste to endeavour, as I have been doing ever since, to put an end to them, than to profit by them.

---

[1] Bentham's marked copy of this pamphlet is in the British Library, shelf-mark C.T. 80 (5). There are some minor inaccuracies in the rendering of the passages; more substantial discrepancies are recorded in editorial footnotes. The italics, unless otherwise noted, are Bentham's. Samuel Compton Cox (1757–1839), having been called to the bar in 1781, and served as a Commissioner of Bankrupts 1787–98 and as Second Justice of Carmarthen 1798–1804, was a Master in Chancery from 1804 to 1831.

[2] See *Théorie des peines et des récompenses*, ii. 54–66, and *The Rationale of Reward*, (published in 1825) pp. 54–66 (Bowring, ii. 208–12), which deal with occasions on which remuneration is mischievous, and refer to the example of the Masters in Chancery.

from it are the following alleged samples: samples of the improvements made in the arts and sciences of fraud and extortion, by Masters in Chancery and others, under the Noble and Learned Lord's so assiduously fostering and protecting care.

I. *In regard to attendances on and by Masters, money exacted by them as above, when no such services are performed.*

P.12. 'The issuing of warrants is another subject which requires consideration. These are issued frequently upon states of facts, abstracts of titles, charges and discharges, &c. *not according to the time consumed* in going through the business before the Master, *or his Clerk*[a], but according to the *length of the statement*. The Clerk *takes it for granted*, that the investigation of a state of facts of a given length may be *expected* to occupy a given number of hours. The Solicitor, therefore, in drawing such[1] his bill of costs, *after the statement has been gone through*,[2] leaves a blank for the number of warrants 'to proceed on the state of facts.' *The Master's Clerk fills up the blank*, by inserting such a number, as *might, if* there had been much contention between the different parties, have by *possibility* been issued. Thus, where *two* or *three* are all that, in fact, have been taken out, *ten* or *fifteen* are charged and allowed. The Solicitor produces those he has *actually received* in the course of the business, and *the Clerk* delivers to him so many *more* as are necessary to make up the requisite number.[b]'

P.12.[3] 'A similar process takes place with respect to *the Report*. If the charge for the warrants alone were all that was to be complained of, the mischief would not be so great. But *you are aware, Sir*,[c] that an attendance on each of these warrants is charged for and allowed, and

---

[a] Of the business charged for, as if done by the Master the greater part, Masters taken together, is done by the Master's clerk. The officers stiled Six-clerks have long ascended into the Epicurean heaven, the region of sinecures: the Masters are jogging on in the road to it. I have known instances of Masterships given to common lawyers, to whom the practice of the court was as completely unknown as any thing could be.

[b] Thus exacting, for the Master, payment for that same number of attendances not bestowed; and as to Solicitors, not only allowing but forcing them, on both sides— and there may be any number on each side—to receive payment, each of them, for the same number of attendances on his part.

[c] Thus saith the nameless Barrister to the Master, who has taken care all this while to know no more of the matter than Lord Eldon does. He is one of the thirteen Commissioners, commissioned by Lord Eldon, to enquire, along with Lord Eldon into the conduct of Lord Eldon.[4]

---

[1] *Letter to Samuel Compton Cox* 'out'.
[2] This phrase is italicized in *Letter to Samuel Compton Cox*.
[3] This passage is in fact at pp. 12–13.
[4] Cox was one of the fourteen Royal Commissioners, including Eldon, appointed to inquire into the practice of Chancery.

that frequently by several different solicitors,[a] so that the expense to the suitors is grievously increased.'

II. *Of the sinister profit made by the Solicitor, the greater part has for its cause the rapacity of the Master, supported by the Chancellor.*

P.9.[1] 'Copies of proceedings of all sorts, of states of facts, of affidavits, of reports, of every paper in short which is brought into the office, are multiplied without the least necessity; and, in many instances, are *charged for, though never made*. For instance, in an amicable suit, where the only object is to obtain the opinion of the Court on some doubtful point, and the Master's report is previously necessary to ascertain the facts of the case clearly, each solicitor concerned is required, in most instances, to take, or at least to pay for, a copy of the state of facts carried in, of the affidavits in support of it, and of the draft of the report; and in the event of his not taking these copies, he is not allowed to charge for any of his attendances in the Master's office.'

P.10. 'The draft of the report is kept with the other papers relating to the suit, in the Master's office; and to such a length is the system of charging for copies carried, that in amicable suits it not unfrequently happens, I believe, that no copy whatever of the draft report is made, but the Solicitor merely looks over the original draft in the Master's office. Yet, even in this case, two or more copies will be charged for[b] as made for the plaintiff and defendants.' pp. 10, 11.

III. *How, by breach of duty as to attendance on the part of Masters and their clerks, delay and expense are manufactured by them, and profit out of it, over and above what is exacted by them on mendacious grounds, as above.*

P.15.—'The Masters seldom, I believe, make their appearance in Southampton-buildings before *eleven*, and are mostly to be seen on their way home by *three* o'clock at the latest.'

P.16.—'Another evil, is that of issuing warrants to different parties to attend at the same hour.'

'With some exceptions (says another pamphlet, with a high and responsible name to it, page 32.)[2] I find a general understanding prevails, that the *earliest* appointment for a Master must be *eleven*,

---

[a] Though no cause has more than two sides—the plaintiff's and the defendant's—yet on each side there may be as many different Solicitors as there are different parties, and to the number of them there is no limit.

[b] By, and for the profit of, the Master.

---

[1] This passage is in fact at pp. 9–10.

[2] See William Vizard (1774–1859), *Letter to William Courtenay, Esq. One of the Commissioners for Inquiring into the Practice established in the Court of Chancery*, London, 1824. Bentham's

and the *latest* at *two* o'clock.' Consequence—warrant sent for, frequent answer—'Master full for a week:' page 31. 'Court sits from ten to four.' So far the authority. Court, sitting as yet in public, cannot convert *itself* into a sinecurist: this accommodation it cannot afford to any but its feudatories, who, so long as they act, the shorter the proportion of time in a day they sit on each cause, have the greater number of attendances to be paid for.

The attendance, stiled *the Master's*, is, after all, in many instances, only the *Clerk's:* so that it may be matter of calculation at the end of what period, under the cherishing care of Lord Eldon, all Masterships may have ripened into sinecures, and thus completed the course completed by the Six-Clerkships. Per pamphlet, intitled [Review],[1] &c. p. 49. of which presently. Average emolument of one of the Master's *Clerks*, in 1822, 1823, and 1824, 2,300*l.* a year.

IV. *Strict community of sinister interest between the judicial and professional lawyers; the judicial, principals, the professional, forced accomplices.*

P.13.[2] 'Their bills will be less rigidly examined. Under these circumstances it is not the interest of a Solicitor to quarrel with the Master's clerk.'[a] Both are alike gainers by the existing system.— p. 14. 'In cases where the costs come out of a fund in court, *much less strictness* is likely to prevail. If the plaintiff's Solicitor be allowed for attendances on more warrants than are actually taken out during the progress of the business, a similar allowance must be made to the defendant's Solicitor. But even if it were both the interest and the inclination of the Solicitor to amend this practice, it is not in his power so to do. He might indeed amend it so far as his own charges go, but no farther. Over those of the Master's clerks,[3] he has no controul; and

---

[a] 'Since writing the above, I have been informed that in *one* office[a] the clerk is not allowed to receive gratuities, but is paid a stipulated salary; and I understand that the business of that office is conducted as well, as expeditiously, and as satisfactorily in all respects as in other offices. It might seem invidious to say more so.'—*Barrister.*

---

[a] Worth knowing it surely would be by the House of Commons, what that *one* office is.—J.B.

---

marked copy of this pamphlet is in the British Library, shelf-mark C.T. 80 (6). There are some minor inaccuracies in the rendering of the passages. The italics are Bentham's.

William Courtenay (1777–1859), later tenth Earl of Devon, MP for Exeter 1812–26, was a Master in Chancery from 1817 to 1826.

[1] 1825C, 1825D, 1826, 1830 'Rewards' is a slip. The following information is in fact given in *Review of the Delays and Abuses occasioned by the Constitution and Present Practice of the Court of Chancery*, p. 49n, for which see Postscript, §1, pp. 271–3 below.

[2] The following extracts are again from *Letter to Samuel Compton Cox*.

[3] *Letter to Samuel Compton Cox* 'clerk'.

he is moreover at the mercy of the clerk. If he quarrels with the clerk, he must expect to be thwarted and delayed in every suit which comes into that office, and to have his bills rigorously taxed. The Master's clerk, with the assistance of a clerk in court, taxes the Solicitor's bill; but there is nobody to tax the Master's bill.'—p. 14.

V. *Corruption and extortion, by bribes, given to and received by Master's clerks, in addition to the sinister profit, carried as above to the account of the Master.*

P.13. 'The gratuities at present allowed to the Master's clerks ought to be done away with altogether. . . . Solicitors, who are in the habit of giving large gratuities to the clerks, will at any rate be looked upon favourably. Their business will be readily attended to, and often-times to the delay of others, who, in strictness, are entitled to priority.'

VI. *Anno 1814, Lord Eldon's eyes, forced to open themselves to fraud and extortion in one portentously scandalous instance, kept shut in all other instances before and since.*

P.11. 'With regard to copies of particulars of sale, where an estate is sold in the Master's office, a material alteration has of late years been made. To such a height had these charges amounted, that in one instance (Casamajor *v.* Strode) 700*l.* were claimed for *compensation-money*,[1] in lieu of *written* copies of *particulars of sale*. In consequence of that charge, the *general order of 24th March*, 1814, was made, by which the Master is allowed sixpence a side for so many printed copies of the particulars as there are *actual* bidders, *and no more*.[2] There seems no good reason for making even this allowance. It would be fair enough, *if the Masters are to continue to be paid by fees*, to allow the expense of copying the particular for the printer, and even a fee, if thought necessary, for settling it; but beyond that, as there is no actual trouble, there should be no charge on the suitor.'—p.12.

Of the particulars above given, a general confirmation may be deduced from the contents of the (I now see) *named*, but not promis-cuously published pamphlet, above alluded to—Mr. Vizard's.[3]

What is above is a small sample of that which is said to have place. Of what follows in sections 4, 8, and 9,[4] the design is—to show how that which has place, came, and comes to have place.

---

[1] *Letter to Samuel Compton Cox* 'composition money'.
[2] For the Order of 24 March 1814 see John Beames, *The General Orders of the High Court of Chancery: from the year 1600 to the present period*, London, 1815, pp. 483–4.
[3] See pp. 209–10 above.
[4] See pp. 213–15, 222–5 below.

§ III. *Anno 1807. Order by Chancellor and Master of the Rolls, augmenting the fees, of offices in the gift of one of them.*

It consists of a printed pamphlet of 25 pages, bearing in the title page the words following:

'List of Costs in Chancery, regarding Solicitors, and also Clerks in Court, as increased by orders of Court, dated 26th February last; issued under the joint signatures of the Right Hon. the Lord Chancellor, and Master of the Rolls: being exact copies of those orders. The same having been collated with the original Lists of the Court.'

'London: printed for Heraud and Co. Law Stationers, Carey-street, corner of Bell-yard. By J. and W. Smith, King-street, Seven-dials, 1807.'[1]

In the preamble to that part which regards the 'Clerks in Court Fees,' the order speaks of itself as establishing 'a schedule of—increased fees.' Thereupon follows the schedule, and the number of the fees is forty-three.[2]

Anno 1814. In pursuance of certain orders of the House of Commons,[3] returns were made, amongst other Chancery offices, from that of the *Six-Clerks*, and another from that of the *Sworn and Waiting Clerks*. These are comprised in pages 5, 6, 7, 8, of a paper intitled 'Fees in Courts of Justice.' Dates of order for printing, 13th May, and 11th July, 1814. Nos. 234 and 250.[4]

In the return relative to the Sworn Clerks, are reprinted the contents of the pamphlet above mentioned.[5]

---

[1] There are some minor inaccuracies in the rendering of the title page.

[2] Bentham's marked copy of the pamphlet is in Lincoln's Inn Library, shelf-mark L.P. 262, where he has enumerated the list of fees of the Clerks in Court (the schedule is at pp. 19–25). Although there are forty-four fees listed, he has conflated two of them to give his total of forty-three. As Bentham mentions below, the Order of Court of 26 February 1807, insofar as it related to the Clerks in Court, is reproduced in *Commons Sessional Papers* (1813–14) xiii. 39–40.

[3] On 31 March 1814, the House of Commons ordered, 'That there be laid before this House, a Return of any Increase of Rate of the Fees demanded and received in the several superior Courts of Justice Civil or Ecclesiastical, in the United Kingdom, by the Judges and Officers of such Courts, during twenty years, on the several Proceedings in the same: together with a Statement of the Authority under which such Increase has taken place', and further ordered on 2 May 1814, 'That the said Return be laid before this House forthwith'. See *Commons Journals*, lxix. 175, 225.

[4] See *Commons Sessional Papers* (1813–14) iii. 33–84 (pp. 5–8 of the return are at xiii. 37–40).

[5] i.e. the Order of Court of 26 February 1807.

§IV. *Profit to subordinates was profit to superiors;*
so, in course, to successors.

Here begins the proof of the fact—that a twopenny loaf costs two-
pence: in Honourable and Right Honourable House, the proof will be
insufficient; in any other, unless it were a Right Honourable one, it
would be superfluous: for information, yes: but, for reminiscence, it
may have its use.

1. Wherever an office has any money value, so has the patronage of
it. By the patronage, understand the power of determining the
individuals by whom, together, or one after another, it shall be
possessed:—the whole power or any share in it.

Take any office singly, compared with the value of the possession,
that of the patronage may be less or greater. It is most commonly
less; but it may be many times greater. Patron (say) a father near the
grave; son, in early youth: value of the office if occupied by the father,
not one year's purchase; if by the son, a dozen years or more.

Present income of a Six-clerkship, about 1,000*l.* a year: so stated to
me by gentlemen belonging to the office.[1] It is regarded as a sinecure;
patron, the Master of the Rolls. One of these Judges was Sir Thomas
Sewel; children, numerous.[2] No further provision for this one, without injustice to others. Suppose it sold, what would it have been worth
to him? Not a fifth of what it was by being given.—2,000*l.* the price
usually got by patron. So at least said, by gentlemen belonging to the
office. This for the information of Mr. Robinson: the Mr. Robinson
who, as far as I understand hitherto, to secure purity interdicts sale,
leaving gift as he found it.[3]

Say *patron* and *grandpatron*, as you say *son* and *grandson*. Grand
patronage is not so valuable as patronage. True: nor yet valueless. In
the King's Bench, is an office called the Clerkship of the Rules. Annual
value, as per Finance Reports, 1797–8, 2,767*l.* Nominal joint patrons

---

[1] Bentham's source of information was Samuel Hawtayne Lewin (d. 1840), a Sworn Clerk in a
Six Clerk's Office (see UC xix. 121–2; the latter sheet is dated 6 May 1825).

[2] Sir Thomas Sewell (c.1710–84), MP for Harwich 1758–61 and Winchelsea 1761–8,
Master of the Rolls 1764–84, had four sons and three daughters by his first wife, and a further
child who died in infancy by his second wife.

[3] Frederick John Robinson (1782–1859), later first Viscount Goderich and first Earl of
Ripon, Chancellor of the Exchequer 1823–7, Secretary for War and Colonies 1827, 1830–3,
First Lord of the Treasury 1827–8, Lord Privy Seal 1833–4, in a debate in the House of Commons on 16 May 1825 on the increase of judges' salaries, proposed to prevent the sale of offices
in the Courts of King's Bench and Common Pleas on the grounds that the practice was 'inconsistent with the dignity and personal independence of the judges' (see *Parliamentary Debates*
(1825) xiii. 612–18).

in those days, Earl of Stormont and Mr. Way; grand patron, Earl of Mansfield, Lord Chief Justice. Trustee for the Lord Chief Justice, said Earl of Stormont and Mr. Way: price paid 7,000*l.*: circumstances led me to the knowledge of it.[1] But for grand patron's cowardice (that cowardice which is matter of history) more might have been got for it. That or thereabouts was got for it a second time.[2]

Would you know the money value of an office, exclusive of the emolument in possession? to the aggregate value of the patronage belonging to it, add that of the grand patronage. Nor is that of great grand patronage nothing. Wherever you can see a grand patron other than the king, seeing the king, you see a great grand patron.

A Mastership was a fortune to a daughter of Lord Erskine.[3] Had he held the seals long enough, a Six-Clerkship might have been a provision for a son, supposing the matter settled with Sir William Grant, who had no issue.[4]

If either patronage, grand patronage, or great grand patronage of the office are valueless, so is the possession of it.

In case of abuse, profit to individuals is one thing; mischief to the public, another. Profit from fee-gathering offices may be made either by sale or by gift. When by sale, small is the mischief in comparison of what it is when by gift. But this belongs to another head.[5]

Neither by the Chancellor, nor by the Master of the Rolls (it may be said) are nominated any of the officers to whose fees the Order gives increase. True: nor by this is the additional value, given by it to the patronage, lessened. Along with the values of the Sworn-clerkship and the Waiting-clerkship, rises that of the Six-clerkship. *Ten-pence*

---

[1] The Clerk of the Rules at this time was Bentham's step-brother, Charles Abbot, who had been appointed to the office in 1794 on the death of his elder brother, John Farr Abbot (1756–94): he gives an account of his motives for accepting the post in *The Diary and Correspondence of Charles Abbot, Lord Colchester*, ed. Charles, Lord Colchester, 3 vols., London, 1861, i. pp. xv–xvi, but makes no mention of any payment. The Clerk of the Rules was appointed by the Chief Clerk of the Pleas, who in turn was appointed by the Lord Chief Justice. At the time of Abbot's appointment, the Chief Clerkship had been held jointly by David Murray (1727–96), seventh Viscount Stormont and second Earl of Mansfield (he was Chief Justice Mansfield's nephew and heir), and John Way, a long-serving official of the Court; they in turn had been appointed by Chief Justice Mansfield in 1778. See the Twenty-Seventh Report of the Finance Committee, *Commons Sessional Papers of the Eighteenth Century*, cxi. 184–7.

[2] The occasion to which Bentham is referring is unclear, though he perhaps had in mind Abbot's resignation of the office in 1801 on his appointment as Chief Secretary to the Lord Lieutenant of Ireland.

[3] As he was about to leave office as Chancellor in April 1807, Erskine persuaded Sir William Weller Pepys (1740–1825) to resign his Mastership in Chancery, and appointed his son-in-law Edward Morris (1768–1815), MP for Newport 1803–12, in his place.

[4] Grant, as Master of the Rolls, was responsible for the appointment of Six Clerks during Erskine's Chancellorship.

[5] For such a discussion see Appendix A, 'Indications respecting Lord Eldon', Postscript §3, pp. 307–33 below.

per folio is paid to Sworn and Waiting-clerks; *ten-pence* per *ninety words*, called a *folio*, for copies taken by them: out of each such ten-pence, the Six Clerks, for doing nothing, receive four-pence.[1] This is all they receive: an *all* which, to some eyes, may not appear much too little.

The measure was one of experiment: direct object, that project of plunderage, which will be seen continued and extended by the hands of Lord Eldon in [1820],[2] and sanctioned by Parliament in 1822: collateral, or subsidiary object on his part, giving additional strength to the dominion of Judge-made over Parliament-made[3] law. Full butt did this order run against a special statute, made for remedy against this very abuse: not to speak of the general principle laid down, and thus vainly endeavoured to be established, by the Petition of Rights. But as to this, see next section.

Of the price the public was made to pay for this sinister profit, not more than half has, as yet, been brought to view. The other half went to stop mouths. Waste, all of it, as well as productive of correspondent delay, is what is exacted for all three sorts of clerks. Thus felt, and even yet say, the solicitors. The plunderable fund is composed of the aggregate property of all those who can afford to buy a chance, for the article sold under the name of Equity. The greater the quantity taken by the one set, the less is left for the other—see an experience of this shewn in §13.[4] Preceded accordingly by the bonuses given to these more immediate cointeressees of the Chancellor and his feudatory, was a like bonus given to the fraternity of solicitors.

§V. *Contrary to law was the order.*

Not to speak of clauses of *common*, that is to say, *imaginary law*, called *principles*, borrowed or made by each disputant for the purpose of the dispute—full butt does the order run against indisputable *Acts of Parliament*:—acts of general application, applying to taxation in any mode without consent of Parliament;—acts of particular application, applying to taxation in this particular mode:

[1] Bentham had again received this information from Lewin: see UC xix. 122.
[2] 1825C, 1825D, 1826, 1830 '1807' is presumably a slip, since Bentham appears to be referring to the remarks attributed to Eldon in Donnison v. Currie, discussed in §VIII, pp. 222–4 below.
[3] 1826, 1830 'over-Parliament-made'.
[4] See pp. 238–42 below. Bentham's reference to this section, however, is unclear: perhaps he had in mind the complaint made by James Lowe concerning the exaction of fees he believed illegal mentioned in §X, pp. 225–30 below.

1. First comes the *generally*-applying act, 25 Ed. I. c.7. anno 1297. 'We have granted for us and our heirs, as well to Archbishops . . . . as to Earls . . . . and to all the commonalty of the land, that for no business from henceforth we shall take such manner of aids, tasks, nor aprises, but by the common assent of the realm.'

2. Next comes 34 Ed. I. stat. 4, c.1. anno 1306. 'No Tallage or Aid shall be taken or levied by us, or our heirs, in our realm, without the good-will and assent of Archbishops, Bishops, Lords, Barons, Knights, Burgesses, and other freemen of the land.'

3. Now comes the *specially*-applying act, 20 Ed. III. c.1. anno 1346. 'First, we have commanded' (says the statute) 'all our justices to be sworn, that they shall from henceforth do equal law and execution of right to all our subjects, rich and poor. And we have ordained and caused our said Justices to be sworn, that they shall not from henceforth, as long as they shall be in the office of justice, take fee nor robe of any man but of ourself, and that they shall take no gift nor reward, by themselves nor by others privily or apertly, of any man that hath to do before them by any way, *except meat and drink, and that of small value.*'[a]

4. Lastly comes the all-comprehensively applying clause in the Act commonly called the Petition of Rights, 3. [Ch.][1] 1, c.1, § 10, 'That no man hereafter be compelled to make, or yield any gift, loan,

---

[a] The exception—*the meat and drink of small value* (need it be said?) speaks the simplicity of the times: roads bad, inns scantily scattered, judges, in their progresses in the suite of the monarch starved, if not kept alive by the hospitality of some one or other, who, in some way or other, '*had to do before them.*'

A few words to obviate cavil.

Objection. Immediately before this last-mentioned clause in the statute, runs a sort of special preamble, in these words,—'to the intent that our justices should do every right to all people, in the manner aforesaid, without more favour showing to one than to another.' Well then: fee, the same to all, shews no such favour.

Answer, 1. Preamble limits not enacting part:—a rule too generally recognized to need reference; disallow it, the whole mass of statute-law is shaken to pieces.

2. Fee the same to all, *does* show such favour in the extreme. A. has less than 10*l.* a-year to live on: B, more than 100,000*l.* a-year: on A. a 5s. fee is more than ten thousand times as heavy as on B. Of the B.'s, there are several: of the A.'s, several millions. By the aggregate of the fees exacted on the plaintiff's side, all who cannot afford to pay it, are placed in a state of out-lawry: in a still worse state those, who, having paid a certain part of the way, can pay no further. Ditto on defendant's side, sells to every man, who, in the character of plaintiff, is able and willing to buy it, an unlimited power of plundering and oppressing every man, who cannot spend as much in law as he can.

---

[1] 1825C, 1825D, 1826, 1830 'ch.'

benevolence, tax, or such like charge, without common consent by Act of Parliament.'[1]

Turn back now to the Judge-made law, and the enactors of it. Could they have had any doubt as to the illegality of what they were doing? Not unless these sages of the law had forgot the A, B, C of it.

But a pretence is made,—and what is it? 'Whereas the same' (speaking of the fees of the offices in question) 'have been at different times regulated by the orders of this Court, as occasion required.'[2]

The 'different times,'—what are they? They are the *one* time, at which, by a like joint order, anno 1743, 17 Geo. II. Lord Chancellor Hardwicke, his Master of the Rolls, Fortescue,[3] 'did order and direct that the Sworn-clerks and Waiting-clerks, do not demand, or take any greater fees or reward for the business done or to be done by them in the Six-clerks' office, than the fees and rewards following:' whereupon comes a list of them.[a]

In any of the many reigns in which Parliament never sat but to give money, and in which, could Kings have kept within bounds, there would have been an end of Parliaments,—as the value of money sunk, augmentation of subordinates'[4] fees by superiors might have had something of an excuse. But Lord Hardwicke—while he was scheming this order, he was receiving in the House of Lords, money-bills in profusion, brought up by the House of Commons. This tax of his—would the Commons have given, or would they have refused

[a] House of Commons paper, 1814, intituled 'Fees in Courts of Justice,' p. 5.[5]— Returns to orders of the Honourable House of Commons of 31st March and 2nd of May, 1814:[6] for 'a return of any increase of rate of the fees, demanded and received in the several superior *Courts of Justice*, civil or ecclesiastical, in the *United Kingdom*, by the Judges and Officers of such Courts, during twenty years, on the several proceedings in the same, together with a statement of the authority under which such increase has taken place.'

1. England, 2. Scotland, 3. Ireland, 234 and 250.—Ordered by the House of Commons to be printed, 13th May and 11th July, 1814.[7]

---

[1] The Petition of Right was presented by Parliament to Charles I (1600–49), King of England, Scotland and Ireland from 1625, who gave his assent to it on 7 June 1628.

[2] This phrase occurs in the preamble of the Order of Court of 26 February 1807: see *List of Costs in Chancery*, p. 18, and *Commons Sessional Papers* (1813–14) xiii. 39.

[3] 1825D, 1830 'Fontescue,'. Philip Yorke (1690–1764), first Baron and first Earl of Hardwicke, Lord Chancellor 1737–56; William Fortescue (1687–1749), Master of the Rolls 1741–9.

[4] 1825D, 1826, 1830 'subordinate's'.

[5] 1830 omits closing speech mark after 'Justice,' adds opening speech mark before 'p.5.'

[6] 1830 '184:'.

[7] For details of the Return see §III, p. 212 above. For the Order of 1743 see *Commons Sessional Papers* (1813–14) xiii. 37–9 (this is pp. 5–7 of the Return).

their sanction to it? Under either supposition, this tax of his imposition was without excuse.

Well, and suppose that Chancellor and his Master of the Rolls *had* done what Lord Chancellor Erskine and his Mentor[1] did, — '*order and direct* that the said schedule of fees be adopted.'? (p. 18.)[2] But they did no such thing: they were too wary: the time was not ripe for it. George the Second had a Pretender to keep him in check: George the Third had none.[3] True it is, that by their adroitly-worded *prohibition*, all the effect of *allowance* was produced. But, had anything been said about the Order, *there* were the *terms* of it: — all that these models of incorruption had in view by it was *repression: allowance* was what it was converted into, by underlings acting out of sight of superiors. Thus, on a ground of rapacity, was laid an appropriate varnish: — a coating of severe and self-denying justice.

The caricature-shops used to exhibit divers progresses: Progress of a *Scotchman*, Progress of a *Parson*, and some others. In these pages may be seen that of a *fee-gathering Judge*. Seen already has been the first stage of it.

If Lord Erskine, or rather the unfledged Equityman's Mentor, had any doubts of the illegality of what they were doing, no such doubts had Lord Eldon: for now comes another motion in the gymnastics of lawyer-craft—the last stage, or thereabouts, which for the moment we must anticipate.

The last stage in the progress, is that which is exhibited in, and by that which will be seen to be *his* Act—the Act of 1822—3 Geo. IV. c. 69, as per § 13, of these pages:[4] the assumption per force recognized to be *illegal;* because, as will also be seen, the Court of King's Bench had just been forced to declare as much: whereupon came the necessity of going, after all, to Parliament: *illegality* recognized, but a different word, the word *effectually*, employed,[5] that from all who were not in the secret, the evil consciousness might be kept hid. 'Whereas' (says the preamble) 'it is *expedient* that some provision should be made for the permanent regulations and establishment of the fees of the officers, clerks, and ministers of justice of the several Courts of Chancery, King's Bench, Common Pleas, Exchequer, and

---

[1] i.e. Sir William Grant, Master of the Rolls during Erskine's Chancellorship.

[2] In fact, the schedule of fees was 'ordered and decreed' to be adopted: see *List of Costs in Chancery*, p. 18, and *Commons Sessional Papers* (1813–14) xiii. 39.

[3] James Francis Edward Stuart (1688–1766), the Old Pretender, and Charles Edward Stuart (1720–88), the Young Pretender, both survived into the reign of George III, but any threat to the Hanoverian succession was thenceforward perceived to be small.

[4] See pp. 238–42 below.

[5] 1825D, 1826, 1830 '*effectually*-employed,'.

Exchequer Chamber, at Westminster, and of the clerks and other officers of the Judges of the same Courts; but the same cannot be *effectually* done but by the authority of Parliament'[1]. . . . thereupon, comes the first enactment, enabling Judges to deny and sell justice for their own profit, and giving legality and permanence (and, by the blessing of God!—Mr. Justice Bailey and Mr. Justice Park! eternity) to the things of which we have been seeing samples.

As to the *effectuality* of the thing, what had been done in this way without Parliament and against Parliament, had been but *too effectually* done; and, but for the so lately disclosed *illegality*, might and would have continued to be done, as long as matchless Constitution held together. At the same time, what is insinuated is—that, although what *had* thus been done without Parliament, *had* hitherto and all along been done *legally*, yet, for want of some *machinery*, which could not be supplied but by Parliament, it could not *in future* be so effectually done, as it would be with the help of such machinery, which, accordingly, the Act was made to supply. Not an atom of any such subsidiary matter is there in the Act. All that this Act of Lord Eldon's does, is to authorize and require himself, and the other Judges in question—the Westminster Hall Chiefs—to do as it had found them doing: taxing the injured—taxing them on pain of outlawry—taxing the people, and putting the money into their own pockets. In § 13, the reader will see whether what is here said of the absence of all machinery is not strictly true. Nothing whatever, besides what is here mentioned, does the Act so much as aim at.

§ VI. *By it, Increase and Sanction were given to Extortion.*

The illegality of the order supposed, taking money by colour of it, is *extortion;*—either *that* is, or nothing is.

Ask Mr. Serjeant Hawkins else. As good common law as Mr. Anybody else, or even my Lord Anybody else makes, is that made by Mr. Serjeant Hawkins; so says everybody. Look to ditto's Pleas of the Crown, vol. ii, b. i, ch. 68, § 1.[2] In the margin especially, if you take

---

[1] There are some minor inaccuracies in the rendering of the passage, as well as the following more substantial one: 'without the authority' is rendered here as 'but by the authority'. The italics are Bentham's.

[2] For the following quotation see William Hawkins (1673–1746), *A Treatise of the Pleas of the Crown; or a system of the principal matters relating to that subject, digested under proper heads*, 4 vols., 7th edn., ed. Thomas Leach, London, 1795, ii. 79. The two books of the original work were expanded into four volumes in this edition, hence Book I is comprized of the first two volumes. There are some minor inaccuracies in the rendering of the following passage and that in § VII, p. 221 below. The italics are Bentham's.

Leach's edition, or any subsequent one, you will see a rich embroidery of references: if the ground does not suit you, go to the embroidery, and hard indeed is your fortune, if you do not find something or other that will suit you better.

'It is said' (says he) 'that extortion, in a *large* sense, signifies any *oppression* under colour of right; but that in a *strict* sense, it signifies the taking of money by any officer, by colour of his office, either where none at all is due, or not so much is due, or where it is not yet due.' So much for the learned manufacturer. For the present purpose, the *strict* sense, you will see, is quite sufficient: as for the *large* sense, this is the sense you must take the word in, if what you want is nonsense. If you do, go on with the book, and there you will find enough of it; and that too without need of hunting on through the references; for if, with the law-making Serjeant, you want to enlarge *extortion* into oppression, you must strike out of *extortion* the first syllable, and, with it, half the sense of the word; which done, you will have tortion—which will give you, if not the exact synonyme of oppression, something very little wide of it; and here, by the bye, you have a sample of the sort of stuff on which hang life and death under *Common Law*.

§ VII. *So, to Corruption.*

Corruption? No: no such head has the learned aforesaid manufacturer and wholesale dealer in crown-law. No matter: he has *bribery*.[1] Rambling over that field, he picks up *corruption*, which he takes for the same thing. Had he lived in present times, well would he have known the difference. Bribery is what no Judge practices: would you know what prevents him, see 'Observations on the Magistrates' Salary-raising Bill:'[2] Corruption—self-corruption—is what, as you may see there and here, every Westminster Hall Chief Judge has been in use to practice; and is now, by Act of Parliament, anno 1822, 3 Geo. IV. c. 69, allowed to practice.

For bribery too, Hawkins has his *strict* sense and his *large* sense. It is in its *large* sense that he fancies it the same thing with *corruption*. Neither to bribery, however, nor to corruption, does this law of his apply itself, in any other case than that in which he who commits it

---

[1] Bribery is the subject-matter of Ch. 67, ii. 73–7.

[2] Bentham's reference is to that part of 'Observations on Peel's Speech' which deals with 'the announced Judges' Salary Raising Bill': see especially pp. 186–7 above.

has something or other to do with the administration of justice.[a] But, as before, this is all that is wanted here.

'Bribery' (says he) 'in a *strict* sense, is taken for a great *misprision* of one in a judicial place, taking any valuable thing whatsoever, *except meat and drink of small value*,[b] of any one who has to do before him any way, for doing his office, or by colour of his office, but of the King only.

'§2. But bribery in a *large* sense' (continues he) 'is sometimes taken for the receiving or offering of any undue reward, by or to any person whatsoever, whose ordinary profession or business relates to the administration of public justice, in order to incline him to do a thing against the *known rules of honesty and integrity*; for *the law abhors* {inuendo the common law, that is to say, it makes the Judges abhor} *any the least tendency to corruption in those who are any way concerned in its administration.*'[1]

Here the learned Serjeant waxes stronger and stronger in sentimentality, as he ascends into the heaven of hypocrisy, where he remains during the whole of that and the next long section.[2]—'Abhor corruption?' Oh yes, even as a dog does carrion.

Be this as it may, note with how hot a burning iron he stamps bribery and corruption on the foreheads of such a host of sages:—of Lord Erskine (oh fie! isn't he dead?) Sir William Grant (oh fie! was he not an able Judge?) and Lord Eldon, the Lord of Lords,[3] with his *cæteras* the inferior Chiefs.

---

[a] By Lord Chief Justice Raymond,[4] or by somebody for him, *Bench* law was afterwards made to explain and amend this *Inn of Court* law of the learned Serjeant, in addition to judicial law: corporation election bribery was thereby made bribery likewise. See the embroidery as above.[5]

[b] To Serjeant Hawkins (we see) to Serjeant Hawkins, though he never was a Judge—the Statute of Edward the Third[6] was not unknown, though so perfectly either unknown or contemned by the host of the under-mentioned Judges.

---

[1] Hawkins, *Pleas of the Crown*, ii. 73.
[2] The following section of Ch. 67 deals with 'the taking or giving of a reward for offices of a public nature'.
[3] See 1 Timothy 6: 15; Revelation 17: 14, 19: 16.
[4] Robert Raymond (1673–1733), first Baron Raymond, Chief Justice of King's Bench 1725–33, produced reports of the Common Law Courts dating from 1694 to 1732.
[5] Hawkins gives 2 Ld. Ray. 1377 (i.e. Robert, Lord Raymond, *Reports of Cases argued and adjudged in the Courts of King's Bench and Common Pleas, in the Reigns of the late King William, Queen Anne, King George the First, and King George the Second*, vol. II, 2nd edn., London, 1765, pp. 1377–9) as one of the sources for a note to this effect which follows §2 quoted below.
[6] 20 Ed. III, c.1, referred to in §V, p. 216 above.

§ VIII. *How Lord Eldon pronounced the Exaction contrary to Law—
all the while continuing it.*

The following is the tenor of a note obtained from an eminent barrister present, who had particular means and motives for being correct as to the facts, and who does not, to this moment, know the use intended to be made of it.[1] In the Court of Exchequer, February 5, 1820.

'DONNISON *v.* CURRIE.

'A question was made upon a petition, whether certain allowances, made to a solicitor on the taxation of his bill of costs, were regular, which they would have been, if the Court of Exchequer adopted in its practice the additional allowances made by Lord Erskine's order, otherwise not.

'It was objected that those additional allowances were not adopted by the Exchequer, inasmuch as Lord Erskine's order was not legal, and that Lord Eldon had intimated an opinion that he did not consider it as legal.

'The Chief Baron (Richards)[2] admitted that he understood *Lord Eldon had said that he did not consider Lord Erskine's order as being legal, but that it had been now so long acted upon, that the Court must be considered as having sanctioned it*, and that he (Richards) should follow what had been said by Lord Eldon.' Thus far the Report.

As to its being for his own benefit—see § 4.[3]

Thirteen years, and no more, having sufficed thus to set Bench above Parliament, anno 1820, quære what is the *smallest* length of time that will have become sufficient before the reign of John the Second[4] is at an end?

Objector.—Idle fears! how inconsiderable in all this time, the utmost of what the people can have suffered from the exercise of this power!

Answer.—True, the plunderage has its limit. Thank for it, however—not learned moderation, but a very different circumstance, which will be explained in § 13,[5] when the Act by which the last hand put to the plan comes to be considered: moreover, what makes fees

---

[1] The barrister was Bentham's former secretary, John Herbert Koe (1783–1860), who acted in the case for the plaintiff. A draft of the following note in Koe's hand, dated 21 October 1824, is at UC xix. 25a.

[2] Sir Richard Richards (1752–1823), Puisne Baron of the Exchequer 1814–17, Chief Baron of the Exchequer 1817–23.

[3] See pp. 213–15 above.

[4] i.e. Eldon.

[5] See pp. 238–42 below.

so stickled for in preference to salary is—that as plunderable matter increases, so will plunderage.

As to its being for his own profit that Lord Eldon thus continued the exaction, see §4.[1]

Bravo, Lord Chancellor Eldon! bravo, Lord Chief Baron Richards! '*So long!*' that is to say, just thirteen years: assuming what of course is true—that of the course of illegality begun under Lord Erskine, and pursued under Lord Eldon, the continuation commenced with his reaccession.[2] Years, thirteen! Here then is [*one*][3] length of time which suffices to entitle the Westminster Chiefs, all or any one of them, to set aside any Act or Acts of Parliament[4] they please: and in particular any Act of Parliament, the declared object of which is to prevent them from plundering, without stint, all people, who can and will buy of them, what they call *justice*, and from denying it to all who cannot.

But Bar? . . . what said Bar to this? Oh! Exchequer is a snug Court: small the quantity of Bar that is ever there. But, were there ever so much, Bench cannot raise itself above Parliament but it raises Bar along with it. Between Bench and Bar, even without partnership in money or power, sympathy would of itself suffice to make community of sinister interest. The same fungus, which, when green, is made into Bar, is it not, when dry, made into Bench?

No want of Bar was there, anno 1801, when Lord Eldon, as per next section,[5] laid the ground for the decision, thus pronounced anno 1820; as little, when, the next year (1821) as per §12,[6] ground and all were laid low by the shock of an earthquake. Matchless Constitution (it will be seen) may be turned topsy-turvy, and *lay-gents* know nothing of the matter: Bar looking on, and laughing in its sleeve.

Note here the felicity of Lord Eldon: the profit reaped by him from his *Hegira* of a few months.[7] We shall soon see, how, from one of the most unexpectable of all incidents, the grand design of the Grand Master of delay experienced a delay of six years: a delay, which, like so many of his own making, might never have found an end, but for the short-lived apparent triumph and un-quiet reign of the pretenders to the throne. When, upon their expulsion, the legitimates resumed their due omnipotence, it seemed to all who were in the secrets of

[1] See pp. 213–15 above.
[2] Eldon had been reappointed Lord Chancellor in April 1807.
[3] 1825C, 1825D, 1826, 1830 '*on*'.
[4] 1825D, 1826, 1830 'Parliaments'.
[5] See pp. 224–5 below.
[6] See pp. 231–7 below.
[7] Eldon was out of office from February 1806 to April 1807, during the Ministry of All the Talents, the only 'Whig' ministry between 1783 and 1830.

providence—and neither Mr. Justice Bailey nor Mr. Justice Park, nor any other chaplain of Lord Eldon's, could entertain a doubt of it—that it was only to give safety and success to this grand design of his, that the momentary ascendency of the intruders had been permitted. The Chancellor, by whom the first visible step in the track of execution was taken, being a Whig,—not only was a precedent set, and ground thus made for the accommodation of Lord Eldon, but a precedent which the Whigs, as such, stood effectually *estopped* from controverting. Poor Lord Erskine—all that he had had time to do, was to prepare the treat: to prepare it for his more fortunate predecessor and successor. Scarce was the banquet on the table, when up rose from his nap the 'giant refreshed,' and swept into his wallet, this, in addition to all the other sweets of office. As to poor Lord Erskine, over and above his paltry 4,000*l.*[1] a-year, nothing was left him, but to sing with Virgil—*Sic vos non nobis mellificatis apes.*[2]

§IX. *How the Chancellor had laid the ground for the more effectual corruption of himself and the other Chiefs.*

For this ground we must, from 1821, go as far back as the year 1801. In the explanation here given of the charges, it seemed necessary to make this departure from the order of time: for, till some conception of the design, and of a certain progress made in the execution of it, had been conveyed, the nature of the ground, so early, and so long ago laid for it, could not so clearly have been understood.

In nonsense (it will be seen) was this ground laid: plain sense might have been too hazardous. The document in which the design may be seen revealed, is another reported case, and (what is better) one already in print: *Ex-parte Leicester, Vesey Junior's Equity Reports*, VI. 429.[3] Buried in huge grim-gribber folios, secrets may be talked in print, and, for any length of time, kept. The language nonsense, the design may be not the less ascertainable and undeniable. Nonsense more egregious was seldom talked, than, on certain occasions, by Oliver Cromwell.[4] Whatever it was to the audience *then*, to us the design is no secret *now*.

---

[1] 1830 omits full stop.

[2] 'Thus you bees make honey not for us.' An adaptation (*nobis* instead of *vobis*) of Virgil's attributed response to Bathyllus fraudulently claiming the authorship of certain lines Virgil himself had written, containing advice to the Emperor Augustus.

[3] See Francis Vesey, Jun., *Reports of Cases argued and determined in the High Court of Chancery*, vol. VI, London, 1803. The report of Ex-parte Leicester is at pp. 429–34, Eldon's remarks at pp. 432–4, and the passage reproduced below at p. 433.

[4] Oliver Cromwell (1599–1658), Protector of England 1653–8, renowned for his falsehood and hypocrisy.

Here it follows—that is to say, Lord Eldon's.

Vesey Junior, vi. 429 to 434. Date of the report, 1801, Aug. 8. Date of the volume, 1803, p. 432.—LORD CHANCELLOR (p. 433)[1]—'A practice having prevailed, for a series of years, *contrary to* the terms of *an Order of the Court*, and sometimes *contrary to an Act of Parliament*, it is more consistent to suppose some ground appeared to former Judges, upon which *it* might be rendered *consistent with the practice:* and therefore, that it would be better to correct *it* in future, *not in that particular instance*. Upon the question, whether that order is to be altered, or to be acted upon according to its terms, which are at variance with the practice, I am not now *prepared* to deliver a decisive opinion: for this practice having been ever since permitted to grow up as expository of the order, if my opinion was different from what it is as to the policy of the order according to its terms, I must collect, that there is in that practice testimony given, that, according to the terms, it would be an inconvenient order.'

No abstract this—no paraphrase—*Verba ipsissima*. Eldon this all over. None but himself can be his parallel.[2]

Nothing which it could be of any use to insert is here omitted. Those who think they could find an interpretation more useful to Lord Eldon by wading through the five or six folio pages of his speech, let them take it in hand and see what they can make of it. All they will be able to do is to make darkness still more visible.

§X. *How the Design was stopt short by a Solicitor, till set a-going again, as above.*

The deepest-laid designs are sometimes frustrated by the most unexpected accidents. From the hardihood of a man whose[3] place was at his feet, we come now to see a design, so magnificent as this of the Chancellor's, experiencing the above-mentioned stoppage of six years.

Before me lies an unfinished work, printed but not published: title, 'Observations on Fees in Courts of Justice:' date to the Preface, Southampton Buildings, 17th November, 1822. In that street is the residence of Mr. Lowe, an eminent solicitor.[4] The work fell into my

[1] There are some minor inaccuracies in the rendering of the passage. The italics are Bentham's.

[2] See Lewis Theobald, *Double Falshood; or, The Distrest Lovers*, London, 1728, p. 25: 'None but Itself can be its Parallel'.

[3] 1825C 'hardihood of a man, whose'; 1830 'hardihood, of a man whose'.

[4] Bentham had an incomplete and unbound copy of this work, which had been printed anonymously in 1822, but had not been published. His notes on it and a copy of the extract para-

hands without his knowledge.[1] He is guiltless of all communication with me. This said, I shall speak of him as the author without reserve. From that work I collect the following facts. Year and month, as above, may be found material.

1. Page 20. Early in Lord Eldon's first Chancellorship, to wit, anno 1801, his Lordship not having then been five months in office, Mr Lowe, in various forms, stated to his Lordship, in public as well as in private, that *in his Lordship's Court, 'the corruption of office had become so great, that it was impossible for a solicitor to transact his business with propriety.'* This in general terms: adding, at the same time what, in his view, were particular instances, and praying redress. Note, that to say *in his Lordship's court*, was as much as to say, *under his Lordship's eye:—after* such information, at any rate, if not *before*.

2. Page 20. Argument thereupon by counsel: Mansfield, afterwards Chief Justice of the Common Pleas; Romilly, afterwards Solicitor-General.[2] On the part of both, assurance of strong conviction that the charge was well founded; proportionable fears, and not dissembled, of the detriment that might ensue to the personal interest of their client from the resentment of the noble and learned judge.

3. Page 20, 21. Proof exhibited, of the reasonableness of these fears:—'*Judge angry*.' . . . . Petitioner 'bent beneath a torrent of power and *personal abuse*.'

4. Page 21. Five years after, to wit, anno 1806—Lord Erskine then Chancellor—similar address to his Lordship: a brief again given to Romilly (at this time Solicitor-General) but with no better fortune: further encouragement this rebuff—further encouragement, to wit, to Lord Eldon, when restored.

5. Page [20].[3] In a note, reference to the above-mentioned case, *Ex-parte Leicester*, in Vesey, junior, with quotation of that portion of his Lordship's speech, which may be seen above in §9.[4] Hence a conjecture, that in that same case, Mr. Lowe himself, in some way or other, had a special interest. From the reference so made to that case, and his Lordship's speech on the occasion of it, it should seem that

phrased below, and reproduced in full at pp. 229–30 below, are at UC xix. 38–42 (10 March 1825), where he refers to its author, James Lowe, as 'a veteran and eminent Chancery Solicitor'.

[1] Bentham apparently acquired his copy of the work from Koe (see Koe to Bentham, 10 February 1825, UC xix. 5 and Bentham's note of 23 February 1825 at UC xix. 25a).

[2] Sir James Mansfield, originally Manfield (1733–1821), Solicitor General 1780–2, 1783, Chief Justice of Common Pleas 1804–14; Sir Samuel Romilly (1757–1818), MP for Queenborough 1806–7, Horsham 1807–8, Wareham 1808–12, Arundel 1812–18 and Westminster 1818, Solicitor General 1806–7.

[3] 1825C, 1825D, 1826, 1830 '21'.

[4] See p. 225 above.

the design of it, as above, was not a secret to Mr. Lowe, and that his Lordship knew it was not.

Here ends the history of the *stoppage*.

6. Preface, pp. 6, 7. Upwards of eighteen months antecedently to the above-mentioned 17th November, 1822, say accordingly, on or about 17th May, 1821, page 6, on the occasion of two causes—Limbrey against Gurr, and Adams against Limbrey,—laid by Mr. Lowe before the Attorney-General of that time, to wit, Sir Robert Gifford,[1] matters showing 'that the increasing amount of fees and costs was like *a leprosy rapidly spreading over the body of the law*.'

7. Preface, p. 3. Anno 1821, Trinity vacation—day not stated—to wit, sometime between July and November, mention made of his Lordship's[2] courtesy, and of 'a promise which his Lordship' (wrath having had twenty years to cool) 'very condescendingly performed.' On this occasion, *hearing* before his Lordship, Master of the Rolls[3] sitting with him: proof presumptive, not to say conclusive, that, on this occasion, Lord Erskine's Order was under consideration: 'Controverted' by Mr. Lowe, a fee that had received the confirmation of one of the sets of Commissioners, appointed by Lord Eldon for this and those other purposes that every body knows of.[4]

8. Preface, p. 5. Anno 1822, Easter term. Observations on the same subject, laid before the 'Master in Ordinary,' meaning doubtless one of the officers ordinarily stiled *Masters in Chancery*, ten in number, exclusive of the Grand Master, the Master of the Rolls. With as good a chance of success might the gentleman have laid them before the Master of the Mint.

9. P.5. Anno 1822, soon after the above, 'Information and Bill' filed against Mr. Lowe, by Mr. Attorney-General, and said to be fully answered. Solicitor to the Treasury, 'Mr. Maule.'[5] Answer put in by defendant, attachment for contempt in *not* answering. Quære, what means '*Information*' and '*Bill?*' Information in King's Bench? Bill in Chancery? But what *answer* can an information in King's Bench admit of?

---

[1] Sir Robert Gifford (1779–1826), later first Baron Gifford, Solicitor General 1817–19, Attorney General 1819–24, Chief Justice of Common Pleas 1824, Master of the Rolls 1824–6.

[2] i.e. Eldon's.

[3] Sir Thomas Plumer (1753–1824), Solicitor General 1807–12, Attorney General 1812–13, Vice-Chancellor 1813–18, Master of the Rolls 1818–24.

[4] The Royal Commission for examining into the Duties, Salaries and Emoluments, of the Officers, Clerks and Ministers, of the several Courts of Justice, in England, Wales, and Berwick-upon-Tweed, had been appointed on 9 February 1815, and continued to sit until 1824, in which time it produced eight reports. The first two of these dealt with the Court of Chancery (see *Commons Sessional Papers* (1816) viii. 91–257 and (1818) vii. 225–41.

[5] George Maule (1776–1851), Solicitor to the Treasury 1818–51.

10. P.6. Shortly afterwards, Observations laid by him before the Lords of the Treasury, soliciting the investigation of the charge laid before the Attorney-General (Sir Robert Gifford) *eighteen months before*, on the occasion of the cases of Limbrey and Gurr, &c. as per No. 6.

Containing, as it does, pages between 5 and 6, this same preface is too long for insertion here. Carefully have the above allegations been culled from it. Of the passage contained in the body of the work, the matter is too interesting and instructive to be omitted: it will be found below.[1]

Here then is *one* source, from which, had it ears for corruption, Honourable House might learn at any time, whether, from the above alleged corruption, Lord Eldon has not, during the whole of his two Chancellorships, been reaping profit, and whether it was possible so to have been doing without knowing it. By Lord Eldon's present set of nominees, evidence from Mr. Lowe has, I hear, been elicited.[2] Little, if any fruit, I hear, has been obtained from it. Anything unacceptable to their creator they could not be very desirous to receive; nor, perhaps, Mr. Lowe, since the experience had of his Lordship's 'courtesy,' to give.

Astonished all this while at the stoppage—astonished no less than disappointed—must have been the goodly fellowship—the solicitors and clerks in court; importunate for six long years, but not less vain than importunate, had been their endeavours to obtain from Lord Eldon and his Sir William Grant—yea, even from Lord Eldon!—that boon, which with the same Sir William Grant for mediator and advocate,—at the end of six short months, we have seen them obtaining from Lord Erskine:—the said Sir William Grant being, as per §4,[3] in quality of patron, in partnership with the said clerks in court.[a]

[a] Since writing what is in the text, a slight correction has come to hand. Not the whole of John the Second's first reign, only the two last years of it experienced this disturbance. There was an old Sixty-Clerk named *Barker*,[4] who was a favourite at Court, and had his *entrées*. Cause of favour, this—after pining the exact number of years it cost to take Troy,[5] Mr. Scot, junior, had formed his determination to pine no longer, when providence sent an angel in the shape of Mr. Barker with the papers of a fat suit and a retaining fee. Him the fellowship constituted for this purpose Minister

[1] See pp. 229–30 below.

[2] Lowe gave evidence to the Royal Commission on Chancery practice on 9 and 18 August 1824: see *Commons Sessional Papers* (1826) xv. 160–72, 217–23.

[3] See pp. 213–15 above.

[4] Henry Barker (d. 1807) was a Sworn Clerk in the division of William Luther Sewell (d. 1832), one of the Six Clerks in Chancery.

[5] According to Homer's *Iliad*, the city of Troy was besieged for ten years by the Greeks.

P.19.[1] *'An attempt in* 1801 *to reform practice.'*

Whilst Lord Thurlow held the great seal,[2] tables of *fees* taken by *officers in the Court of Chancery* remained set up or affixed in their respective offices, and the most trifling gratuity was received with a watchful dubious eye, and cautious hand; but soon after the great seal was resigned by his lordship, those tables began to disappear, and (in 1822)[3] have *never since been renewed:* gratuities then augmented, until they had no limits: and so early as the year 1801, when increased fees and costs had attained little of the strength and consistency *at which they have since arrived*, the Author of these observations stated to the Court *'that*[4] *the corruption of office had become so great, that it was impossible for a solicitor to transact his business with propriety;'*[a] to justify such statement he, by petition, set forth certain payments made, which he insisted ought not to have been demanded or received, and prayed for redress; and he wrote a letter to one of the Lord Chancellor's secretaries, in which he stated an opinion, which (until the great charter, and the before-mentioned statutes of King Edward III. and King Richard II. are repealed,)[5]

Plenipotentiary at the Court. Upon an average of the two years, every other day, it was computed, the Minister sought, and as regularly obtained an audience: answer, no less regular—'to-morrow.' On this occasion, observation was made of a sort of competition in the arena of frugality between the potentate and his quondam protec-tor, now sunk into his humble friend. Without an extra stock of powder in his hair, never, on a mission of such importance, durst the plenipotentiary approach the presence; consequence, in that article alone, in the course of the two diplomatic years, such an increase of expense, as, though his Excellency was well stricken in years, exceeded, according to the most accurate computation, the aggregate expen-diture in that same article, during the whole of his preceding life.[6]

[a] 'On hearing the case *ex-parte* Leicester, 6th Vez. jun. 429, where it was said, 'that a practice having prevailed for a series of years, contrary to the terms of an order in Court, and sometimes contrary to an Act of Parliament, it is most convenient to suppose some ground appeared to former judges upon which it might be rendered consistent with the practice; and therefore that it would be better to correct practice in future, not in the particular instance.' Whereas, the Author of these observations thinks that all practice which is contrary to an Act of Parliament, or to the terms of a standing order of Court, originates in corruption, and ought to be abolished in the particular instance complained of, or when, or however, a practice, at variance with law or order, is first made known to the Court.'

---

[1] The following extract, which for the sake of clarity is here displayed, is taken from pp. 19–21 of Lowe's 'Observations on Fees in Courts of Justice'. There are some minor inaccuracies in the rendering of the passage. The italics, unless otherwise noted, are Bentham's.

[2] Edward Thurlow (1731–1806), first Baron Thurlow, was Lord Chancellor 1778–83, 1783–92.

[3] This parenthesis is added by Bentham.

[4] This phrase is italicized by Lowe.

[5] i.e. 20 Ed. III, c.1 (see §V, p. 216 above) and 12 Ric. II, c.2, outlawing the sale of those offices in the appointment of the King's justices, referred to by Lowe at pp. 3–4 of his 'Ob-servations on Fees in Courts of Justice'.

[6] According to Bentham, then, the officers of the Court used Barker as an intermediary with Eldon in an attempt to persuade him to raise their fees.

he is disposed to maintain: and which, (though otherwise advised by his counsel) he then refused to retract.[a] The petition came on for hearing, and was supported by Mr. Mansfield and Mr. Romilly, with a spirit, and in a manner, peculiar to those advocates, and satisfactory to the feelings of the petitioner; and resisted by Mr. Attorney-General (Sir Spencer Percival)[1] and Mr. Richards.

In vain did Mr. Mansfield urge that *'gratuity was the mother of extortion,'*[2] and Mr. Romilly state the intrepidity of his client. On that occasion, the Author of these observations, who never heard an *angry judge* give a just judgment, bent beneath a torrent of power and *personal abuse*.

On the coming in of a new administration, in the year 1806, the Author of these observations addressed a letter to Lord Erskine, and prepared to further hear his petition; but he was given to understand, by those who had once applauded his efforts,[b] that *a change of men did not change measures; and since that time the irregular increase of fees and costs* has introduced much confusion into the law.

§ XI. *How the other Chiefs were corrupted accordingly.*

As to what regards the Chief of the Exchequer Judicatory, an indication has been seen in § [8].[3] As to what regards King's Bench and Common Pleas, the like may be seen in § 12.[4] Invitation, — 'Take and eat.'[5] Seen it has been and will be, whether there was any backwardness as to acceptance.

[a] 'Mr. Mansfield sent for the Author of these observations to his chambers, and there told him, that the Lord Chancellor *had expressed displeasure* at something said in a letter to his secretary, and advised an apology to be made. In reply, the Author of these observations told his counsel, that he was prepared to maintain what he had written, and that he would not make an apology; and, having read to Mr. Mansfield the draft of the letter, Mr. Mansfield said that he recollected when Lord Thurlow was made Lord Chancellor, his Lordship had mentioned to him in conversation, that he had been told that he was entitled to receive some fees, which he doubted his right to take. And Mr. Mansfield added, that such fees must have been those alluded to in the letter.'

[b] 'The letter to Lord Erskine was delivered to the late Mr. Lowton,[6] who had a conversation with the Author of these observations thereon, and Sir Samuel Romilly sent for and had his brief to reconsider.'

---

[1] Perceval was Attorney General 1802–6.
[2] This phrase is italicized by Lowe.
[3] 1825C, 1825D, 1826, 1830 '6'. For § VIII see pp. 222–4 above.
[4] See pp. 231–7 below.
[5] In the Anglican service of Holy Communion, the priest, when delivering the sacrament of the body of Christ, invited the communicant to 'Take and eat this in remembrance that Christ died for thee'.
[6] Unidentified.

Forget not that these men were, all of them, his creatures: breath of his nostrils; sheep of his pasture.[1]

§XII. *How the illegality got wind: and how Felix trembled.*[2]

Of the spread of the contagion from Chancery to Exchequer, indications were given in §8:[3] mention was there made of its having completed the tour of Westminster Hall. What is there said is no more than general intimation: the manner *how*, comes now to be set forth.

Anno 1821, lived a broken Botanist and Ex-Nursery-man, named *Salisbury*.[4] To distinguish him from a namesake of the gentleman-class,[5] *Salisbury minor* is the name he goes by among the Fancy. At the end of a series of vicissitudes, he had sunk into one of those sinks of misfortune, in which, to help pamper over-fed judges, debtors are squeezed by jailors, out of the substance that should go to creditors. As from Smithfield an over-driven ox into a china-shop—breaking loose one day from his tormentors, Salisbury *minor* found means, somehow or other, to break into one of the great Westminster Hall shops; in which, as often as a demand comes for the article so mis-called *justice*, bad goods are so dearly sold to all who can come up to the price, and denied, of course, to those who cannot. The china-shop scene ensued. Surprised and confounded, the shopmen exhibited that sort of derangement, which the French express by *loss of head—Ils ont perdu la tête*. Under the notion of defence, confessions came out, which come now to be recorded.

Anno 1821, Nov. 21. (The date is material.) Barnewall and Alderson's King's Bench Reports, Vol. v. p. 266.[6]

---

[1] See Lamentations 4: 20; Psalm 74: 1.

[2] Marcus Antonius Felix, Roman Procurator of Judaea c.52–60, before whom the Apostle Paul was sent to be tried. He allowed Paul to speak on faith in Christ, but as Paul 'reasoned of righteousness, temperance, and judgment to come, Felix trembled'. He continued to keep Paul in custody for two years without coming to any decision (see Acts 24). Felix is Bentham's pseudonym for Eldon.

[3] See pp. 222–4 above.

[4] Probably Richard Anthony Salisbury (1761–1829), botanist and author, Secretary of the Horticultural Society of London 1805–16, who cultivated a garden at Mill Hill, and then in Queen Street, Edgware Road.

[5] Probably William Salisbury (d. 1823), botanist, who owned the London Botanical Garden, Cadogan Place, Sloane Street.

[6] See Richard Vaughan Barnewall and Edward Hall Alderson, *Reports of Cases argued and determined in the Court of King's Bench*, vol. V, London, 1822. There are some minor inaccuracies in the rendering of the passage. The italics, apart from the words 'Gurney', 'Platt' and 'Michaelmas', are Bentham's.

'IN THE MATTER OF SALISBURY (IN PERSON!)[1]

'Salisbury *in person* had obtained a rule *nisi*, for one of the tipstaffs of the Court, to answer the matters of his affidavit. The affidavit stated, that the tipstaff had taken a fee of half a guinea, for conveying him from the Judge's chambers, (to which he had been brought by habeas corpus) to the King's Bench prison, such fee being more than he had a right to demand, according to the table of fees *affixed in the King's Bench, in pursuance of a rule of this court*.'

'*Gurney* and *Platt*[2] shewed cause, upon *affidavits*, stating that the fee had been taken *for a very long period of time by all tipstaffs in both courts*, and that it was *allowed* by the *Master* in costs.'

'The Court, however, adverting to the statutes 2 Geo. II. c.22, §4, and 32 Geo. II. c.28, §[5],[3] and the rule of court of *Michaelmas* term, 3 Geo. II. and the table of fees settled in the following year,[4] said, that it was *clear*, that the tipstaff had no right to take any other fee for taking a prisoner from the Judge's chambers to the King's Bench prison, than six shillings, which was the fee allowed him in that table. They, therefore, ordered the fee so taken to be *returned* to the complainant.'[a]

'Figure to himself, who can, the explosion. *Bancum regis* shaken, as by an earthquake. *Bancum regis* in an uproar! the edifice it had cost Lord Eldon twenty years to rear, laid in ruins. *We are above Parliament*, had said, as above, Lord Eldon—*Alas! no:* at the first meeting cried Lord Abbot,[5] *I could not, for the life of me, keep where you set us. I had not nerve for it. That fellow . . . . such impudence! who could have thought it? As to the fees, it is from Parliament, you see, we must have them now, if at all. It may take you some little trouble; but you see how necessary it is, and you will not grudge it.*'

---

[a] 'See the table of fees in the rules of the King's Bench, p. 241.'[6]—Here ends the report.

---

[1] The parenthesis is added by Bentham.

[2] John Gurney (1768–1845), called to the bar 1793, King's Council 1816, Baron of the Exchequer 1832–45, and Thomas Joshua Platt (1790?–1862), called to the bar 1816, King's Council 1834, Baron of the Exchequer 1845–56.

[3] 1825C, 1825D, 1826, 1830 '8' is a miscopy. According to the fourth clause of 2 Geo. II, c.22, only lawful fees were to be taken of prisoners, and tables of fees were to be hung in every gaol; and according to the fifth clause of 32 Geo. II, c.28, the Chief Justices of the Westminster Courts and groups of local magistrates were to settle the table of fees to be taken by gaolers.

[4] See 'Rules and Orders for the better Government of the King's Bench Prison, made and signed the 25th. of Nov. 1729', and 'A Table of Fees to be taken by the Marshal of the King's Bench Prison', dated 17 December 1730, reproduced in *Rules, Orders and Notices, in the Court of King's Bench, from the Second of King James I. to Trinity Term the Twenty-first of King George II. 1747 inclusive*, 2nd edn., London, 1747 (to which Bentham refers in §XIII, pp. 240–1 below).

[5] i.e. Lord Chief Justice Abbott.

[6] Presumably the table of 17 December 1730.

This is not in the report; but it is in the nature of the case, and that is worth a thousand law reports, drawn up by toads under harrows.

Think now of the scene exhibited in and by King's Bench;—culprit and judge under one hood—Guilty or not guilty?—Not guilty? O yes, if the Master, whose every-day business it is to *tax* costs, knows not what they are: if the Chief Justice, whose every-day business it is to *hear discussions* about costs, knows not what they are, or what they ought to be.—See now how the account stands:—the money account. Of the 10*s.* 6*d.* legalized, say 6*s.*: remains confessed to have been extorted, 4*s.* 6*d.*: sub-extortioner's profit, the 4*s.* 6*d.*: hcad-extortioner's, the 4*s.* 6*d.*, minus ×: to find the value of × see above, §4,[1] and forget not, any more than Lord Eldon and Lord Abbot forgot, that pounds and thousands of pounds are made of pence and shillings.

Mark now another sort of account. Case, a criminal one. Co-defendants, had the list been complete, Tipstaff, Master, and Chief Justice. Had it been as agreeable to punishers to punish themselves as others, what a rich variety of choice was here! Motion for imprisonment by *attachment*, as above: for this is what is meant by *answering affidavits:* Indictment for extortion, Indictment for corruption, Indictment for conspiracy; Information for all or any of the above crimes.

Mark now the *denouement*. The case, as above, a criminal one: the crime not punished, but without the consent of the sufferer *compounded* for: of the fruit of the crime the exact nominal amount ordered to be restored:—not a farthing even given to the hapless masterman by whose sad day's labour thus employed, so much more than the value had been consumed in thus sueing for it: with cost of affidavits several times as much. After seeing in this precedent the utmost he could hope for—what man, by whom like extortion had been suffered from like hands, would ever tax himself to seek redress for it? Redress—administered in semblance, denied in substance. With not an exception, unless by accident, such or to an indefinite degree worse, is matchless Constitution's justice!

But the punishment?—where was the punishment? This is answered already. Had the order for redress comprised a sixpence beyond the 4*s.* 6*d.* the inferior malefactor might have turned upon his principal, and the fable of the young thief, who at the gallows bit his mother's ear off, have been realized.[2] *Isn't it you that have led me to*

---

[1] See pp. 213–15 above.

[2] For the fable of 'The Boy and his Mother' see *Select Fables, in Three Parts. Part I. Fables extracted from Dodsley's. Part II. Fables with Reflections, in Prose and Verse. Part III. Fables in Verse*, Newcastle, 1784, Part II, Fable lxiv, pp. 218–21. The boy, having been commended by his mother for a minor theft, was led on to commit greater crimes, until at last he was condemned to be hanged for a felony. At the gallows, blaming his fate on his mother, he bit off her ear to express his resentment.

this? These four and sixpences that I have been pocketing—is there any of them you did not know of? Had it not been for this mishap, would not my place have been made worth so much the more to you, by every one of them? *Is there any one of them that did not add to the value of the place you will have to dispose of when I am out of it?* Why do you come upon me then? Can't you afford it better than I can? Pay it yourself.

But—the two learned Counsel, who thus fought for the 4*s.* 6*d.*—*by whom* were they *employed?* by Tipstaff, Master, or Chief Justice? Not by Tipstaff, surely: seeing that his cause was so much the Chief Justice's, he would not thus have flung away his money: he would not have given six, eight, or ten guineas to save a 4*s.* 6*d.*: these, if any, are among the secrets worth knowing, and which House of Commons will insist on knowing. Insist?—But when? when House of Commons has ceased to be House of Commons.

Well, then, this four-and-sixpenny tripartite business—is it not extortion? Is it not corruption? If not, still, for argument sake, suppose, on the part of all three learned persons—all or any of them—suppose a real desire to commit either of these crimes; can imagination present a more effectual mode of doing it? Till this be found, spare yourself, whoever you are, spare yourself all such trouble as that of crying out Shame, Shame! Contempt of Court! Calumny! Blasphemy!

Contempt of Court? forsooth! If contempt is ever brought upon such Courts (and, for the good of mankind too much of it cannot be brought upon them) it is not in the telling of such things, but in the doing of them, that the culpable cause will be to be found.

Here then, we see, were Statutes—here (according to Lord Eldon's instructions) laid down as per §9,[1] at the outset—here were Rules of Court disposed of in the same way, and at one stroke. Anno 1801, in the first year of his reign—disposed of at one stroke, and in the same way. A liberty which might so easily be taken with Acts of Parliament—hard indeed it would have been, if a Judge might not take it with the Rules of his own Court. Conformable (we see here exactly) was this operation to the instructions laid down by him, as per §9, just 20 years before, anno 1801, in the first year of his reign. As to the Rules of Court, it was not in the nature of the case that they should present any additional difficulty; Rules which, if it were worth the trouble, and would not make too much sensation, he might have repealed in form at any time.

Be this as it may, here was the exact case, so long ago provided for by Eldonic providence: the case, which, being the principle laid down,

---

[1] See pp. 224–5 above.

with virtual directions given, for the guidance of his next in command, had been made broad enough to fit. 'You need not be told (say these directions) how much more obedience-worthy Common is than Statute law:—law of our own making, than any of the law we are forced to recieve from Lay-gents. But, though you should find one of our own laws in your way—nay, though with one of *their's*, you should find in your way one of *our's* to give validity and strength to it—never you mind that; your business is to make sure of the fees. At the same time, for decency sake, while our underlings, who get more of them than we do, are screwing them up (and you may trust *them* for *that*) you of course will know nothing of the matter. Should any unpleasant accident happen—such as the having the Table with the lawful fee, in company with the proof of the additional money habitually exacted, bolted out upon you in the face of the public, you will of course be all amazement. Though the thing can never have taken place, but under your own eye—while the prisoner was beginning to be conducted from your own chambers, where you had just been examining him—never had you so much as suspected the existence of any such difference.'

As to Lord Abbot, whatever want of disposition on his part there may have been to pay regard to Acts of Parliament, no such want could there have been as to any such instructions as these of Lord Eldon's. But whether it was that he had not got them by heart, or that when the time came to repeat them and apply them to practice, his heart failed him,—so it was—they were not followed: and so, out came the confession that has been seen: the confession in all its nakedness.

This is not all: not more than three years before, this very fee had been taken into consideration by specially-appointed authority, and the 4*s.* 6*d.* disallowed. Under the head of "Tipstaff," 'the Table of 1760' (say[1] certain commissioners, of whom presently) 'directs the fee of 6*s.* to be paid to the Tipstaff that carries any prisoner committed at a Judge's chambers to the King's Bench prison.' . . . . 'The fee of 10*s.* 6*d.* we conceive, to have been taken in respect of these commitments . . . . for twenty-five years, and probably longer: but *we recommend* 'that the fee of 6*s.* only be received in future.'[a]

[a] Report printed for the House of Commons—Date of order for printing, 14th May, 1818. Sole subject of it: 'Duties, salaries, and emoluments as to the Court of King's Bench.'[2]

---

[1] 1825C, 1830 omit opening bracket.

[2] See the third Report of the Royal Commission on Officers of Courts of Justice, *Commons Sessional Papers* (1818) vii. 243–430. There are minor inaccuracies in the rendering of the above passage, which is at vii. 426–7.

Mark now the regard manifested by these commissioners—by these commissioners of Lord Eldon's—for the authority of Parliament. Recommendation soft as lambskin: of the extortion, and contempt of Parliament, impudent as it was, not any the slightest intimation, unless the rotten apology, thus foisted in instead of censure, be regarded as such. Of this recommendation the fruit has been already seen: the fee taken, and for aught that appears uninterruptedly taken, notwithstanding. What?—In all the three intervening years, the Chief Justice, had he never heard of any such recommendation? never heard a *Report*, of which his own court, with the fees belonging to it, were the subject? never seen any thing of it?

And the commissioners? For what cause disallow the 4s. 6d.? Only because the Act of Parliament, and the contempt so impudently put upon it, and the extortion and corruption for the purpose of which the contempt was put, had been staring them in the face. Men, who from such hands accept, and in this way execute, such commissions—is not some punishment their due? Yes surely: therefore here it is. Public—behold their names! 1. John Campbell, Esq. Master in Chancery;—2. William Alexander, Esq. then Master, now, by the grace of Lord Eldon, Lord Chief Baron of the Exchequer;—3. William Adams, Doctor of Civil Law;—4. William Osgood, Esq.—5. William Walton, Esq.[1]

Accompanied are these recommendations by certain *non-recommendations*. From those as to Tipstaffs, reference is made to ditto as to Marshal: and there it is, that, after stating (p. 172) that his profit arises chiefly out of two sources, of which (be it not forgotten) *the tap* is one[2]—with this source before them it is that (after ringing the praises of it) another of their recommendations is—'that this matter be left in the hands of the court to which the prison more immediately belongs.'[3] In plain English, of the Chief Justice, whose

[1] John Campbell (c.1750–1826), MP for Ayr Burghs 1794–1807, Master in Chancery 1801–19, Accountant General 1819–26; Sir William Alexander (c.1761–1842), Master in Chancery 1809–24, Chief Baron of the Exchequer 1824–31; William Adams (1772–1851), Advocate of Doctors' Commons 1799–1825; William Osgoode (1754–1824), Chief Justice of Upper Canada 1791–4, Chief Justice of Lower Canada 1794–1801; William Walton (d. 1833), Attorney General of the Duchy of Lancaster 1810–33.

[2] According to the third Report of the Royal Commission on Officers of Courts of Justice, *Commons Sessional Papers* (1818) vii. 418 (this is p. 172 of the Report), 'The marshal's chief sources of profit at the present time, arise from the sale of porter and ale, and from the granting of the rules.' The granting of the rules was a practice whereby the Marshal, who was custodian of the King's Bench Prison, would, in return for a security, allow debtors to live out of the prison.

[3] In regard to the emoluments of the Marshal 'not derived from fees', the Report states: 'It appears to us upon the whole, to leave this matter where the statute 32 Geo. 2, cap. 28, has placed it; together with all matters conducive to the better government of the prison, in the hands of the court to which the prison more immediately belongs' (ibid., vii. 417–18).

interest it is to maximize the profit in all manner of ways, and of whose emoluments they saw a vast portion, rising in proportion to the productiveness of *this* source. Throughout the whole of the Report, except for a purpose such as this, not the least symptom of thinking exhibited: '*fees taken so much, we recommend so much:*' such throughout is the product of the united genius of these five scholars of the school of Eldon.[a]

See now, Mr. Peel, and in its genuine colours, this fresh fruit of the consistency of your consistent friend.[1] See, in this rich fruit, the effect and character of his commission. Oppose now, Mr. Peel, if you have face for it; oppose now, Mr. Attorney-General, if you have face for it; oppose now, Mr. Attorney-General Copley[2]—for neither must your name be covered up—the permitting of the House of Commons to exercise the functions of the House of Commons.

Oppose now, if you have face for it, 'the dragging the Judges of the land' before the Catos[3] whom you are addressing—the tribunal of Parliament. Fear no longer, Mr. Peel, if ever you feared before, the obtaining credence for your assurance—that it was by Lord Eldon his Majesty was advised to commission Lord Eldon to report upon the conduct of Lord Eldon. Mr. Canning—you, who but two years ago— so light in the scale of sentimentalism is public duty weighed against private friendship, (and such friendship!)—you who, so lately uttered the so solemn promise never to give a vote that should cast imputation upon Lord Eldon,[4] watch well, Sir, your time, and when, *these* imputations having come on, votes come to be given on them, repress then, if possible, your tears, and, wrapping yourself up in your agony, hurry out of the House.

---

[a] Report of the commissioners on the duties, salaries, and emoluments in Courts of Justice;- - -As to the Court of King's Bench, 'Ordered by the House of Commons to be printed 14th May, 1818.'

---

[1] For Peel on Eldon's consistency see 'Observations on Peel's Speech', p. 177n above.

[2] John Singleton Copley (1772–1863), first Baron Lyndhurst, Solicitor General 1819–24, Attorney General 1824–6, Master of the Rolls 1826–7, Lord Chancellor 1827–30, 1834–5, 1841–6, Chief Baron of the Exchequer 1831–4.

[3] An allusion to Marcus Porcius Cato (234–149BC), Roman Censor and Senator, proverbial for his brusque manners, bluntness of speech and opposition to luxury.

[4] In the House of Commons on 4 June 1823, in opposing John Williams' motion to appoint a Select Committee to inquire into the delays in Chancery (for which see below), Canning had stated that he could not 'give a vote which might appear to call the noble and learned lord's [i.e. Eldon's] character, judicial or personal, into question' (see *Parliamentary Debates* (1823) ix. 791–4).

§ XIII. *How the Chancellor went to Parliament, and got the Corruption established.*

The explosion has been seen. Blown by it into open air, was the scheme of taxing without Parliament, and in the teeth of Parliament. At the same time, a handle for denunciation was left prominent; and it has been seen how broad an one: a handle too, which some *Williams*[1] or other might at any time lay hold of, and give trouble: the trouble which the driver of pigs has with his pigs—the trouble of collecting Honourable Gentlemen together, and whistling them in when the question is called for. Delay, therefore, was not now in season. Nov. 21, 1821, was the day on which the breach, as above, was made: a session did not pass without providing for the repair of it: the 10th of June, 1822, is the day on which the first stone was laid;[2] and how thorough and complete the repair is, remains now to be shown. The hand of Parliament being the only applicable instrument, stooping at last to employ it could not but be more or less mortifying to a workman to whom, for so many years, it had been a football. But, to Lord Eldon, the part of the reed is not less familiar than that of the oak; and what was lost in universally applicable power will be seen gained in ease and tranquillity, reference had to this special and most valuable use of it.

Act, 22 July 1822,[3] 3 Geo. IV. c. 69. Title, 'An Act to enable the Judges of the several Courts of Record at Westminster to make regulations respecting the fees of the Officers, Clerks, and Ministers of the said Courts.'

The preamble has been seen:[4] business of it, skinning over the past illegality, section[s] 6.[5] Business of the first, empowering these same Judges to screw up to a maximum, and without stint, the accustomed fees: of the second, to add any number of new ones: of the third, making it to this effect, the special duty of all underlings to do whatever their masters please: of the fourth, anxiously easing them of the trouble of regulating Solicitors' fees, forasmuch as nothing was to be

---

[1] John Williams (1777–1846), MP for Lincoln 1822–6 and Winchelsea 1830–2, Baron of the Exchequer 1834, Justice of King's Bench 1834–46, a supporter of legal reform, and particularly interested in the correction of abuses and delays in Chancery, had brought forward motions on the subject in the House of Commons on 4 June 1823 and 24 February 1824. In response to the latter, Peel had announced the proposed appointment of the Royal Commission on Chancery practice (see *Parliamentary Debates* (1824) x. 372–437).

[2] The Bill was in fact ordered by the House of Commons to be brought in on 11 June 1822.

[3] 1825C 'Act 22 (July 1822)'; 1825D 'Act 22 July 1822,'; 1826, 1830 'Act 22, July 1822,'.

[4] See § V, pp. 218–19 above.

[5] 1825C 'section 1, six.'; 1825D, 1826, 1830 'section 6.'

got by it: of the fifth, providing, as has been and will be seen, for the concealment of the fees as before, should more be to be got at any time by their being concealed than by their being known: of the sixth, which is the last, providing compensation for any the smallest fee, which, by accident, should happen to slip out: should any such misfortune ever happen, the losers are not only authorized, but '*required,*' to tell '*his Majesty*' of it.

For every possible additional *duty*, an additional fee or batch of fees: Good. In § 14,[1] or elsewhere, it will be seen how it is that, by multiplying such *duties* under the rose, equity pace, and equity cost, have been rendered what they are.

Everything at '*discretion:*' (§ 1:) everything as they '*shall see fit:*' (§ 1:)[2] the people of England, all who have redress to seek for injury from without doors—all who have to defend themselves against any of those injuries of which these same Judges are the instruments—all who have to defend themselves against injuries, the seat of which is in the pretended seat of redress—all who have to defend themselves against the attacks of any of those villains with whom Lord Eldon has thus placed these Judges, together with himself, in partnership—all, all are thus delivered up bound, to be plundered in secret, without stint or control, by the hand of these same Judges. Never could more solicitude have been demonstrated: never more appropriate talent, as well as care, expended in satisfying it: so exquisite the work, the most exquisitely magnifying microscope might be challenged to bring to view a flaw in it. In the stile of English legislation, it may be given as a model: as a study—for a young draughtsman, who, for sections a yard long, looks to be paid at so much a word. The same hand, which, had no better interest than the public's been to be provided for, would have left loop-holes, through which the entire substance of the measure might be extracted, has, in this its darling work, as if by an hermetic seal, closed all such crannies. Could this pamphlet have been made to hold it, I should have copied it, and pointed out the beauties of it. For comprehensiveness it has but one rival, and that is in the law called *Civil Law. Quod principi placuit legis habet vigorem.*[3] For *principi*, put *judici*, you have the Act of *English law*—the Act of George the Fourth.

The enacting part could not be too clear of equivocation: and not a

---

[1] See p. 250 below, where Bentham, however, postpones discussion of this topic.

[2] The first clause of the Act gave powers to the judges 'to establish and ordain, by their Discretion, Tables of Fees . . . which Tables of Fees shall be entered or inrolled in the public Books or Records of the Courts . . . in such manner as the Persons establishing the same shall think fit'.

[3] 'A decision given by the emperor has the force of a statute.' *Digest of Justinian*, I. iv. 1.

particle is to be found in it. The preamble presented an irresistible demand for equivocation; and here it is. Seen already (in §5)[1] has been this same preamble, with its essential word *effectually*. Note here the use of it: it is this. The more *effectually* to turn men's minds aside from the idea of the illegality,—causing them to suppose, that though nothing had been done but what was *legal*, strictly legal, yet, to give to what had been done its full effect, legal *machinery* in some shape or other was needed, in addition to such as learned workmen stood already provided with: and that, to give existence to such additional machinery, was accordingly the object of the Act. Now, the fact is, that no such additional machinery does the Act provide or attempt to provide: not an atom of it. What it does, is—easing the hands of the criminals, of whatsoever check they felt applied by the consciousness of their so lately divulged criminality,—thus giving to them the undisturbed power of taxing the people for their own profit, without stint; and, for this purpose, rendering that power which had so long been arbitrary in *fact*, at length arbitrary by *law*.

Remains the clause about keeping the table of fees exposed to view. They are to be 'kept hung up'—these tables of fees—'hung up in a *conspicuous part* of the' room.[2] Good: and while there hung up, what will be the effect of them? The same as of those hung up in virtue of those former statutes of George II., with the King's Bench Rule that followed them.[3] The *place* they are hung up in, is to be a conspicuous one. Good: but the *characters?* of these nothing is said; so that here is a loophole ready made and provided.

In the above-mentioned case,[a] which produced the demand for this act, a document, referred to as a ground of the decision, is—a Rule of Court of Michaelmas Term, 3 Geo. II.[b] and 'the Table of Fees settled in the following year.' In article 8, of the document intituled 'Rules and Orders,' &c. mentioned in that same Rule of Court, which, without any title, is in Latin, in speaking of the Table of Fees, it is said, that it shall be 'fairly written in a plain and legible hand.' With this clause lying before him—and he could not but have had it lying before him—with this clause lying before him it is, that the penner of

---

[a] 1821. Barnewall and Alderson, vi. 266.[4]

[b] See the book intituled 'Rules, Orders, and Notices, in the Court of King's Bench . . . to the 21 Geo. II. inclusive.' 2nd edit. 1747. Page not referable to, there being no paging in the book!

---

[1] See pp. 218–19 above.

[2] According to the fifth clause, 'Extracts of the Table of the Fees . . . shall be kept hung up in some conspicuous Part of the Office or Place of Business of the Officer, Clerk, or Minister respectively, whom the same may concern'.

[3] See §XII, p. 232 above.   [4] See §XII, pp. 231–2 above.

this same Act of Lord Eldon's contents himself with speaking about the *place*, and says nothing about the *hand*.

What the omission had for its cause, whether design or accident, judge, whosoever is free to judge, from the whole complexion of the business. Not that even in this same Rule of Court, with its '*fair and legible hand*,' there was any thing better than the semblance of honesty. Tables of Benefactors to Churches and Parishes—Tables of Turnpike Tolls—were they, even in *those* days, *written in a fair and legible hand?* No: they were painted in print hand, as they are still, in black and gold. But, if instead of *fair and legible*, the characters should come to be microscopic, and as illegible a scrawl as can be found— suppose in the grim-gribber hand called *Court hand*—a precedent of this sort will not be among the authorities to be set at nought: this will not be among the cases, in which, according to Lord Eldon's consistency, as per page [225],[1] 'It would be more consistent to suppose some ground appeared to former Judges, upon which it' (the Act of Parliament, or the Rule of Court, or both) 'might be rendered consistent with the practice'—meaning, with the practice carried on in violation of them.

Lord Eldon's Act, or *The Eldon Act*, should be the stile and title of this Act. Precedent, *Lord Ellenborough's Act*,—so stiled in a late vote paper of Honourable House:[a] Lord Ellenborough's Act, sole, but sufficient and characteristic, monument, of the legislative care, wisdom, and humanity of that Peer of Parliament, as well as Lord Chief Justice.[b]

---

[a] May 17th, 1825.[2]

[b] Note, that '*effectually*,' as all *future* corruption is sanctioned, nothing is said of any that is *past*. If, in the situation in question, the word *responsibility* were anything better than a mockery, the fate of Lord Macclesfield[3]—and on so much stronger grounds—would await Lord Eldon, his instruments, and accomplices. But, forasmuch as all such responsibility *is* a mere mockery, the only practical and practicable course would be—for some Member (Mr. John Williams, for example,) to move for a *Bill of Indemnity* for them: which motion, to prove the needlessness of it, would call forth another stream of Mr. Peel's eloquence: a reply might afford no bad occasion for Whig wigs, could a decent cloak be found for their departed saint.[4]

---

[1] 1825C, 1825D, 1830 blank; 1826 '18'.

[2] See *Votes and Proceedings of the House of Commons* (1825) no. 64, p. 462. Edward Law (1750–1818), first Baron Ellenborough, Attorney General 1801–2, Chief Justice of King's Bench 1802–18. Bentham elsewhere characterized the so-called Ellenborough Act of 1803 (43 Geo. III, c.58) as 'the Act for the extension of capital punishment, and encouragement to perseverance in murder, by applying to the *attempt* the punishment which is found confined to the *consummation*' (see Parcus, 'Peel and Munificence;—Bentham and Niggardliness', *Morning Herald*, 15 April 1828).

[3] Thomas Parker (1667–1732), first Baron and first Earl of Macclesfield, Chief Justice of Queen's Bench 1710–18, Lord Chancellor 1718–25. Following investigations by a committee of

 [*See p. 242 for n. 3 cont. and n. 4.*]

As to the Chancellor's being the *primum mobile* of the Act,—only for form's sake, and to anticipate cavil, can proof in words be necessary. The Bill being a Money Bill, it could not make its first appearance in the House in which Lord Eldon rules these matters by his own hand. The Members, by whom it was brought into the only competent House, were the two Law Officers:[1] and that, by these two official persons, any such Bill could, consistently either with usage or propriety, have been brought in otherwise than under the direction of the Head of the Law, will not be affirmed by any one. The Act, then, was LORD ELDON'S Act.

§ XIV. *How the Head of the Law, seeing Swindling at work, continued it, and took his profit out of it.*

Swindling is an intelligible word: it is used here for shortness, and because familiar to everybody. Look closely, and see whether, on this occasion, it is in any the slightest degree misapplied.

By statute 30 Geo. II. c. 24. § 1:[2] '*All persons who knowingly or designedly, by false pretence, or pretences, shall obtain from any person, or persons, money. . . . with intent to cheat or defraud any person, or persons, of the same, . . . shall be fined or imprisoned, or . . . be put in the pillory, or publicly whipped, or transported . . . for . . . seven years.*'[a]

1. *All persons*, says the Act. If then a *Master in Chancery*, so com-

[a] Let it not be said, that to come within this Act it is necessary a man should have proposed to himself the pleasure of being, or of being called, a *cheat:* the man the Act means, if it means any man, is he who, on obtaining the money by any false pretence, intends to convert it to his own use. Instead of the words *cheat* and *defraud*, words which,—and not the less for being so familiar—require a definition, better would it have been, if a definition such as the above had been employed. But logic is an utter stranger to the Statute-book, and without any such help from it as is here endeavoured to be given, the Act has been constantly receiving the above interpretation in practice.

the Privy Council into the funds of suitors in the hands of the Masters in Chancery, and the improper use of suitors' money, Macclesfield was impeached in 1725 for a variety of abuses in the Court of Chancery, subsequently found guilty, and sentenced to pay a fine of £30,000 to the King and committed to the Tower until the fine had been paid.
[4] Presumably Erskine.

[1] Robert Gifford, later Baron Gifford, Attorney General 1819–24, and John Singleton Copley, later Baron Lyndhurst, Solicitor General 1819–24.
[2] 'An Act for the more effectual Punishment of Persons who shall attain, or attempt to attain, Possession of Goods or Money, by false or untrue Pretences; for preventing the unlawful Pawning of Goods; for the easy Redemption of Goods pawned; and for preventing Gaming in Public Houses by Journeymen, Labourers, Servants and Apprentices.' There are some minor inaccuracies in the rendering of the passage.

porting himself as above, is not a person, he is *not* a *swindler:* if he *is* a person, *he is.*

2. And so, in the case of a *Commissioner of Bankrupts*, if any one there be who has *so* comported himself.

3. So likewise in the case of any other functionary, holding an office under Lord Eldon.

4. So likewise in the case of every *Barrister*, practising in any of the Courts in or over which Lord Eldon is judge: in the case of every such Barrister, if *so* comporting himself.

5. Add every *Solicitor*.

If, however, it is true, as indicated in the samples given in §2,[1] that in the case of the Solicitor, in respect of what he does in this way, he is, by the subordinate Judge (the aforesaid Master) not only to a great extent *allowed*, but at the same time to a certain extent *compelled*,—here, in his case, is no inconsiderable alleviation: in the guilt of the official, that of the non-official malefactors is eclipsed, and in a manner swallowed up and drowned.

So far as regards Masters in Chancery, to judge whether, among those same subordinate Judges under Lord Eldon, there be any such person as a *swindler*, and if so, what number of such persons, see the sample given in §2.[2]

Same question as to Commissioners of Bankrupts, concerning whom, except as follows, it has not as yet been my fortune to meet with any indications. Lists of these Commissioners, 14: in each list, 5: all creatures, all removable creatures—accordingly, all so many virtual pensioners during pleasure—of Lord Eldon. Further subject of enquiry, whether these groupes likewise be, or be not, so many gangs of his learned swindlers.

Indication from the Morning Chronicle, Friday, April 15, 1825:—[3]

At a Common Council, Thursday, April 14, Information given by Mr. *Favel*. Appointment made by list 2 of these Commissioners, for

---

[1] See pp. 206–11 above.

[2] See ibid.

[3] The passage to which Bentham refers is as follows: 'Mr Favell called the attention of the Court to what he conceived to be a most serious grievance to the mercantile and commercial interests of the City of London. It was not his intention to conclude by making a motion, and he therefore requested the indulgence of the Court whilst he brought forward a complaint against the Commissioners of Bankrupts. A short time ago he attended to prove a debt before the Commissioners, and he found that they had appointed twelve for one to prove debts, etc. He waited till above half-past one, and no Commissioner made his appearance. He was about to quit the place, when one Commissioner (Mr. Horace Twiss) made his appearance, and before him he proved his debt. He now understood that he should have to dance attendance again before the Commissioners, because the proof being made before one Commissioner only, was not legal. He was aware, that as Mr. Twiss was a Member of Parliament, some excuse might be made for him; but the other Commissioners on the list, Messrs. Glynn and Whitmore, were not Members

proof of debts in a certain case: hour appointed, that from 12 to 1: Commissioners named in the instrument of appointment, Messrs. *Glynn, Whitmore*, and Mr. M.P. *Horace Twiss*.[1] Attendance by Mr. *Glynn*, none: by Mr. *Whitmore*, as little: consequence, nothing done: by Mr. *Horace Twiss*, an hour and a half after the commencement of the appointed time, half an hour after the termination of it, a call made at the place. Had he even been in attendance from the commencement of the time, instead of stepping in half an hour after the termination of it, still, Commissioners more than one not being present, no business could (it seems) have been done. To what purpose, then, came he when he did, unless it was to make a title to the attendance-fee? Moreover, for this *non-attendance* of theirs, Messrs. *Glynn* and *Whitmore*, have they received their *attendance* fees? If so, let them prove, if they can, that they are not swindlers. Mr. *Horace Twiss*, who does not attend any part of the time, but steps in half an hour after, when his coming cannot answer the purpose, has *he* received for that day any attendance fee? If so, then comes the same task for him to perform. Mr. *Favel's* candour supposes some excuse may be made for Mr. *Twiss*: if so, a very lame one it will be. An option he should have had to make, is, to do his duty as a Commissioner of Bankrupts, and not be a Member of Parliament, or do his duty as a Member of Parliament (oh, ridiculous!) and not be a Commissioner of Bankrupts:—a Commissioner of Bankrupts, and, as such, one of Lord Eldon's pensioners. Convinced by his commissionership of the immaculateness of his patron, Commissioner makes a speech for patron, much, no doubt, to the satisfaction of both. Should a Committee be appointed to inquire into Chancery practice, there, Mr. Peel, there, in Mr. *Twiss*, you have a *Chairman* for it.

Meantime, suppose, for argument sake, Mr. *Twiss* comporting himself in any such manner as to give just cause of complaint against him—be the case ever so serious—to what person, who had any command over his temper, would it appear worth while to make any such complaint? To judge whether it would, let him put the question to *Mr. Lowe*, as per § 10.[2]

These men—or some (and which?) of them—being so many

of Parliament, and it was important that their duties as Commissioners, should not be neglected. He knew many complaints had been made of the want of punctuality on the part of the Commissioners of Bankrupts, and if the evil was not remedied, it would be the duty of the Court to bring the subject before the highest legal authority.' A copy of this passage is at UC xix. 27.

[1] Thomas Christopher Glyn (1789–1827); Horace Twiss (1787–1849), MP for Wootton Basset 1820–30, Newport I.o.W. 1830–1 and Bridport 1835–7, Under Secretary of War and Colonies 1828–30, and later the biographer of Eldon. Whitmore has not been identified.

[2] See pp. 225–30 above.

swindlers,—he who, *knowing* them to be so, *protects* them in such their *practices*, and shares with them—with all of them—in their *profits*, what is *he?* Is not he too either a *swindler*, or, if distinguishable, something still worse? If, with strict grammatical or legal propriety, he cannot be denominated a receiver of *stolen* goods,—still, the *relation* borne by him to these swindlers, is it not exactly that which the *receiver* of stolen goods bears to the *thief? Masters* in Chancery, 10: *Commissioners of Bankrupts*, 90;[1] together, 100; and, upon the booty made by every one of them, if any, who is a swindler, does this receiver of a portion of their respective gains make his profit: these same swindlers, every one of them, made by him what they are.—Stop! Between the two sorts of receivers,—the thief-breeding and the swindler-breeding receivers,—one difference, it is true, there is. The *thief-breeder*, though, in so far as in his power, he gives *concealment* to his confederates, he does not, because he cannot, give them *impunity:* whereas, the *swindler-breeding* receiver, seeing that he can, gives both.

Masters in Chancery—creatures of this same creator, almost all, if not all of them—is there so much as one of them who is not a swindler? an habitual swindler? Say no, if you can, Lord Eldon! Say no, if you can, Mr. Secretary Peel! Deny, if you can, that your Mentor is in partnership with all these swindlers. Deny it, if you can, that, out of those who have accepted from him the appointment of reporting him blameless, two are of the number of these same swindlers![2]

'Oh! but,' by one of his hundred mouthpieces, cries Lord Eldon, 'nothing has he ever known of all this: nothing, except in those instances in which his just displeasure at it has well been manifested. Whatever there be that is amiss, never has been wanting the desire to rectify it—the anxious desire. . . . But the task! think what a task! think too of the leisure, the quantity of leisure necessary! necessary, and to a man who knows not what it is to have leisure! Then the wisdom! the consummate wisdom! the recondite, the boundless learning! Alas! what more easy than for the malevolent and the foolish to besputter with their slaver the virtuous and the wise!'

Not know of it indeed? Oh hypocrisy! hypocrisy! The keeper of a house of ill fame . . . to support an indictment against him, is it necessary that everything done in his house should have been done in his actual presence? Ask any barrister, or rather ask any solicitor, whom retirement has saved from the Chancellor's prospect-destroying power—ask him, whether it be in the nature of the case, that of all the

---

[1] There were in fact only seventy Commissioners of Bankrupts.
[2] Of the Commissioners appointed to inquire into Chancery practice, Samuel Compton Cox and William Courtenay were Masters in Chancery.

modes in which depredation has been practising in any of his courts, there should have been so much as one, that can ever have been a secret to him?

No *time* for it, indeed! Of the particular *time* and *words*, employed by him in talking backwards and forwards, in addition to the already so elaborately-organized general mass, as if to make delay and pretences for it, a thousandth—a ten thousandth part—would have served an honest man anywhere for a reform: a reform, which, how far soever from complete, would suffice for striking off two-thirds of the existing mass, and who can say how much more?

Have you any doubt of this, Mr. Peel?—accept then a few samples.

1. Reform the first. (Directed to the proper person.) *Order* in these words. *Charge for no more days than you attend.* Number of words, eight. At the Master's office off go two-thirds of the whole delay, and with it of the expense.

2. Reform the second. *Text. On every attendance-day attend ten hours. Paraphrase.* Attend these ten, instead of the five, four, or three, on which you attend now. For your emolument, with the vast power attached to it, give the attendance which so many thousand other official persons would rejoice to give for a twentieth part of it.

3. A third reform. *In the year there are twelve months: serve in every one of them. Months excepted for vacation, those in which no wrong that requires redress is practised anywhere.*

4. A fourth reform. You are one person: any clerk of your's, another. The business of any clerk of yours is to serve *with* you, not *for* you. Serving by another is not serving, but swindling.

Small as is the number of words in the above proposed Orders, any body may see how many more of them there are than are strictly needful to the purpose of directing what it is desired shall be done.

Numerous are the reforms that might be added: all of them thus simple; many of them still more concisely expressible.

Oh, but the *learning* necessary! the recondite lore! fruit of mother Blackstone's twice twenty years' lucubrations![1] Learning indeed! Of all the reforms that have been seen, is there a single one that would require more learning than is possessed by his lordship's house-keeper, if he has one, or any one of his housemaids?

Wisdom necessary for anything of all this? Oh hypocrites! nothing but the most common of all common honesty.

Of those whom, because unsuccessful, poor, and powerless, men

---

[1] The phrase 'viginti annorum lucubrationibus', from Sir John Fortescue, *De Laudibus Legum Angliae*, Ch. VIII, referring to the twenty years experience of the law necessary for judges, is repeated by Blackstone, *Commentaries on the Laws of England*, i. 69. Bentham perhaps had in mind the forty years between Blackstone's beginning his legal studies upon entering the Middle Temple in 1741, and his death in 1780.

are in the habit of calling *swindlers*, the seat—that of many of them at least—is in the *hulks:* of those hereby supposed swindlers, whom, because rich and powerful, no man till now has ever called *swindlers*—the seat—the seat of *ten* of them at least—is in the *House of Lords*.[1] As between the one class and the other, would you know in which, when the *principle of legitimacy* has given way to the *greatest happiness principle*, public indignation will press with severest weight? Set them against one another in the balance.

1. *Quantity of mischief* produced? is that among the articles to be put into the scale?

Nothing, in comparison, the mischief of the second order:— nothing the *alarm* produced by the offence of him whose seat is in the *hulks*. Against all such offences, each man bears what, in his own estimation, is little less than an adequate security—his own prudence: a circumstance by which the *swindler* is distinguished, to his advantage, from the *thief*. No man can, for a moment, so much as fancy himself secure against the hand of the swindler, if any such there be, whose seat is in the *House of Lords*. United in that irresistible hand, are the powers of fraud and force. Force is the power applied to the victim; fraud, the power applied to the mind of the public; applied as, with but too much success, it has been hitherto, to the purpose of engaging it to look on unmoved, while *depredation*, in one of its most shameless shapes, is exercised under the name of *justice*.

2. [*Unpremeditatedness*][2]—is it not in possession of being regarded as operating in extenuation of moral guilt? *deliberateness*, as an aggravation? deliberateness, does it not, in case of homicide, make to the offender the difference between death and life, under the laws of blood so dear to Honourable Gentlemen—Noble Lords, and Learned Judges? Of those swindlers, whose seat is in the hulks, how many may there not be, whose delinquency may have been the result of a hasty thought begotten by the craving of the moment? Answer and then say—of the swindler, if any such there be, whose seat is in the House of Lords, the offence is it not the *deliberate*, the *regularly repeated*, the *daily* repeated, the *authentically recorded* practice?

3. *Quantity of profit* made—is that among the circumstances that influence the magnitude of the crime? For every penny made by the swindler whose seat is in the *hulks*, the swindler, if any, whose seat is in the *House of Lords*, makes six-and-eight-pence. Six-and-eight-pence?[3] aye, six-and-eight-pences in multitudes.

---

[1] In fact, at the time Bentham was writing, of the thirteen members of the Cabinet, eight were peers.

[2] 1825C, 1825D, 1826, 1830 '*Premeditatedness*' contradicts the evident sense of the passage.

[3] 1825D, 1826, 1830 '6*s*. 8*d*. six-and-eight-pence?'

4. *Indigence*—is it not in possession of being regarded as operating in extenuation of moral guilt? all have it of those whose seat is in the *hulks*. No such extenuation, but on the contrary, the opposite aggravation have they, if any, whose seat is in the *House of Lords*.

5. *Uneducatedness*—is it not in possession of being regarded as operating in extenuation of moral guilt? Goodness of education, or, at least, the means of it, as an aggravation? The extenuation, you have in the case of those whose seat is in the *hulks:* the aggravation, in the case of those, if any, whose seat is in the *House of Lords*.

6.[1] *Multitude of the offenders*—does *that* obliterate the crime? Go then to the hulks and fetch the swindlers who serve *there*, to sit with their fellows, if such there be, who serve in the House of Lords.

7.[2] *Long continuance* of the practice—is it in the nature of that circumstance to obliterate the crime? Much longer have there been swindlers out of the Master's office than there can have been in it. The earliest on record are those who 'spoiled the Eygptians:'[3] but with them it was all pure fraud: no force was added to it.

Learning—appropriate learning—of demand for this endowment, assuredly there is no want: and not only for this, which every lawyer speaks of, but for original and originating genius—an endowment which no lawyer ever speaks of. Adding to the mass in the *Augean Stable*, every *ox* had wisdom enough for: every ox that ever was put into it: to employ a river in the cleansing of it, required, not the *muscle*, but the *genius* of a Hercules.[4]

Wisdom? Yes, indeed: but of what sort? Not that which is identical with, but that which is opposite to, Lord Eldon's. Years spent in the pursuit of those which we have seen to be the *actual ends of judicature*, four and twenty.[5] True: but by every year thus spent, a man will have been rendered, not the more, but so much the less apt, for pursuing the *ends of justice*. Lord Eldon serve the ends of justice? He knows not even what they are. Ask him what they are—at the end of half an hour employed in talking backwards and forwards, he will conclude with his speech in *Ex-parte Leicester*, and the passage that has been seen in it.[6] Ask what are the ends of justice?—Thirty paces are more than I need go, to see boys in number, any one of whom, when the question had

---

[1] 1825D, 1830 '5.'
[2] 1825D, 1830 '6.'
[3] i.e. the Israelites: see Exodus 12: 36.
[4] One of the twelve labours of the Greek hero Hercules was to cleanse in a single day the stables of Augeas, King of Elis, which housed his great herd of oxen, and which had not been cleaned for thirty years. He accomplished his task by diverting the rivers Alpheus and Peneus through the stalls.
[5] Since 1801, when Eldon had been first appointed Lord Chancellor.
[6] See §IX, p. 225 above.

found him mute, or worse than mute, could answer and take his place.

Yes: in that man, in whom the will has been vitiated as his has been, the understanding—sure as death—has been vitiated along with it. Should a pericranium such as his ever meet the hand or eye of a Gall or a Spurtzheim,[1] they will find the organ of justice obliterated, and the organ of *chicane*,—a *process* from their organ of *theft* grown up in the place of it.[a]

[a] How to grant licence under the guise of censure:
Extract from the Examiner, Nov. [8],[2] 1824:—[3]
'*The Six Clerks*.—In the Court of Chancery, on Monday, the following conversation occurred. An affidavit having been handed to the Lord Chancellor, his Lordship asked, "What is the meaning of 'Agent to a Six-Clerk,' which I see there? What is his business?"—Mr. Hart's client stated, that the Agent was a person who manages the business for a Six-Clerk.—Lord Chancellor: "And what does the Six-Clerk himself?"—Solicitor: Attends the Master.—Lord Chancellor: "Then he is entirely out of the business of his own office: he does nothing in it?"—Solicitor: Nothing, my Lord.—The Lord Chancellor (after a pause): "When I came into this Court, the Six-Clerks were the most efficient Solicitors in the Court of Chancery. Some of the most eminent Solicitors were Clerks of that class, and used to transact their business, and draw up minutes with such ability, that we had few or no motions to vary minutes. But now the Six-Clerk abandons his business to a person who knows nothing at all about it. 'Tis no wonder then that delays have crept into the practice, which we formerly knew nothing of. However, before it proceeds further, I'll take care that Solicitors in this Court shall be obliged to transact their business in person."'

"When I came into this Court:" that is to say, four-and-twenty years ago. Good, my Lord, and where have you been ever since? Incessant have been such threats: constant the execution of them with the same punctuality as in this case. What Solicitor, what Barrister, is there, that does not understand this? Who that does not know, that, where official depredation is concerned, what in English is a threat, is in Eldonish a licence?

When, as per sample in §2, page [211],[4] 700*l.* was exacted in reduction of a demand of we know not how much more, for office copies of a Particular of Sale—office copies for which there was as much need, as for those which, according to the story, were once taken of the Bible—on that occasion was there any of this vapouring? Silent as a mouse was this Aristides,[5] who could not endure the existence of the harmless Agent, whose agency consisted in looking over the books, to see that his employers, the Six-Drones, were not defrauded of the per centage due to them from the labours of the Sixty working-bees.[6] But this summer-up of six-and-eightpences was an intruder. Lord Eldon's patronage was not increased by him, while official secrets were open to him. Such was his offence.

---

[1] Franz Joseph Gall (1758–1828), anatomist, physiologist and founder of phrenology, and his one-time friend and associate Johann Christoph Spurzheim (1776–1832).

[2] 1825C, 1825D, 1826, 1830 '7'.

[3] There are some minor inaccuracies in the rendering of this passage.

[4] 1825C, 1825D, 1830 blank; 1826 '7'.

[5] Aristides (c.520–467BC), surnamed 'the Just', Athenian statesman and soldier, Archon 489–488BC.

 [*See p. 250 for n. 6.*]

If I misrecollect not, this section has been referred to for something to be said, as to the profit capable of being derived from the source here spoken of:[1] if so, the reader's indulgence must be trusted to for a respite, till the entire of the Judges' Salary-raising measure has been found ripe for a view to be taken of it.

§XV. *How King George's Judges improved upon the precedent set by King Charles's, in the case of Ship-money.*[2] See above, §9.[3]

The improvement was an altogether simple one. The pocket, which received the produce of the tax imposed by King Charles's judges, was the King's. The pocket, which received and receives the produce of the tax imposed by King George's Judges, was and is their own.

Now for consistency—now for the use of this same principle as a precedent: a precedent set, and with this improvement, in the seats and sources of what is called justice, and thence offered to the adoption of the other departments. But what applies to this purpose will be better understood when the consummation given to the system by the pending measure comes to be brought to view.

What *they* did, they contented themselves with doing, as it were, by the *side* of Parliament: giving indeed their sanction to the operations of an authority acting without Parliament,—but not, of their own authority, taking upon themselves to obstruct and frustrate the operations of Parliament. Never did *they* levy war against the authority of Parliament. Never did *they* make known by express terms, that whatever Parliament had ordained should, as they pleased, go for anything or for nothing. Never did they adjourn obedience *sine die*. Never did they say—'*A practice having prevailed ... contrary to an Act of Parliament ... it would be better to correct it in future*, not *in that particular instance*.'[a]

---

[a] Lord Eldon, in vi. Vesey, jun. p. 433, as above, p. [225.][4]

---

[6] i.e. the Sworn or Sixty Clerks, of whom each Six Clerk was allowed to appoint a maximum of ten.

[1] See §XIII, p. 239 above. Bentham does not return specifically to this point.
[2] This ancient tax had been revived by Charles I in 1634, but by the Ship Money Act of 1640 (17 Car. I, c.14) it had been declared illegal.
[3] See pp. 224–5 above.
[4] 1825C, 1825D, 1826, 1830 blank.

§XVI. *How to be consistent, and complete the Application of the Self-serving Principle.*

Now as to consistency. You, Lord Eldon, you who practice consistency,—you, Mr. Peel, you who admire it,[1]—go on as you have begun. Assisted by your official instruments, you have planted in the statute-book, after having established it in practice, the self-serving, the self-corrupting, the self-gorging principle. You have rooted it in one department: plant off-sets from it in the others. You have covered with it the field of justice: go on with it, and cover with it the field of force.

Repair, in the first place, the ravage so lately made by the fabled dry-rot; that dry-rot which, not content with timber, rotted the china and the glasses. Give to the Duke of York[2] the power of settling the pay of his subordinates, and levying, by his own order, the amount of it. . . . What! do you hesitate? Not to speak of loyalty, all pretence then to consistency is at an end with you. Dignity is, in your creed, the one thing needful: your judges are brimful of it, at least if it be in the power of gold to make them so. So far, 'everything is as it should be.'[3] But the Commander-in-chief—not to speak of the Heir to the Crown—has he not, in his situation, demand enough for plenitude of dignity? And, forasmuch as, in your mathematics, Mr. Robinson— applied to administration of justice, aptitude is *as* dignity,[a]—say, if you can, how the same proposition should fail when applied to the still more dignified function of wielding military force?

---

[a] In Mr. Robinson's speech of 16th May, 1825, as per *Globe and Traveller* of the next day, no less than *ten* times (for they have been counted) was this *ratio* assumed in the character of a *postulate:*[4] assumed by the Finance Master, and by his scholars, *nemine contradicente*, acknowledged in that character: every one of them, for self, sons, daughters' husbands, or other *et cæteras*, panting, even as the hart panteth after the water-brooks,[5] for the benefit of it. Number of repetitions, *ten* exactly: for Mr. Robinson had not forgot his Horace—with his *decus repetitu placebunt*.[6]

---

[1] See 'Observations on Peel's Speech', p. 177n above.

[2] Frederick Augustus, Duke of York and Albany (1763–1827), Commander in Chief 1798– 1809, 1811–27, heir presumptive to the throne from the death of his father, George III, in 1820 until his own death in 1827.

[3] A favourite allusion of Bentham's, referring to Blackstone's opinion that, with regard to the offence of heresy, 'Everything is now as it should be' (see 'Defence of Economy against Burke', §VI, p. 72n above).

[4] In his speech in the debate on the regulation of judges' salaries, as reported in the *Globe and Traveller* of 17 May 1825, Robinson used the word 'dignity' not on ten, but twelve occasions.

[5] Psalm 42: 1.

[6] See Horace, *Ars Poetica*, 365: 'haec placuit semel, haec deciens repetita placebit', i.e. 'this pleased but once; that, though ten times repeated, will always please'.

Apply it next to the Navy. For the benefit of Lord Melville and his Croker,[1] give legality to ship-money, as, for the benefit of Lord Eldon and his Abbott, you have given it to extortion and denial of justice. Legalizing that mode of supply, now in the 19th century, you will add to it the improvements you have found for it in your own genius and your own age. You will not, as did the creatures of Charles I. make the *faux pas* of putting the produce into the King's pocket. No; you will remember what that experiment cost his Majesty's predecessor. You will, if you can get leave of envy,—you will put it into the pockets of Lord Melville, Mr. Croker, and their friends, and thus, in the navy department likewise, 'will everything be as it should be.'

Rhetoric and fallacy all this (says somebody). Fallacy?—Not it, indeed: nothing but the plainest common sense. Suffer not *yourself* to be blinded by one of those fallacies which timidity and self-distrust are so ready to oppose to indisputable truth. Say not to yourself, *all this is strong, therefore none of it is true*.

What *I do not* say is that, in the two supposed cases, the *mischief* of the application is as great as in the real one.

What I *do* say is, that the *principle* would not be *different*.—The principle different? no: nor the course taken more palpably *indefensible*.

§ XVII. *How Lord Eldon planned and established, by Act of Parliament, a Joint Stock Company, composed of the Westminster Hall Chiefs, and dishonest Men of all Classes.*

In general, Joint-stock Companies are no favourites with Lord Eldon;[2] but general rules have their exceptions.

That between dishonest men of all classes, Judges taking payment to themselves out of a fund common to both, the strictest community of interest has place, has been proved, if any thing was ever proved, over and over. A tax, into what pocket soever the money goes, cannot be imposed on *judicial pursuit*, but, to all who cannot advance the money, justice is denied, and all those who fail to do what has thus been rendered impossible to them, are delivered over to injury in all

---

[1] Robert Saunders-Dundas, formerly Dundas (1771–1851), second Viscount Melville, First Lord of the Admiralty 1812–27, 1828–30, and John Wilson Croker (1780–1857), Secretary to the Admiralty 1809–30.

[2] In the House of Lords on 3 February and again on 7 February 1825, Eldon announced his intention of bringing in a bill to check the dealings in shares of joint-stock companies before they were formed, but on 25 March 1825 apologised for having done nothing (see *Parliamentary Debates* (1825) xii. 31, 127–8, 1195–6).

shapes, at the hands of all persons who are dishonest enough to take advantage of the licence so held out. A tax, into what pocket soever the money goes, cannot be imposed on the necessary means of *judicial defence*, but it offers, to all who can advance the money, and are dishonest enough to accept the offer, an instrument, wherewith, by the power of the Judges, yet without their appearing to know anything of the use thus made of it, injury, in almost every imaginable shape, may be inflicted,—inflicted with certainty and impunity, and the correspondent sinister profit reaped, at the charge of all those who are not able to purchase the use of that same instrument for their defence. Thus, in so far as the produce of the exaction goes into the Judge's pocket, the interest of the dishonest man cannot, in either of those his situations, as above, be served, but the interest of the Judge is served along with it.

Of a partnership contract, whatever else be among its objects, one object, as well as effect, is the establishing a community of interest between the several members: and, if the persons acting so described are not dishonest; and if, between them and the Judge in question, a community of interest is not formed; let any one say who thinks he can, in what more indisputable way it is in the power of man to be dishonest; and whether, between such a set of men and a set of dishonest Judges, it would be possible for a community of sinister interest to be formed.

Not less difficult will it be found to say, how any man, Judge or not Judge, can fail to be dishonest, who, receiving money in proportion, consents, and with his eyes open, to the habitual promotion and production of injury in all imaginable shapes, in both or either of the situations described as above.

True it is that, in general, Joint-stock Companies, any at least that can be named on the same day with this for magnitude, have not been formed without *a charter:* and that, on the occasion here in question, no charter has been employed. Not less true is it, that in the establishment of other Joint-stock Companies, the power of Parliament has been employed; and that, in the establishment of the Joint-stock Company in question, that hand, so superior to all morality, has, in the manner shown in §13,[1] most diligently and effectually been employed. In the concession of a charter, the hand of the Chancellor is regularly employed: and, in the passing of the Acts of Parliament in question, it has been shown, how that same learned hand has not been less primarily and effectually employed.

Such being the *partnership*, now as to the terms of it. A species of

---

[1] See pp. 238–42 above.

partnership as well known as any other is.—A. finds money; B. skill and labour. Of the partnership here in question, such are the terms.

Head of the firm, beyond all dispute, Lord Eldon. Found by him, in by far the greatest abundance, skill, labour, power, and example. Looked for by him, and received accordingly, profit in correspondent abundance. Behold then, the firm of Eldon and Co. By what other name can the firm, with any tolerable degree of propriety, be denominated?

Apprized of the existence of this partnership, *Judge and Co.* is the denomination, by which, for I forget what length of time—some thirty or forty years probably—in print as well as in conversation, I have been in the habit of designating it: not a pen, not a voice having ever raised itself to controvert this undeniable truth. But, though established by intrinsic power—by that power which is so much in the habit of setting at nought that of Parliament—never till Lord Eldon stood up, and with so much ease carried the matter through as above, was this Coryphæus of Joint-stock Companies established by an express Act of Parliament.

One all-embracing and undeniable truth, when the public mind is sufficiently familiarized with it, will remove doubts and difficulties in abundance; it will serve as a key to every thing, that, in this country, has ever been done in the field of judicial procedure. From the Norman conquest down to the present time, diametrically opposite to the ends of justice, have been the actual ends of judicature: judicial establishment and judicial procedure included, but more especially judicial procedure. Paid, as Judges have been, by fees,—paid by taxes, the produce of which has all along been liable to be augmented, and been augmented accordingly by themselves, at no time could the system have been in any better state. Suppose that in those their situations, and *that* in the most barbarous times, Judges would have for the end of action the happiness of suitors?—As well might you suppose that it is for the happiness of negroes that planters have all along been flogging negroes; for the good of Hindoos that the Leadenhall Street Proprietors[1] have all along been squeezing and excoriating the sixty or a hundred millions of Hindoos.

---

[1] The stockholders of the East India Company, whose headquarters were in Leadenhall Street in the City of London.

§XVIII.[1] *How the King's Chancellor exercised a dispensing Power.*

To those who have read §§9 and 10 or §9 alone,[2] this can be no news. But of the nature and magnitude of the dispensing power thus assumed and exercised by Lord Eldon, conception may be helped by a few words more.

James the Second and his advisers operated openly and rashly. Prerogative in hand, they ran a-tilt against Parliament law.[3] Lord Eldon was Lord Eldon. In a cause of no expectation, out of sight of all *lay-gents*,—out of sight of all men but his co-partners in the firm, of which he is the head; he laid down the fundamental principle. When, under a so unexpected opposition, his good humour, habitual and pre-eminent as it is, forgot itself for awhile,—not so his prudence. Taking instruction from the adversary, he made a full stop: nor, till the impediment ceased, could he be made to move a step, by all the importunity we have seen employed, in the endeavour to urge him on towards the consummation of his own schemes.

Still out of the sight of *lay-gents*, when on the cessation of the inter-regnum, he remounted the throne, and, like Louis XVIII. reaped the benefit of whatever had been done for the consolidation of it by the usurper,[4]—the obstructor, persevering as we have seen him, being for the time dispirited by the rebuff received from Lord Erskine, under the tuition of the learned Jack-of-both sides,[5]—still, he imposed not any fresh tax, contenting himself with increasing—in the manner and to the extent, samples of which have been seen in §2[6]—the produce of those he found established. Nor was this the whole of his labour or of his success: for we have seen how (still out of sight of *lay-gents*) at times and in ways altogether invisible to unlearned eyes (at what tables and over what bottles, must be left to imagination) he had succeeded in completely impregnating his Westminster Hall creatures, and, in their several Judicatories, giving complete estab-lishment to his plan, as well in principle as in practice.

[1] 1825C, 1825D, 1830 '18.'

[2] See pp. 224–30 above.

[3] One of the major grievances brought against James II in the Bill of Rights of 1689 was his assumption and exercise of a dispensing and suspending power: see 1 W. and M., sess.2, c.2.

[4] The reign of Louis XVIII (1755–1824), King of France from 1814, marked the restoration of the French monarchy after its abolition by the National Convention in 1792 and the sub-sequent rule of Napoleon Bonaparte (1769–1821), First Consul of France 1799–1804, Emperor of the French 1804–14. Eldon's 'interregnum' was, of course, during the Ministry of All the Talents 1806–7, when Erskine was Lord Chancellor.

[5] i.e. Sir William Grant, Master of the Rolls, who had practised in both the Common Law and Equity Courts.

[6] See pp. 206–11 above.

Then again, when another unexpectable mishap befel him, and the webs, which the united strength of so many learned spiders had, for such a length of time, been employed in weaving, were broken through and demolished altogether by the irruption of one poor hunted fly,—even this shock, severe as it could not but be, did not make him relinquish his high purpose. Bold, where boldness was requisite, pliant where pliancy, all the sacrifice it brought him to was—the accepting from Parliament, and that too with improvement, the consummation of the ambitious and rapacious plan, at the commencement of which the nature of the case had obliged him to act, though with all prudent and practicable secrecy, against Parliament.

Thus much as to the *mode*—now as to *effect:* and the *extent* given to it. *James the Second*, with his dispensing power, placed a catholic priest in the Privy Council, and a catholic or no less obsequious protestant fellow, in an Oxford college.[1] *John the Second*[2] gave the dispensing power not only to himself but to all his underlings, covering thus, with a so much more profitable power, the whole field of judicature.

§ XIX. *Character Evidence.*

Against specific indications such as these, Honourable House and the Old Bailey receive a sort of evidence, which is neither quite so easily obtained, nor quite so efficient when obtained, in the Old Bailey as in Honourable House. It may be called, and, for aught I know, is called, *character evidence. Quantity*, in pretty exact proportion to that of the hope and fear, of which he, who is the subject of it, is the object. *Quality*, determined by the same causes. *Colours*, two—white and black.

But for my old friend Mr. Butler, no such evidence as this would have been offered—no such section as this have been written. Nor yet, if in the laud heaped up by him upon Lord Eldon, he had contented himself with using his own hand. But the hand, to which he has assigned this task, is the hand of Romilly: that confidence-

---

[1] Using his power to dispense with statute law, James II, in violation of the Test Act excluding Roman Catholics from public office, appointed his confessor Edward Petre (1631–99) to the Privy Council in 1687, and in the same year appointed Samuel Parker (1640–88), Bishop of Oxford, sympathetic to Roman Catholicism and an advocate of the repeal of the Test Act, and then, upon Parker's death, Bonaventure Giffard (1642–1734), Roman Catholic Bishop, as President of Magdalen College, Oxford.

[2] i.e. Eldon.

commanding and uncontradictable hand, which for this purpose, resurrection-man like, he has ravished from the tomb.[1]

Having, in the course of between thirty and forty years' intimacy, been in the habit of hearing sentiments of so widely different a tendency, on every occasion, delivered in relation to this same person,—silence, on an occasion such as the present, would have been so little distinguishable from assent, that I could not sit easy without defending myself against what might otherwise have appeared a contradiction, given to me by my departed and ever-lamented friend.

In relation to Lord Eldon, I have no doubt of Romilly's having used language, which, at a distance of time, and for want of sufficient discrimination, might naturally and sincerely enough, by a not un-willing hand, have been improved into a sort of panegyrick thus put into his mouth. But, by the simple omission of one part of it, the strictest truth may have the effect of falsehood.

With a transcript of the panegyrick in question, or of any part of it, I will not swell these already too full pages. Suffice it to mention my sincere wish, that it may be compared with what here follows.

By my living friend,—my departed friend, I have reason to think, was never seen but in a mixt company: assured I well am, and by the declaration of my departed friend, that between them there was no intimacy. Between my departed friend and myself, confidence was mutual and entire.

Romilly was among the earliest, and, for a time, the only efficient one of my disciples.[a]

---

[a] He was brought to me by my earliest—the late *George Wilson*, who, after leading the Norfolk Circuit for some years, retired with silk on his back to his native Scotland.[2]

---

[1] Charles Butler (1750–1832), Roman Catholic barrister, had possibly known Bentham since his admission to Lincoln's Inn in 1775. In his *Reminiscences of Charles Butler, Esq. of Lincoln's-Inn*, London, 1822, pp. 141–3, he had written: 'In profound, extensive and accurate knowledge of the principles of his court, and the rules of practice which regulate its proceedings,—in complete recollection and just appreciation of former decisions,—in discerning the inferences to be justly drawn from them,—in the power of instantaneously applying this immense theoretical and practical knowledge to the business immediately before the court,—in perceiving almost with intuitive readiness, on the first opening of a case, its real state, and the ultimate conclusion of equity upon it, yet investigating it with the most conscientious, most minute, and most edifying industry,—in all, or in any of these requisites for a due discharge of his high office,—*Lord Eldon*, if he has been equalled, has assuredly never been surpassed by any of his predecessors.—He has other merits:—He has often opposed popular clamour,—yet he has always been popular; but, to use the words of lord Mansfield, "it has been with that popularity which follows, not with that which is run after." He has almost always supported administration, but has never been subservient to any minister; and among those, who by dignity of character attach public opinion to the British government, and thus secure its stability, his lordship is universally allowed to be eminently conspicuous. On all this, there is no dissentient voice: All, which these

 [*See p. 258 for n. 1 cont. and n. 2.*]

To Romilly, with that secrecy which prudence dictated, my works, such as they are, were from first to last a text-book: the sort of light in which I was viewed by him, was, in Honourable House, in his own presence, on an ever memorable occasion, attested by our common friend, Mr. Brougham.[a]

Not a *reformatiuncle* of his (as *Hartley* would have called it)[1] did Romilly ever bring forward, that he had not first brought to me, and conned over with me. One of them—that in which Paley's love of arbitrary power was laid open—was borrowed from my spiders, under whose covering they may still be found.[2] The project so successfully opposed by Lord Eldon's Sir William Grant—the endeavour to prevail upon Honourable Gentlemen to divest themselves of the power of swindling in their individual capacities,—was, to both of us, a favourite one.[3] Nothing of this sort could ever come upon the

---

[a] Hansard's House of Commons Debates, 2nd June, 1818. 'He (Mr. Brougham) agreed with his hon. friend, the member for Arundel, Sir S. Romilly, who looked up to Mr. Bentham with the almost filial reverence of a pupil for his tutor.'[4]

---

lines have expressed, or attempted to express, the Reminiscent has heard often, and much better said by the late sir Samuel Romilly, both in public and in private:—testimony goes no higher.'

[2] Wilson (d. 1816) had introduced Bentham to Romilly in 1784 (see Bowring, x. 186; *The Correspondence of Jeremy Bentham*, vol. iv, ed. A.T. Milne, London, 1981 (*CW*), p. 17n). In 1810 an attack of palsy had forced Wilson to quit the bar, whereupon he had retired to Edinburgh (see *The Correspondence of Jeremy Bentham*, vol. i, ed. T.L.S. Sprigge, London, 1968 (*CW*), p. 293n).

[1] See David Hartley (1705–57), *Observations on Man, his Frame, his Duty, and his Expectations*, 2 vols., London, 1749, Part I, Ch. I, Section II, Prop. 9, p. 58: 'Sensory vibrations, by being often repeated, beget, in the medullary Substance of the Brain, a Disposition to diminutive Vibrations, which may also be called Vibratiuncles and Miniatures, corresponding to themselves respectively.' A vibratiuncle being a diminutive vibration, then by analogy a 'reformatiuncle' would be a minor measure of reform.

[2] William Paley (1743–1805), Archdeacon of Carlisle, had defended capital punishment in his influential treatise *The Principles of Moral and Political Philosophy*, first published in 1785 (see Book VI, Ch. IX). In an unpublished essay, 'Law versus arbitrary power:—or, A Hatchet for Dr. Paley's Net', written mainly in January and February 1809 (see UC cvii. 199–266 for the original essay, cvii. 278–343 for a copy, and cvii. 193–8, 267–77 for related MSS), Bentham subjected Paley's defence to a detailed critique. Bentham's arguments were taken up by Romilly in his speech on capital punishment in the House of Commons on 9 February 1810 (see *Parliamentary Debates*, xix, Appendix, pp. i–xliii, where a corrected version of Romilly's speech is reproduced).

[3] Presumably the Freehold Estates Bill which Romilly, as Solicitor General, introduced into the House of Commons on 28 January 1807. The measure, which would have made freehold estates, upon the death of the possessor, liable for the payment of simple contract debts, was opposed by Grant, the Master of the Rolls, on its third reading on 18 March 1807, whereupon it was defeated (see *Parliamentary Debates* (1806–7) viii. 561–3 and (1807) ix. 159–65). Romilly reintroduced the measure in 1814 and 1815; on both occasions it passed the Commons, but was lost in the Lords after meeting opposition from Eldon (see *Parliamentary Debates* (1814) xxviii. 748–50 and (1815) xxxi. 1036–9).

[4] Brougham's reference to Bentham, in the debate on Sir Francis Burdett's motion for parliamentary reform, was not entirely complimentary. Opposing the motion, and referring to

carpet, but the character of Lord Eldon came of necessity along with it: a few lines will give the substance of volumes. The determinate opposer of everything good; the zealous, able, and indefatigable supporter of everything evil, from which, to the ruling one or the ruling few, reputed good, in any the smallest quantity, at the expense of the many, appeared derivable.

'Well! and what chance do you see of the evil genius's suffering it to pass?' This, on one part was the constant question. 'Why. . . . just now things are so and so:' stating, or alluding to, some hold, which, at the moment, he thought he might have upon Lord Eldon. A favourable circumstance was—that, though regarding the M.P. with the eye with which he could not but regard one of the most troublesome of his political opponents,—the Chancellor—such, in his estimation, was the legal knowledge and judgment of Romilly—was in the habit of paying to the arguments of this advocate not less, but even more, deference, than, in the eyes of the profession, was always consistent with justice; so at least I have heard, over and over again, from various professional men. In Romilly's acquirements and character he beheld a leaning-stock, the value of which he knew how to appreciate.

Now for the like, through channels less exposed to suspicion:—

'The state of the Court of Chancery is such, that it is the disgrace of a civilized society.' These are the words furnished me, in writing, by a friend, as among the very words used by Romilly, but a few months before his death, in a mixed company. It was at a *place* which, for several days of his last autumn (a place I occupied in Devonshire), afforded to the relator various free conversations, besides those at which I was present.—General result:—'Lord Eldon himself the cause of many of the abuses; of the greater part of the others, the remedy always in his own hands.'[1]

Bentham's *Plan of Parliamentary Reform, in the form of a Catechism, with reasons for each article, with an Introduction, shewing the necessity of radical, and the inadequacy of moderate, reform*, London, 1817 (Bowring, iii. 433–557), he commented: 'He agreed with his hon. friend, the member for Arundel (Sir S. Romilly), who looked up to Mr. Bentham with the almost filial reverence of a pupil for his tutor, in wishing that he had never written that work.' (See *Parliamentary Debates* (1818) xxxviii. 1164.)

[1] Bentham's informant was James Mill, whose note (endorsed by Bentham, 'Written by James Mill, and delivered by him to Jeremy Bentham', and dated 13 June 1825) is at UC xix. 32: 'In a pretty large company, at the table of a common friend, when a free conversation on the abuses in the court of chancery, and the share in these abuses which the conduct of the Lord Chancellor appropriated to him, Sir Romilly, as I distinctly remember, used these words, the state of the court of chancery is such that it is the disgrace of a civilized country. The general result of various conversations I had with him was, that not only was Lord Eldon himself the cause of many of the abuses, but that [he] had the remedy of the greater part of them in his hands.' These conversations presumably occurred at Bentham's retreat, Ford Abbey, near Chard in Devonshire, on Romilly's visit there on 25–9 September 1817, when Mill was also

'If there is a hell, the Court of Chancery is hell.' Words these, given as the very words uttered by Lord Erskine but a few weeks before his death, in conversation with another person, from whom I have them under his own hand.[1]

Both relators most extensively known, and not more known than trusted. On any adequate occasion, both papers should be visible.

Judex à non judicando, ut lucus à non lucendo,[2] the sort of service of all others for which Lord Eldon is not only most eminently but most notoriously unfit,[a] is the very service for the performance of which his

---

[a] I would willingly have said *most unfit*, but Truth, as will be seen, forbids me.

Saul and Jonathan were Lord Eldon and Lord Redesdale. Lord Eldon, Attorney-General; Lord Redesdale, Solicitor-General: Chancellors—Lord Eldon, of England; Lord Redesdale, of Ireland.[3] Scholars of the school of Fabius,[4] but with one difference:—by the Roman cunctation, everything was perfected; by the English and Irish, marred.

The London laid a wager with the Dublin Chancellor, which should, in a given time, do least business. Dublin beat London hollow.

Witness, Earl Grey,—in those days Lord Howick.[a]

'When he' (Mr. Ponsonby) 'succeeded to the office,' (succeeded to Lord Redes-

---

[a] Cobbett's Debates, ix. 731. July 3, 1807. House of Commons. *Pensions to Chancellors.* From the Speech of Lord Howick, now Earl Grey.[5]

---

present (see Bentham to John Herbert Koe, 29 September 1817, *The Correspondence of Jeremy Bentham*, vol. ix, ed. S. Conway, Oxford, 1989 (*CW*), pp. 65–9).

[1] Bentham's informant was his disciple and future literary executor, John Bowring (1792–1872), whose note (dated 2 November 1824) is at UC xix. 30: 'Lord Erskine who was in the habit of railing furiously against the Court of Chancery used to me (John Bowring) this language "If there be any hell the Court of Chancery is hell".' Erskine had died on 17 November 1823.

[2] Roughly translated, 'A judge is so called from being not judicious, because a grove is so called from not being lucent.' The proverb 'Lucus a non lucendo' conveyed the notion of an object deriving its name from a quality which it did not possess. The source of the proverb was Quintilian, *Institutionis Oratoriae*, I. vi. 34: 'lucus, quia umbra opacus parum luceat', i.e. 'a grove is so called because, from the dense shade, there is very little light'.

[3] The story of Saul, the first King of Israel, and his eldest son Jonathan, is told in the first book of Samuel. Eldon was Attorney General 1793–9 and Lord Chancellor 1801–6, 1807–27, while John Mitford, afterwards Freeman-Mitford (1748–1830), first Baron Redesdale, was Solicitor General 1793–9 and Lord Chancellor of Ireland 1802–6.

[4] Quintus Fabius Maximus (d. 203BC), Roman statesman and general, named Cunctator, 'the delayer', on account of his cautious tactics in the war with Hannibal.

[5] Charles Grey (1764–1845), second Earl Grey, styled Viscount Howick 1806–7, First Lord of the Admiralty 1806, Foreign Secretary 1806–7, First Lord of the Treasury 1830–4. The debate in question concerned the pension granted to George Ponsonby (1755–1817), Lord Chancellor of Ireland 1806–7, upon his dismissal from office. On 2 July 1807 William Huskisson (1770–1830) had asked whether the grant contained the usual limitation clause providing that the pension should cease if he resumed his office or any other of equal profit (*Parliamentary Debates* (1807) ix. 729). On the following day Huskisson reported that he had received information that the grant did contain such a clause, which led Howick to praise Ponsonby's conduct in office in the passage reproduced below (see *Parliamentary Debates* (1807) ix. 731–2). There are some minor inaccuracies in the rendering of the passage. The italics are Bentham's.

dale) 'the Chancery Court of Dublin was in arrears for *six* years of *notices*, for *six hundred motions*, and for *four hundred and twenty-seven causes:* when he' (Mr. Ponsonby,) 'quitted office, he had got under *all* the *notices* and *motions*, and had brought down the *causes* to *two hundred*, besides going through the current business. Had he remained in office a few months longer, not a single *cause* would have been left undetermined.'[1]

This single incident speaks volumes: it paints *matchless constitution* to the life. Take two traits, out of more.

1. Profundity and universality of the contempt of human happiness and justice, in the breasts of the ruling and would-be-ruling few.

During the whole six years, during which Lord Redesdale, with his unfitness, staring him and everybody in the face, was paralyzing justice and manufacturing misery by wholesale[2]—not only his creator silent, but every member of the *Aristocracy* on both sides, in Ireland as well as in England. Down to this moment, never would anybody have heard of it, but for a personal squabble about Mr. *Ponsonby*, and a clause in his pension of retreat.

Mr. Ponsonby, with his matchless, and, but for admission, incredible aptitude,—turned out in Ireland! Lord Eldon, after his six years perpetually demonstrated inaptitude, restored, and continued with continually increasing influence!

As to *delay*, think from hence, whether, though in that, as well as all other shapes, abuse runs through every vein in the system—think whether, of that delay which drew forth the *present* complaints, there was any other cause than the difference, in point of dispatch, between this one man and every other; and whether, while this one man is where he is, deliverance from evil in that shape, any more than in any other, be possible.

Henceforward, in Honourable House, or in Right Honourable House,—on the one side, or on the other,—should any man have the hardihood to stand up and declare, that, on either side there is any more real regard for justice there than in the hulks—or in men's breasts any more sympathy for the sufferings of the people than in the cook's for the eels she is skinning—tell him of this!

2. Double-bodied monster, Head Judge and Head Party-man, back to back: fitter to be kept constantly in spirits in an anatomy school, than one hour in the Cabinet and the next hour on the Bench. Behold in this emblem one of the consequences of having one and the same man to sit as sole highest Judge, with all the property of the Kingdom at his disposal, and in the Cabinet to act as chief organizer of intrigues, and moderator of squabbles about power, money, and patronage: the Cabinet situation being the paramount one,—the most transcendent aptitude for the judicial situation cannot keep him in it, the most completely demonstrated inaptitude remove him out of it! This, under matchless constitution, under which the most loudly trumpeted tune is— *the Independence of the Judges*.

Practical lesson. Never by any other means than the making the ruling few *uneasy*, can the oppressed many obtain a particle of relief. Never out of mind should be the parable of the *Unjust Judge*.[3]

Such was the *alter idem* appointed by Lord Eldon to sit with *idem* and report the non-existence of delay, together with the most effectual means of removing it.[4]

Keeping Falstaff in his eye,—inefficient myself, I am the cause (said Lord Eldon to

---

[1] 1825C, 1830 omit closing speech mark.

[2] Redesdale was Lord Chancellor of Ireland for nearer four years than six.

[3] See Luke 18: 1–8.

[4] Redesdale and Eldon both sat on the Royal Commission on Chancery practice appointed in 1824.

unexampled power may have been originally placed, but if pretended, so falsely pretended, to be still kept in his hand.

This being premised, and admission made of the facility with which, for purposes such as have been brought to view, he can wrap his misery-breeding meaning up in clouds, such as while transparent to accomplices and natural allies, shall be opaque to all destined victims,—I must, for shortness, refer my readers to Mr. Butler's panegyrick.[1] Sending them to a work which has already had ten times as many readers as any of mine can look to have, I secure myself against the consciousness of injustice, and, I hope, from the reproach of it.

I will advance further in my approach to meet him.

On any of those nice points on which, expectation being equally strong and sincere on both sides, the difference between right and wrong being scarce discernible, decisions, were it not for appearances, might, with as little prejudice to the sense of security, be committed to lot, as to reflection holding the scales of justice,—on any of those sources of doubt and display, which, in any tolerable system of legislature-made law, a line or two, or a word or two, would have dried up—Lord Eldon, at the expense of years, where another man

himself) that inefficiency is in other men.[2] In Dublin my foil,[3] in London my Mitford[4] shall be at the head of my securities, that nothing shall be done, in the Commission, which with my disciple Peel, to laud and defend me,—I will establish for that purpose.

As to Lord Redesdale, digression upon digression as it is, candour and sympathy compel the mention—he, like Mr. Peel, has committed one act of rebellion against his creator: he, too, has made one departure from *consistency*. Mr. *Peel's* is the *Special Jury Act*: *Lord Redesdale's*, the *Insolvency Act*[5]—Should the day of repentance ever come,—each, with his Bill in his hand, may cry, like *Lovelace* under the avenging sword—Let this expiate![6] But Lord Eldon!—where will be his atonement? One alone will he be able to find, and that he must borrow of *Lord Castlereagh*.[7]

---

[1] See pp. 257–8n above.

[2] See Falstaff's comment in *Henry IV, Part Two*, I. ii. 11: 'I am not only witty in myself, but the cause that wit is in other men.'

[3] Thomas Manners-Sutton (1756–1842), first Baron Manners, was Lord Chancellor of Ireland 1807–27.

[4] i.e. Redesdale.

[5] For Peel's Jury Act (6 Geo. IV, c.50) see 'Observations on Peel's Speech', p. 197 above. Redesdale had been responsible for the Insolvent Debtors Act of 1813 (53 Geo. III, c.102), creating a permanent court to which prisoners for debt could, under certain conditions, apply for discharge.

[6] Robert Lovelace, a character in Samuel Richardson's novel *Clarissa*, first published in 1747–8. Having been seduced by Lovelace, Clarissa died of shame. Seized with remorse, he was killed in a duel with her cousin, Colonel Morden. As he died, he exclaimed: 'Let this expiate!'

[7] Castlereagh had committed suicide in 1822 by cutting his throat.

would have taken days, has given to the amateurs of difficulty a degree of satisfaction beyond what any other man could have given to them: to them, satisfaction; to himself, reputation—instrument of power applicable to all purposes. This, by the having stocked his memory with a larger mass than perhaps any other man (Romilly possibly excepted) of the cases known to have sprung up within the field of Equity,—and the having also enabled himself, with correspondent facility, to make application of them to the purpose of each moment, whatsoever be that purpose, whether it be to lead aright, to mislead, or to puzzle and put to a stand, himself or others.

So much for intellectuals: now for morals. Beyond all contro-versy,—recognized not less readily by adversaries than by depen-dents, one politico-judicial virtue his lordship has,—which, in his noble and learned bosom, has swelled to so vast a magnitude, that, like Aaron's serpent-rod, it shews as if it had swallowed up all the rest.[1] In the public recognition of it, trembling complaint seeks an emollient for vengeance; decorous and just satire, a mask. After stabbing the *Master of the Abuses* through and through with facts, Mr. Vizard takes in hand the name of this virtue—and, *innuendo*, this is the only one that can be found, lays it like a piece of goldbeater's skin on the wounds.[2] That which beauty, according to Anacreon, is to woman,[3]—*courtesy*, according to everybody, is to Lord Eldon: to armour of all sorts—offensive as well as defensive—a matchless and most advantageous substitute. With the exception of those, whom, while doubting, he is ruining, and, without knowing anything of the matter, plundering,—this it is that keeps everybody in good humour: everybody—from My Lord Duke, down to the Barrister's servant-clerk. Useful here, useful there, useful everywhere,—of all places, it

---

[1] See Exodus 7: 12.

[2] Vizard does not in fact mention Eldon's courtesy, but does refer to his 'urbanity and kindness': see *Letter to William Courtenay*, p. 36.

[3] The odes attributed to Anacreon, Greek lyric poet of the sixth century BC, were best known through the verse translation of Thomas Moore, *Odes of Anacreon, translated into English verse, with notes*, London, 1800. For Bentham's allusion see Ode XXIV in this collection:

> To man she [Nature] gave the flame refin'd,
> The spark of heav'n—a thinking mind!
> And had she no surpassing treasure,
> For thee, oh woman!—child of pleasure?
> She gave thee beauty—shaft of eyes,
> That every shaft of war outflies!
> She gave thee beauty—blush of fire,
> That bids the flames of war retire!
> Woman! be fair, we must adore thee;
> Smile, and a world is weak before thee!

is in the Cabinet that it does Knights' service. It is the *Court sticking-plaister*, which, even when it fails to heal, keeps covered all solutions of continuity: it is the *Grand Imperial cement*, which keeps political corruption from dissolving in its own filth. Never (said somebody once) never do I think of *Lord Eldon* or *Lord Sidmouth*, but I think of the aphorism of *Helvetius—Celui qui n'a ni honneur ni humeur est un Courtisan parfait.*[1]

When this virtue of the Noble and Learned Lord's has received its homage, the rest may be most effectually and instructively made known by their fruits. These fruits will be his *res gestæ:* exploits— performed, throughout, or in the course of, his four-and-twenty years' dominion over the fields of judicature and legislation. Enterprizes consummated—enterprizes in progress—measures not originating with him, but taken up by him and improved—exploits performed by his own hands, exploits performed by the hands of his creatures, or other instruments;—under one or more of these heads, were any such exactness worth the space and trouble, would some of these exploits be to be entered,—under another or others, others. But, forasmuch as all *judicial* censure is altogether out of the question, and the space and research necessary for such distinctions altogether unaffordable, they must unavoidably be omitted. Under each head, it will be for the reader, from what he has seen or heard, or may choose to see or hear, to consider whether, and, if yes, how far, the imputation attaches. To improve upon these hastily collected hints, and complete the investigation, would, if performed by a competent hand, assuredly be a most interesting as well as useful work.

1. Nipping in the bud the spread of improvement over the habitable globe, ruining fortunes by wholesale, and involving in alarm and insecurity a vast proportion of the vast capital of the country, by wantonly scattered doubts, leaving the settlement of them to a future contingent time that may never come.[a]

---

[a] Of this broadcast dissemination of uncertainty, one obvious cause may naturally be found in the profit made in the two great shops—the *Private Act of Parliament shop* and the *Charter Shop*, in which the right of associating for mutually beneficial purposes is sold at so enormous a price,—for the benefit of men, by whom nothing but obstruction, in this and other shapes, is contributed.

Wheresoever, in the case of a public functionary, remuneration wears the shape of fees, there, abuse in every shape is sure to have place. Not only in judicial offices so

---

[1] The aphorism was attributed by Claude Adrien Helvétius (1715–71) to Philippe, duc d'Orléans (1674–1723), Regent of France 1715–23. See *De l'Esprit*, Paris, 1758, Discours IV, Chapitre XIII, p. 586: '*Quiconque est sans honneur et sans humeur*, disoit M. le duc d'Orléans régent, *est un courtisan parfait.*'

2. Rendering all literary property dependent upon his own inscrutable and uncontrolable will and pleasure.[1]

3. Establishing a censorship over the press, under himself, with his absolute and inscrutable will, as censor: inviting, after publication with its expense has been completed, applications to himself for prohibition, with profit to himself in these, as in all other instances.[2]

4. Leaving the line of distinction between cases for *open* and cases for *secret* judicature, for so long as there is any, at all times dependent on his own inscrutable and uncontrovertible will and pleasure, establishing and continually extending the practice of covering his own proceeding with the cloak of secrecy.

5. Rivetting, on the neck of the people, the continually pinching yoke of an aristocratical magistracy, by rendering all relief at the

called, but in all offices whatsoever, such cases excepted, if any, in which for special adequate cause, special exception can be shown, salary should be substituted for fees.

In the case of patents for invention, exaction in this shape has swelled to an enormous magnitude. Justice, in the shape of reward for inventive genius, denied to the relatively poor, that is to say, to probably the far greater number;—sold at an enormous price to the relatively rich: all inventions,—the authors of which are not themselves rich enough to carry them through, nor able to find a capitalist to join with them,—nipt in the bud. Official men, lawyers and non-lawyers in swarms, who contribute nothing but obstruction, murdering invention thus in the cradle, ravish from genius its reward, and in case of failure, aggravate the pressure of ill success. To see the use of *matchless constitution*, on this occasion, compare the price, paid by inventive genius, for this security, in the United States and in France. Note, that on these occasions, that plunderage may be tripled, the three kingdoms are disunited.[3]

In all, or most of these cases, Lord Eldon, after having had a little finger in the pie when Attorney General, has a finger and thumb in it, now that he is Chancellor: adding to the pleasure of licking in the sweets, the gratification of obstructing improvement—called for this purpose *innovation*.

A set of motions, calling for returns of these several sources, and of the masses of emolument derived from each by the several functionaries, could scarcely be negatived.

---

[1] Eldon had introduced and developed the doctrine that the Court of Chancery would not grant an injunction against literary piracy if, in the opinion of the Judge, the publication contained anything of an immoral, seditious or irreligious tendency (see John, Lord Campbell, *The Lives of the Lord Chancellors and Keepers of the Great Seal of England, from the earliest times till the reign of King George IV*, 7 vols., London, 1845–7, vii. 655–62).

[2] Under the Common Law, no previous restraints were placed upon publication, but after publication, the publisher could be prosecuted and punished for any matter deemed libellous. Prosecutions however would take place in the Common Law courts, and not in Chancery.

[3] Separate patents had to be sought for England and Wales, Ireland, and Scotland; the cost could amount to several hundred pounds. Under the French Law of Patents of 1791, and the United States Law of Patents of 1793, the cost of taking out patents was considerably cheaper. See the Report on the Law relative to Patents for Inventions, *Commons Sessional Papers* (1829) iii. 415–676.

hands of the Chancellor as hopeless, as, by artificial law expenses, and participation in sinister interest and prejudice, it has been rendered, at the hands of the Judge.

6. On pretence of heterodoxy, by *ex post facto* law, made by a single Judge for the purpose,—divesting parents of the guardianship of their own children.[1]

7. Injecting into men's minds the poison of insincerity and hypocrisy, by attaching to pretended misdeeds, sufferings, from which, by an unpunishable and unprovable, though solemn act of insincerity, the supposed misdoer may, in every case, with certainty exempt himself.[a]

[a] Questions allowed to be put to a proposed witness. Do you believe in the existence of a God? If he, who does not believe, answers that he does,—thus answering falsely, he is received: if his answer be, that he does not believe—speaking thus truly, he is rejected of course.

It is by exploits such as this, that rise has been given to this appalling question— 'Which, in the capacity of a proposed witness, is most trustworthy—the Christian, Priest or Layman, who, for a series of years, has never passed a day without the commission of perjury,—or the Atheist, who—when at the instance of Lord Eldon, or any one of his creatures in the situation of Judge, interrogated as to what he believes—submits to public ignominy, rather than defile himself with that abomination in so much as a single instance?'[2] Christians! such of you as dare, think of this and tremble!

Question, as to this virtual Statute, the source and seat of which is in the breast of Lord Eldon:—if this is not a subornation of perjury, what is or can be? Lord Eldon— is his mind's eye really so weak, as, throughout the whole field of legislation, to be kept by words from seeing things as they are?[a] Decide who can, and give to head or heart,—sometimes to the one perhaps, sometimes to the other,—the credit of this blindness.

[a] As to the constant and all-pervading habit of perjury, see '*Swear not at all*.'[3] For cleansing judicature of this abomination, a not unpromising course is in the power of individuals. Any suitor, who sees a witness of whose testimony he is apprehensive— if the witness belongs to any of the classes in question, let his counsel have in hand a copy of the statutes in question, asking him whether he did not swear observance to every one of these statutes, and whether, in the breach of this or that article, he did not constantly live:[4] on denial, he will be indictable for perjury: on admission, it will be a question whether he can be heard.

Lord Eldon! did you never take that oath? Lord Eldon! did you never violate it? Think of this, Lord Eldon!—*Mr. Peel!* did you never take that oath? Mr. Peel! did you never violate it? Think of this, Mr. Peel!

[1] The Court of Chancery, exercising the authority of the King as *parens patriæ*, possessed jurisdiction to remove children from the custody of their parents.

[2] 1825C, 1826, 1830 omit closing speech mark.

[3] For details of this work, and a further discussion of perjury, see 'Defence of Economy against Rose', §XII, pp. 150–1 above.

[4] Bentham perhaps had in mind the 'classes' who had subscribed to the Thirty-nine Articles of the Church of England, which would have included Eldon and Peel upon their entering the University of Oxford.

8. In all manner of shapes, planting or fixing humiliation and anxiety in the breasts of all, who, on points confessedly too obscure for knowledge, oppose him, or refuse to join with him, in the profession of opinions, in relation to which there is no better evidence of their being really his, than the money and power he has obtained by the profession of them.

9. Pretending to establish useful truth by the only means by which success to pernicious falsehood can ever be secured. Proclaiming, in the most impressive manner, the falsehood and mischievousness of every thing that is called *religion*,—by punishing, or threatening to punish, whatsoever is said in the way of controverting the truth or usefulness of it.

10. Bearding Parliament, by openly declaring its incapacity to render unpunishable anything to which the judges, with the words *Common Law* in their mouths, shall have been pleased to attach punishment, or take upon them to punish:—thus by the assumed authority of himself, and those his creatures, keeping men under the rod of punishment, for habits of action, which, in consideration of their innoxiousness, had by Parliament been recently exempted from it: as if Parliament had not exempted men from *declared* and *limited*, but for the purpose of subjecting them to *unconjecturable* and *unlimited*, punishment. Witness the Unitarians, and all others, who will not, at his command thus signified, defile themselves with insincerity, to purchase the common rights of subjects.[1]

11. Doing that which even Parliament would not dare to do, and because Parliament would not dare to do it: doing it, with no other warrant, than this or that one of a multitude of words and phrases, to which *one* import as well as *another* may be assigned at pleasure. Witness *libel, blasphemy, malice, contra bonos mores, conspiracy, Christianity is part and parcel of the law of the land:* converting thus at pleasure into crimes, any the most perfectly innoxious acts, and even meritorious ones: substituting thus, to legislative definition and prohibition, an act of *ex post facto* punishment, which the most consummate legal knowledge would not have enabled a man to avoid,

---

[1] In the House of Lords on 3 June 1825, Eldon had opposed the Unitarian Marriage Bill, which would have allowed Unitarians to marry according to their own ceremonies, and therefore not be constrained to declare their belief in the Trinity. He had argued that even though by an Act of 1813 (53 Geo. III, c.160) so much of the Blasphemy Act of 1689 (9 and 10 W.III, c.32) as related to the denial of the doctrine of the Trinity had been repealed, and the provisions of the Toleration Act of 1689 (1 W. and M., sess.1, c.18) extended to the Unitarians, such a denial remained an offence at Common Law.

and as to which, in many an instance perhaps, it[1] was not intended that it should be avoided.[a]

All this—which, under a really existing constitution, grounded on the greatest-happiness-principle, would furnish matter for impeachment upon impeachment,—furnishes, under the imaginary matchless one, matter of triumph, claim to reward, and reward accordingly.

12. Poisoning the fountain of history, by punishing what is said of a departed public character on the disapproving side—while, for evidence and argument on the approving side, an inexhaustible fund of reward is left open to every eye: thus, by *suppression,* doubling the effect of *subornation, of evidence.* This by the hand of one of his creatures: his own hand, without the aid of that other, not reaching quite far enough.[2]

---

[a] But Parliament—contempts[3] of its authority all the while thus continually repeated—what does it say to them? Say to them? why nothing at all to be sure: Cabinet, by which the wires of Parliament are moved, desires no better sport. Chancellor,—by whom the wires of Cabinet are moved, and by whom the acts of contempt are committed or procured,—looks on and laughs in his sleeve.

Contempt of Parliament indeed! Parliament desires no better than to be thus contemned: and, to be assured of this, observe whether, of the indications given in these pages, it will suffer any, and what use to be made. Contempt of Parliament! Why, all this is the work of Parliament itself. That which, with its own forms, it could not do without a world of trouble—what it might even be afraid to do—(for, where guilt abounds, so does cowardice) it does by simple connivance, without a particle of trouble. But why talk of *fear?* On each occasion, whatever is to be done, the object with all concerned is to have it done with least *trouble* to themselves. By the hand of a judge, those by whom Parliament is governed do, without any trouble, that which without trouble in abundance could not be done by the hand of Parliament.

In flash language, *Common Law*—in honest English, *Judge-made Law*—is an instrument, that is to say, Judges are instruments—for doing the dirty work of Parliament: for doing in an oblique and clandestine way, that which Parliament would at least be ashamed to do in its own open way.

Nor, for the allotment of these parts, is any such labour as that of concert or direction necessary. Nothing does the purpose require that an English Judge should do, more than what in his situation human nature and habit effectually insure his doing: giving, on every occasion, to his own arbitrary power every possible extent, by all imaginable means. While this is going on, so long as what he does suits the purposes of his superiors, it is regarded of course with that approbation of which their silence is such perfectly conclusive evidence. On the other hand (to suppose, for argument sake, an effect without a cause) should he ever, in any the smallest degree obstruct their purposes, any the least hint would suffice to stop him. What could any Judge do—what could even Lord Eldon hope to do—against the will of Monarchy and Aristocracy in Parliament?

---

[1] 1830 omits 'it'.

[2] Presumably an allusion to the prosecution and conviction of John Hunt for libelling the memory of George III, discussed in 'Observations on Peel's Speech', pp. 189–90 above.

[3] 1830 'contempt'.

The title *Master of the Abuses*, which occurs in one page,[1] may perhaps have been thought to require explanation. It was suggested by that of *Master of the Revels*, coupled with the idea of the enjoyments in which he and his have for so many years been seen revelling, by the exercise given to the functions of it.

The *Mastership of the Revels* being abolished or in disuse,—the *Mastership of the Abuses* appears to have been silently substituted, and Lord Eldon presents himself as having been performing the functions of the office, as yet without a salary:—with his Masters in Chancery, serving under him in the corresponding capacity, and on the same generous footing, on the principle of the *unpaid Magistracy*. A subject for calculation might be—at what *anno domini*, the business of all the *denominated* Offices, possessed by those Masters and their Grand Master respectively, will have been brought into the state, into which, under his Lordship's management, that of the *Six Clerks*, has already been brought, together with that of the *Six*[2] *Offices*, with which the future services of his Honourable Son have been so nobly and generously remunerated?[3]—at what halcyon period, those superior offices will, with the inferior, have been sublimated into sinecures, and the incumbents apotheosed into so many *Dii majorum*, or *Dii minorum*, *gentium*[4] of the Epicurean heaven.

To help conception, a short parallel between the Noble and Learned Lord, and his Noble and Learned predecessor, Jefferies,[5] may be not altogether without its use.—*General Jefferies* had his *one 'campaign:'* *General Eldon*, as many as his command lasted years. The deaths of Jefferies's *killed-offs* were speedy: of Eldon's, lingering as his own resolves. The deaths of Lord Jefferies's victims were public—the sufferers supported and comforted in their affliction by the sympathy of surrounding thousands: Lord Eldon's expired, unseen, in the gloom of that solitude which wealth on its departure leaves behind it. Jefferies, whatsoever he may have gained in the shape of royal favour—source of future contingent wealth,—does not present himself to us clothed in the spoils of any of his slain. No man, no woman, no child, did Eldon ever kill, whose death had not, in the

---

[1] See p. 263 above.

[2] 1830 '*Nine*'.

[3] Eldon's son, William Henry John Scott, held six sinecures, two of which were in reversion. See Postscript, §2, p. 279n below.

[4] i.e. 'Gods of the superior, or Gods of the inferior, people'. The phrase 'maiorum gentium di' is found in Cicero, *Tusculan Disputations*, I. xiii. 29, but is derived from the division of Roman senators into *patres maiorum et minorum gentium*.

[5] George Jeffreys (c.1648–89), first Baron Jeffreys, Chief Justice of King's Bench 1683–5, Lord Chancellor 1685–8, had attained notoriety for his part in the 'Bloody Assize' following the Battle of Sedgemoor in 1685, when he condemned several hundred persons to death.

course of it, in some way or other, put money into his pocket. In the language, visage, and deportment of Jefferies, the suffering of his victims produced a savage exultation: in Eldon's, never any interruption did they produce to the most amiable good humour, throwing its grace over the most accomplished indifference. Jefferies was a tiger: Eldon, in the midst of all his tears, like Niobe, a stone.[1]

Prophet at once and painter,—another predecessor of Lord Eldon, Lord Bacon, has drawn his emblem. Behold the man (says he) who, to roast an egg for himself, is ready to set another's house on fire![2] So far, so good: but, to complete the likeness, he should have added—*after having first gutted it*. One other emblem—one other prophecy. Is it not written in the Arabian Nights' Entertainments?—Sinbad the Sailor—*Britannia:* Old Man of the Sea,[3] the Learned Slaughterer of pheasants,[4] whose prompt deaths are objects of envy to his suitors. After fretting and pummelling, with no better effect than sharpening the gripe,—the Arabian slave, by one desperate effort, shook off his tormenting master.[5] The entire prophecy will have been accomplished, and the prayers of Britannia heard, should so happy an issue, out of the severest of all her afflictions, be, in her instance, brought to pass.

---

[1] According to Greek legend, Niobe, daughter of Tantalus, wife of Amphion, King of Thebes, and the mother of twelve children, boasted that she was superior to Leto, who had only two, Apollo and Artemis. In response, Apollo and Artemis slew all her children. Thereupon Niobe, who had gone to Mount Sipylon, was metamorphosed into a stone, which was said to shed tears for her children.

[2] See Sir Francis Bacon, *The Essayes or Counsels, Civill and Morall*, ed. M. Kiernan, Oxford, 1985 (first published 1597–1625), Essay XXIII, 'Of Wisdome for a Mans selfe', p. 74: 'And certainly, it is the Nature of Extreme *Selfe-Lovers*; As they will set an House on Fire, and it were but to roast their Egges'.

[3] 1830 'Woods,'.

[4] Shooting was one of Eldon's favourite pastimes.

[5] For the story of Sindbad and the old man of the sea see R.F. Burton, *A plain and literal translation of the Arabian Nights' Entertainments, now entituled The Book of the Thousand Nights and a Night*, 16 vols., Benares, 1885–8, vi. 50–3. Bentham seems to have been in the habit of describing the old man of the sea as the 'old man of the woods' (see *First Principles* (*CW*), p. 189n).

POSTSCRIPT.

§ 1. *Under Lord Eldon, Equity an Instrument of Fraud and Extortion.—Samples continued.*

WHILE writing what is above, came to hand a 'Review of Chancery Delays,' &c. signature, 'The Authors.'[1] When what they say is seen, the reason for such their concealment will be sufficiently manifest. Read this work of theirs, whoever you are,—you who, thinking for the public, have any regard for justice: so rich the mass of abuse, it not merely denounces in general terms, but spreads out in detail, bringing it at the same time within the conception of non-lawyers: the matter ranged under some nine or ten heads, following one another in the chronological order of the proceedings in a suit.

'Proper subject of every honest man's indignation,' according to them (p. 42) not only 'the system which allows,' but 'the Judges who *encourage* such conduct:'[2] and with a little attention, every solicitor who has had twenty-five years' practice, and a few over, in the Equity Courts, as well as many a man who has had none, will be able to draw the line, and say to himself, whether, by any former Judge, anything like so much *encouragement* has been given to the sort of conduct therein held up to view. Ask, with so many learned gentlemen, whether it be to Lord Eldon, or to the system, that the phœnomena are due? Ask first, whether it is to the father or to the mother that the birth of a child is due?

From this most instructive publication, take a few hastily-picked-up samples. Pages 48, 49. 1. Master's attendance (as everybody knows) never more than one hour in one day in the same cause.

2. Between attendance and attendance, distance commonly three or four days, frequently a week.

3. For every such actual attendance, payment for that and two others exacted by the Master, he declaring in writing that on both days he has attended, whereas on neither day has he, or anybody for him, attended.

---

[1] See *Review of the Delays and Abuses occasioned by the Constitution and Present Practice of the Court of Chancery; with practical hints as to the remedy: in a Letter to the Commissioners of Inquiry*, London, 1825. Bentham's marked copy of this pamphlet is in the British Library, shelf-mark C.T. 80 (8).

[2] Outlining the procedural delays which defendants could make use of in Chancery, 'The Authors' comment: 'It is the system which allows, and the Judges who encourage such conduct, that ought to be the subject of every honest man's indignation.'

4. For each such falsely alleged, and unjustly charged attendance, fees exacted by the Master, not only for himself, but for every solicitor employed in the suit a separate one; there being in every Equity suit parties in any number, having, as many as please, each of them a separate solicitor.

5. Hours of such attendance in a day seldom more than five (other accounts generally make it less.) Per Mr. Vizard, see above, §2, p. [209–10],[1] with '*some exceptions*' only, not more than three.

6. Months in which such attendances are to be had, out of the twelve, not more than seven.

Page 52. Recapitulation of the means of delay, employable in ordinary, over and above the additions employable in extraordinary cases: to wit, employable by dishonestly-disposed men on the two sides of the suit respectively, thus enabled and invited by Lord Eldon, with or without predecessors for stalking-horses, to carry that same disposition into effect.

I. By dishonesty on the *Defendant's* side; to which side, in a common law-suit, dishonesty is of course most apt to have place.

Years.

1. Before the time for what is called *appearance* (the defendant not being *permitted to appear*, but forced to employ in appearing for him a solicitor, whom, likewise, without a train of barristers to speak for him, the Chancellor will not see) .... $1\frac{1}{2}$

2. By not appearing before the cause is ultimately called on for Judge's *hearing* 2

3. After *hearing* 'wasted by reference to a Master, years from 4 to 6:' oftener a much longer period .... 4 to 6

4. Between Master's report made, and Judge's second hearing .... 2 to 3

Total, 9 to $12\frac{1}{2}$

II. By dishonesty on the *Plaintiff's* side, that is to say, on the part of him, who, at common law, had been on the Defendant's side; one half of the business of Equity consisting in stopping or frustrating the application of the remedy held out by common law; and at any stage, down to the very last, this stoppage may be effected.

N.B. This combination of two sorts of judicatories, proceeding on mutually contradictory principles, is by Lord Eldon, and by so many others, professed to be regarded as necessary to justice.

---

[1] 1825D, 1830 '9'.

	Years.
1. By amending Bills, from	4 to 6[1]
2. Between the suit's being *set down* for hearing by the Judge, and its being by that same Judge *called on* for hearing	2
3. After hearing, wasteable in reference to a Master, as in the Defendant's case, as above, from	4 to 6
4. Between Master's report and Judge's second hearing, as above	2 to 3
Total,	12 to 17

Note that (as has been often stated, and never denied) delay on the Plaintiff's side, as here, has been in use to be employed as a regular and sure source of profit by dishonest men with other men's money in their pockets, where the quantity of it in the shape of capital has been deemed sufficient, by means of the interest or profit on it, to pay for the delay sold by the Judges of the common law and Equity courts together: they, with their creatures and other dependents in office, and their friends and connections in all branches of the profession, sharing, by means of the fees, with these dishonest men in the profit of their dishonesty.

Comes in, at the same time, 'Letter to Mr. Secretary Peel on Chancery Delays, by a Member of Gray's Inn.' Pages, 25.[2]

[1.][3] Page 20.[4] Subject-matter of the most common and seldomest-contested species of suit—account of a testator's estate.

Number[5] of useless copies taken of said account, ten.

N.B. Cost of each, ten-pence for every ninety words.

2. Pages 15, 16, 17.[6] Under Lord Eldon, irrelevance, technically stiled '*impertinence*,' thence useless lengths of pleadings perpetually increasing—'laxity of pleadings, quantity of impertinent matter—a subject-matter of general complaint, and general observation *by Lord Eldon.*' Punishment being all this while unexampled; encouragement in the shape of reproof in the air, or threats, of which it is known they will never be executed, are at the same time frequent. Before Lord

---

[1] From 'three to six years', according to 'The Authors'.

[2] See *A Letter to the Right Honourable Robert Peel; upon the delays in the Court of Chancery. By a Member of Gray's Inn*, London, 1825. Bentham's marked copy of this pamphlet is in the British Library, shelf-mark C.T. 80 (11).

[3] 1825D, 1830 'I.' Bentham's enumeration has been rendered consistent with the sense.

[4] The following information is in fact given at pp. 20–1.

[5] 1825D, 1830 '1. Number'.

[6] The following passage which Bentham paraphrases is in fact at pp. 15–16.

Eldon, the practice was, to saddle the counsel with costs. Per the Authors, as above, (p. 9) by '*late decisions* this abuse has received positive encouragement and increase.'

Pages of all five pamphlets, taken together (Mr. Vizard's included) 157.[1] Compressed into perhaps a third of the number, the substance would compose a most instructive work. By detaching from the abuses the proposed remedies, the compression might perhaps be aided: the remedies, in a narrow side column or at bottom, in form of notes.

But neither should the defences, whatever they are, pass unexamined: for of the charges, with such premiums for defence, whatsoever is passed over unnoticed or slurred over, may, with unexceptionable propriety be regarded as admitted.

§ 2. *Lord Eldon Squeaking.*

Drama (not to say *farce*), — '*The Courts of Law Bill.*' Time, — June 28, 1825. Editor, — *Globe and Traveller*. Scene, — Right Honourable House.[2] Enter Lord Liverpool, Prime Minister, Bill in hand. Lord Eldon, Chancellor, in the back ground. Motion by Lord Liverpool for proceeding in the Bill.[3] Enter Lord Grosvenor[4] with a digression—a dissertation on sinecures: Lord Liverpool, in answer: — determined to save fees from commutation during the incumbency of the present incumbents; determined to save the Head Fee-eater from all hardships imposed on inferior ones: determined to give the Puisne Judges

---

[1] In fact, this is the total number of pages of only four pamphlets: *A Letter to Samuel Compton Cox*; Vizard, *Letter to William Courtenay*; and the two mentioned above.

[2] For the debate in the House of Lords on 27 June 1825 see *Parliamentary Debates* (1825) xiii. 1378–80. Though each of the three judges' salaries-raising measures (for which see §I, p. 205n above) received their third reading on that day, it seems that the more general Bill dealing with the Master of the Rolls, Vice-Chancellor, Chief Baron of the Exchequer and puisne Judges and Barons was the occasion for this debate. Bentham's source is the report of the debate which appeared in the *Globe and Traveller* of 28 June 1825.

[3] Bentham evidently intended the following note at UC xix. 332 (22 July 1825) to be inserted at this point (see the Editorial Introduction, p. xxxviiin above): 'The system of hypocritical corruption and sham reform, of which the announcement above made, when compared with others, afford[s] but too strong an indication, is such as rendered it impossible to me to refrain from bestowing a few observations upon it. But, not being relevant with relation to the subject of this section, they are postponed to a concluding one. According to present appearances, I can see nothing in it better than a perseverance in and continuation of the plan of judicial corruption established by the Statute mentioned in §| |.' Bentham's reference is to 3 Geo. IV, c.69, discussed in 'Indications respecting Lord Eldon', §XIII, pp. 238–42 above. The 'concluding' section is presumably that published in Appendix A as § 3 of the Postscript, pp. 307–33 below, which deals with the prohibition of the sale of offices in the Courts of King's Bench and Common Pleas, and the eventual commutation of fees.

[4] Robert Grosvenor (1767–1845), second Earl of Grosvenor and later first Marquis of Westminster.

the proposed 5,500*l.* a year, because there were others, who, for doing less, were paid more. Mr. Robinson having previously (to wit, in Honourable House) demonstrated the necessity of the increase, appropriate aptitude being, in his mathematics, as *dignity*, and *dignity as opulence:* the proof being composed of repetitions, ten in number, (for they have been counted) of the word *dignity*.[1]

Whereupon,[2] up rises Lord Eldon, finger in eye, answering Lord Grosvenor's digression, with a digression on calumny and firmness. Addresses, two: one to the people, the other to Noble Lords.[3] For better intelligibility, behold these same addresses, in the first place, in plain English: after that, for security against misrepresentation, in Lord Eldonish.

1. *Lord Eldon to the people, in plain English.* Have done! Have done! Let me alone! Nay, but don't tease me so. You had best not; you won't get anything by it. This is not the way to get me out, I can tell you that. Come now, if you will but let me alone, I'll go out of my own accord. I should have been out long ago, had it not been for you. It's only your teazing me so that keeps me in. If you keep on teaze— teaze, I'll never go out: no, *that* I won't.

Note that this was on the 28th of June 1825:[4] ten days after the day on which, without authority or expectation on the part of the Author, the Editor of the Morning Chronicle, with whose stripes the noble and learned back is so well acquainted, had given an article on these *Indications*.[5]

The original in Lord Eldonish.[a] 'Perhaps it is thought that this mode of calumnious misrepresentation is the way to get me out of office. They are mistaken who think so: I will not yield to such aspersions; nor shrink from asserting what I owe to myself. Had I been treated with common justice, I should not, perhaps, have been Lord Chancellor this day; but, I repeat it, I will not be driven out of office by calumnious attack. Let me only be treated with common justice, and my place shall be *at any man's disposal*.'

Calumnious indeed! Look back, cautious and justice-loving reader.

---

[a] For greater fidelity, and to avoid some circumlocutions, the third person is here all along retransmuted into the first.[6]

---

[1] See §XVI, p. 251 & n above.

[2] 1830 'Wherepon,'.

[3] 1830 'Lords,'.

[4] The debate of course occurred on 27 June 1825, though the report appeared in the *Globe and Traveller* on the following day.

[5] A review had appeared in the *Morning Chronicle* of 18 June 1825.

[6] There are other minor inaccuracies in the rendering of this and the following passages from Eldon's speech; more substantial discrepancies are recorded in editorial footnotes. The italics are Bentham's.

Look back at the *Indications:* see what any of them want of being *proofs:* see whether anything but a formulary or two is wanting to render them proofs, and conclusive ones. Suppose, for argument's sake, the defendant guilty, and see whether, on that supposition, anything more convincing than what is there brought to view, could have been adduced. Say whether, in case of misstatement anywhere, there can be any ground for regarding it as wilful: any ground for attaching to it any such epithet as *calumnious*.

2. *Lord Eldon to Lordships in plain English.* Help! help! help! Going, going! Can't stand it any longer. What! nobody lend me a hand? Nobody speak a word for me? Do not you see how it is with me? What! and will *you* turn against me? Better not: I can tell you *that*. You'll be all the worse for it. When I am put down, it will be your turn next. What will become of your privileges—think of that! I'll tell you what, so sure as they take away my seals, so sure will they take away your privileges.

Squeaking, staggering, blustering, crying out for help—all in a breath! What an exhibition!

Original in Lord Eldonish. 'The feelings and fate of an individual are in themselves of small importance to the public, and I may be sacrificed to the insults I daily receive. But I beg noble Lords to reflect, that I may not be the only sacrifice. If the object is, as it appears to be, to pull down the reputations, and throw discredit on the motives and conduct, of men in high official situations—if every man who occupies a high situation[1] in the Church' {turning of course to the Bishops'[2] Bench} 'in the Church or State is to become the object of slander and calumny, then your Lordships may lay your account with similar treatment, and be convinced that your privileges or power[3] cannot long be respected, when such characters have been sacrificed.'

N.B. At what words the tears began to flow is not reported. When a crocodile comes on the stage—*Tears, tears*, should be added to the *Hear! hears!*

No, my weeping and fainting and firmness-acting Lord. How purblind soever the eyes you are accustomed to see around you, blindness is not yet so near to entire, as to make Lordships see no difference between your seals and their privileges. Their privileges! Who is it that is to take away these same privileges? The King? or the People? or the Pope of Rome? Your seals! Yes, the King can take away these pretty playthings of yours and not improbably will, so soon

---

[1] *Globe and Traveller* 'an eminent station'.
[2] 1830 'Bishop's'.
[3] *Globe and Traveller* 'privileges as peers'.

as in his estimation there will be more uneasiness from keeping them where they are, than from placing them elsewhere. But Lords' *privileges!* they are a sort of a thing not quite so easily disposed of. To bring his hand in, his Majesty will first take away from himself his own *prerogatives*.

The people? Yes: supposing guards and garrisons were all annihilated in a day, the people, that is to say a mob, might not find much more difficulty in dealing with these accoutrements of yours than the King would: after burning your bags, they might throw your seals into the Thames, where your predecessor, *Littleton*, threw his.[1] Yes: all this a *mob* (for this is what you always have in view when you speak or think of the people) might indeed do. But could they either burn or throw into the Thames their Lordships' privileges?

As to the Pope, I say nothing of him here: what regards him, belongs to Catholic Emancipation.

Seriously, it was found impossible, by anything but extravagance, to comment upon such extravagance. What must have been the state of that mind which could rely upon it as argument?

In this place, without aid either from witchcraft or from treachery, I had actually gone on and given the substance of the argument, with which, in cabinets and over bottles, the noble and learned Lord has for these five-and-twenty years, and more, been occupying himself in the endeavour—no very difficult one, it must be confessed—to keep up, and if possible to increase, the aversion to improvement in so many shapes, and to reform in every shape. But relevancy seeming questionable, and mischief from overweight unquestionable, the papers have been put aside.

The *Indications* are before the reader: some original, others copied. In both cases, how determinate they are, he can scarcely have failed to remark. As well as the proofs, he shall now have before him the answers. From a clear conscience, accompanied by a clear and well-exercised conception, *they* would have been correspondently determinate. In generals, at any rate, and in particulars, according as time and occasion admitted, and importance required, every charge would have been noticed; and, lest omission should be taken for confession, no one left altogether without notice.

So much as to what the answers might have been, and, in the

---

[1] The Great Seal was in fact thrown into the Thames by James II on 10 December 1688, as he attempted to flee to France. Edward Littleton (1589–1645), first Baron Lyttelton, Chief Justice of Common Pleas 1640–1, Lord Keeper of the Great Seal 1641–5, fled from Parliament in May 1642, taking the Great Seal with him, and joined Charles I at York. Parliament eventually passed an ordinance for a new Seal in November 1643.

momentarily supposed case, would have been. Behold now what, in the actual case, they are.

First, as to the general heads of defence. They will be found composed of uncharacteristically-vituperative matter, applied at every turn to the accusations, and expressed in these terms:—

1. 'Misrepresentation and calumnies.'
2. 'Calumnious misrepresentation.'
3. 'Such aspersions.'
4. 'Calumnious attacks.'
5. 'Misstatements and misrepresentations of every kind.'
6. 'Much misrepresentation.'
7. 'Calumny and misstatement.'
8. 'Slander and calumny.'[1]

What the noble and learned Defendant's perturbation did not permit him to perceive is, how strongly this sort of language smells of *'the Old Bailey:'* of the place he was looking to be 'sent to by their Lordships,' (as per *Globe*, June 21, 1825) there to be *'put to death:'*[2] and that when a man can find nothing to say that shall tend to his exculpation, this sort of unmeaning outcry is what he vents his anguish in, rather than be seen to make confession in the shape of silence.

So much for generals. Follow now all the several specific attempts at defence, with an observation or two upon each.

LORD ELDON.[3]

I. *'From the accounts which have been furnished to me of my emoluments as Lord Chancellor from those who best know the amount,'* {Lordship himself being nobly careless of all such things} *'apart from my income, as Speaker of the House of Lords, I am happy to say, that the Lord Chief Justice of the King's Bench has received a larger sum from his office: I speak from the average accounts of the last three years.'*

OBSERVATIONS.

1. What is this to the purpose? Not of the *quantum* do we complain, but of the *sources:* of which sources he dares not say a syllable.
2. Whatever it be that you receive, is it the less because you receive it from a number of *places*, instead of one?

---

[1] 1830 omits closing speech mark.

[2] According to the report in the *Globe and Traveller* of 21 June 1825, in a debate in the House of Lords on the previous day, Eldon had stated: 'Much had been said about common law and common law lawyers, but if there was any lawyer who would say that this country could go on without a court of the nature of the Court of Chancery, he would say that their lordships might as well expect to send him to the Old Bailey, and put him to death.'

[3] The following extracts are also from the debate in the House of Lords on 27 June 1825.

3. Of the patronage, nothing said: whereas, from a small portion of it, you receive, in the person of your Son, according to the undisputed calculation of Mr. Miller,[a] 3,500*l*.[1] a year, and, unless in case of untimely death, will receive in the whole, 9,000*l*.

4. What is it to the purpose what the Chief Justice has? If the emolument of the man in question is excessive, does the greater excess of another man's make it less so?

5. Since he knows, then, what his emoluments are, why will he sit to be thus badgered, rather than produce them? Why, unless it be because they would be seen not to agree with the account thus given of them? and because he fears that, if Honourable Gentlemen knew the whole amount, they would grudge giving him full value for it?

LORD ELDON.

II. '*And I will further say, that, in no one year since I have been made Chancellor, have I received the* same *amount of profit as I enjoyed while at the Bar.*'

OBSERVATIONS.

1. The *same?* No, most probably not; for, so long as there is a farthing's-worth of difference, this is strictly true. But how is anybody to know whether it is?

2. If everybody knows it, what would it be to the purpose?

3. While the Chancellor declares himself *happy*, that the Chief Justice's profits out of other men's misery are so great, may a suitor be permitted to confess himself not quite so *happy*, that Barrister's profits, drawn by insincerity, out of the same impure source, are, if so it really be, so enormous?

[a] 'Inquiry into the Present State of the Civil Law of England,' pp. 79, 80.[2]

---

[1] 1830 '3,500*l*,'.

[2] See John Miller, *An Inquiry into the Present State of the Civil Law of England*, London, 1825, pp. 79–80: 'It appears from a return made to the House of Commons in 1822, that a near relation of the Chancellor has received from him a grant of the six following offices: 1. Register of Affidavits in the Court of Chancery, — 2. Clerk of the Letters Patent to the Court of Chancery, — 3. Receiver of Fines in the Court of Chancery, — 4. One of the Cursitors for London and Middlesex, — 5. The Clerkship of the Crown in Chancery in reversion, — and 6. The Grant of the Office for the Execution of the Laws and Statutes concerning Bankrupts in reversion likewise. All of these offices are for life, and all of them executed by deputy. . . . Of the four first he is now in actual possession, receiving from them probably not much less than £3500. a year; and if he should survive the occupant of the other two, the reversion of them may swell his income to about £9000. a year.' The 'near relation' was, of course, his son, William Henry John Scott. Miller's source was the Report of the Select Committee on the Returns made by Members of the House of Commons (see *Commons Sessional Papers* (1822) iv. 41–60), where MPs were required to list the offices they held: Scott's sinecures are listed at iv. 52–3.

LORD ELDON.

III. *'Had I remained at the Bar, and kept the situation I held there, I solemnly declare I should not have been a shilling the poorer man than I am this moment, notwithstanding my office.'*

OBSERVATIONS.

1. Believe who can: evidence none. Disprobative counter-evidence, as to the official side of the account, obstinacy of concealment: evidence, circumstantial indeed, but not the less conclusive.

But, possibly, here as before, of his cluster of offices, with their emoluments, he shuts his eyes against all but one: and thus, by a virtual falsehood, thinks to keep clear of a literal one.

2. Again—what is all this to the purpose?

Oh, had he but kept to the Bar! or, instead of the Bench, been sent to that Bar to which, as above, he so lately looked to be sent by their Lordships on his way to another place[1]—what a waste of human misery would have been saved! Of human misery, for which who ever saw or heard him exhibiting any the slightest mark of regard? Men, women, and children—widows and orphans being treated by him as if composed of insentient matter, like the stones from which the gold exacted from them was extracted.

LORD ELDON.

IV. *'No charge of delay can fairly be brought against me.'*

OBSERVATIONS.

1. Now well done, Lord Eldon! To a host of witnesses continue to oppose a front of brass!

2. Not to speak of the mountains of manufactured delay opened to view by the samples, as if by a particular providence, in opposition to this plea of *Not Guilty*, behold, prepared by anticipation, six months antecedently to the pleading of it, a special piece of criminative evidence: a statement, the manifestly trustworthy result of a course of observation, the commencement and continuance of which was a phenomenon not much less extraordinary than the course observed upon. It is here copied, word for word, from a Morning Paper.[a]

[a] *Morning Herald*, Thursday, 2nd December 1824.[2]

---

[1] i.e. the Old Bailey: see p. 278 above.

[2] There are some minor inaccuracies in the rendering of the following passage; more substantial discrepancies are recorded in editorial footnotes. The italics, apart from the foreign phrases, unless otherwise noted, are Bentham's.

Whence it came from is unknown: neither to the whole nor to any part of it whatsoever has any contradiction been ever heard of.

3. Under the eyes of so vast a posse of retainers, retained by every tie of interest in the defence of this giver of good gifts,—is it in the nature of the case that anything to which the name of misrepresentation could have been applied with any chance of being regarded as properly applied, should in all this time have passed unnoticed?

'COURT OF CHANCERY.—(*From a Suitor.*)—Term ended on Monday:[1] the Lord Chancellor, when he was rising, apprised the gentlemen of the Bar and the suitors of the Court, that he would not come down till Thursday. His Lordship is no doubt entitled to two day's recreation after his learned labours of a month. In order that the public may duly appreciate those labours, let us briefly review them:—the calculation may appear curious—the time which his Lordship sat—the number of cases *heard*—not *decided*—and the *quantum* of relief afforded.

'His Lordship commenced his sittings on the 1st November, and from that to the 29th, both inclusive, he sat in Court 24 days. In no day but *one*, did he sit before *ten* o'clock; on *one* day only did he remain till *three:* indeed he could not during Term, for as he has often said, "*the students should have their dinner.*"[2]

---

[1] 29 November 1824.

[2] Bentham evidently intended the following note, based on the original draft at UC xix. 331 (21 July 1825) and the additions made by him to the copy at xix. 398 (n.d. July 1825), to be inserted at this point (see the Editorial Introduction, p. xxxviii in above): 'The shew of justice to be at an end at *three*, lest otherwise they should not have time to get to their dinners by $\frac{1}{2}$ after 4! Lest these unfledged harpies should have to wait a few minutes for their dinners, (which, by the bye, is before the usual hour for their condition in life, in consequence of which many sit without eating) suitors in such unhappy numbers bereft of *theirs*? By heart as well as in his heart, had this man (it should seem) the verse *Let wretches hang, that Jurymen may dine!* If in that heart there be really any such thing as a particle of sympathy, it is of the very narrowest kind, while antipathy or insensibility is of the broadest: the sympathy, *that* by which, that the units may be over-comforted, the thousands are tormented. Like a cat's, the fondness of this man, if he has any, takes different courses, according as it is awakened by different objects: for students, that of a cat for her kittens: for suitors, that of a cat for mice. During the whole of his five-and-twenty years' reign—who, in all his exhibitions, ever observed him vouchsafing so much as to counterfeit any the smallest particle of remorse or of so much as regret at the thoughts of the sufferings, to which, on the most transparent pretences, he was continually occupied in giving encrease?

'Not that by all this it is in any considerable degree probabilized, that as between Students and Suitors, there has been, in his feelings towards them, any very marked difference. But the unfledged, as well as the fledged, Barrister class, were those he was surrounded with and living with: the suitor class, those he was killing by inches at a distance.

'And why, to all his other pretences has he never added that of something like sensibility as towards the people? Why?—but because, whether it was to Bar, to Lords, or to Cabinet, that he turned his eyes,—what he never ceased to observe was—that, by being thought to harbour any such feelings, what in those places a man gained would be—scorn and contempt, not reverence.'

The quotation, 'And Wretches hang that Jury-men may Dine', is from Alexander Pope, *The Rape of the Lock*, iii. 22.

'His Lordship out of the 24 days, spent in Court $79\frac{1}{2}$ hours!!!

For 4 days his Lordship sat $4\frac{1}{2}$ hours each, equal to 18
For 6 ditto 4 24
For 8 ditto .... $3\frac{11}{2}$ 26
For 4 ditto .... $2\frac{1}{4}$ 9
For 2 ditto .... $1\frac{1}{4}$ .... $2\frac{1}{2}$

_____

24 days $79\frac{1}{2}$ hours

'This statement is correct, if the Court *Clerk* can be depended on. On two of those short sitting days his Lordship had to attend in Council to hear the Recorder's Report of the Old Bailey convicts; on another of them, he rose before twelve o'clock, in indignation that there was *no business:*—No business in Chancery! On some of the other short days he was called on *business elsewhere*. But let us now see how this time was occupied.

'The case of the *Rev. A. Fletcher* is entitled to the first place in this enumeration. Indeed the flight of Paris *with*[2] Helen was not destined to give more employment for the Grecian heroes,[3] than the flight of Mr. Fletcher *from*[4] his Caledonian lassie is to cut[5] out for the gentlemen of the long robe: thus may we fairly exclaim, — *Cedent arma togæ!*[6] In the King's Bench we had only a skirmish, from which the parties[7] retired *æquo Marte*.[8] The great fight was reserved for the arena of Chancery: for four days the contending parties fought, and four times did night, or preparations for the students' dinner, put an end to the contest. On the fifth day,—after hearing[9] from eight Counsel nine speeches, the reply included,—his Lordship decided that he would not become an officer of police for a Scotch Synod, to pull the Rev. Preacher from the pulpit.[a]

'This case consumed 17 hours out of $79\frac{1}{2}$. But is it decided?—No— the contrary, for his Lordship more than once intimated "that, *if it were worth while by a longer term of suspension to bring the question before the Court in a more regular form*, his opinion *might* incline the

_____

[a] Sarcasm and false wit, instead of calm judgment!

_____

[1] *Morning Herald* '$3\frac{1}{4}$'.
[2] This word is italicized in the *Morning Herald*.
[3] Homer's *Iliad* tells the story of how Paris carried off Helen, wife of Menelaus, King of Sparta, and fled with her to Troy, thus precipitating the Trojan Wars.
[4] This word is italicized in the *Morning Herald*.
[5] *Morning Herald* 'carve'.
[6] 'Let arms yield to the toga', or 'Let war yield to peace.' Cicero, *De Officiis*, I. xxii. 77.
[7] *Morning Herald* 'Justices'.
[8] i.e. 'on equal terms'.
[9] *Morning Herald* 'having'.

other way." His intimations will not be lost on the Synod; therefore, Mr. Fletcher, that you may not be pulled down by the skirts, you had better, like *Mawworm*,[1] wear a spencer.[2]

'Fourteen hours more were consumed, from day to day, in two cases which were new to the Court. These were—petitions, from *Latham* and *Abbotts*, bankrupts, praying that his Lordship, by virtue of the enlarged jurisdiction conferred on him by the new Bankrupt Law, would grant them their certificate, which the required number of their creditors refused. His Lordship, after many observations, referred one to be re-examined by the Commissioners; and, to determine the fate of the other, he demanded more papers. The cases of these parties are therefore *in statu quo*,[3] and we are again fated to listen to half a dozen long-winded orations.

'Next after these in point of duration, is to be placed the motion to commit the *Glamorganshire Canal Proprietors*, for violating his Lordship's injunction. After hearing eight counsel for ten hours on different days, his Lordship decided that four of the Defendants were not to be committed; but the liberty of the fifth is *adhuc sub judice*.[4] To balance the mildness of the judgment with a sort of trimming policy, vengeance was denounced against the[5] refractory *watchmen;* therefore *they* had better look sharp. *Discite justitiam moniti et non temnere*.[6]

'We have now accounted for 41 hours out of the $79\frac{1}{2}$. Of the rest, the old cases of *Grey* v. *Grey*, and of *Garrick* v. *Lord Camden*, in which no progress was made, took up 5 hours; 5 more were devoted to *Hale* v. *Hale*, to determine the sale of mother's estates,[7] to be commenced *de novo;* and 10 from day to day were given to the *Attorney-General* v. *Heales; Sims* v. *Ridge;* the matter of *Bayles*, and the matter of *Blackburns;* to[8] *Honey* v. *Honey*, *Wilcox* v. *Rhodes*—appeals from the Vice-Chancellor, in the latter of which *his Honour's decree* was pronounced to be "*nonsense, incapable of being executed.*" Not one of them is a jot advanced.

---

[1] This word is italicized in the *Morning Herald*.

[2] Maw-worm, a character in Isaac Bickerstaffe's play *The Hypocrite*, first published in 1769, had become proverbial for a sanctimonious hypocrite. He had got up to preach on Kennington Common, but reported that, 'the boys threw brick-bats at me, and pinn'd crackers to my tail; and I have been afraid to mount ever since'. Presumably he wore a spencer in order to avoid suffering again the same indignity.

[3] i.e. 'in the condition in which it was'.

[4] i.e. 'as yet under the consideration of the court'.

[5] *Morning Herald* 'all'.

[6] *Morning Herald* 'temnere divos.' 'From my example learn to be just, and not to despise the gods.' Virgil, *Aeneid*, vi. 620.

[7] *Morning Herald* 'the line of six mothers' estates,'.

[8] *Morning Herald* 'Ridge, in the matter of Baylis, of Blackburns, to'.

'*Lunatics* and the *Elopement of a Ward*, took up $2\frac{1}{2}$ hours. The *New Alliance Company* took up 3: and then 9 more were wasted in disputes between Counsel and Court about priority of motions.

'The opening of the eternal *Opera House* cases (of which there are now three) took up 3 hours, and the remaining 7 were consumed from time to time on bankrupts' petitions, and miscellaneous orders.[1]

'To recapitulate the whole, the business and time are balanced thus:—

The Attorney General *v.* The Rev. A. Fletcher	17
Exparte Latham *in re* Latham and Parry, bankrupts, and Ditto Abbots	
in re Abbots and Abbots, ditto	14
Blackmore *v.* The Glamorganshire Canal Company	10
Grey *v.* Grey; Garrick *v.* Lord Camden and Hale *v.* Hale	10
The Attorney-General *v.* Heales; Sims *v.* Ridge; *in re* Baylis, and *in re*	
Blackburns, with Honey *v.* Honey and Wilcox *v.* Rhodes	10
Lunatics, Elopement of Ward, Alliance Company, and disputes about	
priority of motions	$8\frac{1}{2}$
The Opera House cases	3
Miscellaneous	7

$79\frac{1}{2}$

LORD ELDON.

V. '*It is a mistake to suppose, that because the drudgery of some offices is performed by deputies, they are therefore to be called sinecures.*'

OBSERVATIONS.

1. Nebulous-gas—confusion-gas—evasion-gas, from the Eldon laboratory. Eldon junior's six sinecures—four in possession; two more in reversion;—of course here in view.[2] Never, where common honesty is an object of regard—unpunishable swindling, of indignation,—never will they be anywhere out of view.

2. Mark here the division. Business of official situation, *drudgery* and non-drudgery. Drudgery, doing the business of the office: non-drudgery, receiving and spending the emoluments of it; paying for the doing of the business (unless it be of a particular connection) no more than a pittance, the smallest that any one can be found to take.

Note that, with few, if any exceptions, when from any one of these offices, you have separated the drudgery, you have separated all the

---

[1] *Morning Herald* 'matters.'
[2] For William Henry John Scott's sinecures see p. 279n above.

business from it. For, laying out of the case those which are *judicial*, such as the *Masterships* and the Commissionerships and the Examinerships,—the business of them amounts to little or nothing more than ordinary clerk-business, such as copying or making entries under heads: business not requiring a tenth part so much appropriate knowledge and judgment and active talent, as that of an Exciseman does.

3. Note that what his Lordship here does, consists in putting a *possible* case, that those who are eager to lay hold of every supposition favourable to him and his system, may, without proof, set it down in their minds an *actual* case: an actual case, to a considerable extent exemplified; and in particular, in the instance of the rich cluster of sinecures, out of the profits of which, without troubling himself with the drudgery either of writing or thinking, his Honourable Son is acting the part of a fine gentleman; and, if rumour does not over-flatter him, testifying filial gratitude by good dinners.

4. The *possible* case is this:—a situation in which one man and no more is placed, though the business of it is more than one man can adequately perform: the business being at the same time of such a nature, as to be capable of being divided into two branches: one, requiring extraordinary appropriate acquirements, the other requiring none beyond ordinary ones; for example, shopkeepers' clerks' acquirements. In this state of things, the extraordinary-talent-requiring part of the business is reserved by the principal official person for himself (his appropriate aptitude, considering the dignity of him of whose choice he is the object, being unquestionable:) the no-more-than-ordinary-talent-requiring part (that, to wit, which is meant by the *drudgery*) being turned over, or rather turned down, by him to the deputy. Of the thus wisely and carefully made division and distri-bution, sole object of course—the good of the service.

5. Now then—supposing an enquiry into this matter included in the enquiries of a House of Commons' Committee, is there so much as a single instance in which any such over-weight of business, together with any such division made, would be found exemplified? Whoever is a layer of wagers, might, without much danger, venture a consider-able one to the contrary.

6. In the case of *Eldon junior*, what I would venture to lay for is—that, of his four places in possession, there is not one, the business of which requires so much appropriate knowledge, judgment, and active talent as that of an Exciseman does; and that there is not one for which he himself does any business other than signing his name, with or without the trouble of looking over the accounts of the deputies (if in name or effect there be any) to wit, for the purpose of ascertaining

whether the principal receives the whole of what is his due. And so in regard to the *reversions:* the existence of which, by the bye, is a separate one, and that an abominable and altogether indefensible abuse.

7. True, my Lord. An office, in which, for the public service, a something, an *anything*, is done—is not in strictness of speech a sinecure: though that something were no more than any charity-school boy is equal to; and although it took up but a minute in doing, once out of each of the seven months in a year, during which your Masters (your Lordship's Son-in-law included)[1] serve.

8. This being conceded to you, what are you the better for it?

Would you have the amount of the depredation exercised by the maintenance of an office allowed to be executed by deputy? I will give you a rule by which, in every case, you may obtain it. From the sum received by the principal, subtract that received by the deputy or deputies: the difference is, all of it, depredation. Of thus much you may be sure; whether of this which the deputy or deputies receive, there be any and what part that belongs to that same account, is more than you can be sure of, otherwise than by applying to this case, that matchless criterion of due proportion as between reward and service, fair competition—competition, as in the case of goods sold, and under the name of *work done*, service, in all shapes, sold to individuals: and, if good in those cases, what should render it otherwise in this?

9. Casting back an eye on the matter thus employed in effecting the explosion of the Eldon gas, I cannot but regret the quantity. If, by any instruction contained in it, the labour of looking into it be paid for, it will be by the applications capable of being made of this concluding rule.

LORD ELDON.

VI. '*I will pledge myself to be as active as any Noble Lord in correcting abuses, but I will perform my duty with a due regard to the rights of others.*'

---

[1] Neither of Eldon's son-in-laws, George Stanley Repton (c.1781–1858), architect and designer, who married Lady Elizabeth Scott (d. 1862) in 1817, and Edward Bankes (1795–1867), Rector of Corfe Castle 1820–67, who married Lady Frances Jane Scott (d. 1838) in 1820, were Masters in Chancery. However, Bankes' elder brother, George Bankes (1788–1856), MP for Corfe Castle 1816–23, 1826–32 and Dorset 1841–56, was appointed a Commissioner of Bankrupts in 1822 and Cursitor Baron of Exchequer in 1824. Moreover, James William Farrer (1785–1863), who in 1811 had married Henrietta Elizabeth White-Ridley, the widow of Eldon's eldest son John Scott (1774–1805), was appointed to a Mastership in Chancery in 1824, an office he held until its abolition in 1852.

OBSERVATIONS.

1. Pledge himself? Yes: but giving a pledge is one thing—
redeeming it, another. In the whole five and twenty years, during
which this has been swagging, like an incubus, on the breast of
Justice, in what instance has he ever meddled with abuse in any
shape, unless it be by the endeavour to give perpetuity and increase to
it?

Not that, as thus worded, this desire amounts to any great matter
beyond what he might have credit given him for, and this without any
very wide departure from the exact line of truth. Noble Lords,—if in a
situation such as theirs it were possible for men to feel any such
desire,—would not have far to look for the gratification of it. Your
Majesty (said somebody once to a King of Spain who was complaining
of ceremonies) is but a ceremony.[1] Your Lordships (the same person
might have said to their Lordships) are but an abuse.

As an *argumentum ad hominem*, nothing against this challenge can
be said. But, the organs, for which it was designed, were the ears of
Noble Lords, not the eyes of the public: to which, however, I hereby
take the liberty of recommending it. *Abuses* are neither *hares* nor
foxes. Noble Lords are too well born, and under Noble and Learned
Lords too well bred, to take any great delight in *hunting* them.

LORD ELDON.

VII. '*The reason why in the present Bill there appeared no clause regulating offices in the Court of Chancery is—that a Commission is now sitting
on the state of the Court.*'[2]

OBSERVATIONS.

1. Now sitting? O yes, and for ever will be, if his Lordship's
recommendation to the people is taken by the people, and the operation of *teazing* ceases or relaxes—*Sedet, æternùmque sedebit*.[3]

2. A Commission? Yes: and what Commission?—A Commission
which never could have sat at all—which never could have been
thought of at all—had it been supposed that, in either House, there
exists any such sense as a sense of shame.

---

[1] This response of a Spanish Ambassador, who had been criticized by Philip II (1527–98),
King of Spain from 1556, for neglecting a piece of business on account of a dispute with the
French Ambassador over a point of honour, is related in *The Life of Edward Lord Herbert of
Cherbury, Written by himself*, ed. Horace Walpole, Strawberry Hill, printed in 1764, p. 141.

[2] The Royal Commission on Chancery practice which had been appointed in April 1824.

[3] 'He sits, and he will sit for eternity.' Virgil, *Aeneid*, vi. 617.

3. An enormous dilatory plea, set, like a gun, in a self-judication system; a transparent veil for corruption; a snug succedaneum to the still apprehended and eventually troublesome inquisition, of a not quite sufficiently corrupt Honourable House,—such is this Commission:—a subterfuge, which, more than perhaps all others, has damaged the reputation of the principal, not to speak of the accomplices. In matchless Constitution, that all-pervading and all-ruling principle, the self-judication principle, has now to that *local habitation*, which it has so long had, added *a name:* a name which, so long as the mass of corruption in which it has been hatched continues undissolved, will never cease to be remembered—remembered, in time and place, by every lover of justice and mankind, as occasion serves.

LORD ELDON.

VIII. '*I am uncorrupt in office; and I can form no better wish for my country than that my successor shall be penetrated with an equal* desire *to execute his duties with fidelity.*'

OBSERVATIONS.

1. *I am uncorrupt!* And so a plea of *Not Guilty* was regarded by this Defendant as sufficient in his case to destroy the effect of so matchless a mass of criminative evidence, and supersede the need of all justification and exculpative evidence!

Incorrupt? Oh yes: in every way in which it has not been possible for you to be corrupt, *that* you are. So far, this negative quality is yours. Make the most of it, and see what it will avail you. Remains, neither possessed, nor so much as pretended to, the whole remainder of appropriate moral aptitude, appropriate intellectual aptitude, and that appropriate active aptitude, without which, a man possessed in the highest degree of appropriate aptitude in both those other shapes *may* in your situation be, *has* in your situation *been*—a nuisance.

Desire! And so in an office such as that of Chief Judge, and that but one out of a cluster of rich offices fed upon by the same insatiable jaws, *desire* is sufficient: *accomplishment*, or anything like an approach to it, supervacaneous!

Yes: that he *does* form no better wish for his country—this may be conceded to him without much difficulty: for, whatever be the situation, when a man has been disgraced in it by inaptitude, the least apt is to him, but too naturally the least unacceptable successor. But, as to the *can*, this is really too much to be admitted: for, even a Lord Eldon—after rubbing his eyes, for the length of time necessary to rub out of them, for a moment, the *motes*, which keep so perpetually floating in them in the shape of doubts,—even a Lord Eldon might be *able* to see that desire and accomplishment are not exactly the same thing; and that, where the object is worth having, *desire* without *accomplishment* is not quite so good a thing as desire *with* accomplishment at the end of it. Put into this Chancellor's place, his housekeeper, supposing her to have any regard for the money it brings, would have this same desire—which, except the uncorruption, is all he can muster up courage to lay claim to, and which is so much more than can be conceded to him—the desire, in respect of *fidelity* and everything else, so far to execute the duties of it as to save herself from losing it.

Next to this, comes what has been seen already in his Lordship's concluding address to their Lordships.[1] Of the visible condition of the Defendant, no intimation is given in the report: to judge from what is given, a man who could with such a peroration close such a defence, must have been at the verge of a fainting fit: in which condition he shall, for the present, be left.

---

[1] See pp. 275–6 above.

ON THE MILITIA.

WHAT regards the militia, considered as a source, seat, or subject-matter of retrenchment, having been already brought into a determinate shape, and printed, Anno 1828 or 1829, in a newspaper,[1]—is here reprinted: reprinted in the form in which, when Vol. II. of the Constitutional Code now in the press, and in some advance, comes to be published, it will be seen in *Ch.*X. DEFENSIVE FORCE, §3, *Radicals, who*. Articles from 21 to 35, both inclusive; pages 40 to 49, both inclusive.[2]

---

[1] See the *Morning Herald*, 27 April 1829.
[2] Bentham printed, but did not in the event publish, Ch. X of *Constitutional Code*. For the text of this Paper see *Constitutional Code*, Ch. X, §3, Arts. 21–35 (Bowring, ix. 345–8).

ON PUBLIC ACCOUNT KEEPING.

COMPLAINTS have of late been made, of the method at present pursued, for making recordation and appropriate publication, of the transactions of the several classes of functionaries, of whom the official establishment of the British Government is composed; and of the pecuniary and *quasi-pecuniary* transactions more particularly. By high authority, it has been pronounced inadequate and ill-adapted to its professed purpose. To this, by that same authority, a substitution has been proposed, and *that* in the character of a well-adapted and adequate one. It consists in simply substituting, to the *method* and *phraseology* at present employed, the method and phraseology, which is called sometimes the *Italian*, sometimes the *double-entry* mode or system; and the use of which is confined to the case in which pecuniary profit and loss are conjunctly presented to view.[1]

Against this change, so far as regards the use of this peculiar and technical phraseology, I protest on two grounds—1. that, instead of being conducive to, it is incompatible with, the design which, on this occasion, whether it actually be or no, ought to be entertained; namely, that of rendering the state of the accounts in question more effectually and extensively understood—2. that, if introduced, it would of itself produce deterioration, to an unfathomable degree, in a form of government which assuredly stands not in need of any *such* change.

These evils will, when examined, be seen coalescing into [one].[2]

First, as to the *design*. What ought it to be?—Answer, as above. To render the transactions in question as effectually *understood* as may be, and to that end as *intelligible* as may be, to those whose interests

---

[1] The Select Committee on Public Income and Expenditure of 1828 had recommended to the Treasury that a commission be appointed to examine the practice of keeping public accounts: see their Second Report, *Commons Sessional Papers* (1828) v. 3–475 (especially 5–6, 475). In consequence, the Treasury appointed a Commission consisting of three members, Thomas Constantine Brooksbank (d. 1850), a Treasury official and Private Secretary to the First Lord 1811–27, Samuel Beltz of the Commissariat Department, and Peter Harris Abbott, a professional accountant. In February 1829 a majority report was produced by Brooksbank and Beltz, who proposed a substantial overhaul of the accounts, using in part a modified version of the mercantile or Italian system of double-entry, but opposing its unqualified adoption, and a minority report by Abbott, who advocated the adoption of the double-entry system without qualification (see *Commons Sessional Papers* (1829) vi. *passim*).

[2] 1830 'use'.

are at stake upon them: that is to say, in the first place, to the *representatives* of the people, in the next place to the *people* themselves, constituents of those same representatives.

Now, then, in respect of *intelligibility*, what would be the effect of the introduction of this same Italian mode? So far from augmentation, it would be little less than destruction: and this, relation had as well to *constituents* as to *representatives*.

Method is one thing; phraseology is another—1. First, as to *method:* that, by means of it, any addition would be made to the number of those by whom the transactions in question would be understood, remains to be proved: no determinate reason for thinking so have I anywhere been able to find. Whatsoever, if anything, this same addition would be, might it not, to equal effect and with equal conveniency, in every respect, be made, by the phraseology in use with everybody, as well as by that which is peculiar to merchants? With little or no hesitation I answer in the affirmative: at any rate, that which may be asserted without even the smallest hesitation is, that whatsoever may be the advantage derivable from the *method*, never can it compensate for the evil inseparably attached to the unintelligibility of the *phraseology*.

2. Next and lastly, as to the *phraseology*. To the whole community, with the exception of the single class designated by the appellation of *merchants*, this phraseology is utterly unintelligible: to all those for whose use it is, or ought to be, designed, by those by whom the substitution of it to that which is universally intelligible, is proposed: Members of Honourable House, and people without doors, included.

Of the number of those to whom it is unintelligible, compared with the number of those to whom it is intelligible, what is the amount? To any person whatsoever the answer may be intrusted. Be it what it may,—say who can, that it will not suffice to ground the putting a decided exclusion upon the proposed change.

Now then for the other objection:—deterioration of the form of Government. To a universally intelligible mode of giving expression to the transactions of the functionaries of Government, and in particular to the plan which consists in the collection of the produce of the taxes, and the disposal made of it, substitute an almost universally unintelligible mode; what is the consequence? *Answer*—Exit Public Opinion: enter Darkness: such as that which forms the characteristic of absolute Government. To matchless Constitution may be substituted the Government of Spain, Portugal, or Turkey: and this without responsibility, or danger in any shape, on the part of the authors of the change.

Obvious as these effects can scarcely fail to appear when once mentioned, to none of those persons by whom the subject has been taken into consideration do they appear to have presented themselves: neither to those by whom the change has been proposed, nor yet even by those by whom it has been opposed.

First, as to those by whom it has been *opposed*. These are—Messrs *Brooksbank and Beltz*, two of the three Commissioners for enquiry into the state of the Public Accounts. '*A wide difference exists* (say they) *between the business and circumstances of a trader and those of a* government department:'[1] in the observation thus vague and unapplied consists the only objection made by them to the introduction of the Italian mode: of the distinction between *method* and *phraseology*, no intimation whatever is conveyed by it.

Next and lastly, as to those by whom the change has been *proposed*. Not without sincere regret is it, that, on this occasion, and for such a purpose, I hold up to view a production on so many other accounts so highly estimable as the work entitled '*Financial Reform, by Sir Henry Parnell, Baronet, M.P.*' late Chairman of the Committee on Finance.[2] *Pure*, once (p. 196), *purest*, twice (pp. 192 and 197):[3]—in these two words are contained all the arguments I can find in that work, in favour of this same phraseology. 'Mr Abbot's proposal is' (he says, p. [192])[4] 'to establish the Italian system in its *purest* form; and to those persons who are *practically* acquainted with the Italian system of accounts, the reasons on which Mr Abbot founds his opinion of its being applicable to all official accounts, cannot but be (he says, p. [193])[5] completely satisfactory.'[a]

[a] Session of 1830. House of Commons Report, No. 159. 'Copy of a Letter from Mr Abbot, late one of the Commissioners,' &c.[6]
Parnell.—Purest, p. 192—Pure, 196—Purest, 197.

---

[1] This view is repeatedly stated in the Report by Brooksbank and Beltz, though these exact words are in fact used in their 'Observations' on Abbott's letter to the Treasury of 27 November 1829 referred to in the note below (see *Commons Sessional Papers* (1830) xxix. 3).

[2] Sir Henry Brooke Parnell (1776–1842), first Baron Congleton, Chairman of the Select Committee on Public Income and Expenditure of 1828, Secretary at War 1831–2, Treasurer of the Navy 1835–6, Paymaster-General 1835–41. He advocated the adoption of the Italian method in *On Financial Reform*, London, 1830. Bentham's marked copy of this work is in the British Library, shelf-mark Cup. 403. a. 37.

[3] Bentham had in mind the following passages: 'Messrs. Brooksbank and Beltz propose a plan which sacrifices the security of the pure Italian system to the minor object of saving the trouble of referring to a regularly kept journal in making out accounts for Parliament' (p. 196); 'Mr. Abbot's proposal to establish the Italian system, in its purest form, in all the public offices, deserves to have great weight with Government and Parliament' (p. 192); 'In that country [France] the Italian system is acted upon, in all the public departments, in its purest form' (p. 197).

[4] 1830 '194'. See above.

[5] 1830 '173'. 'To those persons who are practically acquainted with the Italian system of

 [*See p. 296 for n. 5 cont. and n. 6.*]

'Applicable?'—Unquestionably. But what is that to the purpose? Just nothing. Applicable means *capable* of being applied. But, of the truth of this proposition what need of opinion from that gentleman or any body else, to make us fully satisfied? Applicable, or not applicable *with advantage?*—that is the question. And, to that question answer has *not* been given by Mr Abbot; answer *has* been given *here*.

That of the desire of these so highly intelligent and well-informed statesmen above-mentioned, unintelligibility on the part of the subject-matter in question, and ignorance, next to entire, on the part of the persons in question, were not amongst the objects—I, who write this, am altogether satisfied. But of the desire of those by whom the recommendations made by the Committee over which he presided were set at nought, and the existence of that same Committee cut short, were or were not these among the objects?[1] Relieved should I be from an anxiety eminently painful, were it in this paper, consistently with sincerity, to answer in the negative.

'To bring forward a motion for the emolument of the persons in question,' was, according to Mr Chancellor of the Exchequer (if the account of the debate is to be believed[a]) '*treating* them' (it should perhaps have been *placing* them) 'in an invidious point of view:'[2]—and, in effect, he, accordingly, on that same occasion, did what depended on him towards preventing their being placed in that same point of view.

---

[a] *Morning Chronicle*, May 15, Debate of May 14.[3]

---

accounts, the reasoning on which Mr. Abbot founds his opinion of its being applicable to all official accounts cannot fail to be completely satisfactory.'

[6] The disagreement between Abbott on the one hand, and Brooksbank and Beltz on the other, was continued in 'Copy of a Letter from Mr. Abbott, late one of the Commissioners, for inquiring into the state of the Public Accounts, addressed to the Right honourable the Lords Commissioners of His Majesty's Treasury, dated the 27th November 1829; together with the Explanations and Observations of Messrs. Brooksbank and Beltz thereupon, dated 18th Dec. 1829', *Commons Sessional Papers* (1830) xxix. 1–20.

[1] The Committee on Public Income and Expenditure had not been revived by the Wellington administration in the 1829 session of Parliament.

[2] The *Morning Chronicle* reported Goulburn as saying, 'To bring forward a motion for the emoluments of the Members of the Privy Council, was not, as it appeared to me, treating with sufficient respect a body composing the Council of the Sovereign, and a high judicial Court—it was treating them in an invidious point of view'.

[3] The *Morning Chronicle* of 15 May 1830 reported a debate in the House of Commons on the previous day, when Sir James Robert George Graham (1792–1861), First Lord of the Admiralty 1830–4, 1852–5, Home Secretary 1841–6, brought in a motion for returns to be made of the salaries of members of the Privy Council. Henry Goulburn (1784–1856), Chancellor of the Exchequer 1828–30, 1841–6, Home Secretary 1834–5, proposed an amendment that returns be made of the salaries of all public officers with salaries exceeding £2,000. The amendment was carried by 231 votes to 147. (See also *Parliamentary Debates* (1830) xxiv. 731–58.)

But these same persons—who were they? *Answer*, 'Members,' (says he) 'of the Privy Council,'—'a body composed of the Council of the Sovereign;' and afterwards, 'the first Judge in the land was included in it.'[1]—Prodigious! And so, in the opinion of this member of the Cabinet Council, be the man who he may, the servants of the Crown have but to obtain the placing of him in a situation which affords them the means of putting into his pocket an indefinitely large portion of the produce of the taxes,—this done, nobody but themselves is to be informed of the amount of it. What the amount is of the booty thus determined to be screened from detection, the Right Honourable guardian of the public purse has not informed us. But if the imputation couched under the word *invidious* be all that he objects to, a sure and easy receipt for the wiping it off is at his command. It consists—in the giving publicity to the information in question, in the instance of every public functionary without distinction.

In and by the original Committee on Finance, of which the late Charles Abbot, afterwards Speaker, and not long ago ennobled by the title of Lord Colchester,[2] was Chairman, extensive were the disclosures of this sort made; and, as far as appeared, in endeavours to narrow them. This was in the years 1797, 1798. Thirteen or fourteen years after, came the Committee on Finance, of which the Chairman was the still living Mr Henry Banks,[3] the Lord Eldon of Honourable House. From the Report made by that Committee,[4] no possibility was there of learning the aggregate of the emoluments received, in the instance of any one of the functionaries occupying the situations mentioned in it. So exquisite was the ingenuity by which the deed of darkness was accomplished.

In the eyes of the Right Honourable persons in question, is the imputation of harbouring this same design of darkness regarded as matter of importance? is the clearing themselves of it considered by them as an object worth their regard? The means at their command are most effectual.

For and during many years in the latter part of the last century, for the use of the Directors of the Life Insurance Company called the *Amicable Society*, was annually published, in conjunction with an

---

[1] According to the *Morning Chronicle*, Goulburn commented: 'The Hon. Baronet knows that the first Judges in the land are included in his Motion.'

[2] Abbot was created Baron Colchester in 1817, upon his retirement as Speaker of the House of Commons.

[3] Henry Bankes (1756–1834), MP for Corfe Castle 1780–1826 and Dorset 1826–31. The Committee on Public Expenditure sat from 1807 to 1812, and produced thirteen Reports; Bankes was Chairman 1807–9 and again from 1810.

[4] i.e. the Third Report on 'Pensions, Sinecures, Reversions': see *Commons Sessional Papers* (1808) iii. 257–459.

almanac, a list of the situations of which the official establishment was composed, with the emolument attached to each in the shape of salary. At present in the annual publication, intituled the *Royal Calendar*, of these situations, or at any rate the greatest part of them, a list is published; but, of emolument in the shape of salary, or in any other shape, in no such publication, or in any other publication, is any mention to be found.[1]

Now then, by order of some one of the constituted authorities, let a complete list be published of all those several situations, with the amount of the aggregate of the emolument respectively attached to them: and to the columns in which these aggregates are inserted, let be added another, exhibiting the total of the emoluments received by the functionary in question, from all public sources taken together; with numeral figures, expressive of the pages, in which the several situations, with their respective masses of emolument, are presented to view.

Against the proposition for throwing the light of day upon this part of the den of Cacus,[2] the only argument adduced by the Right Honourable Gentleman is composed of the word *invidious*. In the import of this same word the idea of *distinction* is included. Do away the distinction—set fire to the gas—illuminate *uno flatu* the whole den, as above proposed,—extinguished is this argument. Some dictionary, dead or living, he will have to turn over for another such.

On the present occasion,—after what has been said on the subject of *unintelligibility*, is it worth while to say anything more of that same branch of art and science (for *science* I see it called)[3] to which the attribute of *purity* has so unhappily been ascribed? Of fiction, and nothing else is it composed: of a tissue of misrepresentations—of departures from truth—and these not merely useless, but much worse than useless. To *things*, relations all along ascribed, of which *things* are not susceptible: to *persons*, relative situations in which, on the occasion in question, these same persons are not placed. *Wine* is said to be *debtor* to *cloth*.[4] To what use this absurd falsehood? What explanation, if

---

[1] See further p. 301 below.

[2] In classical mythology, Cacus was a savage three-headed monster. His den was a cave on Mount Aventine, from where he plundered the surrounding countryside. He was killed by Hercules for stealing some of his oxen and hiding them in his cave.

[3] The Italian method is so described by Brooksbank and Beltz at p. 5 of their Report.

[4] Bentham expanded on this point at UC cxii. 384 (9 May 1830): 'Some 30 or 40 years ago I remember advertized and published by subscription, with no small parade and anxiety for previous secrecy, a pamphlet of two or three sheets under the name, if I misrecollect not, of Jones. From this I learnt that in those days . . . Wine was in the habit of running in debt to Cloth: on which relation the author took occasion to crack a joke: recommending it to Cloth to call upon wine for payment. From this joke I learnt the inaptitude of the institution for its professed purposes: and from the whole of the work this was all I learnt.' The pamphlet in question was

anything, does it give? To what human being who has not been drenching himself with this and the kindred falsehoods for weeks or months, can it present any idea, unless it be an illusive one, unless it be translated into the vulgar tongue? True it is, that, had this locution been originally applied to the presenting to view the ideas annexed to it by the professors of this art-and-science,—it might have served as well for the purpose as does the correspondent part and parcel of the vulgar tongue: but, having once been fixed in the habit of being applied to so different a purpose, thence comes the confusion, and the useless difficulty which stands opposed to all endeavours to understand it.

So much for confusion-spreading *proposition:* now (to speak in logical language) use for a delusive *term*. Enter *Waste-book, cum totâ sequelâ suâ:*[1]—*Waste-book*, a book, composed of paper the value of which is that of waste paper. To an unadept mind, what other idea than this is it in the nature of this appellation to suggest. Yet is this one book the corner-stone, on which the truth and usefulness of all the others rest:—a book, error in which infects with correspondent error all the rest:—the original, of which, though in different forms, all those others are but copies. Call this book the *original* book, those others the *derivative* books, the delusion vanishes. Call this book the *chronological*,—those others the *logical* books, the matter being traced in different *orders*, according to the different purposes,—a further instruction is afforded.

It is one of the branches of that art-and-science, which teaches how to make plain things difficult. A curious and not altogether uninstructive parallel, is that which might be made between this *regular* and *technical* mode of account keeping (for by both these epithets do I see it honoured)[2] and the technical and regular system of judicial procedure. It would show to what a degree, by the leading-string held by blind Custom, without any additional one tacked on by Sinister Interest, aberration from the rule of right is capable of being effected.

[Edward Thomas Jones], *Jones's English System of Book-Keeping, by single or double entry, in which it is impossible for an error of the most trifling amount to be passed unnoticed; calculated effectually to prevent the evils attendant on the methods so long established; and adapted to every species of trade*, Bristol, 1796. Bentham's memory of the passage (see p. 24) was not quite accurate: 'why should a Merchant's, or Tradesman's Books be stuffed with such ridiculous and mysterious nonsense, as appears on every leaf of those kept by Double Entry.—Such as "*Sundry Accounts Debtor to Sundry Accounts;—A.B.* D^r *to Wine;—Wine* D^r *to Profit and Loss:—C.D.* D^r *to Deals, etc. etc.* Now if A.B. owes Wine money, why not let Wine call for payment? But if A.B. do not owe Wine money, why make the entry in such way as only tends to confuse the mind of a person who is not a good acccomptant?' Bentham also discussed the Italian method of book-keeping in *Constitutional Code*, I (*CW*), Ch. IX, §7, Bis§6, Art. 5, pp. 266–7n.

[1] i.e. 'with all its retinue'.

[2] The Italian method is so described in several passages in the Brooksbank and Beltz Report.

Of this phraseology, if any use it have, the use consists in giving *brevity* to the mode of expression. Analogous is the use, in this case, to that of *short-hand*, as a substitute to ordinary hand,—to that of arithmetical notation as a substitute to ordinary orthography,—and to that of algebraic, as a substitute to arithmetical, notation. But, small in comparison is the utmost service, which, in this character, can be rendered by it: and on this ground, not on an imaginary one, by those who teach it, should the usefulness of it be placed.

In my *Constitutional Code*—to wit, in the already published volume of it—may be seen a section, in which, in the compass of sixty-eight pages, what is designed for an all-comprehensive set of books, for the exhibition of the accounts, pecuniary and quasi-pecuniary, of any Government whatsoever, is presented to view.[1] But for the bulk of it, it would have been included in this present miscellany. Official establishments, which it embraces in its view, are—not only those of this country, but those of any other country whatsoever.

To any attention, bestowed upon it by the only persons from whose attention to it any good to the community would ensue,—two objections there are, to the potency of which the author is duly sensible. No title had he, having the effect of a warrant from authority, for the undertaking of it. Instead of the 1,600*l.* a-year, or some such matter, from all the members of the community taken together,—16*s.* from each of such of them as may vouchsafe to purchase it, is the remuneration he will receive from it: by which remuneration, in the case of this work, as in the case of almost all others by which he has endeavoured to render his labours useful to his own country and mankind,—his profits will, to a large amount, be left on the *minus* side.

Two objections there are, to its being regarded as worth the 16*s.* by those with whose title to receive money out of the taxes, Mr Chancellor of the Exchequer is so effectually satisfied, by the consideration of the quantity thereof so received by them.[2] Two objections, and each of them an unconquerable one. No such remuneration will be offered; and, were it offered, no such remuneration,—nor any remuneration, other than that which would be afforded by the acknowledgment of the usefulness of the work,—would be received.

But, let but a title, such as that of *Privy Councillor*, or were it even no other than that of *Commissioner*, with 1,600*l.* a year or some such

---

[1] See *Constitutional Code*, I (*CW*), Ch. IX, §7, pp. 218–67 (this section formed pp. 274–341 in the edition published by Bentham in 1830).

[2] In the debate on Graham's motion, referring to the Privy Council, Goulburn had said: 'They are a body comprising persons who, undoubtedly, receive emoluments from the public, on the whole, perhaps, to a very large amount'. (*Morning Chronicle*, 15 May 1830.)

matter, be added to it—oh what a treasure it would be! Multiply the
1,600*l.* by ten,—multiplied by the same number would be the value
of the work! Multiply it by a hundred,—the value would be multiplied
an hundred fold! Multiply it by 10,000, its value would outstrip that of
Holy Writ;—and prostrate before it would lie the whole population of
the Cabinet, accompanied and sanctified by his Grace of Canterbury,
and all those other paragons of piety, whose regard for that same Holy
Writ is manifested by the fineness of their sleeves, and the Tyrian dye
of their servants' liveries. Included are all these propositions, in that
mathematical axiom, which is the key-stone of matchless Constitution—*Aptitude is* AS *opulence*.

* Since the proof of this sheet came in, a Royal Calendar has been taken in
hand, of so recent a date as the year 1808; and in it are seen names of official
situations, with salaries annexed, as in the case of the Almanack mentioned
in page [297–8].[1] What was the year in which this mention of salaries was
for the first time omitted, and what the state of the Administration in that
same year, may be curious enough subjects of inquiry.[2]

[1] 1830 '8'.
[2] Salaries had last been listed in the *Royal Kalendar* in the 1818 edition, during Liverpool's
administration.

CONSTITUTIONAL CODE.— TABLE OF CONTENTS.[1]

---

[1] For this table see *Constitutional Code*, I (*CW*), prefixed to p. 1. In 1830, the table is prefixed to the title page.

APPENDICES

APPENDIX A
INDICATIONS RESPECTING
LORD ELDON
POSTSCRIPT

§3. *Warning—intended system of abuse anticipated*

The Eldon Act[1]—with the bustle that preceded and followed it—
having, during this discussion, become productive of a sort of reform
which is nothing but a new sauce poured over the overdone abuse,[2]
the indications already given threatened to appear incompleat, unless
something were done, towards putting *lay-gents* in a way to smell out
the true character of it. 'But', (says somebody) 'if this will not do what
it undertakes for, what is it that will? And, what chance, if any, does
the nature of the case afford for its being effected? Never yet has it
been your practice to aim at pulling down, but for the purpose of
building up. Never till now: and shall it be so now? Necessary as is to
reform the removal of the implacable and unsubduable enemy to all
reform, at the same time shall *reform* itself—the still superior and
only ultimate object—remain altogether without notice?'—Such are
the considerations which have given birth to this and the next ensuing
section.

Again. 'Of the plan thus pronounced upon, a part only' (it may be
said) 'has been as yet in view; other part remains still undeveloped.'
True. But, of that which is in front, there is quite enough, to shew the
object and leading features of that which is behind.

Be this as it may, to Lord Eldon nothing but convenience can be the
result of the course thus taken, and the anticipations here brought
forward.

Of the undisclosed part of his own plan, is any thing here brought to
view, which after the exposure made of it, is deemed untenable? Up
rises a second cry of 'misrepresentation' and 'calumny:'[a] and this time

---

[a] Postscript §2: p. [274–89].

[1] The Act of 1822 enabling judges to regulate fees (3 Geo. IV, c.69), so characterized by
Bentham in 'Indications respecting Lord Eldon', §XIII, pp. 238–42 above.

[2] Bentham is referring to the three Bills which together increased the salaries of judges,
abolished the sale of offices in the Courts of King's Bench and Common Pleas, and commuted
into salaries the fees of the Chief Justices and newly appointed officials of those Courts: see
ibid., §I, p. 205n above.

with a pretext altogether wanting to the first. Is there any thing, which, notwithstanding exposure, he remains determined to persevere in? Instead of being taken on the sudden, he has as many months as he pleases to raise up his doubts for the defence of it. Of what is here brought forward, does there happen to be any thing which it suits him to make use of?—'what use' (it may be asked) 'in giving us what is our own already, and what, if it were not, any body else might in better form have given us?'

To search out and make distinct references to every thing that has been done already, as also the grounds of the several conclusions deduced, would require more time than the commentator could or the reader would care to bestow. After these explanations, for argument sake, and subject to correction, his Lordship's real plan is in substance this—

1. To continue to as great an extent as possible, for the benefit of Judges and their subordinates, the faculty of receiving money from suitors in the shape of fees.

2. In so far as this cannot, it is thought, with sufficient decency be done, to make commutation for them in the shape of salary: but so to order the matter that the commutation shall not take place till after the death or removal of the present incumbents.

3. When thus the fees cease to be received by the incumbents on their own account, not to extinguish them but to cause them to be received on public account, and, at stated periods, to be transferred to the use of the public.

4. As to those fee-yielding offices which, though the incumbents have been in a state of subordination to the Judges, have not been in the gift of the Judges,—in so far as they form perfect and acknowledged sinecures, to abolish them: making compensation for the value: if in so far as they are regarded as being in any degree efficient offices, to place them in the gift of the Judges: and with the fees continued; or if that can not conveniently be managed, with salaries in lieu of fees.

5. As to offices which have been sold by and for the benefit of Judges, whether sinecure or efficient, to inhibit the future sale of them: but to retain them—such as are regarded as efficient—in the gift of the Judges, with fees annext, or if that can not conveniently be managed, with salaries in lieu of fees.

6. In particular, not to substitute salary to fees in the case of the offices held by the Masters in Chancery.

7. In the case of Lord Eldon, to preserve to the greatest practicable extent to all offices in his gift, whether sinecure or efficient, as well as to his own, the faculty of receiving fees to the use of the incumbents.

In regard to the effects of this plan, I will venture to advance two all-embracing positions:

1. That, from the existing mass of abuses and imperfections, the defalcation which, in so far as carried into execution, it will make, will, if any, be very inconsiderable.

2. That it will of itself suffice to render impracticable, during the life of the longest liver of the functionaries allowed to receive fees, so much as the commencement of any system of judicial procedure having really for its ends the ends of justice.

On this occasion I shall shew:

I.[1] That the receipt of so much as a single fee by any official person at the expence of suitors is in direct and irreconcileable repugnancy to the ends of justice: and accordingly the desire to give continuance to this exaction, incompatible with the desire of giving fulfilment to the ends of justice.

II. That, on the part of Judges, the cause of the adherence to remuneration in this shape is an apprehension, and *that* a perfectly well-grounded one, that their interest would suffer very materially in case of a determination to give, in lieu of fees, salaries not exceeding such as in the eyes of the donors, for want of such explanations as in the present state of things can not be given, would appear equivalent and sufficient.

III. That, for removal of this apprehension and consequent opposition on the part of Judges and Advocates looking to become Judges, it is highly expedient that, in the shape of salary, ample and more than equivalent compensation should be given to the several persons interested: compensation—not only for all monies habitually received, but for all monies that can really be at present expected to be received in the course of the time in question, by the continuance and encrease of the system of abuse sanctioned by the Eldon Act.

IV. That all abuses which have been produced by, or could arise out of, fees received by means of offices which have been the subject-matter of *sale*, will, instead of being lessened, be necessarily and to an indefinite degree encreased, should they be made the subject-matter of *gift*: that is to say by the hands of the Judges or other functionaries, by whom alone in ordinary cases any controul is exercised over the subordinates in question.[2]

---

[1] For the sake of clarity, Bentham's Arabic numerals have been changed to Roman.

[2] The text was originally continued by the following passage at UC xix. 310 (n.d. July 1825):
'V. That so long as fees are admitted to be received for judicial services from the hands and at the charge of Suitors, transference of the money to the use of the public would still leave the system in a state of repugnancy to the ends of justice.

'VI. My position as above is universal in its application—to wit, that whatsoever systems of

I. First, as to the mode of remuneration in question—its repugnancy to the ends of justice. Every fee or mass of fees operates as a denial of justice to all those who are unable to pay it, and, in England, by reason of the aggregate of the fees exacted, whether on the one side or on the other, on the occasion of an ordinary suit at law, in any one of the ordinary Courts, the number of the persons to whom in that way justice is denied constitutes a vast majority of the whole people.

By this denial of justice, it contravenes the direct ends of justice: and by encrease of delay, expence and vexation, it contravenes the collateral ends of justice. Delay, besides its own mischiefs, produces additions to expence: to wit, by means of the intervening incidents by which fresh services are called for at judicial hands; and by deparition of means of proof or means of satisfaction for wrong, it produces failure of justice, having the effect of denial of justice, in contravention of the direct ends of justice.

Whatever be the amount of the exaction thus imposed, these effects are in equal degree produced by it, in whatsoever pocket the money, in so far as it is received, rests. What makes the law fees in question worse than law taxes is—that in the case of the law fees, the motives for giving indefinite encrease to them are in the same hands with the power. This is not so in the case of the law taxes. The money which the fee-fed Judge puts into his pocket, he exacts, on each individual occasion, from each individual suitor: not so the man of finance.

Whosoever therefore persists in the endeavour to exact money from suitors as such, can not but see that by so doing he is producing denial of justice, and inflicting on the people all the evils correspondent and opposite to all the several ends of justice.

II. As to the insufficiency of salaries to produce an adequate equivalent for fees, without taking into account sources which can not be taken into account but by means of such disclosure as in the present state of things can not officially be made.

The cause of difficulty is here the illegality and turpitude of these

judicial procedure are capable of being conducive to the ends of justice, the execution of [the] above supposed plan would be incompatible with it and effectually prevent it from having place.

'VII. In this position is included the position that the existing system is repugnant with the ends of justice: and according to my conception of the matter, as on various occasions advanced, it never can have had for its ends the ends of justice; nor, consistently with the essential condition of human nature, ever could have had.

'VIII. Thereupon for greater clearness to conception, I will endeavour to convey in as few words an idea of the only system of procedure which in my eyes is compatible with the ends of justice: stating only so much of it as [is] indispensably necessary for the present purpose.'

Bentham did not go on to discuss any of these four points, apart from a fragment on 'Transference' at UC xix. 371–5 (see the Editorial Introduction, p. xln above).

sources: stains which can not be washed out but by the hand of Parliament.

To make this clear it will be necessary to bring to view the ways or some of the ways in which fees *not* avowedly intended to be exacted are let in by fees avowedly intended [to be] exacted. They are as follows.

1. Under the name of *a fee*, on an occasion on which a fee is avowedly intended to be exacted, a sum added to the sum avowedly intended to be exacted. Witness the 4ˢ· 6[d.] exacted by Lord Chief Justice Abbot by the hand of his tipstaff in addition to the 6ˢ· allowed by the Table of fees.[1]

2. Under the name of a fee, money exacted on *an occasion* on which, it not being in the number of the occasions mentioned in the Table, it was not intended, or at least was not *avowedly* intended, to be exacted.

3. Under the name of a fee, to a fee originally, as per N⁰· 2, unauthorized *in toto*, an unauthorized addition made.

4. Not under the name of a fee, but under the name of a *gratuity*, or under no particular name, in consideration or on pretence of extra service, in this or that shape, with or without mention of specific extra service: as for example for extra labour bestowed or dispatch given.

5. To a sum habitually taken as per N⁰· 4, addition made as per N⁰· 1.

6. Giving encrease to the number of occasions productive of a demand for judiciary services to which fees are attached. By Judges this power is possessed and exercised to an extent to which there are no limits.

Of these manufactured occasions, some may be made intelligible without entering into the way of the details of procedure. Witness the case where a cause is made to stand over, put off to a distant period, or struck out of the paper, and then reinstated: or a thirst for affidavits with fees adhering to them gratified: or a special case made for argument at a distant time: or a verdict taken subject to the opinion of the Court. So much for samples. But as to enumeration, an enumeration of all the occasions capable of being thus created would include in it an enumeration of all the steps capable of being taken on both sides in the course of a suit.

Partly in the natural and necessary course of things, partly with the assistance of *delay*, is every case pregnant with *fee-yielding occasions*.

---

[1] See 'Indications respecting Lord Eldon', §XII, pp. 231–7 above.

What gives to this source of fees, as compared with those above-mentioned, a peculiar value, is—that by employing it, instead of the reproach so justly merited, honour is frequently and habitually not only claimed but received for the employment given to it.

A wholesale manufacture of delay is that which was originally set up, and with such prodigious success has been carried on, by the distinction between *terms* and *vacations*. Born and bred under the reign of this abuse, the deluded people regard the four terms, with their intervening length of factitious delay, with the same patient acquiescence as if it came from the same hand along with the four seasons.

When sleeps Injustice so may Justice too

is a verse, which, clumsy as it is, should never be out of mind. At each judicial station, every day on which the judicatory is not sitting is a day of triumph given to Injustice.

Delay manufactured in this way may be manufactured independently of whatever is produced by insufficiency in the number of the judicatories, or in the number of days or hours of attendance on the part of those same judicatories. Take ten suits and suppose two days, if contiguous, sufficient for the dispatch of each. If, instead of being gone on with the next day, each suit is put off for six months, in this way a six month manufactured delay may be given to suits in any number while judicatories in sufficient number are sitting all of them during a sufficient length of time.

Such is the manifest and undeniable effect, such the equally undeniable object and end of the establishment and continuance given to Terms and Vacations, Circuits, Assizes and Quarter Sessions. In a criminal case, commencement given one day, continuance instead of the next put off to that day six or twelve months, in the course of which time the party dies or is ruined in prison, or the prosecutor or a material witness, on the one side or the other, dies, or is bought off, or makes his escape, or has forgot what passed.

7. Precipitation itself is pregnant with delay. If, in the first instance, a time within which an operation necessary to justice can not be performed is appointed for performance, thereupon comes the necessity of an application for enlargement: the application opposed or unopposed, and in either case, in correspondent proportion, production of fresh fees.

Thus do the opposite vices walk hand in hand and give assistance to each other. When, by a fixt rule, the same interval of time is allotted for an operation or set of operations for the performance of which, according to circumstances, different lengths of time will be necessary, especially when the parties, by whom they are to be performed, are resident at different distances from the seat of business and source of notice, a proportionable mixture of delay and precipitation is a necessary consequence. Of precipitation, producing in this way the effects of delay, the proceedings in the Equity Courts in the case of an Injunction present a notable example recently offered to public view.

8. Between delay and fees so perfectly is the connection understood by all lawyers, and in particular by the most experienced class of them, the Judges, that on each occasion to consider whether on that particular occasion delay would be productive of an addition to fees would require more time than it would be worth. Both by Bench and Bar every the slightest pretence for delay is accordingly eagerly laid hold of: not with least eagerness where lamentations on the score of delay are loudest.

In comparison of the delays which in a covert way are the work of Judges, whether of the whole fraternity or of this or that individual Judge, the delays which are manifestly the work of an individual Judge in particular are very inconsiderable. In this case, if no apparent possibly adequate cause can be pointed to for a justification, the delay created, for example by a Lord Eldon, is ascribed to the time requisite for deliberation and the constant and constantly self-tormenting anxiety to do justice.

If, instead of being gained, money were lost by these mixtures of delay and precipitation, some title to credence might belong to these pretensions of self-sacrifice. Moreover, here may be seen one natural source at least of Eldonic dubitation. In this way it is, that the more enormous the quantity of mischief and misery his Lordship produces, the more enormous is the quantity of laud he receives, in the first place from his own learned lips, in the next place from the chorus of his dependents.

9. Note, that whatsoever be the quantity of profit, extracted or extractible, from the aggregate of all these sources at the present time, proportioned to the encrease received by the prosperity of the country will naturally be, and be expected to be, the encrease given to the quantity of the above sinister profit.

Of this exposure the practical object has been—to put it out of doubt that, for the mass of fees in question, no compensation, which in appearance is no more than equivalent, can fail of being in reality, in a very large proportion, short of being so: and that accordingly, if, on the part of Judges and Barristers looking to be Judges, opposition is to be bought off, this difference, whatever it may amount to, must be made up.

[III.]¹ Now as to the buying off the above explained sinister interest of the Judges and, in so far as possible, of the professional class of Lawyers.

If, in my breast, as towards those who profit from the abuses of the judicial and procedure system antipathy were stronger than sympathy for mankind, no such proposal could I make. But sympathy for mankind is the source of the highest enjoyments I am capable of, and towards no one of those individuals have I any such feeling as that of antipathy any other than that which I keep alive as well as I can for the moment as a stimulus [to] the exertions necessary to the engaging those on whom it depends to put an end to the abuses.

The point to be compassed is, on the part of the persons in question, the persuasion that, after as well as during the removal of the abuses in question, they will upon the whole find themselves at least as well off as during the continuance of those same abuses.

But to this purpose not only money is necessary but amnesty. Expected receipts can not be compensated for, but except in so far as they are known: and they can not be universally made known unless all who are at present in the habit of receiving them are universally secured against all punishment for the past. Amnesty is an expedient resorted to upon occasion by every government: and this for the prevention of the very highest and most mischievous crimes. It might be mischievous in those cases, and still be beneficial in the case of the comparatively lighter misdeeds here in view.

Invitation must be given to all official men acting in judicial offices, and in particular in all offices in the gift of Judges, to give in a full account of their past receipts during such length of time as they respectively choose, together with any such additions as they expect to have made at the end of any and what time, stating the grounds of those same expectations—the invitation being coupled with an assurance that in case of commutation, the value of the commutation given will not be less than the greatest value which it is believed they themselves really set upon the pecuniary emolument of their respective offices. Upon no other terms than these can the Judges, in whose gift the subordinate offices respectively are, be as well off in this respect as they are at present.

The Masters in Chancery may serve for exemplification. Amongst the delinquents in question, I have without reserve denounced the whole fraternity as a gang of swindlers, and the Chancellor, as the

---

¹ MS 'V.' The following sequence, originally headed 'Prospect as to remedy', develops Bentham's third point at p. 309 above. A further fragment on this theme is at UC xix. 357 (26 July 1825).

head of the gang, sharing in the plunderage made by them: and such I have shewn them to be by indications which I challenge them to controvert, and which from the nature of the case any body may stand assured they will not any of them controvert. It is with that scene full in view that I propose for them, as well as for all minor delinquents, what has been seen: to wit, the completest indemnity as against punishment and more than compleat indemnity as against all loss, under whatever name—fees, perquisites or any other.

'What then?' says somebody, 'would you reward men for having been swindlers?' Answer. No: not swindlers at large: only the gang of swindlers thus particularly circumstanced. In the case of swindlers at large, such indemnity for past delinquency would, in the character of a bounty, produce future, and so on without end. But in the case of this particular gang, the bounty, if such it is to be called, could not be productive of such effect. Inhibited from taking money of suitors on any account, they would no more take it than Judges at present take bribes: by every fee taken henceforward, the functionary in question would place himself, fortune and reputation, at the mercy of the giver in the transaction, as well of every other person privy to it.

Of punishment as applied to a mischievous act, the sole use is the prevention of the like in future. In the case of ordinary misdeeds, in so far as they are capable of being prevented, it is by the fear of punishment, and thence of necessity, for keeping up the fear, by the actual application of punishment, reward being employed (for procurement of evidence for example) so far only as punishment is inapplicable. In the present case, punishment can not be employed, and even if it could be employed would be too expensive: while on the other hand reward may be applied with less expence and full assurance of success.

For an example of the magnitude of the disorder, and thence of the magnitude of the remedy necessary, the case of these functionaries will serve more effectually than that of any other. In this situation the delinquent not [only] cheats assignable individuals out of their money, but unassignable individuals out of a vast quantity of time which is their due. Of a Judge so-called, the disposable time is fully occupied in the business of his Office. Of the sort of subordinate Judge called a Master in Chancery, the disposable time is not near so much as half occupied. To make him as well off after the reform as before it, he must either be suffered to continue in his present degree of idleness, paying others for supplying the deficiency, or he must be paid what will satisfy him for whatever additional quantity of time he is really obliged to expend. To compleat the reform in his case, whatever attendance he engages to give, he must be made to give. Only in one way can he [be] made to do so: and that is by making his receipt of the money depend every penny of it upon the fact of his having bestowed the requisite attendance. But for this, after the augmentation of his salary he will continue to cheat the public of the time due to it, as he does at present. In the effecting of this dependence between service and reward there is not any the smallest difficulty. None is ever found as between individual and individual. It is always effected wherever it is intended: and in every instance its not being effected is a most conclusive proof of its not being intended.

The quantity of time desirable being determined, so it were but given, and by an individual possessed of equal aptitude, it would not matter what the stile and title of the individual were, whether a Master, Master's Clerk, Master's Assistant or Master's Depute: except that the word Clerk importing inferiority of aptitude with reference to the person to whom he is Clerk, either of those other titles would on that account be preferable. In how many instances has it not happened that while the Master has yielded his name and nothing else, the Clerk and he alone has yielded whatever there has been of aptitude? and that at whatsoever time the business was done, the worst thing that could happen to the party in the right was its being by the Master that it was done?

Distributed in a manner not prejudicial to health, a quantity of time not greater, or even perhaps less, than the quantity employed by a Lord Chief Justice would suffice in the case of Master. Suppose this to amount every day to 8 hours: and, though according to Mr Vizard it is not so much,[1] the quantity of time upon an average at present bestowed by a Master to be four hours. The public would still be a great gainer if, on this consideration, his present emolument from all sources were doubled, he being at the same time bound to provide a Depute who should sit whenever he did not sit: in this condition there need not be any vacation, in which case, instead of the present 7 months in the year, every Master, by himself or Depute, would serve all twelve.

At this expence, supposing it made worth a Judge's while to be honest, it would be made worth the while of the highest rank of professional men to be honest: meaning by the highest rank those whose expectations look to the Bench. Less, considerably less, than the mass of emolument received by a man in the situation of Counsel would suffice to render the same man desirous of the situation of a

---

[1] See Vizard, *Letter to William Courtenay*, p. 32, 'I now find a general understanding prevails, that the earliest appointment for a Master must be eleven, and the latest at two o'clock', quoted in 'Indications respecting Lord Eldon', §II, pp. 209–10 above.

Judge. Supposing the quantity of time bestowed in the two situations the same, in the situation of Judge the [. . .?] of [. . .?] is altogether inconsiderable. The Judge, in the exercise of his function, says as much or as little as he pleases. In no instance is there any use in his saying so much as has been said by the leading Counsel who has said most. In the situation of the Judge, the quantum of the emolument would, by the supposition, be throughout certain: in the situation of the Counsel, health of itself suffices to render it constantly precarious. Be the appetite for money ever so sharp—be it as sharp as in the breast of a Lord Eldon or a Chief Justice Abbot, power and dignity— whether to that which is natural to the situation any thing factitious be or not added—can never be altogether without value. To Lord Eldon in particular, in his situation of Chancellor, the power of keeping every thing tolerably quiet in the Cabinet, and added to that intolerably unquiet every where else, could not, in case of an estimate made, fail to be in a pecuniary [view] worth something, unknown as that something necessarily is to every body else, and great as the doubts could not fail to be in his own Noble and learned Dubitation-machine. Scarcely in any other breast, official or professional, could these two conjunct powers operate with quite so much weight as in that: but is it too much to hope for, that in this or that professional breast the prospect of doing good upon the largest scale may operate with equal force: Henry Brougham, what say you to this? And what, think you, will other men say for you?

Only to this highest reach of professional men can apply this possibility of the extinction of sinister interest by purchase. Of sinister interest wherever else seated, by exposure alone can any thing be done towards weakening it.

Different classes of men here present themselves as being each of them in possession of a separate sinister interest with different masses of power employable in support of it.

1. Barristers, the rhetorical class. Whatever be the state of the law, the question of fact must, so long as the world stands, continue to supply no small quantity of business to professional men of this description. The law in all its branches might be put upon the best footing possible, and the quantity of emolument enjoyed by the leading and influential men of this [class] not suffer any decided defalcation.

2. Writing Advocates. To this head may be referred the special pleading tribe at Common Law, as well as the Draughtsman tribe in Equity. On a final settlement as above, great would be the defalcation. But whenever commenced, great would be the length of time elapsed before a radical judicial reform could have been brought to its termination: and

while business was on the [one] hand lessened by the reform, on the other hand it would be encreased by the doubts, difficulties and disputes produced by the change. In the mean time, as profit to the occupants of the situation decreased, influx into the situation by rivals would decrease also, and thus the decrease of profit would, to individuals, be moderated, and they would every one of them have time to look about him and prepare for the decrease.

In the case of the writing men considered as such, by no formidable influence would their sinister interest be supported. Howsoever void of sympathy for lay-gents, they themselves might be objects of sympathy to that same ignorant and contemptible multitude, but need not in respect of their sinister interest be objects of apprehension.

3. Conveyancers. In a similar predicament possess themselves the conveyancing tribe. By a system of law having the security of property for its object, ultimately their profit migh[t] be brought down to a level not a great deal superior to that of a Country Schoolmaster. No such nuisance as an English Conveyancer is to be found in France under Bonaparte's Code,[1] nor even in the Anglo-American[?] United States, infested as they still continue with the greatest part of the English Judge-made law. But so strong and so numerous are the chains in which, by the existing ones and their predecessors, landed property in particular has been bound, that long, too long, would be the time elapsed before they could have been loosened, whatsoever limits might be put to the application of future ones. Here would be the like mixture as above—decrease of business, or rather of profit of business, by reform—encrease by the transition from the bad system to the good one.

So much for the Barrister classes.

4. Now as to the Solicitor Class. In respect of judicial reform, these men occupy a particular situation. In one way they would be gainers. In another way they would be losers. Their gain would be immediate: their loss remote—certain indeed, but indefinitely remote.

Their gain immediate—why and how? Because [in] the case of the official men the conversion of fees into salary might be immediate: and the suitors being exonerated of this expence, so much more of the quantity of money expendable in litigation would remain to be expended in the purchase of their services. Many a suit which could not now be brought would then be brought: many a suit which can not now be defended would then be defended. By no inconsiderable number of men in this situation has this connection between reform

---

[1] The Napoleonic Codes were *Code Civil* (1804), *Code de Procédure Civile* (1806), *Code de Commerce* (1807), *Code d'Instruction Criminelle* (1809) and *Code Pénal* (1810).

and their particular interest been clearly enough viewed; as may be seen in a variety of publications. This source of profit, it may perhaps be observed, belongs also to the Barrister class. But it belongs in a peculiar degree to the Solicitor class: their profit commencing at, or rather before, the commencement of a suit; that of the Barrister class not till such an advance has been made as in many a suit will not have been made. By this circumstance has been produced the otherwise inexplicable and to many an eye, naturally enough, surprizing phæno-menon: a wish for reform having place in the breasts not only of lawyers, but of the lowest rank of lawyers.

But were the reform to stop there, small indeed would be the relief to lay-gents in the character of suitors. This is but one in the train of necessary measures ere the end could be accomplished. But as before, this accomplishment would in every possible case be a waste of time.

Remains as the only other class of sinister interests, that of the aristocracy of wealth divided into its two branches—the landed aristocracy and the moneyed aristocracy.

First as to the aristocracy of wealth.[1] Here too may be seen the like mixture of profit and loss by reform. Unfortunately loss being most extensively shared, the first place is the place demanded by the nature of it.

The thing in respect of which the loss would take place is the conjoined faculty of oppression and depredation, resulting in pro-portion to the substitution of justice to the denial of justice: of oppres-sion in a direct and universally visible way: of depredation in a way less direct and conspicuous, but of late days with singular talent as well as patriotism laid open by the liberal part of the public press.

In this shape the existence [of] sinister interest is universal: scarcely perhaps will that individual breast be found in which its influence is not more or less operative and efficient.

As to the gain, it is confined to the situation of those to whom the expence of a lawsuit, present, past or future, is a cause of more or less serious chagrin. The more intense and extensive the sense of insecurity in the breasts of this class, the stronger is the correspond-ing rightly-operating interest, acting in alliance with the universal interest and in opposition to the abovementioned particular and sinister interest. In this way, by the salutary torments they have planted in the breasts of Noble Lords and Honorable Gentlemen, the conveyancing tribe, guiltless as they are of any such intention as that of serving the interests of the ignorant and indigent multitude, have

---

[1] i.e. the landed aristocracy.

actually rendered to those same despicable interests no inconsiderable service.

The thing to be prayed for, if praying were the instrument by which it could be performed, is—that till Coke's Littleton, with all the embroidery wrought upon it,[1] were burnt in ceremony in one of the Palace Yards, no Noble Lord and Honorable Gentleman should regard his estate as worth two years' purchase, or be able to borrow the value of a sovereign upon a Mortgage of it.

Lastly as to the monied aristocracy. Here neither would the loss by reform be so great, nor on the other hand the gain by it, as in the case of the more opulent branch.

The pleasure of tyranny, the desire of exercising it, is not so great, is not so intense or universal. Sympathy for the great body of the community is not so completely wanting. Among the moneyed men, no man is born to the possession or assured prospect of a degree of opulence approaching to that possessed by the highest class of landholder. No one is so entirely destitute of that sympathy of conception which is so necessary to the existence of sympathy of affection. If his occupations are of the mercantile class, the pursuit of them brings him into contact with the less opulent of all classes.

On the other hand, those whose pursuits as above are mercantile are on that account more exposed than the landed class to the misfortune of being obliged to have recourse to litigation for the protection of their property, whether in the character of Plaintiffs or Defendants: to the service that would be done to their interests by the reform in question they will naturally therefore be more acutely sensible. The landed man is perhaps more exposed than the other to the misfortune of seeing his property the whole of it in Chancery, as the phrase is: but if he escapes this misfortune, he may pass on quietly through his whole life, without experiencing that misfortune: while to the moneyed man it can scarcely happen [to] avoid from first to last being or under the apprehension of being thus subjected to pillage.

In the case of the vast majority of the people, no such conflict of opposite interests has place. Thus the only distinction is that between the honest man and the dishonest man. Of the honest man it is the interest in all cases that delay, expence, vexation and uncertainty be

---

[1] The famous first part of *The Institutes of the Laws of England*, by Sir Edward Coke (1552–1634), Chief Justice of Common Pleas 1606–13, Chief Justice of King's Bench 1613–16, first published in 1628, which was a commentary on the standard work on the law of real property, the *Tenures* of Sir Thomas Littleton (c.1415–81), Justice of Common Pleas 1466–81. *Coke on Littleton*, with its substantial glosses, remained the principal textbook on property law in Bentham's age.

minimized. Of the dishonest man the interest is served in so far as by the means of the mass of delay, vexation and expence which he is able to endure, he is able to subdue those whom for any purpose it is his desire to subdue, their shoulders being at the same time unable to abide it.[1]

[IV.][2] Gift more pernicious than Sale.

Causes three.

1. On the part of *locatees* (persons appointed), the degree of probable inaptitude greater, and indeed maximized: so the probability of it in that same degree.

2. In case of abuse and misconduct in every shape, redress much more improbable: and indeed the improbability of it maximized.

3. In case of misconduct, the apparent improbability of redress still greater than the real: so great as to be altogether hopeless; and upon the whole, on the part of the functionary, the assurance of impunity compleat.

1. As to inaptitude. In case of purchase, the *locatee* is a stranger to the patron—the *locator*: or at least the probability of his being so is at the highest point. Proportioned will be the weakness of his hope of undue favour. Under these circumstances, he will not pay his money for the place, unless the employment belonging to it is more or less agreable to him: he will not enter upon it with a formed design to neglect the business of it, or under the assurance of connivance, to apply it to the purpose of extortion or oppression.

Just the contrary in the case when, sale being excluded, gift with the fees belonging to the office is preserved. Excluded from the faculty of putting the money in his pocket in an immediate way, the patron will be on the look out for the means of making the most of the thing in an unimmediate way: that is to say, through the medium of his nearest relatives and his and their connections, whether in the way of self-regarding interest or sympathy: parliamentary-corruption interest of course not forgotten. If the locatee is one for whom he would otherwise have made provision at his own expence, the profit of the office is as to so much a clear addition made to it.[3] Is it not, Lord Eldon? Is it not, Lord Chief Justice Abbot?

As to aptitude on the part of the locatee, it is a question which in this state of things will not so much as present itself to the thoughts of

---

[1] A sequence headed 'Aristocratical sinister interest continued' is at UC xix. 380–7 (31 July 1825). A further fragment is at UC xix. 388–9 (31 July 1825).

[2] MS '12 or 13.' The provenance of the original enumeration is unclear. The following sequence develops Bentham's fourth point at p. 309 above. A related fragment is at UC xix. 413 (6 August 1825).

[3] i.e. 'his own income' as per MS del.

either party—locator or locatee. On the part of the locator, his own persuasion of the most consummate inaptitude on the part of the locatee will not prevent the location from taking place. As little will the locatee's own consciousness of his own inaptitude oppose any impediment to acceptance: against all uneasiness through aversion to the business, and at the same time against all fear of exposure by manifestation of inaptitude, an easy remedy is at all times at his hands: and that is—to let the business shift for itself, and not to trouble his head with it.

As to appropriate aptitude, no such question ever enters[?] the thoughts of either the one or the other. The only question is whether the thing is worth the locatee's acceptance. It is so in either of two cases. One is where the thing is so good a thing, that out of it a Deputy can be paid for doing the business: in this case it is worth any gentleman's acceptance: it may even be worth a Nobleman's acceptance: the other is where, though it will not afford pay for a Deputy, still rather than refuse it, the man in question will prevail upon himself to do the business of it.

What may happen to the same office is—to be sometimes in an integral state, sometimes in a state of decomposition: at any given time whether it be in the one state or the other will depend on a combination of circumstances—the profitableness of the office, the irksomeness of the business, the pecuniary circumstances, endowments and temper of the great man's favorite by whose acceptance it is to be honored.

To give validity to what is done, is it necessary that the principal should make his signature, or is it sufficient if made by the Deputy? Only in the latter case will the existence of a sinecure be acknowledged. Signing is one thing; thinking is another. If, to the receipt of the fees, the signature of the person whose name is in the red book is necessary, the Chancellor or other patron or grand patron, whoever he be, will, if questioned, stand up and, looking as fierce as he can, pronounce the office an Efficient office, and every intimation to the contrary, 'calumny and misrepresentation.'[1]

As to offices, those excepted which, with or without the name, involve the exercise of judicial authority, such as Masters in Chancery, Examiners in Equity, and the functionaries by whom costs are taxed in the Common Law Courts, nothing that can bear the name of appropriate aptitude can well be said to be necessary: moral aptitude such as consists in not leaving the business altogether undone, active aptitude such as is possessed by every Shopkeeper's

---

[1] See 'Indications respecting Lord Eldon', Postscript § 2, pp. 274–89 above.

Clerk who, having been engaged in that capacity, is not turned off, this, with here and there an exception, would on enquiry be found sufficient to keep a man in these situations unexposed to any determinate charge.

The importance of a situation—thence the magnitude of the mischief liable to be produced by non-exercise or undue-exercise of the functions belonging to it—is but an erroneous measure of the magnitude of the acquirements necessary on the part of the functionary by whom it is possessed. Little if any more skill in arithmetic is exercised in keeping the accounts of an empire than of a Chandler's shop.

As to moral inaptitude, the maximum of audacity and shamelessness is exemplified in the case of an act of extortion, committed in the teeth of a universally notorious Table of fees: on one of the occasions mentioned in the Table, a fee taken greater than the one so mentioned. Why?—because in that case, no possibility of mistake can have place, nothing in the capacity of an excuse can be brought forward. It is not like non-attendance, misperformance of the business, insolent behaviour manifested for the gratification of pride or the expectation of being mollified by service: by service in one of the thousand ways in which service need not, and accordingly would not, by a Judge having an interest in the abuse, be adjudged to be *a bribe*. Lord Chief Justice Abbot, what says Your Lordship to this? Lord Chief Justice Abbot!

But where abuse of power in this most palpable of all shapes is connived at, and by connivance invited, abuse of power in all other shapes should to every purpose but that of the infliction of punishment on individuals be regarded as proved. If it does not absolutely follow that in all those shapes it has actually [been] committed, it is because under *matchless constitution* neither individuals, nor functionaries acting in subordination to Judges, have at any time been so flagitiously wicked as those great dignitaries have at all times striven to make them. It is from what liberty which, in the teeth of what is called law, is enjoyed by the press, that depravity in those high situations has experienced whatever limits it has ever found in its way: hence one cause, and that the principal one, of the implacable war which they have at all times waged, and so long as the judiciary system continues on its present footing, never will cease to wage, against that sole palliative of the evils of which matchless constitution is composed.

As against any incommodious severity on the part of his locator (his father perhaps or wife's father or uncle or wife's uncle) he will be still more at his ease than an Honorable County Member or Noble Lord in his Magisterial capacity under the protection of the Chief Justice and the Chancellor when the Chief Justice is a Sir Abbot and the Chancellor a Lord Eldon.

Even in the case where, but for this opportunity, provision at locator's own expence would have been made for him, adequate motives for acceptance will not be wanting to him: for either the profit of the place of itself will exceed what the locator would have allowed him, or by allowance and place together he will find himself better provided for than he would have been without the place.

According to the magnitude of the income, instead of locator's son or nephew etc. put superannuated Clerk, superannuated servant, relative's relative, connection's connection, and so on in a continually decreasing series till the interest becomes equal 0, the superior probability of inaptitude will vary only in degree.

2. In case of abuse, says a foregoing observation, redress is much more improbable. In the case of sale, be the locatee ever so perfect a stranger to him, disposition to severity will not on the part of the locator be naturally very alert: for the greater the facility for extortion[?] and abuse in every other beneficial or agreable shape the office affords, the greater the sum a purchaser will naturally be disposed to give for it. But, whatsoever indulgence, on this or any other account, the locator might be disposed to give to a mere stranger, greater and greater indulgence will he be disposed to give to a particular connection of his own, according to the nature and nearness of the connection.

A Chief Justice who can give such licence as has been seen given by Lord Chief Justice Abbot to his Tipstaff,[1] what is the licence that he will not at all times have given to his son?

3. The apparent improbability of redress will naturally be still greater in this case than the real.

Whether from natural severity of disposition, or from some innate and not altogether extinguished regard for justice, suppose in this or that instance a locator not disposed to bear out his locatee in every sort of misbehaviour. This supposed, on the part of persons in general, and in particular, persons exposed to become sufferers by such misbehaviour, by any such casual circumstance can any general assurance or hope of redress be maintained or produced? No such thing. That which is present to all minds is the situation of the two functionaries: that which, if to any eye, only to this or that eye by accident can be visible is the particular and supposed beneficent disposition on the part of the locator. But to every eye to which the

---

[1] See ibid., §XII, pp. 231–7 above.

situation and that alone is visible, the improbability will seem entire, redress altogether hopeless.

In this case, among the persons most exposed to suffer from mis-behaviour on the part of the locatee will be those who, in case of displeasure on the part of the locator, on whose pleasure all chance of redress depends, will feel themselves most exposed to suffer from that same displeasure.[a]

Mark now the advantage taken on this occasion of vulgar errors, the result of indistinct conceptions, and the admirable accord established betwixt deluders and deluded, betwixt knaves and their dupes.

If disposed of by sale, there may be a want of sufficient scrutiny into the aptitude of the locatee: the less apt, if he gives most, being preferred to the more apt, if he will not give so much. True: but there will be no motive, nor consequently propensity, to give the preference to inaptitude: which in the case of gift, as has been seen, there can not fail to be.

In private service, an employer has every [thing] to lose, nothing to gain, by inaptitude on the part of his *employee*. In public service in many branches, and in this more particularly than in any other, he has, as has been seen, every thing to gain by that circumstance, nothing to lose.

Thus is sale, even for the benefit of the locator, less mischievous than gift: what would be beyond comparison less bad is sale for the benefit of the public. But sale for the benefit of the public would be a tax on and thence a denial of justice, and as such be the very worst of all taxes: it would involve that *transference* which has just [been] spoken of.[1]

Be it here noted as a corollary, sadly unapt must that Constitution [be] in which the power of dislocation is in no other hands than those of the locator, or some person or set of persons connected with him in particular interest, self-regarding or sympathetic. It may with safety be lodged in the hands of a number of persons or sets of persons, one in default of another, provided always that none of them have any share, or considerable influence, in the location of the successor.

[a] In the case of a locatee who is in by the gift of a predecessor of the great man in office, the expectation of undue protection will not (it is obvious) be quite so strong as in the case of a person located by the actual incumbent. This is mentioned lest it should be supposed to be overlooked. But what is no less obvious is—that to a person in office, especially in an office in which abuse is so abundant as has been seen, every intimation of it as existing in any particular instance will of course be odious and, in this case, respect for the memory of the venerable predecessor, who-soever he be, will throw over the convenient vice the cloak of virtue.

[1] See pp. 309–10n above.

Full in the mind of the reader, unless more than commonly inattentive, must all this while have been the cases of Lord Eldon's Masters, his Son, and the Son of Chief Justice Abbot.[1]

In the Masters' Offices, altogether natural, not to say necessary, will be seen to be that scene of turpitude, which, to a foreigner, no common degree of confidence in the trustworthiness of the narrator will suffice to render credible.

On the part of the Honorable possessor of the rich cluster of the Six-Offices—that so well-afforded reward for the real authorship of the *Six Acts*,[2] let any one imagine what degree, if any, of inaptitude or criminal misconduct would draw down upon him so much as a frown from the Noble and learned author of his being:[3] and if [in] any one of those precious gems there be any room for extortion at the charge of individuals, or public mischief in case of neglect, let all who care for individuals or the public please themselves with the thought that they are so many perfect sinecures, and no otherwise capable of being made instruments of mischief than by and in proportion to the settled exaction of which they are the instruments.

Services there are, which ought not to be sold: and from this circumstance, where such or such other services are mentioned, it is concluded or said that they ought not to be sold, without considering that all payment for labour in any shape includes sale of services, and that without such sale civilized society could not have place.

In the case of service, whether the venality of it is beneficial or mischievous depends upon the application given to it.

A representative of the people ought not to sell to the Minister his services, in such sort as that they shall be employed in aiding him in exercising depredation and oppression. But there is no reason why he should not sell his services to the people—sell them for the purpose of their being employed in guarding the people against those same enormities, nor why they the people should not accordingly purchase of him those same services, unless so it be that for the purpose in question they can get them better or cheaper from some other hand.

The vulgar error has been seen: a word as to its cause: of the use made of it in the present instance.

While from gift as compared with sale more sinister advantage is to

---

[1] For the six sinecures held by Eldon's son, William Henry John Scott, see 'Indications respecting Lord Eldon', Postscript §2, p. 279n above. Abbott's eldest son, John Henry Abbott (1796–1870), later second Baron Tenterden, held the office of Associate and Marshal at the Sittings of Nisi Prius in London and Middlesex, the duties of which were executed by a deputy.

[2] Bentham is again alluding to William Henry John Scott, though the reference to the so-called Six Acts of 1819 is problematic. Eldon himself is usually credited with a part in the drafting of this legislation.

[3] i.e. Eldon.

be gained, less obloquy is feared. Vulgar error confines censure to the case of sale: under the guidance of hypocrisy it throws its cloak over the case of gift.

Conjugates to the word sale, are to sell and saleable. Synonymous or nearly so to the word sale, is the word *vent*, and perfectly to the conjugates of sale, the words to vend, and vendible. Pseudo-conjugates to vendible are venal and venality. The sense in which *vent* and *to vend* are used is merely physical, neither importing approbation nor disapprobation in relation to the practice: the sense in which venal and venality are used is moral, and dyslogistic or say cacologist, imputing disapprobation in relation to the practice. But the physical, having been the original sense, has been altogether expelled by the moral and cacologist sense which has fastened on it, and by degrees come to adhere to it. The office being vendible, venality is a quality which can not with propriety be denied to belong to it. But between the office and the possessor of it, the relation is intimate: from the idea of the one to the idea of the other, the transition easy and immediate. Of the office *venality* being an indispensable attribute, to the possessor of it this same attribute is without reflection, and for want of reflection, wont to be applied—and thereupon by a congenial confusion is brought on the reflection, what the man buys he will naturally be disposed to make the most of.

How opposite is the case of gift. Not more intimate is the connection between sale and venality than between gift and generosity: generosity with its amiable synonyms *liberality*, *bountifulness* and *bounteousness*. In the practice of sale, where is the ingenuity that would be able to find so much as a grain of virtue? On the other hand, if generosity be not intituled to a place in the list of virtues, what other quality can be? But why talk of virtues—mere human endowments? Bounteousness, is it not among the attributes of the Almighty? Who but he is the giver of all good gifts?[1] He by whom good gifts are given, imitates the Almighty and shares with him in this attribute. In a word, when it is his pleasure to part with any thing good, is it ever in any other way than that of gift? Who ever heard of his doing any thing in the way of sale? In a word, is not this the only way in which the Almighty ever part[s] with any [thing] that is worth having? for so many good things as he has been giving us was he ever known to receive in return the value of a sixpence? Not he indeed. To assert any such thing of him, would it not be an act of blasphemy? Ask any of those learned and reverend persons who have so highly distinguished themselves as connoisseurs in blasphemy. Would it not, Lord Chief

---

[1] See Matthew 7: 11, Luke 11: 13.

Justice Abbot? Would it not, Mr Justice Baily? Would it not, Mr Justice Park? The King, who, as Blackstone has shewn us, is God upon earth,[1] does he not by every penny that he gives approach by so much the nearer to that God which is in heaven? Is it not in this way, that, as Mr Justice Baily has shewn us, he makes us even so much the richer by every penny he takes from us in taxes?[2]

But if the act of giving gifts, provided they be good ones, is thus meritorious, can the act of receiving them fail of being so too? To pass censure on the act of giving would be to pass censure on the act of [receiving].[3] If nothing were ever received, nothing could ever be given. To wish that gifts be given and no receipts be received is a self-contradictory wish. True it is, for we have it upon the highest authority—true it is—that to give is more blessed than receive:[4] but though to give is the more blessed, still it could not be so unless the act of receiving were so, though in an inferior degree.

But if from stranger, gift, when compared with sale, is thus blessed, how much more when from father to child? especially if to plain *father* and plain *son* an appropriate pair of sentimental appellatives be substituted? To whatsoever merit, how brilliant so ever, it might manifest in the general case, it adds fulfilment of duty in the more particular case: a duty on the fulfilment of which the very existence of society depends. But the better the gift, the more meritorious the act of giving: and if this is true of each one of six good gifts, how can it be otherwise of the aggregate of all?

To the case of Lord Eldon with his son's six Sinecures, few readers, it is hoped, are so dull as not to have already made application of this argument.

But if, of carnal gifts, such as Masterships, Tipstaffships and the like, the possession and exercise constitute such ample stocks of merit, what is to be thought of spiritual ones? If of any single sacred benefice, what shall be said of the 500 well-told which are at the disposal of Lord Eldon? not to speak of those Bishopricks and Bishops which he has been heard to call his.[5]

The reader has here the essence of those arguments by which Honorable House will be, and if it were worth while the people of

---

[1] See Blackstone, *Commentaries on the Laws of England*, i. 230–70, which deals with the King's prerogative, and where the attributes of '*sovereignty*, or pre-eminence', 'absolute *perfection*' and 'absolute immortality' are said to be ascribed to him by the law.

[2] Bayley had outlined what he regarded as the beneficial effects of high taxation in his charge to the Grand Jury of York on 26 July 1819 (reported in *The Times*, 29 July 1819).

[3] MS 'giving'.

[4] See Acts 20: 35.

[5] Eldon, as Lord Chancellor, had a considerable amount of ecclesiastical patronage in his gift.

England would be, to be satisfied of the more-than-wisdom of the measures by which, while the selfish and too-long tolerated system of sale is to be suppressed, the noble, the generous, the pious practice of gift is to be preserved: preserved over the whole field of judicial office to as great an extent as possible, but at any rate, and at any price, to preserve from the new-fangled limitations the field of the munificence of Lord Eldon.

Of this sort are the arguments with which his Majesty's Attorney General, according to announcement, and his Majesty's Solicitor General, according to duty,[1] with the support of Mr Peel, will have to persuade Honorable House. Were it possible, it would be alike curious and instructive to make the catalogue of those individuals in Honorable House, Right Honorable House, Common Council of the City of London and Worshipful the Court of Aldermen respectively, by whom upon occasion these arguments, without their being persuaded of the soundness of them, would be ready to [be] urged and made to pass, and on the other hand of those on whom they have been used to pass, or at the expence of a word or two would at any time be made to pass. The particular good is perpetually presenting itself to every mind's eye, is of a pleasing colour, and the narrowest pupil is not too narrow to give admission to it; the general good does not as yet present itself in any distinct form to one eye out of a thousand, is of a sombre hue, and not one pupil out of ten thousand cares to open itself for the reception of it.[2]

Concluding fallacy

Of all these arguments the most triumphant is this—it is established, self-sufficient and conclusive. When a man buys a place his endeavour will be to make the most of it: he has a right so to do, his money has given him this right. So says the man himself: and howsoever mistakenly, so say others along with him: every body feels the force of it.

He will endeavour to make the most of it. True enough: against this nothing can be said. But under the cover of this affirmative lies a negative, which he to whom the affirmative is addressed is expected to tack to it of himself: otherwise the affirmative would amount to nothing. This is—that the man who gets the place for nothing will not endeavour to make the most of it. Not make the most of it? Why not?

---

[1] John Singleton Copley, later first Baron Lyndhurst, Attorney General 1824–6, and Charles Wetherell (1770–1846), Solicitor General 1824–6, respectively. By the time Bentham was writing, the Acts in question had received the Royal Assent. Robinson, the Chancellor of the Exchequer, had taken responsibility for steering the measures through the House of Commons.

[2] In the text, Bentham noted at this point, '☞ Add on another sheet exercise of patronage in the City of London', but no corresponding material appears to have been written.

If for this negative there be so much [as] the shadow of a reason, it lies in a circumstance purely accidental: if so it be that he who possesses the office by gift is an idler averse to all business and his income, including that from the office, is so ample as to release him from the need of paying any attention to business of any kind, then indeed, along with the duties of the office, he will neglect the care of making profit out of it to himself by sinister devices. And thus by accident, whatsoever be the evil resulting from the accumulation of offices thus converted into Sinecures, out of this absolute evil may result a diminution of the evil which an attention to business might otherwise have produced.

Not that even from this circumstance the argument has much to gain. For the fine gentleman who, neglecting the public business, neglects his own business, the mischievous part of it included along with the rest, to this fine gentleman will belong a deputy: which deputy, not being a fine gentleman, will attend to the business in all its parts, beneficial and mischievous together: the profit, sinister as it is, if he is a man like other men, will occupy rather more of his attention and endeavours than the, to him, unprofitable duty: and whether it goes the whole of it into his own pocket, or is in any proportion shared with his principal, to the public the result is the same.

Apply this for example to the case of Lord Chief Justice Abbot and his Tipstaff. Suppose the office of Tipstaff vacant. If brought already into such a state as to be capable of being executed by deputy, it will of course pass into the hands of his Lordship's Son, if he has no more than one, and when it is three will not make the number of offices held by one hand half so great as the number of those held by the son of Lord Eldon. Had the business of the $4^{s.}$ $6^{[d.]}$ addition been yet to do, a gentleman so *appointed* as he would scarcely have given himself the trouble of picking up the $4^{s.}$ and sixpence. But what would the poor debtors and their suffering creditors be the better: what the principal neglected, the deputy would have performed. Complaining to the Lord Chief Justice of the Deputy would have been complaining to the same Lord Chief Justice of the principal—of his beloved Son, with whom, as to a matter of this sort at any rate, he could not fail to be well-pleased.[1] No man who had any thing to fear or hope from the Lord Chief Justice would, if master of himself, be guilty of such rashness.

---

[1] See Matthew 3: 17.

Comparative view of the several modes of payment

Follows now a comparative view of the several different arrangements which are in existence, or are likely to be [in] contemplation, on the subject of official remuneration combined with that of patronage. They will be brought to view by ringing the changes in the several influencing circumstances that will be seen.

Circumstances common to all the cases:

[1.] Locator, the Judge.

[2.] Locatee, an officer acting under the Judge.

3. Sole functionary exercising in ordinary cases a controul over the demeanour of the locatee in the office in question, the aforesaid Judge.

I. Case I. 1. Shape of the remuneration, fees received from suitors by and retained to the use of the locatee.

2. The locator inhibited from taking payment for the act of location—inhibited from selling the office.

This case, as above, exhibits the maximum of inaptitude. Reasons abovementioned. None locable but persons more or less connected with the Judge.

II. Case II. 1. Mode of remuneration, fees received as above to the use of the receiver—the locatee.

2. The locator not inhibited from selling the office.

This case stands second in the order of inaptitude. Reasons as above. In this case what may happen is that between the locator—controuling superior as he is, and the locatee, no particular connection antecedent to the time of location had place.

III. Case III. 1. Mode of remuneration, salary: but coupled with fees received by the locatee to his own use for a time, but charged with the obligation of accounting for them, and transferring them periodically to the use of the public.

2. The locator inhibited from selling the office, as above.

This case stands third and next in the order of inaptitude. The quantum of sinister interest given to the Judge not so great as in Cases I and II, but still great enough to give a sinister bias to his conduct: opportunity being given for extortion by fees not allowed, and peculation by non-transference of fees allowed.

IV. Case IV. 1. Mode of remuneration as per Case III.

2. The locator *not* inhibited from selling the office as above. Reasons as per Cases II and III.

V. VI. VII. VIII. Cases I. II. III. and IV. repeated with no other difference than that the Judge, instead of being immediately, is more or less remotely the locator of the subordinate functionary in

331

question: to wit, locator of his locator—grand-locator of the functionary in question—or great-grand-locator, as we say grandfather and great-grandfather etc.: for example the Chancellor, with reference to an office in the gift of his locatee, the Master of the Rolls, or of his locatees the Masters in Chancery, they having respectively the appointment of those Clerks by whom a large portion of the business is performed.

IX. Case IX. 1. Remuneration by salary without fees.

2. Locator, the sole controuling Judge, as above.

3. The locator inhibited from Sale.

Reasons. No unlimited faculty of extortion as per Case I: no faculty of peculation, as per Case IV: but a sinister interest in choosing persons, how unapt so ever, by thus providing for whom he may save to the amount of a more or less considerable portion, or even the whole, of the salary, or gratify his connections more or less intimate in the way of self-regarding or sympathetic interest: so likewise in continuing them uncontrouled, any degree of inaptitude manifested subsequently to location notwithstanding.

X. The locator [not] inhibited from sale.

Reasons. The probability of mischief not so great as in Case IX: on account of the chance that between the locator and locatee no corruptive connection may antecedently to the act of location have place.

XI. The locator a person other than the controuling Judge, for example the Secretary of State.

Reasons. This an improvement upon the last preceding case: the chance of sinister connection between the locatee and the controuling Judge being less than in the last preceding case.

XII. Case XII. The locatee determined by competition, the office with the established salary sold for the benefit of the public: the chance of sinister connection, as above, is thus minimized: so likewise the net expence produced to the public by the office.

Viewing every functionary serving under him an intruder, a Judge who, under the arrangement N°· 1, would be a Lord Eldon, marring and reposing into Sinecures for the benefit of self and family and connections of all sorts, Masterships, Clerkships, Registrarships, and all sorts of ships, might exhibit himself a very Cato: exercising over the servants of the public, his subordinates, a degree of vigilance exceeded only by that which the most ordinary Merchant, Manufacturer or Shipman exercises over the several sorts of persons whom he employs on his account.

Should his patience have carried him this far, at the sight of this highest step in the ladder of Utopianism, in which all the wildness of the Voyage to the Houhynms manifests itself without any of the delectableness,[1] the passion of the Courier[2] will be to such a degree excited, that those on whom it depends might not do amiss in taking some precautionary arrangements for fear of accidents. Lord Eldon's largest lachrymatory should likewise be ready for the occasion should these pages ever receive the honor of coming under his eyes.

§4. *Proper Question what: Uses of these Indications*[3]

Time joins with Space to command brevity. Look round, reader. Defence none any where. Attempts at *diversion* several. Would you escape delusion—look steadily at the true question.

Behold it in the shortest and quickest form possible: Does or does not the good of the community require, that by this man the office he now holds should cease to be filled? The affirmative is the answer the above indications have been employed to support as well as indicate. Whoever agrees in this answer will, according to the degree of his regard for the good of the community, and the nature of the means he feels to be in his hands, contribute his endeavours towards a consummation so devoutly to be wished.

Before speaking of the means, a word or two as to the above-mentioned diversions.

Diversion 1. Inaptitude of the system itself, the application of which is in his hands. Conclusion—amend the system; leave the man at the head of it. This is the course taken by the authors of two anonymous tracts:

1. One who styles himself '*A Member of Gray's Inn*' and addresses himself to *Mr Peel*: pages 25. A°· 1825.[4]

2. The other intitules his work '*An Inquiry into the causes of the delay, attending proceedings in the Court of Chancery,*' pages 50. A°· 1824.[5]

Answer. Admitted as abundantly demonstrated. But, in regard to the removal, this instead of being a reason *contrà* is an additional reason *pro*. Melioration in any shape, call it *improvement*, call it *reform*, so long as he is where he is, is impossible. By that consideration, in addition to the ever-encreasing and boundless mass of positive evil apprehended, was birth given to the present Indications.

---

[1] 'A Voyage to the Country of the Houyhnhnms' is described in Part IV of Jonathan Swift's *Gulliver's Travels*, first published in 1726.

[2] Bentham seems to mean the person who he hopes will deliver the 'Indications' to Eldon.

[3] Related fragments are at UC xix. 303 (2 July 1825) and xix. 328–30 (19 July 1825).

[4] See 'Indications respecting Lord Eldon', Postscript §1, pp. 273–4 above.

[5] *An Inquiry into the Causes of the Delay, attending proceedings in the Court of Chancery*, London, 1824. Bentham's marked copy of this pamphlet is in the British Library, shelf-mark C.T. 80 (7).

The fact is two changes are indispensable: change of the man, change of the system. Neither would suffice without the other. But without change of the man, sensibly effective change in the system is altogether hopeless.

Diversion 2.[1] *Attack on Common Law.* 'Nay, Mr John Williams—this Dulcimer of yours is no better than she should be: so you need not talk. A dear enough bargain is she to those who have to do with her: you can not deny *that*. And pray now, do you think she would ever be able to maintain herself, or go through her business, if it were not for her younger Sister—that sweet beautiful creature, Equity? Not she indeed.' Thereupon comes a tritical Essay on *Fraud*, *trust* and *accident*, and another thing or two taken from the A.B.C. book which every Solicitor puts into his Clerk's hands. This occupies not much less than the whole of the '*Letter*,' and is to make people think that Mr John Williams had never heard a syllable of all this. As to delay in Equity business, not an atom of it is ever to be seen except what the parties themselves make, or what the nature of the case absolutely requires. Then as to the *law of real property*, nothing can be clearer. *I understand it* Mr Williams, says his correspondent (page 13)[2] *and if you don't, the more is the pity*. Then as to the *blending* them together (Your Common Law and our Equity) (p. 7)[3] was there ever any thing so ridiculous? At present they are both of them in their proper places: Common Law undermost: Equity uppermost. Yes: if it were a salad you were making, and they oil and vinegar. But really this is too bad. Not that I would have you suppose that, if there be really any thing amiss in either of them, I should not be as glad as any body to see it set right. But then it must be upon this condition. Nothing must ever be said that can tend to make lay-gents suppose that there is any thing wrong about any of those by whom they have been made what they are (page 20).[4]

[1] In this and the following paragraph, Bentham parodies Edward Burtenshaw Sugden, *A Letter to John Williams, Esq. M.P. In reply to his observations upon the abuses of the Court of Chancery*, London, 1825 (also published in *The Pamphleteer*, xxv (1825), 445–54). Bentham's marked copy of this pamphlet is in the British Library, shelf-mark C.T. 80 (9).

Sugden (1781–1875), first Baron Saint Leonards, Solicitor General 1829–30, Lord Chancellor of Ireland 1835, 1841–6, Lord Chancellor 1852. For Williams' motions in the House of Commons calling for the reform of Chancery see 'Indications respecting Lord Eldon', §XIII, p. 238n above.

[2] In the passage at pp. 12–14, Sugden explains the nature of the jurisdiction of equity in compelling the specific performance of contract, particularly in regard to the sale of landed estates.

[3] 'Whether it was originally desirable that the jurisdictions should have been divided is not the question, but whether now, that both jurisdictions are defined and ascertained by known boundaries, they should be blended? No man who understands the bearing of the question would venture to attempt the task.'

[4] 'I have thrown these observations hastily together, with a warm feeling of the indispensable

If any such thing as a wen or a wart is really to be found in any part of their sweet persons (Oh how comfortable am I with the youngest of them! p. 2.)[1] cut, and welcome: but, remember this! cut away what flesh you will, not a drop of the dear sweet blood of either of them must come with it.[2]

This is Mr Sugden. So skilful a piece of generalship combined with so generous an act of self-devotion can seldom have been exhibited. Sole object: saving what could be saved of the wreck of Lord Eldon's reputation. Yet from first to last, neither by name nor in the way of allusion, is any so much as the slightest mention of the Noble and learned defendant to be found.[a] There we see the generalship:—an attack made on the assailant's flanks, to draw off his fire: all direct defence being hopeless.

Now for the generosity. From divers impartial quarters it has happened to me to hear of this Gentleman's professional talents, as also of his expectations, as being notoriously of the very first order: and from the same quarters I have heard this exhibition spoken of as forming a no less remarkable anomaly when compared with them. Here then is the generosity. By the attack thus made, to call off the attention of the enemy is the sole imaginable object of this display: in which, by one desperate effort, to save the reputation of his friend, he has sacrificed as much of his own as a man could easily contrive to sacrifice in the compass of one and twenty pages.

Could he but have made a sufficiently early transfusion of his own wisdom into the breast of his Noble and learned protegé, how much better would his Lordship's condition have been than what it has been seen to be! He would not have exposed his flank to any such annoyance

---

[a] O yes! once: to wit on page 7: and it is in this wise. Rules 'given to us' by 'Bacon, Nottingham,[3] Hardwicke, Thurlow, Eldon.'[4] In this latter case, quære has not Mr Sugden reckoned up *doubts* as *rules*?

---

necessity of upholding the jurisdiction of equity, and of not diminishing the reverence of the people for the administration of justice in that court; and if they shall operate to make you hesitate in the attacks which you so strongly make against the court, and which must lessen its authority, and the value of its decisions in the eyes of the country, my labour will not have been thrown away.'

[1] Bentham is parodying the passage at pp. 2–4.

[2] Bentham's allusion is to *The Merchant of Venice*, IV. i.

[3] Heneage Finch (1621–82), first Baron Finch and first Earl of Nottingham, Lord Chancellor 1675–82.

[4] 'If you did blend them [i.e. courts of law and courts of equity], or if you established a new jurisdiction, you would be compelled to have new courts and additional judges, *who must first learn* the present rules of equity, or now establish better than the successive experience of ages—of Bacon, Nottingham, Hardwicke, Thurlow, Eldon, *assisted in all times by the Judges of England*—have given to us.'

as he so pathetically complains of at the hands of pamphleteers, Newspaper Editors, and so many other men, who (he says) '*mean well*, though they do not understand what they are talking about.'[1]

Not to them assuredly is this merit of well-meaning confined. To combatants on the opposite side may it with no less justice be ascribed, though the end meant is so different. Oh yes! Well-meant Mr Member of Gray's Inn! Well-meant, yes and well done, Mr Sugden! The best course that could be taken for a *protegé* in his situation, you have, both of you, taken for yours. Still however, so unfortunate is his case, not an atom of advantage has been gained by it. In default of every thing else that runs on all fours, a pack of hounds may be set a running after a red herring. But when an old fox is already in full scent and the dogs in full cry, not all the red herrings that were ever cured at the exhortation of De Wit,[2] would suffice to draw them off from the true game to the counterfeit.

Mr Sugden concludes with a wish, which, if I live, I shall ere long have great pleasure in meeting: it is 'that they who attack the wisdom of the law will . . . first shew in what particulars they object to the law as it stands, and secondly what improvements they suggest.'[3]

This challenge I had prepared myself for, before it reached me. Not that it is to the wisdom of the law (of the *lawyers* I would say, for it is not my way to contend with *abstraction*) not that it is to their wisdom that my objections, generally speaking, point. The great source of them is—the object or end in view to which that same wisdom has been directed: instead of the ends of justice, the ends of judicature; instead of the comfort of that greatest number, for whose use the article has of course always been professed to be made, the comfort of the manufacturers, derived from the torment of their customers.

In the mean time what is but too certain is—that the learned gentleman and the unlearned radical are not predestinated to agree near so well on this subject as they once did on that of *Usury*.[4] My

---

[1] In the House of Lords on 20 June 1825, Eldon was reported in the *Globe and Traveller* of the following day as saying, 'there had been much clamour and calumny on the subject of proceedings in Chancery—not by persons who meant ill, but by persons who did not well consider the consequences of what they talked about'.

[2] John de Witt (1625–72), Dutch statesman, Grand Pensionary of Holland 1653–72. The question of the right of the Dutch to catch herring off the British North Sea coast had been a source of friction between the two countries through much of the seventeenth century.

[3] See Sugden, *Letter to Williams*, p. 21. There are some minor inaccuracies in the rendering of the passage.

[4] Sugden had commended Bentham's *Defence of Usury; shewing the impolicy of the present legal restraints on the terms of pecuniary bargains*, London, 1787 (Bowring, iii. 1–29), when sending him a copy of his own *A Cursory Inquiry into the expediency of repealing the Annuity Act and raising the legal rate of Interest*, London, 1812: see *Correspondence (CW)*, viii. 287.

learned friend (if he will allow me the honor of calling him by that name) will find the sharpest of Mr Williams's attacks upon the sister Goddesses little more than scratches in comparison of mine. At the same time, as to any endeavour on his part to set me right in any part, it is a benefit I altogether despair of receiving: I am not worth his notice. By laying me still lower than I am, nothing would be to be gained of that which has been so well earned by his skirmish with Mr Williams. Were it possible he should ever be disposed to bestow upon so fruitless an object any part of his valuable time, I could put him into a method of husbanding it to a degree beyond what he himself could naturally have thought of. At the shops of certain Booksellers, though not of any Law Booksellers, is to be found a certain Book intituled *The Book of Fallacies*.[1] In it may be seen drawn up in array whatsoever arguments any person would find applicable to the defence of those existing arrangements of which I shall have exposed the mischievous effects after having proposed substitutes of an opposite nature. All then he will have to do is—to put the book into the hands of one of his Clerks or of some stuff-gowned and Case-hunting junior friend, with instructions to pick out a few of the arguments such as seem most apposite, and setting down their names, with reference to the pages where they are found, send them to the Editor of some Law periodical who, understanding from what quarter they come and what it is they are employed to defend, will of course be proud to give them a place in his miscellany with some such title as that of a *Defence of the Judicial Establishment and Judicial Procedure of England against the lately published calumnies*. As to the looking into the work, against which these arguments will serve as the most effectual, indeed the only applicable, defence, far be it from me to attempt putting his Clerk or his learned friend to any such needless trouble. It is the characteristic and matchlessly useful property of those same arguments, that no sort of relation is necessary between them and the work, be it what it may, which they are employed to overthrow. In a word, there is no use in their having any more direct and visible connection with it, than Mr Sugden's most ingenious and generous Defence of his Noble and learned friend has with the *life, character or behaviour* of that same Noble and learned friend.

The Noble and learned Defendant's original answer being to a degree which in general terms has been seen insufficient, waving the

---

[1] *The Book of Fallacies: from unfinished papers of Jeremy Bentham*, London, 1824 (Bowring, ii. 375–487). This version, based on Bentham's manuscripts, which had been earlier published as 'Traité des sophismes politique' in the second volume of Dumont's French recension, *Tactiques des assemblées législatives*, was edited by Peregrine Bingham (1788–1864), barrister and legal writer, subsequently a police magistrate at Great Marlborough Street.

formality of *exceptions*, I will venture to submitt to his consideration the idea of such an answer as, if the nature of his case admitted of a sufficient one, or any approach to a sufficient one, he would make: and the instruction thus submitted to his Lordship will serve at the same time for the kind learned Gentleman of Gray's Inn, as also Mr Sugden if, after the failure experienced, it should happen to him to be disposed to substitute a pertinent and unexceptionable answer to one which, in the character of an answer for and as from Lord Eldon, has been shewn to be composed exclusively of that sort of matter which in *technical* language is characterized by the name of impertinence.

To return to his Lordship. To him it can not be unknown what sort of a thing a Bill in Equity is—what sorts of things the charges on such a Bill are: what sort of things the interrogatories grounded on those charges are: or what sort of things Exceptions, when taken to such a Bill, are.

This being premised, that every thing may be done in form and order such as practice has rendered familiar and fees pleasant, let him be pleased to take in hand and consider in the character of *Instructions* (in Solicitor's language) for the drawing up an appropriate Bill the printed paper styled *Indications etc.*, together with the present Postscript now added: let him cause to be put into the hands of Mr Sugden, with or without a fee as he shall be advised, the said paper of Instructions, with directions to give to the matter of them the form of a Bill of Equity with the initiatory pet[it]ions, complaints, charges and corresponding interrogatories thereto belonging, not omitting the history of the Defendant's turnings, windings, and false pretences, or the oblique [. . .?] confederates of his, whose case, so soon as they are discovered, will be added to his: taking care that the interrogatories be drawn in form so pressing as leave to evasion as small and narrow a set of loop-holes as possible. When the ground [has been][1] thus prepared and laid out, he will feel himself quite at home: he will feel as some 70 years ago he may have felt when playing at Beat Knave out of doors with Grandmama or Dominie on the other side. To all these several charges and interrogatories, drawing up an answer will be a revisit of the pastures of his youth. It will be child's play to him. He will thus be master of the facts of the case together with the arguments.

Now then as to the time and place for putting this stock of valuable information to appropriate use. The House of Lords will not open again these five or six months: to wit, at as late a time as he can

---

[1] MS 'being'.

contrive to give to it.[1] The highest and brightest theatre of his Glory—the Cabinet—has an hermetic seal upon it: nor in that place and from him, for any thing in the way of defence, can there at any time be any so much as the smallest demand. But Lincoln's Inn Hall will every now and then be open. There, instead of private letters and answers, let him take in hand the above interrogatories (distinguishing them by numbers as in the case of the Examiners' questions) and make answer to them seriatim. On this occasion he may have the advantage of making a second display of his already manifested courtesy to Mr Brougham and Mr John Williams: to each of those his learned tormentors, he may have furnished a previous copy of the charges and the correspondent interrogatories: thus may they bear him witness that nothing has remained unanswered.

As to a demurrer, he need not trouble himself with putting in any such instrument. This case is not of the number of those stiled criminal cases. The applications made of the self-judication principle have been quite numerous enough. The people want no more of them. The last impeachment so-called the History of England will ever have exhibited is that of Lord Melville.[2] The case of Lord Eldon has shewn them what it is to proceed, according to law, against one who is above those whom (as per § 9)[3] he has placed above all law. The judicatory is not the House of Lords. It is the Public Opinion Tribunal: and in that judicatory no demurrer is received. The plea *Nemo tenetur seipsum accusare*[4] is thus taken as a plea of Guilty: and judgment is pronounced accordingly.

Here then will be something like an ordeal: an ordeal out of which, if his Lordship's character be as uncorrupt as in his own noble and learned eyes he has certified it to be, it will come out with redoubled splendor, like gold out of the refiner's fire.

In lieu of, or in addition to, so rare a shew, I would venture to recommend a similar and corresponding course to Mr Sugden. What I mean is—not that like his Noble and learned Client he should stand up and deliver *vivá voce* his answer or his arguments or his evidence, no matter which they are called, but that he should committ them to the press in the form of an amendment to his first printed speech or Letter addressed to Mr John Williams: following on this occasion the course so frequently taken in Honorable House by leaving out

---

[1] Parliament had been dissolved on 6 July 1825. In the event, it reassembled on 2 February 1826.

[2] Melville was impeached in 1806 for financial irregularities during his tenure as Treasurer of the Navy (1782–3, 1783–1800), but acquitted on all charges.

[3] See pp. 224–5 above.

[4] i.e. 'no one is compelled to accuse himself'.

whatsoever presents itself in the original document after the word *that*.

On the occasion of the humble recommendation thus hazarded, care has been taken to pay every regard possible to the convenience of these learned persons, to put them as little out of their way as possible: to give to the work proposed for them no other form than one as familiar to them as possible, and with which the most pleasing ideas can not fail to stand associated in their learned eyes.

The time expended on this humble proposal is the less regretted, inasmuch as at the same cost the same ordeal may serve for placing in correspondent lustre the virtues of the virtue-professing portion of the population of Honorable House. Inseparably included in this enquiry is the character not only of Lord Eldon, but of Honorable House, Right Honorable House and the worthy object of their conjunct worship, Matchless Constitution, a divinity of which, to the shame of our artists, no sensible image has yet been pourtrayed. After such indications as have been given, will not silence be connivance, and connivance complicity?

What is more—should it unfortunately happen that within a reasonable time no such Quasi-Bill with Quasi-Answer shall have made their appearance,—out of the original documents in question might be framed petitions in any number, and from any description of persons desirous of relief from that virtual outlawry of the vastly greatest number, that denial of justice and that all-embracing insecurity to which all classes stand devoted, so long as Lord Eldon continues where he is. Petitions to the effect in substance have already found their way into Honorable House, and may be seen among the Votes.

'*Surrounding nations*'—of whose *envy* matchless constitution is, they are so authoritatively informed, the object—surrounding nations, when they have looked at these *Indications* and seen the result—these same surrounding nations (for neither is the name at the commencement of these pages altogether unknown to any of them) will then have before them a more than commonly instructive test and exhibition of the real value of the so indefatigably boasted treasure. The French in particular, among whom, in matters between man and man, since Bonaparte's Codes have reigned,[1] Judicial corruption is in a manner unknown, will see what *uncorruptness* means when applied to English judicature.

Sooner or later, after half a year's time or thereabouts given to grievances of all sorts to rage without controul, petition to Parliament will again be possible. Petitions on this subject may then be presented

---

[1] See § 3, p. 318n above.

to Right Honorable House, should Right Honorable House be in any want of waste paper. Petitions to Honorable House may be presented not altogether without use: petitions from anxiously separate individuals the only channel through which the people can communicate with one another on a political subject, without being *exposed* to be fined, imprisoned, banished, sabred or hanged for it.

Meantime two single persons there are, to each of whom petitions in this view might be presented at any time.

1. One is the King: to wit through the medium of I remember not at this moment what official person or chain of persons: nor is it worth while to expend five minutes in looking or enquiring.[1]

2. The other is Lord Eldon himself: and in this case, reference had to his Lordship's implied offer as above, petitioners might make offer, with conditional provision, to have done teazing, if his Lordship, according to the hope given by him, would be pleased to have done staying where he is.[2]

To that virtue of his in which he is so matchless, his indefatigable courtesy—additional exercise might then be given, and a refiner's fire, of any warmth requisite for the giving to it its utmost lustre, provided. The cause is it not that of every one, whose wish it is to see abuse in any form removed—improvement in any form suffered to come into existence—security for every thing the possession of which depends upon that system of judicature which assumes and presumes the name of justice, substituted to the as yet triumphant insecurity.[3]

---

[1] At the beginning of each Parliament, the Lord Chancellor, on behalf of the King, nominated Receivers of Petitions, who were to examine petitions to ensure that they complied with certain forms, and Triers, who were to ascertain the reasonableness of the remedies sought.

[2] See 'Indications respecting Lord Eldon', Postscript §2, p. 275 above.

[3] In the text, Bentham noted at this point: 'End of Section 3: and of the whole Postscript.' For the renumbering of this section see the Editorial Introduction, p. xxxixn above.

APPENDIX B
ON RETRENCHMENT

§1. *Disappointment-prevention principle—what: its connection with Greatest happiness principle*

1. Proportioned to profusion is the demand for retrenchment.

2. For the conduct of this operation, one subordinate principle, and that the only one justifiable, is presented by the all-ruling and all-comprehensive principle—the greatest happiness principle.

3. Undenominated as yet, though so extensively acted upon, is this alike unobjectionable principle. Call it the *Disappointment-prevention* principle.[a]

4. Corresponding proposition, this proposition or say *aphorism*: this aphorism fit to serve as an *axiom*:

In the distribution made and maintained of the several separable portions of the aggregate subject-matter of property in the state, let the object or end in view be, on each occasion, *minimization*, and so far as possible *exclusion*, of the sensation of *disappointment*.

5. *Reason*. Never can any such sensation have place without being accompanied with a correspondent *pain*: call it the *pain of disappointment*.

6. Possession or expectancy—in either of those two relative situations will be the subject-matter in question: and in every case it will be in either the one or the other.

7. Correspondent to the import attached to the word *disappointment* is the import attached to the word *loss*. By the word *loss* is denoted that state of things which, reference to the happiness of the individual in question, has place when, after having been the object of his

---

[a] Use of the principle, bringing to view the axiom: contributing—to *conciseness*, by the difference between the number of words entering into the composition of the substantive with its compound adjective; to clearness, by the employment of a locution constantly the same instead of one for the expression of which assemblages of words indefinite in number and diversity are liable to be employed: and as often as the assemblages of words are different, doubts will be liable to arise whether so many different imports may not have been intended to be expressed by them.

By this same principle, so far as regards the modification of justice termed civil in contradistinction to penal—justice applied to cases called *civil* in contradistinction to cases called *penal*—may moreover be attached, also for the first time, a clear idea to the denominations *justice* and *principle*, say rather *principle* of *justice*.

342

expectation, any thing considered in the light of [a][1] benefit fails of actually being, or of being about to be, in his possession.[a]

8. Proportioned to the value of the interest in the subject-matter in the breast of the individual in question will be, in each of the two cases, the pain of disappointment. As to the circumstances on which that value depends, they belong not, in any especial manner, to the present purpose.

9. With few exceptions, by this principle, under the existing system, are the allotments made of the several subject-matters of property regulated. By this principle, notwithstanding its not having till now been ever heard of: and by this undenominatedness are called to mind the species of contract termed innominative in Rome-bred law, and the Bible text *Quem vobis ignoranter colitis hunc vobis annuncio*.[2]

§2. *Offences in the case of which this principle constitutes the sole reason for constituting them such*

10. On looking over the several sorts of acts regarded as maleficent, and on that account by appropriate prohibitions, by the laws of civilized nations, generally speaking inserted in the catalogue of *offences*, and combated by punishment and the appropriate remedies, the sole reason for so dealing by them, though that an amply sufficient one, may be seen to be the pain denominated as above: the pain of which, by every one who [puts][3] to himself the question, and

---

[a] N.B. Disappointment can not have place without loss or belief of loss on the part of the individual said to be disappointed. Loss may have place without disappointment: it actually has place in so far as the benefit lost had not been an object of expectation antecedently to the loss. Where, antecedently to the loss, no expectation had place, the result is—not *disappointment*, but *regret*: and the pain, whatever it be, which in the breast of the loser is produced by contemplation of the loss, is termed a pain—not a *pain of disappointment*, but a *pain of regret*. But of the case where regret without disappointment has place the exemplification being so unfrequent in comparison of that where disappointment is the result, it seems scarcely worth while to establish a separate principle for the case where regret, without disappointment, is the result.

---

[1] MS 'the'.
[2] This passage from the Vulgate is properly rendered, 'Quod ergo ignorantes colitis, hoc ego annuntio vobis', and appears in the Authorized Version as, 'Whom therefore ye ignorantly worship, him declare I unto you' (Acts 17: 23). These were Paul's words to the Athenians, after seeing the altar dedicated to the unknown God.
[3] MS 'putting'.

[deduces][1] the answer to it from his own feelings and experience, it may be seen and felt to be productive.

11. Offences affecting the use of a corporeal subject-matter of property, moveable or immoveable: but not the title thereto, otherwise than in so far as title, defeasible or indefeasible, is conferred by simple *possession*.

i.[2] Wrongful *detention*, or say *detainer*, applicable alike to moveables and immoveables.

ii. Wrongful asportation—applicable to moveables alone.

iii. Wrongful destruction—applicable to moveables alone.

iv. Wrongful deterioration—applicable to moveables and immoveables.

v. Wrongful disturbance of occupation—applicable to moveables and immoveables.

vi. Wrongful interception of occupation.

vii. Wrongful occupation.

viii. Theft: i.e. wrongful asportation without supposition of title.

ix. Embezzlement: i.e. wrongful detention without supposition of title.

x. Fraudulent obtainment: i.e. obtainment of the subject-matter with consent obtained by deception.

xi. Peculation: i.e. obtainment of benefit in any shape by a trustee, accompanied with loss to the intended benefitee.

xii. Wrongful damnification: i.e. wrongful production of loss in any shape, from any source, to the party wronged.

xiii. Wrongful interception of profit in any shape, from any source, to the party wronged.[a]

xiv. Extortion: i.e. wrongful obtainment of a corporeal subject-matter of property, or of profit, in any shape to the loss of the party wronged by means of intimidation: i.e. production of fear of eventual evil in any other shape than that of corporal vexation: in which case the offence is called *robbery*.

12. Offences affecting title to subject-matters of property, or to a benefit in any other shape.

i. Wrongful non-collation of title.

---

[a] ☞ In these two cases, though by previous non-expectation coupled with subsequent non-information, disappointment is excluded, and with it the evil of the first order, yet ditto of 2d· order has place.[3]

---

[1] MS 'deducing'.

[2] For the sake of clarity, in the enumeration of these sub-categories, Bentham's Arabic numerals have been replaced by Roman numerals.

[3] For the distinction between evil of the first and evil of the second order see §3, p. 353n below.

ii. Wrongful ablation of title.

iii. Usurpation of title.

iv. Wrongful transference of title.

v. Wrongful interception of title.

vi. Wrongful depretiation of title.

13. Offences of these same denominations have place with regard to *condition in life* in so far as beneficial, or considered as such.

Conditions in life are:

i. Domestic.

ii. Profit-seeking occupations.

iii. Power-conferring situations.

iv. Rank- or Dignity-conferring situations.

14. Domestic conditions are those of:

i. Husbandship.

ii. Wifeship.

iii. Fathership.

iv. Mothership.

v. Sonship.

vi. Daughtership.

vii. Natural Relationship in remoter degrees.

viii. Guardianship.

ix. Wardship.

15. Offences affecting the enjoyments from condition in life considered as beneficial.

i. Wrongful detention of Child, Ward, Servant, or Wife.

ii. Wrongful asportation of ditto.

iii. Wrongful disturbance of beneficial occupation of ditto.

iv. Wrongful occupation of ditto: wherein of *adultery* in the case of wife.

v. Wrongful disobedience on the part of ditto.

vi. Wrongful desertion, or say elopement, on the part of ditto.

16. Offences affecting property and reputation: property, by means of reputation.

i. Usurpation of inventorship: in particular in the case of any profitable or profit-seeking invention.

ii. Usurpation of fabricatorship: as where in regard to a certain corporeal subject-matter of property, a man pretends that it was made by him, whereas it was not: or that in the making of it he bore a certain part, whereas he did not.

iii. Wrongful ascription of fabricatorship: as where a man sells, as fabricated by another fabricator whose reputation as such is superior to his, a subject-matter made by him, or by some other fabricator of inferior reputation.

iv. Usurpation of vendorship: as where a subject-matter is offered to sale and sold as if belonging to the stock of a vendor superior in reputation, whereas the stock it belonged to was that of a vendor inferior in reputation.

In all these several cases, the benefit by the loss of which the disappointment is produced consists of profit—pecuniary or quasi-pecuniary profit—or of relative and appropriate reputation, or of both.

17. When the benefit in question has for its efficient cause human service in this or that particular shape, the rendition of that service being the subject-matter of obligation, and the obligation having for its efficient cause agreement of two or more parties one with another, promising the one to render to the other service in this or that shape, the other to render to the former, in consideration of service in that same shape, service in this or that other shape—in this state of things the species of *convention* called a contract has place: in which case in so far as a benefit, the expectation of which was produced by the making of the contract, fails of being received, correspondent loss, actual or supposed, with correspondent disappointment takes place.[1]

Thus it is that under the direction of the greatest happiness principle the practice of compelling the fulfilment of contracts has for its sole reason, though that, exceptions excepted, a sufficient one, the disappointment produced by the non-fulfilment.

As to the exceptions, it is in like manner to the greatest happiness principle that a benevolent mind will address itself for such exceptions as the nature of things furnishes.

The period during which the imaginary *original contract* was by liberalists in general resorted to as affording the sole reason why what was regarded as good government should be instituted or maintained, may be considered as constituting a special period in the history of the progress of society in civilization—in the arts of life.

---

[1] A passage at UC cxii. 145 (3 June 1828), which Bentham inserted in the text, but which interrupts the sense of the essay, and appears to have been abandoned in mid-sentence (see the Editorial Introduction, p. xliin above), is reproduced here: 'As a test of the propriety of the above-mentioned theory—and of the usefulness of the denomination thence given to so indisputably influential a principle, let any one make upon himself the following experiment. Let him take in hand any arrangement, existing or proposed, which to him is an object of disapprobation, and if his disapprobation have not for its efficient cause and ground the notion of its being detrimental in respect of national subsistence, national abundance, or national equality, let him see whether, in his view of it, the effect of it will not be the production of the pain of disappointment somewhere.

'Different (it may be said)—widely different—the quantities of pain produced in different breasts by the same loss. True: but, notwithstanding all this diversity, if for any purpose, on any occasion, an estimate is preferable to blind caprice, and the making of it a duty incumbent on government'.

Since the bringing to view the greatest happiness principle, whether under this its name or under that of the principle of utility, that period may be considered as having terminated, and this other as having succeeded it.

The time is now come when the utter inaptitude of the original contract principle in the character of a ground and source of practice in the constitution of government has been placed and stands in a light too clear and strong to be resistible. For:

1. The alledged fact of the formation of such a contract is a mere fiction.

2. The formation of such a contract, supposing it to have had place, would not, in the eyes of a being endowed with self-regard and sympathy, be upon consideration accepted as being *of itself* a fit ground for and source of practice. For:

3. Suppose, be the contract what it may, to the community in general, more happiness from the breach than [from][1] the observance—more unhappiness from the observance than from the breach[2]—what human being, endowed with feeling self-regarding and sympathetic, would, after due consideration, say—'Let the contract, however, be observed'?

Accordingly under all existing systems of law, cases are found—cases ample in extent and number—in which, without difficulty, the Legislator, or in his place the Judge, has said—'Let not this contract be observed'. And of this inhibitory exception, what has been the ground—the declared ground? always evil, in this or that particular shape, stated as eventually about to have place, if, of the whole contract in question, or of this or that clause in it, observance should happen to have place.

Correspondent to the several subject-matters of the several species of contract will be the evils of which, but for the requisite and appropriate inhibition, observance given to the contract would to a certainty, or with more or less probability, as supposed, be productive. Accordingly under the head of every such species of transaction, one sub-head requisite to be inserted is that of Cases of exception as to observance.

And note that where for the purpose of securing observance, the application of the power of the government is not thought fit to be made, either of two courses may be taken by it.

1. The option between observance and non-observance may be left to the free choice of the party in question: or,

---

[1] MS 'for'.

[2] An echo of *Hamlet*, I. iv. 15–16: 'it is a custom More honour'd in the breach than the observance'.

2. The observance of it may be made the subject-matter of positive interdiction.

Obvious are the sorts of cases in which the demand for positive interdiction has place. Witness the case in which the subject-matter of the contract is—an act of homicide in a case in which the act has received the appellation of an act of murder. General Rule: whatsoever act is by the law treated on the footing of an offence, observance of a contract for the bearing a part in the commission of such offence is neither compelled nor so much as permitted, but inhibited: inhibited, and accordingly dealt with on the footing of an act of *co-delinquency* with relation to such offence.

Note well the course taken by human reason in this track.

Assuming that in every political community it is right and proper that all but one should be, at all times and in respect of all acts, subject to the will of that one, Filmer held up to view, in the character of an adequate ground, reason or justificative cause, the fictitious fact, the existence of which is asserted by the proposition—Of this community (naming it) all the members but one were begotten by that one.[1]

To this reason, the mind of Locke, having taken it into due consideration, found itself unable to subscribe.[2] Of the arrangement in question, according to him, the propriety was still to be assumed. But, for the support of it on the ground of reason, some other principle was to be assumed, and was assumed accordingly. That principle, what was it? The *original contract*.

Here then for the overthrow of one phantom—not Reason, but Imagination was to be applied to. The champion furnished by Imagination was of course—not a truth, but another such phantom— another fiction. Resorted to by this philosopher was the device employed, as the story goes, by an ingenious Law-adviser: who, when by his client information was given to him of a document which presented itself as a forgery, said, 'Don't set about making proof of the forgery: but, what will be much less trouble to you—forge a release.'

The philosopher having had for his patron Sir Anthony Ashley Cooper, who, being originally a lawyer, became, with the title of Earl of Shaftesbury, Lord High Chancellor,[3] hence a probability that it was from lawyercraft that this fiction was borrowed. Fiction, the most

[1] See Filmer's *Patriarcha*, first published in 1680.

[2] In his *Two Treatises of Government*, first published in 1690, Locke attempted to refute Filmer's views.

[3] Anthony Ashley Cooper (1621–83), first Baron Ashley and first Earl of Shaftesbury, was Lord Chancellor 1672–3.

efficient of all the instruments invented by lawyercraft, was an instrument of all work, presenting itself to every hand that had boldness enough to take it up.

Bad as compared to the greatest happiness principle, compared with Filmer's fiction, and the correspondent principle, the principle adopted by Locke, though from lawyercraft, was good. Under Filmer's principle, the propriety of submission to the absolute sway of one admitted not of any exceptions. Not so under the original contract principle. For, the existence of a contract being admitted, remained to be settled—settled by so many fictions of detail—the terms of that same contract. But in the settling of those terms, the interest of the subject many [is][1] the interest which would of course be taken for the object of endeavour on the part of the subject many—that is to say of all who were not, by the power of corruption or that of delusion, engaged in the path of absolutism. Here then, and thus far, in a sort of twilight, the greatest happiness principle, though not under that name or under any name, would be taken for a guide: so many occasions for the application of it, so many imaginary clauses in the imaginary contract.

But what sort of an argument is that for the explosion of which two words are, at any time on each occasion, sufficient—*Not true!*

Feign a reason for the support of your position? why be at the trouble of any such expedient? As well might you claim the liberty of feigning the truth of your position, whatever it be, as that of feigning the truth of any other position adduced by you for the support of it.

The original contract had not only taken possession of that part of the public mind at large which, adhering to Monarchical Government, had not adopted it in its purest form but looked for limitations and checks to it, but had even been adopted by the new Government—the Whig Government, which took place on the occasion of the Revolution of 1688.

As to the partisans of a Republic, from no such fiction could their purpose receive support. Whether they had any fixt principle with a determinate name to it does not appear. As an avowed member of that party, till comparatively of late years no man had ever ventured to shew himself.

It was at the very conclusion of a small pamphlet, title at present not remembered, that in the character of the only defensible end in view in government Joseph Priestly held up in view 'the greatest

---

[1] MS 'being'.

happiness of the greatest number'. Date of that same pamphlet, 1767, or a few years before or after.[1]

In the year 1776 was published, by the author of these pages, the 8vo· Volume intituled *Fragment on Government etc.*[2] In that work the principle expressed as above by Priestly was taken in hand and employed in form in waging war against the *Original Contract* principle.

But the denomination there employed was not an exactly apt one. The denomination given to it was that which had presented itself to his view as being established: not only as one that was found established by authority too respectable to be opposed: but as one the aptness of which had been exemplified and demonstrated by the instructive and useful application that had been made of it.

In France the denomination of the principle of Utility had by Helvetius, in his work intituled *de l'Esprit*,[3] been given to this same principle. Clearness had at the same time been given to the import of it: the import of the word happiness had been brought down from the region of vague generalities, anchored on *terra firma* by means of its relation to that of the words pain and pleasure: in happiness he viewed a compound—composed of the presence of pleasure in any of its forms coupled with the absence of pain in all its forms, the mass of pleasure being at the same time regarded as being in a considerable degree *intense*. This being established, he proceeded, as the course of instruction required, to frame a catalogue of the several observable modifications of pleasure on the one hand, of pain on the other: but had not travelled far in that track when he stopt. After his death a work of his was published—a posthumous work under the title of *De l'Homme*.[4] But in this, but little if any advance was made beyond that which, as above, had been [made] in his abovementioned first work.[a]

---

[a] By the author of these, Anno 18., the investigation of the several distinguishable modifications of pleasure and pain of which human nature is susceptible having been pursued, the catalogue of them has (it is believed) been rendered little, if any thing, short of completion; and in conjunction with it have been given lists of the several

[1] See Joseph Priestley, *An Essay on the First Principles of Government; and on the nature of Political, Civil, and Religious Liberty*, London, 1768, p. 17: 'the good and happiness of the members, that is the majority of the members of any state, is the great standard by which every thing relating to that state must finally be determined'. The pamphlet in fact had 191 pages.

[2] See *A Comment on the Commentaries and A Fragment on Government*, ed. J.H. Burns and H.L.A. Hart, London, 1977 (*CW*), especially pp. 439–48.

[3] *De l'Esprit* had been first published in 1758.

[4] Helvétius' posthumous *De l'Homme, de ses facultés intellectuelles et de son éducation*, was first published, in two volumes, in 1773.

Some years before this, so long before as the year 1742, came out the *Essays* of David Hume. In this work the locution *the principle of Utility* presents itself. But by Hume, no such precise idea was attached to the word *Utility* as by Helvetius. Witness the title to one of those same *Essays*—namely, *Why Utility pleases?*[1] Attached in his mind to the word *utility* appears to have been the idea of *conduciveness to an end*, whatsoever it might happen to that end to be productive of: pleasure indeed if pleasure: but production of positive pain, if so it happened that *such* was the end in view: or another meaning capable of being attached to it was—that of conduciveness to a more valuable future contingent, in preference to less valuable present or speedily expected, pleasure.

So far was this appellative from being the most apt one, that by thinking men in considerable proportion (so it has fallen in the way of the author of these pages from time to time to hear) the import attached to it has been understood to be confined to that of a principle employed for the purpose of prescribing the giving preference to future pleasure of greater value or exclusion of future pain of greater value, or both, to present pleasure or exemption from pain, or both.

In particular, in the case of a lady of great celebrity, notice having been taken that the principle of utility was to her an object of declared distaste, a reason or efficient cause that had been assigned for such distaste was—that it had been wont to present itself to her view as putting an exclusion upon *pleasure*.

Long after the publication of the *Fragment* as above, Dr Paley, in his work on Morals,[2] took up and employed the locution *principle of Utility*. But for reasons too obvious to need explanation, it did not suit his purpose to make any such particular application of it as had been made of it, nor therefore to attach any such clear and precise import to it as had been attached to it by Helvetius.

---

other names of fictitious entities the import of which [have][3] for [their][4] basis the respective imports of so many correspondent modifications of pleasure or pain: that is to say *interests*, *desires*, and *motives*: by which means has been given what by no other means could be given—a correspondently fixt and precise import to these same additional names of fictitious psychological entities.[5]

---

[1] David Hume (1711–76) had published the first version of his *Essays, Moral and Political* in two volumes in 1741–2. However the 'essay' to which Bentham refers is in fact Section V of *An Enquiry concerning the Principles of Morals*, first published in 1751.

[2] In the margin, Bentham noted at this point: '☞ Quere the title of it?' William Paley had first published *The Principles of Moral and Political Philosophy* in 1785.

[3] MS 'has'.

[4] MS 'its'.

[5] See *A Table of the Springs of Action*, first published in 1817, in *Deontology* (*CW*), pp. 79–115.

Impressed by the above considerations with the persuasion of its comparative inaptitude, for several years past the author of these pages has, in his writings, substituted to the locution *the principle of utility* that of *the greatest happiness principle*.

For some time however, and indeed till very lately, the catalogue of his aberrations from the line of exact propriety was not yet at an end. As occasion called, to the locution *greatest happiness* he had substituted the locution (copied as above from Priestley) *the greatest happiness of the greatest number* (always understood of the members of the community in question): regarding the longer locution as the apt expression in its compleat state, and the shorter as nothing different from an abridgment of it.

Lately however—by it is not remembered what particular incident—a closer degree of attention having been called down upon the subject, a conviction was obtained that by this mode of expression, if applied to practice, effects widely different from those intended—in a word mischief to an almost indefinite amount—might be produced. For, note what is capable of being understood to be the result.

Bring to view in supposition two communities. Number of the individuals—in the one, 1,000: in the other, 1,001: of both together, 2,001. By the greatest happiness, the arrangement prescribed would be that by which the greatest happiness of all together would be produced. But wide indeed from this effect might be the effect of the application of the principle, if the arrangement productive of the greatest happiness of the greatest number—no regard being shewn to the happiness of the smallest number—were understood to be the arrangement prescribed by that same principle.

So long as the greatest number—the 1,001—were in the enjoyment of the greatest degree of comfort, the greatest possible degree of torment might be the lot of the smallest of the two numbers—the 1,000: and still the principle stating as the proper object of endeavour the greatest happiness of the greatest number be actually conformed to—not contravened.[1]

---

[1] On the corresponding marginal summary sheet at UC cxii. 77, Bentham made the following 'Addendum' dated 10 June 1828: 'Note that, to be at once appropriate and all-comprehensive, a deontological principle designed for giving direction to human conduct should apply alike to conduct in public and private life.

'This does the greatest happiness principle:—*original contract*, not.

'Original contract, if good for any thing, would have been applicable to private life.'

§3. *Evil of 2ᵈ order from disappointment*

Hitherto no *other* consequences have been brought into consideration—no other evil consequences of an arrangement considered as liable to be productive of disappointment have been brought into account. But before the account can with propriety be closed—before the instructions for the application to be made to practice of the disappointment-prevention principle can be presented as compleat—the consequences of the *2ᵈ order*—the *evil consequences of the 2ᵈ order*—must be brought to view.[a]

For this purpose a distinction will require to be made between the cases where, in the breast of the party in whose instance the disappointment is regarded as having place, his title to the subject-matter of loss is, by supposition, *out* of doubt, and those in which it is capable of being the subject-matter of doubt.

Take for instance the case of *theft*. In this case, at the time of the theft, the lawful proprietor, from whom the thing was taken, was in the undisturbed expectation of continuing, as long as he should be so pleased, to derive from it whatsoever benefit it presented itself to him as affording to him in his situation the means of deriving from it. In these circumstances, no sooner is the loss of it discovered by him, than the disappointment, with the pain inseparable from it, is experienced by him. On his part, from the first to the last of the time during which his possession of the thing had had place, an assurance had had place, not only that such means as it was in the power of the law to afford him for the continuing of the thing in the state in which it would be at his disposal would, upon occasion, be afforded to him, but that such means would be effectual: excepting always the cases in which it might happen to his possession to be cut short by any one of those accidents of which the one in question (loss by theft) is one: accidents the occurrence of which is comparatively so rare, that by the contemplation of the whole assemblage of them put together the strength of the assurance as to the continuance of the possession experiences, in the ordinary state of things, no more than a scarcely sensible degree of diminution.

[a] See Bentham per Dumont, *Traités de Législation &c.*[1]

---

[1] The distinction between evil of the first and evil of the second order is discussed in *Traités de législation*, ii. 251–5. See also *An Introduction to the Principles of Morals and Legislation* (*CW*), p. 143, where Bentham defines 'primary mischief' as that 'sustained by an assignable individual, or a multitude of assignable individuals', and 'secondary mischief' as that 'which, taking its origin from the former [i.e. primary mischief], extends itself either over the whole community, or over some other multitude of unassignable individuals'.

Not so in the cases where, as between a party on one side and a party on the other, the title to the thing is the subject of doubt: each of them regarding himself as having the right to the possession of, and benefit derivable from, the thing, to the exclusion of the other as well as of all besides. In this case a natural question is—in what way is it that, in this case, the disappointment-prevention [principle] can afford a sufficient indication of the course which, consistently with the conceptions associated with the word *justice*, justice requires to be taken?—for in this case, by the very supposition, whatsoever of the two opposite courses it may be that is taken, disappointment will take place: to both the contending parties the thing can not be allotted, and in the breast of that one of them, whichsoever it be, to whom it is not allotted, the sensation of loss will be experienced, and that of disappointment will, by the supposition, be sure to have place.

Answer. The object, or say end in view, which the Judge, acting in conformity to his duty, will have in view and his endeavours directed to the attainment of—at any rate the main object is—the prevention, or at least the termination, of that evil of the $2^{d.}$ order, which, in the breasts of such other members of the community to whose cognizance it might happen to the case to come, might naturally be expected to have place in the event of an allotment made of the thing in question different from that which would be dictated by the conception commonly attached to the word justice, but without correspondent consciousness, directed by the idea of the eventual *disappointment*.

This, let it be observed, is the *main* object. For, as to the evil of the first order, it *has* already taken place, and can not, by the Judges or any other human power, be made *not* to have taken place: what remains, generally speaking, possible is the administering to the sufferer in some shape or other *good—benefit*—in satisfaction and compensation for it. But whether in the nature of the case such satisfaction can be afforded depends upon the circumstances of the individual parties, and other particular circumstances, such as are apt to be different, one from another, in each individual case: whereas, by apt judicial arrangements, the evil of the $2^{d.}$ order is in every case capable of being either prevented or any rate in a considerable degree diminished: and, by the extent of which it is susceptible, this in other cases remediable evil is in the scale of importance much superior to that other which is in such a degree liable to prove irremediable.

Under these circumstances, for the purpose of doing what the conceptions attached to the word *Justice* require to be done, what is the course which a well-intentioned Judge will take? Answer. He will take into joint consideration, and compare the one with the other, the respective situations which the two parties present themselves to his conception as being respectively in as to strength of expectation with reference to the possession of the thing—of expectation as likely to have had place in their respective breasts with regard to the enjoyment of the mass of benefit which the proprietorship of the thing is capable of conferring. He will put himself in idea successively into the two relative situations which present themselves to him as being occupied by the two parties: this done, he will put a question to himself, and the question will be—on which of the two sides, were you on that side, would your expectation of being ultimately in possession of the thing be the strongest? To this question let an answer [have][1] been given, so will thereby an answer have been given to the question, to which of the two parties does the disappointment-prevention principle require that the ultimate possession of the thing be allotted: for, in exact proportion to the strength of the expectation of the benefit derivable from the thing, will be that of the disappointment produced by the loss of it.

§4. *Estimate of loss—difficulties attending it*

Two cases require here to be distinguished: that in which graduation as between quantity and quantity has no place, and that in which such graduation has place. Of the case where graduation has not place, an example is afforded by the case where the question is which of the two parties it is that has a right to the benefit—say the thing moveable or immoveable in dispute. Of the case where graduation has place, an example is afforded by the case where the question is concerning the *quantum* of the damage done to the subject-matter in question, to wit person, subject-matter of property, moveable or immoveable, and the like. In the non-graduation-exhibiting case, the task of the Judge, under the guidance of the disappointment-prevention principle, will be a comparatively easy one: nothing of idiosyncracy in regard either to persons or to things will have place, perplexing the judgment with degrees indefinite perhaps in number, between all which, without any criterion exclusively applying to any one of them, he will have to decide. In the graduation-exhibiting case he will have to labour under this same difficulty.

In respect to the degree of this difficulty two cases require again to be distinguished: 1. that in which, whether in respect of mind or body, person is the subject-matter of the damage; 2. that in which some thing, corporeal or incorporeal—moveable or immoveable, is

---

[1] MS 'being'.

the subject-matter of the damage. The case where the difficulty is at its maximum is that in which *mind* is the subject-matter of the damage. For in this case are liable to have place, each of them presenting a demand for mensuration, the several circumstances affecting sensibility:[a] and of the whole number of these, a great part, perhaps the greater,[1] will be found exposed to exaggeration—either on the side of infra-appretiation,[2] or on the side of super-appretiation,[3] or on both sides.

§5. *For estimation of loss, parties' attendance needful*

To this case bears reference one of the many circumstances by which the importance of the appearance of parties in the presence of the Judge, in contradistinction to the appearance of their respective advocates, is established. Where the personal condition of the party himself is present to the perception of the Judge, the probability of deception on the one part by misrepresentation on the other is at its minimum: not only is evidence capable of being checked immediately without the intervention of any refracting medium, but deportment—a circumstance speaking so strongly in explanation of reported evidence—is presented to the observation of the Judge. In this case, where the object presented to the senses of the Judge is the party, the object so presented is the original itself: in the case where it is the professional representative of the party, it is but the picture of that same original: and that a picture in the painting of which the utmost skill and energy of the experienced artist will be employed in effecting the utmost degree of misrepresentation possible: the consequence is that in each individual case, taken individually, the probability of misrepresentation and consequent and correspondent deception is at its maximum: and in the aggregate of the whole number of individual cases the degree of probability as to success between the best cause and the worst approach[es] to a level with a degree of propinquity depending conjunctly on the degree of appropriate aptitude on the part of the advocate, and the degree of deficiency in respect of appropriate

---

[a] For a detailed list and explanation of them see *Introduction to Morals and Legislation*, Ch.| |.[4]

---

[1] In the margin, Bentham noted at this point: '☞ Examine.'
[2] MS orig. 'depretiation'.
[3] MS orig. 'ultra-pretiation'.
[4] See *An Introduction to the Principles of Morals and Legislation* (*CW*), Ch. VI Of Circumstances Influencing Sensibility, pp. 51–73.

aptitude, and in particular in respect of *judicial* aptitude, on the part of the Judge. Think in this case of the chance which an ordinary Jury has for the not being deceived by a first-rate Advocate opposed by an inferior Advocate of ordinary rate.

True it is—that, in this case, [in] the breast of the party, there is the particular and sinister interest operating with greater strength than in the breast of his Advocate. But, on the other hand, supposing on the part of the Judge a sincere desire to come at the truth, the efficiency of the power he has for eliciting the truth in spite of concealment and misrepresentation, and at the same time for detecting and exposing falshood, will be much greater where the subject-matter on which it operates is the unexperienced and unskilled individual than where it is the well-experienced and well-skilled advocate. In case of wilful misrepresentation, on the part of the Advocate no such sensibility to the sudden reproach of contradictory conscience has place as that which has place commonly in the breast of the party.

§6. *Existing system*—peculiar case of *Vested rights*

Vested rights! vested rights! On an occasion on which an arrangement is proposed having for its object the exsiccation of a source of expence regarded as needless, if the case be such that on the part of the present possessors of a benefit derived from the expence the locution *vested rights* is regarded as being applicable, strong is the reliance placed on the influence and effect expected from it. Here then we have two sorts of rights, vested and unvested, in opposition to one other. Practical effect of the distinction this. Of a possessor of a vested right, in case of extinction, altogether indisputable is the claim of the possessor to compensation, and *that* altogether an adequate one. Of the possessor of a right not coming under the denomination of a vested right, it may happen to the claim to be sufficiently grounded or not sufficiently grounded, according to circumstances.

This being the case, and supposing it admitted that in case of competition a vested right possesses a claim to compensation operating in preference to any which can be possessed by a right not vested—this admitted, what, under the guidance of the greatest happiness principle, is the ground capable of being assigned for such preference? Answer. This, beyond dispute. Under the circumstances under which a vested right is understood to have place, the expectation is regarded as being more intense than in the other case, so therefore the correspondent disappointment.

Set aside the ill effects to which the disappointment-prevention principle bears reference, wheresoever, on the ground of the needlessness of the official situation to which the service, if any, is attached, the situation is abolished, no compensation at all ought to be allowed: so much money employed in compensation, so much money expended in waste. Take into account those same evil effects, thereupon comes in the demand for compensation, and that compensation an adequate one.

In the so frequently exemplified case where, for the use of the public, property in immoveables is taken out of the hands of the proprietor, and lodged in the hands of government, the propriety of the demand for compensation, and that to an amount fully adequate, is universally acknowledged. Between this case and that of an official situation regarded as the subject-matter of a vested right, is there, in any and what respect, a difference? Answer. So far as regards the evil of the 1[st.] order, expectation of situation being regarded as equally strong, disappointment in case of loss correspondent and proportionable, none.

To the evil effects of the 2[d.] order bears reference what difference has place between the two cases: proportioned to the extent of the class on which the evil of the 2[d.] order—the danger and alarm—applies itself is the magnitude of this branch of the evil. The class to which it extends in the case where it is land that is thus, and by the supposition without compensation, taken into the hands of government, is the class composed of all who have any interest in land. The class to which it extends in the case in which it is official profit that is thus, and on the same terms, taken into the hands of government, is the class composed of those alone who are in possession of such official profit, and among these of those alone in whose instance the interest possessed is understood to come under the denomination of a *vested interest*.[1]

§7. *Creation of needless Offices for compensation in contemplation of revolutionary retrenchment—how to obviate*

Two cases require now to be put in conjunction.

Case 1[st.] The progress of depredation, corruption and waste so rapid, as to have driven on the vessel of government to a near-

---

[1] The text continues with the following paragraph, which Bentham appears to have abandoned in mid-sentence: 'Among those whose interest is commonly understood to come under the denomination of a *vested interest* are the possessors of offices, the existence of which belongs to the catalogue of the most mischievous of established nuisances: offices, that is to say, by which, in proportion to the amount of the fees attached to them and'.

approaching revolution: understand by a revolution, the sudden substitution of a system in which equal regard is paid to the interest of all, to the existing system in which the interest of the many, of the vast majority, is made a constant sacrifice of to the particular and sinister associated interest of the one and the few.

Case 2[d.] In contemplation of the vastness of the burthen thus fastened or sought to be fastened on the shoulder of the community, those who take the lead in the reform-seeking enterprize have in contemplation the suppression of the alledged needless offices, or some of them, without compensation.

Note that, in the natural course of things, the profused institution of needless lucrative offices is at once a cause and an effect of the sort of change in question. In the character of an efficient and not improbably effective cause, it has long been in progress: and of whatsoever efficient causes may be found assignable, it presents itself as the most strongly operative.[1]

On the other hand, suppose such a change to present itself, to those whose interest is bound up with the existing system, as in a *paulo-post-futurus*[2] state, nothing is more natural than that, by observation made of the punctuality of the regard paid to vested interests, they should take instruction from the proverb by which the policy of making hay while the sun shines is recommended.

A design of this sort being (by supposition) acted upon,—for defeating it, here would be a case in which the evil produced by disappointment applied to the expectations thus generated would be outweighed by the evil that would be produced by the giving effect to the design: and [by] the apprehension of the appropriate remedy, that is to say the resumption, the peculation [which] the supposed design has for its object would naturally be, if not altogether prevented, at any rate checked.

§8. *Quantity of emolument given, gradations in value*
in respect of certainty—Offices considered
with a view to compensation on abolition

In a state of things by supposition presenting an irresistible demand for retrenchment, two classes of functionaries, placed in strongly contrasted situations, have now been brought to view: possessors of

---

[1] The sense of the marginal summary (see the marginal summary sheet in Bentham's hand at UC cxii. 78) differs from that of the text at this point: 'Creation of Needless Offices is the natural cause of a revolution: suppression of them the natural effect.'
[2] i.e. 'a little in the future'.

situations the interest in which passes under the denomination of a *vested interest*, and possessors of situations to which no such favour-conferring denomination is attached.

Thus far, as to supposition. In point of fact, among the former are to be found at all times, and will naturally be found, the possessors of needless offices, useless offices, overpaid offices, and sinecure offices—offices these last in which no labour whatever, serviceable or unserviceable, being performed, the possession of the office is but a pretence for receiving the emolument attached to it, the act of receiving that same emolument being accordingly an obtainment of money on false pretences to every effect but that of being dealt with in consideration of it [on] the footing of a criminal delinquent—that which in the language of existing penal law is *visited* (as the word is) with punishment in a variety of shapes, all of them having the effect of imprinting infamy. This class being composed of persons coming under the description of the ruling few, themselves possessors of political power in this or that shape, or retainers of those who are, the class they belong to may be distinguished by the appellation of the aristocratical class.

To the latter of the two classes belong those by whom in no instance is emolument received without labour performed, and in whose instance the quantity of labour is maximized, the quantity of remuneration minimized. The individuals thus situated being neither themselves possessors of power, nor by any community of particular interest linked with the possessors of power, the class they belong to may be distinguished by the appellation of the democratical class.

To this class belong the sort of Clerks denominated Writing Clerks: functionaries whose functions consist in little or nothing more than writing and performing the operations of common arithmetic. Upon these plebeians, in any number, without a thought of any such thing as a Retired allowance, when retrenchment is the order of the day, the process of elimination, it is believed, [has] been commonly performed with as little scruple or hesitation as upon privates in Army or Navy service.

Consistently with the greatest happiness principle—consistently with its immediate subordinate, the disappointment principle—can this distinction thus acted upon be defended? Let him who thinks he can without exposure to the imputation of inconsistency—and in consequence to merited disapprobation, answer in the affirmative.

As applied to this class, as between adequate compensation and no compensation at all, a sort of middle course presents itself as not being, in appearance at least, altogether destitute of ground for its support—ground derived from the greatest happiness principle.

These, it may be said, possess an attainment for which other occupations besides official ones present a demand: eliminated from their official situations they will accordingly have it [in] their power to obtain other situations in the service of individuals. This case being realized, of the utmost pay they will find obtainable, in point of quantity and certainty of continuance taken together, the value will not be so great as that of the pay attached to their respective official situations—'Give them then the amount of the difference: such is the allowance prescribed by justice.'

True: provided always that, and in so far as, the correct value of that same difference shall have been ascertained. But can it be ascertained? how it can be seems not very easy to determine.

So far as, an allowance being proposed, the individual in question prefers the acceptance of it to the continuing in the service, it is well: no disappointment produced; no injustice suffered. But suppose this is not the case? In this case, on his being disbanded from the service, disappointment will have place; to defend the arrangement from the imputation of injustice does not present itself as practicable.

In return for his labour, will he have it in his power to obtain any pay at all? Even of this, if the number thus eliminated at once is to a certain degree considerable, scarcely can any adequate assurance be had: at any rate in that state of over-population, the pressure of which seems destined to indefinite encrease.

Supposing the attainment of the proper temperament not absolutely impracticable, the accomplishment of it can not but necessitate a minute enquiry into idiosyncratical circumstances. In a word, nothing less than a judicial enquiry, carried on by a judicatory acting in the way of antitechnical procedure, could answer the purpose: and, under the existing system, where is any such judicatory to be found? at any rate a judicatory capable of being applied to this same purpose?

§9. Existing System—gradations as to dislocability, thence as to value as depending on certainty

Under the existing system, gradations may be observed in the value of regard considered as due to the claim for compensation. At the head of the scale stands the sort of office on which vested rights are rivetted: next to that, the office holden during good behaviour: lowest, the office holden during pleasure.

Not so great in reality and effect as in shew is the difference between Office with vested rights and Office during good behaviour.

Office held during good behaviour is, in plain English, Office held unless and until removal shall take place at the suit of the King by sentence of the King's own Bench: and unless the prosecution were carried on in pursuance of the known wishes of the Right Honorables who govern in his Majesty's name, supposing remorse to have produced in the breast of a delinquent possessor of such an office a desire, with a view to atonement, to see himself convicted, it would not be a matter altogether easy to him to find the means of giving accomplishment to so pious a purpose. Under matchless Constitution, functionaries of the highest order have a vested interest in the impunity of all subordinates under them, in the impunity, that is to say, at any hands but their own.

Witness the case of a Justice of Peace who, for giving encrease to the value of a publick House of his own, refuses to grant or continue a licence to the occupant of a neighbouring house. Under Lord Tenterden's law in particular, no punishment without a corrupt motive, no knowing that a corrupt motive has had place unless the party accused makes declaration to that effect.[1] Be the gain ever so enormous, no defensible reason assigned or assignable, if his wish is to be put upon his trial, the worshipful Gentleman must make affidavit, and say my motive for refusing the licence was corrupt: and even [then] might be found to remain a question garnished with great doubts—the question whether the rule *nemo tenetur seipsum [accusare]*[2] might not be found applicable to this case.

No accusation, no conviction: no conviction, no dislocation, no punishment. Be the place a place during good behaviour or only during pleasure, in rebellion to those who govern in the King's name, will a man in a subordinate office dare to prefer accusation, or so much as to give information, against the occupants of a superordinate authority in a certain higher sphere? If, on the part of this informant, a peccadillo can, by an appropriate microscope, be discovered, how vast so ever the mass of waste, depredation and corruption proved in the higher regions, how extensive the conspiracy by which it has been effected, [. . .?] will be [the] lot of the informant, a peerage that of the arch-delinquent. A case which may at any rate be consulted for illustration, may be seen in the letters of Mr Sedgwick and the Reports of

---

[1] The Court of King's Bench would not proceed against a Justice of the Peace for an alleged illegal act, unless it appeared that he had been influenced by a partial, corrupt or malicious motive. This applied to the granting of alehouse licences. It is unclear however what Bentham means by 'Lord Tenterden's law': it does not appear that Tenterden (as Abbott had been created in April 1827) made any innovations, either in Parliament or on the bench, in this area of the law.
[2] i.e. 'no one is compelled to accuse himself'.

the Committee which had for Chairman the Right Hon. | | Wallace:[1] whether for proof, would be for any person to answer to whom it should appear worth his while, for any practical purpose, to give perusal to those instructive documents.

At any rate one thing is still wanting in that case; for Mr Wallace's Noble relative Lord Melville, an advancement in the peerage.[2]

So far as regards strength of expectation, small in some situations is the difference between tenure during good behaviour, and tenure during pleasure. In name no longer than during pleasure, in effect (says the man to himself) my tenure is during life: for, during life, I shall, for I will, continue to please.

§ 10. *Existing System, custom as to self-dislocation on dislocation of patrons*

Always be it remembered, however, that, on the present occasion, the behaviour of the individual does not come in the question, belongs not to the subject under consideration. This subject is dislocation in the wholesale way for the purpose of frugality: not dislocation in retail, with a view to appropriate aptitude.

In the entire list of Offices held during pleasure, instances however are found, in no small number and of no small value, in which, upon the dislocation of a superordinate, subordinates, one or more, go out of course. In this case the dislocation has for its efficient cause—in some instances the act of a superior paramount to both, in others the act of the dislocatee himself. In this latter case, the suicidal act has for

[1] Thomas Wallace (1768–1844), first Baron Wallace, Lord of the Admiralty 1797–1800, Commissioner of the Board of Control 1800–6, 1807–16, 1828–30, Vice-President of the Board of Trade 1818–23, Master of the Mint in Ireland 1823–7, was Chairman of the Commission of Inquiry into the Collection and Management of the Revenue, whose Thirteenth and Fourteenth Reports dealt with the Board of Stamps, recommending substantial alterations to its organization and procedures (see *Commons Sessional Papers* (1826) x. *passim*). In particular, the Commissioners were critical of the inadequate supervision and control exercised over officials in Scotland by the Board, especially its Chairman, James Sedgwick (1775–1851), who had been appointed to the office in 1817. As a result, the Treasury decided to dismiss the existing Board and appoint a new one, giving allowances in compensation to all the members except Sedgwick (see the Treasury Minute of 6 October 1826 in *Commons Sessional Papers* (1826–7) xvii. 1–14.) Sedgwick vigorously defended himself in a series of letters published in the *Morning Chronicle*, and republished in three pamphlets: *Twelve Letters addressed to the Right Hon. Thomas Wallace, M.P. Chairman of the Commission of Revenue Inquiry*, London, 1826; *Letter the Thirteenth*, London, 1826; and *Letter the Fourteenth*, London, 1827.

[2] In 1814 Wallace had married Jean, Lady Melville (1766–1829), second wife and widow of Henry Dundas, first Viscount Melville, and step-mother of Robert Dundas, second Viscount Melville. Sedgwick had criticized the system of patronage in Scotland, in which Melville, Lord Privy Seal of Scotland 1814–51, had considerable influence. Bentham was perhaps unaware that Wallace himself had been raised to the peerage in February 1828 as Baron Wallace.

its internal cause, in outward shew gratitude, or a sense of honour: in reality, most commonly self-regarding prudence—if of my own accord I follow my patron in his retirement, the consequence is—that in the event of his reinstatement I shall by him be reinstated with him: if I stay behind, I may be ejected at any time by those by whom he is ejected; in which case I shall not be reinstated with him: serving under the banners of his adversaries, I shall be regarded as hostile to his interests, or at best indifferent.

In no small degree curious and instructive would be a list of these Official situations, accompanied, confronted and contrasted by a correspondent list of situations in regard to which the efficient cause of mortality has not had place.[a] Thereupon an object for enquiry,

---

[a] Pitt the first it was who for the first time placed in office the Earl of Shelburne of that day, afterwards Marquis of Lansdowne, constituting him one of the Secretaries of State.[1] Shelburne being at that time a personal favorite of George the third—as such he has often spoken of himself to the author of these pages—with whom the choice originated can not be affirmed with any degree of assurance. Shelburne, when he became Minister-in-Chief in the situation of First Lord of the Treasury, constituted Pitt the second, son of Pitt the first, his Vice-Minister, in the situation of Chancellor of the Exchequer.[2] When, in 1783, upon the conclusion of the peace, the Whig Aristocracy, of which the Marquis of Rockingham was the head, Edmund Burke the life and soul, out-voted the Earl of Shelburne and thus rendered his resignation necessary, the simultaneous resignation of his protegé and locatee, Pitt the second, was looked for by him as a matter of course.[3] Pitt the second, young as he was, was not so young as not to see that on the part of his patron the chance of reintegration was = 0—the Whigs of that time being a strong, numerous, well-compacted and disciplined phalanx, while Shelburne had scarce any adherents besides personal ones; [he] accepted the offer made him by the Royal master and to the Vice-Ministership added the Ministership-in-chief.[4] Perfidy and ingratitude—perfidy by breach of a virtual contract—were the stains cast by this conduct upon the character of the young Statesman. So, at least, was the conception of the Ex-Premier, as more than once expressed by him, and with no slight energy, in discourse with, or in the hearing of, the author of these pages.

---

[1] William Petty (1737–1805), second Earl of Shelburne and first Marquis of Lansdowne, had in fact been appointed to office as First Lord of Trade (April–September 1763) by George Grenville (1712–70), First Lord of the Treasury 1763–5, before serving under Chatham (Pitt was raised to the peerage as Earl of Chatham in August 1766) as Secretary of State for the Southern Department from July 1766 to October 1768.

[2] Pitt was Chancellor of the Exchequer in Shelburne's administration from July 1782 to April 1783.

[3] Shelburne was defeated in the House of Commons on 17 and 21 February 1783 on the preliminary articles of peace, agreed with the United States of America, France and Spain, at the conclusion of the American War of Independence. After several weeks of negotiation, George III eventually accepted the resignation of Shelburne, and with him Pitt, whereupon the Fox-North Coalition came into office. Rockingham had in fact died in July 1782.

[4] When forming his own ministry in December 1783, Pitt took the offices of First Lord of the Treasury and Chancellor of the Exchequer, but did not give office to Shelburne.

proof, and explanation, would be—the *principle* in which the distinction has had its source.

§11. *Existing System. Inconsistencies as to undislocability and dislocability of Judges*

Among the boasts of matchless Constitution is the undislocability, so delusively termed the independency, of the Judges. This quality being a declared indispensable requisite to and of upright judicature, it accordingly has place in the case of the 12 high-seated Common Law Judges and one of the three highest-seated Equity Judges, to wit the Master of the Rolls. At the same time, either it is not an indispensable requisite to upright judicature, or upright judicature is not necessary to good government or to the well-being of the community. For it has not *place* in the situation of Lord High Chancellor, nor in that of Justice of the Peace: and the said Chancellor is, amongst other things, head of the law, the functionary by whom, to so vast an extent, the proceedings of all the other great Judges are controuled, and at whose recommendation the occupants of their several situations are located. As little has it place in the case of the situation of Justice of the Peace: a situation of which there [are] at all times several thousands in existence—situations in which some scores or perhaps hundreds as many suits, of one sort or other, are heard and determined as by all the Judges of the superior class put together. Thus it is that, for instances in which the boast is consistent with truth, instances there are to the amount of scores or hundreds in which it is repugnant to truth. It is [untrue][1] in regard to the top and bottom of the scale; it is [true][2] in regard to the intermediate degrees of the scale.

From a recent occurrence, to the list of the cases in which either that which goes by the name of independence is not necessary to upright judicature—or upright judicature is not necessary to the well-being of the community, it appears that addition must be made of the situation of Judge Advocate.[3]

[1] MS 'true'. Bentham of course meant to say that the 'boast' was 'untrue' in its application to the Lord Chancellor and Justices of the Peace, 'true' in its application to the twelve 'high-seated Common Law Judges' and the Master of the Rolls.

[2] MS 'untrue'.

[3] This paragraph appears to supersede a previous passage at UC cxii. 173: 'A curious enough particular is—that among these situations in regard to which, according to the practice of matchless Constitution, dislocation in retail ought to be expected to ensue in the event and in virtue of the dislocation in gross termed a change of Ministry or a change of administration, a sort of judicial office is one. This is the Office of *Judge-Advocate*, Justice Minister of the Army— of the Land-branch of the Defensive Force.'

The Judge Advocate General had not traditionally been a political appointment. However upon

In the person of the Judge Advocate may be seen a mongrel in another form. Impartiality is an indispensable quality in a Judge: partiality is an inseparable quality in an Advocate. Accordingly, in the person of every Judge Advocate, as the very appellation declares and acknowledges, the two qualities, each of them the negation of the other, are united. But here too comes into action the King's Prerogative, the universal solvent of all difficulties. In each case that comes before them, let my Judges be every one of them impartial; let my Attorney General be partial; let my Judge Advocate be at once impartial and partial, both in the most perfect degree. So saith the royal worker of all needful miracles; so saith he, and the miracle is wrought according to his word.

Not that in this case the arrangement is in so high a degree absurd as, upon the face of the statement, it may naturally be supposed to be. In military service, as in every branch of service, high in the scale of importance stands *justice*: but in military service, still higher, it may be said, stands *obedience*. For the anomaly, from this same plea, so it is that excuse may be found derivable: excuse, yes: but justification, not. For the necessary obedience, provision equally, or rather still more, effectual might be made by other arrangements, and those standing clear from an objection so palpable, placing upon the arrangement the imputation of inconsistency with so strong a glare.

§ 12. *Existing System. Inconsistencies as to the union of Law and Equity Jurisdiction in one person*

Among official situations, some pairs of situations may be seen which ought to be and are said to be to each other as oil and vinegar: vinegar occup[y]ing the under, oil the upper: mixture of the two, but for some intermediate substance, for example a hard egg, serving as a bond of unity, impracticable.

Thus are circumstanced in relation to one another Common Law and Equity law: Common Law the vinegar, Equity the Oil. But in this case the King's Prerogative possesses the virtue, and performs the

---

the formation of Canning's administration in April 1827, the incumbent Judge Advocate General, John Beckett (1775–1847), MP for Cockermouth 1818–21, Haslemere 1826–32 and Leeds 1835–7, had been replaced by James Abercromby (1776–1858), later first Baron Dunfermline, MP for Midhurst 1807–12, Calne 1812–30 and Edinburgh 1832–9, Speaker of the House of Commons 1835–9. Abercromby retained his place during Goderich's administration (September 1827—January 1828), but was in turn dismissed and Beckett reinstated upon the formation of Wellington's administration.

function, of the hard egg. Accordingly, in the case of each one of the four Judges called Barons of the Exchequer Judicatory, Common Law and Equity law may at all times be seen condensed in equal perfection and perfect union.

APPENDIX C

ON THE MODE OF REMUNERATION
AS BETWEEN SALARY AND FEES

§ 1. *Official Remuneration—which the best mode? Salary or Fees?*

By salary understand a mass of emolument periodically afforded, and generally at all times the same: or if on any occasion in any degree varied, not lessened without timely notice in such sort as to minimize, if it be not practicable to exclude altogether, the attendant pain of disappointment: the elementary portions of it in any case not being attached to the several times and occasions on which this or that individual portion of the aggregate mass of service, rendered or supposed to be rendered in virtue of the situation, is performed.

By a fee understand a portion of emolument received on the occasion or in consideration of a particular service rendered by a functionary in virtue of this or that particular situation occupied by him, or occupation followed by him.

As a means of engaging appropriate and apt service of the ordinary kind in official situations by pecuniary remuneration, which of the two modes is the most apt—salary or fees? Answer—salary: fees being in an eminent degree unapt: and that in the case of every official situation whatsoever: though more in certain situations than in others. Reasons, these, the heads of which here follow.

Follows in general terms the enumeration of the evil effects, not produced, any of them, by salary; produced, all of them, by fees.

1. To the public at large, delay in the business whatsoever it may be.

2. To individual suitors at the several offices, expence, vexation and delay: the whole augmented to an indefinite amount, comparison had with salary.

3. To the functionary so remunerated, the value of the remuneration lessened, by the uncertainty of its amount.

4. To the functionary, pain of disappointment liable to be produced, on the unexpected sinking of the amount below the expectation produced by antecedent habitual experience or calculation.

The judiciary is the department in which the badness of the first and second of these evil effects will be seen to have swollen to a paramount magnitude.

All these several evil effects will be more particularly brought to view and their existence rendered manifest in and by so many ensuing Sections.[1]

Of whatever good effects have ever been or can be regarded as produced by this mode of remuneration, the conception will be shewn to be illusory. These are:

1. Good effects looked for in the circumstance that the burthen imposed rests on an individual to whom the service performed by the functionary is rendered. See §| |.[2]

2. Good effects looked for from the alacrity supposed to be produced on the part of the functionary on the occasion of the performance of each service, and the consequent receipt of the remuneration attached to it. See §| |.

In conclusion,[3] a view will be given of the efficient causes by which the practice of giving this shape to official remuneration has been produced. Among them, any thing rather than any experience of the usefulness of this institution will be seen perceptible: usefulness— understand to persons other than the authors and persons linked with them by a community of particular and sinister interest.[4]

§ 2. *Evil effect the first—to the detriment of the public service, delay augmented*

In itself evil in this shape constitutes, it will be seen, an item distinct from, and in many cases to an indefinite degree greater than, the aggregate of the evils produced at the charge of individual suitors. Therefore it is, that it is stated as a separate evil, and that the place assigned to it is the first place. But the nature and magnitude of it can not be made apparent but by and in the course of the statements and observations by which the evil effects in relation to suitors individually taken are held up to view: and moreover its nature is variously

---

[1] The evils enumerated above are dealt with in §§2, 4, 6 and 5 respectively. Bentham inserted two additional sections dealing with further 'evil effects', namely §3 on 'Expence to Suitors' (see p. 371 below) and §7 on 'Effect on the Judiciary system' (see pp. 374–81 below).

[2] No material for the sections dealing with these 'good effects' appears to have been written, though it seems from the plan at UC cxii. 245 (12 June 1828) that Bentham intended to consider the topic of alacrity in §11 (see p. 391 below). For an earlier discussion of this topic however see UC cxii. 257–61 (25, 29 May 1828).

[3] See §10, pp. 386–91 below.

[4] On the marginal summary sheet at UC cxii. 249 (13 June 1828), Bentham made the following 'Addenda' at this point: 'The evil how, and how far, remediable. 1. In all official situations, by Salary of equal value. 2. Competition will minimize the expence *in futurum*. 3. In lawyers' professional situations, remedy none.'

modified by the nature of the services belonging to the different departments of the entire official establishment.

The delay is produced by individual functionaries, by the sinister interest, as will be seen, of the individual functionaries, to the detriment of individual suitors: and from the delay produced on this occasion is liable to result, in this or that branch of the public service, as will be seen, correspondent detriment to the public service.

It will be shown in § [4][1] how under the fee-system, for the sake of the profit by the expence, delay to the business is manufactured by functionaries: and the business of suitors being, at the same time, the business of government, thus it is that delay to the suitors is in a correspondent degree delay to the business of government.

By the mere operation of telling the money of which the fee is composed, and examining into the goodness of it, and, on each individual occasion, ascertaining the coincidence between the sum demanded for the service in question and the sum allowed or supposed to be allowed by regulation or custom, additional quantities of time can not but be consumed: and forasmuch as for every part of the functionary's time remuneration is not less requisite than for any other, here may be seen a perennial source of delay and expence to government, such as, in the aggregate, can not but be considerable.

The occasions on which a fee is due, and on each occasion the quantum of what is due, being in the nature of the case more or less involved in uncertainty, every now and then disputes and even quarrels can not fail to arise: and by all these contestations, an additional and extra consumption of time can not fail to be produced.

The greater the number of these discussions, the greater the number of the occasions on which the suitor and the functionary are brought into contact with each other: the greater the length of them, the closer the contact. The situation of the suitor being on every occasion, in a greater or less degree, that of dependence on the good-will and agency of the functionary, the closer this contact, the more strongly sensible will the suitor be to the necessity of conciliating in his favour the goodwill of the functionary.

On this occasion a distinction will require to be made between two sorts of occasions: one on which, by undue favour shewn to the suitor, detriment to the public service is capable of being produced; another on which evil in that shape is not capable of being produced. To the former class for example will be found those which are presented by various branches of the revenue: in particular that derived from exports and imports of commodities that have been ren-

[1] MS blank.

dered subject-matters of taxation or prohibition: to the latter class some of those which are afforded by various offices belonging to the department of justice.

But in respect of the delay and vexation in other shapes to which, in a greater or less degree, the suitor can not but be exposed to experience at the hands of the functionary, his state can not but be a state of correspondent dependence.

[§ 3. *Evil effect the 2ᵈ Expence to Suitors*]¹

§ 4. *Evil effect the 3[d.] To suitors, expence, delay and vexation augmented*

1. By suitors, understand individuals of all sorts considered as having or capable of having business to transact at the office in question with any functionary or other person in relation to that branch of the public

---

¹ Bentham inserted this section into the essay after drawing up the original list of evil effects at §1, pp. 368–9 above. The text has not been found, but the following copy of the marginal summaries is at UC cxii. 250 (15 June 1828): 'Of Salary, exact amount ascertainable: not so of remuneration by fees.

'Result, enormous excess to which the amount of remuneration by fees may rise unknown to any but those whose interest it is to maximize it.

'Example, emoluments of Prerogative office of the Archbishop of Canterbury.

'Principal Registrars, sinecure situations, increasing in value as population and wealth—present amount £| |.

'Deputy Registrar, each office $\frac{2}{3}$ds· of a sinecure.

'Archbishop's office itself a sinecure, excepting occasional approvals of other functionaries, and visits to the House of Lords, when it suits his convenience.

'Only in the case of the principal Registrars, the sinecurism compleat.

'[Their] names do not appear from the returns.

'Two Principal Clerks, also pure sinecurists.

'But one seat for the two, in which however they neither of them sit.

'Labour of the other Principal Clerks not much more severe.

'Deputy assistant Clerks—neither name nor number mentioned in the Returns.'

Bentham's source of information was the Report of the Royal Commission on Officers of Courts of Justice dealing with the Court of Arches, the Prerogative Court and the Court of Peculiars of the Archbishop of Canterbury (see *Commons Sessional Papers* (1823) vii. 27–109, especially 55, 80–2). The Report did not however give the annual incomes of the three principal Registers of the Prerogative Court, whose emoluments were derived from fees. Each principal Register appointed a Deputy, hence Bentham's calculation that each Deputy performed the duty of one-third of an office. Of the five Clerks of the Seats, four were appointed by the principal Registers, and the fifth was appropriated to the Deputies. The Deputies appointed two Clerks to perform the duties of their seat, while the four other Clerks of the Seats appointed Clerks to act under them: according to the Report, the Clerks of the Seats appointed by the Registers (presumably 'the other Principal Clerks' referred to by Bentham) 'almost entirely perform their duties by Deputies, or assistant Clerks'. It appears however that the two Clerks appointed by the Deputies (presumably Bentham's 'two Principal Clerks') were efficient officers, and not sinecurists.

service to which the office belongs. In general this appellation has not been [used] in any case except that in which the department the office belongs to is the judiciary, and the business, business done in the course of litiscontestation. In the case of every department however and every office in it, individuals there are who have business in this or that shape to transact in that same office: for individuals, in so far as considered in this respect, a common denomination is needed, and this may serve at least as well as, and in virtue of the analogy, still better than any other.

2. By expence, on this as on other occasions, under[stand] expence in all shapes—expence as applied not only to money but to all subject-matters of expenditure: human labour and time in particular—that being the main source of the matter of wealth in all its shapes—of money's worth as well as money.

In the articles of time and labour, expence is equivalent to expence in the article of money.

What if the suitor in question be so circumstanced that he neither does obtain, nor ever endeavours to obtain, money or money's worth by the correspondent employment given to his labour and his time? Between the two cases, in words, yes: but in effect, no difference is there except in so far as employment given to labour and time is in the case of one class necessary to the subsistence of the individual; in the case of another class, not thus necessary. This case allowed for, expence in labour and time, if not employed in obtaining or en-deavouring to obtain money or money's worth in a permanent shape, is employed in the enjoyment of or endeavour to enjoy pleasure, or in the exclusion of or endeavour to exclude pain: and only in so far as it is productive of these effects—one or other of them, are money, or money's worth in a permanent shape, possessed of any value.[1]

With truth may it be said—that fees receivable by functionaries [have] among their effects the maximization of expence at the charge of suitors. Why? Answer. Because in the instance of each such func-tionary, to effect such maximization is his interest: and on the part of every such functionary, according to the nature of the office in a degree more or less considerable, it is in his power, in this or that shape, in this or that way, to make addition to the net aggregate value

---

[1] The following paragraph, the sense of which is unclear, has been excluded from the text at this point: 'With truth it may be said that fees to functionaries have for their effects maximiza-tion of expence, delay and vexation to suitors. Why? Answer. Because in the first place they have for their effect maximization of expence and production of delay having for its effect production of expence, expence thus produced having among its efficient causes production of delay, and vexation to an individual having among its efficient causes production of expence at the charge of that same individual and production of delay in the transaction of the business of that same individual.'

of those same fees, or what comes to the same thing, to the aggregate of the net emolument, in all shapes taken together, derivable by means of them, and in the case of every individual, if the interest and the power are united, the correspondent *will*, and in consequence the correspondent *agency*, takes place of course.

In regard to expence at the charge of the suitor, remains to be shewn how it is that the power of giving encrease to it is in every case in the hands of the functionary. Through the medium of the power of giving encrease to delay, this power exists in every case: and of this presently.[1] But, for the most part, even in a direct way, this pernicious and predatory power has, and at all times has had, and, unless appropriate measure and effectual arrangement, of which elsewhere,[2] shall have been employed for the extinction of it, will at all times continue to have, place.

For the purpose of seeing how it is that this state of things has been produced, two correspondent and inseparably connected official situations must be taken into view. These are those of *incumbent* and *patron*: incumbent, the functionary by whom the official situation is filled: patron, the functionary by the result of whose will, in a direct or indirect way, the incumbent is located: and note that, under the existing system, generally speaking, to a great, perhaps the most considerable, extent, by the same individual by whom the location is performed, so also, and by him alone, is the dislocation performable: so also is the direction given to the operations which, on the rendering of the service or supposed service, come to be performed.

By whatsoever interest the incumbent has in the production of evil in any of these shapes, the patron has a correspondent interest.

In the case of an office belonging to the department called spiritual or ecclesiastical, and in particular in regard to those offices the patronage in regard to which is openly and without attempt at restriction an object of sale, this connection in respect of interest is not only seen, but universally acknowledged to be seen, by every eye. In the case of offices in general it is perhaps not in every instance seen, certainly not in every instance acknowledged: acknowledged or not acknowledged, its influence is not the less effective.

---

[1] Bentham does not go on to discuss this topic here, but for a discussion of the relationship between delay and remuneration see *Constitutional Code*, I (*CW*), Ch. IX, § 25, Arts. 13–25, pp. 423–6.

[2] For Bentham's detailed proposals regarding official remuneration see ibid., Ch. IX, § 15, pp. 297–310.

§5. *Evil effect the 4ᵗʰ· To functionaries, value of the remuneration lessened by incidental disappointments*

In the Reports of the Account Commission Aᵒ· 1780, Vol. II. p. 185,[1] may be seen an instance in which between the amount of the remuneration of one year and that of the remuneration of the next year there was a difference of one half:[2] suppose the difference to be on the side of encrease, so far to the purpose here in question it is well: but suppose it to be on the side of decrease, think of the situation of one who, having adjusted his expenditure to the amount of his income of the first of the two years, finds the half of it slipping through his fingers in the second.

§6. *Evil effect the 5ᵗʰ· To functionaries, the value lessened by the uncertainty of the amount*

This evil effect, though so intimately connected with the one just mentioned, is still distinguishable from it. By the former evil, as often as it is experienced, and on each occasion in proportion to the quantity of it, the party suffering is—the individual functionary. But that which one man has experienced, another, whose interest engages him to pay more or less attention to the case, will anticipate: and in so far as his conduct is determined by the suggestions of prudence, comparing the uncertainty attached to the income by the fee system with its certainty under the salary system, he will prefer, to the average annual amount of the remuneration receivable from fees, a less amount paid in the shape of salary: and the public may be made a gainer by the amount of the difference.

§7. *Evil effect the 6ᵗʰ· Effect on the Judiciary system*

Whatsoever be the department, remuneration in the shape of fees (as hath been seen) is, to the whole extent of it, a bounty upon the

---

[1] The Commission on Public Accounts sat from 1780 to 1787 and produced fifteen Reports. Bentham had a three-volume edition of the Reports (see §8, p. 381 below), which has not been traced. The Reports are reproduced in *Commons Sessional Papers of the Eighteenth Century*, xli–xlv.

[2] See the Twelfth Report (June 1784), *Commons Sessional Papers of the Eighteenth Century*, xliii. 144, where the income of an Auditor of the Imprest is reported as increasing from £10,331 5s. 11d. in 1782 to £16,373 3s. 4d. in 1783.

production of expence, delay and vexation. As in all other departments so in this, parties by whom the evil effects are experienced: the public, the suitors, and the functionaries belonging to the department.

But so far as the functionaries are concerned, the evils, though as above shewn to be real, are in comparison so minute, as to constitute no more than an evanescent quantity: while to functionaries taken in the aggregate, the benefit is to such a degree enormous, that to every eye but of a minute observer, the evils—the evils as above—are compleatly hid.

At the same time, vast as they are, compared with the evils by which assignable individuals are separately affected, still so small are those by which the public in its aggregate capacity is the sufferer, so small, and at the same [time] so much less conspicuous, that in bringing the aggregate of both branches of the evil to view, there will be a convenience in giving the first place to those by which individuals are more manifestly affected.

Various are the occasions on which, by the author of these pages, industry has been employed in the endeavour to hold up to view the state into which the business of the Judiciary department has been brought by the giving of this form to judicial remuneration. Of so large a quantity neither can repetition nor so much as any thing like an adequate abridgment be afforded here. *Law unknowable, justice inaccessible*: by these four words may however some conception, how general and faint, be given of the practical result. Justice inaccessible: in these two words may be seen the state of things expressed by the general rule: the case where it is accessible being no more than an exception, and that comparatively a very narrow one. In the number of the individuals to whom justice is accessible compared with the number of those to whom it is inaccessible would be expressed in figures the ratio between the extent of the exception as compared with that of the general rule.

Justice rendered inaccessible—of this effect what are the efficient and final causes? Answer: efficient cause, the tax imposed in the name of fees. From the one cause, two exquisitely agreable effects: sale of justice to all who can find wherewithal to pay the tax: denial of justice to all who can not: that is to all besides. From the denial of justice, results to the fee-fed Judge, correspondent ease: to the man of opulence, in one word to the aristocrat, member of the so intimately associated though not in form incorporated body of the ruling few, the conjoint and correspondent powers of depredation and oppression.

On the condition of the member of the body composed of the

relatively indigent, the effect produced by this inaccessibility, coupled with the venality of the powers of judicature, is differently modified, according as the situation in which he has need of it is that of plaintiff or that of defendant.

1. By the denial of the faculty of acting in the character of plaintiff, the Judge delivers him up to all the several members of the relatively opulent body, to be oppressed and plundered, or in one word to be tormented, in all imaginable ways at pleasure. In so doing, no exercise does the learned functionary give in any shape to his active faculty, in any other way than by refusing to act—unless he receives the fee which the individual is unable to give. Whatsoever be the suffering produced, no otherwise is it contribute[d] to by him than a murder would be contributed to by a surgeon, who, seeing a wounded man wilting in his blood, and being in league with a murderer by whom the wound had been given, should refuse to save his life without a fee which he saw would not be given.

2. By the denial of the faculty of acting in the character of defendant, the Judge employs his active faculty in inflicting on the unoffending whatever sufferings are professed to be intended to be inflicted, whether in the shape of punishment or in the shape of the burthen of affording satisfaction, upon offenders: partly in the way of unproductive oppression, partly in the way of depredation, as the case may be: where it is in the way of depredation, in consideration of the share he has in the booty, he employs his irresistible power in exacting from the relatively indigent individual whatsoever is demanded at his expence by the relatively opulent. In this case the part he acts is that of the surgeon who, for a fee given him by a murderer, should lend his hand for the purpose of the mortal stab.

Whatsoever villainy is practiced by, or to the benefit of, the ruling few, a veil for it, the least transparent that the nature of the case affords, will, by or for the said ruling few, of course be found. The villainy here in question is the venality, coupled with the inaccessibility, of justice. The veil employed in this case is composed of the words, *discouragement to litigation*. Litigation is a dyslogistic term which has for its correspondent neutral associate, litiscontestation. Those whose purpose it is on the occasion in question to cause litiscontestation to be regarded with displeasure employ instead of it the word *litigation*, a word designative of an action on the idea of which the stamp of general disapprobation is seen to stand affixt. Litigation is a bad thing: this admitted, discouragement opposed to it is a good thing.

Not that this statement is altogether correct. In it are contained two positions, one of which is indeed true, but the other false. Applied to the case of him whose character, were he able to sustain it, would be that of plaintiff, true it is that the mass of unpayable fees do discourage litiscontestation and therein and with it litigation: not simply do they discourage it, they impossibilize it. But applied to the case of him whose character, were he able to sustain it, would be that of defendant, so far from impossibilizing litiscontestation and therein litigation, they give birth to it: they cause it to have place in instances in which it would otherwise not have place. Of the sword called the sword of justice, the Judge, at the price which he has set upon it, to every body who, for the pleasure of oppression or the profit of depredation, feels disposed to put it to use, offers the use of it accordingly: if in consequence of this advertisement no person becomes a customer for the article, it is no fault of the Judge: what depends upon him to do for the prosperity of this branch of trade has been done.

In what is it that the slavery under which the subject many are held by the ruling few differs from that in which the blacks are held by the whites in the tropical regions, and that in which the Catholics are held by the Protestants in Great Britain and Ireland? Answer—in this: to wit, that there exists not in this case as in those any invariable or determinate line of demarcation between those [who] are under subjection to the tyranny and those who derive the benefit of it. In the case of the blacks, and others in which that tint is discernible, the mark of distinction and justificative cause of oppression is the colour: in the case of the hereticks abovementioned, it is their creed. On the other hand, it not being found possible to keep all men of the class in question at all times in the state of the requisite degree of indigence, neither is the slave kept for ever out of all hope of relative emancipation, nor is the tyrant altogether exempted from the fear of experiencing[1] resistance.[2]

True it is that a power thus commodious and extensive is not obtained by them [from][3] the learned manufacturers gratis: a price is set upon it: the price constituted by the payment of their fees. But in the amount of the fees no distinction being in any case produced by the degree of opulence on the part of him of whom it is exacted, the greater the opulence of the public enemy, the lighter is the burthen, and the more delicious the correspondent benefit: hence the more enormous his opulence, the more closely is his sinister interest connected with that of the men of law: with that of the fee-fed Judge

---

[1] MS 'of no longer experiencing' contradicts the evident sense of the passage.

[2] The marginal summary differs slightly from the text at this point: 'By this incompleat separation of interests are produced the exceptions to the total denial of justice to the subject many.'

[3] MS 'by'.

under the existing system; with that of the professional Advocate in a greater or less degree under every possible system.

Were it not for this[1] and a few other obstacles which, how insufficient separately, collectively taken have for some ages constituted a nearly effectual bar, the lives and fortunes of the male part, the chastity of the female, would be compleatly at the mercy and disposal of the ruling few.

By a Noble Lord, an Honourable Gentleman, and a Gentleman in a way to become Honourable, an ordinary gun would be employed upon all vulgars who stood in the way of his pleasure in any shape with as little hesitation or difficulty as at present upon those who stand in the way of his pleasure in the shape of field sports: in every such distinguished person would be to be seen a Miguel and a Constantine.[2]

A learned Judge on his part, looking round from [his] country [seat],[3] would make observation of the instances on which the [regularity][4] of his demesne was interrupted by the intrusion of this or that village Naboth. By a motion of course the irregularity would be obliterated, and with as little difficulty, should the peasant have proved troublesome, the lot of Naboth would be his.[5] The head of a wolf (learned Judges know how) would be sat upon his shoulders:[6] and the sooner the wolf is [in] the appropriate manner disposed of, so much the better for sheep, not forgetting the shepherd. To effect this or any other desirable transplantation would but cost one fiction more in addition to so many others already established for congenial purposes and with congenial effects.

Of the female sex, the whole of the desirable portion would constitute a Harem of which Noble Lords, Honorable Gentlemen, Gentlemen in a way to become Honorable, and Learned Judges would be Tenants in common. Tenants in common in the first instance, unless and untill by a writ of partition, or a partition by treaty without writ,

---

[1] i.e. 'this imperfect separation of the interests' of the ruling few and subject many, as per marginal summary.

[2] Presumably Maria Evarist Miguel (1802–66), usually known as Dom Miguel, usurper of the Portugueze throne 1828–34, and Constantine Pavlovich (1779–1831), Grand Duke and Cesarevich of Russia, *de facto* ruler of Poland from 1815, both notorious for their personal excesses.

[3] MS 'their country seats'.

[4] MS 'regularly'.

[5] King Ahab coveted the vineyard of Naboth, which was near to his palace, but Naboth refused to sell or exchange it. Ahab's wife, Jezebel, then arranged the execution of Naboth, allowing Ahab to take possession of the vineyard. See 1 Kings 21: 1–16.

[6] The maxim applied to outlaws was *Utlagatus est quasi extra legem positus: caput gerit lupinum*, i.e. 'An outlaw is, as it were, placed outside the law: he bears the head of the wolf'. According to *Coke on Littleton*, 128b, until the reign of Edward III, this had been taken to mean that an outlaw might be put to death by any man as he would a wild beast, but thereafter such killing had been declared to be unlawful. Where the outlaw had been charged with treason or felony, he forfeited his whole estate, real and personal, to the Crown.

[or] by an equitable adjustment such as the Equity Judges in their wisdom might approve, a separation shall have been made—a separation the probable terms of which are not on this occasion necessary to be ascertained.

Mere satire, extravagance, unground[ed], arbitrary, licentious, uncandid, etc.: to the supposition here brought to view, can any such epithets of reprobation with reason and justice be applied? Not they indeed. Fable, no part of it: history, all of it.

Wolf-head transplanting practice.

First as the sort of conquests made by learned Judges by so simple an expedient as the clapping of a wolf-head on the shoulders of whatever landholder was destined to be vanquished. This in the reign of Henry the 6[th.1] was *practice*: so, by a Statute of that [reign][2] we are informed. Not being such perfect admirers of practice in those days as in these, Honorable Gentlemen and Noble Lords, it appears, objected to this. By His Majesty in Parliament intimation was accordingly given that the continuance of this practice would not be approved of.[3] As for anything in the shape of punishment or so much as removal of the Judges of those good old times for the obtainment of land on this false pretence, it was no more in the order of things than would now be the calling Lord Tenterden in question for the impunity given by him to his partner in the profit of the transaction, the learned Tipstaff, who, with the Table of allowed fees before his eyes, confessed the having taken almost the double of it: as to which see *Indications respecting Lord Eldon*, § [XII].[4]

Next as to the precedent for the establishment of the Harem. Not being so generally known as the Metamorphoses for the knowledge of which we are indebted to Ovid,[5] the wolf-head leger-de-main required proof. Of the Harem-authorizing precedent so extensive is the notoriety, a simple allusion will in this case suffice. Howsoever it may be with Christianity, the feudal system beyond all dispute is part and parcel of the law of England. Under that system, if not to an all-comprehensive, at any rate to a considerably wide extent, the first night of a tenant's bride was numbered among the subject-matters of vested rights.

At present, such has been the disregard shewn [to] these matchless, invaluable privileges, not only has the exercise of them been

---

[1] Henry VI (1421–71), King of England from 1422 to 1461.
[2] MS 'year'.
[3] See 6 Hen. VI, c.1, which was confirmed by 8 Hen. VI, c.10 and 10 Hen. VI, c.6.
[4] MS blank. See pp. 231–7 above.
[5] The *Metamorphoses* of Ovid (43BC–AD17) were a collection of mythological stories about transformations, including those of men and women who became animals.

subjected [to] a limitation by the circumstance of colour, but to enable himself to enjoy the benefit of them, a gentleman, howsoever worshipful, must confine himself to this or that particular spot in another hemisphere.[1]

By grievances thus afflictive a reflecting mind can not but be thrown back to those times of antient wisdom in which, by the hardness of them, the powers of learned Doctors of Physic had been subjected to so restrictive a limitation as that which was imposed by a prohibition to dissect bodies until the life had left them: *pro duritie temporum ubi vivos homines dissecare non licet.*[2]

This is not yet enough. Under the cover, and for the benefit, of the same learned fraternity, with its Noble and Right Honorable and Honorable members and allies, with their exertions for its efficient cause, it is that all approach to any thing like a[n] acquaintance with that rule of action, for the non-observance of which the subject many are punished and otherwise afflicted in an endless variety of ways, has been rendered and kept physically impossible; and by the blessing of God, as drawn down upon the nation by Reverend, Right Reverend and Most Reverend Divines, will be kept in that state so long as the blessing inflicted on the nation of matchless constitution continues to be enjoyed by it.

Be the subject what it may, to its being known a condition precedent is—its possession of existence. This attribute, the determination is, that to an infinite portion of its extent it never shall be in possession of. Ductility by proper hands being a quality regarded as indispensable, fictitiousness, a quality of a secondary nature admirably suited to the purpose of such ductility, is accordingly secured, and by God's blessing for ever, by this all-regulating rule. 'That which you assert to be true, namely the existence of an imaginary being which you call Common Law, is to your own full knowledge contrary to truth.' This is what to every learned gentleman may with undisputable truth be said by any unlearned individual. But by this consideration will any learned Gentleman be ever stopped either from appealing to this imaginary standard, or from trumpeting forth the excellence of it? No: not till general and public indignation puts effrontery to shame, and mendacity to silence.[3]

[1] Bentham seems to suggest that the *jus primae noctis* had been limited to slaveowners in the West Indies: however it is unlikely that such a right ever existed at all under feudal law.

[2] i.e. 'on account of the harshness of the times when it is not permitted to dissect living men'. Bentham perhaps had in mind a quotation from Celsus, *De Medicina*, Prooemium, 74–5: 'Incidere autem vivorum corpora et crudele et supervacuum est, mortuorum discentibus necessarium', i.e. 'But to lay open the bodies of men whilst still alive is as cruel as it is needless, that of the dead is a necessity for learners'.

[3] The following sentence appears in the margin at this point, but it is unclear where it should

Of this state of the rule [of] action—this state in which it stands placed by the substitution of fees to salary on the occasion of re-muneration for official service in the judiciary department—in a word by the fee-gathering system—[the result is] that not only to the subject many, but even to the very authors of the evil themselves, the ruling few, security by virtue of the law is for every thing dear to man an empty name. Yet such on the nature of men is the effect of the possession of power—that rather than part with the pleasure of hold-ing others in a state of greater torment, they choose to remain in a similar state of torment themselves. To turn their eyes to the evil, for the purpose of remedy, would require trouble: to turn their eyes from the evil requires none.

§8. *Reprobation of the fee system by the*
Account Commission *of 1780 to 1787*

So much for principles. Now for inferences deduced by authority from practice: authority, that of the Commissioners of Accounts: Commis-sion dated | | 1780.[a] Of Reports, three Volumes: published Vol. I. A°· 1783; Vol. II. A°· 1785; Vol. III. A°· 1787.[1]

[a] For the existence of this instrument of economy and security against abuse, the community was indebted to the then Earl of Shelburne, afterwards first Marquis of Lansdowne.[2] '*Accounts can not be too public*' is an aphorism inserted by him, in the course of his too short Premiership, into the King's Speech.[3] Having in early youth a distinguished place in the perfect favour of George the third, this was one use he made of it. For throughout the whole field of legislation his affections were on the side of the subject many: in one word, he was a radical. Throughout, and in particular in relation to economy, he was what Edmund Burke pretended to be. That, in this part of the field, Burke was an impostor—a purposed betrayer of the cause he pretended to advocate—is shewn in the tract N°· [V][4] intituled *Defence of Economy against*

be inserted in the text: 'Still better than a rule which nobody can sufficiently understand, is a rule which any body whose place is among the select can make on each occasion into a shape which best suits his purpose.'

[1] The three-volume edition of the Reports used by Bentham has not been traced.

[2] In notes to himself, Bentham queried the accuracy of this statement: '☞ Consult the *Annual Register* of 1782, 1783 for the day of commencement and d°· of termination of Shelburne's Premiership.

'☞ Quere as to this. Though this *publication* was A°· 1783 during Shelburne's administration, the year when this Commission was instituted was 3 years earlier—viz. 1780.'

The Commission on Public Accounts was in fact instituted in 1780 during North's administra-tion (1770–82), when Shelburne was in opposition. Shelburne however, during his brief ministry from July 1782 to April 1783, did actively pursue measures of administrative and financial reform.

[3] See *Commons Journals*, xxxix. 4, for the King's Speech on 5 December 1782 at the opening of the 1782–3 session: 'Matters of Account can never be made too public.'

[4] MS blank.

Here follow certain extracts, being all those which have for their subject-matter remuneration in the shape of fees. Nothing can be more decided than the condemnation there passed upon this mode. On no occasion does the field of observation extend beyond one department—that department some branch of the financial. But unless some specific reason can be assigned to the contrary, the observation may without much danger of error be regarded as applying alike to all.[a]

Sympathetic intercourse between suitor and functionary, corruptive and detrimental to the interest of the public.

Vol. III. pp. 187. 188.[1] With whatever strictness a line of conduct under these circumstances may be watched, it behoves, as a primary precaution, to fix the mode of Reward upon the purest foundation. The practice of allowing the officer to be paid by the Merchant, for the performance of Official Business, appears to be repugnant to that maxim. It occasions an intercourse unfit and dangerous, and brings them into a mutual relation, in which they should never stand. Habits of pecuniary obligation or Exchange of

Burke.[2] Edmund Burke being the organ, and in respect of talent and acquirements the grand support, of the particular and sinister interest of the ruling few, Whigs as well as Tories, and Shelburne not having in either House any party for his support, and moreover, in advocating the interest of the subject many, in effect counteracting the particular and sinister interest of the ruling one—a truth of which George the third could not fail to have sooner or later a perception—the fall of the only friend the people ever had in that situation was a speedy and necessary consequence. In the House of Commons he was outvoted:[3] and the subject many, for supporting whose cause he was sacrificed, were not at that time far enough advanced in moral strength to give him their support.

[a] In the reprinting of these extracts the order pursued is—what may be termed the logical order: namely that which presented itself as best adapted to the purpose of conception: the preference being given to this order as compared with the chronological order, as deduced from the consideration of the times at which it happened to the general observations to be called forth by particular branches of the subject-matter. Those which here follow in the first place, occupy the last place in the Official work, and present accordingly the result of the reflections in their matured state.[4]

---

[1] These extracts are from the Fifteenth Report (January 1787): see *Commons Sessional Papers of the Eighteenth Century*, xlv. 67–8.

[2] See pp. 39–94 above.

[3] Shelburne resigned after two defeats in the House of Commons, on 17 and 21 February 1783, on the peace treaties he had negotiated to end the American War of Independence.

[4] On the corresponding marginal summary sheet (UC cxii. 251), Bentham re-arranged the order of these extracts. The original order however has been retained. The extracts are in the hand of a copyist; Bentham added marginal summaries, which are here used as headings to the extracts. There are some minor inaccuracies in the rendering of the extracts: more substantial discrepancies are recorded in editorial footnotes.

private Interest, ought not to mingle with the execution of such Public Duty.—The subsistence of the Officer who collects Revenue, should in no wise depend upon the person who contributes. . . .

The fee is incapable of being made variable in its quantum according to the value of the service.

It is not to be overlooked, that the Fee has in itself an inherent Defect. That method of payment can not be so adjusted as to bear exact proportion to the value of the subject which it affects. The fee is a given sum paid upon a certain Document, or for a certain service: whether it be upon an entry, or by the Package, or Tale, or such like measure, the different value of the goods does not produce any corresponding variation in the Fee. And this is not barely a speculative imperfection: it has hurtful consequences. We have it in evidence, that orders, when but to small amount, have been very frequently left unexecuted on account of the heaviness of the Fees which must have been paid upon them: and further, that these orders, there was great reason to believe, were thereby diverted into the channels of Foreign Trade.

Throughout the Customs, fees and gratuities ought to be abolished.

We are accordingly of opinion, that every payment by Fee or Gratuity, or in any shape whatsoever, by the Merchant or others to the Officer, for or on account of business done in the discharge of his official duty, ought to be abolished throughout the whole department of the Customs; and that the reward of the Officer (except in what arises from seizures) should be by salary alone.

All fees ought to be abolished.

Vol. I. p. 111. 112.[1] Fees[2] of every kind should be suppressed and totally abolished. . . .

Gratuities. At the charge of the suitors, custom swells them into fees.

The remaining head is that of gratuities: a species of Emolument very liable to Abuse: It may be a Reward for Civility, Favour, or extra service: it may be also the Purchase of undue Preference, Expedition, and, in some cases, of Procrastination: flowing, at first, from the Liberality of Opulence, the Ostentation of Vanity, or the design of cunning, it very soon assumes the name of Custom, and becomes a claim, submitted to, to avoid the imputation of

---

[1] These extracts are from the Sixth Report (February 1782): see ibid., xli. 267–8.
[2] Sixth Report 'all Poundage Fees'.

meanness, and frequently to the great inconvenience of contracted circumstances:

So, at the charge of the public.

nor is it confined to individuals only; the Public pay their share: In the payments out of the deductions of Twelve pence in the pound, there are two articles, making six hundred fifty three pounds twelve shillings and eight pence, distributed by the Paymaster General of the Forces in Gratuities: The Public voice unites with that of Individuals, in demanding a suppression of a species of Emolument so easily perverted to purposes injurious to the Interest of both.

By fees, functionary interested in making delay: delay a necessary and actual consequence.

. . . . During the time the Treasurer or Paymaster General has continued in office, not one of his year's accounts has ever been made up; and it has been the Interest of the officers not to make them up: if they had, it must have been considered as part of their official Business, and paid for by their yearly emoluments; but by delaying it for ten or fifteen years, they crave, on the ground of custom, and obtain of the Treasury, a special allowance for this business, as for extra service they were not bound to perform.

Fees in a special instance reprobated.

Vol. II. p. 78.[1] The proper payment for this Clerk is a salary only. The acceptance of any Fee, Gratuity, or other Reward, ought to be strictly prohibited.

Honor of government etc.

It is not for the honor of Government that his Majesty's Bounty should be curtailed by Gratuities and Fees of Office: no part is to be intercepted: it should pass to the Object as liberally and as entire as it flows from the Royal Beneficence.

Greatest happiness principle.

Vol. II. p. 134.[2] The principle which gives existence to and governs every public office, is the Benefit of the State. . . .

---

[1] These extracts are from the Tenth Report (July 1783): see *Commons Sessional Papers of the Eighteenth Century*, xlii. 154.
[2] These and the following extracts are from the Eleventh Report (December 1783): see ibid., xliii. 26 and 27 respectively.

Public interest paramount to private.

The officer has Powers delegated to him necessary for the Execution: but he has no other right than to the reward of his Labour: He has no right to any specific quantity of business: that quantity must fluctuate according to circumstances, or may be regulated by the convenience of the State.

Public interest paramount to private.

Vol. II. p. 135. Hence, in every proposed official Regulation, the advantage or disadvantage of the officer can never be properly a subject of Discussion; the only question is, whether the necessity or good of the State actually requires it?

One fixt Salary alone should be substituted to all partial salaries, fees and gratuities.

Vol. II. p. 186.[1] The profits of the Auditors of the Imprest rise in proportion to the increase of the Public Distress. Upon these reasons we ground our opinion that the Public Good requires that all Fees and Gratuities in the Office of the Auditors of the Imprest should be forthwith abolished; that the Profits of the auditors themselves should be reduced to a reasonable standard: and that every officer and Clerk in the said office should be paid, by the public, a certain fixed annual salary, in proportion to his Rank and Employment, in lieu of all Salaries, Fees and Gratuities whatsoever:

Vested rights should not *be* withstanding.

And we continue to adhere to the opinion we have stated in our last Report, seeing no reason to depart from it, That no Right is vested in the Auditor, either by the Letters Patent by which he holds his office, or by usage, that can be opposed to this Reduction and Regulation.

Payment by fees is capable of being made an instrument of delay or undue dispatch, therefore ought to be abolished.

Vol. II. p. 184. The allowance of the Auditor being necessary to every article both of the Receipt and Expenditure, the State of the account, as between the Public and the accountant, must continue unknown until the Balance is ascertained by the Auditor at the completion of his Examination: and consequently, that Balance, however great it may be, if in favour of the Public,

---

[1] These and the following extracts are from the Twelfth Report (June 1784): see ibid., xliii. 144–5 and 143 respectively. In the third extract, the italics are Bentham's.

remains with the accountant: if in favour of the accountant, remains with the public, until that period. Hence it may be the *interest* of the accountant *to purchase*, at a high price, either *delay or Expedition* in passing his accounts; and, should an officer be corrupt, the *permission to receive fees and gratuities* is an obvious method to obtain it: and therefore we are of opinion, that the payment of Fees and gratuities by the person accounting, however confined by usage as to the quantum, is a mode ill adapted to the constitution of this Office, and to the Nature of the Business there transacted.

Where abuse is probable, reform should not wait actual instances. Prevention is better than cure.

We do not say or mean to insinuate, that we have discovered any instance of such abuse in this Office; but the mode is open to it: and a wise Government does not wait for the mischief: It guards, as far as human prudence can guard, against the possibility of the Evil: it prevents or removes the Temptation.

§9. *Complaints of the fee system in British India by the Grand Jury of Calcutta*[1]

§10. *Causes of the attachment to the fee system, no proof of its aptitude. Origin of the practice*

The arrangement being thus pernicious, quere—to the influence of what causes may the prevalence of it be ascribed?
Answers.
1. Sinister interest.
2. Vague conception of economy produced by narrow views.
3. Application made of the *Imitation principle*—subject-matter of imitation, the practice of antient and relatively different times.[2]
[1.] Cause the 1st. Sinister interest: seat of it, the breasts of all those on whose power the choice between this mode of remuneration and that by salary has all along depended. To such a degree have the existence and the potency of this cause been brought to view, as above, that nothing further in relation to it under this head [will] be, it is supposed, looked for as needful.

---

[1] No material on this topic appears to have been written: the title is taken from the plan at UC cxii. 245 (12 June 1828). Bentham's source of information respecting the controversy in Calcutta over legal fees (see his note at UC cxii. 262) was 'Letter of General News from Bengal', published in the *Oriental Herald*, vol. vii, no. liv (June 1828), 548–53, especially 552–3.
[2] Bentham does not go on to consider this third cause.

2. Cause the 2$^{d.}$ Vague conception of economy produced by narrow views.

Seeing an office to which acceptance is given, of the remuneration attached to it, salary or other allowances attached to it at the expence of government—that is to say of the national fund—not making any part, a man concludes that to the *public* the whole of the remuneration in that shape, paid and received, is so much saved.

Seeing another office in which the remuneration is composed in part of salary, in part of fees, he forms the correspondent inference.

True: if the individuals, the *suitors*, formed not, any one of them, any part of the *public*, and if while salary [had]^{1} no innate tendency to encrease, so neither had self-remuneration by fees.

But, on every occasion the interest of individuals in general, and thence of suitors in particular, should (it may be said) give way to, and in a word be *sacrificed* to, that of the public at large.

True: upon each occasion, if necessary that one or other should be sacrificed, it is the lesser interest that ought to be sacrificed to the greater, not the greater to the lesser: but where the case is such that both may be promoted, neither sacrificed, this is the course which the greatest happiness principle, and the principles of arithmetic when employed under it, concurr in dictating.

The case in which both interests together are promoted, neither sacrificed, is that in which at the expence of the more extensive, the public interest, out of its profit from the arrangement, compensation fully adequate—rather more than equivalent—is given to the private, the less extensive interest, for the loss sustained by it from that same arrangement.

In so far as the quantities can be ascertained, in compensation for the loss, more rather than less than the exact amount of it should be given to the less extensive interest. Why?—Answer. Because, from the arrangement in question profit is, by the supposition, made by the more extensive interest: and, while by one of two parties profit is made, why profit should not at the same time be made by the other, let him say who regards himself as able.

Supposing both parties alike free, such is the arrangement which, on exhibition and collision of the two interests, would naturally be the result: and wherever power interferes, and comes to be exercised by an all-powerful party over a party incapable of making resistance, the turn of the scale should rather be in favour of the weaker party: lest in the minds of the similarly situated, the sense of security should be shaken, and thence to a proportionable amount the evil of the 2$^{d.}$

---

^{1} MS 'has'.

order (to wit danger and alarm) be produced: that evil—in the avoidance of which may be seen the sole though so amply sufficient reason for securing to every man the possession of, and benefit from, whatever is his own.

Take on each occasion out of the universal fund the quantity of the matter of good requisite to be made over to the functionary, to operate in remuneration of the service on that occasion rendered [by][1] him,—take this course, the conditions above-mentioned are observed: in the burthen of remuneration the suitor in question bears his proportionate and apt share, and from the particular service which on the individual occasion in question he receives the benefit of, he receives the especial benefit which it happens to him to stand in need of.

Under despotic sway, the feelings of individuals form an object too minute to be capable of attracting the regards of the high-seated personages by whom their destiny is disposed of: it is by some vague conception of public good, that is to say the good of the ruling one and the ruling few, that their opinions and conduct are directed: if not their opinions as entertained, at any rate their opinions as professed and expressed.

In France under the *ancien* regime, when by government land belonging to individuals was taken for the purpose of being converted into a public road, it was for individual losers all of them to reconcile themselves to the loss as they could: to make compensation for the loss was too minute for royal dignity.

Scarcely less effectually beneath the dignity of the Monarch is the care of justice in England than in France. When a criminal suffers the punishment allotted to his crime—when for robbery for example a man is hanged—satisfaction is thereby made to the Monarch for the affront put by it upon his royal dignity: and moreover whatsoever property, if any, belonged to the criminal takes its course into the pocket of the said Monarch or of those to whom he has been pleased to grant the product of this forfeiture. Well, but the individual robbed—who, having suffered this loss, is moreover by this same law saddled with the burthen, personal, temporal and pecuniary, of prosecuting to conviction and delivering evidence. What, to this doubly injured individual, nothing in the way of satisfaction? Oh no: needless, according to Blackstone, is justice in any such shape. Why needless? because (says he) the satisfaction to the public is so very great.[2]

---

[1] MS 'to'.

[2] See Blackstone, *Commentaries on the Laws of England*, iv. 6: 'In . . . gross and atrocius injuries the private wrong is swallowed up in the public: we seldom hear any mention made of satisfaction to the individual; the satisfaction to the community being so very great.'

Ere as yet from the Bar the learned Judge had stept up to the Bench, had it occurred to his several Clients to pay into the Royal treasury the fees employed in remuneration of his professional services instead of delivering them into the hands of his Clerk, would this arrangement have to his feelings been a satisfactory one? Be this as it may, it would have been still more flagrantly hostile to justice than in the other case.

In whatever place you see *dignity*, especially dignity in company with crown—in a word royal dignity, think not in that place to see justice.

Thus again in the case of costs. Payment of costs is beneath royal dignity: so moreover to receive them. The word *dignity*, a word which follows the word crown and the word *royal*, constituted in the mind of Blackstone a compleat justification for whatever arrangement he saw his convenience in hanging it to.[1]

The case is of the number of those in which an accusation or other demand made in a course of judicial enquiry has by the competent authority been pronounced ungrounded, and, by reason of the burthen cast on the defendant in the shape of expence and vexation, injurious. For this infliction, were the wrongdoer an individual, he would, in so far as able, be compelled (such at least is what is professed) to make compensation such as is regarded, or professed to be regarded, as adequate. But instead of being an individual, and as such under the law, being the ruling one, and as such above the law, no compensation—not a tittle of satisfaction in any shape—will he make. No, nor ought he (declares Blackstone in the lesson of morality delivered to young Students). No, nor ought he. Indeed why need he? For as the God which is in heaven is unable to committ sin, so is his Vicegerent here upon earth under the correspondent and godlike incapacity of doing wrong.[2] Under the like incapacity is the weathercock—under the like incapacity of going against the wind. Why? because whithersoever the wind turns, the weathercock turns along with it.

According to the congenial and corresponding notion entertained concerning justice or, what is still more amiable if not respectable, *Equity*, neither does his Majesty receive costs: for this too is beneath his royal dignity. Beneath this same dignity to receive from the maleficent compensation for this part of the evil produced by their maleficence? Why so! Beneath this same dignity it never is to receive

---

[1] Ibid., iii. 400: 'The king (and any person suing to his use) shall neither pay, nor receive costs: for . . . as it is his prerogative not to pay them to a subject, so it is beneath his dignity to receive them.'

[2] For Blackstone on the maxim 'The King can do no wrong' see ibid., i. 238–41.

money to the utmost amount capable of being exacted from individuals to whom no maleficence in any shape is so much as imputed.

These are among the *arcana imperii*.[1] But the time for pervulgation is now come.

[1.] First as to the needlessness of satisfaction to any party wronged by the loss, coupled with the needfulness of it to the party by whom no wrong, no loss, had been sustained.

Dulcis odor lucri ex re qualibet.[2]

Under the advice and by the hands of English lawyers, this maxim, ascribed to a Roman Emperor, has at all [times] and upon the largest scale been established, avowed and acted upon for the benefit of English Monarchs (themselves not forgotten) by English lawyers. No laystall so foul that to extract money out of it the lawyers scrupled to rake into it. By means of the law of forfeitures so assiduously and fondly cultivated by Chancellor York, profit to the common father was made to grow out of the loss to his beloved children: the sever[er] the loss on the one part, the richer the profit on the other. Crimes were accordingly sown—sown by the hand of this common father—sown that forfeitures might be reaped.[3]

By the hand of the *par nobile fratrum*[4]—Empson and Dudley,[5] the reign, nor that a short one, of the only Monarch who had not been prodigal (for Elizabeth was a Queen)[6] was employed in this mode of culture. Employed, and with such success, as sufficed to render Henry the seventh the richest of all Monarchs by whom society was ever afflicted; and to enable his son and successor to be the most profuse: extending to immovables the rapine exercised by his father

---

[1] i.e. 'secrets of empire'. See Tacitus, *Histories*, I. iv (here 'imperii arcano'), and *Annals*, II. xxxv.

[2] Presumably a misrendering of Juvenal, *Satires*, xiv. 204–5: 'lucri bonus est odor ex re qualibet', i.e. 'the smell of gain is good whatever the thing from which it comes'. Juvenal does not, however, ascribe the maxim to an Emperor, as Bentham suggests, but to a father advising his son.

[3] Philip Yorke, first Baron and first Earl of Hardwicke, Lord Chancellor 1737–56, had been responsible for an Act of 1744 (17 Geo. II, c.39) by which correspondence with the sons of the Pretender had been declared to be high treason, and the punishment of corruption of blood, which would otherwise have lapsed on the death of the Pretender, extended to the time of the death of the sons of the Pretender. As Lord High Steward, Hardwicke had presided at the trials of the rebel Jacobite lords in 1746–7, and had then been responsible for the legislation by which the forfeited estates were annexed immediately to the Crown without the usual inquisitions (20 Geo. II, c.41).

[4] i.e. 'famous pair of brothers'. Horace, *Satires*, II. iii. 243.

[5] Sir Richard Empson (c.1450–1510) and Edmund Dudley (1462?-1510), agents of Henry VII (1457–1509), King of England from 1485, for whom, it was claimed, they amassed a vast sum of coin and bullion through extortion. On his accession, Henry VIII (1491–1547), King of England from 1509 and King of Ireland from 1541, in the face of a popular outcry, committed Empson and Dudley to the Tower, and subsequently executed them for treason.

[6] Elizabeth I (1533–1603), Queen of England and Ireland from 1558.

upon moveable property: and in so doing, and for the purpose of so doing, planting the reformation and begetting upon the Church of Rome the richest and most illustrious of all her daughters, the Church of England.

2. Secondly as to the not paying costs. It is more blessed (says the most exalted authority) to give than to receive.[1] True. But it is more convenient to receive than to give. Sums equal, it is still more convenient to avoid giving. His Majesty paid no costs: why? because he would not: and his Majesty being Lord of all—Sovereign Lord, means of compelling him to pay money there were none. By compelling others to pay money, he and his got money for themselves: but by compelling themselves or one another to pay money, no money was to be got. By the forfeiture the whole property was already transferred to the proper coffers: without much prejudice to good economy, magnanimity was thus displayed by the forbearance which left untouched each part.

3. Thirdly and lastly, as to the not receiving costs. For abstinence in this form in the case of treason and felony the best reason imaginable had place: and in the good old times, when the star of ancestor wisdom shone brightest, these cases were by far the richest: and were as numerous as industry in the hands of power could cause them to be.[2]

§ 11. *Insufficiency of the conception brought to view in support of the fee system—supposed production of alacrity on the part of the functionary*[3]

---

[1] Acts 20: 35.

[2] In the text, Bentham noted at this point, 'Go on as to inferior causes', but no further material appears to have been written.

[3] No material on this topic appears to have been written: the title is taken from the plan at UC cxii. 245 (12 June 1828).

COLLATIONS

The collations print all variants (including variations in punctuation, spelling, italics and capitalization) between the 1830 edition of *Official Aptitude Maximized; Expense Minimized*, on which the present text is based, and all the published versions of its component Papers which appeared during Bentham's lifetime. The following points should, however, be noted. In the text, double inverted commas indicating quotations are replaced with single inverted commas, and single inverted commas usually indicating quotations within quotations are replaced with double inverted commas: the same convention has been adopted in the collations—consequently where a single quotation mark appears in this collation, the original employs double; and *vice versa*. The variants mentioned in editorial footnotes at the appropriate place in the text are not reproduced in the collations.

In the first column of the collations, the first figure refers to the page number(s), the second figure to line number(s): hence 41, 3 refers to page 41, line 3.

A. EXTRACT FROM
CONSTITUTIONAL CODE COLLATION

Collation: Extract from the proposed Constitutional Code, entitled Official Aptitude Maximized, Expense Minimized. By Jeremy Bentham, Esq. Bencher of Lincoln's Inn. London: MDCCCXVI.

Note. 1826 *Extract* and 1830 are mis-dated MDCCCXVI. In 1830, the title page is bound after the 'Introductory View'. 1826 *Extract* and 1830 give the following publication details on verso of title page: 'London: printed by C.H. Reynell, Broad Street, Golden Square.'

There are no variations in the text of the 'Introductory View'; for variations in Ch.IX, §§15–17 and Supplements see *Constitutional Code*, I (*CW*), pp. 520–8.

B. DEFENCE OF ECONOMY
AGAINST BURKE COLLATION

Collation: Defence of Economy against the late Mr. Burke. By Jeremy Bentham, Esq. *The Pamphleteer*, vol. ix, no. xvii (1817), 3–47.

Note: The following minor variations, based on printing conventions, are not recorded in the collation: (a) variations in the form of footnote markers: 1817 employs suprascript Arabic numerals, 1830 symbols; (b) variations in the section headings: 1817 employs section symbol and Arabic numeral (e.g. §1), and replaces small capital letters with italicized lower-case letters.

39, 3–5	LATE MR. BURKE. BY JEREMY BENTHAM, ESQ. ORIGINAL. 1817.
41, 3	*Honorable*
41, 5	*Honorable*
42, 1	found,
42, 1 *omits note*	
42, 4	seem that
42, 19	any where to recognize; every where
42, 20	profiting,
42, 21	from the
43, 5	for the office,
43, 10	difficult to
43, 22	error or
43, 27	and,
43, 39	any thing
44, 3	loss,
44, 3	Yes:
44, 5	four:
44, 17	another,
44, 23	case and
44, 25	us good your
44, 32	every thing
45, 2	by the rougher
45, 8	any thing,
45, 11	any thing,
45, 13	any thing,
45, 20	1782,
45, 29	most noble son
47, 1	principles,
47, 3	tracts;
49, 1	ECONOMY.
49, 2 *omits*	AGAINST BURKE.
49, 19	colors,

49, 20	splendor
49, 25	shewing
50, 8–9	the intimately connected though antagonizing
50, 28	hands so is it with
50, 34	and,
50, 35	admitted, —
50, 38	favor:
51, 9	favorable
51, 14	unfavorable
51, 18	favorable
51, 22	them in
51, 32	preserved, —
51, 36	(1811.)
51, 37	Dumont under
52, 6	cruize
52, 8	amount seek
52, 11	fact,
52, 18	Principles
52, 19	any thing
52, 20	any thing
52, 26	Lord looking
52, 29	favorites
52, 30	ever have to say
52, 34	honorable
52, 37	*well deserved! well deserved!*
53, 2	honorable
53, 4	shew,
53, 4	alike,
53, 6	orator they
53, 18	*wrestling match*
53, 23	Thus
53, 26	developement
53, 30	3rd—year
53, 34	color,
54, 24	*order,*
54, 33	part,
54, 34	transcendently
55, 3	*public money—what the proper uses*
55, 10	individuals:
55, 23	*honors.'*
55, 26	Dodsley 1780.
56, 16	31 years,
57, 2	honors.'
57, 3	Anne,
57, 3	went,)
57, 19	any thing
57, 24	But,
57, 30	liberties,
57, 31	*Law;*
57, 37	any thing
57, 37	*theory,*

57, 39	which,
58, 3	4,000l.
58, 3	4,000l.
58, 3	12,000l.
58, 6	2,100l.
58, 11	4,000l.
58, 11	2,100l. a year,
58, 11	12,000
58, 16	Honorable
58, 20	2nd,
58, 22	12,000l.
58, 26	settled. V.
58, 26	5.
58, 31	22,624l.,
58, 31	1,500l. a year.' Journals
59, 1	of,)
59, 16	'honorable
59, 20	not.'—
59, 21	dishonorable
59, 21	any thing
59, 31	that,
60, 3	public, understand
60, 4	people, remains
60, 8	(Observations.)
60, 10	that,
60, 21	'honorable
60, 22	imagination as
60, 29	or,
60, 38	favorites
60, 40	favoritism)
61, 1	upon: yes,
61, 7	p. 62.
61, 7	quoted—
61, 11	humanity that
61, 13	compensation,)
61, 14	now,
61, 22	(3rd. Report, p. 126.)
61, 23	only to the
61, 23	words, 'at
61, 29	copy;
61, 31	which,
61, 32	power of
61, 35	taxes, exacted
61, 38	vigor;
61, 41	into,
61, 41	imposer and
61, 41	assembly,
61, 42	share, have
62, 7	justice,
62, 8	otherwise,)
62, 9	Honorable

62, 14	favorites,
62, 15	*honors,*'
62, 17	the
62, 25	Sinecures granted
62, 26	reports
62, 31	Reports:
63, 26–7	Honorable Louisa
63, 27	Honorable Lady
63, 42	84 85—
63, 42	72 p, 280.
63, 43	K.3a K.3b p. 62,
63, 48	1,994l.
63, 48–9	1792. 27th
63, 50	5d a
63, 51	uncertain.' 27th
63, 51	N. 29.
64, 3	record,
64, 5	fixt.
64, 14	*justice* would
64, 20	worked,
64, 21	private,
65, 11	whichever
65, 13	master of the rolls
65, 19	rolls
65, 24	*fees'* is
65, 37	Chancery,
66, 4	In
66, 12–13	Rhetorician's
66, 17	parliament,
66, 23	*money* all
66, 30	*Pensions* some
66, 37	bestowed;—
67, 16	now in
67, 28	power,
68, 2	bestowed.—
68, 26	When
68, 31	Rhetorician)
69, 3	common place
69, 18	honorable
69, 18–19	Rhetorician
69, 22	cut down
69, 30	Honorable
69, 33	York and his honorable
70, 2	that 'purpose;'
70, 24	*have,*
70, 25	dependence,'
70, 27	Crown' (says he)
71, 1	good call
71, 7	requires, that to
71, 8	corruption he
71, 29	Men,

72, 26–7	*favorite* shouldered
72, 31	intolerable.
73, 4	The
73, 15	Townshends,
73, 18	Note)
73, 29	believe),
74, 17	*e* appendages
74, 18	from the
75, 10–11	ejaculation poured
75, 29	object we
76, 6	£4,000
76, 6	£6,000
76, 7	£23,000
76, 7	£38,000
76, 16	do and
77, 2	one 'of
77, 11	But,
77, 28	him,)
77, 36	38,000l.
77, 37	20l.
77, 38	10l.
78, 5	or any sort
78, 12	38,000l.
78, 33	If
78, 34	expence,
79, 3	Proof.—
79, 3	p. 67,)
79, 5	p. 66,)
79, 9	honorable
79, 13	*Observations.*—
79, 14	*(says he)*
79, 16	Tract
79, 24	*services,*'
79, 24	Orator,)
79, 37	application,)
80, 2	takes,)
80, 16	p. 66,)
80, 19	p. 67,)
80, 21	he,)
80, 25	is that,
80, 33	such,
80, 34	*in effect*
80, 36	unhesitating,
81, 21	expence?
81, 29	money,
81, 35	all-comprehensive body of
81, 37	labor
82, 24	before,
82, 37	dont
83, 6	*Comparisons!*
83, 6	and,

83, 7	which,
83, 10	*Unity and Agreement*
83, 13	people,
83, 14	a destruction of
83, 15	casual check
83, 18	said—
83, 24	and, behind
83, 25	peculation should
83, 35 *adds*	*Proposition* 17.
83, 36 *omits*	*Proposition* 17.—
83, 36	The King,
84, 1	p. 67.)
84, 5	'profits,')
84, 6	true,'
84, 6	he,)
84, 9	extravagancies
85, 3	is according
85, 7	wit in
85, 30	*power* with
86, 6	The
86, 20	passage:
86, 33	*law,'* no
86, 37	idea,
87, 5	alledged
87, 7	*unity*, have
87, 19	up?
87, 39	this a sort
88, 2	*mine;*
88, 10	necessity,
88, 10	*self-defence*,
88, 16	plan,
88, 18	any thing
88, 24	Sham-economy,
88, 39	*shew*
89, 2	every body.
89, 5	every thing
89, 6	dramatized,
89, 10	(£60,000
90, 5	future-contingencies,
90, 8	any body
90, 17	*show bread*,
90, 18	temple of corruption—
90, 20	*pension*,
90, 28–9	establishments and
91, 4	After
91, 14	second
91, 26	contracts.
92, 28	auction
92, 29	*smirk*
92, 30	hammer.—
93, 6	Erasmus

93, 13	any thing
93, 14	abhorrence, let
94, 15	any thing
94, 23	regard;

C. DEFENCE OF ECONOMY AGAINST ROSE COLLATION

Collation: Defence of Economy against the Right Hon. George Rose. By Jeremy Bentham, Esq. *The Pamphleteer*, vol. x, no. xx (1817), 281–332.

Note: The following minor variations, based on printing conventions, are not recorded in the collation: (a) variations in the form of footnote markers: 1817 employs suprascript numerals, 1830 symbols; (b) variations in the section headings: 1817 omits section symbol and replaces small capital letters with italicized lower-case letters.

95, 3–4	HON. GEORGE ROSE. BY JEREMY BENTHAM, ESQ. ORIGINAL. LONDON. 1817.
97, 7	Honorable
97, 11	extent,
97, 12–13	occasions in his instance,
97, 28	May 1810.
98, 1–2	ECONOMY, &c. &c.
99, 6	The
99, 10	Britain,
99, 10–11	Honorable Gentleman, (p. 62.) is
99, 16	saving continues he, *we*
100, 26	that,
101, 13	them as
101, 19	*a callus*
101, 28	Honorable
101, 30	you)
101, 36	to'
101, 36	p. 62.)
102, 5	here is—
102, 9	imagine is
102, 9	Honorable
102, 14	then as
102, 14	error;
102, 17	Honorable
102, 20	any thing
102, 25	*extent'*
102, 30	error;
102, 35	Honorable
102, 35	any thing
102, 37	every thing
102, 41	Honorable or Honorable
103, 4	must in the first place impute to him,
103, 11	mixt

103, 15	The next
103, 17	list,'
103, 17	Honorable
103, 18	p. 63.)
103, 21	Something,'
103, 22	favor;
103, 28	Honorable
103, 37	expence
104, 11	place as
104, 13	Honorable
104, 18	made to wit by
104, 19	Honorable
104, 26	families, then it
104, 26	families it
104, 31	Honorable
104, 34–5	profitable,
104, 43	Honorable
105, 1	families satisfied
105, 5	limited, some
105, 9	Honorable
105, 15	Honorable
105, 19	families for
105, 24	Honorable
105, 25	Honorable
105, 29	Honorable
105, 38–9	parochially supported
106, 3	plenty,
106, 6	Honorable
106, 7	families let
106, 10	observation
106, 12	Honorable
106, 14	Scotland,
106, 31	beams upon
106, 31–2	Honorable gentleman.
106, 34	any thing,
107, 4	vigor
107, 6	Honorable
107, 7	any where
107, 7	True:—
107, 10	Honorable
107, 11	candor)
107, 11	favor.'
107, 12	favor,
107, 13	service,
107, 17	E.O.,
107, 17–18	is nobility
107, 18	is respectability
107, 23	disfavor,
107, 26	Rt. Honorable
107, 28	candor
107, 34	1,200*l*.

107, 38	honorable
108, 4	sir:
108, 13	candor
108, 13–14	Honorable Gentleman) must
108, 14	*favor.'*
108, 15	candor
108, 26	Honorable
108, 27	*or*
108, 30	Honorable
108, 37	Honorable
109, 2	'now' *so*
109, 6	third
109, 9	Honorable
109, 16	*indefiniteness,*
109, 21	any thing
109, 35	Honorable
109, 37	Honorable
110, 6	patrimony if
110, 11	The next
110, 15	quoted), 'may
110, 21	Honorable
110, 24	is that
111, 7	Honorable
111, 10	boldly:
111, 20	honor
111, 25	theirs,
111, 31	limits as
111, 36	Honorable
111, 41	Honorable
112, 2	thus, and *then,*
112, 3	Honorable
112, 4	*erotesis;* that
112, 11	Honorable
112, 21	Honorable
112, 22	Honorable
112, 23	Honorable
112, 23	gallant general
112, 29	Burke, 65.
113, 4	Honorable
113, 6	any thing
113, 7	endeavor
113, 14	far this
113, 21	Honorable
113, 21–2	of[a] regularly
113, 24	favorable
113, 27	Honorable
113, 33	p.p.
114, 3	shall from time to time have
114, 18	towards the destroying
114, 20	money received
114, 29	Honorable

114, 34		crown
114, 37		is—
114, 40		§.
115, 3		Honorable
115, 6		Honorable
115, 7		*'reasonable'*—
115, 8		*'politic,'*
115, 13	*omits*	5.
115, 13		fifth
115, 18		he p. 64.)
115, 22		author),
115, 23		indeed),
115, 32		honorable
115, 35		Honorable
115, 36		Honorable
116, 7		Honorable
116, 13		wise?'
116, 13		be it:
116, 16		But,
116, 29		Honorable
116, 34		necessary. What,
117, 1–2		*buying off*
117, 26		plea,
117, 29		Honorable
117, 33		*honors,*
117, 34		Honorable
117, 41		Honourable
117, 43		honorable
118, 8		Honorable
118, 13–14		is, in his eyes, so powerful that
118, 15		de-obstruent
118, 16		removing it:
118, 18		some body or any body,
118, 18		any body
118, 21		*country,'*
118, 35		Honorable
118, 42		Honorable
119, 2		*honorable*
119, 9		Honorable
119, 14–15		who with
119, 16		Honorable
119, 20		*maximum* taking, then,
119, 25		Honorable
119, 28		this, in short,
119, 33		him,
119, 39		Honorable
119, 41		not uow indeed
119, 42		Honorable
120, 3		author'
120, 4		Honorable
120, 11		Such,

120, 12	Honorable
120, 16	Honorable
120, 18–19	Honorable Gentleman's—
120, 22	Honorable
120, 27	Honorable
120, 30	body:
120, 32	Honorable
120, 37–121, 1	Honorable Author,
121, 5	extensive,
121, 8	any thing
121, 9	Honorable
121, 17	Honorable
121, 26	Honorable
121, 32	Honorable
121, 38	man:
121, 39	Honorable Gentleman himself:
122, 5	any thing
122, 9	is—
122, 13	which,
122, 16	himself;
122, 25	gain.'—
122, 26	power (I
122, 37	Explanations.
123, 3	Honorable
123, 5	impossible
123, 6	No:
123, 9	Treasureships!
123, 14	humor
123, 16	laboring
123, 19	Honorable
123, 24	sixth
123, 24	alledged
123, 33	any thing
123, 34	Honorable
123, 37	p. 65.
124, 14	favorable
124, 14	*honors*
124, 16	Honorable
124, 20	laboring
124, 21	one,)
124, 25	*Liverpool*, seing
124, 28	every body
125, 3	Honorable
125, 4	laboring,
125, 6	majesty,
125, 9	Honorable
125, 13	Honorable
125, 18	betrayed,
125, 21	which,
125, 23	laboring
125, 33	say—)

125, 34	Honorable
126, 4	pensions;'
126, 5	condition,
126, 8	'and consequently,
126, 9	dispute:
126, 13	in this his 66th page,
126, 19	them, (and
126, 27–8	I am, I,
127, 8	Honorable
127, 12	Honorable
127, 25	Honorable
127, 32	Honorable
128, 3	*Perceval*,
128, 4	Honorable,
128, 8	Honorable
128, 12	it if
128, 19	a-year,
128, 28	seventh
128, 31	Honorable
129, 2	every thing)
129, 5	but,
129, 10	come,
129, 12	Honorable
129, 22	*for*':
129, 26	Honorable
129, 29	need,
129, 31	Honorable
129, 32	candor
130, 3	yet, —
130, 4	implication, —
130, 9	which,'
130, 10	without a liberal
130, 14	any thing
130, 16	Honorable
130, 17–18	*debtor and creditor*,
130, 19–20	any thing
130, 28	Honorable
130, 33	Honorable
130, 40	unlawfully,
130, 41	seats,)—
131, 4	then,
131, 7	Honorable
131, 16	any body
131, 22	any thing
131, 27	society,'
131, 28	Honorable
131, 32	*Commons*:
131, 35	not, (so
132, 2	*dignity*. Having this dignity;
132, 4	*Dignity*—such,
132, 4	higher species

132, 8	Honorable
132, 11	Honorable
132, 11–12	Honorable
132, 18	Immediately
132, 19	ascertainment of
132, 23	Honorable
132, 24	expenditure, (private expenditure),
132, 25	Honorable
132, 27	he) 'who was,[a]
132, 29	honorable
132, 37	p. 67.
133, 4	Honorable
133, 8	one:
133, 10	comprized
133, 24	Honorable
133, 30	mass, amount not mentioned, of
133, 33	Honorable
133, 34	is that
133, 34	*'honorable'*
133, 36	expences
134, 1	Honorable
134, 4–5	*dishonor*
134, 34	Honorable
134, 36	imitation;—for
134, 38	offices, an
134, 40	Honorable
135, 7	*honorable,*
135, 10	*honorable:*
135, 12	*honorable*
135, 14	*'necessity,'*
135, 15	Honorable
135, 16	convenience that
135, 17	same being
135, 19	Honorable
135, 23	thought),
135, 33	5,032l. 11s. 0d.
135, 35	6,930 6 1
135, 36	select
136, 1	Honorable
136, 3	*'parsimony;'*
136, 12	description,—
136, 13	intriguer:—
136, 16	and, nobly,
136, 16	heroically,
136, 19	Honorable
136, 26	any thing
136, 28	Honorable
136, 28	person,—
136, 29	honor,
136, 30	supply,—
136, 33	any where

137, 2	*necessity,'*
137, 4	Honorable
137, 8	annext
137, 24	Honorable
137, 28	8,000*l.*
138, 2	loath
138, 8	endeavor
138, 9–10	was in the Duke's case actually
138, 11	failed is
138, 16	supply:—
138, 29	any thing
138, 31	any thing
139, 3	ministers
139, 9–10	Honorable
139, 11	done,—
139, 11	encouraged,—
139, 25	Honorable
139, 26	Honorable,
139, 27	Honorable
139, 30	Honorable
139, 31	Honorable, Honorable,
139, 34	situations?—one
139, 37	ministers.
140, 14	*contracts,* assistance
140, 15	things in
140, 19	5,000*l.*
140, 22	*that* may
140, 23	*seats* for
141, 8	Honorable
141, 8	Honorable and Honorable
141, 12	*ministers*
142, 13	Honorable Panegyrist:
142, 18	Honorable
142, 28	On
142, 28	Honorable
143, 3	things,
143, 9	Honorable
143, 11–12	Honorable Accountant multiplied
143, 13	arithmetic are
143, 21	understand,
143, 26	Honorable
143, 30	his,
143, 32	candor
143, 33	Honorable
144, 6	considering,
144, 6	Honorable
144, 13	Honorable
144, 14	avoided—
144, 15	his,
144, 16	aim:
144, 17	are that

144, 19	this,
144, 21	manner,
144, 26	p. 60:
144, 27	publication,' 'In
144, 33	Honorable
144, 36	(p. 62.)
145, 2	Honorable
145, 9	(p. 74.)
145, 9	Honorable
145, 10	favored
145, 12–13	are? Because
145, 15	what?
145, 17	Honorable
145, 19	it,
145, 20	no
145, 23	all this delicacy,
145, 28	persuasion,
145, 30	developement
145, 37	activity, (p. 66.)
146, 4	Honorable
146, 6	(p. 61.)
146, 15	Honorable, who in
146, 16	favor
146, 19	mind,
146, 21	received
146, 26	favor
146, 29	him,
146, 29–30	Solicitor-general,
146, 35	(p. 66.)
146, 36	(p. 66.)
146, 38	argument, they could, for a moment,
147, 1	any thing
147, 2	would one
147, 7	Before
147, 8	endeavoring
147, 9	Honorable
147, 15	reader,
147, 22	Honorable
147, 24	Pitt.
147, 25	us p. 25.) . . .
148, 1	savings . . . . . and
148, 5–6	measures . . . . in
148, 6	lotteries . . . . . proceeding
148, 14	Honorable
148, 16	(p. 34.)
148, 19	reign for
148, 20	but in
148, 24	made,
148, 30	Anne.
148, 31	crown
148, 32	1,500*l*.,

411

148, 33–4	2,228*l*., a year. Journals, vol. xxv.
149, 2	favorable
149, 5	4000*l*.
149, 12	*favor*
149, 14	treasury
149, 26	Honorable
149, 29	But
149, 37	mode,
149, 38	C.75.
150, 7	survey, ... made
150, 11–12	Honorable Gentleman endeavors
150, 12	(p. 35.)—is that
150, 13	can . . . . take
150, 13	favor
150, 18	*perjury* the
150, 31	are,
150, 33	*viva voce*,
150, 34	cross examination:
151, 2	Honorable Gentleman endeavors
151, 3	argument
151, 5	surprize
151, 23	one side,
151, 24	some how
151, 32–3	which with
151, 38–9	favorable
151, 39	accommodation let any one who
151, 40	loss,
152, 3	*saving*—
152, 4	acquisition—
152, 7	(p. 37.),
152, 9	members
152, 12–13	minister's favor.'
152, 17	correct,
152, 20	can not
152, 22	change for
152, 26	Honorable
152, 26	*members*
152, 30	present:
152, 31–2	Honorable arguer
152, 32–3	Honorable or Right Honorable
153, 5	Honorable
153, 11	Honorable
153, 13	exist, *at bottom*,
153, 15	Honorable
153, 18	Honorable
153, 23	favorable
153, 30	price,—
153, 31	success in
154, 4	*without-doors*,
154, 5	Honorable
154, 6	voyage Economy

154, 7	*lands* she
154, 15–16	Honorable
154, 21	Honorable
154, 28	Honorable author,
154, 29	p. 35.)
154, 31	directed,
154, 32	knowing,
154, 37	to,
154, 37	Honorable and Right Honorable
154, 39	boys,
154, 40–1	*crown*, and of whom, certain *sceptics*,
154, 43	hero—there can not
155, 1	existence,—
155, 1–2	this as on so many
155, 5	submit:—

D. OBSERVATIONS ON PEEL'S SPEECH COLLATION

Collation: Observations on Mr. Secretary Peel's House of Commons Speech, 21st March, 1825, introducing his Police Magistrates' Salary Raising Bill. Date of Order for Printing, 24th March, 1825. Also on the Announced Judges' Salary Raising Bill, and the Pending County Courts Bill. By Jeremy Bentham. London: Published by John and H.L. Hunt, Tavistock Street, Covent Garden. M.DCCC.XXV.

Note: Both 1825A and 1830 contain the following printer's imprint on the verso of the title page: 'London: printed by C.H. Reynell, Broad Street, Golden Square.'

157 *adds*	BY JEREMY BENTHAM. LONDON: PUBLISHED BY JOHN AND H.L. HUNT, TAVISTOCK STREET, COVENT GARDEN. M.DCCC.XXV.
182, 15	few eaves.
187, 7	day, carried
190, 17	fie, fie,
190, 20	and though
195, 25	think,
196, 22	Establishment,
197, 15–16	which in
197, 16	elsewhere has
198, 6	endeavours such
200, 34	police magistrate
200, 2nd col., 37	told that
201, 11–12	the importance ones
202, 26	justice of the peace,

Collation: Observations on Mr. Secretary Peel's House of Commons Speech, 21st March, 1825, introducing his Police Magistrates' Salary Raising Bill. Date of order for printing, 24th March, 1825. Also on the Announced Judges' Salary Raising Bill, and the Pending County Courts Bill. By Jeremy Bentham. London:—1825. *The Pamphleteer*, vol. xxv, no. 1 (1825), 405–43.

Note: The following minor variation, based on printing conventions, is not recorded in the collation: for footnote markers, 1825B employs suprascript Arabic numerals, 1830 symbols.

157 *adds*	BY JEREMY BENTHAM. LONDON:—1825.
159, 2	Clauses,
159, 6	police magistrates.

159, 16	all-sufficient:
160, 6	minister.
160, 18	below).
160, 38	parliament.
161, 6	barristers
161, 7	secretaries,
161, 10	parliament
161, 12	virtue,
161, 14	tinge,)
161, 18	parliamentary
161, 28	take on
161, 31	police magistrates'
161, 32	knowlege,
162, 24	any thing
162, 27	jest book,
162, 30	Honorable
162, 35	color,
163, 1	labor
163, 4	cabinet minister's
163, 6	act
163, 9	test and corporation acts:
163, 17	laid on
163, 20	parliamentary
163, 35	subject matter
164, 4	*Chron*.) 'almost
164, 5	Hereon
164, 12	invidious,
164, 13	gentlemen,
164, 17	barristers
164, 18	barristers
164, 25	*barrister*.
164, 27	being
164, 32	inn of court;
164, 35	taste,
164, 37–8	another on
164, 41	*barrister:*
165, 4	may
165, 5	like!
165, 15	noble and learned oracle,
165, 17	expended on
165, 18	years
165, 19	successor
165, 24–5	ministers, not to say kings
165, 35	barristers,
165, 37	magistrates—
165, 37	magistrates
166, 12	barristers,
166, 15	inn of court
166, 22	magistrate.
166, 24–5	course on
166, 25	conversation on

166, 26	conversation on
166, 30	barristers
166, 30–1	gentleman
166, 32	building act,
166, 33	Honorable
166, 36	magistrate
166, 37	barrister?
166, 38	magistrates,
167, 5	act of parliament,
167, 6	act.
167, 7	employed what
167, 9	speech (No.
167, 11–12	endeavors
167, 14	all barristers
167, 18	so,
167, 21	barristers
167, 26	barristers:
168, 2	barrister,
168, 2	police magistrate
168, 19	*refuse?'*
168, 23	hoped soften
168, 29	labor,
168, 30	barrister,
168, 30	police magistrate.
169, 17	barrister;
169, 21	cabinet minister,
169, 22	depends on
169, 23	as on
169, 28	reporter,
170, 5	barrister
170, 6	police magistrate.
170, 7	barristers
170, 17	furnishing, on
170, 26	labor,
170, 37	honorable house
171, 1	Being barristers,
171, 14	*non-barristership*.
171, 16	barrister
171, 28–9	hon. house—
171, 32	ex-barrister
172, 10	magistrates,
172, 11	magistrates
172, 18	major,
172, 18	clergymen,
172, 19	major?) starch dealers,
172, 19	trader,
172, 20	clergymen
172, 22	magistrates
172, 30	major, being a major,
172, 31	ensign
172, 31–2	lieutenant, captain:

172, 34	starch dealers,
172, 37	depended on
173, 3	trader.
173, 13	barrister-magistrates,
173, 14	a year,
173, 17–18	directly on
173, 27	favor
173, 28	favor
173, 31	trader,
174, 4	laboring
174, 5	1800,
174, 13	learned gentleman
174, 17	board
174, 18	board
174, 20	trader:
174, 23	clergymen,
175, 2	a year as
175, 5	magistrates
175, 7	Honorable
175, 20	a year, so incompetent,)—
175, 23	barrister
175, 26	any thing
175, 30	Honorable
176, 1	Honorable
176, 2	Honorable
176, 10	Honorable
176, 11	Honorable
176, 18	magistrates
176, 18–19	imposed on
176, 26	any thing
176, 28	Honorable
176, 32	Honorable
176, 33	Honorable and Right Honorable
176, 40	worked on
177, 3	Honorable Member of Honorable
177, 27	endeavor
177, 28	Honorable
178, 28	altogether on
178, 31	honorable,
178, 32	labor,
178, 35	cannot
179, 1	non-honorable
179, 1	honorable
179, 2	non-honorable
179, 3	honorable
179, 4	honorable
179, 8–9	non-honorable,
179, 9	honorable
179, 10	labor of the honorable
179, 11	non-honorable
179, 22	endeavor

179, 22–3	endeavoring
179, 23	favor
179, 24–5	exemplified on
180, 9	*right*, and
180, 15	knowlege
180, 23	Honorable
181, 28	is on
182, 22	Honorable
182, 28	honored
182, 29	endeavored
183, 30	labor?
183, 32	*protégé*
184, 8	chief
185, 23	Honorable
185, 25	irresistible,
185, 30	Honorable
186, 3	thereon,
186, 10	profit on
187, 2	favor—
187, 3	honor'—
187, 7	day, carried
187, 37	full on
187, 37	laboring
188, 14	whereon
189, 21–2	Honorable
190, 10	bow on
190, 17	fie, fie,
190, 20	and though
190, 28	unfavorable
190, 30	favorable
190, 32	favor
190, 33	favor
191, 3	cast on
191, 4–5	cast on
191, 14–15	*parliament-law*
191, 21	acknowleged
191, 25–6	sat on
192, 11	Honorable
192, 29	Honorable
193, 3	learned
193, 11	honorable gentleman,
193, 21	favor
194, 2	opposition member
194, 4	honorable
194, 4–5	stand on
194, 5	*calculation*
194, 16	Thereon
194, 27	While on
195, 3	mother),
195, 13–14	bias on
195, 19	one, on

195, 21	connexion;
195, 24	turned on
195, 25	think,
195, 26	increased,
195, 29	increase
195, 32	inquiry, —
195, 36–7	equity, put above law,
196, 8–9	Honorable
196, 13	insisted on,
196, 16	entered on
196, 19	speaking on
196, 22	Establishment, on
196, 24	turn on
197, 12	endeavored
197, 15–16	which in
197, 16	elsewhere has
197, 20	author
198, 5	Honorable
198, 6	endeavors,
198, 6	themselves: yet,
198, 8	Courts'
198, 17	stands),
198, 30	feefed
199, 3	*The Times*
199, 3	*22d:*
199, 1st col., 9	institution
199, 1st col., 18	proposition on
199, 2nd col., 18	proposition on
199, 26	devolved on
199, 28	laid on
200, 34	police magistrate
200, 2nd col., 37	told that
201, 4	Country
201, 19	called on
201, 21–2	knowlege.
201, 25	called on
201, 38	provisions on
202, 9	On those
202, 18	*knowlege,*
202, 23	Honorable
202, 26	justice of the peace,
202, 30 *omits*	THE END.

E. INDICATIONS RESPECTING
LORD ELDON COLLATION

Collation: Indications respecting Lord Eldon, including History of the Pending Judges'-Salary-Raising Measure. By Jeremy Bentham, Esq. Bencher of Lincoln's Inn. London: printed for John and H.L. Hunt, Tavistock Street, Covent Garden. MDCCCXXV.

Note: This version does not include the Postscript. The following printer's imprint is at the end of the text: 'London: printed by C.H. Reynell, Broad Street, Golden Square.'

205, 2	*Enquiry*
206, 2	fees of
206, 11	Chiefs
206, 29	*Equity an*
206, 37	1772,
208, 32	exacting for
208, 38–9	Eldon, into
209, 25	*Clerks*,
210, 14	1824,—
211, 7	*Clerks*,
211, 16	*instance—*
211, 35	in § .4,
212, 2	*fees of*
213, 30	1797–8,—2,767*l*.
216, 6	stat. 4.
216, 15	Justice,
216, 21	1, c.1, § 10:
216, 35	B.
216, 38	outlawry:
217, 5	C,
217, 25	March,
218, 5	adopted?'
218, 10	it: all
218, 15	'progresses:'
219, 6	God! Mr.
219, 6	M. Justice
219, 13–14 *omits*	Parliament, *had* hitherto and all along been done
219, 32	ii. b.i.
220, 21	*Increase and Sanction to Corruption.*
220, 23	Crown-law.
221, 16	Sergeant
222, 8	petition whether
222, 13	objected,
223, 10–11	or any of them,

223, 16	Bar—what
223, 21	fungus which
223, 24	pronounced,
223, 32	Master of Delay
223, 34	unquiet
224, 17	*Corruption*
224, 27	*junior's*
224, 27	vi.
225, 2	junior,
225, 3–4	—'Lord CHANCELLOR (p. 433)—A
225, 9	*tha particular*
225, 14	order,
225, 18	'None
225, 18	parallel.'
225, 19	any us to
225, 31–2	title 'Observations
226, 2	author,
226, 6	Mr.
226, 12	in his *Lordship's Court,*
226, 19	Judge.
226, 20	Pages
226, 21	*angry'* . . . Petitioner
226, 30	above,
227, 4	pp. 6.7.
227, 5	above mentioned
227, 5	November 1822,
227, 6	May 1821,
227, 7	'Limbrey *v.* Gurr,' and 'Adams *v.* Limbrey,'—
227, 12	some time
227, 12	November—
227, 27	9. Page 5.
227, 27	'Information' and 'Bill'
227, 29	Mr. Maule. 'Answer'
227, 31	*Information* and *Bill?*—
228, 1	10. Page 6.
228, 1	observations
228, 22–3	Solicitors and Clerks in Court;
228, 29–30	Clerks in Court.
229, 2	Tables of *Fees*
229, 6	Tables
229, 10	Court,
229, 15	Great Charter,
229, 16	repealed)
229, 19	regular,—'To-morrow.'
229, 27	Ves.
229, 33	thinks,
229, 34	Order
229, 36	Court.
230, 1	which (though
230, 9	*Judge*
230, 13	understand by

230, 21	been,
231, 3	*Illegality*
231, 15	china shop—
231, 19	justice,
231, 23	*perdu, la tète*.
232, 2	Tipstaffs
232, 4	Tipstaff
232, 4	half-a-guinea,
232, 7	Table of Fees
232, 8	*court*.
232, 10	*Tipstaffs*
232, 11	costs.
232, 14	3. Geo.
232, 14	Table of Fees
232, 15	Tipstaff
232, 17	Table.
232, 24	*us, I*
232, 29	Table of Fees in the Rules
233, 3	Bench:—
233, 4	Judge
233, 4	Guilty, or Not Guilty?—Not guilty!
233, 14—15	Co-defendents,
233, 22	but,
233, 22	sufferer,
234, 21	Shame, shame!
234, 37	difficulty,—
234, 41	principal
235, 3	obedience worthy
235, 31	1760,'
235, 31	commissioners (of
235, 37	Commons. Date
236, 7	and,
236, 7	appears,
236, 8	What! In
236, 9	Justice—
236, 10	Never
236, 11	Never
236, 12	commissioners—for
236, 27	the *tap*
237, 5	*much*,—
237, 26—7	agony hurry
237, 28	Commissioners
237, 29	Justice:—
238, 17	foot-ball.
238, 24	Regulations
238, 24	Fees
238, 32	solicitors'
239, 12	Every thing
239, 24	exquisitively
240, 17	*fact* at
240, 18	Table of Fees

240, 19	Tables of Fees—
240, 25	loop-hole
240, 26	above mentioned
240, 29	8 of
240, 32	hand,'
241, 2	hand.
241, 4	judge whosoever
241, 6	anything
241, 10	But if
241, 12	*Court-hand*—
241, 20	the *Eldon Act* should
241, 21	*Act*, so
241, 22	Act,—
242, 6	that by
242, 10	ACT.
242, 12	*Profit*
242, 16	c.24,
243, 1	*Swindler:*
243, 16	eclipsed and
243, 25	5;
244, 13	*attendance*-fees?
244, 17	attendance-fee?
245, 7	*theif?*
245, 8	10;
245, 20	swindler—an
245, 30	necessary—necessary,
245, 34	bespatter
245, 35	indeed!
246, 1	Courts,
246, 3	him.
246, 14	eight At
246, 24	yours,
246, 27–8	anybody
246, 33	lucubrations!—
246, 35	Lordship's
247, 6–7	*greatest-happiness-principle*,
247, 9	produced—
247, 15	circumstunce
247, 22	shamless
247, 25	*Deliberateness*,
247, 26	Deliberateness,
247, 28	Gentlemen, Noble
248, 2	All
248, 4	House of Lords.
248, 7	extenuation you
248, 10	does that
248, 13	*of the practice*—
248, 22	for—every
248, 30	justice! He
249, 7	*chicane*, a
249, 7	*theft*—

249, 9	license
249, 9	censure:—
249, 11	'THE SIX CLERKS.—
249, 13	Six-clerk,'
249, 16	"Attends the Master."—
249, 17–18	"Nothing, my Lord."—
249, 24	fomerly
249, 26	'When
249, 26	Court:'
249, 33	sale—
249, 36	endure to existence
249, 39	six-and-eight-pences
250, 6	*Precedent*
250, 7	*Ship-Money.*—
250, 9	Judges,
250, 29	in Vesey, jun. vi. p. 433,
251, 3	practise
251, 4	aemire
251, 19	Commander-in-Chief—
251, 25	May 1825 (as
251, 26	day)
251, 29	*et ceteras*,
252, 7	*faux-pas*
252, 10	Navy
252, 11	likewise, will 'everything
252, 14	self-distress
252, 20	different! No:
252, 23	*Parliment, a Joint-Stock*
252, 24	*Westminster-hall*
252, 24	*Dishonest*
258, 16	fo A rundel,
267, 14	anything,
267, 14	Judges,
267, 16	thus,
267, 21–2	*unlimited* punishment.
267, 29	*contra*
268, 1	instance,
268, 18	commited
268, 24	cowardice)—
268, 27	Judge,
269, 1	*Abuses* which occurs in page 76, may
269, 4	*revelling* by
269, 6	abolished,
269, 7	substituted;
269, 9	salary: with
269, 11	principal
269, 17	*future*
269, 18–19	period, these offices will, with the rest, have
269, 20–1	*minorum gentium*
269, 21	heaven?
269, 23	predecessor Jefferies,

269, 26	*killed-off*
269, 30	solitude,
269, 34	child did
270, 7	painter, another
270, 7–8	Eldon—Lord
270, 10	far so
270, 13	Sailor, *Britannia:*
270, 14	Pheasants,

Collation: Indications respecting Lord Eldon, including History of the Pending Judges'-Salary-Raising Measure. By Jeremy Bentham, Esq. Bencher of Lincoln's Inn. London: published by Robert Heward, Wellington Street, Strand. 1825.

Note: The following printer's imprint is on the verso of the title page and on the final page of the Postscript: 'London: printed by C. and W. Reynell, Broad Street, Golden Square.'

203 *adds*	LONDON: PUBLISHED BY ROBERT HEWARD, WELLINGTON STREET, STRAND. 1825.
205, 2	*Enquiry*
205, 14	not,
205, 16	cap. 6,
205, 23	may perhaps receive
205, 28	styled
206, 2	augmenting the fees of
206, 3	so, in course,
206, 29	*Equity an*
206, 29	*Fraud and Extortion.*
207, 33	things,
207, 34	profession;
208, 11	Clerk,[a]
208, 27	Master,
208, 28	styled Six-Clerks
208, 31	anything
208, 33	solicitors,
210, 8	styled
210, 13	p. 49,
210, 18	P.13.—
210, 19	circumstances,
210, 27	charges,
211, 9	P.13.—
211, 18	P.11.—
211, 23	*March* 1814,
211, 33	Mr Vizard's.
212, 2	*fees of*
212, 9	Court.
212, 10	Co.,
212, 10	Carey street,

212, 11	Bell yard, by
212, 11	King street, Seven Dials,
212, 20	entitled
212, 22	July 1814.
213, 1	*Subordinates was Profit to Superiors;*
213, 2	*Successors.*
213, 11	possessed;—
213, 17	Six-Clerkship,
213, 20	Sewell;
213, 24	Mr Robinson: the Mr Robinson
214, 1	Mr Way;
214, 3	Mr Way:
214, 3	paid,
214, 4	grandpatron's
214, 9–10	great-grand
214, 10	grandpatron
214, 11	great-grand
214, 16	great-grand
215, 1	Waiting Clerks;
215, 4	which to
215, 27	*Law was the Order.*
215, 31	*Parliament;—*
215, 31	application applying
216, 1	c.7,
216, 21	c.1. §20,
216, 25	monarch,
216, 35	5*s.*
217, 14	Six-clerk's
219, 6	Mr Justice Bailey
219, 6	Mr Justice Park!
219, 32	vol. ii., b. i.,
220, 5	extortion in
220, 16	word,
220, 26	practises:
221, 27	corruption election
222, 31	Learned
223, 1	salary,
223, 16	Oh;
223, 32	Master of Delay
224, 1	Mr Justice Bailey
224, 1	Mr Justice Park,
224, 4	ascendancy
224, 14	4000*l.*
224, 20	time;
225, 4	(p. 423)—
225, 22	hand,
225, 23	do,
225, 34	Mr Lowe,
226, 12	say *under*
226, 24	Lordship;
226, 28	3. Page

226, 31	Mr Lowe
227, 1	Mr Lowe
227, 7–8	Mr Lowe
227, 16	say,
227, 17	consideration;
227, 18	Mr Lowe,
227, 20	everybody
227, 23	styled
227, 27	above 'Information
227, 28	Mr Lowe,
227, 28	Mr Attorney-General,
227, 29	'Mr Maule.'
228, 16	Mr Lowe
228, 18	receive:
228, 19	Mr Lowe,
228, 33	*Barker* who
228, 34	*entreés*.
228, 35	Mr Scot,
228, 36	Mr Barker,
229, 16	III and
229, 16	II are
229, 28	"that
229, 32	instance."
230, 3	Mr Mansfield
230, 3	Mr Romilly,
230, 5	Mr Attorney-General
230, 6	Mr Richards.
230, 7	Mr Mansfield
230, 8	Mr Romilly
230, 23	'Mr Mansfield
230, 27	Mr Mansfield
230, 28	Mr Mansfield
230, 31	Mr Mansfield
230, 32	letter.
230, 33	Mr Lowton,
231, 22	*ils*
231, 25	21.—
232, 2	obtain a
232, 8	*court*.
232, 9	*affidavits* stating
232, 11	costs.
232, 20	Figure
232, 23	Eldon,—'*Alas!*
232, 24	*not for*
232, 30	Report.
233, 9	6*s.*.
233, 23	for;
233, 25	master-man
235, 6	way, nay,
235, 10	screwiug
236, 12	6*d.*?—

237, 10	Mr Peel,
237, 28	Commissioners
237, 29	Justice;—As
237, 29	Bench.
238, 12	without proving for
238, 22	c.66.
238, 29	ones;
238, 30	underling
239, 8	additional feel or
239, 21	hy the hand
239, 25	style
239, 35	*Law*—
240, 11	is that
240, 22	II,
240, 28	II,
240, 30–1	which without
241, 6	anything
241, 20	style
241, 21	styled
241, 32	(Mr John
241, 34	Mr Peel's
242, 16	II,
242, 23	*cheat;*
243, 8	Judge:
243, 29	1825.
243, 31	Mr *Favel*.
244, 3	Mr M.P.
244, 3–4	Mr *Glynn*,
244, 4	Mr *Whitmore*,
244, 5	Mr *Horace*
244, 12	Messrs *Glynn*
244, 14	Mr *Horace*
244, 18	Mr *Favel's*
244, 19	Mr *Twiss:*
244, 27–8	Mr Peel,
244, 28	Mr *Twiss,*
244, 29	Mr *Twiss*
244, 34	*Mr Lowe,*
245, 14	power he
245, 21	Mr Secretary
245, 36	ill-fame
246, 11	Mr Peel?—
246, 25	your's
246, 27–8	anybody
246, 33	indeed?
247, 6–7	*greatest-happiness-principle*,
247, 11–12	order: nothing
248, 28	four-and-twenty.
249, 14	Mr Hart's
249, 16	"Attends the Master."—
249, 17–18	"Nothing, my Lord."—

249, 38	Six Drones,
249, 38	per-centage
250, 7	*Charles's in*
250, 27	*future* not
251, 4	Mr Peel,
251, 9	Justice:
251, 21	And forasmuch
251, 21	Mr Robinson—
251, 25	Mr Robinson's
251, 25	May 1825,
251, 30	exactly;
251, 31	Mr Robinson
252, 6	I,
252, 10	Mr Croker,
252, 19	*different*. The
252, 29	anything
253, 19	say,
254, 1	is,—
254, 11	denomination by
254, 14	But though
254, 22	everything,
254, 25	justice have
255, 2	10,
255, 18	XVIII,
255, 22	Jack-of-both-sides,—
255, 26	of the *lay-gents*)
256, 29	Mr Butler,
257, 14	panegyric
257, 17	panegyric
257, 22	declation of
258, 5	Mr Brougham.
258, 6	called in)
258, 15	June 1818.
258, 15	(Mr Brougham)
258, 17	Mr Bentham
260, 19	(Mr Ponsonby)
261, 2–3	(Mr Ponsonby,)
261, 15	Mr *Ponsonby*,
261, 17	Mr Ponsonby,
262, 7–8	Mr Butler's panegyric
262, 17	lot as
262, 21	Mitford,
262, 22	commission,
262, 23	me—I
262, 26	Mr Peel,
262, 27	Mr *Peel's*
263, 14	has, which,
263, 16	shows
263, 19–20	Mr Vizard
264, 12	years dominion
264, 35	*Charter shop*,

265, 29	Attorney-General,
265, 29	it now
266, 11	witness, 'Do
266, 12	God?'
266, 13	believe,—
266, 17	Priest,
266, 18	commmission
266, 38	*Mr Peel!*
266, 38	Mr Peel!
266, 39	Mr Peel!
267, 1	3. In
267, 10	everything
267, 14	Judges,
267, 16	thus,
267, 21–2	*unlimited* punishment.
267, 29	*contra*
268, 1	instance,
268, 5	'matchless'
268, 20	and to
268, 24	cowardice)—it
268, 27	Judge,
268, 38	regarded, of course,
269, 1	*Abuses* which occurs in page 76, may
269, 4	*revelling* by
269, 6	abolished, or in disuse—
269, 7	substituted:
269, 9	salary: with
269, 15	*Clerks* has
269, 17	*future*
269, 18–19	period these offices will, with the rest, have
269, 20	*majorum* or
269, 20–1	*minorum gentium*
269, 21	heaven?
269, 23	predecessor Jefferies,
269, 26	*killed-off*
269, 30	solitude,
269, 34	child did
270, 7	painter, another
270, 7–8	Eldon—Lord
270, 10	far so
270, 13	Sailor, *Britannia:*
270, 14	Pheasants,
270, 16	gripe—
272, 7	Mr Vizard,
273, 16	equity
273, 21	Mr Secretary
273, 28	styled
274, 2	above (p. 9),
274, 4	(Mr Vizard's
274, 13	propriety,
274, 15	Time, June

275, 2	Mr Robinson
275, 14	teaze
276, 6	mis-statement
276, 24	conduct of
276, 24	situations,—
276, 25	church'
276, 26	State,
277, 6	People?
277, 32	conception *they*
278, 10	'Mis-statements
278, 10	exery
278, 12	mis-statement.'
278, 19	angnish
278, 26–7	*income as*
278, 34	*places* instead
279, 3	Mr Miller,
280, 13	bar!
281, 2	whatsoever,
282, 18	Mr Fletcher
283, 2	Mr Fletcher,
283, 6	*Abbots*,
283, 20	rhe refractory
284, 9	Attorney-General
284, 13	Camden,
285, 23–4	extraordinary talent-requiring
286, 7–8	charity-school-boy
287, 3	five-and-twenty
288, 1–2	self-judication-system;
288, 29	shapes,

Collation: Indications respecting Lord Eldon, including History of the Pending Judges' Salary-Raising Measure. By Jeremy Bentham, Esq. Bencher of Lincoln's Inn. London:—1825. *The Pamphleteer*, vol. xxvi, no. li (1826), 1–55.

Note: This version does not include the Postscript. The following minor variation, based on printing conventions, is not recorded in the collation: variations in the form of footnote markers: 1826 employs suprascript Arabic numerals, 1830 symbols.

203, 4	JUDGES' SALARY-RAISING
205, 2	*inquiry*
205, 4	inquiry
205, 15–16	3d Geo. IV. cap. 6,
205, 26	Equity,
205, 28	styled
206, 11	Chiefs
206, 18	stepped
206, 20	improved on
206, 21	Charles's in

207, 11–12	displeasure of
207, 35	endeavor,
208, 8	frequently on
208, 27	Master,
208, 28	styled
208, 31	Court
208, 38	inquire,
208, 38	Eldon,
209, 1	Solicitors,
209, 11	Solicitor
209, 18	suit in
209, 25	*Clerks*,
209, 28	P.15. 'The
209, 29	Southampton buildings
209, 31	P.16. 'Another
209, 34	32,)
209, 35–210, 1	*eleven* and
210, 2–3	from en
210, 8	styled
210, 13	p. 49,
210, 25–6	and inclination
210, 28	control;
211, 11–12	looked on favorably.
211, 13	intitled
211, 36	place came,
212, 3	pages bearing
212, 3	title-page
212, 10	Law-stationers,
212, 15	Thereon
213, 3	twopenny-loaf
213, 4	Honorable and Right Honorable
213, 5	Honorable
213, 17	Six-Clerkship,
214, 4	knowlege
214, 23	said),
215, 13	endeavored
215, 23	shown
216, 25	monarch,
216, 30	favor
216, 31	shows no such favor.
216, 32	recognised
216, 34	favor
216, 35	B.
216, 35	5*s*.
216, 38	outlawry:
217, 1	such-like
217, 5	C,
217, 14–15	whereon
217, 21–2	Lords money-bills
217, 25	Honorable
218, 5	adopted?'

218, 26	recognised
218, 28	whereon
218, 29	recognised,
219, 3	thereon,
219, 5	(and by
219, 19	authorise
219, 27	color
220, 6	color
220, 7	color
220, 26	practises:
220, 30	practise;
220, 31	practise.
220, 32	*large sense*.
221, 6	color
222, 6	it?
222, 8	made on
222, 19	*acted on*,
223, 10	intitle
223, 35	When, on
224, 22	early and
225, 7	Judges, on
225, 8	*practice;*
225, 9	On the
225, 10	acted on
225, 24	*design*
226, 1	knowlege.
226, 6	Mr.
226, 10	time,
226, 12	*Court*,
226, 14	thereon
226, 20	exhibited of
226, 25	Solicitor-General),
227, 23	styled
228, 12	Honorable
228, 24	endeavors
228, 33	favorite
228, 34	favor,
229, 4	eye and
229, 17	On an
229, 26	article during
229, 28	"that
229, 30	judges on
229, 32	instance."
230, 1	maintain; and which (though
230, 3–4	spirit and in a manner peculiar
230, 31	take: and Mr Mansfield
231, 8	forth,
231, 14	jailors out
232, 5	chambers (to
232, 6	habeas-corpus)
232, 9	showed cause, on

232, 17	prison than
232, 27	*all It*
233, 9	legalised,
233, 25	labor
233, 35	turned on
233, 37	realised.
234, 3	you by
234, 5–6	come on
234, 23	brought on
234, 24–5	brought on them),
235, 1	given for
235, 5	lay-gents.
235, 11	*that*),
235, 14	out on
235, 31	1760,'
235, 31	presently,)
235, 34	conceive to
235, 36	"that
235, 36	future.'"
236, 13–14	put on
236, 17	Yes,
237, 8	colors,
237, 19	report on
237, 22	you, who so
237, 23–4	imputation on
238, 9	Honorable
238, 17	foot-ball.
239, 6	authorised,
239, 12	Every thing
239, 12	every thing
239, 25	style
240, 21	them!
240, 25	loop-hole
240, 29	intitutled
240, 36–7	Bench . . . . to
240, 37	inclusive:'
241, 16	Judges, on
241, 20	style
241, 21	styled
241, 22	Honorable
242, 18–19	*persons of the same,* . . . . *shall*
242, 28–9	endeavored
243, 19	judges
243, 27	inquiry,
243, 29	1825:
244, 11	attendance fee?
244, 18	candor
244, 27	there Mr.
245, 3	or if
246, 6	elaborately-organised
247, 28	Honorable

434

249, 10	1824:
249, 16	intirely
249, 25	person."
249, 32	When as
249, 39	labors
250, 4	intire
250, 11	judges,
250, 21	taking on
251, 28	acknowleged
252, 4	Legalising
252, 23	*Joint-Stock*
252, 25	favorites
254, 1	is: —
254, 2	labor.
254, 5	labor,
254, 10	Apprised
254, 21	familiarised
255, 11	humor,
255, 15	endeavor
255, 25	labor
256, 21	Honorable
256, 24	Honorable
256, 27	*Colors*,
256, 31	him on
257, 14	panegyric
257, 17	panegyric
257, 21	mixed
257, 24	intire.
258, 3	Honorable
258, 11–12	endeavor to prevail on Honorable
258, 14	favorite
258, 14	come on
259, 10	have on
259, 10–11	favorable
259, 14	knowlege
259, 22	civilised
261, 12	paralysing
261, 18	years'
261, 26	Honorable House, or in Right Honorable
261, 35	organiser
262, 8	panegyric.
262, 25	digression on
262, 25	candor
262, 28	*Act.*—Should
263, 13	recognised
263, 16	shows
263, 24	armor
263, 27	humor:
263, 28	Duke down
264, 5	once),
264, 11	performed throughout,

264, 12–13	Enterprises consummated—enterprises
264, 15	hands—exploits
264, 19	But forasmuch
264, 24	improve on
264, 34	*Shop*
265, 1	dependent on
265, 15	cause special
265, 19	number; sold
265, 24	failure aggravate
265, 25–6	price paid by inventive genius for
265, 29	Attorney-General,
265, 29	it now
266, 1–2	expenses and
266, 24	perujry,
267, 3	knowlege,
267, 14	Judges,
267, 16	take on
267, 16	thus,
267, 18	punishment for
267, 21–2	*unlimited* punishment.
267, 23–4	insincerity to
267, 29	*contra*
267, 31	crimes any
267, 32	thus to
267, 33	prohibition an
267, 34	knowlege
268, 1	instance,
268, 4–5	impeachment on
268, 11	*subornation of*
268, 24	cowardice)—it
268, 27	Judge,
268, 33	labor
268, 40	cause), should he ever in
269, 1	*Abuses* which occurs in page 49, may
269, 4	*revelling* by
269, 6	abolished,
269, 7	substituted;
269, 9	salary: with
269, 15	*Clerks* has
269, 17	*future*
269, 17	Honorable
269, 18–19	period these offices will, with the rest, have
269, 20–1	*minorum gentium*
269, 21	heaven?
269, 23	Lord and
269, 23	predecessor Jefferies,
269, 26	*killed-off*
269, 32	favor—
269, 34	child did
270, 4	humor,
270, 7	painter, another

270, 7–8	Eldon—Lord
270, 10	far so
270, 13	Sailor, *Britannia:*
270, 14	Pheasants,

INDEX OF SUBJECTS

Note. The following is a unified index which refers to the texts of all the essays included in the volume, without identifying the particular work in question.

References to Bentham's notes and to editorial notes are given by means of the page numbers(s) followed by the letter 'n'.

The symbol 'v.' is used to indicate 'as distinct from' or 'as opposed to'. Other abbreviations for frequently occurring words and phrases are as follows:

app. apt. appropriate aptitude
f(s). functionary(ies)
govt. government
gtst. h. greatest happiness
inapt. inaptitude

ABLATION: offence affecting title to property, 344–5
ABSOLUTISM: interest of subject many taken for object of endeavour on part of all not engaged in path of, 349
ABUSE(S): charge Eldon with creation of, he names inquisitors, 186; Eldon as Master of, 263, 269; where remuneration wears shape of fees, sure to have place, 264–5n; in Court of Chancery, 271–4; existence of reversions an abominable, 286; Eldon's desire to correct, 286–7; Eldon's plan will make inconsiderable defalcation from existing mass of, 309; produced by fees received by offices which have been subject-matter of sale v. gift, 309, 321; antipathy towards those who profit from, of judicial and procedure system, 314; amnesty necessary to purpose of persuading judges and lawyers that after removal of, they will find themselves as well off, 314; ways in which service would not be adjudged bribe by judge having interest in, 323; greater facility for, office affords, greater sum purchaser will give, 324; intimation of, odious, 325n; cause that of everyone whose wish to see, removed, 341; Account Commission instrument of economy and security against, 381n; where, probable, reform should not wait actual instances, 386
ACCIDENT(S): success in profession of barrister depends upon, 169; deepest-laid designs sometimes frustrated by, 225; tritical essay on, 334
ACCOUNT(S): of expense bestowed on democratical v. aristocratical class of paupers, 15; complaints made of method of, keeping, 293–6; Italian system of, keeping composed of fiction, 298–9; regular and technical mode of, keeping v. technical and regular system of judicial procedure, 299; all-comprehensive set of books for exhibition of, of any govt., 300; Eldon's plan to cause fees to be received on public, 308; invitation to all in judicial offices to give in, of past receipts, 314; little more skill in arithmetic exercised in keeping, of empire than of chandler's shop, 323; locatee charged with obligation of accounting for fees, 331–2; reprobation of fee system by, Commission, 381–6
ACTION: none against judges, 186; suppose that judges have for end of, h. of suitors, 254. *See* SPRING OF ACTION
ACTIVE APTITUDE: problem how to prove that by exclusion of non-barristers as police magistrates, will be produced, 164; of experienced magistrates v. unfledged barristers, 180–1; neither possessed nor pretended to by Eldon, 288; sufficient to keep man in judicial situations unexposed to any determinate charge, 322–3
ACTIVE TALENT: required in office of Exciseman, 285. *See* TALENT

essential to apt., 27; benefit of whatsoever degree of apt. given to instructors open
to non-fs., 29; objection to publicity of examination: timid apt. excluded, 29;
objection to probationary period proposed for instruction: apt. insufficient, 29; to
monarch neither apt. on part of servants nor frugality of pay allotted to them
naturally unacceptable, 29–30; form of govt. in which maximization of apt. object
of horror to rulers, 30; maximizing official apt. intimately connected with minimizing official pay, 41; maximizing official apt. irreconcilably opposite to particular
interest of ruling few, 42–3; deficiency in apt. of police magistrates, 161–70,
175–7; apt. of original police magistrates, 170–5; loss in article of apt. in instance
of police magistrates, 178; plan serving for apt. of police magistrates, 179–80;
value of office to patron directly as inapt. of protégé he has power to put in, 183–4;
official apt. in direct ratio of official remuneration, 194; apt. of police magistrates
to be proved as well as disproved, 195; in patronage of County Court judges, no
hands in point of apt. would bear a thought in comparison of Peel's, 198; apt. is as
dignity, 251 & n, 275, 285; apt. of Ponsonby v. inapt. of Eldon, 261n; transcendent apt. for judicial situation cannot keep Lord Chancellor in it, 261n; without
active apt., man possessed of app. apt. in other shapes may in Eldon's situation be
a nuisance, 288; when man disgraced in situation by inapt., least apt is to him least
unacceptable successor, 288; apt. is as opulence, 301; apt. of clerk v. Master in
Chancery, 316; on part of locatees, degree of inapt. greater in case of gift than
sale, 321, 321–4; scrutiny into apt. of locatee, 325; degree of inapt. on part of
Eldon's son, 326; comparative inapt. of arrangements of official remuneration
combined with patronage, 331–2; inapt. of system, 333–4; utter inapt. of original
contract principle, 347–8; comparative inapt. of locution principle of utility, 352;
app. apt. of advocate v. deficiency in app. apt. of judge, 356–7; dislocation in retail
with view to app. apt., 363; causes of attachment to fee system no proof of apt.,
386. *See* ACTIVE APTITUDE, INTELLECTUAL APTITUDE, MORAL APTITUDE

ARCHBISHOP(S) OF CANTERBURY: incompetence of clergymen as police magistrates to be settled with, 174; prostrate before *Constitutional Code*, 301; emoluments of Prerogative Office of, 371n

ARCOT: debts of Nabob of, 140–1

ARISTOCRACY: aristocratical v. democratical paupers, 15–17; form of govt. no
where exemplified to any considerable extent, 30; in mixture of monarchy, aristocracy and democracy, expense of official emolument maximized, 30; relation
between money and, of talent and virtue, 123–4, 127–8, 145; silent while
Redesdale paralyzing justice, 261n; yoke of aristocratical magistracy rivetted on
neck of people, 265–6; what could judge do against will of monarchy and, in Parliament, 268n; sinister interest of, 319–20; aristocratical v. democratical classes of
fs., 359–61; Whig, out-voted Shelburne and rendered his resignation necessary,
364n; powers of depredation and oppression result to aristocrat from denial of
justice, 375–6

ARMY(IES): security provided by proportional diminution of, 13–14; maintenance of
standing, 30; list fills no small book, 108; barristers may not know anything more
of business of police magistrate than, officer, 180; process of diminution
performed upon writing clerks with as little scruple as upon privates in, 360

ASPORTATION: offence affecting use of corporeal subject-matter of property, 344;
offence affecting enjoyments from condition in life, 345

ASSIGNMENT: of wealth v. merit, 74, 75

ASSIZES: delay effect and object of establishment given to, 312

ATHEIST: or Christian most trustworthy, 266n

ATTENDANCE(S): evil proposed to be remedied by increase of police magistrates' salaries: deficiency in, 160–1, 163–4, 175–7; police magistrate cannot be altogether eased of, 178–9; plan serving for, of police magistrates, 179–80, 181; before Master in Chancery, 206–7, 208–9, 210–11; on part of Masters in Chancery, 209–10, 271–2, 286; of Commissioners of Bankrupts, 243–4; reforms as to, 246; delay manufactured independently of whatever produced by insufficiency in, of judicatories, 312; Master in Chancery must be made to give whatever, he engages to give, 315–16; for estimation of loss, of parties needful, 356–7

ATTORNEY(IES): situation of Sixty Clerks intermediate between officer of Court of Chancery and, 64–5n; service as clerk to, as security for apt. in office of police magistrate, 165; success in profession of barrister depends upon opinion of, 169. *See* LAWYER(S), SOLICITOR(S)

AUCTION: and public service, 91–3; when no fraud, in form only and not in effect any difference between competition and, 153–4. *See* PECUNIARY COMPETITION

AUTHORITY: Eldon's setting his own, above that of Parliament, 205; regard manifested by Eldon's commissioners for, of Parliament, 236; judges and, of Parliament, 250; app. apt. not necessary to offices which involve exercise of judicial, 322–3

BANKER'S CASE: argument of Holt, 55–7, 57–60n, 60, 64n

BANKRUPTCY: if Commissioner of Bankrupts not a person, not a swindler, 243–4

BAR: will be seen arguing while Court writes dockets, 188; community of sinister interest between Bench and, 223; amount of profit enjoyed by Eldon while at, 279–80; contempt of, for sensibility towards people, 281n; every pretence for delay eagerly laid hold of by, 313. *See* BARRISTER(S)

BARONETCIES: invitation to obtain, at expense of public, 140

BARRISTER(S): exclusion of non-barristers and, of less than three years' standing as police magistrates, 161, 164–70; non-barristership as proof of incompetence of original police magistrates, 170–4; Peel has manufactured apt. in instance of three-year-old, 177; plan excluding, from office of police magistrate, 179–80; contrast between experienced magistrates and unfledged, 180–1; if not a person, not a swindler, 243; ask any, whether any mode in which depredation practised in courts can ever have been secret to Lord Chancellor, 245–6; understand that where official depredation concerned, threat in English is licence in Eldonish, 249n; Eldon surrounded with, class, 281n; for removal of opposition on part of, looking to become judges, ample compensation should be given, 313; sinister interest of, 317–18; and increase in quantity of money expendable in litigation, 318–19. *See* ADVOCATE(S), BAR, LAWYER(S)

BENCH: set above Parliament, 222–3, 232; community of sinister interest between, and Bar, 223; Lord Chancellor in Cabinet and on, 261n; every pretence for delay eagerly laid hold of by, 313; highest rank of professional men those whose expectations look to, 316. *See* JUDGE(S)

BENEFICENCE: only by accident can beneficent disposition on part of locator be visible, 324; whether venality of service beneficial or mischievous, 326

BENEFICE(S): yielding £800 a year not object of disdain, 178; merit of gifts such as, 328

BENEFIT: v. burden of govt., 6; evil apprehended from desire of vengeance produced in mind of evil-doer by loss of, 7; taking, of instruction matter of choice, 28; Eldon's plan for screwing up fraud and extortion for own, 205; office sold for, of public, 332; loss has place when, after having been object of expectation, fails to be in possession, 342–3; offences affecting title to, 344–5; by loss of which disappointment produced consists of profit or reputation, 345–6; loss of, where

aberration from rule of right capable of being effected by blind, 299; as to self-dislocation on dislocation of patrons, 363–5; swells gratuities at charge of suitors and public into fees, 383–4
CUSTOMS: fees ought to be abolished throughout, 383

DAMAGE: graduation has place where question concerns quantum of, done, 355–6
DAMNIFICATION: offence affecting use of corporeal subject-matter of property, 344
DANGER: if police magistrates born in Ireland or United States, 168; as evil of second order, 358, 387–8
DEAD WEIGHT: *See* PENSION(S)
DEBTOR(S): money squeezed out of, by jailor, 184; squeezed by jailors to pamper judges, 231, 330; wine said to be, to cloth, 298–9
DEBT(S): time at end of which aristocratical pauper-list will have out-run national, 15; interest of, paid without money, 102; Pitt's, 132–42
DECAY: plea in bar to economy: necessity of provision for noble and respectable families fallen into, 103–9, 110–11
DEFENCE: forms for instruments of, included in procedure code, 34–5; tax imposed on judicial, 253
DEFENDANT: in equity, to ask question of, impute to him having told some story, 103; fees exacted on side of, sells unlimited power of plundering and oppressing, 216n; means of delay by dishonesty on side of, 272; effect produced by inaccessibility coupled with venality of powers of judicature on indigent in situation of, 375–6; applied to case of, mass of unpayable fees give birth to litigation, 377; by burden cast on, in shape of expense and vexation, accusation pronounced injurious, 389
DEFINITION: *per genus et differentium* ordinary mode of, 33; *ex post facto* punishment substituted to legislative, and prohibition, 267–8
DELAY: board an instrument of intrigue and, 27; of justice forbidden by Magna Charta, 62n; manufactured by trading justices v. judges, 185; tripled for sake of profit, 207; profit out of, manufactured out of breach of duty as to attendance by Masters in Chancery, 209–10; waste productive of correspondent, 215; Eldon's grand design experienced, 223–4, 225–30; at office of Master in Chancery, off go two-thirds of, and expense, 246; in English v. Irish Court of Chancery, 260–2n; means of, employable in ordinary cases, 272–3; Eldon's plea that no charge of, can be fairly brought against him, 280–4; with assistance of, every case pregnant with fee-yielding occasions, 311–12; manufacture of, set up by distinction between terms and vacations, 312; precipitation pregnant with, 312–13; connection between, and fees understood by lawyers, 313; not an atom of, in Equity business except what parties make, 334; evil effect produced by fees, 368–71; through medium of power of giving increase to, power of giving increase to expense exists, 373; by fees, f. interested in making, 384; payment by fees capable of being made instrument of, or undue dispatch, 385–6. *See* DELAY EXPENSE AND VEXATION
DELAY EXPENSE AND VEXATION: maximized for sake of profit, 184; charge Eldon with creation of, he names inquisitors, 186; by increase of, remuneration by fees contravenes collateral ends of justice, 310; interest of honest man that, be minimized, 320–1; evil effect produced by fees, 368–9, 371–3; remuneration in shape of fees, a bounty upon production of, 374–5
DELIBERATENESS: regarded as aggravation of moral guilt, 247
DELUSION: those labouring to inculcate erroneous opinion themselves involved in, 12; security by means of delusive show, 14; by which judges exhibited as models of

DESPOTISM: for security against anarchy, people of Britain driven into arms of, 90; mixture of waste, corruption and dark, exemplified, 97; under despotic sway, feelings of individuals form object too minute, 388

DESTRUCTION: offence affecting use of corporeal subject-matter of property, 344

DETAINER: *See* DETENTION

DETENTION: offence affecting use of corporeal subject-matter of property, 344; offence affecting enjoyments from condition in life, 345

DETERIORATION: offence affecting use of corporeal subject-matter of property, 344

DIGNITY(IES): without effect as incitement to virtuous ambition, 68–70; plea in bar to economy: need of money for support of official, 128–32; apt. is as, 251 & n, 275, 285; never without value, 317; dignity-conferring situations as conditions in life, 345; in France under *ancien* regime, to make compensation for loss beneath royal, 388; in England, care of justice beneath, of monarch, 388–91. *See* HONOUR(S), TITLE(S)

DISAPPOINTMENT: pain of, produced by taking away of anything valuable, 36; no expectation, consequently no, 170; in distribution of property, let object be minimization of, 342–3; sole reason for inserting acts in catalogue of offences may be seen in pain of, 343–6; evil of second order from, 353–5; more intense in case of vested than unvested right, 357–8; evil produced by, outweighed by evil produced by creation of needless offices, 359; salary not lessened without notice to minimize pain of, 368; evil effect of fees: pain of, to f., 368

DISAPPOINTMENT-PREVENTION PRINCIPLE: guide for resumption and original distribution, 8–10; and pensions of retreat, 14; connection with gtst. h. principle, 342–3; offences constituted such by, 343–6; and evil consequences of second order, 353–5; task of judge, under guidance of, in graduation v. non-graduation exhibiting case, 355–6; set aside ill effects to which, bears reference, no compensation ought to be allowed, 357–8; and distinction between aristocratical and democratical class, 360–1

DISGRACE: receipt of money at public expense without danger of, 78–80

DISOBEDIENCE: *See* OBEDIENCE AND DISOBEDIENCE

DISPATCH: fee exacted for extra, 311; payment by fees capable of being made instrument of delay or undue, 385–6

DISPOSITION: govt.'s title to confidence depends on, to press retrenchments, 144–5; no reason for supposing that so far as, goes, barristers who get least business are behind-hand in insincerity, 167; in House of Commons to keep influence within bounds, 192; want of, on part of Abbott to pay regard to Acts of Parliament, 235; means of delay employable in cases by dishonestly-disposed men, 272; only by accident can beneficent, on part of locator be visible, 324–5

DISREPUTE: men operated upon by fear of, in concert with love of power, 122

DISTANT DEPENDENCY(IES): navy and defence of colonies, 13; interests of metropolis and, 13; kept up to make places, 43–4

DOUBLE ENTRY SYSTEM OF BOOK-KEEPING: *See* ITALIAN SYSTEM OF BOOK-KEEPING

DOUBT(S): sources of, which legislature-made law would have dried up, 262–3; capital of country involved in alarm and insecurity by Eldon's, 264; Sugden reckoned up, as rules, 335n; and title to subject-matter of loss, 353–5

DRAUGHTSMEN: sinister interest of, 317–18

DUCTILITY: quality regarded as indispensable to rule of action, 380

DUPES: admirable accord betwixt knaves and, 325

DUTY(IES): manner of bringing into coincidence conduct prescribed by private interest and public, 15–16n; performance of, of office, 24; concerning ministers and, to themselves, 73–8; salary and offices of, 79–82; Peel puts from him such magistrates as have been in use to perform, of office, 165–6; deficiency in time employed by magistrates in fulfilment of, 175–6; in judges, interest at daggers drawn with, 183; breach of, as to attendance on part of Masters in Chancery, 209–10; by Canning, in scale of sentimentalism public, weighed light against private friendship, 237; for every additional, additional fee, 239; as Commissioner of Bankrupts v. Member of Parliament, 244; Eldon's desire to execute, with fidelity, 288–9; to merit, gift from father to child adds fulfilment of, 328; along with, of office, idler will neglect making profit out of it, 329–30. *See* OBLIGATION

EASE: titled imbecility at, behind screen of secrecy, waste, oppression and peculation, 83; stipendiary magistrates not disinclined to be attended for since, would increase, 181; what was lost in power gained in, 238; locatee at, against severity on part of locator, 323–4; results to fee-fed judge from denial of justice, 375. *See* UNEASINESS

EAST INDIA COMPANY: and debts of Nabob of Arcot, 140–1; suppose that proprietors have been squeezing Hindoos for good of Hindoos, 254

EAST INDIES: *See* INDIA

ECCLESIASTICAL DEPARTMENT: connection in respect of interest between patron and incumbent, 373. *See* SPIRITUAL DEPARTMENT

ECONOMY: exclusion of board essential to, 27; public, object of contempt, 42; Burke's anti-economical principles, 50–3; of service rendered to state by minister v. that by individual to individual, 77; Burke's Economy Bill, 85–6, 88–9; due regard for, furnished by Rose's practice, 97; Rose's pleas in bar to, 99–120, 123–32; impropriety of, how far proved by Pitt's expenditure, 132–42; cause of, left to take its chance for finding advocate among low people, 146–7; competition made subservient to, 147; and sale of Crown lands, 151–2, 154; such, as form of govt. admits of applied to some of administration offices, 192–3; Liverpool's love for, 196–7; Account Commission instrument of, and security against abuse, 381–2n; prevalence of fee system ascribed to vague conception of, 386, 387–91. *See* FRUGALITY

EDUCATION: assistance which arrangements proposed for instruction of fs. would give to national, 28–9; means of, regarded as aggravation of moral guilt, 248

EGYPT: earliest swindlers on record those who spoiled Egyptians, 248

ELOPEMENT: *See* DESERTION

EMBEZZLEMENT: offence affecting use of corporeal subject-matter of property, 344

EMOLUMENT(S): expense of official, maximized, 30; offices with, greater in war than peace, 44; in shape of sinecure v. pension, 61n; list of law sinecures with, 62–3n; greater the value of Six Clerk's place, greater, of Master of Rolls, 65n; attached to permanent place does not operate as corruption, 70–1; attached to efficient v. inefficient offices, 75–8; men serving without, 79; reduction of exorbitant, 85–6, 86n; reduction of official, contended against, 87–8; official persons should determine for themselves mass of, sufficient for expenses, 113–15; plea in bar to economy: want of wisdom in failing to allow official men as much money in shape of, as anybody can gain by trade or manufactures, 115–20; as reward for public service, 129–32; Rose's proof of insufficiency of official, 133–42; office in man's gift has no less decided value than office of same, in possession, 183; value of office to incumbent directly as, 183; average, of one of Master in Chancery's clerks, 210; value of office exclusive of, in possession, 214; and attendance of Masters in Chancery, 246; Eldon's, as Lord Chancellor, 278–80; non-drudgery is

community of interest between dishonest men of all classes and, 252–4; Eldon notoriously unfit for service of, 260–2; Lord Chancellor as head, and head party-man, 261n; relief at hands of Lord Chancellor rendered as hopeless as at hands of, 265–6; by *ex post facto* law made by single, parents divested of guardianship of children, 266; incapacity of Parliament to render unpunishable anything to which, pleased to attach punishment declared by Eldon, 267; instruments for doing dirty work of Parliament, 268n; delay sold by, of Common Law and Equity courts together, 273; Eldon's real plan to continue faculty of receiving fees for benefit of, 308; on part of, cause of adherence to remuneration in shape of fees, 309; power of giving increase to occasions productive of demand for judiciary services, 311–12; connection between delay and fees understood by, 313; for removal of opposition on part of, ample compensation should be given, 313; buying off sinister interest of, 314–21; ways in which service would not be adjudged bribe by, having interest in abuse, 323; under Matchless Constitution, individuals not so flagitiously wicked as, striven to make them, 323; comparative view of arrangements of official remuneration combined with patronage where, locator, 331–2; cases in which, has said let not contract be observed, 347; main end in view of, prevention of evil of second order, 354–5; task of, in graduation v. non-graduation exhibiting case, 355–6; importance of appearance of parties in presence of, 356–7; inconsistencies as to undislocability and dislocability of, 365–6; ease results to fee-fed, from denial of justice, 375; delivers member of indigent body up to members of opulent body to be oppressed, 376; offers use of sword of justice, 377; more enormous his opulence, more closely his sinister interest connected with that of fee-fed, 377–8; wolf-head clapped on shoulders of landholder by, 378, 379; tenants in common of harem of desirable portion of female sex, 378–9, 379–80. *See* BENCH

JUDICA-TEIPSUM PRINCIPLE: *See* SELF-JUDICATION PRINCIPLE

JUDICATORY(IES): security for testimony in open, 150; on which life and death depend not court of justice, 187–8; combination of two sorts of, proceeding on contradictory principles professed to be regarded as necessary to justice, 272; every day on which, not sitting is day of triumph to injustice, 312; in Eldon's case, is public opinion tribunal, 339; under existing system no, acting in way of anti-technical procedure, 361. *See* COURT(S)

JUDICATURE: under Matchless Constitution, judicial establishment directed to ends of, 178; necessary before kings had money to pay salaries, 184; influence of public opinion tribunal weakened by giving certain size and form to chambers of, 188; mendacity licence held up to view as one of pillars of English, 197; ends of, v. ends of justice, 248–9, 254; Eldon covered whole field of, with dispensing power, 256; Eldon's exploits during course of dominion over field of, 264–8; wisdom of lawyers directed to ends of, instead of ends of justice, 336; French will see what uncorruptness means when applied to English, 340; system of, which assumes name of justice, 341; independency declared indispensable to upright, 365; effect produced by inaccessibility coupled with venality of powers of, on indigent, 375–6

JUDICIAL ESTABLISHMENT: directed to ends of justice, 177–8; Peel would not consent to pay, in England upon same scale as paid in United States, 196; in England, ends of, diametrically opposite to ends of justice, 254

JUDICIAL PROCEDURE: *See* PROCEDURE

JUDICIARY: and boards, 27; separation of matter in part of constitutional code which regards, establishment, 33; evil effect of fees in, department, 368, 374–81; appellation suitor not used except case in which department is, 372

JURISDICTION: of trading justices v. judges, 185; inconsistencies as to union of law and equity, in one person, 366–7

of judge-made over Parliament-made, 215; Chancery Order contrary to, 215–19; Eldon pronounced exaction contrary to, 222–4; power so long arbitrary in fact rendered arbitrary at, 240; head of, continued swindling and took profit out of it, 242–50; James II ran a-tilt against Parliament-law, 255; sources of doubt which legislature-made, would have dried up, 262–3; relief at hands of Lord Chancellor rendered hopeless by artificial, expenses, 265–6; by *ex post facto*, parents divested of guardianship of children, 266; judge-made, is instrument for doing dirty work of Parliament, 268n; by reason of fees exacted on occasion of suit at, justice denied to vast majority of people, 310; fees worse than taxes, 310; whatever state of, question of fact must continue to supply business to barristers of rhetorical class, 317; by system of, having security of property for object, profit of conveyancers might be brought down, 318; liberty enjoyed by press in teeth of, 323; nothing clearer than, of real property, 334; wisdom of, directed to ends of judicature instead of ends of justice, 336; Eldon above those whom he has placed above all, 339; sorts of acts inserted in catalogue of offences by, of civilized nations, 343–4; under all systems of, cases in which legislator or judge has said let not contract be observed, 347; inconsistencies as to union of, and equity jurisdiction in one person, 366–7; unknowable, justice inaccessible, 375; more enormous his opulence, more closely his sinister interest connected with that of men of, 377–8; feudal system part and parcel of, of England, 379; security by virtue of, an empty name, 381; ruling one above, 389. *See* CIVIL LAW, COMMON LAW, EQUITY, LEGISLATION, PENAL LAW, ROMAN LAW, STATUTE(S)

LAWYER(S): particular interest of, and rule of action, 32; successors of Gavestons, Spencers and Mortimers forced to enter partnership with, 64n; under guidance of, people made to perjure themselves, 150; as many Equity as Common, 180; cannot be altogether prevented from betraying secrets of court, 188; Masterships in Chancery given to Common, 208n; strict community of sinister interest between judicial and professional, 210–11; learning endowment which every, speaks of, 248; in case of patents for invention, contribute nothing but obstruction, 265n; connection between delay and fees understood by, 313; buying off sinister interest of professional class of, 314–21; wisdom of, directed to ends of judicature instead of ends of justice, 336; fiction of original contract borrowed from lawyercraft, 348–9; maxim established for benefit of English monarchs by English, 390–1. *See* ADVOCATE(S), ATTORNEY(IES), BARRISTER(S), SOLICITOR(S), SPECIAL PLEADERS

LEARNING: necessary for reform, 245, 246, 248

LEGISLATION: under guidance of priests and lawyers, of country fond of causing men to perjure themselves, 150; consistently with, impeachment physically impossible, 186; for purpose of, look to situation, 190; model in style of English, 239; Eldon's exploits during course of dominion over field of, 264–8; throughout whole field of, Shelburne's affections on side of subject many, 381–2n. *See* ACT(S) OF PARLIAMENT, STATUTE(S)

LEGISLATOR: purpose of instructional matter giving instructions to, 31; in England, disposition to raise language of, 31–2; cases in which, has said let not contract be observed, 347

LEGISLATURE: experienced magistrates engaged in support of what, pronounced right, 180; sources of doubt which legislature-made law would have dried up, 262–3

LEGITIMACY: when principle of, given way to gtst. h. principle, public indignation will press with severest weight on swindlers in House of Lords, 247–8

LIBEL: that which Parliament would not dare, done by Eldon with no other warrant than word, 267

LIBERTY(IES): reason sufficient for trusting King with, 57n; strife between, and love, 169; of press sole palliative of evils of Matchless Constitution, 323

LICENCE: how to grant, under guise of censure, 249n; Justice of Peace refuses to grant, to occupant of public house, 362

LIE: everyday employed instrument of judges, 182

LIFE: reason sufficient for trusting King with lives, 57n; judicatory on which, and death depend not court of justice, 187–8; sort of stuff on which hang, and death under Common Law, 220; in case of homicide, deliberateness makes to offender difference between death and, 247; Eldon's plan will render impracticable commencement of system of judicial procedure having ends of justice during, of fs. allowed to receive fees, 309; in name no longer than during pleasure, in effect tenure is during, 363; lives of male part of subject many at mercy of ruling few, 378, 379; prohibition to dissect bodies until, had left them, 380

LINCOLN'S INN: place for putting indications to use, 338–9. *See* INN(S) OF COURT

LITIGATION: quantity of money expendable in, 318–19; mercantile more exposed than landed class to misfortune of, for protection of property, 320; discouragement to, as veil for villainy of ruling few, 376–7. *See* LITISCONTESTATION, SUIT(S)

LITISCONTESTATION: appellation suitor not used except case in which department is judiciary and business done in course of, 372; correspondent neutral associate of term litigation, 376–7. *See* LITIGATION, SUIT(S)

LOCATION AND DISLOCATION: wish to see located individual in whose instance maximum of app. apt. has place, 25; by reason of responsibility, choice determined in favour of one locator, 27; on part of locatees degree of inapt. greater in case of gift than sale, 321–4; disposition to severity on part of locator, 324–5; scrutiny into apt. of locatee, 325; constitution unapt in which power of dislocation in hands of locator, 325; gradations as to dislocability, 361–3; custom as to self-dislocation on dislocation of patrons, 363–5; inconsistencies as to undislocability and dislocability of judges, 365–6; same individual by whom location performed is dislocation performable, 373. *See* MANAGEMENT, PATRONAGE

LOGIC: subject-matter confined to dictates of understanding, 16n; Rose's skill in, 110, 112, 133; made to share in expense of repair to Pitt's reputation, 135; problem Peel's, has undertaken for solution of, 164; leading talent of judge, 169; Peel sets out with history to prepare House of Commons for, 170–1; logical field of jurisdiction of trading justices and judges too irregular for measurement, 185; utter stranger to statute-book, 242n. *See* NOMOGRAPHY

LOGICAL BOOKS: v. chronological book, 299

LORD CHANCELLOR(S): profits of office, 57–8n; fees increased by Orders signed by, 65n; incompetence of clergymen as police magistrates to be settled with, 174; is head over himself, 186; and corruptive intercourse, 190; and patronage of County Court judges, 198; greater part of sinister profit made by solicitor has for cause rapacity of Master in Chancery supported by, 209; Orders by, and Master of Rolls augmenting fees, 212, 214–15, 217–18; laid ground for more effectual corruption of himself and other Chiefs, 224–5; design stopt short by solicitor, 225–30; went to Parliament and got corruption established, 238–42; whether any mode in which depredation practised in courts can ever have been secret to, 245–6; hand of, regularly employed in concession of charter, 253; how, exercised dispensing power, 255–6; wager laid whether English or Irish, should do least business, 260n; as head judge and head party-man, 261n; relief at hands of, rendered hopeless, 265–6; wires of Cabinet moved by, 268n; Eldon's emoluments as, 278–80; sharing in plunderage made by Masters in Chancery, 314–15; power of keeping everything quiet in Cabinet and unquiet everywhere else, 317; as grand-locator, 332; independency has not place in situation of, 365

LORD LIEUTENANTS: incompetence of clergymen as police magistrates to be settled with, 174–5; and patronage of County Court judges, 198

LORDS: fashioned into philosophers and patriots by force, 45; banker and merchant made, 140; learned, above shame, 193; are but an abuse, 287; torments planted in breasts of Noble, by conveyancers, 319–20; Noble, tenants in common of harem of desirable portion of female sex, 378–80. *See* HOUSE OF LORDS, NOBILITY

LOSS: distant dependencies productive of, 44; produced to public by mode of sale of Crown lands, 151–2; by waste of public money an evil, in article of apt. still greater evil, 178; pecuniary profit and, presented to view, 293; complete indemnity against, for Masters in Chancery, 314–15; reform and mixture of profit and, to aristocracy, 319–20; correspondent to disappointment, 342–3; benefit by, of which disappointment produced consists of profit or reputation, 346; where contract has place, 346; doubt and title to subject-matter of, 353–5; difficulties attending estimate of, 355–6; for estimation of, attendance of parties needful, 356–7; out of profit of public interest, compensation given to private for, sustained, 387; in France under *ancien* regime, to make compensation for, beneath royal dignity, 388; needlessness of satisfaction to party wronged by, 388, 390–1

LOT: Special Jury Bill and substitution of, to packing, 197; with little prejudice to sense of security decisions might be committed to, 262

MAGISTRATES: conduct affords evidence that power and reputation have value, 130; inaptitude of country, insinuated by Peel, 165–7; plan admitting experienced, to office of police magistrate, 179–80; contrast between experienced, and unfledged barristers, 180–1; trade of Middlesex, put an end to, 184–6; yoke of aristocratical magistracy rivetted on neck of people, 265–6. *See* JUSTICE OF THE PEACE, POLICE MAGISTRATE(S)

MAGNA CARTA: delay, sale and denial of justice forbidden by, 62–4n

MALE: lives and fortunes of, part of subject many at mercy of ruling few, 378, 379

MALEFICENCE: connection between punishment and, 16n; several sorts of acts regarded as maleficent and on that account inserted in catalogue of offences, 343–4; beneath royal dignity to receive compensation from maleficent, 389–90

MALICE: that which Parliament would not dare, done by Eldon with no other warrant than word, 267

MANAGEMENT: power of, with effect as incitement to virtuous ambition, 68–70; according to Rose, to purpose of providing recruits for official establishment power of, without force or value, 117. *See* LOCATION AND DISLOCATION, PATRONAGE

MANDATES: forms for, required to be issued by judge included in procedure code, 34–5

MANUFACTURES: plea in bar to economy: want of wisdom in failing to allow official men as much money as anybody can gain by, 115–20; place occupied by those who engage in, 124–5

MASTER OF THE ROLLS: nominates Sixty and Six Clerks, 65n; fees increased by Orders signed by, 65n; Orders by Lord Chancellor and, increasing fees, 212, 214–15, 217–18; patron of Six Clerkship, 213; locatee of Lord Chancellor, 332; independency has place in case of, 365

MASTER(S) IN CHANCERY: attendance before, 206–7; improvements in arts and sciences of fraud and extortion made by, 207–11; Mastership was fortune to daughter of Erskine, 214; fee taken by Tipstaff allowed by, in costs, 232–4; if not

Bench and Bar, 223; confessed to have been extorted, 233–7; obtaining, by false pretence, 242n; tax not imposed on judicial pursuit but justice denied to all who cannot advance, 252–3; Lord Chancellor as moderator of squabbles about, 261n; no better evidence of opinions being really Eldon's than, obtained by profession of them, 267; delay on plaintiff's side employed as sure source of profit by dishonest men with other men's, in their pockets, 273; objections to worth of *Constitutional Code* by those with title to receive, out of taxes, 300; Eldon's real plan to continue faculty of receiving, from suitors in shape of fees for benefit of judges, 308; exacted by judge v. man of finance, 310; gained by mixture of delay and precipitation, 313; and amnesty necessary to purpose of persuading judges and lawyers that after removal of abuses they will find themselves as well off, 314; Masters in Chancery inhibited from taking, of suitors, 315; Master in Chancery cheats assignable individuals out of, 315–16; be appetite for, ever so sharp, power and dignity never without value, 317; suitors exonerated of expense of fees, more, would be expended in purchase of solicitors' services, 318–19; sinister interest of monied aristocracy, 320; locatee will not pay, for place unless employment agreeable, 321; when man buys place, has given him right to make most of it, 329–30; employed in compensation, 358; act of receiving emolument of sinecure office obtainment of, on false pretences, 360; by operation of telling, quantities of time consumed, 370; labour and time main source of, and money's worth, 372; never beneath royal dignity to receive, from individuals to whom no maleficence imputed, 389–90; no laystall so foul that to extract, lawyers scrupled to rake into it, 390; no means of compelling His Majesty to pay, 391. *See* SHIP-MONEY

MORAL APTITUDE: attendance and moral branch of apt., 163–4; problem how to prove that by exclusion of non-barristers as police magistrates, will be produced, 164; of experienced magistrates v. unfledged barristers, 180; neither possessed nor pretended to by Eldon, 288; sufficient to keep man in judicial situations unexposed to any determinate charge, 322–3; as to moral inapt., maximum of audacity and shamelessness exemplified, 323

MORALITY: made to share in expense of repair to Pitt's reputation, 135; contempt in which sincerity held by one of head guardians of public morals, 167; extenuation and aggravation of moral guilt, 247–8; hand of Parliament superior to all, 253; lesson of, delivered by Blackstone to young students, 389

MOTIVE(S): by which compliance produced, 16n; not in nature of salary to furnish, for ordinary service, 79; sympathy frequently sole, to rendering service, 81–2; in instance of Rose and Pitt real regard for economy an actuating, 97; for creation of abuse: profit upon expense, 186; influence of, on conduct, 190; in case of law fees, for giving increase to them in same hands with power, 310; for acceptance of place where provision at locator's expense would have been made, 324; in case of sale, no, to give preference to inapt., 325; list of, which have for basis correspondent modifications of pleasure or pain, 350–1n; no punishment of Justice of Peace without corrupt, 362

NATIONAL DEBT: *See* DEBT(S)

NATIONS: system of proposed constitutional law for all, professing liberal opinions, 5; Matchless Constitution is envy of surrounding, 340; sorts of acts inserted in catalogue of offences by laws of civilized, 343–4

NATURE: power of masquerade dress to change man's, 185; human, and habit insure judge gives every possible extent to own arbitrary power, 268n; effect on, of men of possession of power, 381

NAVY(IES): and defence of colonies, 13; security procured by proportional

OPPRESSION: standing army instrument of, 30; ease behind screen of, 83; principle of making provision for noble families founded on oppressive extortion, 104; payment by fees pregnant with, 184; for benefit of monarch v. judges, 191–2; fees on defendant's side sells to every man able to buy it power of oppressing every man unable, 216n; v. extortion, 220; only by making ruling few uneasy can oppressed many obtain relief, 261n; loss in conjoined faculty of, and depredation, 319; in case of purchase, locatee will not enter place with formed design of, 321; services of representative of people employed in aiding minister in, 326; powers of depredation and, result to man of opulence from denial of justice, 375–6; judge offers use of sword of justice to everybody who for pleasure of, feels disposed to put it to use, 377; colour and creed as justificative cause of, 377

OPULENCE: objection to pecuniary competition: unopulent classes excluded, 29; public money to raise families to state of, 55, 69; dignity is as, 275, 301; degree of, possessed by highest class of landholder, 320; powers of depredation and oppression result to man of, from denial of justice, 375–8. *See* RICH, WEALTH

ORDINANCE: mode of address where will operating is superior, 16n

ORIGINAL BOOK: v. derivative books, 299

ORIGINAL CONTRACT: period during which, resorted to as affording reason why good govt. should be instituted, 346–7; utter inapt. of, principle, 347–8; principle assumed by Locke, 348–9; not applicable to private life, 352n

OUTLAWRY: by fees exacted on plaintiff's side all who cannot afford to pay placed in state of, 216n; virtual, of gtst. number, 340

OXFORD: James II placed obsequious Protestant in, college, 256

PAIN: *See* PLEASURE AND PAIN

PARLIAMENT: Parliamentary phrase vested rights, 36; so long as offices kept on foot with emolument greater in war than peace, conduct pernicious and corrupt, 44; practical proof that when obedience drops off, power drops off, experienced, 45–6; principles established on public expenditure preached from, 46–7; fees exacted without allowance from representatives of people in, 61–2n; money levied upon suitors without consent of, 65n; modes in which law made by judges without consent of, 65n; and modes of disposing of public money under notion of reward for service, 66–8; pitiable condition of every member of, 69; plea of gratitude protects man in, against charge of corruption, 71; sinecures necessary to secure fidelity at expense of sincerity, 72; obsequiousness principal ingredient of merit in, 78; Parliamentary debate a topic of invidious comparisons, 83; encouragement to spending other people's money by tokens of Parliamentary approbation, 135, 138–41; opinion of, that Pitt's emolument sufficient, 136–7; number of members holding Crown leases, 152–3, 154; expediency as standing reason of, 159–60; means provided for remedying of police magistrates' evils by wisdom of, 160–1; address of both Houses is impeachment under another name, 186; judge-made law more useful to, than Parliament-made law, 191; whatsoever learned in, in state of insurrection, 193; after Parliamentary enquiry into facts, Peel would not consent to pay judicial establishment in England on same scale as paid in United States, 196; Eldon set his own authority above that of, 205; project of plunderage sanctioned by, 215; Bench set above, 222, 232; regard manifested for authority of, by Commissioners on Officers of Courts of Justice, 236; judges dragged before tribunal of, 237; Chancellor went to, and got corruption established, 238–42; duty as Commissioner of Bankrupts v. Member of, 244; judges and authority of, 250; James II ran a-tilt against Parliament-law, 255; Eldon accepted from, consummation of plan, 256; incapacity of, to render unpunishable anything to which judges pleased

viduals by whom situation shall be filled be finally determined, 27; objections to, 29; and use made of principle, 147–55. *See* AUCTION, COMPETITION

PEERAGE(S): invitation to obtain, at expense of public, 140; will be the lot of arch-delinquent, 362–3

PENAL LAW: penal branch of property law founded on disappointment-prevention principle, 8; separation of matter in penal code, 33; by disappointment-prevention principle may be attached clear idea to denomination justice in civil cases in contradistinction to penal cases, 342n

PENSION(S): Brithibernia indebted to Matchless Constitution for, 14–15; of Lord Chancellor, 57–8n; v. sinecures, 61n; mode of disposing of public money under notion of reward for public service: pensions granted by Crown, 66–7; might operate with same effect as sinecure, 70–1; Burke's, 90; charge on revenue for, 99–103, 126; Commissioners of Bankrupts virtual pensioners of Eldon, 243–4; squabble about clause in Ponsonby's, 260–1n. *See* RETIRED ALLOWANCE

PEOPLE: expenditure employed at charge of, in engaging persons to render services, 23; groaning under yoke of ruling few, 45–6; property of, to be at disposal of Burke, 53; King's power to give away people's money, 57n; in disposition of property of, plea of its furnishing reward to public service a false pretence, 66–8; opulence at expense of, 69–70; property of, to be disposed of by Crown, 70; with reference to interests of, destruction of unity among ministers check upon misrule, 83; govt. in which titled imbecility should lord it over King and, Burke's Utopia, 83; burden pressing on, concluded necessary on ground that it is customary, 85; legitimate influence of, manifested in equalized representation, 88–9; for security against anarchy, of Britain driven into arms of despotism, 90; money not to be had without, being forced to part with it, 94; whatsoever at expense of, given without preponderate advantage is waste or peculation, 100; facility of engaging, to submit to increased burdens, 100–1; made to perjure themselves, 150; work of corruption carried on in face of deluded, 187; Liverpool's love for, 197; Westminster Hall Chiefs authorized to tax, 219; of England to be plundered in secret by judges, 239–40; sympathy for sufferings of, in House of Commons v. hulks, 261n; yoke of aristocratical magistracy rivetted on neck of, 265–6; Eldon's address to, 275–7, 287; Eldon never pretended sensibility towards, 281n; design ought to be to render transactions understood to, 293–6; in England, justice denied to vast majority of, 310; regard terms with patient acquiescence, 312; in case of vast majority of, no conflict of opposite interests, 320–1; sale of services of representative of people to, 326; arguments by which, of England would be satisfied of more-than-wisdom of preservation of practice of gift, 328–9; want no more applications of self-judication principle, 339; petitions only channel, can communicate with one another on political subject, 341; Shelburne only friend, ever had in situation of Prime Minister, 382n. *See* PUBLIC, REPRESENTATIVE(S) OF THE PEOPLE

PERJURY: security provided by, 150–2; Bentham never yet convicted of, 166; and questions allowed to be put to proposed witness, 266n; constant and all-pervading habit of, 266n

PERMISSION: disguised as prohibition or punishment, 17n; non-permission of serving without salary, 79. *See* ALLOWANCE

PERSON: graduation has place where question concerns damage done to, 355–6

PETITION OF RIGHT: general principle vainly endeavoured to be established by, 215, 216–17

PETITION(S): mode of address where will operating is inferior, 16n; reduction of emoluments called for by, 85–6; might be framed from persons desirous of relief from virtual outlawry, 340–1

PROHIBITION: variety of ways, producible, 17n; of serving without salary, 79; by adroitly-worded, effect of allowance produced, 218; after publication completed, applications invited to Eldon for, 265; *ex post facto* punishment substituted to legislative definition and, 267–8; to dissect bodies until life had left them, 380

PROPERTY(IES): law of, founded on disappointment-prevention principle, 8; of f. in chief not at stake upon apt. of his choice of helpers, 25; of people to be at disposal of Burke, 53; no limit to quantity of public, disposed of, 55, 60; reason sufficient to trust King with disposal of, 57n; private, in part undisposed of, 60–1; principle of policy and humanity that forbids abolition of sinecures to prejudice of existing rights of, 61n; in Westminster Hall Courts, taking of, of distressed to make fortunes for favourites, 62–4n; in disposition of, of govt. and people, plea of its furnishing reward to public service a false pretence, 66–8; of people to be disposed of by Crown, 70; King will possess himself of whole, of country, 83–6; making provision for noble families capable of effecting revolution in state of, 104; no exclusion put upon candidates who have, of their own, 114–15; aristocracy of talent and virtue v. that of rank and, 127–8, 145; best price for public, 149–55; plunderable fund composed of, of those who can buy chance for article sold under name of Equity, 215; of kingdom at disposal of Lord Chancellor, 261n; literary, rendered dependent upon Eldon's will, 265; by system of law having security of, for object, profit of conveyancers might be brought down, 318; mercantile more exposed than landed class to misfortune of litigation for protection of, 320; nothing clearer than law of real, 334; in distribution of, let object be minimization of disappointment, 342–3; offences affecting use of corporeal subject-matter of, 344; offences affecting title to, 344–5; offences affecting, by means of reputation, 345–6; graduation has place where question concerns quantum of damage done to, 355–6; where, taken out of hands of proprietor and lodged in govt., demand for compensation acknowledged, 358; rapine exercised upon, 390–1; by forfeiture whole, transferred to proper coffers, 391

PROPOSAL: mode of address where will operating is equal, 16n

PROPOSITION: mode of address where will operating is equal, 16n

PROTECTION: possession of wealth regarded as proof of title for purpose of, 74; expectation of undue, in case of locatee in by gift of predecessor of great man, 325n

PROTESTANT(S): James II placed obsequious, in Oxford college, 256; slavery under which Catholics held by, in Great Britain and Ireland, 377

PRUDENCE: might join with sympathy in constructing bridge of gold, 36; operated on Burke's mind towards production of Economy Bill, 85; each man's, security against offences of him whose seat in hulks, 247; when Eldon's humour forgot itself, not so his, 255; to Romilly with secrecy which, dictated, Bentham's works a text-book, 258; suicidal act of dislocation has for internal cause self-regarding, 363–4; insofar as conduct determined by suggestions of, f. will prefer salary to fees, 374

PUBLIC: cognizance taken of proceedings of examiners by, 25–6; expense of instructors drawn from pockets of, 26; information as to merit of candidates in possession of, 27; economy in paying for services to, 77; Necker trusted, with own money, 90n; information and time wanting to, 107–8; Rose stands convicted of charging, with burden necessity of which could not be pretended, 139; loss produced to, by mode of sale of Crown lands, 151–2; profit to individuals v. mischief to, 214; price, made to pay for sinister profit, 215; table with lawful fee bolted out in face of, 235; power of fraud applied to mind of, 247; fees to be transferred to use of, 308; Master in Chancery cheats, of time due to it, 315–16; sale of office for benefit of, would be tax on justice, 325; office with salary sold for benefit

REGRET: where antecedently to loss no expectation, pain produced is pain of, 343n

RELIGION: falsehood and mischievousness of, proclaimed by Eldon, 267

RELISH: apt. for political situation by proof given of, 9

REMUNERATION: in United States, mis-seated or extravasated none, 14; connection between service and, 15–16n; disguised as punishment, 17n; v. apt., 24; of instructors drawn from pockets of those by whom instruction received, 26–7; expense of, to intended fs., 27; pain of disappointment produced by taking away of, 36; and reward for public service, 66–8, 129–32; at expense of people, 69–70; withholding, for public service, 126–7; in eyes of Rose's aristocracy of talent and virtue, to purpose of, nothing but money of any value, 127, 145; in possession of rank and property v. talent and virtue branch of aristocracy, 128; insufficiency of, fund, 193; official apt. in direct ratio of official, 194; Liverpool would not assign to official establishment same rate of, as has place in United States, 196–7; where, wears shape of fees, abuse sure to have place, 264–5n; for undertaking *Constitutional Code*, 300–1; on part of judges, cause of adherence to, in shape of fees, 309; repugnancy of, by fees to ends of justice, 310; comparative view of arrangements of official, combined with patronage, 331–2; in instance of democratical class quantity of, minimized, 360; best mode of official, salary v. fees, 368–91. *See* EMOLUMENT(S), INCOME(S), PAY, SALARY(IES)

REPRESENTATION: legitimate influence of people manifested in equalized, 88

REPRESENTATIVE DEMOCRACY: in proposed arrangements sort of govt. supposed, 29. *See* DEMOCRACY

REPRESENTATIVE(S) OF THE PEOPLE: fees exacted without allowance from, in Parliament, 61–2n; design ought to be to render transactions understood to, 293–4; sale of services of, 326

REPUTATION: of f. in chief at stake upon apt. of choice of helpers, 25; gained to supporters of Burke's plan, 50; without effect as incitement to virtuous ambition, 68–70; when service rendered to public, prospect of gratification to love of, 81–2; according to Rose, to purpose of providing recruits for official establishment, without force or value, 117; value of, admitted by Rose, 130–2; Pitt's, threatened by meanness and rapacity, 135–6; share of, possessed by Pitt, 137–8; in Pitt's instance, value of, 141; Pitt's purchase of, 142; Peel must content himself with, of probity, 197; Eldon given, to himself, 262–3; of Master in Chancery at mercy of giver of fee, 315; Sugden's object: saving what could be saved from wreck of Eldon's, 335; offences affecting property by means of, 345–6

RESISTANCE: tyrant not altogether exempted from fear of experiencing, 377

RESPECT: without effect as incitement to virtuous ambition, 68–70; Burke's, for wealth and honour, 73–5; plea in bar to economy: necessity of provision for respectable families, 103–9, 111; disrespect for official man, 120–3; sources of, 131–2; share of, possessed by Pitt, 137–8; Pitt's purchase of, 142

RESPONSIBILITY: advantages looked for from board better secured by, 27; by reason of, choice determined in favour of one locator, 27; objection to pecuniary competition: pecuniary, diminished, 29; invitation to obtain good things at public expense without risk of being made responsible, 140; of trading justices v. judges, 185–6; if, anything better than mockery, impeachment would await Eldon, 241n; govt. of Spain, Portugal or Turkey may be substituted to Matchless Constitution without, on part of authors of change, 294

RETIRED ALLOWANCE: process of elimination performed upon writing clerks without thought of, 360. *See* PENSION(S)

RETRENCHMENT(S): less the number of sufferers by sum proposed to be retrenched the better, 9; and rulers, 11–12; field of, is whole field of expenditure,

as, against waste and corruption, 93; provided by perjury, 150–2; for apt. in office of police magistrate, 164–5, 169–70; afforded by cancelling quantity of sinecure, 192; prudence as, against swindler, 247; with little prejudice to sense of, decisions might be committed to lot, 262; capital of country involved in insecurity, 264; price paid by inventive genius for, 265n; by system of law having, of property for object, profit of conveyancers might be brought down, 318; more intense and extensive sense of insecurity in breasts of aristocracy, stronger rightly-operating interest, 319–20; all classes stand devoted to all-embracing insecurity, 340; wish to see, substituted to insecurity, 341; by virtue of law an empty name, 381; Account Commission instrument of economy and, against abuse, 381–2n; where power interferes, turn of scale should be in favour of weaker party lest sense of, shaken, 387–8

SELF-JUDICATION PRINCIPLE: characteristic of Matchless Constitution, 19, 288; people want no more applications of, 339

SELF-REGARD: constitution unapt in which power of dislocation in hands of locator or person connected with him in self-regarding interest, 325; sinister interest of judge in choosing persons by whom he may gratify connections in way of self-regarding interest, 332; being endowed with, and sympathy would not accept formation of original contract as being of itself fit ground for practice, 347; suicidal act of dislocation has for internal cause self-regarding prudence, 363–4. *See* REGARD

SENSIBILITY: circumstances affecting, 356

SENTIMENTALISM: by Canning, in scale of, public duty weighed light against private friendship, 237

SERVANTS: to monarch neither apt. of, nor frugality of pay allotted to them naturally unacceptable, 29–30; of Crown habitually employed in disposing of property of public to purpose of remuneration, 67–8; man in Parliament and conduct of, of Crown, 71. *See* FUNCTIONARY(IES), OFFICIAL(S)

SERVICE(S): offers of, 9; connection between remuneration and, 15–16n; expenditure employed at charge of people in engaging persons to render, 23; reward and public, 55–71, 73–83, 86–8, 129–32; of state as bar to reformation, 86n; Necker's serving in office without salary, 90n; auction and public, 91–3; according to Rose, money is to constitute man's inducement to engage in, of country, 117; professions and branches of trade and manufactures enter into competition with official, 117–20; withholding remuneration for public, 126–7; Pitt's extraordinary, 136; whether any preponderant use can be found for influence without prejudice to public, 142–7; as clerk to attorney as security for apt. in office of police magistrate, 165; money exacted by Masters in Chancery when no, performed, 208–9; Eldon notoriously unfit for, of judge, 260–2; object of division of business of office: good of, 285; competition criterion of due proportion between reward and, 286; fee exacted in consideration of extra, 311; judges' power of giving increase to occasions productive of demand for judiciary, 311–12; effecting of dependence between, and reward, 316; suitors exonerated of expense of fees, more money would be expended in purchase of solicitors', 318–19; ways in which, would not be adjudged bribe by judge having interest in abuse, 323; inapt. and private v. public, 325; venality of, 326–30; rendition of, where contract has place, 346; pay attached to official situations v. pay obtainable in private, 361; in military, importance of justice v. obedience, 366; salary v. fees as means of engaging app., 368–9; evil effect of fees: delay augmented to detriment of public, 369–71; fee incapable of being made variable according to value of, 383; from particular, suitor receives especial benefit, 388. *See* SECRET SERVICE

SHAME: by fear of, judges might be driven to punish trading justices, 186; work of

sympathetic intercourse between suitor and f. corruptive and detrimental to interest of public, 382–3

pleasure of, not so great in monied aristocracy, 320; line of demarcation between those under subjection to, and those who derive benefit of it, 377

UNDERSTANDING: subject-matter of logic confined to dictates of, 16n; in Eldon, vitiated along with will, 249

UNEASINESS: spring of action by which constitution will be cleared of morbific matter, 44–6; only by making ruling few uneasy can oppressed many obtain relief, 261n; King will take away Eldon's seals so soon as more, from keeping them where they are than from placing them elsewhere, 276–7; remedy against, through aversion to business in hands of locatee, 322. *See* EASE

UNITARIANS: will not defile themselves with insincerity to purchase common rights of subjects, 267

UNITED STATES OF AMERICA: Brithibernia surrendered dominion to inhabitants of, 13; no pensions of retreat, 14; unpopularity and ill success of American war, 89; danger if police magistrates born in, 168; salary of Chief Justice of Supreme Court, 195–6; Liverpool declared that expense of official establishment less in England than in, 196–7; price paid by inventive genius for security, 268n; no such nuisance as English conveyancer found in, 318

UNIVERSAL INTEREST: points relative to which interest of ruling few coincides with, and in state of implacable hostility with, 42–3; rightly-operating interest acting in alliance with, in aristocracy of wealth, 319–20. *See* INTEREST(S)

USURPATION: offence affecting title to property, 344–5; of inventorship, fabricatorship and vendorship as offences affecting property by means of reputation, 345–6

USURY: Pitt did not put money out to, 141; Sugden and Bentham agree on subject of, 336

UTILITY: and disappointment-prevention principle, 8; no virtue can be made out of, 79–80; necessity in sense of public, never worth a thought, 85; since bringing to view principle of, period of original contract terminated, 347; by Helvétius denomination of principle of, given to gst. h. principle, 350; no precise idea attached to word, by Hume and Paley as by Helvétius, 351; locution gst. h. principle substituted to principle of, 352

VACATION(S): manufacture of delay set up by distinction between terms and, 312; no need for, 316

VALUE: by divesting power of patronage of arbitrariness, it will not be divested of, 27; of Sixty Clerk's place, 65n; measure of, of good things, 77; Burke's caricature of himself as man in whose estimation nothing but money has, 93–4; of money, 117, 120–3, 127; of money, power and reputation, 130–2, 141–2; differences of opinion as to, of Crown lands, 151–2; office in man's gift has no less decided, than office in possession, 183; wherever office has money, so has patronage, 213–15; as, of money sunk, augmentation of fees might have had excuse, 217; of *Constitutional Code*, 301; of commutation, 314; power and dignity never without, 317; instructive test and exhibition of real, of Matchless Constitution, 340; pain of disappointment proportioned to, of interest, 343; principle of utility understood as prescribing preference to future pleasure of greater, to present pleasure, 351; gradations in, of offices in respect of certainty, 359–63; evil effect of fees: value of remuneration lessened by uncertainty of amount, 368, 374; money possessed of, insofar as employed in enjoyment of pleasure or exclusion of pain, 372; power of f. to make addition to, of fees, 372–3; evil effect of fees: value of remuneration

INDEX OF NAMES

Note. The following is an index of names of persons and places appearing in the introduction, text, and notes; the last (whether Bentham's or the editor's) are indicated by 'n'. Under Bentham's name only references to his other works are indicated.

498